PANZERGRENADIERS TO THE FRONT!

THE COMBAT HISTORY OF *PANZERGRENADIER-DIVISION BRANDENBURG* ON THE EASTERN FRONT 1944-45

A. Stephan Hamilton

Helion & Company Ltd

Dedication
For Frank Schwuchow
Your support and enthusiasm has carried many of my projects through the years.

Helion & Company Limited
26 Willow Road
Solihull
West Midlands
B91 1UE
England
Tel. 0121 705 3393
Fax 0121 711 4075
Email: info@helion.co.uk
Website: www.helion.co.uk
Twitter: @helionbooks
Visit our blog http://blog.helion.co.uk/

Published by Helion & Company 2016
Designed and typeset by Farr our Publications, Wokingham, Berkshire
Cover designed by Paul Hewitt, Battlefield Design (www.battlefield-design.co.uk)
Printed by Gutenberg Press Limited, Tarxien, Malta

Text © A. Stephan Hamilton 2016
Photographs © as individually credited
Original maps drawn by Paul Hewitt, Battlefield Design (www.battlefield-design.co.uk) © Helion & Company Ltd 2016

ISBN 978-1-910777-13-8

British Library Cataloguing-in-Publication Data.
A catalogue record for this book is available from the British Library.

For details of other military history titles published by Helion & Company
Limited contact the above address, or visit our website: http://www.helion.co.uk.

We always welcome receiving book proposals from prospective authors.

Contents

List of photographs

Period images of the battlefields and units covered in this book are exceedingly rare. Many of the images are derived from three main sources: pre-war or wartime postcards of the towns and villages where fighting occurred; photos of Bautzen taken by Kurt Arno Lehnert in April and May 1945; and photos taken by the author during a March 1945 trip to Weißenberg and Bautzen. Document images are derived from archival files of *OKH* or *Lage Ost* situational maps. Select leader photographs were graciously sourced and provided by Peter van Holstein and Mark C. Yerger.

List of maps in Map Book

List of terms and abbreviations

Ia	Chief of Operations.
Ic	Chief of Intelligence.
Ib	Chief of Supply/Maintenance.
IIa	Adjutant.
AA	Anti-aircraft.
Abteilung / Abt.	Battalion / Btl.
Alarmeinheiten / Al.	Alarm Units. These were typically ad hoc formations formed from rear area personnel.
Armee Oberkommando / AOK	Army HQ.
Armee	Army.
Armeeabteilung	A reinforced Corps, commanded by a Corps Commander with a Corps Staff.
Armeegruppe	A weak Army Group that was *ad hoc* in its organization. These were typically associated with names like *Armeegruppe Steiner* for example.
Artillerie	Artillery.
AT	Anti-tank.
Aufklärung	Reconnaissance.
Bahnhof	Railway Station.
Bataillon / Btl.	Battalion.
Batterie	Battery.
Brigade	Brigade.
Chef des Generalstabes	The Chief of General Staff.
Chef des Stabes	Chief of Staff.
Division / Div.	Division.
Divisiongruppe	A unit formed by transferring the designation of a partially destroyed division to one of or a consolidation of its regiments.
Ersatzheer	Replacement Army.
Fallschirmjäger	Paratrooper.
Feld-Ersatz-Bataillon / FEB	Field Replacement Bataillon, usually assigned to a specific division and responsible for training new replacements assigned to the unit.
Festung / Fes.	Fortress.
Fliegerabwehrkanone or Flak	Anti-aircraft guns.
Fliegerverbindungsoffizier / Flivo	Air Liaison Officer.
Freiwillige	Volunteer.
Fremde Heeres Ost	Foreign Armies East.
Gau	Nazi Party administrative area.
Gauleiter	Official in charge of Nazi Party administrative area (*Gau*). His control over party matters in his area was complete, and

gradually after 1933, and even more after 1939, he assumed complete control over the entire civilian population.

G.R.	*Grenadier Regiment*
Generalkommando / Gen.Kdo.	*Korps* (Corps) headquarters.
Gruppe	Group.
Guards	Honorific title given to Soviet infantry and tank formations.
Hanomag	*Hanoverische Maschinenbau* German halftrack manufacturer; a reference to the Sd.Kfz 250/251 series of halftracks.
Heer	Army.
Heeresgruppe	Army Group.
Hauptkampflinie / HKL	Main Defense Line.
Hilfswillige / Hiwis	Foreign Auxiliary Volunteers.
Hitlerjugend / HJ	Hitler Youth.
Infanterie	Infantry.
Jäger (division or other size unit)	Light infantry.
Jagdpanzer IV/L70	Tank destroyer built of the Panzer IV chassis. The ones used by *Sturmgeschütz-Artillerie-Brigade 'GD'* were the Panzer IV/70 variant armed with the PAK 42 L/70 gun.
Joseph Stall II / JSII	Soviet heavy tank armed with a 122mm main gun.
Kampfgruppe / KG.	Essentially an ad hoc formation of different arms, organized temporarily for a specific task; often named for its commander.
Kampfwert I	Capable for any offensive action.
Kampfwert II	Capable for limited offensive action.
Kampfwert III	Capable for defense only.
Kampfwert IV	Capable for limited defensive actions only.
Kompanie	Company.
Korps	Corps.
Korpsabteilung	A reinforced division commanded by a (usually senior) Division Commander, with a Division Staff.
Korpsgruppe	Two or three understrength divisions assembled into a tactical unit under a Corps Commander, with an improvised Corps Staff.
Kraft Radfahrzeug / Krad	Motorcycle
Kriegsmarine	German Navy.
Landesschützen / Lds.Sch.	A Territorial unit.
Luftgau	Administrative and supply organization of the German Air Force, its authority was limited to a well defined and permanently fixed geographical area. Those established in Germany were designated by Roman numerals, those in occupied areas by their location.
Luftwaffe	German Airforce.
Marine	German Naval Infantry.
Maschinengewehr / MG	Machinegun.
Nachrichten Abteilung / N.A.	Signals Battalion
Nebelwerfer	Rocket Artillery.
Non-Commissioned Officer / NCO	Senior enlisted soldier, usually holding the rank of Sergeant and above.

Oberbefehlshaber / Ob	Highest ranking officer or higher command of a geographic area or Army Group.
Oberkommando der Wehrmacht / OKW	Armed Forces High Command.
Oberkommando des Heeres / OKH	German Army High Command.
Organization Todt	Paramilitary construction organization of the Nazi Party, auxiliary to the *Wehrmacht*. Named after its founder, Dr. Todt. Consisted of a cadre of engineers, expanded as necessary by the use of hired, conscript, or foreign labor.
Panzerabwehrkanone / PAK	Anti-tank gun.
Panzer / Pz.	Tank, armor or armored.
Panzerfaust	One use, hand-held rocket propelled grenade.
Panzergrenadier / PzGr.	Armored Infantry; usually motorized, occasionally mechanized.
Panzergruppe	Armored force the size of an army, but operating in conjunction with an army (When operating independently, normally re-designated as a Panzer Army).
Panzerjäger / PzJg.	Tank hunter.
Panzerturms	A panzer turret, usually fixed in place atop a concrete bunker, used as an anti-tank strongpoint in the defense.
Pferde	Horses
Pionier	German Army engineer.
Quartiermeister / QM / Qu.	Quartermaster (*Ib*) on a general staff responsible for supply.
Reichsarbeitsdienst / RAD	Reich Labor Force.
Reichswehr	The German national Defense Establishment under the Versailles Treaty.
Regiment / Rgt.	Regiment.
Regimentgruppe	a.) A regiment constituted during operation and consisting of men and equipment from various arms; b.) A reinforced battalion, given a Regimental designation.
Rifle	Soviet designation for regular infantry formations.
Rollbahn	Road designated as a main axis of motorized transportation, from which all animal transport and marching columns were normally barred.
Selbstfahrlafette / S.F.L. or *sfl*	self-propelled gun mount.
Sturmabteilung / SA	Storm Trooper detachment of the *Nazi* party.
Sturmgeschütz IV / StuG	Tank destroyer built on a Panzer IV chassis. Armed StuK 40 L/48 main gun.
Schwere	Heavy.
Sicherung	Security.
Schützenpanzerwagen or SPW	German armored halftrack personnel carrier. See *Hanomag*.
SS / Schutzstaffel	Administrative *SS*.
Stellvertreter / Stellv.	Deputy *Korps* of a *Wehrkreis* (Military District).
Sturmgeschütz / Stug.	Assault Gun.
T-34/85	Soviet main battle tank armed with an 85mm main gun.
Verteidigungsbereich / Vert.Ber.	Defensive Area.
Volksgrenadier	A term first applied in autumn 1944, to reorganized infantry divisions, organized on reduced T/O with increased ratio of automatic weapons; it was also consider a "Honorific" title.
Volkssturm / V.St.	Peoples' militia assembled during the later years of the war.

Wach	Watch or guard.
Waffen-SS	Armed *Schutzstaffel*; combat arm of the *SS*.
Wehrkreis	The basic military area of Germany; had the additional functions of administering conscription and furnishing replacements to specific units (divisions and corps) whose home station was located in the *Wehrkreis*.
Wehrmacht	German Armed Forces.
zur besonderen Verwendung / z.b.V.	For special employment; an ad hoc unit or command established for a specific purpose. In the late war period many *z.b.V.* units became established commands or divisions.

Preface

I never intended to write a book about *Panzergrenadier-Division 'Brandenburg'*. I have no special affinity to the *Division* or its veterans, just the period in time this book covers. However, the choice I made to research and write this book was an easy one.

The background to how this book came about is essential to understanding why it exists at all. In 2012 Duncan Rogers, my editor at Helion, approached me about writing an expanded *Introduction* for a single volume reprint edition of Eduard Bodenmüller's two volume *Diary of a Tank Gunner: in the Panzer Regiment of the Brandenburg Panzergrenadier-Division, February-April 1945* published by Antonio J. Munoz's Axis Europa in 2004 and 2005 respectively. Bodenmüller was a Panther tank commander in the *4.Kompanie* of *Panzer-Regiment 'Brandenburg'*. According to his first volume he served along the Oder River, specifically along the Seelow Heights as part of the *9.Armee*, then later in his second volume, we find him fighting much farther south, along the Neisse River as part of the *4.Panzer-Armee*. Given the overlap in research I was already conducting on the operations of late-war *Wehrmacht* formations for the second volume in my *The Oder Front 1945* series, I immediately agreed.

In preparing to the write the introduction of the reprint I decided to conduct archival research on *Panzergrenadier-Division 'BR'* as my cursory review of secondary sources revealed little about the operations of *Panzer-Regiment 'Brandenburg'* or its relationship to the division of the same name. I soon located and acquired two massive files from the *Bundesarchiv-Militärarchiv* in Freiburg, Germany that belonged to Helmuth Spaeter. Spaeter served as the former Quartermaster of *Panzergrenadier-Division 'BR'* and was the official historian of *Panzer-Korps 'Großdeutschland'* in the postwar years. A review of his collected papers suggested that Bodenmüller's *4.Kompanie* and the *Panzer-Regiment* it belonged to never served with *Panzergrenadier-Division 'BR'*.

I then began to scour the records of *OKH* for additional clues. What I found was that while Bodenmüller's unit, *Panzer-Regiment 'Brandenburg'*, was intended to join its parent unit *Panzergrenadier-Division 'BR'*, it never did because of the pace of operations at the start of the Soviet Vistula-Oder Strategic Offensive in January 1945. The *Panzer-Regiment 'Brandenburg'* was subsequently reassigned accordingly. There was a request to *OKH* by *Heeresgruppe Mitte* to transfer *1.Btl./Panzer-Regiment 'Brandenburg'* to them from *Heeresgruppe Weichsel* based on an *Obkdo. H.Gr. Mitte Ia Nr. 2018/45* dated April 4th. That request was soundly denied by *OKH* the following day in order *Nr. 5546/45* with the response that the request cannot be granted as the unit will remain with *Panzergrenadier-Division 'Kurmark'*.[1] *Panzergrenadier-Division 'Kurmark'* was serving with *Heeresgruppe Weichsel* at that time. Perhaps the final word is *Order Nr. 6239/45* from *OKH/Gen St d H/Op.Abt.* that states the *4.Kompanie* of *Panzer-Regiment 'Brandenburg'* (Bodenmüller's company) from *Panzergrenadier-Division 'Kurmark'* will deploy from Wünsdorf to Müncheberg on April 14th.[2] Clearly the *4.Kompanie* could not serve in the *9.Armee* and *4.Panzer-Armee* at the same time.

Almost simultaneously, I was contacted by Wolfgang Ockert, a German researcher and historian who was in the process of finalizing his own work on *Panzer-Regiment 'Brandenburg'*—Eduard Bodenmüller's unit. Mr. Ockert shared several scans of Bodenmüller's *Soldbuch* and award certificates he acquired as verification of Bodenmüller's assigned unit and areas of deployment. It was clear that

---

1 National Archives Record Administration (NARA) RG242 T-Series 78/Roll 305/Frame 6256926. Hereafter cited as NARA T78/305/6256926.
2 NARA T78/415/6383941.

Bodenmüller's unit stayed with *Panzergrenadier-Division 'Kurmark'* during the last months of the war and not *'Brandenburg'*. Why is this distinction so important? Because Bodenmüller's entire account supposedly takes place with *Panzergrenadier-Division 'BR'* and while Volume I is geographical based on the Seelow Heights, Volume II appears to take place in Silesia. This brought into question the authenticity of his entire second volume, if not much of his entire account altogether. Bodenmüller's own award certificate corroborates this inconsistency as his *Soldbuch* records that he received the Iron Cross Ist Class while assigned to *Panzergrenadier-Division 'Kurmark'* with the *9. Armee* in *Heeresgruppe Weichsel* at the end of March when, according to his second volume, he was supposedly serving with *Panzergrenadier-Division 'BR'* as part of *Heeresgruppe Mitte*.

Further analysis of Bodenmüller's account reveals other issues. His account starts off "Our unit is located somewhere near Litzmannstadt" (Lodz in Poland), sometime between February 1st-5th. That claim is impossible as the entire division had already withdrawn back to the Oder River in Silesia by that date. As previously noted, his unit never deployed with its parent division. What I believe occurred is that whoever sold his account to the original publisher, Antonio J. Munoz of Axis Europa Press, simply did not do their historical research and assumed that Bodenmüller served in the parent division of the same name—*'Brandenburg'*. Knowing the basic deployment of *Panzergrenadier-Division 'BR'*, whoever doctored Bodenmüller's account attempted to set up the story accordingly, with an intent to extend his account beyond what Bodenmüller originally kept as a diary. It is likely that Bodenmüller did pen a substantial portion of his own first volume before his death in 1990, but that his so called "second volume" was fictionalized and penned after he passed away by someone utterly unscrupulous, and with questionable historical credentials. This is revealed by the lack of any mention of a unit transfer or redeployment to a geographic area some 50 kilometers to the south, which is not an insignificant event in a soldier's world. As primary documents demonstrate, his *4. Kompanie* never left *Panzergrenadier-Division 'Kurmark'* and *'Kurmark'* never left the area around the Seelow Heights outside of Berlin.

This collected evidence was shared with the original publisher of Bodenmüller's account, Mr. Antonio J. Munoz. He agreed with the conclusion that he was likely sold a fictionalized second volume by someone looking to make a fast buck.

While I have focused my comments on the historical location of Bodenmüller's unit, specific exaggerations by Bodenmüller appear prevalent in what is believed to be his original diary entries. A discussion about Bodenmüller's potential exaggerations is beyond the scope of this work. However, there is a lesson to be learned when dealing with veteran accounts, German or otherwise. There is a huge publication market for first person perspective from World War II. These works are often billed as "authoritative" and this current work is no exception. However, the author or compiler of such works has a responsibility wherever possible to fact check the veracity of those accounts against the established, documented record of the time—unfortunately, few do. As appropriate, they should note discrepancies in veterans' accounts and offer alternative explanations based on official documents. Doing so does not necessarily undermine the veteran's credibility, but offers the reader an opportunity to evaluate the account and make a final decision for themselves on its veracity.

Where did all this leave my Publisher and I? I immediately recommend that any re-publication of Bodenmüller's two volume account cease. I incorporated the bulk of Bodenmüller's verified account from his first volume into my *The Oder Front 1945 Volume 2: Documents, Reports, and Personal Accounts* then proposed to my editor that I write a comprehensive history of *Panzergrenadier-Division 'BR'* based on the collected veteran accounts of Spaeter and other original research I had by then undertaken. After a careful review of the acquired primary documents, my publisher agreed, and this current book was born.

Panzergrenadier-Division 'Brandenburg' to the Front! is the first in-depth look at this division's five months of combat along the Eastern Front during World War II. This book draws on the previously unpublished personal papers and individual accounts by division veterans collected by Helmuth Spaeter, a former *Division* member, and supplemented by primary documents from the archival files of *Oberkommando der Wehrmacht*, *Oberkommando des Heeres* and *Lage Ost* maps of *Heeresgruppe Mitte*. This book represents the most complete and accurate treatment of *Panzergrenadier-Division 'BR'* published to-date. However, the book offers far more than the recounting of a single combat division. Drawing on an array of archival and related source material, this book provides a look into the often chaotic defensive fighting of *Heeresgruppe Mitte*. Detailed for the first time in English are the combat operations around Weißenberg and Bautzen where *Panzergrenadier-Division 'BR'* participated in the last *Wehrmacht* operational victory during the war.

 Panzergrenadier-Division 'BR' formed in the fall of 1944 out of the battered regiments of *Division 'Brandenburg'* scattered across southeastern Europe. This new late-war division maintained a lineage in name only to the earlier famous commandos whose remnants were sent from the Balkans to East Prussia where, along with its sister unit *Panzergrenadier-Division 'Großdeutschland'*, they formed the nucleus of the new *Panzer-Korps 'Großdeutschland'*.

 Panzer-Korps 'Großdeutschland' was the only operational reserve along the Eastern Front available to *Oberkommando des Heeres* (Army High Command or *OKH*) when the Soviet Vistula-Oder Strategic Offensive began in January 1945. The *Korps* was barely a month old in its formation. Both *Panzergrenadier-Divisions* were still forming. *'Brandenburg'* was worse off than its sister division as it had never operated as a single conventional combat formation before. Many of its officers and soldiers were new and had not been in combat before. Others were veterans that came from a half-dozen different combat units that had no previous association with *'Brandenburg'*. Much of the *Division's* equipment was new and unfamiliar. Training was limited to tactical maneuvers at the company level. Not all authorized weapons, equipment, and vehicles had arrived by mid-January. Some of its key divisional components were still forming or awaiting deployment from training grounds in the west, as in the case of its *Panzer-Regiment*. *Panzer-Korps 'Großdeutschland'* and its assigned divisions were not ready for battle.

 On orders of *Chef des Generalstabes des Heeres* (Chief of the General Staff of the Army) Heinz Guderian, who was in charge of *OKH*, the *Panzer-Korps 'Großdeutschland'* was deployed into the maw of one of the most powerful Soviet offensives of the war. The month long effort to forge a new *Korps* staff together with its two assigned divisions was immediately undone. Guderian broke up the *Korps* when he ordered it deployed south. *Panzergrenadier-Division 'Großdeutschland'* was left behind in East Prussia, as the still forming *Panzer-Korps* Command Staff and the incomplete *Panzergrenadier-Division 'BR'* deployed with the equally reorganized and unfamiliar *Fallschirmjäger-Panzer-Division 1 'Hermann Göring'* to Litzmannstadt (Lodz). These newly reorganized divisions were unrealistically expected to halt the advance of Marshal Georgy Zhukov's 1st Belorussian Front and Marshal Ivan Koniev's 1st Ukrainian Front despite the fact that both the *9.Armee* and *4.Panzer-Armee* failed to do so at the start of the Soviet winter offensive. It is no surprise that Guderian's intent met with operational failure.

 Panzergrenadier-Division 'BR' went into the defense immediately upon deployment. The only success it achieved was to maintain a brief corridor open for the withdrawing elements of the shattered *XXIV.Panzer-Korps* and *XXXXII.Armee-Korps* known as *Gruppe Nehring*. *Panzergrenadier-Division 'BR'*, along with the rest of the cut off German formations, had no choice but to conduct a 200 kilometer retreat west behind Soviet lines. The *Division* fought for survival against overwhelming odds each kilometer of the way. After its arduous trek west to the border of the Reich, it found itself defending along the Neisse River as part of the *4.Panzer-Armee* when the final Soviet assault on Germany began on April 16th, 1945. The grenadiers of *Panzergrenadier-Division 'BR'* were split into three separate groups cut off from their higher headquarters within the first several days of the Red Army's unprecedented land offensive against Germany. The men of the *Division* fought hard despite their desperate situation. Less than a week later the divisional elements recombined against the odds to participate in the *Wehrmacht's* last operational victory of the war against overextended Soviet formations. The successful counterattack of *'Brandenburg'* helped stabilize the frontline of the *4.Panzer-Armee* through the Reich's capitulation and prevented Dresden's capture by the 2nd Polish Army. Subsequently ordered into Czechoslovakia to support the withdrawal of the *1.Panzer-Armee*, the soldiers of *'Brandenburg'* found themselves caught in hostile territory between the advancing Red Army in the east and U.S. Army in the west during the last days of the war. With the Reich's capitulation imminent, they had to choose to either put down their arms and surrender to the Red Army, or withdraw west across Czechoslovakia to reach U.S Forces. For the men of *'Brandenburg'* their choice was an easy one. They selected to withdraw west against the terms of the Reich's capitulation to reach U.S. forces. By mid-May the *Division* had split into increasingly smaller groups that moved west and south by foot across hundreds of kilometers of increasing hostile territory without basic supplies or weapons. Some succeeded in their journey, but most did not.

The final months of the war in Europe continue to captivate my attention as a researcher and historian. The personal accounts by *'Brandenburg'* veterans contained in the following pages offer a rare glimpse into the brutal combat conditions in the winter and spring of 1945. They fill an important void in the historical record of the time and reveal much detail about how men serving in late war *Wehrmacht* divisions continued to fight long after the pendulum of victory inexorably swung against them.

A. Stephan Hamilton
Virginia, 2016

Acknowledgements

First and foremost, I need to thank Duncan Rogers for his support with this project. Had Duncan not reached out to me with the idea to write a historical introduction to the planned reprint of Eduard Bodenmüller's two volume *Diary of a Tank Gunner* this book would never have been researched, written or published. Wolfgang Ockert's prompting to do some historical digging on Bodenmüller's *4.Kompanie* accelerated the work that eventually led to the conclusions outlined in the Preface and terminated any further reprint of what can best be described as the semi-fictitious *Diary of a Tank Gunner*. Dr. Jürgen Vollbrecht, Director of Museum Bautzen, graciously researched and supplied select images of the city taken shortly after *Panzer-Korps 'GD'* liberated it from the 7th Guards Mechanized Corps in late April 1945. I greatly appreciated the time he spent discussing the history of Bautzen and the region during my very brief—and impromptu—visit to the city in late March, 2015. Duncan, Peter van Holstein and Mark C. Yerger sourced unique leader photographs for many of the central characters in the narrative that follows. Lastly, thanks go to my wife Kim who has endured my unending passion for research and writing along with my multitude of other hobbies.

Introduction

Few army, corps or division level records exist for German combat units that fought along the Eastern Front in the last year of the war in Europe. The documents that were kept during the hectic defend-and-retreat combat actions of 1945 were either destroyed by their own commands to prevent capture, or if captured by the Soviets, remain locked up in various Russian archives awaiting to be located or released into the public domain. What is left for the historian to recreate this past are the relevant documents scattered throughout the thousands of pages of *OKH* files, operational deployments depicted on the numerous *Lage Ost* maps, and the personal accounts of veterans.

By the end of World War II, Helmuth Spaeter found himself a *Major* in charge of the *Ib* (Quartermaster Section) of *Panzergrenadier-Division 'Brandenburg'*. Spaeter was a combat veteran and Knight's Cross winner who served in the original *Panzergrenadier-Division 'Großdeutschland'* during the fighting at Kursk in 1943. After the war he was an active member who ultimately rose through the administration to become President of the *Großdeutschland* Veterans Association in Germany. He authored several books on the history of *'Großdeutschland'* and *'Brandenburg'* after the war, collecting numerous personal accounts and documents along the way. It was by pure accident that I uncovered nearly 500 pages of collected and loosely organized first-person accounts by veterans of *Panzergrenadier-Division 'BR'* in the *Bundesarchiv-Militärarchiv* in Freiburg, Germany during a search for documents that I will outline later in this Introduction.

Spaeter used the collected accounts of his former comrades for his three volume *Geschichte des Panzerkorps Großdeutschland* (*History of Panzer-Korps Großdeutschland*) self-published in 1958. It is in Volume 3 that Spaeter covered the formation of *Panzergrenadier-Division 'BR'*. In comparing his collected first person accounts to his own published work, I determined that he utilized less than a third of the rich source material. Within the material he did use, it became obvious that he sometimes found himself confronted with conflicting veteran's perspectives of the same event. This is not uncommon in oral histories of war, as a soldier's mind often records the narrowest of views during conditions of intense combat where survival is paramount. Spaeter had to make content choices accordingly, and often selected a single perspective without reconciling both. But what Spaeter was most apt to do was to summarize much of the accounts at his disposal, sacrificing the potency of his companions' own words and experiences.

Spaeter wrote in Volume 3 that "to record the unique history of this unit in a non-dramatic, factual way based on documents and operational reports was the goal of the publisher and his co-workers. A conscious effort was made to avoid over-glorification, which could only have falsified the true picture of this unit."[1] Spaeter achieved that goal for the most part. As a member of the division who took on the role of its historian, he was prone to editorial decisions that served to maintain a certain storyline—one of sacrifice and honor. Yet the accounts he had access to reveal much more than the simple virtues of all wartime soldiers. Many of his comrades kept diaries during the war and recorded their memories right after the moment experienced. One aspect worth mentioning is the state of morale of this "elite" unit. Spaeter was careful in how he wrote about the morale and motivation of his comrades. He leads one to believe that a breakdown in morale only occurred in early May, and only among the new recruits of *'Brandenburg'*. Yet the words of many longtime veterans of

---

1   Hans Spaeter, *The History of Panzerkorps Großdeutschland, Volume 3* (J.J. Fedorowicz Publishing, Inc.: Winnipeg, 2000), p. 113.

his *Division*, reveal a continuous psychological struggle during the devastating battles in the winter and spring of 1945. *Oberleutnant* Eric Röseke wrote of his experiences during his withdrawal across Poland in January while cut off from his division that:

> When I wonder now, right after these difficult days in Poland, what gave me the ability to hold on and what gave me physical strength that I would never have imagined I had, I must say that some of it was the fear of becoming a prisoner of the Russians, but especially it was the responsibility I had as the leader of this group of eight dispersed soldiers and the more doubts that arose from my comrades, the stronger my will was to see my homeland with them again.

Fahnenjunker-Unteroffizier Held-Kleingründlach was a witness to the summary executions delivered to German soldiers who showed any signs of defeatism in the face of continued Soviet attacks during February-March by the commander of *Heeresgruppe Mitte, Generaloberst* Ferdinand Schörner.[2] "I can accept the lack of self-control of this army commander only because the fighting spirit of the German East Front soldiers was to some extent already very bad" he recorded. In some cases, Spaeter's comrades wanted it all to end. They couldn't face the continued battles, the endless withdrawals. Some charged straight into battle one last time, while others put a pistol to their head and pulled the trigger. *Obergefreiter* J. Klingenschmid recalled his desire to die during the massive Soviet bombardment that began their final offensive into Germany on April 16th:

> Here we had all come to terms with our lives when one shell after another howled past our ears, the air was hardly breathable and we were all just praying for the final shell. But fate still had something good in mind for some of us. However, we will never forget these hours, which demoralized even the strongest of us down to the core.

And upon the notification that their *Führer*, Adolf Hitler had died, and that all members of the *Wehrmacht* were to swear another oath to the new *Führer, Großadmiral* Karl Dönitz, *Hauptmann* Müller-Rochholz recalled thinking in those early days of May: "We will not swear a new oath. We are a sworn out bunch!"

The fellow veterans that Spaeter corresponded with shortly after the war were human. They were dealing with the fact that their country was defeated, split in two, and many of their comrades were still in Soviet prisoner-of-war camps. Their wartime experiences seemed, perhaps, better than the peace they had to endure. In some cases raw emotions were penned and forgotten. For example, left out was *Hauptmann* Müller-Rochholz's lament about letting a number of prisoners go after he captured some 600 soldiers of the 9th Polish Infantry Division during a successful counterattack in late April 1945 around Bautzen. He was subsequently sentenced to 25 years in a Soviet POW camp for the successful combat action, not for any atrocity committed on the battlefield. Writing in the 1970s after his release, he penned "I received 25 years in Russia for this battle. I should have given the order to shoot 300 prisoners of war!!" *Major* Kurt Steidl stated in his letters to Spaeter in the 1950s how he experienced some particularly cruel treatment at the hands of a Czech "Jewish" Guard when he went into captivity after the war, and wrote "Don't talk to me just about atrocities by the evil Germans!" All of these accounts are important contributions to the historiography of the period, and should not be ignored despite their arguably sensitive, if not personal nature.

Many wrote fondly of their wartime experiences despite the horror of brutal war unleashed by Nazi Germany on its neighbors that reaped a harvest of vengeance when the war reached the borders of the Reich. While the accounts by members of *'Brandenburg'* talk about the very real atrocities perpetrated on German soldiers and civilians alike in graphic terms, Spaeter sanitized or ignored much of that

---

2   Schörner was not promoted to *Generalfeldmarschall* until April 5th, 1945.

detail, tending to focus on operations and tactics. Further discussion of atrocities is required because of their prevalence during the fighting in Silesia. Significant academic work has been done on the nature of the Red Army's behavior when it first reached Eastern Europe in 1944 and throughout its advance into Germany during 1945. While it is easy to write off Red Army behavior as revenge for the atrocities committed by the *Wehrmacht* and *SS* on Soviet soil, this conveniently ignores the reality that the outright plunder, rape and murder by the Red Army began against citizens of Romania, and continued in Hungary, Yugoslavia, Czechoslovakia, and even Poland some six months before a single Soviet soldier touched the German soil of East Prussia.[3] Soviet officers and senior officials had months to issue orders and instill discipline among the Red Army before German territory was entered, however, the behavior was all but ignored. In some cases it was encouraged. Stalin himself dismissed his subordinates concerns outright using an old Russian proverb that "In every family there is a black sheep" and later by exclaiming he would not address the issue at all as he "will not allow anyone to drag the reputation of the Red Army in the mud."[4] As research continues in this largely ignored area of World War II history, more evidence has come to light regarding specific directives issued by Soviet commanders that incited their men to acts of violence contrary to the accepted laws of war. Senior Soviet commanders like Marshal Georgy Zhukov and Marshal Ivan Koniev issued documented orders that some have argued are similar in intent to those that earned prominent Nazis like Alfred Rosenberg and Fritz Sauckel death sentences for crimes against humanity at the Nuremberg War Trials.[5] Marshal Koniev's 1st Ukrainian Front political officers "were constantly trying to step up hatred towards Germans" and a "passion for revenge", as stated by Koniev's own political department.[6]

Much of the fighting contained in the following pages occurred in Saxony and the former German province of Silesia (now a part of Poland). These areas, like all other German Eastern provinces, experienced a high level of brutality by the Red Army. The liberated town of Striegau portended of things to come. The town was occupied by Soviet soldiers for just a few days, but when it was liberated in a counterattack, German soldiers were genuinely shocked. Everything in the town was destroyed. Around 6,000 German civilians were in the town before its occupation by the Soviets. Only 56 survivors were found when the *Wehrmacht* forced reoccupied the town. The survivors reportedly wandered the streets in a "psychologically broken" state due to the atrocities committed by Koniev's soldiers. Rape, murder, and plunder prevailed as the bodies of 200 civilians were uncovered in the houses and streets. These were not military age males. They were children, women and the elderly. The rest were expelled, likely to work camps.[7] Much of Silesia was already agreed to be turned over to Poland after the war, so there was no incentive for Soviet authorities to treat the subjected population with any humanity. In the accounts of 'Brandenburg' contained in this book they often credit the atrocities they saw in reoccupied villages in Silesia and particularly Saxony to "Russians", however, they

3   Norman M. Naimark, *The Russians in Germany: A History of the Soviet Zone of Occupation*, 1945-1949 (Harvard University Press Paperback Edition: Cambridge, 1997), pp. 69-71.
4   Ibid., p. 71. See Giles Macdonogh, *After the Reich* (Basic Books: New York, 2007), pp. 45-59. Giles argues that the Red Army rage was fueled by what they saw in the Nazi camps and prisons liberated during their drive across Poland. He also notes correctly that while rape and murder were rampant, not all Russians (or Poles) were rapists or child murders. There are noted cases where Russian commanders exercised martial justice by shooting the soldier perpetrators, sometimes right in front of their victims. Despite the caveat, the documented behavior by the Red Army and its Polish satellite forces to German civilians and military personnel was generally poor.
5   Alastair Noble, *Nazi Rule and the Soviet Offensive in Eastern Germany, 1944-1945: The Darkest Hour* (Sussex Academic Press: Portland, 2009), p. 226. Noble is quoting specific German research in making this point. Alfred Rosenberg was convicted at Nuremberg for, among other offensives, the systematic plundering of Europe, and Fritz Sauckel was convicted of crimes against humanity for the use of unpaid forced laborers who often were worked to death in German industry. In both cases, the argument goes, senior Red Army commanders like Zhukov and Koniev issued orders or were responsible for activities that achieved the same results both during and after the war.
6   Anthony Beevor, *The Fall of Berlin 1945* (Viking Press: New York, 2008), p. 169. See also Naimark, p. 72.
7   Noble, p. 228.

never realized at the time, or in most cases even after the war, that the soldiers that committed the rapes and murders were Polish.

The main area of advance between Weisswasser and Rothenburg starting on April 16th, 1945 was given to the newly formed 2nd Polish Army. This area was where the veterans of *Panzergrenadier-Division 'BR'* fought from the start of the final Soviet offensive into Germany until April 30th. Their accounts are replete with scenes of rape, murder and empty villages that simply cannot be conveniently disentangled from their tales of combat. Atrocity was a part of the battlefield in a way never experienced by British, American, or French soldiers on the Western Front. More detail is provided on the 2nd Polish Army in Chapter 16, but a brief comment on its formation and leadership is required for context. The Polish officers and soldiers for this formation were recruited from towns and villages that long suffered under the genocidal occupation policies of Nazi Germany and were recently liberated by the Red Army. They had an understandably intense desire for revenge.[8] The formation was established in the late fall of 1944 and had not gone into combat prior to April 16th. Its commander, General Karol Świerczewski, was a committed Communist and anti-Fascist who joined the Bolshevik Party in 1918, and saw service with the Red Army during the Russian Civil War and the Soviet invasion of Poland in 1919. He fought on the side of communists in the Spanish Civil War and rose to the rank of General in the Red Army by the outbreak of World War II in Europe. Despite his military experience he proved to be a particularly poor tactician and was temporarily relieved of command by Koniev during the fighting. His personal desire for glory combined with a desire for revenge among his soldiers, cut a swath of destruction across the frontline of *Panzer-Korps 'Großdeutschland'*. Captured German prisoners-of-war were often shot. German civilians were raped, brutalized, and murdered. Homes and business were routinely plundered or destroyed. Vehicles of the 2nd Polish Army were painted with slogans like "For Majdanek!", "For Warsaw!", "Death to every German!" or "Revenge for 1939!"[9]

Recent scholarly research into the various church burial records throughout the towns and villages that dot the area of Saxony within the former East German State known as the *Deutsche Demokratische Republik (DDR)* revealed the long covered up and forgotten brutality. The church burial records combined with extensive first person interviews conducted by Theodor Seidel corroborate the accounts by *'Brandenburger'* veterans of what they saw and experienced. In the town of Jauer for example, 31 captured German soldiers were executed through a shot to the base of their neck by Polish soldiers. In Niesky more than a dozen children, old men and women were murdered. In See a dozen civilians were murdered, with one father shooting himself after witnessing the rape of his daughter. Female refugees passing through the area were captured by Polish soldiers and raped, often with their children watching. These scenes were repeated in Förstgen, Weißenberg, Königswartha, Neschwitz, and Burk. When Russian and Polish soldiers captured the city of Bautzen, they plundered, raped and murdered freely, often while drunk. The city was retaken by soldiers of the *20.Panzer-Division*, *Fallschirm-Panzer-Division 1 'Hermann Göring'* and elements of *'Brandenburg'* after only a few days of Soviet occupation. What they found was gruesome. Like Steinau, survivors roamed the streets in shock. Civilians were just not found murdered, but tortured, as in the case of a woman left to lie in the open with her breasts bayoneted. Children's skulls were crushed by the butt of a rifle or their throats slit in their beds. Age was no deterrent as a retirement home was not spared vengeance.[10] One

---

8   Naimark, p. 75.

9   Theodor Seidel, *Kriegsverbrechen in Sachsen. Die vergessenen Toten von April/Mai 1945* (Leipziger Universitätsverlag GMBH: Leipzig, 2013), p. 41, 46 and Kazimierz Kaczmarek, *Polacy w bitwie pod Budziszynem* (Wyadawnictwo Interpress: Warsaw, 1970), p. 28.

10   I decided not to include any images of dead civilians for this book as this topic is not the main focus of my research and would likely only serve as a distraction. However, pictures of violence against German civilians in Bautzen by Soviet soldiers do exist. They were taken by the city's residents shortly after the battle and are catalogued in the Bautzen city archives and on permanent display in Museum Bautzen.

particularly brutal incident occurred as members of the 2nd Polish Army captured nearly 200 men of the *33.Volkssturm-Bataillon* just outside the city. They were placed in a locked barn in Niederkaina that was then set on fire. Anyone who tried to escape the burning barn was shot down by machineguns. All were killed.[11]

How did the men of *Panzer-Korps 'Großdeutschland'* and *Panzergrenadier-Division 'BR'* respond to the excesses of the Red Army and 2nd Polish Army? This is less clear. In several accounts, the veterans themselves lamented the fact that despite what they saw they were still required to capture prisoners. Accounts are clear that during the fighting thousands of Russian and Polish prisoners were taken. In the case of one high ranking Soviet General who was captured severely wounded, he was given medical treatment and ultimately released during the Soviet offensive south to capture Prague in early May. Clearly the desire to shoot captured prisoners existed. Shooting of captured prisoners most certainly occurred during and shortly after the heat of battle, often in retaliation for what was witnessed in recaptured villages and towns. Wounded were particularly easy targets as they could not walk on their own and neither side afforded them required transportation or medical care. Specific cases of retaliatory atrocities are not well documented outside "official" sources of the former *DDR* that routinely trumped up the excess of "Nazi" or "Fascist" troops while purposely obfuscating any committed by the "Heroes" of the Red Army that "liberated" Eastern Germany. Recent Polish scholarship does corroborate certain communist era reports and they are provided here for balance. According to former *DDR* sources a medical battalion of the 7th Guards Mechanized Corps was captured in the area of Weißenberg. The medical personnel and wounded were reportedly bayonetted and crushed by the treads of tanks. While it is not known who perpetrated this atrocity, what is known is that Weißenberg was recaptured by *Panzergrenadier-Division 'BR'* during a counterattack in late April. In Bautzen, where elements of *Panzergrenadier-Division 'BR'* along with *Fallschirm-Panzer-Division 1 'Hermann Göring'* and *20.Panzer-Division* fought, the medical battalion of the Soviet 254th Rifle Division was captured and their medical staff as well as wounded were also found "tortured and shot". In Spreefurt (today Uhyst) 102 Soviet and Polish POWs were found shot, and in Horka, north of Crostwitz, (not to be confused with Wehrkirch (today Horka) farther east near the Neisse, some 200 Polish wounded soldiers of the 9th Polish Infantry Division were reportedly killed on April 26th.[12] We know from German accounts that *Kampfgruppe Wiethersheim* of the *20.Panzer-Division* operated in this area at that time, along the left flank of *'Brandenburg'*. This level of battlefield brutality and counter-brutality between armed combatants should be viewed through the prism of Nazi racial policies carried out among the occupied territories of Poland and the Soviet Union during the period 1939-1944. Unfortunately, such heinous human behavior during war was not left behind on the Eastern Front at the end of World War II. Far from being unique to this time period or its combatants, such wartime brutality has manifested itself through radical political ideology, racial hatred, and religious intolerance on other fields of battle across the world despite the existence of the Geneva Conventions and internationally accepted laws of war.

Writing in the 1950s, Spaeter had no access to the vast amount of primary documents now available to even the most amateur of researchers. Their lack of accessibility was the reason that some technical errors occurred in his writing as he occasionally misidentified units or placed them in the wrong location. He also knew little of the overall Soviet operational picture that confronted *Panzergrenadier-Division 'BR'*. When his three volume history was translated into English and published by J.J.

11 Seidel, pp. 23-30, 39-54, 57, 59, 62, 65, 66, 68-70, 88-97. There is some suggestion that the atrocity in Niederkaina may have been conducted by troops of the 13th Guards Tank Regiment under the command of Major Alexander Lukitsch Fomenko during his unit's initial advance in the area. Lukitsch's unit fought in Bautzen, where additional atrocities against German civilians occurred. In 1972 he was awarded the title of "Honorary Major" of Bautzen. The source for this information comes from the Museum Bautzen.
12 Ibid., p. 40. The number fluctuates to as much as 300 according to Czesław Grzelak, Henryk Stańczyk and Stefan Zwoliński, *Armia Berlinga, I Żymierskiego* (Wyadawnictwo Neriton: Warsaw, 2003), p. 277.

Fedorowicz between the years 1992-2000, they were not updated to resolve inconsistencies in the text or reflect new research available at the time.

The accounts of *Panzergrenadier-Division 'BR'* veterans contained in the following pages are derived primarily from the letters, diaries, and personal notes of the following unit members:

Oberarzt Dr. Braune, Troop Physician of *Heeres-Flak-Artillerie-Abteilung 'BR'*
Oberleutnant i.G. Hamburg Bröker, *IIb* of the *Division*
SS-Sturmbannführer Graf von Egloffstein, commander of *Fahrschwadron 'BR'*
Obergefreiter R. Felhofer of *1.Kompanie* of *Regiment 2 'BR'*
Oberfeldwebel Goller, of *3.Kompanie* of *Regiment 1 'BR'*
Leutnant Grosser, *O1* of *Jäger-Regiment 1 'BR'*
Fahnenjunker-Unteroffizier (later *Wachtmeister13*) Held-Kleingründlach, *2.Batterie* commander
    in *Sturmgeschütz-Brigade 'GD'* subordinated to the *Division*
Leutnant Kass, commander *2.Kompanie* of *Panzerjäger-Abteilung 'BR'*
Obergefreiter J. Klingenschmid of 3rd Platoon, *1.Kompanie* of *I.Btl./Jäg.Rgt.2*
Hauptmann Herbert Noeres, *Adjutant* of *II.Bat./Pz.Rgt. 'BR'*
Hauptmann Friedrich Müller-Rochholz, commander of *Panzer-Sturm-Pionier Bataillon 'BR'*
Oberleutnant (later *Hauptmann*) *der Reserve* Eric Röseke, commander of *6.Kompanie* of
    Jägerregiment 1 'BR' until February 8th
Leutnant (later *Oberleutnant*) Schmalbruch, commander *3.Kompanie (mot)* of *I.Btl./Jäg.Rgt.2*
Gefreiter Siebert-Göttingen, member of a *Fahnenjunker-Kompanie* as part of *Kampfgruppe*
    Spornring dispatched as field replacements for the *Division*
Leutnant G. Simons, company commander in *II.Btl./Jäg.Rgt. 2 'BR'*
Major Helmuth Spaeter, *Ib* (Quartermaster) of the *Division Hauptmann der Reserve* (later *Major*)
    Konrad (Kurt) Steidl, commander *I.Bataillon* of *Jägerregiment 2 'BR'*[14]
Fahnenjunker-Unteroffizier Hans Stübling, member of *Panzer-Sturm-Pionier Bataillon 'BR'*

These veterans' accounts offer a wide and useful cross-section of the entire *Division's* experience from formation to surrender. All major combat formations are represented. While the above names represent the main contributors to the accounts collected by Spaeter, he also introduced references apparently acquired through conversations with other veteran acquaintances. These accounts referenced in his notes are not delineated by the usual "person X stated. . . ." This made it difficult to identify what division member provided the account. While Spaeter knew who he was talking about, he left no reference to the person's name. Thankfully, these were few and far between and I have incorporated them accordingly.

As noted earlier, when Spaeter wrote his history he did not have the benefit of access to an enormous amount of both primary documents and published reference material. The first person narratives in this current work are supplemented by available primary documents located in Germany's *Bundesarchiv-Militärarchiv* (hereafter cited as BAMA) and the United States' National Archives Records Administration (hereafter cited as NARA). Among the records accessed were various division status reports available from the files of *Generalinspekteur der Panzertruppen* (General Inspector of Panzer Troops) the daily situation reports in the vast collection of *Oberkommando des Heeres* files (*OKH*). The previously unpublished postwar study of the initial defense and retreat of the *4.Panzer-Armee* during January-February 1945 written by *Generalmajor s.Zt. Kommandeur des Sperrverbandes* Hans von Ahlfen in 1946 for the U.S Army Europe Historical Division titled *Rueckzug von der Weichsel*

---

13   First Sergeant in the Cavalry; *Feldwebel* equivalent.
14   Steidl's given name was Konrad, but in every account used for this book, including those he gave himself, he used the name Kurt. I have selected to use Kurt throughout this book in accordance with his own apparent preference.

zur Oder im Januar 1945 infolge des russischen Durchbruchs aus dem Baranov und Pulawy Brueckenkopf (*Retreat from the Vistula to the Oder in January 1945 as a result of the Russian breakthrough from the Baranov and Pulawy Bridgeheads*) and the final surrender of the *Heeresgruppe Mitte* documented by *Generalleutnant* Oldwig Otto von Natzmer who served as the *Chefs des Generalstabes* for the *Heeresgruppe* were both translated and integrated into the text. Newly discovered "Z" series postwar studies were located in the *Bundesarchiv-Militärarchiv*. Specific "Z" studies accessed for this work include *ZA1-2058 Der Feldzug Gegen Die Sowjetunion Im Mittelabschnitt Der Ostfront 1941-1945, Zehnter Teil* (*The Campaign against the Soviet Union in the Central Portion of the Eastern Front 1941-1945, Part Ten*) by *General der Infanterie a.D.* Rudolf Hofmann and *ZA1-2759 Versorgungsführung der H.Gr. Mitte bei Rückzug und Verteidigung März-Mai 1945* (*Supply Management of H.Gr. Mitte during Retreat and Defense from March-May 1945*) author unknown. In addition to the primary documents, the daily situation maps for *Heeresgruppe A* and *Heeresgruppe Mitte* known as *Lage Ost* maps were re-discovered in the U.S. National Archives Records Administration in College Park, Maryland after being misfiled for more than 40 years. In the 1980s the National Archives Records Administration retuned all the original *Lage Ost* maps in their collection back to Germany after creating a microfiche image of each. That never happened with nearly 500 misfiled maps. The act of opening the archive box and unfolding the *Lage Ost* maps for *H.Gr Mitte* revealing their near 6 foot by 4 foot hand pencil marked surface likely occurred only a few times, if at all, between their wartime capture and my February 2014 visit. Each map was prepared by intelligence officers of *Fremde Heeres Ost* (*FHO*-Foreign Armies East) at *OKH* each evening based on the submitted reports received from the various *Heeresgruppe* Headquarters and overlaid directly with the positions of enemy units. Information from prisoners-of-war and other details were often added in pencil or by typed notes glued to the maps. In the absence of the actual *Heeresgruppe Kriegstagebuch* (War Diary) for both *Mitte* and *A*, these maps are essential for understanding the operational picture in their areas of command.

I utilized select secondary sources to provide both background and context. Among the most useful secondary sources was Spaeter's *Die Brandenburger, eine deutsche Kommandotruppe: zbV 800* (*Commando Troops: Special Division 800*) published in Germany in 1991. This excellent work has yet to be translated into English.[15] *Die Brandenburger* provided the background for each of the 'Brandenburg' regiments fighting in the Balkans and south east Europe in the fall of 1944. This book ends with the formation of *Panzergrenadier-Division 'BR'* in the fall of 1944. David Glantz's impressive 1986 *Art of War Symposium: From the Vistula to the Oder: Soviet Offensive Operations, October 1944-March 1945* two volume proceedings transcript was essential for deconstructing the Soviet Winter Offensive that led to the destruction of *Heeresgruppe A*. His work provided both Soviet and German operational perspectives that were essential in reconstructing the events that led to the *4.Panzer-Armee* and *Panzer-Korps 'Großdeutschland'* being cut off, and tracing their withdrawal back to the Oder and Neisse Rivers. No published work to-date can match Glantz's thorough treatment of Soviet operations during the winter offensive of 1945. Also used was Glantz's *Red Army Officers Speak! Interviews with veterans of the Vistula-Oder Operation (January-February 1945)* that offers an unparalleled first person Soviet perspective on both their own and German operations, to include what went well and what did not. Hans von Ahlfen published an account of the fighting in Silesia in 1963 titled *Der Kampf um Schlesien, 1944-1945*. Von Ahlfen's recorded experiences during the withdrawal across Poland and as Fortress commander of Breslau, coupled with the veteran accounts he included in his book, provided firsthand knowledge of *Heeresgruppe Mitte* operations for a period in time that lacks primary documents. Eberhard Berndt's original research for his 2012 *Die Kämpfe um Weißenberg und Bautzen im April 1945* brought to light many new aspects of the fighting in Saxony. His work was instrumental in developing a clear narrative of the fighting around Weißenberg and

---

15   The original veteran's accounts that this work was based upon were also located in the *Bundesarchiv-Militärarchiv*.

Bautzen in late April.[16]

Additional research into the organization and combat actions of the 2nd Polish Army was necessary given the prominence of this unit in the fighting opposite *Panzer-Korps 'Großdeutschland'* during the final Soviet offensive into Germany. *Polacy w bitwie pod Budziszynem* (Poland in the Battle of Bautzen) written by Kazimierz Kaczmarek was published in 1970 while Poland was under the influence of its pro-Soviet Communist regime. It provides excellent background and context from the Polish perspective of the battle, despite using the typical Communist jargon of the time. The most useful Polish work consulted was *Armia Berlinga, I Żymierskiego* (*The Army of Berlinga and Żymierskiego*) by authors Czesław Grzelak, Henryk Stańczyk and Stefan Zwoliński. Published in 2003, this is a superb study that covers all aspects of the 1st and 2nd Polish Armies. Particular attention is given their wartime establishment during the occupation of Poland by the Soviet Union to include training, leadership, supply and combat operations. It proved an essential source to understand how *Panzer-Korps 'Großdeutschland'* and other elements of the *4.Panzer-Armee* were able to achieve such an overwhelming operational victory in the last days of World War II.

A note on terminology is in order. German town names utilized during World War II are cited in the text. Given that these accounts were in German and often based upon maps of the time period, it made it ahistorical to use modern day, or even prewar names, especially when referring to Polish and Czechoslovakian towns. For consistency and historical accuracy I use the German names and place the Polish or Czech names in parentheses, as in the case of Litzmannstadt (Lodz). In several cases German town names were changed as they were themselves renamed during the Nazi period. German units are cited using their original German nomenclature with several modifications. English translations are used for German units at the platoon level or below. For example, instead of writing *Erkundungs Zug*, you will see Reconnaissance Platoon. Many of the accounts referred to other units using shorthand or slang, so for clarity I included the actual unit name. For example, almost everyone universally referred to the *I.(gep)Bataillon/Jägerregiment 1 'BR'* as the "SPW Bataillon". I kept the original designation *I.(gep)Bataillon*. Reconnaissance Platoon refers to one or more unspecified platoons from *Panzer-Aufklärungs-Abteilung 'BR'*. Typical German abbreviations used the scheme company (numbers), battalion (roman numerals) followed by a forward "/" then the regiment. So that the *1.Kompanie, I.Bataillon* of *Jägerregiment 1 'BR'* will be abbreviated as *1./I./Jäg.Rgt. 1 'BR'*. In order to make it easier for the reader I abbreviated the formation type in this format *1.Kp./I.Btl./Jäg. Rgt. 1 'BR'*. Other slang used by the veterans was clarified where possible. Two examples were the use of "sleds" and *Geschütz* in place of *Sturmgeschütz*. In terms of plurals, I tried to keep to a normal use of "e" like in *Sturmgeschütze* and "en" as in the case of *Kompanien*. I italicize the word *Division* when used alone to represent *Panzergrenadier-Division 'BR'* as many of the veterans often just state "the division". This helps to avoid confusing the reader as to what division is referenced.

Readers will come across the term "Seydlitz" or "Free Germany" referred to by the veterans of *'Brandebourg'*. These German soldiers appeared on the East Front battlefield increasingly from 1943. By 1945 they were a part of every major Soviet offensive. These German men were former prisoners-of-war in Soviet captivity that conducted both covert and direct combat actions against the *Wehrmacht* to assist the Soviets in gaining intelligence, mislead German forces, and launch attacks. These German soldiers were known to *Oberkommando der Wehrmacht* (*OKW*) universally as "Seydlitz Troops." They were named after *General der Artillerie* Walther von Seydlitz-Kurzbach who was captured in the battle for Stalingrad. Seydlitz was a key Soviet collaborator and soon became the leader of the *Bund deutscher Offiziere* (League of German Officers) and a prominent member of the *Nationalkomitee Freies Deutschland* (National Committee Free Germany). There appears to be some debate in Germany today of the existence of an organized group of ex-*Wehrmacht* officers and soldiers fighting their own

---

16   Berndt's book also features rare images of the fighting, to include destroyed German and Soviet vehicles, in and around Weißenberg and Bautzen.

countrymen under Soviet command. While documentary evidence is scarce to non-existent in Russian Archives on the movement, the hundreds of first-person accounts by former *Wehrmacht* veterans of the direct use of "Seydlitz Troops" in combat operations at war's end cannot be denied. Many of the "Seydlitz Troops" became ranking members of the postwar *Deutsche Demokratische Republik* and participated in establishing one of the most brutally repressive regimes in post-World War II Europe.

Another term that requires a brief explanation is "Cossack". There was a large recruitment effort late in the war to create combat units from Soviet prisoners-of-war to help make up for battlefield losses. The history of the Soviet peoples serving in organized military formations under command of the *Wehrmacht* is complex and diverse. The use of former Soviet prisoners by the *Wehrmacht* started back in 1942 with the creation of the Russian National Army of Liberation (RONA), and the employment of native Cossacks. National Socialist racial policy precluded the full mobilization of any native forces from the Soviet Union to help defeat the Communist state, and internal politics between the *Heer* and the *SS* also caused friction in the creation and employment of such forces. Only late in the war were full combat divisions fielded that were made up of former Soviet prisoners. A number of Cossack Battalions fought alongside *'Brandenburg'* in the final months of the war. While there was initially skepticism in their loyalty and ability to fight, they proved themselves every bit as capable as their German counterparts.[17]

No single volume history of *Panzergrenadier-Division 'BR'* exists. Outside of Helmuth Spaeter's multi-volume history of the family of *'Großdeutschland'* units already discussed, three other historical works should be mentioned. Two are discussed below, while a third work, *Division Brandenburg: Die Haustruppe des Admirals Canaris*, written by Will Berthold and published in 1959 is discussed in the Conclusion. There is Franz Kurowski's *Deutsche Kommandotrupps 1939-1945 (German Commando Troops 1939-1945)* that was translated into English and published under the title *The Brandenburgers Global Mission* in 1997 by J.J. Fedorowicz and Eric Lefevre's 1983 *La Division Brandebourg 1939-1945*, translated into English and published under the title of *Brandenburg Division: Commandos of the Reich*, published by Histoire & Collections in 2000. At the time of this writing, both books are nearly 20-30 years old. As an observation, both works read like adventure novels more than works of history, and both were based on little more than a few dozen English, French and German secondary sources. Both works recount the earlier period of *'Brandenburg'*, when it was employed as a commando unit in some detail. While claiming to cover the last year of the war, the authors reserve a scant 20 and 10 pages respectively to cover eight months of formation and combat history of *Panzergrenadier-Division 'BR'*. While it is tempting to trace a seamless lineage of the *'Brandenburgers'* from *Sonderkommandos* to *Panzergrenadiers*, it is ahistorical to do so in a single book. Spaeter knew this, which is why we wrote an entire book on the *'Brandenburg'* commandos that ended in September 1944. While he included some of the earlier commando experiences of *zbV Division 'Brandenburg'* in his multi-volume history of the *'Großdeutschland'* units, he did so for context only. He knew there was a clear break in lineage between these two very different formations that in the end, shared little more than a name and some of its veterans. Spaeter noted this fact regarding *Panzergrenadier-Division 'BR'* when he wrote "Its battalions and *Kampfgruppen* were characterized by outstanding fighting spirit and were extremely familiar with the fighting methods of the Soviets and the Soviet-led partisan units of the southeast (Balkans), however they were not used to participating in division-size operations."[18] Furthermore, while the division is grouped under the umbrella of *'Großdeutschland'* Spaeter also notes that it "shared little in common with its new sister division, *Panzergrenadier-Division 'Großdeutschland'*, in terms of the origins of its personnel or the nature of its tactical employment."[19]

---

17 Werner Knop, *Prowling Russia's Forbidden Zone: A Secret Journey into Soviet Germany* (Alfred A. Knopp: New York, 1949), pp. 85-86.
18 Spaeter, *The History of Panzerkorps Großdeutschland, Volume 3*, p. 5.
19 Ibid.

Panzergrenadier-Division 'BR' was one of the many late war combat divisions fielded from the burnt out carcasses of other units. The *Wehrmacht's* ability to continue the war against all logic was rooted in its ability to masterfully reform, refit, and redeploy combat divisions from the barest nucleus of various staffs or destroyed units; stitched together through its ingenious replacement system in support of a doomed Third Reich. Most of these new formations established in 1944 and 1945 were shadows of the combat divisions fielded in 1940 and 1941. *'Brandenburg'* was no exception and yet its men fought to the end of the war and beyond. The bonds of camaraderie that held this group together can be traced to the late war improvisations of the *Wehrmacht's Ersatzheer* (Replacement Army). Many historians have attempted to credit the continued resistance of the *Wehrmacht* despite its many battlefield setbacks to a host of reasons like ideology or better weapon systems (See Chapter 4 and Chapter 14). These reasons, however, simply sit at the periphery of the core reason often missed in attempts at an explanation. It was the *Ersatzheer* more than any other factor that kept men in the field and maintained Nazi Germany as a political entity until the very end. Through the improvisations of the *Ersatzheer* once destroyed units like *zbv Division 'Brandenburg'* were able to take to the field of battle again in another form.

The famous commandos of *'Brandenburg'* were no more by December 1944. Their ranks were depleted during the bitter combat actions across the Balkans during the fall months. For those veterans that did remain, the irregular combat tactics that characterized small unit anti-partisan warfare had to be replaced with conventional division level tactics and operations. New and unfamiliar equipment had to be integrated into the unit. Coordinated operations between armor, infantry, and artillery elements had to be learned. New officers and NCOs had to prove capable to lead and earn the trust of their men, while new replacements that arrived had to be trained. Trust and camaraderie had to form across a diverse set of backgrounds and experiences. The monumental process of re-forging the *Sonderkommandos* of *'Brandenburg'* into a conventional *Panzergrenadier-Division* occurred in only a few short weeks before it deployed into the path of one of the largest land offensives conducted during World War II. The odds of survival were not in their favor, yet the *Division* did survive and a strong bond of camaraderie forged among the men during those harrowing first months. The camaraderie that emerged fostered an effective fighting force that secured a series of improbable victories at war's end.

What follows is their story.

1

The Evolution of 'Brandenburg'

Panzergrenadier-Division 'Brandenburg' and *Division 'Brandenburg'* shared little in common beyond their names. *Division 'Brandenburg'* was an umbrella organization that comprised an assortment of special purpose units known as *Sonderkommando* that were established to carry out tailored military missions behind enemy lines. *Panzergrenadier-Division 'BR'* was a regular *Panzergrenadier-Division* formed for conventional frontline combat. The political-military evolution of the *Sonderkommandos* is critical to understand the circumstances of its final transformation from an unconventional to conventional force.

The formation of what became *Division 'Brandenburg'* is traced to the vision of *Hauptmann* Dr. Theodor Von Hippel. Von Hippel served under *General* Paul von Lettow-Vorbeck during World War I. Von Lettow-Vorbeck conducted one of the most brilliant guerilla campaigns in military history against the British in East Africa. A small well trained force of approximately 3,000 German officers, non-commissioned officers, and 12,000 East African askaris tied up a force of nearly 200,000 British Soldiers for more than four years across German East Africa, Portuguese East Africa and Rhodesia. The end result was that this diminishing unconventional force kept an increasingly larger conventional force off the battlefields of Western Europe where they were needed.[1] During the inter-war period von Hippel attempted to convince the *Reichswehr* of the value in establishing small elite teams with expertise in infiltration to conduct acts of sabotage behind enemy lines. Their mission was to disrupt command-and-control, communications, and logistics. The small interwar *Reichswehr* was in no position to support the creation of such a radical force, and he found no support among the traditional military minded command. With the establishment of the *Wehrmacht* and expansion of various military services, von Hippel took his concept to *Konteradmiral* Wilhelm Canaris, who in 1935 was in command of the *Abwehr*, the German intelligence service.[2]

Canaris gave von Hippel permission to establish a small force of saboteurs that fell under control of the *Abwehr/Abteilung II Sonderdienst* office led by then *Oberst* Erwin von Vivremont Lahousen. This small force was given the cover name of *zbV Lehr und Bau Kompanie* (Special Purpose Training and Construction Company)—a fitting cover for an organization designed to destroy rather than build.

The *zbv Lehr and Bau Kompanie* were soon expanded in the fall of 1939 after a series of successes in Czechoslovakia and Poland. Its members were German speaking volunteers from across Europe, as well as the German diaspora in Africa and the Americas. They brought diverse experiences and skills well beyond that of traditional military recruits. The unit was given the official name of *Baulehr-*

---

1   Some estimates run as high as 250,000. The East African Campaign was the genesis for the ideas that gave rise to the *'Brandenburgers'* of World War II. The campaign is largely unknown in the west outside the communities of historians who study guerilla campaigns and special operations. Several dated yet excellent books on the topic include Charles Miller, *Battle for the Bundu: The First World War in East Africa* (Macmillan Publishing Co., Inc: New York, 1974), Brian Gardner, *On to Kilimanjaro: The bizarre story of the First World War in East Africa* (Macfadden-Bartell: New York, 1964), and Leonard Mosley, *Duel for Kilimanjaro, Africa 1914-1918: The Dramatic Story of an Unconventional War* (Ballantine Books: New York, 1963).

2   Established in 1938, *Ausland/Abwehr* was organized as follows in 1939: *Abteilung Ausland* (Abroad); *Abteilung I Nachrichtenbeschaffung* (Information Gathering); *Abteilung II Sonderdienst* (Special Service); *Abteilung III Abwehr* (Defense); *Auslandsprüfstelle* (Foreign Assessment); and *Auslands-Telegramm-Prüfstelle* (Signals Assessment).

Battalion zbV 800 (Special Purpose Construction Battalion 800) and based in of Brandenburg on der Havel (hereafter referred to as Brandenburg/Havel). However, being referred to as a "Special Purpose Construction Battalion" did not resonate well among its diverse assemblage of unit members. According to an undocumented account, this atypical military unit adopted the name *'Brandenburg'* over the course of a 1939 Christmas Eve celebration, referring to its home base. The name stuck. For the rest of the war until late 1944, the name *'Brandenburg'* referred to the ever increasing number of special operations soldiers fielded by the *Abwehr*, then *OKW*.

The training of *'Brandenburg'* soldiers fell into two parts. They received traditional combat engineering training that focused on demolition, to include emplacing and removing charges. Mission specific training was conducted in long-range reconnaissance and the infiltration of enemy territory undetected. To capture their assigned objectives efficiently, but more importantly, quietly, the men of *'Brandenburg'* trained in hand-to-hand combat techniques. Even a *Fallschirmjäger* (parachute) platoon was incorporated giving *'Brandenburg'* a nascent capability (and largely unproven at that time) to infiltrate deep behind enemy lines undetected. *'Brandenburg'* received special skills that set the men of this unit apart from their traditional counterparts in the *Wehrmacht*. While their *Wehrmacht* comrades trained in conventional combat that focused on the integration of infantry, armor, and supporting fires (artillery and air support) at the battalion and regimental level, *'Brandenburg'* focused on small team and individual combat. This became an issue in 1945 as many of these men found themselves in a new *Panzergrenadier-Division* fighting as regular infantry in the frontline without any of the skills or experience necessary to excel in conventional combat.

The hallmark of the unit was its pioneering use of camouflage in order to carry out their missions successfully. They either adapted the use of semi-camouflage or full camouflage through the use of enemy uniforms. These skills came into use during the campaign in the west in 1940 where the seizure of bridges ahead of the advancing *Panzer* columns was important, especially against those that crossed the Maas River. The use of an enemy uniform layered over one's actual uniform to infiltrate behind enemy lines was fraught with both legal and practical challenges. Legally, The international Hague Convention II, "Convention with Respect to the Laws and Customs of War on Land" that went into effect on September 4th, 1900 contained specific language regarding the classification of soldiers who donned enemy uniforms. Article 23 Regulations Respecting the Laws and Customs of Land Warfare, subsection (f) reads: "Besides the prohibitions provided by special Conventions, it is especially prohibited: . . . (f.) To make improper use of a flag of truce, the national flag, or military ensigns and the *enemy's uniform*, as well as the distinctive badges of the Geneva Convention. . . ." [emphasis added]. In a Europe dominated by conservative Victorian Era monarchies, the use of camouflage to gain an advantage in combat was viewed as an ungentlemanly, if not radical form of warfare. An additional provision in Article 29 on spies stated "An individual can only be considered a spy if, acting clandestinely, or on false pretenses, he obtains, or seeks to obtain information in the zone of operations of a belligerent, with the intention of communicating it to the hostile party." The Hague Convention's ruling meant that soldiers of one nation captured behind the lines of another not in uniform could be treated as spies. The determination of who was a combatant or a spy was in practice left up to the capturing authorities, and being labeled a spy meant likely execution. Execution was often the case even when soldiers claimed to be conducting a legitimate military mission like seizing a bridge. Given that little distinguished between someone caught wearing an enemy uniform over their true uniform or just wearing the former made little difference legally if caught. Soon after the war started the use of multiple layers of uniforms during a mission was halted by the men of *'Brandenburgers'* as impracticable. Whatever uniform or disguise was necessary to complete the mission would be worn.

While the use of infiltration and spies was frowned upon in legal convention at that time, the use of disguise as a means to carry out a military mission during wartime was accepted and rewarded throughout military history. During the 19th Century it was used by both the Union and Confederate forces during the American Civil War, nearly 40 years before the new conventions were signed. It is a little known fact that the United States Medal of Honor was first granted to Union commandos, who were labeled "spies" by the Confederate authorities, and not to soldiers who distinguished themselves in conventional battle. The original recipients of the Medal of Honor were the 19 out of 22 Union Army volunteers led by James J. Andrews who donned civilian clothes and infiltrated the Confederacy in April 1962. Their military purpose was to destroy the rail links to the key transportation hub of the city of Chattanooga, isolating it from Atlanta. It was their intent to make the city vulnerable to attack by the forces of Union Major-General Ormsby M. Mitchel through this act of sabotage. Many of the soldiers who were eventually captured by the Confederacy were tried as spies and executed. This prompted others to escape and make their way back to Union lines often by again disguising themselves and traveling behind enemy lines. While this clandestine operation using disguise pre-dated The Hague Convention, it illustrates the military importance and danger of what is now accepted in modern warfare as special operations. The Andrews Raid (as it was known) during the American Civil War, underscores that the establishment of *Brandenburg* was simply the formalization of long accepted military practice going back to the Trojan Horse of Greek History that other countries pursued during World War II. For example, the United Kingdom established the "L" Detachment, Special Air Service Brigade in 1941 to conduct commando raids behind enemy lines less than two years after *Brandenburg*. After the war this unit was reorganized into the well-known elite Special Air Service (SAS). The United States also conducted similar operations through the Office of Strategic Services (OSS). Captain Aaron Bank organized and led the aborted Operation Iron Cross. Operation Iron Cross was designed to send a company of men (recruited from former German *SS* and *Fallschirmjäger* prisoners of war) disguised as *Wehrmacht* soldiers into Bavaria to capture or kill Adolf Hitler. The rapid collapse of the Western Front in 1945 made the plan obsolete. After the war Colonel Aaron Bank went on to establish the United States Army's Special Forces. These developments demonstrate that the formalized practice of sending small, highly trained teams behind enemy lines was not unique to the *'Brandenburgers'* or the Third Reich, and that this has become an enduring capability in every modern military force across the world.

After the campaign in the west was completed in 1940 it was determined that an expansion of *Brandenburg* was required. A combination of issues in command-and-control as well as a desire to expand the units' capacity to conduct missions led to its growth into a regiment with three battalions. The responsibility to oversee this expansion was given to the new regiment's first and only commander, *Oberstleutnant* Lanzenauer von Haehling in November 1940. Another effective change made was to disperse various sub-headquarters regionally throughout Germany in order that these units could quickly respond to taskings by *OKH*. This led to the following geographic dispositions: Berlin for the command and signals element and for operations at the request of *Ausland/Abwehr*; *I.Btl./zbV 800* at Brandenburg/Havel for interregional and main effort operations; *II.Btl./zbV 800* at Baden (near Vienna) for missions in eastern and southeastern Europe; and *III.Btl./zbV 800* at Aachen (later Düren) for follow-on missions in western Europe and the planned invasion against England known as Operation Sea Lion. This logical separation of *zbV 800* into regional areas began the process of even further specialization of the battalions reflected in their training and personnel composition. Over the course of the next year *'Brandenburg'* operations took its soldiers into the mountains of Afghanistan, the oil fields of Romania and into the Balkans. On the eve of the invasion of the Soviet Union in June 1941 the unit expanded further to include a regiment with the exception of two regional companies with one designated to conduct operations in Africa and one for Finland.

As the war progressed the soldiers of *'Brandenburg'* were soon caught in a series of political cross-currents. Canaris and other members of his organization demonstrated disagreement to the occupation policies of the National Socialist regime. This caught the attention of Himmler who moved to limit Canaris' influence. Himmler, always looking to grow his *Reichssicherheitshauptamt* (Central Security

Department of the Reich or *RHSA*) organization, saw in the *Ausland/Abwehr* a rivalry with his own Branch III (*Ausland*) of the *Sicherheitsdienst* (Security Service or *SD*), and he took all opportunities to erode the authority of Canaris.[3] Within Himmler's *SS*, there was a strong advocate for taking over the '*Brandenburgers*'. *SS-Hauptsturmführer* Otto Skorzeny, always the opportunist, saw in the elite '*Brandenburgers*' a capability he wanted for his own nascent *SS-Sonderkommandos*. Simultaneously *OKW* also saw in '*Brandenburg*' a capability they could use in the growing anti-partisan war in the Balkans.

The invasion of the Soviet Union was a defining moment for '*Brandenburg*'. Dramatic success in special operations occurred on the battlefield for the men of the unit, but a broad fissure between Canaris and the policies of the Third Reich opened that swallowed him and almost swallowed '*Brandenburg*' later in the war. Canaris and much of the *Abwehr* professed a passive anti-Nazi sentiment and were shocked by Nazi occupation policies. As early as September 12th, 1939 Admiral Canaris raised objections to *OKW* about the intended executions of a certain ethnic-political nature after the invasion of Poland.[4] Again the issue of occupation policies was raised after the invasion of the Soviet Union in 1941. Canaris gave instructions to his men to focus their efforts on military targets and avoid being utilized in the execution of political objectives, figuratively and literally. In July of 1941 the *SS-Obergruppenführer* Reinhard Heydrich and the *Wehrmacht's Generalleutnant* Hermann Reinecke came to agreement to allow the *Gestapo* and *SD* to sift through Soviet prisoners of war and identify commissars and other Bolshevik sympathizers so that they could be removed and executed. This was confirmed by *Oberst* Erwin von Lahousen in a subsequent meeting on the topic.[5] The intended

---

3   *Abwehr Hauptmann* Otto Kurrer who served as *SD* Liaison Officer stated "There was enormous rivalry between the Abwehr, Gestapo and SD … " Georg Duesterberg, former head of *Abwehr* Finance Branch (*Abwehr ZF*) and later part of *RSHA Amt II* after the Himmler's takeover of the *Abwehr* in the wake of the July 20th Assassination Plot against Adolf Hitler stated "The antagonism between the *Abwehr* and the *SD* went at times so far that agents of *Abwehr II* inside Germany were used to sabotage Intelligence operations of the *SD* when they were considered prejudicial to the German cause by Admiral Canaris who always insisted that all Intelligence operations were to be kept within the limits of International Law and Usage." See Vol. CV 02. Office of Strategic Services Mission for Germany. United States Forces European Theatre. "Dissensions in German Intelligence Services". 7 July 1945, pp. 2-3.

4   Peter Longerich, *Heinrich Himmler* (Oxford University Press: New York, 2012), p. 433.

5   After the war *Oberst* Erwin von Lahousen, former head of *Abwehr* under Admiral Canaris, turned witness for the prosecution at the Nuremburg War Crimes trials. He supplied the Allied War Crimes Tribunal with evidence of the murder of hundreds of thousands of Soviet POWs, and the operations of the *Einsatzgruppen* that carried out the liquidation of Jewish communities. On September 15th 1945, Erwin Lahousen was interrogated by U.S. Army Colonel Amen as a witness for the Nuremberg Tribunal. Below is a summary of the interrogation:

   Witness was a professional officer in the Austrian Amy from 1915 to 1938. In that year he was taken over by the German Amy and worked in Intelligence. He became a full colonel in 1940 and a Major General, equivalent to Brig, General in the American Army, 1 January 1945. In his work, witness was immediately under Canaris, consequently he had contact also with Keitel, Jodl, and others. In the fall of 1941, witness attended a conference, as a representative of Canaris, at which General Reinecke [sic] was chairman. Mueller represented RSHA. There was a representative for the Office for PW's [Prisoners of War]. The purpose of the meeting was to discuss certain orders which had been issued and were to be issued, concerning the treatment of Russian PW's. The effect of these orders was that a soldier of the Red Army was to be treated not as a PW, but as a political prisoner and "that the war between Germany and Russia, was not to be looked on as a war between two states, but as a war between two political conceptions, and thus, it was that Russians were considered as beasts, sub-human, or whatever they called them". The only outcome of the meeting was that executions would not take place where troops could see them. Witness believes the orders were in effect issued before the war ever started. Witness's mission was, on behalf of Canaris, to say that the orders in question had undesirable effects on the work of his office and on morale and on prospective future PW's. Selection of those to be killed as communists was entirely arbitrary. In one instance, some Mohammedans [Muslims] were captured and were executed under the mistaken notion that they were Jews. The term "special treatment" in German *Sonderbehandlung* in official papers always meant 'condemned to die'.
   Disturbed by the conduct of the war by the National Socialists, *Oberst* Erwin Von Lahousen became involved in Operation Spark, the failed March 13th, 1943 plot to assassinate Hitler. From *Cornell University's Donovan Nuremberg*

occupation policy generated a complaint by Canaris to *Generalfeldmarschall* Wilhelm Keitel, Chief of *OKW*, through his *Abwehr* superior *Admiral* Leopold Bürkner in writing due to its contrary nature of the international laws of warfare. Additionally, the political and international repercussions against Germany were raised. This letter was in keeping with the *Ausland/Abwehr* office's responsibility for the monitoring of issues of international law. Keitel's response echoed what *Oberst* Erwin von Lahousen reportedly heard from *Generalleutnant* Reinicke: that they were now involved in a total war of the destruction of a world view—communism—and that international law no longer applied. The open questioning of what amounted to core Nazi political-racial policy certainly did not go unnoticed. Himmler's distrust in Canaris and his organization began to grow, and he raised suspicions with Hitler that Canaris and his organization were in league with the anti-Nazi resistance.[6]

Over the course of the next two years the men of *'Brandenburg'* found themselves involved in operations in Iraq, Iran, Africa, across Russia and throughout mainland Europe. They moved well beyond their original training as saboteurs to include commando raids, liaison and training of local forces, and anti-partisan operations, especially in the Balkans. The extent of their missions and the unforeseen length of the war required *'Brandenburg'* to fill growing mission requirements. At the end of 1942 it was decided to expand the regiment into a division with control still under Canaris. The expansion was slow, particularly due to the growing shortage of manpower and specialized equipment caused by the war. With Germany's strategic culmination underway in 1942, the need to employ *'Brandenburg'* soldiers in far reaching special operations also waned. By June 1942 new guidelines issued by von Haehling outlined that *'Brandenburg'* operations were now to fall in line with the needs of the frontline commanders. As he noted in his *Report No. 1509/42* titled *General Duties*: "In view of the significance of movement in modern war, the taking of transportation facilities, especially bridges, is of primary importance." He set the ground rules that his men were to be employed exclusively "in the vanguard of motorized and armored units [as the] the rule." Once combat transitioned to positional warfare they were to be removed from the frontline.

The new *Baulehr-Division zbV 800 'Brandenburg'* was authorized four regiments, a number of independent companies, a separate Tropical Battalion, a Coastal Raider Battalion, and a Parachute Battalion. By mid-March 1943 the expansion to a division was complete organizationally, though manpower and equipment levels were still being staffed. *Regiment 1* was initially formed under the name *Sonderverband 801* from the *I.Btl./Lehr-Regiment 'Brandenburg'* in Freiburg, in *Wehrkreis V*; *Regiment 2* was formed initially under the name *Sonderverband 802* from the *II.Btl./Lehr-Regiment 'Brandenburg'* at Baden bei Wein, then later Admont in *Wehrkreis XVIII*; *Regiment 3* was initially formed under the name *Sonderverband 803* from the *III.Btl./Lehr-Regiment 'Brandenburg'* in Düren/Rheinland in *Wehrkreis VI*; and *Regiment 4* was initially formed under the name *Sonderverband 804* from sections of the *V-Abteilung, Abteilung 'von Koenen'* and the rest from the so called *'Donaufahrer'* in Brandenburg/Havel in *Wehrkreis II*.

As the *Division* expanded, both the *SS* and *OKW* saw utility in owning a unique combat capability embodied by *zbV 800*. Himmler had already created a nascent special operations

Trials Collection: Witness: Erwin Lahousen/Office of U.S. Counsel for the Prosecution of Axis Criminality/Document Rom Interrogation Analysis. Reinhard Heydrich was the founding head of the *SD*, played a key role in the organizing the Holocaust and ruled part of Czechoslovakia as the Reich Protectorate of Bohemia and Moravia. His racial policies and brutal reaction to the nascent Czech resistance generated Operation Anthropoid by Czech exiles in England. Trained by the British Special Operations executive (SOE), two Czech exiles re-entered occupied Czechoslovakia in December 1941 and mortally wounded Heydrich on May 27th 1942 during an ambush. Hermann Reinecke was an ardent supporter of National Socialism. During the war he became head of the new *Nationalsozialistische Führungsoffiziere* (NSFO), who were responsible for increased National Socialist indoctrination of the *Wehrmacht* after the unsuccessful July 20th 1944 Plot to assassinate Adolf Hitler. He was convicted of war crimes and crimes against humanity during the Nuremberg Trials after the war.

6   David Kahn, *Hitler's Spies: German Military Intelligence in World War II* (Macmillan Publishing Co., Inc.: New York, 1978), p. 268.

capability in 1942 under *Amt VI, Ausland-SD* (the foreign intelligence service department of the *SS-Reichssicherheitshauptamt*) in Oranienburg commanded by *SS* officer Otto Skorzeny. Skorzeny's unit was called *Waffen Sonderverband zbV 'Friedenthal'*. Designated Group S (for sabotage), Skorzeny's men were trained to handle a variety of missions that often included the infiltration of enemy lines while wearing enemy uniforms. As the *SS* grew its own special operations capability and Skorzeny began to eye the *'Brandenburgers'* with increasing interest, the *Wehrmacht* stepped in to take control. In early 1943 *'Brandenburg'* was transferred out of *Ausland/Abwehr* and its office was moved from Berlin to the underground *OKW* command complex at Zossen.

On February 12th, 1943 command of *'Brandenburg'* passed to *Oberst* Alexander von Pfuhlstein who previously led *Infanterie-Regiment 154* in Russia. He won the German Cross in Gold on February 14th, 1942 followed by the Knight's Cross on August 17th 1942. During April 1943 the *'Brandenburgers'* were renamed *Division 'Brandenburg' zbV 800* and placed under the control of the *Wehrmacht* Operations Staff. Now that the unit was elevated to a division, von Pfuhlstein was promoted to *Generalmajor* on July 1st. This conventional *Heer* officer brought with him the skills necessary to take the motley group of commandos and integrate into regiments under a unified command. One of von Pfuhlstein's first proposals was the formation of a single training regiment based in Brandenburg/Havel from the remnants of *zbV 'Brandenburg'* training cadre still left under the control of the *Abwehr*. Canaris approved the recommendation and the *Lehr-Regiment 'Brandenburg'* was formed that consisted of two battalions to provide specialized training. One was assigned to Admont in Italy where members received specialized mountain warfare training and the other went to Baden in Vienna where there was a focus on anti-partisan warfare. With the change in operational authority came discussions about how best to employ the newly acquired capability. Strategically, the Reich had shifted over to the defense. The need for experts in infiltration and sabotage became a second priority to the need for trained light infantry to conduct anti-partisan operations, which had become a persistent threat in the Balkans and across south east Europe. By July 1943 almost all of *'Brandenburg'* was engaged in anti-partisan warfare. This was a growing concern outlined in a radio message between *Heeresgruppe Südost* and *Division 'Brandenburg'* in *WFST/Op(H)/Südost F.H.Qu.*, dated October 10th, 1943 where they noted that increasingly the men of the division were ordered by local commanders to remain in the frontline after they completed their special operations mission to be employed as "elite infantry". This situation was unwelcome by the staff of *Division 'Brandenburg'* that saw their authority over their men eroded. Spending more time in the frontline meant losses subsequently increased among the specially trained cadre of *'Brandenburg'* that could not easily be replaced. Gone were the days of seizing bridges and tactical objectives ahead of the advancing *Panzer* formations, or conducting operations in far flung corners of the globe. As the war progressed and Germany went on the defensive, operations transformed as required.

Generalmajor von Pfuhlstein was relieved from command due to "political unreliability" sometime in late March (see Chapter 2 for a complete account of the event). The 52 year old *Generalleutnant* Friedrich Kühlwein was then assigned command of the division on April 14th 1944. He continued as commander through October 16th 1944, overseeing the administrative transition of *'Brandenburg'* from a *Sonderkommando* to a *Panzergrenadier* division. His last command was that of the *45.Infanterie-Division* serving in *Heeresgruppe Mitte* on the East Front from February 1942 through April 1943, followed by an entire year in the *Führer-Reserve*. Kühlwein's selection as division commander was likely a deliberate decision given his lack of active *Wehrmacht* involvement during the last year. He would have come into command with no political allegiances and no agendas, though this assessment is speculative. His prior commands were frontline conventional infantry units, and he had just spent the last year sitting out the war. It just may be that his lack of special operations experience was what was called for by *OKW* knowing that the days of the units' special operations were long over.

Within a month of taking command Kühlwein generated two memos designed to preserve the integrity of *Division 'Brandenburg'*. First was *Abt.Ic Nr.22/44 g.Kdos. Kampfdolmetacher und Leg. Wesen in der Division Brandenburg und Aufstellung von "Streifkorps"* to the *Wehrmacht Führungsstab* (Operations Staff) on May 26th, and *Abt.Ic Nr.23/44 g.Kdos. Landeseigene Streifkorps der Division Brandenburg* on May 27th proposing the reorganization of *'Brandenburg'* around a *Streif-Korps* (Patrol Corps) with light infantry regiments and special units. The second memo began "The *Division 'Brandenburg'* was created as a special unit for offensive operations. Since the *Wehrmacht* has been fighting on the defensive, it has adapted to this changed situation and has become the *'OKW's* standing anti-partisan unit'" Kühlwein went on to argue that *'Brandenburg'* had transitioned from a special operations unit into a light infantry force that specialized in anti-partisan warfare—specifically in the Balkans—as the demands of the war dictated. Noting the change in mission and experience, he believed that the next evolutionary step for the *Division* was to establish a presence in each theatre of war, not just the Balkans, with the responsibility to conduct fast, limited duration, on-demand combat missions as required. That meant most of the division's men had to be employed specifically as light infantry, while only select elements would retain their special operations capabilities. Only one *Streif-Korps* was established. The *8.Kp./III.Regiment* was sent to Southern France as *Streif-Korps 'Süd Frankreich'* to guard the Pyrenees. Another was planned for Slovakia but it was not formed. The events of July 20th, 1944 soon put an end to Kühlwein's proposal.

2

From *Sonderkommandos* to *Panzergrenadiers*

The failed July 20th, 1944 attempted assassination of Adolf Hitler sent shock waves through the Reich. Among the conspirators arrested were Canaris and other members of the *Abwehr*. Much of Canaris' organization was dismantled in the process and *RFSS* Heinrich Himmler moved in to assert his control. Among the questions on the table was whether or not *Division 'Brandenburg'* would stay under *OKW* control or become part of the *SS*.

The failed assassination plot was only the final nail in the coffin for Canaris and his *Abwehr*. As early as January 1944 Himmler had moved directly against Canaris. The *SD* had previously broken up a circle of anti-Nazis and found one of its members served in the *Abwehr*. Two other officers, *Oberst* Hans Oster, Canaris' Chief of Staff, and Hans von Dohnanyi, were investigated for anti-Nazi activities. Oster resigned (to be later arrested), but Dohnanyi was arrested in April 1943. Finally at the end of January 1944 a member of the *Abwehr* post in Istanbul defected to the British. Hitler became furious upon hearing the news. On February 12th Hitler ordered Canaris sent to a backwater post, and transitioned operational control of the *Abwehr* to Himmler's *RSHA*.[1] *Division 'Brandenburg'*, however, remained operationally under *OKW* control.

The case of Hans von Dohnanyi is both interesting and relevant to the overall development of *'Brandenburg'*. Von Dohnanyi grew up a Berliner of Hungarian descent, who earned a Doctorate in Law and entered the Germany Justice System in the 1920s. He was a vocal opponent of Nazi racial policies against the Jewish citizens of Germany, especially after the Night of the Long Knives in 1934. He was subsequently marginalized by Martin Bormann and relegated to a lower judicial post outside of Berlin. He immediately began to cultivate contacts in the resistance community and later helped a number of Jews to emigrate from Germany to Switzerland and avoid deportation. At the outbreak of war it was Hans Oster that recruited him into the *Abwehr* to become his Deputy. In early 1943 von Dohnanyi was directly involved with active plotting to assassinate Hitler. His subsequent arrest on April 5th 1943 was not related to the assassination plot, but was based on a currency charge of transferring money to a Swiss bank account on behalf of Jews he helped to emigrate.

The judge in von Dohnanyi's case was the notorious *Oberkriegsgerichtsrat* Dr. Manfred Roeder. He served as a Judge Advocate in the *Luftwaffe* and was particularly ruthless in prosecuting members of the German resistance. He gained the reputation as "Hitler's Blood Judge" according to those he sentenced. During his investigation into the Von Dohnanyi Case, Roeder wrote despairingly of *'Brandenburg'* calling it a "Quitters Club". Canaris became upset with this "judgment" being entered into an official trial against one of his own. In a conversation with von Pfuhlstein he urged that this matter should not go unchallenged. A man of action, von Pfuhlstein boarded a plane to Lemberg (Lviv) in western Ukraine in January 1944 where he paid a visit to Dr. Roeder, who at that time was serving as Chief Judge of *Luftflotte 4* and slapped him in the face. In response to this incident *Feldmarschall* Keitel placed von Pfuhlstein under arrest on January 23rd. Canaris informed Keitel that he put von Pfuhlstein up to this task, and he placed himself into self-imposed "house arrest" until von Pfuhlstein was released. Keitel released von Pfuhlstein just over a week later, but this case would bring retribution by those in Nazi circles that questioned Canaris and his supporter's motivations.

---

1   Ibid.

Generalmajor von Pfuhlstein was subsequently relieved from command of *Division 'Brandenburg'* due to "political unreliability" in late March and went into the *Führerreserve*. He served in the *50.Infanterie-Division* during the month of May before again being sent back into the *Führerreserve*. He was subsequently arrested by the *SD* in connection with the July 20th plot to assassinate Hitler and sent to prison where he was placed in a cell in the basement of the Gestapo Headquarters on Prinz-Albrecht-Strass in Berlin with Canaris and Oster, both of whom were also arrested. Von Pfuhlstein was only convicted of "association" to the conspiracy and avoided the death penalty. He was stripped of his rank and discharged from the *Wehrmacht* on September 14th. He surrendered to U.S. Forces on April 2nd, 1945 and gave testimony at the Nuremburg Trials. At least one other member of *Division 'Brandenburg'* arrest was sought in connection with von Pfuhlstein (see below Chapter 3).

Concern quickly grew after the formal arrest of Canaris and other members of the *Abwehr* in the wake of the failed assassination plot against Hitler that Skorzeny, with Himmler's support, might attempt to take over all of *Division 'Brandenburg'* and absorb the unit's members into his *SS Sonderkommandos*. The concern was well founded. Skorzeny, through Himmler, inquired about the status of *Division 'Brandenburg'* as the *Abwehr* was dissolved. *Oberstleutnant i.G.* Dr. jur. Johannes (Hans) Erasmus, who served as the *Ia* (Operations Officer) of the division, quickly drafted memo *Abt. Ia No. 362/44* that was submitted to *OKW* on August 30th 1944.[2] Erasmus did not hide his intent that he wanted to keep the division's members together under the *Heer*, and he offered *General* Alfred Jodl who was serving as Chief of the *Wehrmacht's* operation staff, a line of argument to use with Himmler. The memo argued to establish *Division 'Brandenburg'* under the *Heer* as a conventional *Jäger* or *Panzergrenadier-Division*, with the specific intent to avoid complete conversion into an *SS* unit. His argument was that the *Division* was already operating as a conventional force, and only a few of its remaining members were in fact conducting special operations. A key element of his argument was that the *Division* had suffered heavy attrition in terms of equipment and special operations personnel. If the *Division* was transferred over to the *SS*, then Himmler would have to incur the cost of rebuilding the unit as a special operations unit from the ground up. With luck, that cost might be too high a price for Himmler. Erasmus' memorandum *Abt.Ia No. 362/44* read:

> The units now belonging to the Division have been employed on anti-partisan duties behind our front for years. With the exception of minor elements, they carry out their combat duties as normal *Panzergrenadiers* or *Jägers* regiments. The weak forces still carrying out special combat duties are the commando platoons with the battalions and regiments of the Patrol Corps. From a total strength of 14,056 German soldiers they comprise only 900 Officers, NCOs and enlisted men. They contain the bulk of the available language experts. These consist of 210 Russian-speaking, 181 English-speaking, 185 Serbo-Croatian-speaking and 310 Italian-speaking soldiers and 610 who speak other languages.
>
> The bulk of the division today consists of motorized *Jäger* units that in terms of firepower, training and fighting spirit are at the top of their form but that share the fate of all the shattered units. The planned transfer by *WFSt* of 14,000 of our soldiers into units of the *RFSS* would mean the end of the efforts to keep together the personnel suited to special operations.
>
> The following solution is proposed in the event that the release of these 14,000 soldiers proves unavoidable: Remove all units of the *Division* suited to special operations and transfer them to the *RFSS* for the formation of a large-scale unit for these roles.

---

2   Dr. jur. Johannes Erasmus held a Doctorate in legal jurisprudence, which likely was a great benefit in this case. He was an experienced staff officers having served in a variety of *Division* and *Korps* positions since early 1940. He earned the Knight's Cross on April 13th, 1944 while serving as *Ia* of the *XXXXVII.Panzer-Korps* During the defense battles that occurred along the Eastern Front in spring of 1944. He was appointed as Ia of *Panzergrenadier-Division 'Brandenburg'* on June 15th, 1944 and subsequently promoted to *Oberstleutnant i.G.* on August 1st, 1944.

The memo gave Jodl the argument he required. He subsequently informed Himmler's office that to take on the entire *Division 'Brandenburg'* meant the *SS* would have to become responsible for its restructuring. If he just wanted those soldiers carrying out "special operations", then he should take on the 900 soldiers Erasmus recommended. At a time of growing resource constraints within the Reich, Himmler realized Skorzeny's grab for *Division 'Brandenburg'* constituted more effort than originally thought. He backed down from absorbing the entire *Division*. *OKW* agreed to convert *Division 'Brandenburg'* into a conventional force and maintain its integrity. With the losses on both fronts mounting during the summer of 1944, *OKW* could not afford to lose any manpower.

What followed were two orders that relieved *Division 'Brandenburg'* of its special-operations status and reorganized it into a conventional division. The first order was a formal declaration of intent by Jodl issued by *OKW* on September 8th, 1944 under *Nr.0010994/44 g.K.WFSt/Op. Division 'Brandenburg'* was ordered to end all current assignments as a special operations unit and be placed directly under command of the *Heer*. Its units dispersed across the Balkans were ordered to assemble around Belgrade in the command area of *OB Südost*. This included a number of the special purpose units like *Küstenjäger-Abteilung, Fallschirmjäger-Bataillon* and *II.Btl./Regiment 3 'BR'*. Jodl specified that the goal was to accelerate the integration of artillery, a *Pionier-Bataillon, Sturmgeschütz* for anti-tank defense, service support troops and reorganize as a *mot.Jäger-Division* and rapidly deploy into the current conventional fight. While the division was saved from being absorbed into the *SS*, Jodl specified that the 900 linguists conducting special operations were to be absorbed into the *Waffen-SS* under the command of Skorzeny, in agreement with Himmler. However, they were authorized to continue operations in the Balkans for the time being.

This was followed up with a final communication by Jodl directly to the men of *Division 'Brandenburg'* on September 11th, regarding the reorganization of the division. Jodl thanked the soldiers of *'Brandenburg'* for the work they had done under his command, after *OKW* took operational and administrative control from the *Abwehr* earlier in 1944. He also explained in military terms the benefit of brining all the soldiers together into a unified command in the regular infantry role.

Der Chef   F.H.Qu., dem 11.9.44
Des Wehrmachtführungsstabes

Soldiers of *Division 'Brandenburg'*!
The division is being relieved of its duties as a special operations unit and reorganized as a *mot. Jäger-Division*. You are therefore leaving the area of my direct command.
    I thank you for the readiness for action and the willingness to sacrifice that you have shown. The division has fulfilled all my expectations in the infantry role and in the area of special operations.
    That orders for your reorganization as a *mot. Jäger-Division* have nevertheless been given, is so that all forces have proved themselves in the area of special operations might be employed en masse under a unified command and thus achieve new successes.
    The name *'Brandenburg'* is an obligation! I am certain that in its new form the division will do its duty and continue its glorious tradition.

Heil der Führer!

Despite Jodl's memo, most soldiers were likely not aware that their special operations status had been in jeopardy for some time or that this reorganization was a way to prevent Himmler from absorbing *Division 'Brandenburg'* into the *SS*. Many soldiers viewed their conversion to a *Panzergrenadier-Division* with disdain. In spite of the agreement to transfer all 900 linguists to Skorzeny, few actually transferred to the *Waffen-SS*. Only around 350 left *'Brandenburg'*, some being ordered and others volunteering to serve under the *SS-Sonderkommando*. The exception was the *Lehr-Regiment zbV 'Brandenburg'*. According to the division *Adjutant Oberleutnant iG* Bröker the struggle for control of the *"Kampfschule"* (Combat Schools) began in the summer of 1944 between the *Wehrmacht* and the *SS*. With Himmler now in command of the *Ersatzheer*, he moved to control the flow of newly trained personnel. *'Brandenburg'* staff wanted the trainees currently in the schools to be sent to their intended company organizations, but the *SS* did not concur with the thinking now that Skorzeny had established the *SS-Jagdverbände*. Skorzeny began to "fish" around for officers and soldiers to join his new *SS*-Commandos. The conflict reached its height when the decision came to reclassify the training and replacement schools from *zbV* (special action) status to conventional *Panzergrenadier*. In the end 1,800 young trainees of *Lehr-Regiment zbV 'Brandenburg'* elected to convert to the *SS* and join Skorzeny's *SS-Sonderkommando*. This included Freiherr Adrian von Fölkersam who led a group of *'Brandenburgers'* behind Soviet lines in the disguise of Soviet NKVD personnel in 1942 to capture the Maikop oil fields. He converted over to a *SS-Standartenführer*. The other men that converted over joined the ranks of *SS-Jagdverband Mitte*, *SS-Jagdverband Ost* or as part of the *SS-Jäger-Bataillon 502*. Former *'Brandenburgers'* served with Skorzeny during his takeover of the Budapest Government Quarter on Castle Hill in October 1944 known as *Operation Panzerfaust*, and with *Panzer-Brigade 150* during *Operation Grief* in the Ardennes Offensive launched in December 1944.[3]

Discussions continued for the next three days on how best to employ the new *Division*. It was finally decided on September 13th that the division was to become a *Panzergrenadier-Division*. The order was communicated through *OKH/GenStdH/Op.Abt.I/SU, Nr. 19280/44 G.Kdos. 13.9.44.* By September 28th, as already noted above, the new *Panzergrenadier-Division 'Brandenburg'* was subordinated under the new *Panzer-Korps 'Großdeutschland'*. Each regiment was ordered to send a liaison to Baden, near Vienna, where they would assist in the transiting of unit personnel from the Balkans to East Prussia. All efforts were directed to consolidate the disparate subunits of *Division 'Brandenburg'* scattered across southern Europe and reform them into the *Panzergrenadier-Division 'BR'*. This was no easy task given the military situation confronting each of *Division 'Brandenburg'* regiments fighting in south-east Europe.

---

3   Hans Spaeter, *Die Brandenburger, eine deutsche Kommandotruppe: zbV 800* (Karl-Heinz Dissberger: Düsseldorf, 1991), p. 436. Hans Spaeter in *The History of Panzerkorps Großdeutschland, Volume 3*, p. 5. *Bundesarchiv-Militärarchiv* (BAMA) RH 26-1002/File 1002-4. It was revealed during the interrogation of *Generalmajor* Pfuhlstein, the former *Division 'Brandenburg'* commander, during the Nuremberg Proceedings that the *SS-Jagdverbände* replaced the *Wehrmacht's 'Brandenburg' Division* in special operations. As early as 1942-43 members of the *SS* trained and served with *'Brandenburg'* and Himmler used them as spies in foreign countries. By the summer of 1944 all *SS* men serving with *'Brandenburg'* that were still considered "reliable" were requested to report back to the *SS*. See 23 June 1945, Sections of the R.S.H.A. Possibly Involved in War Crimes, p. 10 and Vol CV 01: Vol XCIX 31 10 April 45, Source *Generalmajor a.D.* Alexander von Pfuhlstein. Seventh Army Interrogation Report.

3

Attrition and Consolidation

(Reference Map 3)

Wallen *'Brandenburg'* was ordered to reorganize as a *Panzergrenadier-Division* on September 15th its component regiments were involved in heavy fighting across the Reich. The situation in southeast Europe was difficult for *Heeresgruppe E* under command of *Generaloberst* Alexander Loehr. In late August 1944 Romania surrendered to the Soviet Union, and Bulgaria decided on a path toward neutrality ahead of the advancing Red Army. This would in effect put Loehr's forces in Greece in jeopardy of being cut off. To the north were *Heeresgruppe Südost* and *Heeresgruppe F*. Both *Heeresgruppe* were under command of *Generalfeldmarschall* Maximilian von Weichs who ordered a withdrawal of forces from Greece into southern Serbia on August 26th, though he was under *OKW* orders to avoid giving the impression that a general withdrawal was under way. The withdrawal was in part done to affect a strengthening of the main north-south lines of transportation, particularly the only rail-line that ran from Athens-Salonika-Belgrade and the two main roads that ran north through Bulgarian occupied Macedonia.

When Bulgaria declared neutrality on September 2nd the Soviets, with an eye to the postwar political landscape, declared war on Bulgaria citing a paltry reason that it was a refuge for retreating German forces. They invaded five days later. The new Bulgarian government quickly declared war on Germany as the Soviet 3rd Ukrainian Front advanced across the border. This move prompted the Germans to quickly disarm the Bulgarian occupation force in Macedonia to ensure control of the lines of transportation toward Belgrade. Most of the German formations deployed in the rugged terrain of Greece and the Balkans had little to no motor transportation. Movement north was conducted by rail, horse, or foot, making control of the roads essential. Evacuations of the Aegean Islands began in earnest by airlift to Athens and by sealift to the Greek mainland. This forced *Heeresgruppe E* to maintain a presence in Greece longer than Loehr liked, but suited Weichs and *OKW*. Throughout September the Soviets began building up forces along the western part of Bulgaria and in Romania. Meanwhile the Western Allies conducted a bombing campaign of the bridges and exit routes from Greece, hampering the limited withdrawals authorized by Weichs and *OKW*. The bridges over the Nis River were damaged as well as those crossing the Danube and Sava Rivers at Belgrade.

Josip Tito's communist partisans now began to advance from their mountain strongholds toward the west with an eye on Belgrade. They advanced into Serbia along with Soviet and Bulgarian forces. On October 4th the Soviets crossed Pancevo on the north bank of the Danube River, just a dozen kilometers downstream from Belgrade, forcing Weichs to move his headquarters from the city. On October 8th elements of the Soviet 57th Army's 68th Rifle Corps advanced well behind the German lines and established a bridgehead across the Morava River to the southeast of Belgrade. Marshal F.I. Tolbukhin staff quickly presented the commander of the 3rd Ukrainian Front with a bold plan to use the 4th Guards Mechanized Corps to advance across the new bridgehead, through the winding mountain roads, and capture Belgrade on the 14th where the Soviet mechanized force would hold until the arrival of the 57th Army. Tolbukhin was unsure that such a bold move was possible, but his staff convinced him and he issued the orders to General V.I. Zhdanov's corps to start their attack on the 9th.[1] By October 10th the German evacuation from Greece toward Belgrade was in full swing and largely successful. This freed combat divisions for Weichs to deploy into the area of Belgrade to assist in the defense. Unfortunately their arrival was estimated to take weeks, so Weichs had little choice but to consolidate his forces around Belgrade and authorize them to launch an attack east to the mouth of the Morava where they would join with *Kampfgruppe Wittmann* and the *1.Gebirgsjäger-Division*, then advance along the west bank of the Morava River to strike the Soviets assembling for an attack north. All Weichs could muster around Belgrade was a *Kampfgruppe* known as *Armeeabteilung 'Serbia'*. The attack was launched as planned on October 12th but was called off with the arrival of the Soviet 57th Army that had already established itself *en masse* on the west bank of the river, southeast of Belgrade. The operational situation for the Germans soon went from bad to worse.

Kampfgruppe Wittmann had been established to hold the Morava River from its mouth along the Danube south to Velika Plana. The *Kampfgruppe* consisted of the combined *I.* and *II.Btl./Reg. 4 'BR'*, and the bulk of the *92.Grenadierregiment (mot.)*. Further to the east was *Kampfgruppe Müller* that consisted of the *Regiment 2 'BR'*, *7.SS-Freiwilligen-Gebirgs-Division 'Prinz Eugen'*, the *1.Gebirgs-Division* and an assortment of other units heading toward Belgrade from the east. Heading north from Greece were the withdrawing units of *H.Gr. E*. The Soviets had cut through the German lines splitting *Kampfgruppe Müller* in half and established themselves across the Morava, at the southern end of *Kampfgruppe Wittmann*. They were now poised to advance on Belgrade and along the southern bank of the Sava cutting off all German formation south and east of there.

The Soviets readied for their attack northwest into Belgrade. On October 12th the 17,000 men and 180 tanks of Zhdanov's 4th Guards Mechanized Corps rolled out from its positions around Velika Plana toward Topola and Mladenovac with the 68th Corps and 5th Independent Motorized Brigade in support.[2] The Soviet force was assisted by Tito's 1st Proletarian Corps and later the first 1st Army Group moving from the west. Upon reaching the main road north-south road toward Belgrade at Topola the 4th Guards Mechanized Corps entered into fierce fighting with German elements defending the road. Here German Flak and *Panzers* put up fierce resistance until they were destroyed by the Soviets, opening the road north and cutting off the German force to the south. German forces in the Morava Valley were now cut off. Tolbukhin decided that the German forces to the south must be prevented from reaching Belgrade and ordered General Zhdanov to capture the heights of Avala outside of the city. Weichs placed all forces in the Morava Valley under the command of *Generalleutnant* Walter Ritter Stettner von Grabenhofen who commanded the *1.Gebirgsjäger-Division*. *Armeeabteilung 'Serbia'* was given orders to hold Belgrade until Stettner's forces could withdraw from the valley and cross the Sava River.

The next phase of the Soviet advance on Mt. Avala and Belgrade began on October 14th. The 4th Guards Mechanized Corps was to lead the assault with two Soviet infantry divisions in support. Tito's men of the Yugoslav Liberation Army were to be part of the liberation of Belgrade, riding into the city on the backs of the Soviet tanks. After an initial artillery preparation, the Soviet attack was to develop toward Avala, then into Belgrade, followed by the capture of all bridges over the Sava River to prevent the escape of German forces to the northwest. Specific orders were given not to use Soviet heavy weapons to destroy German defensive positions in the city in order to preserve the bullrings for Tito to quickly occupy and establish political control. Instead, German defenders were to be fought hand-to-hand in the city streets.[3] On the night of October 14th a combined force of Soviets and partisans entered Belgrade and by the next day this force reached the center of the city. Stettner's forces advanced west from Smederevo and reached a point 20 kilometers south of Belgrade on October 15th. The Soviet force inside the city grew concerned that if the Germans reached Belgrade they could

1   John Erickson, *The Road to Berlin* (Yale University Press: New Haven, 1999), p. 385.
2   Ibid., 385-86.
3   Ibid., 387.

supplement the exiting defenders and re-establish control of the city. Inside Belgrade the Soviets had to switch tactics and begin to use heavy weapons to clear out the staunch German defenders. Outside the city elements of the 57th Army setup a cordon around Stettner's forces and issued an ultimatum: surrender or be destroyed. Stettner made a decision not to launch a final coordinated attack toward Belgrade that the Soviet's feared, or to surrender. He ordered all heavy equipment destroyed and to withdrawal west toward the Sava where he hoped his force would reach Sabac. Over the course of the next four days of bitter fighting among the steep valleys and peaks south of Belgrade Stettner's dwindling force reached their goal. On October 21st approximately 12,000 troops crossed over the river. In Belgrade, *Armeeabteilung 'Serbia'* withdrew from the city and surrounding area on October 19th now that its original mission was obsolete. Soviet soldiers and Tito's Partisans celebrated their victory on the 19th in the city streets, though sporadic fighting continued for several days. The withdrawal from Greece was completed over the course of the month delay, with all German troops crossing the Greek border into Yugoslavia by November 1st.

It was in the midst of this desperate fighting in the Balkans that the various regiments of *'Brandenburg'* found themselves when the order came to regroup in East Prussia to form a new *Panzergrenadier-Division*.

Regiment 1 'Brandenburg'

The battalions of *Regiment 1* were scattered. The *I.Bataillon* and *II.Bataillon* were located in Croatia where they were deployed since early 1944. *I.Btl./Rgt. 1 'BR'* was under the command of *Leutnant* Hebeler while *II.Btl./Rgt. 1 'BR'* was under the command of *Major* G. Pinkert. Both battalions began a movement to Belgrade on September 4th that lasted until the 20th. When they arrived, the men turned in their Tropical Uniforms and received Filed Gray, as the summer months now gave way to the fall. The units found out about their reorganization into a *Panzergrenadier-Division* on September 23rd. They were not happy. The war journal of the *3.Kp/I.Btl. 'BR'* noted on September 24th: "*Brandenburg* sold out." The two battalions could not be sent to Baden for consolidation as they were desperately needed to reinforce the area around Belgrade. *I.Btl./Rgt 1 'BR'* was sent via Obrenovac to Sabac where it set up a bridgehead on the southern bank of the Sava River and secured the crossings against potential partisan breakthroughs. *II.Btl./Rgt. 1 'BR'* was ordered to the east bank of the Danube near Theiß to defend against a Soviet advance across the river.

The *III.Bataillon* under command of *Oberleutnant* Wandrey was already southeast of Belgrade on September 25th. With the dual approach of the Soviets toward the Sava, and Tito's partisans from the south, the main line of communication of *Heeresgruppe F* between Macedonia and Greece was in jeopardy of being cut. The *III.Btl./Rgt. 1 'BR'* was ordered to occupy a defensive position on Mt. Vencac, near the town of Arandelovac, and hold the road open. The mountain was already occupied and fierce hand-to-hand fighting occurred. It was during the fighting that *Oberleutnant* von Gußstedt was killed while advancing in a captured Italian armored car. Orders were received the day before to arrest him in conjunction with the July 20th plot to assassinate Hitler because he had served as *O1* under *Generalmajor* von Pfuhlstein (see Chapter 2). The *II.Bataillon* subsequently deployed south of the *II.Btl./Rgt. 2 'BR'* to defend against a Soviet attack north of Belgrade. During October 1st through the 13th all three battalions fought in heavy engagements around Belgrade. While checking on his battalions, *Oberstleutnant* Walther was wounded on October 13th and evacuated back to Germany. His replacement was *Oberst* Erich von Brückner from the *23.Panzer-Division*. Each of the battalions suffered heavily in the fighting. He was not the only leader of the regiment that became a casualty. *Hauptmann* Wandrey, who commanded the *III.Bataillon*, was wounded and replaced by *Hauptmann* John, who in turn was wounded for a second time, and replaced by a third commander *Oberleutnant* Friedrichsmeyer.

The Soviets finally managed to link up with Tito's communist partisans and breach the German lines to the south. On the night of October 14th-15th Soviet tanks broke through German lines and entered southern Belgrade. Street fighting immediately broke out with elements of both the *I.Btl.* and *III.Btl./Rgt. 1 'BR'*. The Germans tried to hold the bridges over the Sava to allow *Generalleutnant* Stettner's *Kampfgruppe Wittmann* through. Stiff resistance by the Soviets forced the bridges to be evacuated to the north, and Stettner tried to attack directly west, south of Belgrade, suffering heavy losses in the process. The *I.Btl./Rgt. 1 'BR'* lost its commander *Oberleutnant* Hebler temporarily after he was cut off behind Soviet lines with members of his battalion. *Rittmeister* Martens took his place, but was soon killed in action during the fighting. Hebler managed to breakout out west, then north, over the Sava to rejoin his unit. The following is a brief account of the fighting for Belgrade by *Oberfeldwebel* Goller who was a member of *3.Kp./I.Btl.* In 1958 we wrote the following from memory:

On October 11th, 1944, we went back to Belgrade from our last deployments to Valjewo into the Sabac area through Ruma/Semlin (the support elements for the *I.Btl.* continued to be in India, a suburb of Belgrade), and we waited for a new deployment order in a park.

At about 2:00 p.m. on October 12th, 1944, we got an order to secure the "Bozsieder" with the *Armee* headquarters. There was barbed wire everywhere among marvelous villas. Excitement coming and going. To some extent there was nervous packing and loading onto vehicles coming and going.

On the morning of October 13th, we had nothing else to guard because the "nest" became empty overnight. The *Armee* Headquarters had "moved" across the Sava during the night. So we got another stretch of road [to defend], where the military court was, as a security sector. People of all ranks, jovial gentlemen, gave us lots of cigarettes, Schoka-Cola and other items while packing and transloading with the request to take good care of them. They asked us repeatedly whether we had enough ammunition; we told them it would suffice for now. And they brought out entire packages of pistol ammunition, which we accepted and stored because this was definitely something in short supply with us.

During the night, all the "precious" stuff also left and moved with its new vehicles over the Sava as well. There would be firefights on both nights. The staff wanted to cross, but the Battle Commandant wanted to defend—finally they moved over there and he was here with us. We spent the remainder of the night in the highest state of readiness in and near the vehicles.

When I place the events of those days in my mind's eye after nearly 12 years, they force me to note the following:

The battle for Belgrade was a tragic symbol in the war, like Stalingrad. I participated in the battle in Stalingrad until October 18th, 1942. At Stalingrad there were front troops deployed with experience in the hardest battles. Everything was systematic; it made sense and had a purpose. Everything was broken down into squares there. Our *Stukas* and military aircraft showed up right at the minute they were supposed to and bombed one or two squares. Then we fought more on the ground. Everyone knew that he could rely on himself and the man beside him—and on his leaders!

In Belgrade, there were no plans or direction. Everything was strange there. So many soldiers, but no fighters! The mass included soldiers of all branches that, in their offices and headquarters or supply warehouses, had forgotten that war is fighting! Aside from their well-regulated work, all they knew about was wine, women and song!

Now they were faced with naked pitiable worry in the open. It made both officers and enlisted soldiers lose their heads!

They wanted to avoid fate by burying their heads in the sand; when they did that, they were eaten alive, without discretion, brutal.

After the evacuation of Belgrade the *III.Btl./Rgt. 1 'BR'* was shifted north in early November to the bridgehead at Apatin.

Fighting continued for the regiment continued through November and into December. The *II.Bataillon* was destroyed in fighting at the end of November with only its commander, *Hauptmann* Heine and seven other soldiers, able to break out of a Soviet encirclement. In early December *I.Bataillon* found itself in Kaposvar engaged in close quarter fighting against Soviet tanks at the rail station, claiming 15 knocked out. Finally on December 8th the *I.Bataillon* was able to withdraw from the frontline and sent by rail to Angerburg, East Prussia. The *III.Bataillon* reached Rechnitz slightly earlier, and was in the process of reorganizing to become a second battalion of the *Korps-Füsilier-Regiment 'GD'*.

Regiment 2 'Brandenburg'

The battalions of *Regiment 2 'BR'* were reduced to three companies during the course of 1943. The regiment was scattered with the *I.Bataillon* sent to Greece. The regiment was ordered to support the 11th Italian Army in September of that year, then ordered back to Greece in October as part of *Heeresgruppe E*. From November 1943-August 1944 the regiment saw action in Montenegro. During the month of September all three battalions were ordered to assemble at Negotin on the border with Bulgaria. The *I.Bataillon* under command of *Hauptmann* Steidl fought its way through partisan-infested mountains where it reached the city by September 22nd. The *II.Btl./Rgt. 2 'BR'* under command of *Hauptmann* Renner reached and secured the city on the 18th. The *III.Bataillon* held the access roads to the west open against potential partisan attacks. By the end of September the *I.Bataillon* suffered significant losses, and was classified a *Kampfgruppe*. It was later encircled by Soviet forces at Don Milanovac and barely made it out. The entire *Regiment* along with the *I.Btl./Rgt. 4 'BR'* now fell under *Kampfgruppe Wittmann*. It fought its way west, south of Belgrade, toward Sabac on the Sava River. The regiment found itself encircled by October 17th/18th. The roving pocket contained about 30,000 Germans. The Soviets surrounded them and gave the Germans several hours to surrender or be killed. Many members of the *II.Bataillon* took their chances on the run and in small groups worked their way west under heavy Soviet fire, with some reaching German lines on October 22nd.

Obergefreiter R. Felhofer offers an account of the regiment during those days. Felhofer was a former member of the *I.Bataillon* and the lead driver of the *1.Kompanie* under the command of *Oberleutnant* Auer.

> Our unit went to Greece in July 1943, then to Albania and in November of that year, where we were transloaded and off we went to the land of the Montenegrin Mountains. We were quartered in Priepolije and from there, we were sent all over the place. There were so many hard battles to fight and many of our old comrades had to give up their lives here.
>
> Finally, the order to move out came in September 1944 and we were glad to be rid of this anti-partisan warfare once and for all. Off we went to Belgrade, but the very next day we went further on to the Iron Gate in an area with a lovely landscape. But no one had any time for gazing at it because war was being waged here in force in this area. We had to fight the Russians here, as well as the partisans. The partisans were all very cocky because the Russian army was right next to them. In the area where Yugoslavia, Bulgaria and Romania came together near the city of Negotin, German *Luftnachrichten-Helferinnen* were released from us and were allowed to start their trip home.
>
> In the vicinity of Milanovac on the southern bank of the Danube, our unit was encircled and our *Bataillon* under the wizened leadership of our Knight's Cross bearer, *Major* Kurt Steidl, was taken out of the 'kettle' to the area of Smederevo.[4]   Everyone knew that there was

---

4   At the time of the actual fighting, Steidl was only a *Hauptmann*. Felhofer was referring to him after his promotion to

only one road from this city to Belgrade that wasn't yet occupied and so naturally, the entire retreat was along this road. Only someone who participated in something similar can imagine how chaotic it was until all the horse-drawn and foot units made it through. Finally we came with the motorized vehicles. However, the road was already partially visible from the other bank of the Danube and of course it was fired on constantly. I made it through well everywhere with the car, but often there was nothing to do except drive across dead horses, because the main idea was to get out of the danger area as fast as possible. About 20 km outside of Belgrade, the *Kompanie* took up position again.

From Ruma, we took the train on to Darda, Hungary, where our support units were. There were only 6 men out of 120 left in my *Kompanie* that made it through. *Hauptfeldwebel* Goller immediately hugged us out of joy because at least some of us had made it back. Unfortunately our reunion was blemished by the knowledge that almost the entire *Kompanie*, including the Commander, were considered missing. It all had to be told, because the support unit people had no idea what we had just gone through. We were hosted and given presents and everyone rejoiced with us that we had survived so well.

We then had 14 days of rest. We were reassigned, given new clothes, our feet were healthy again and after these two weeks, we were redeployed and there was so much difficult time left to get through.

At any rate, the retreat from the Belgrade 'kettle' had demanded everything from everyone. But I would have preferred to try anything rather than become a prisoner. I was just lucky and could wait until the end of the war until I also had the opportunity to march as a prisoner in the vicinity of Olmütz (Olomouc), an opportunity that only lasted a few months.

Hauptmann Kurt Steidl, commander of *I.Bataillon*, offers another view of the fighting south of Belgrade from inside the pocket of *Generalleutnant* Stettner starting on October 12th:

After the transport for wounded had left in the late evening hours and I was now subordinated to the *1.Gebirgsjäger-Division*, I received orders to march 30 km at night to the nearest large town in order to set up quarters there.

The march became a torture; the feet hurt terribly. In the town, everything was crowded with troops and we were able to lay our tired legs down on open streets in the cold again. It was not until it was day that some makeshift quarters were freed up by troops moving out and we could rest a bit. I had the battalion of Russian volunteers and my troops with foot problems move towards Belgrade and I remained with my weaker units subordinate to *Major* Dode as a rear guard. I also found out that *Oberstleutnant* Oesterwitz with his units was not far away.

An unsuccessful flank attack by a regiment of the *1.Gebirgsjäger-Division* to the south gave us an idea of how serious the situation was. The enemy had reached the road to Belgrade on a broad front.

Were we going to be washed down the rainspout by the rain? We decamped in the early morning and marched on muddy roads without any paving. The column seemed endless; we assumed there was enemy contact in the next town. We still had artillery, *Panzer*, *Sturmgeschütz* and ammunition again as well. Just outside of Passarovic (Pozarevac), the Russians were in a town along the road we were using to retreat. We made quick work of sweeping them out of there and the *Kampfgruppe Major Dode* continued on its way toward Passarovic. We broke through the Russians' positions outside the city in heavy fighting.

Right behind me, a *Sturmgeschütz* flew through the air where the rubble had just hit us. Tired and haggard, we made our way into the city at night. A heavy battle for it was in progress.

Major at the end of the war. "kettle" refers to a pocket surrounded by the enemy.

The Russians were attacking from the south and the east. We got through the artillery fire without any losses and my people moved into a large school.

I found out that Oesterwitz also had his command post in the city. While it was still night, I sought him out. He couldn't believe that I and my people were still alive when Milanovac came out; he believed that we were already absolutely destroyed. I also met my old friend Sepp Schmid here. Our reunion was sufficiently celebrated. Jork Adolf, who never made it back from Belgrade, was also there. Unfortunately, I found out about the other painful losses of the other regimental units, including the loss of *Leutnant* Toni Schmid.

We realigned the regiment and formed two battalions. I received parts of the *Bataillon Renner* [Author's Note (AN): members of *II.Bataillon*] and what had formerly been the *Bataillon Oesterwitz* [Author's Note (hereafter cited as AN): *I.Bataillon*] and gave up my *1.Kompanie* with *Leutnant* Auer to get it. I was deployed on the main battle line the very next day. My command post was in the basement of the school building.

Jork turned over his positions to me and he was moved to the *Regiment*. In the courtyards in front of the school building, there was heavy artillery fire and the Katyusha Rockets frequently fired into the city. My new *Kompanie Leutnant* Kopp lay alongside the railway embankment and I was also given a few 8.8cm Flak-Gun.

We stayed a few more days and then broke camp one evening. We went over the bridge across the Morava, which was blown up behind us by our own engineering troops. Right beyond it, we set up positions again in the open air. The Russians were already behind us on the other bank of the Morava and were glad to fire on us! We went further back because the threat from the south became more and more serious and the Russians' first tank forward units were right outside Belgrade.

In a rather large town outside of Semendria (Smederevo), I got more orders to stay as a rear guard until the other troops had made it through. Fortunately, I had vehicles again. A few kilometers outside of Semendria, we were attacked by Russian forces. We managed to stop them. While it was still morning, we moved into the city of Semendria on the Danube. There were heavy battles for the city in progress.

The city was clogged with troops of various units; it was pretty chaotic. I got new orders from Oesterwitz and moved to the edge of the city to secure it and relieve other units. I myself was made the city commandant by Oesterwitz and was supposed to regulate the troops' retreat. We were supposed to move camp in the afternoon. From the northern bank of the Danube, the enemy was firing at our departing troops with all its artillery. Only the road planned for the retreat was still free. The enemy had made its way into the southern part of the city. There was heavy street fighting underway. At the last minute, I got my companies out of there and was getting out in a *Panzerspähwagen* myself. I ran into *Major* Dode again en route. Now off we went to Belgrade on clogged streets. There was wild pushing and shoving underway. There were multiple *Divisions* marching.

On our way, after expenditure of a lot of effort and force and nerves, we reached a place from which one couldn't go any further.

It appears that panic was starting because everyone knew that everyone knew that the Russians were sitting in Belgrade and putting together a kettle for us again. I had no contact with Oesterwitz, so I set off with my people cross country next to the road.

The next morning, we went further down the road, fired on from left and right. Belgrade could be seen far off in the mist. Thick clouds of smoke lay over the city. I could clearly see the suburb of Mokri Lug, from which we had left for Negotin some weeks earlier. On the southern heights, we occupied positions and had strong enemy attacks to repel. The next morning, we attacked toward Belgrade. Regiments of the *1.Gebirgsjäger-Division* and *Oberst* Hildebrand with his *92.Grenadierregiment (mot.)* participated in that. Jork and I observed the attack from the hill. The enemy was sitting at the edge of the city with dug-in tanks and didn't surrender a single meter of ground. The enemy was pressing significantly from the east and the south as well—in the north the Danube put a bar in our way. We no longer hand any freedom of movement; crowded together on a road, we were on a stretch about 20 km long with about 30,000 men facing extermination. *Geschütz* and heavy weapons had no ammunition and *Generalleutnant* Stettner had lost his nerve. In the evening, Jork and I were taken to Oesterwitz's command post. We forced our way through thick columns under heavy antitank fire and reached the place. At Oesterwitz's place, I found out that we would try to break out to the south that evening. We met in a small village near the road at nightfall. Jork Adolf left me, because he was supposed to take over a battalion of the *Regiment 1 'BR'*. This was the last time I ever saw him. The previous afternoon, there had been rolling air attacks that hit thousands of vehicles and people. In the evening, all of the vehicles and the tubes were blown up; a real panic broke out among the other troops and their leaders were nowhere to be found. So thousands of soldiers were wandering around during the night and hundreds of wounded shot themselves. It was a ghastly picture of annihilation. The burning vehicles flamed up in the night sky and the enemy fired without ceasing into the chaos from all sides.

Generalleutnant Stettner spread the word, "if you can save yourself, do so" instead of daring to do an organized breakout. My people were firmly with me and I consulted with Oesterwitz. We joined a column of the *1.Gebirgsjäger-Division* and in a bold night attack broke through the surrounding cordon and just before it became slightly light were able to cross the highway in front of Mt. Avala between individual enemy vehicles. There was also a *General* Wichmann with us.

We were fired on in a town south of Belgrade and hit by artillery fire from the heights above us. We were only a small piece of the 30,000 men that were out. There were Tito units milling around us in the terrain; they usually thought we were Russians. We sent them packing each time when they were close enough. Behind us in the vicinity of Avala Russian T-34 tanks were banging into a canyon stopped up with masses of people.

Words are not sufficient to tell this story. Kieffer and his company were missing and they ran into us a few days later to our great joy after we had made our way further and further south going through Wader.

Our beards became longer and longer and the drudgery got greater; we often moved up to 70 km per day going uphill and downhill. We wanted to cross the Sava going north in the vicinity of Obrenovac. There were supposed to still be friendly troops in Semlin. But there was still no prospect of getting there.

In a small town, we got empty cans and grease together so that we might survive our planned river trip in icy water. Russian tanks were reported in the evening in our vicinity. We moved off in pouring rain. We went on a side road; the mud was up to our knees. We carefully made our way through the darkness. People fell out and were trampled; others lay down off the road out of fatigue. We lost our way and wound up in a place that was full of Tito's troops. After a wild firefight, we got out of the town and the dawning morning saved us from the torture and anguish of this night of ooze. The railway line was crossed. We still had 30 km to go to the Sava. Partisans attacked us and there were some more painful losses. The town on the Sava was taken by storm and stuff to cross the river was built that very evening. The first people make it across as darkness fell. I was with Oesterwitz in a bar on the broad stream, when Russian tanks coming down the road from Belgrade put the crossing site under fire. There was nothing more for us to do except break out of there quickly and reach the city of Sabac, which was 40 km upstream on the Sava and still occupied by friendly troops.

We crawled into the town on all fours and were close to exhaustion. We pushed into quarters and slept for a whole 24 hours.

Nevertheless, we were out of the kettle and the few of us had our lives back. We thought of the thousands of comrades still in the Belgrade kettle, including Adolf Jork and his battalion, *Leutnant* Auer with my brave *1.Kompanie*, *Feldwebel* Steinitz, *Oberjunker* Andre, *Oberleutnant* Wurst and his battalion and many others. New missions again awaited us. The *1.Gebirgsjäger-Division* also no longer existed; it was reconstituted.

Generalleutnant Stettner was killed by partisans during the breakout on October 18th. The remnants of *Regiment 2 'BR'* were reassembled and sent to the Danube at Apatin in late November where *Regiment 1 'BR'* was located. After several more weeks of heavy fighting, the remnants of the regiment were withdrawn, and on December 16th, the tired veterans boarded trains for Angerburg, East Prussia.

Regiment 3 'Brandenburg'

Regiment 3 'BR' was still in Italy mainly fighting partisans in the area of Trieste. When the order to withdraw back to Baden near Vienna for the reorganization was received, *Generalfeldmarschall* Albert Kesselring, who commanded forces in Italy at the time, countermanded them. The men of *Regiment 3 'BR'* remained in Italy and parceled out among several *Gebirgs-Divisions* where they remained until the end of the war. Some members were consolidated to create the *Machinegun-Bataillon 'Kesselring'* in the final months of the war. Despite Kesselring's orders a few members did make their way back to *Division 'Brandenburg'* on their own, without official permission.

Regiment 4 'Brandenburg'

Regiment 4 'BR' commanded by *Hauptmann* Kriegsheim consisted of only two battalions in September 1944. The *II.Bataillon* was combined with the *I.Btl./Rgt. 4 'BR'* in July due to heavy losses. In late August *OB Südost* ordered both *Bataillons* to assemble near Belgrade along with the *Sturmgeschütz-Brigade 201* and *Fallschirmjäger-Bataillon 'BR'* located in Montenegro. This force was being assembled to put down the coup d'état in Romania that occurred on August 23rd. *III.Btl./Rgt. 4 'BR'* did deploy into Romania where it suffered heavy losses in the vicinity of Klausenburg in northern Romania, retreating into the Carpathians in September. The remnants continued to withdraw through Hungary reaching the Danube in late October into early November. They linked up with other units of *'Brandenburg'* in the area between Pees and Novi Sad. *I.Btl./Rgt. 4 'BR'*, commanded by *Hauptmann* Gerlach, never deployed into Romania but remained in Indija, north of Belgrade as a reserve force. It was put on alert in late September to move south and provide cover for *Kampfgruppe Wittmann* advancing to the southeast. *Hauptmann* Gerlach, however, did not deploy with his force and battalion command was passed to *Oberleutnant* Schönherr. The *Kampfgruppe* was ordered to defend against a Soviet advance in the area of Morava and ensure that the *1.Gebirgsjäger-Division* and its accompanying *Regiment 2 'Brandenburg'* could break out of the area between the Danube and the Morawa and head toward Belgrade.

During the night of October 14th/15th the *I.Btl./Rgt. 4 'BR'* found itself in heavy fighting against a Soviet armored force on the west bank of the Morawa driving north along the bank. The Soviet advance threatened to cut off the route of withdrawal and surround the German forces positioned along the west bank. Elements of the *92.Grenadierregiment (mot.)* and the *I.Btl./Rgt. 4 'BR'* were alerted to counterattack the Soviet advance, but those orders were countered the following the day as it was obvious that the Soviet force was too large to stop. On October 15th the *Bataillon* was ordered to deploy to Osipaonica, where it linked up with the parts of the *1.Gebirgsjäger-Division* and *Regiment 2 'Brandenburg'* that had broken through the Soviet positions. With the *I.Btl./Rgt. 4 'BR'* acting as a rear guard, the combined force moved north toward Smederevo on the Danube.

The Soviets were already north of the Danube and in the eastern part of Belgrade where the *I.Btl./*

Rgt. 1 'BR' was engaged in heavy street fighting with Soviet tanks and infantry. The advancing German force was met with heavy artillery fire, but they could not turn back south. The only option was to advance northwest through Soviet lines.

The combined *1.Gebirgsjäger-Division*, *Regiment 2 'Brandenburg'* and *I.Btl./Rgt. 4 'BR'* fought a running battle along the road north to Belgrade against strong Soviets antitank, tank and machine gun positions. The hills between Boleč and Avala, southeast of Belgrade, were the scenes of desperate fighting. The German *Kampfgruppe* became splintered in the hilly terrain, and small pockets of soldiers continued their independent attempts to break through the Soviet lines. In the difficult terrain south of Belgrade, the retreating German soldiers found themselves short on ammunition and physical strength. Many were soon captured by the Soviets. By October 20th the last German remnants surrounded in and around Belgrade surrendered. The *I.Btl./Rgt. 4 'BR'* was split in two during the fighting. The main group of 20 soldiers under the command of *Oberleutnant* Schönherr was captured seven kilometers south of Sava. A dozen or so stragglers of the *Bataillon* broke through north of the pocket assembled in the vicinity of Esseg on the Danube where they were picked up by the Regimental Staff.

Hungary
Shortly after escaping the inferno south of Belgrade, the regiments and other survivors of *'Brandenburg'* were sent (somewhat incredulously given their physical and psychological state) to Hungary where they defended the bridgeheads of Apatin and Batina through November. The heaviest fighting occurred from November 7th-15th. As the survivors of *Regiment 1 'BR'* and *Regiment 2 'BR'* settled into to their positions on the west bank of the Danube River opposite Apatin, the weather conspired to make their defense as miserable as possible, almost rivaling the incessant Soviet artillery and mortar bombardment. According to one veteran "We build foxholes and bunkers; my line is several kilometers long. The ground water is in the positions, heavy rain has transformed the entire forest into a lake." Patrols and small unit combat actions dominated the weeks of November. Casualties mounted. Amidst the foul weather the men dealt with continuous Soviet attacks and the natural process of psychologically dealing with the aftermath of the heavy fighting south of Belgrade, came the rumors that *Division 'Brandenburg'* was no more.

From Southeast Europe to East Prussia
In mid-November the command post of *Division 'Brandenburg'* was located in Darda, north of Esseg, Hungary. The commander, *Generalleutnant* Kühlwein turned over command to *Oberst* Hermann Schulte-Heuthaus. The command elements began leaving Hungary for Baden near Vienna to start restructuring as a *Panzergrenadier-Division*. Subunits of the new division began to form throughout Germany. Only the new *Flak-Abteilung* was ready and sent to the Danube to assist in the defense with the burnt out regiments of *Division 'Brandenburg'*. Starting on November 22nd, and continuing through mid-December, all the regimental remnants began rail movement to Angerburg, East Prussia.

The fighting around Belgrade destroyed the regiments of *'Brandenburg'*. All the battalions of *Regiment 1 'BR'* suffered heavy losses, with the *II.Bataillon* being destroyed. *Regiment 2 'BR'* was largely destroyed. Even before the battle for Belgrade *Regiment 4 'BR'* had suffered such heavy losses in their role as elite infantry that the *I.Bataillon* and *II.Bataillon* were combined as a single force. They were subsequently largely destroyed along with the *III.Bataillon* that deployed to Romania. *Regiment 3 'BR'* never left Italy. Exact numbers of losses do not exist, but if *Regiment 3 'BR'* is excluded from the conservative estimate, it is likely that losses among the other regiments in terms of killed, missing, or wounded exceeded 70%.

Months later as the new *Panzergrenadier-Division 'Brandenburg'* was forming, its soldiers were still dealing with the consequences of the breakout through Belgrade. They not only lost individual comrades, but entire companies went missing. *Leutnant* G. Simons' letter to the father of one his comrades is a fitting epitaph to the destruction of 'Brandenburg' in the Balkans.

Monday, January 8th, 1945

Dear Mr. Mundlos!

A call from the *Division* brought up for me the hard fate of the family of our *Leutnant* Mundlos a few days ago. And the fact that your son has been considered missing since October 21st, 1944 has made his fate such a tragedy that all of us who know him are upset. The fact that you have no news about him is because the news was given to his wife. When his wife died, the news was lost.

Now as your son's comrade, I have taken over the hard task of telling you about his fate. We were in military school together and have been good friends since then. As luck would have it, we were able to serve together in the same *Bataillon*.

This *Bataillon* was deployed against the Russians in October south of Belgrade. And we had to go through difficult battles, though they were successful. And these battles also set your son particularly apart. In many attacks, he and his platoon successfully participated. On October 15th, he gave us all an outstanding example of courage and boldness. He and his assault force got the orders to take an important supply bridge over the Sava in a surprise attach to flock the Russian supply lines to Belgrade. *Leutnant* Mundlos and his men got to the bridge, but found that it was secured by two Russian companies and three tanks. That did not deter him. In a gutsy attack, he caused severe losses to the Russians and he himself destroyed a 52-ton tank with close combat equipment. When the Russians quickly regrouped, however, continuing this enterprise against such an overwhelming force had no prospect of success. *Leutnant* Mundlos got his people back without any friendly losses.

A few days later, the battles to break through to Belgrade began. In the meantime, the enemy took over the city with strong forces and thus set us up to retreat. The battles to break through were unsuccessful. We got orders to fight our way through cross country to the Sava in the west. Your son went missing in the process. Unfortunately there is no one left in his company who could report about his fate.

The last time I saw your son was on October 18th, 1944. We were aware of the hard road that lay ahead. Our two Kompanien were torn apart by the battles. My *Kompanie* found its way out of the "kettle" through a roundabout route. However, nothing more was seen of your son's *Kompanie*. We all assume that your son's *Kompanie* fought its way to the south to somehow find a way out there. Maybe they found a way to hook up with troops returning from Greece.

Even I cannot say anything more about the fate of the missing units. But I do strongly believe that there will be a light one day in this whole matter. And we will certainly get some news someday.

Mr. Mundlos, I will immediately inform you of any news because I know how much of a burden this lack of knowledge can be.

All of those who liked your son because of his open happy personality believe that he will surface someday because there are still men coming back who went missing after the fighting at that time. And we can't imagine an entire *Kompanie* disappearing without a trace.

I am available for any questions you might have about everything that you consider worth knowing. And I still hope that one day the return of your son will answer all the questions and worries.

Mr. Mundlos, please accept these signs of my deep condolences,

Sincerely, *Leutnant* G. Simons

II.Btl./Jäg.Rgt. 2 'BR'

Those who were captured and survived their ordeal as prisoners-of-war in both Tito's and Soviet captivity returned to Germany, sometimes decades later, with stories of how many of their comrades were shot upon capture south of Belgrade by the partisans. The wounded and officers were often the main victims. For example, it was reported by a survivor in 1956 how *Leutnant* Steger of the *1.Kp./I.Btl./Reg. 4 'BR'* was shot by Tito's Partisans after capture once they realized he was a company commander. Others would die as prisoners-of-war in the draconian service of Tito as slave labor. Being a prisoner-of-war in Yugoslavia after the war came with an unusually high mortality rate.[5] One duty assigned to these men was to build Tito's summer palace on Lake Bled (now a hotel in Slovenia). How many *'Brandenburg'* veterans were among the slave laborers that built the palace or who were forced to pose for the artist that painted the wrap-around mural in the double cube room is unknown.[6] Only through these postwar reports by former German prisoners-of-war did family members finally learn of their son's fate.

---

5   Macdonogh, p. 426.
6   Ibid. Former German prisoners of Tito often returned to the villa after the fall of the Soviet Union and communist East European countries to point out their faces in the mural to their wives and children.

4

Genesis of *Panzer-Korps 'Großdeutschland'*

The Soviets launched the Belorussian Strategic Offensive Operation on the 3rd anniversary of the Nazi invasion of the Soviet Union known as Operation *Barbarossa*. Their goal was designed to finally push German armies off Soviet territory. The Soviet offensive was codenamed Operation Bagration. Using deception the Soviet High Command (STAVKA) convinced Adolf Hitler and *Generaloberst* Heinz Guderian that the 1944 summer offensive would strike the area between the Carpathian Mountains and the Black Sea. *Fremde Heeres Ost* (*FHO*-Foreign Armies East) commanded by *Generalmajor* Reinhard Gehlen was the office under Guderian that provided predictions of upcoming Soviet offensives. Gehlen not only confirmed the Soviet deception, but also added that a secondary attack might strike between the Carpathians and Pripet Marshes, on the right flank of *Heeresgruppe Mitte*. This prediction caused a strengthening of the *LVI.Panzer-Korps* during May. By the end of May intelligence reports from the Front appeared to confirm that the upcoming Soviet offensive would miss *Heeresgruppe Mitte* completely causing Hitler to reassign the *LVI.Panzer-Korps* to *Heeresgruppe Nordukraine* along with additional combat resources. In total *Heeresgruppe Mitte* lost 6% of its frontline, 15% of its combat divisions, 88% of its *Panzers*, 23% of its *Sturmgeschütze*, 50% of its *Panzerabwehrkanon* (*PAK*), and 33% of its heavy artillery.[1] With these transfers, *Heeresgruppe Mitte* was still the strongest *Heeresgruppe* in the East on paper, but it also had the longest frontline to defend measuring 785 kilometers (488 miles). The *Heeresgruppe* consisted of 486,000 combat soldiers, not counting rear area personnel, 118 *Panzers*, 377 *Sturmgeschütze*, 2,589 *PAK* and artillery tubes, and 602 aircraft.[2] Across their frontline were the forces of the Soviet 1st Baltic Front, 3rd Belorussian Front, and 2nd Belorussian Front that consisted of 2,331,700 Soviets and 79,900 Polish soldiers, 2,715 tanks, 1,355 assault guns, 24,363 artillery pieces and anti-tank guns of all caliber and 5,327 aircraft.[3]

Based on statistics alone German forces faced incredible odds with the Soviets mustering almost 5:1 in manpower, 8:1 in armored fighting vehicles, 9:1 in anti-tank and artillery guns, and 6:1 in combat aircraft. The Soviets also enjoyed both a high degree of motorization and tactical combat power in their infantry units over their German counterparts. Allied lend lease provided the Soviet Union with hundreds of thousands of trucks and jeeps that motorized the rifle companies and battalions. Soviet infantry were increasingly equipped with semi-automatic rifles and fully automatic submachine guns, while their German counterparts continued to be armed primarily with pre-war bolt-action rifles. The outcome of the Soviet offensive was decided before the attack began.

Operation Bagration decisively defeated *Heeresgruppe Mitte*. The German *3.Panzer-Armee*, *9.Armee*, *4.Armee* and *2.Armee* were crushed and the German frontline in the east was pushed back to the German border in East Prussia and along the Weichsel (Vistula) River in central Poland. Estimates of German losses vary, but losses were approximately 26,300 killed, 109,700 wounded, and 263,000

---

1   Earl F. Ziemke, *Stalingrad to Berlin* (Barnes and Noble Books: New York, ND), p. 313-14.
2   Karl-Heinz Frieser ed. *Das Deutsche Reich und der Zweite Weltkrieg – Vol. 8: Karl-Heinz Frieser, Klaus Schmider, Klaus Schönherr, Gerhard Schreiber, Kristián Ungváry, Bernd Wegner: Die Ostfront 1943/44 – Der Krieg im Osten und an den Nebenfronten* (München: Deutsche Verlags-Anstalt: 2007). p. 531.
3   Ibid, p. 534 and Colonel-General G.F. Krivosheev ed., *Soviet Casualties and Combat Losses* (Frank Cass: Portland, 1998), p. 145.

missing or captured.[4] Soviet losses were also significant, numbering some 771,000[5] killed, wounded or missing, but the Soviets could replace their losses in men and material more readily than the *Wehrmacht*. By mid-September 1944 the frontline in the east stabilized with the exception of the former Baltic Republics where the Soviets continued operations to retake the countries of Estonia, Latvia, and Lithuania.

The defeat in the east was matched by the *Wehrmacht's* defeat in the west during the same summer months of June-August. In the west, German formations under the command of *OB West* likewise fought a difficult summer campaign against the Western Allies who landed along the Normandy coast in June. By early September they were now occupying a frontline that ran through parts of the Low Countries and along the western German border known as the Siegfried Line. During July conspirators consisting of German officers attempted to assassinate Adolf Hitler and failed. Among the repercussions was an increased Nazification of the *Wehrmacht* that included the establishment of National Socialist Political Officers (*Führung Offiziers* or *NSFOs*)[6] and honorary *'Volks'* divisions under the administrative control of Himmler's *SS* organization. Nearly 7,000 individuals, many of whom were officers of the *Wehrmacht* who were considered 'reactionary' by the Gestapo, were arrested and some 5,000 were executed. Hitler ceased to trust his military officers and increasingly relied on his inner circle, specifically Himmler. No decision showed this feeling more than his appointment of *Reichsführer-SS* Heinrich Himmler as the new commander of the *Ersatzheer* (Replacement Army), as it was from within the Replacement Army that the plot to assassinate Hitler was launched. The influence of Himmler's *SS* was growing post July 20th, and it soon reached out to absorb *Division 'Brandenburg'*.

In the wake of the simultaneous defeats on both fronts the *Führer*, Adolf Hitler, decided in early September to launch an attack against the Western Allies in December 1944 using the final operational reserves available to *Oberkommando der Wehrmacht* (*OKW*). It was hoped that this attack would split the Western Allies and force them out of the war. In order to build this offensive force from the shattered remains of both his western and eastern armies, existing combat formations, new recruits, and equipment were sent west from across the Reich to form a new priority *Führerreserve* in western Germany. The Eastern Front would now have to reorganize many of its own battered commands and formations during this strategic buildup of forces in the west. Among the new units formed and re-formed from available forces were *Panzer-Korps 'Großdeutschland'* as well as its new subunits *Panzergrenadier-Division 'Großdeutschland'* and *Panzergrenadier-Division 'Brandenburg'*.

Wehrkreis, Ersatzheer and Primary Groups

Established in 1919 with the founding of the *Reichswehr*, the Military District system known as *Wehrkreis*, provided the manpower that fueled Hitler's war effort until the bitter end. Only seven *Wehrkreis* existed in 1932 but by 1943 nineteen were formed to include two special districts that consisted of General Government (Warsaw) and Bohemia and Moravia (Prague). Each *Wehrkreis* was made up of a headquarters with two headquarter components. One was mobilized and sent to the frontline while the second, known as a *Stellvertreter* (Deputy Commands) remained behind to manage the specific *Wehrkreis*. The duties of the *Wehrkreis* were to mobilize, train, equip, and field new combat divisions. As the war progressed and attrition mounted, these Military Districts became responsible for rebuilding and re-constituting burnt out units. Drawing on the often millions of inhabitants in their area of responsibility, the Deputy Commands became masters of improvisation. The men on these command staffs had an average age in their 60s, being generally ten years older than

---

4   Christopher Bergstrom (2007). *Bagration to Berlin: The Final Air Battles in the East: 1944–1945* (Hersham: Ian Allen Publishing), p.82.

5   Krivosheev, p. 145.

6   *Nationalsozialistischer Führungsoffizier* (*NSFOs*) were established after the failed July 20th, 1944 assassination plot on Adolf Hitler to further National Socialist indoctrination of *Wehrmacht* officers and soldiers.

their counterparts in frontline *Korps* Headquarters. These men were typically veterans of World War I and had significant experience functioning as a military staff. In 1938 the *Wehrkreis* were subordinated to the newly formed *Ersatzheer* in Berlin. The *Ersatzheer* was commanded by *General* Friedrick Fromm who tacitly supported *Oberst i.G.* Count Claus von Stauffenberg's plot to assassinate Hitler on July 20th 1944, then turned against von Stauffenberg and the conspirators executing them that same evening. Fromm was subsequently imprisoned by Hitler and himself executed in March 1945. The importance of the *Ersatzheer*, and its involvement in a plot to bring down the Nazi political apparatus resonated with Hitler who immediately appointed Himmler in charge of the single greatest source of Nazi Germany's continued resistance. Despite the plot and change of leadership, the operations of the *Ersatzheer* and *Wehrkreis* were not interrupted in the least—a testament to their organizational efficiency. Perhaps more to the point, it was the *Wehrkreis* that allowed the *Reichswehr* of 100,000 soldiers in 1935 to rapidly expand into the *Wehrmacht* of more than 4,000,000 soldiers by early 1944, while simultaneously fielding replacement for more than 2,000,000 combat casualties during that same period.

The actions of each *Wehrkreis* Deputy Headquarters in 1945 ensured a continued supply of manpower for the Eastern Front. They also guaranteed a steady stream of casualties as few combat formations were suited for the operational and tactical tasks they were assigned. Many were destroyed in combat against the Western Allies and Red Army in the summer of 1944, then again in Poland, Pomerania, Prussia, or Kurland during the winter of 1945, only to be rebuilt at least once prior to the final Soviet attack on Germany in the spring. The fact that these formations offered as much resistance as they did during the final Soviet assault in the east was an incredible feat of organizational improvisation by the *Ersatzheer*. Such was the conclusion reached in the U.S. Army post war assessment of the German *Ersatzheer*:

> The history of the Replacement Army from 1939 to 1945, in its conscription, replacement, and training system as well as in the changes in the type, number, organization, and location of its units truly reflects the story of the war.
>
> The basic system stood up almost to the end of the war. There were great modifications regarding the affiliation system, the organization of replacement and training units, and the method of transferring replacements to the Field Army during these five and a half years. But there was never a complete new system, and the status of the Replacement Army at any given time, the numbering of its units, etc., could only be understood, and predictions of future developments could only be made, by a study of the Replacement Army from the very start ...
>
> This system was carefully thought out before the war started and was designed to insure maximum efficiency in the utilization of manpower, complete control at all times by an intricate system of administrative records, and the maintenance of the traditions and pride of individual units and districts. Considering the methodical way in which German personnel applied the system, it was ideal for the type of war contemplated by the German High Command in 1939. As the war was prolonged, the fronts became longer and more distant, casualties mounted, and difficulties in communications and in manpower began to multiply, an increasing number of modifications and adjustments had to be made in the operation of the replacement system. As the fighting was carried to German territory by the Allies from the east and the west and, as Goebbels put it, improvisation became infinitely better than organization, the system as originally conceived proved too cumbersome. Characteristically, the Germans nevertheless tried desperately to preserve its essential features to the very end.[7]

---

7   *German Replacement Army Supplement, May 1945* (Washington, DC: Military Intelligence Division, 1945), pp. 12-13. The German *Ersatzheer* and *Wehrkreis* were key elements in rebuilding German combat power in preparation for the Operation *Wacht am Rhein* in the Ardennes. In looking at the 29 German divisions that launched the attack in

The improvisation that maintained the *Wehrmacht* field divisions came in two forms: reduction and reconstitution. The *Wehrmacht* divisions deployed in 1945 were very different from those that existed in 1939. Five years of war radically altered the shape and form of the units that were fielded to the frontline. The combat division became increasingly smaller in size as regiments and battalions were eliminated from their tables of organization in order to cope with manpower and even equipment shortages. By the spring of 1945 it was not uncommon for German divisions to have on average between 5,000-10,000 men, which was a significant drop from the average of more than 16,000 at the start of the war. The *Ersatzheer* and *Wehrkreis* systems could not keep up with the fielding of replacements to form whole new divisions for the frontline and as units were destroyed in battle. The training time required was not compatible with the pace that units were required to deploy against the enemy. Instead, the homogeneous replacement systems of combat divisions were supplanted with an ad hoc reconstitution through the use of other burnt out divisional remnants. We can see just how efficient the *Ersatzheer* was in this improvisation as we examine at the formation of *Panzer-Korps 'GD'* and the re-formed *Panzergrenadier-Division 'GD'* and *Panzergrenadier-Division 'BR'*.

All three formations required the addition of units outside the *'Großdeutschland'* and *'Brandenburg'* replacement battalions to fill out their required organization structures. For example, the *XIII. Armee-Korps* became the basis of the *Panzer-Korps 'GD'* staff organization and the *Panzergrenadier-Division 'GD'* received from the *Heer* the *Panzer-Abteilung (Fkl) 302* and *Sturmpanzer-Kompanie 218*. *Panzergrenadier-Division 'BR'* required the most help in its reorganization. Almost everyone in its training and replacement pipeline was sent to the SS based on the arrangement that kept the majority of the *Division* in the *Heer*. As it began to draw new trainees from the *'Großdeutschland'* replacement system, whole units were assimilated from the *schwere Artillerie-Abteilung 843*, *1.Panzer-Division*, *18.Artillerie-Division*, *78.Sturm-Division*, *258.Infanterie-Division*, *zbV Division 794* and *Sturm-Division 'Rhodos'* to complete its formation. Underscoring the U.S. Army postwar assessment regarding the breakdown of the *Ersatzheer*, *'Brandenburg'* absorbed stragglers from other units into its ranks while in the field to fill in gaps, and recruited and formed its own *Fahrschwadron* without authorization. In many respects, improvisation begets improvisation.

There is an intrinsic benefit to form combat divisions from homogeneous training and replacement units. Men who train together form a bond—a camaraderie—known by social scientists as a "primary group" that provides the psychological support structure relied on by soldiers to survive the strains of combat.[8] Integrating new replacements and their existing primary group bonds into a larger military structure, like a division, is a critical component in fostering what is known as a unit's "cohesion and combat effectiveness". This problem was mastered by the *Ersatzheer* in the early years of the war. Each *Wehrkreis* maintained its own regionally based training battalions. Local new recruits trained together and formed their initial bonds of camaraderie based on months of shared experience. These recruits were then organized into *Marsch Bataillone* (March Battalions) and sent to the frontline as a group—not as individuals—where they were arrived at a designated divisions holding area. Once they arrived at their destination, the *Marsch Bataillone* were dissolved and they entered into the divisional replacement battalion associated with one of the division's combat regiments. Each combat

---

December 1944, 15 were all but destroyed in the August 1944 Mortain-Falaise encirclement, three were reduced in the retreat across France (of which two contributed cadres for new *Volksgrenadier-Divisions*), six were rebuilt *Volksgrenadier-Divisions* that suffered heavy casualties along the Western Front during the fall battles of 1944, and two others were *Volksgrenadier-Divisions* rebuilt from divisions destroyed in fighting on the Eastern Front. The ability to take all but destroyed combat divisions and in several months rebuild them with men and material, or use their staffs as cadres for new divisions, then field these composite units in an offensive, underscores the ingenuity of the *Wehrkreis* system. Unless a German division was captured completely, its remnants were likely going to be reconstituted and placed back into line.

8   The idea of primary group theory was first argued by the social scientists See Edward A. Shils and Morris Janowitz in their article "Cohesion and Disintegration in the Wehrmacht in World War II," Public Opinion Quarterly" *12* (1948): 280-315.

regiment then supplied experienced NCOs and soldiers who picked up the training of the recruits. After a period of time that could last weeks or even months, the new recruits were then integrated into the combat regiment forming a cohesive fighting force. This could be seen in the replacement companies of *zbv Division 'Brandenburg'* who recruited regionally and supplied trained specialists to corresponding battalions of the *Division*. The German system was arguably far superior to the U.S. Army replacement system that made no distinction of the benefit of group bonds. Instead, individuals were fed into units, often without the benefit of a shared background, training or experiences. The Soviet model was closer to the *Ersatzheer* in function and practice.[9] This entire system mutated in the fall of 1944 and experienced additional breakdowns in 1945. With this understanding of the *Wehrkreis* and *Ersatzheer*, the question remains: how did this reorganization affect the combat performance of *'Brandenburg'* in 1945?

Zbv Division 'Brandenburg' was burnt out in November 1944. Its combat battalions were decimated and not only required replacements, but based on the originally proposed organizational structure the *Division* was to expand from four to six combat battalions. While *'Brandenburg'* was organized under a division structure it had none of the support units required in a conventional *Panzergrenadier-Division* like pioneers, artillery, armor or supply. Where was this manpower and equipment to be drawn? From a manpower perspective *'Brandebourg'* lost its core cadre of replacements who were absorbed by the *SS* so it could not draw on the nearly 1,500 men available from this source. It became obvious to the organizers of the new *Division* that six battalions could simply not be formed and the number was immediately reduced to four combat battalions. The survivors from across the four combat regiments of the *zbv Division*—many of whom had not fought with each other in the past— were cross-leveled into two regiments that now made up the core of the *Panzergrenadier-Division*. But this consolidation was not enough to make up for the losses incurred during the fighting in southeast Europe and *'Brandenburgers'* received an infusion of men from other units like *Sturm-Division 'Rhodos'*. The required manpower came from a half-dozen different units, all previously burnt out in frontline combat. The new *Panzergrenadier-Division 'BR'* resembled a patchwork quilt of men whose training and combat experiences were diverse. Gone was the homogeneous makeup of the *Division* and the primary group bonds that served as a critical component to the unit's cohesion and combat effectiveness during the early war years. Despite what might appear to be a breakdown of the essential element of the *Wehrkreis* and *Ersatzheer* system, the reformed *Panzergrenadier-Division 'BR'* proved to be one of the most effective combat divisions fielded in 1945.

Some have argued that a loss of primary groups fostered by the gradual collapse of the *Ersatzheer* demonstrates that the social bond of soldiers, particularly German soldiers, was not critical to the maintenance of cohesion and combat effectiveness. These arguments presuppose that in the wake of a complete breakdown of the *Ersatzheer*, replacements entered into combat divisions as individuals toward the end of the war. In order for divisions to maintain their cohesion and combat effectiveness they had to have a shared belief system. Something had to bond these men together and maintain their will to fight. Some historians have postured in broad terms that varying degrees of ideology embodied in the concepts of National Socialism, *Volksgemeinschaft*, or *Frontgemeinschaft* was the unseen force that maintained cohesive, combat effective units through the bitter end of the war.[10] A look at how

9   See Roger R. Reese *Why Stalin's Soldiers Fought: The Red Army's Effectiveness in World War II* (University of Kansas Press: Lawrence, 2011), pp.217-223 and the dated but still useful Martin van Creveld's *Fighting Power: German and U.S. Army Performance 1939-1945* (Arms and Armour Press: London, 1983), pp. 74-76.

10   Since then, historians have made various attempts to argue that a belief system was also a critical component among German soldiers, given the breakdown of the *Ersatzheer*. See Jürgen E. Förster, "The Dynamics of Volksgemeinschaft: The Effectiveness of the German Military Establishment in the Second World War," in *Military Effectiveness, vol. 3. The Second World War*, ed. Allan R. Millet and Williamson Murray (Unwin Hyman: Boston, 1988), Omer Bartov, *The Eastern Front, 1941-1945: German Troops and the barbarization of Warfare* (St. martin's Press: New York, 1986), pp. 1-6 and his *Hitler's Army: Soldier, Nazis, and War in the Third Reich* (Oxford University Press: New York, 1991), pp.

'Brandenburg' formed and performed in its three combat deployments allows a level of juxtaposition between the competing theories of primary group and ideology in the maintenance of the *Division's* cohesion and combat effectiveness.

The several thousand core veterans of *zbv Division 'Brandenburg'* that made up the new combat regiments were men that shared an elite élan. Even though some members of the old *Division* did not know each other as they reformed companies and battalions, they shared the same training and experiences. Surviving the recent combat in the Balkans fostered fertile ground for camaraderie to grow out of shared combat experiences, transcending most belief systems. When mortars and artillery shells thunder into the ground and the hiss of bullets pierce the air above one's head, soldiers are going to maintain their position in a foxhole to a great extent because of a sense of duty embodied in the camaraderie built between the man to their right and to their left. This core group of 'Brandenburgers' shared that. Into their ranks came men from other units with different combat experiences, as well as new recruits with no shared experiences and little tactical training. Three to four weeks of furious training now began. While there are no available records of the 'Brandenburg' training regime, we can assume it was as intense as possible given the impact of winter weather and available equipment. There was certainly enough time to begin the primary group assimilation and formation process at the squad, platoon, and company level, but not enough to weld the composite force together. Whole units of the *Division* came from outside of the 'Brandenburg' force structure. There was the *Heeres-Flak-Artillerie-Abteilung 'BR'* for example that came from *Heeres-Flak-Artillerie-Abteilung 280* for example. In this case the artillerymen knew one another already and their technical skills of their combat profession. A primary group existed. They did not know the other men of the combat battalions they would be called on to support or the command staff they were now subordinated. The same can be said of *Panzer-Sturm-Pionier-Bataillon 'BR'.* Most officers and men had to acquaint themselves with each other and all the new members. In a few short weeks they had to learn each other's personalities, understand their strengths and weaknesses, and ultimately to build the basic bonds of camaraderie they required to survive the trials of battle. What is clear is that the *Ersatzheer* was working, albeit in an ad hoc way, to forge the basis of new units from a diminishing recruitment pool. Primary groups still existed to varying degrees within the battalions and composite units assigned to forge *Panzergrenadier-Division 'BR'.*

When 'Brandenburg' deployed from the German territory of East Prussia to Poland in January 1945 it was untested as a division in battle—conventional or otherwise. Would the replacements in the combat regiments who shared none of the earlier *Sonderkommando* training or élan of their comrades meet the tasks ahead and be accepted in the ranks? Could the men of the combat regiments trust the crews of the new *Sturmgeschütze* and artillery units to provide them critical support at the right time? Overall did the men, whether old hands or new recruits, receive enough tactical training to foster primary group bonds or develop the conventional tactical skills for the combat tasks ahead?

The first deployment to Poland was a near disaster. Uncoordinated and with little time to react to the overwhelming Soviet forward momentum, the performance of 'Brandenburg' was mixed. Some battalions of the *Division* initially put up stiff resistance and generally demonstrated tactical proficiency, while others displaced without orders, and companies quickly disintegrated. Men broke and ran. Yet, the crucible of combat, where life or death coexist in the same second of time frozen by a nearby explosion or a bullet grazing someone's temple, presents those singular moments where loose primary groups congeal into solid camaraderie. The camaraderie fostered through six weeks of near constant combat exceeded what could be gained through simple training. The new recruits that survived now shared experiences with the old hands. Their beards grew longer together, they struggled through the same snow drifts together, fought off Soviet tank and infantry assaults together. They learned each

---

9-10, and Stephen Fritz, *Frontsoldaten: The German Soldier in World War II* (University Press of Kentucky: Lexington, 1995), pp. 206.

other's strengths and weaknesses together. They entered their first deployment as composite battalions and ended a whole division.

Limited combat continued through March. The *Ersatzheer* continued to function as new replacements made their way to the *Division* This time there was more stability and regularity to the assimilation process. *'Brandenburg'* now enjoyed almost seven weeks of uninterrupted training time that proved critical to hone the existing bonds of camaraderie and forge new ones with the incoming replacements. Unlike the formation period in January, all of the *Division's* components were co-located and functioning and training more like a division. *Panzergrenadier-Division 'BR'* entered its second combat deployment when the final Soviet assault on Germany began in April. *'Brandenburg'* was split into multiple parts almost immediately. The regiments and battalions of the *Division* were placed in a far more catastrophic situation both tactically and strategically then their first deployment, with most of the Reich now occupied. Many men's home towns were bombed during the Allied air campaign in the last few months. Others knew their loved ones were now behind either Western Allied or Soviet lines as the frontline stretched across German territory. Berlin, the Reich capital, was under attack. Communication, command-and-control was disrupted, and many of the cut off regiments and battalions had to temporarily subordinate themselves to other commands. Despite this, the men fought competently to rejoin their *Division* command. When the various combat battalions of *'Brandenburg'* reassembled after being separated behind enemy lines during more than a week (in some cases) of ferocious combat, they delivered devastating tactical defeats against their opponents. The culmination of these victories represented the last operational victory achieved by the *Wehrmacht*, which can be primarily attributed to the combat performance of *Panzergrenadier-Division 'BR'*. It might be argued that the men fought so well because they were fighting in Saxony—on Germany soil—at that time, and that soldiers always fight strongly for their homeland. This argument is hollow given the fact that Germany was all but occupied by mid-April. The men of the *Division* knew there was no military victory achievable on the field of battle no matter how hard they fought and regardless of where they fought. The third combat deployment of *'Brandenburg'* also stands in stark contradiction to this argument.

In the beginning of May *'Brandenburg'* was only an hour or two's drive away from surrender to U.S. Forces and a relatively easy end to the war. Instead, the *Division* was ordered into Czechoslovakia, far to the southeast, into an area of frontline bordered on three sides by an attacking Red Army—far from German soil. *'Brandenburg'* again fought well tactically during the first week of May despite entering into an unknown situation and assigned to a new command it had never been subordinate to in the past. Its defensive actions helped seal off the Soviet penetration in its area. Many German soldiers were given breathing room to withdraw west as a result. The end of *'Brandenburg'* finally came in mid-May, but not due to a defeat in battle or a disintegration of its ranks.

The performance of *'Brandenburg'* suggests that the composite units reformed by the *Ersatzheer* could forge divisional level bonds of camaraderie from disparate primary groups if they survived the crucible of combat. Could a shared ideological belief in some form also contributed to the bonding that fostered cohesion and combat effectiveness in *'Brandenburg'*? It certainly cannot be ruled out, as no historian can divine what lies within the hearts of men, but it is also not easy to prove. When the first person accounts of the *Division* members are surveyed there are no references to the war in ideological terms. The men who kept diaries or wrote letters after the war did so privately without the expectation that their words might be published in total one day. They had no reason to hide their feelings, and in some cases many expressed them openly. When Adolf Hitler's death was announced on the radio on May 1st, it made no recorded difference to the men of *'Brandenburg'*. Who ruled the Third Reich was of little consequence at that late date in the war. They knew the war was over, but they were not going to let their comrades down, nor were they simply going lay down their weapons and surrender. While some began to "disappear" from the ranks, first from the support units, then from frontline combat battalions, most of the *Division* stayed together. Was it because of the camaraderie of shared primary group bonds that continued to form and be reinforced even in the final days of war, or was it some broad ideological belief?

In the last year of war the men of the *Wehrmacht* were bombarded increasingly with ideological education and propaganda provided through routine classes orchestrated by *NSFOs*. Established in 1943, the *NSFOs* did not gain maturity as an organization until after the failed assassination of Adolf Hitler.[11] Their main objective was to instill soldiers with National Socialist ideals, whereby ideological reliability would increase the operational performance of the "reactionary" *Wehrmacht*.[12] The psychological work of these political-indoctrination officers is well documented, but what is less well known is that they were initially deployed primarily on the Western Front where desertion proved more problematic than in the east.[13] After the collapse of the Eastern Front in the winter of 1945 they appeared within the divisions in the east as well, meaning that *'Brandenburg'* may have been spared their direct influence until the front stabilized in mid-March or early April, long after *NSFOs* might have made a difference.

The incorporation of *NSFOs* into the *Wehrmacht* in the last year of war was complimented by a draconian military justice system practiced by many field commanders, especially in *Feldmarschall* Ferdinand Schörner's *H.Gr. Mitte*. As a point of comparison only 150 death sentences were handed out in World War I and of those only 48 were carried out. During World War II, between 15-20,000 German soldiers were executed.[14] Some 75-80% were executed for disciplinary infractions or undermining the spirit of fighting troops.[15] Documented executions show that by the end of 1944 9,732 soldiers had been executed in the first five years of war, while more than 5,000 saw their executions in the last four months of war.[16] In one case, an officer of *'Brandenburg'* shot a member of his unit who seemingly suffered a breakdown and decided to surrender to the enemy. Though the nature of the "desertion" is questionable (discussed in Chapter 16) what it does show is that officers of the *Wehrmacht* had little compulsion to dispense justice on the battlefield when necessary. Even if a soldier was caught in the rear area without "proper" authorization, as one *'Brandenburger'* found himself, summary execution could follow. *Sippenhaft* was also introduced in the fall of 1944.[17] If you were suspected of desertion by your commander, your family would pay the price and have their property confiscated or be sent to a concentration camp. The real fear of immediate execution without a trial might have weighed far more heavily on a soldier's mind when a fight or flight decision arose during combat, more so than the National Socialist indoctrination they may have heard preached by *NSFOs*. However, the *NSFOs* were also used as an outlet for Joseph Goebbels' Propaganda Ministry and in some cases the propaganda issued to the soldiers was a very real source of motivation.

What is revealed in the personal accounts of many *'Brandenburgers'* at the time was the very real fear of unconditional surrender that could lead to Soviet imprisonment. In the final months of the war the use of German soldiers as forced labor to help rebuild the Soviet Union was announced in the open press and capitalized on by the Propaganda Ministry and drummed into the minds of the frontline soldiers through the *NSFOs* (see Appendix C for one such reference). On January 25th, 1945 for example, the New York Times ran an article citing the forcible removal of tens of thousands

---

11 T77/852/5597604. *XVI. Die Mitwirkung der Partei on der Politischen Aktivierung der Wehrmacht.*
12 T77/852/5597556. *I. Einführungs ansprache.*
13 See T77/852/5597631-722 and T77/788/5516842 *Behandlung von Überläufen.*
14 Manfred Messerschmidt, "German Military Law in the Second World War" in *The German Military in the Age of Total War*, ed. Wilhelm Deist (Berg Publishers: Dover, NH, 1985), p. 324.
15 See Wolfram Wette, *Deserteure der Wehrmacht* (Essen: Klartext Verlag, 1995), pp. 31, 74, 141) and Fritz Stern, *Frontsoldaten: The German Soldier in World War II* (Lawrence: The University Press of Kentucky, 1995) p. 90.
16 Messerschmidt, "German Military Law in the Second World War", p. 324.
17 Letter from Himmler to Keitel dated 5.11.44. T77/788/5516835. See also *"Maßnahmen gegen deutsche Überläufer,"* T77/788/5516832-34 dated 6.11.44 and 7.11.44.

of Romanian citizens of German decent (whose only crime was to be German). They were sent east to rebuild the Soviet Union. Again on February 5th, the Soviets made public that Germans must be made to repair all the war damage caused in the Soviet Union after the war. On March 3rd, U.S. President Roosevelt weighed in on the issue, as the British appeared less inclined to support the Soviet demand. Roosevelt's position was to allow Stalin the use of former German veterans to rebuild the Soviet Union providing that Stalin viewed this as payment in kind. As March turned into April the issue of "forced labor" continued to surface in the press prior to the final Soviet assault. If men ever needed a reason to fight, avoiding what was viewed as Soviet "slave labor" was the reason. This fear more than any other tested the limits of their primary group bond. The men who began to desert the *Division* in mid-May fled west to escape the possibility of Soviet captivity.

In the brutal, final months of the war the men of *'Brandenburg'* were likely not exclusively motivated by the ideological preaching of *NSFOs*, draconian punishment, or threat of Soviet "slavery", though all were important factors that made up the milieu of the time. They maintained cohesion and combat effectiveness in the face of overwhelming odds and the stress of constant defeats in January, February, and early March. They performed exceptionally well tactically against larger, better equipped and seemingly victorious Soviet formations in April. They continued to fight long after their "oath" to Adolf Hitler no longer bound them. More than a week after their *Führer's* death and days after the final capitulation of the *Wehrmacht* was announced, the majority of the men of *Panzergrenadier-Division 'BR'* remained together and followed the orders of their commander, *Generalmajor* Schulte-Heuthaus. They did so out of a strong sense of camaraderie found in their various primary groups. Once the *Division* was dissolved by its commander the primary group bonds that held it together during the last four months dissolved in reverse. First, each regiment, then battalion—the basic combat block of a division—moved out on their own. Battalions separated into companies. Then increasingly smaller groups of men who knew each other well formed until they were either captured by the Soviets, or they reached U.S. lines to surrender. As *Major* Steidl wrote in his poem "Our Dead Comrades" (see Appendix J) it was this shared "comradeship that was frequently proven to be a shield and a weapon." *Hauptmann* Müller-Rochholz echoed the same feeling even more poignantly in early May:

> The *Führer* is dead; *Grossadmiral* Dönitz is his successor. We will not swear a new oath. We are a sworn-out bunch! The war can't last much longer. There will be chaos. During these days we want to remain true to ourselves and live through our fate until the end. The battalion's spirit, our comradeship and our dead obligate us to do that. Our shield must remain clean until the last moment. No one is leaving! All of the battles have proven that we will not be defeated if we stand together as one. That is how it will remain until the last order!

This sense of comradeship, fostered in each battalion's primary group, was arguably the strength that the men drew on in impossible situations. In the final analysis it appears to be what maintained their cohesion and combat effectiveness through the end.

Panzer-Korps 'Großdeutschland'

Panzer-Korps 'Großdeutschland' was ordered established on 28 September through the order *OKH/GenStdH/Org.Abt./Nr.II/46843/44 g.Kdos*. There is little information about the decision making process that led to the formation of the new *Panzer-Korps*. The factors that led to its formation are not hard to divine from the strategic situation. Guderian needed an operational reserve in East Prussia and this *Korps Stab* served that purpose. The *Korps Stab* consisted of surviving staff of the *18. Artillerie-Division* that was disbanded on July 27th. Its main staff formed the headquarters of the new *Panzer-Korps* while its regiments formed independent artillery brigades. Addition *Korps* staff was supplied from the remnants of the *XIII. Armee-Korps* that was encircled in the Brody Pocket between July 13th and 18th and destroyed during the Soviet summer offensive against *Heeresgruppe Nordukraine*.

The *Korps* staff established themselves on the southern wing of *Heeresgruppe Mitte* between the *XX. Armee-Korps* on its left flank and the *XXVII. Armee-Korps* on its right flank. The *Korps* was assigned two divisions, the *Panzergrenadier-Division 'Großdeutschland'* and the newly ordered *Panzergrenadier-Division 'BR'*. There is little information about the activities of the *Korps* from September through mid-December and it was during those two and a half months the *Korps* troops were organized in various assembly areas near Praschnitz.

Oberst i.G. Otto Heinrich Bleicken, a talented tactician and one of the youngest officers selected to the General Staff, was reassigned as *Ia* (operations officer) of *Panzergrenadier-Division 'Großdeutschland'* and assigned as *Chef des Stabes* (Chief of Staff) of the new *Panzer-Korps*. He was ordered to Zossen in mid-October where he met with *Generaloberst* Guderian and his staff to discuss the organization of the new *Korps*. Among the topics discussed was the reorganization of the *Korps'* two new divisions, which were still engaged in combat across the Reich.

Panzergrenadier-Division 'Großdeutschland' was ordered to the northern flank of *Heeresgruppe Mitte* in August of 1944 where it fought a series of defensive battles into the early fall. The division was forced back to the coast at Memel and cut off from the rest of the *2. Armee* in East Prussia. The division was ordered to withdraw from Memel on October 26th, 1944 and redeployed to the area of Rastenburg where it was to be reorganized under the new *Panzer-Korps 'Großdeutschland'*. The last troops of the division were shipped by the freighter *Wolta* from Memel to Pillau-Königsberg on December 4th. While reorganization and replenishment was planned for *Panzergrenadier-Division 'Großdeutschland'*, its officers, senior enlisted, and soldiers already enjoyed the benefit of having fought together on the battlefield as a *Panzergrenadier-Division* when it arrived in Rastenburg. The *Panzergrenadiers* of the division were experienced in the conventional battlefield tactics. They knew how to function in company, regiment, and battalion operations. They knew how to coordinate with supporting fires like artillery and aircraft. Perhaps most important, they were familiar with their mechanized equipment and other division assets. The cadre that was to form *Panzergrenadier-Division 'BR'* did not benefit from any of this experience. As the *Panzergrenadiers* of *'Großdeutschland'* were boarding ships in the Baltic, the men of *Division 'Brandenburg'* were fighting for survival across the Balkans.

The final organizational structure of the *Panzer-Korps* and its two divisions was issued on December 13th through *OKH/GenStdH/Org.Abt./Nr.I/21020/44 g.Kdos*. The reorganization had a planned completion date of December 31st. It was also on December 13th that the command staff for the *Panzer-Korps* was officially assigned. *General der Panzertruppen* Dietrich von Saucken became the *Oberbefehlshaber* (commander) or *OB*. Von Saucken was an experienced *Korps* commander and decorated *Panzer* Officer. He previously commanded the *4. Panzer-Division* from 1941-1943, spent nine months as the Commandant of the *Schule für Schnell Truppen* (*Panzer* and *Panzergrenadier* units), and commanded the *III. Panzer-Korps* and *XXXIX. Panzer-Korps*. He was the 46th recipient of Swords to his Knight's Cross with Oak Leaves. His command of *Panzer-Korps 'Großdeutschland'* lasted through March 12th, 1945 when he was subsequently assigned to command the *2. Armee* in East Prussia.[18] Von Saucken was officially replaced as commander of the *Panzer-Korps* by *General der Panzertruppen* Georg Jauer on March 12th. Jauer was also an experienced *Panzer* Officer and Knight's Cross recipient who won the award while commanding the *20. Panzergrenadier-Division* during the spring of 1944. Jauer had experience with *'Großdeutschland'* as the former commander of the *Artillerie-Regiment 'Großdeutschland'* from March-November 1942. Before taking over officially as commander of the *Panzer-Korps* he served as "acting" commander under von Saucken from February 12th to March 12th. This made the transition of command easier for the staff. Jauer served as the *Panzer-Korps* commander through capitulation. The initial *Ia* (Operations Officer) of the *Korps* was *Major*

---

18   He became the last recipient of the Diamonds (27th) to his Knight's Cross on May 8th, 1945 after surrendering the remaining German forces in East Prussia one full day after the official capitulation of hostilities in Europe.

i.G. Beck-Broichsitter who was later wounded and replaced by *Major i.G.* Usener. Usener was initially the *Korps* Quartermaster, but was replaced by *Major i.G.* Volkmar when he assumed the duties of *Ia*.

The *Panzer-Korps* was ordered organized as follows on December 13th with a completion date of December 31st. The *Korps* reorganization, however, was delayed due to constraints related to the reorganization of *Panzergrenadier-Division 'BR'* and other subunits. It continued to reorganize well into January, but did not finish before it deployed out during the Soviet winter offensive began. The following represented its final organization on paper.

Korps-Stab [Headquarters Staff]

Korps-Karte-Stelle (mot) [Mapping Detachment (motorized)]

Korps-Begleit-Kompanie [Escort Company]
Commander: *Oberleutnant* Säuberlich (former *'Brandenburg'* officer). Strength consisted of only 1x motorcycle platoon.

Korps-Aufklärung-Kompanie (gep) [Reconnaissance Company (Armored half-track)]

Stab Artillerie-Kommandeur [Artillery Command Staff]
Commander: *Hauptmann* Burchardt
Adjutant: *Oberleutnant* Mahnke

Artillerie-Regiment 500 [Artillery Regiment 500]
Formed from the *6.(s.F.H. 18) Batterie*, and a battery from *III.Abteilung* of *Pz.Art.Rgt. 'GD'* as well as one battalion *1.F.H.18* from *Pz.Art.Rgt. 'BR'*.

Panzer- Beobachtung-Batterie [Observation Battery (mechanized)]

Panzer-Pionier-Regiment-Stab [Pioneer Regimental Staff (mechanized)]
Commander: *Major* Chrapkowski. It appears that this never had the strength of more than a battalion.

Korps-Panzer-Pionier-Bataillon 500
Commander: *Hauptmann* Eicke.

1.Kompanie
Commander: *Oberleutnant* Meier (While not confirmed, this officer may have been transferred to *Panzerjäger-Abteilung 'BR'* by April).

2.Kompanie
Commander: *Oberleutnant* Wendt (former *'Brandenburg'* officer from *Jägerregiment 1 'BR'*)

3.(Goliath) Kompanie
Commander: [?]

Feldgendarmerie-Trupp (mot) [Military Police Detachment (motorized)]

Korps-Füsilier-Regiment [Corps Fusilier Regiment]

Stab und Stabs-Kompanie [Staff and Staff Company]
Commander: *Major* Fabich.

I. und II. Bataillone [1st and 2nd Battalions]. The *I.Bataillone* was commanded by *Hauptmann* Buse and formed from the *III.Btl./Gren.Rgt. 'GD'*. The *II.Bataillone* was commanded by *Major* Plitt, followed by *Hauptmann* Sprengel and formed from the *III.Btl./Jäg.Rgt. 1 'BR'*.

9.(s.I.G.) [9th Heavy Infantry Gun Company]

Schwere-Panzer-Abteilung [Heavy Tank Battalion]
Commander: *Hauptmann* Hans Bock

Stab und Stabs-Kompanie schwere-Panzer-Abteilung 'Tiger' [Staff and Staff Company for a 'Tiger' Tank battalion]

Schwere-Panzer-Kompanie 'Tiger' [Heavy 'Tiger' Tank Battalion]

Versorgungs-Kompanie 'Tiger' [Supply Company]

Panzer-Werkstatt-Kompanie schwere-Panzer-Abteilung [Tank Workshop for a heavy Tank Battalion]

Schwere-Werkstatt-Kompanie (mot) [Heavy Workshop Company (motorized)]

Panzer-Werkstatt-Zug-Ausführung A [Tank Workshop Platoon, Variant A]
s.Pz.Abt. 'GD' was formed from *III.Bataillone* of the *Panzer-Regiment 'GD'*. Seventeen Tigers were assigned but only four were operational by mid-January. At the end of January the *2.Kp./Panzer-Abteilung 302 (Fkl)* under the command of *Major* Sahmel was subordinated to the unit. Sahmel's *Kompanie* was equipped with remote-controlled *Panzers*. *Hauptmann* Bock became wounded at the end of January after several weeks of hard defensive fighting against the Soviets, earning him the Knight's Cross to the Iron Cross on February 5th. In a final counterattack along the Haff road the Soviets lost sixty-eight tanks. The remaining 4 Tigers of the unit joined a *Kampfgruppe* equipped with assorted *Panzers*. The majority of the original surviving Tiger crews whose tanks were knocked-out in the fighting were transferred to Paderborn for training on Tiger IIs.

Stab Sanitäts-Abteilung [Staff Medical Battalion]

This was formed from the *2.San.Kp. 'GD'*.

Stab Kommandeur eines Feldzeug-Bataillon [Staff Command of an Ordinance Battalion]

Korps-Nachrichten-Abteilung 500 [Signals Battalion]
Commander: *Major* Seek. Strength consisted of 1x telephone and 1x radio platoon.

Versorgungs-Regiment 500 [Supply Regiment]
Commander: *Major* Gericke. This unit was supposed to form from components of both subordinate divisions, but did not happen because of the start of the Soviet winter offensive.

On January 10th, 1945 the staff of *Panzer-Korps 'GD'* produced a report (*OKH/Chef H Rüst u BdE/AHA/Stab Ia (1) Nr. 10 111/44 g.K.v.20.12.1944*) on its current state of reorganization since December 20th, 1944. Overall there were not many issues to report within the *Korps* with minor exceptions. The *Korps-Füsilier-Regiment* was in urgent need of its bicycles to begin training. The *Korps-Panzer-Artillerie-Regiment* was still short specialists for its command staff and batteries. Six light field howitzers still had no tractors. Overall the Staff and *I. Abteilung* was considered ready, while the *II. Abteilung* was only conditionally ready. *Pionier-Regiments-Stab* was considered ready after it received its missing vehicles. The bridging equipment within the battalion was listed as urgently needed. There were still extensive shortages within the *Korps-Versorgungs-Regiment*. The *Korps-Nachschub-Truppen* was only at 50% authorized transport, with several companies considered only 20-30% mobile.

The *Korps* was functioning on the eve of the Soviet winter offensive, but it was far from 100%. What has to be stressed is that it was still forming and had not conducted any known planning exercises among its own staff to prepare many of the new members to work together and function as a team, let alone exercise the two divisions under their command that were themselves still forming. Their first test would come on the field of battle.

5

Reorganization of *Panzergrenadier-Division 'Großdeutschland'*

*P*anzergrenadier-Division 'Großdeutschland' underwent a period of rest and refit in the area of Vasluiui-Bacau Romania as part of the *8.Armee* in June-July 1944. On July 24th the division was ordered north to East Prussia where it was required to help stabilize the frontline of *Heeresgruppe Nord* in the wake of the Soviet summer offensive, Operation Bagration. The division had not completed its refitting due to a lack of available manpower. The manpower shortage was problematic across the *Ersatzheer*, but was even more acute with *'Großdeutschland'* as its single replacement unit, *Panzergrenadier-Ersatz-Brigade 'Großdeutschland'*, was ordered to supply manpower to the *Wacht-Bataillone 'Großdeutschland'* in Berlin, as well as the forming *Führer-Begleit-Brigade* and *Führer-Grenadier-Brigade*. Both of the latter units were to participate in the upcoming offensive in the Ardennes.

Panzergrenadier-Division 'GD' conducted a road march to the Hungarian border and loaded onto special high priority "Blitz" trains during July 26-27th. The division made its way north reaching various East Prussian debarkation stations in the area of Gumbinnen starting on August 3rd, some 40 kilometers from the border with Lithuania. The division now fell under command of the *3.Panzer-Armee* operating on the left wing of *Heeresgruppe Mitte*. *Panzergrenadier-Division 'GD'* was commanded by *Generalleutnant* Hasso von Manteuffel at the time. He later became the commander of the *3.Panzer-Armee* as part of the yet to be formed *Heeresgruppe Weichsel*.

As the division assembled it went into immediate action forcing the Soviets out of Wilkowishken (Vilkavishkis) in a two day battle during August 9th-10th. The street combat was heavy as the *Panzer-Füsilier-Regiment* along with accompanying Tigers conducted fierce street fighting to clear the Soviets out. It was during this battle that the *Panzergrenadiers* used the new *Panzerfaust* for the first time, adopting it for urban combat. Designed as a hand-held, portable anti-tank weapon, German soldiers immediately saw its value in breaching walls and clearing out hardened enemy positions. The division's actions in Wilkowishken were mentioned in the *Wehrmachtberichte* on August 11th, which was the equivalent of a unit citation. The fighting was so heavy that it was also reported in the citation that the Soviets lost 69 tanks and assault guns in two days of fighting. The division, however, was not able to destroy the Soviet salient to the north of the town that was poised to thrust into East Prussia.

Panzergrenadier-Division 'GD' subsequently deployed to northern Lithuania. The *Panzergrenadiers* received orders to capture the town of Schaulen and prevent the Soviets from cutting off *Heeresgruppe Nord* from *Heeresgruppe Mitte* in an operation known as Operation *Doppelkopf*. The Soviets threatened to advance toward the Baltic Coast and cut off *Heeresgruppe Nord* in Courland. On the night of August 14th, *Panzergrenadier-Division 'GD'* crossed the Memel River and advanced northward. During the eight days starting on August 12th the division engaged in heavy fighting against both Soviet infantry and tanks as it advanced north, then north-east toward its objective. By August 20th the division was ordered to pause as its sub-units became spread out across the forested hills of western Lithuania. The operation was called off eight days later on August 28th.

As *Panzergrenadier-Division 'GD'* advanced north, the Soviet 3rd Belorussian Front launched an attack on August 16th with the 5th, 33rd, and 11th Guards Armies that retook Wilkowishken the following day from the German garrison of locally mobilized troops that replaced the withdrawn *'Großdeutschland'*. The Soviet victory was followed up with an advance into East Prussia bringing Soviet troops into German territory for the first time during the war.

The fighting against the Soviets was heavy. The division's battlefield performance earned its members four Knight's Cross awards. While the division failed to capture the town of Schaulen, it did manage to stabilize a 30 kilometer corridor between *H.Gr. Nord* and *H.Gr. Mitte* allowing supplies to move through. Following the offensive *Panzergrenadier-Division 'GD'* went into a defensive position at the end of August. Manteuffel turned command of the division over to *Generalmajor* Karl Lorenz on September 1st. Lorenz remained in command of the division until the end of the war. Hasso von Manteuffel was promoted to *General der Panzertruppen* and sent to command of the *5.Panzer-Armee* fighting on the West Front as part of Operation *Wacht am Rhein* launched in December.

The Soviets launched a follow-on offensive against *H.Gr. Nord* and the left flank of *H.Gr. Mitte* during the month of September using the 1st, 2nd, and 3rd Baltic Fronts. Over the course of the next four weeks the Soviets attempted to split *H.Gr. Nord* and defeat its combat divisions in detail. This main objective failed due to a competent, yet brutal defense under the command of *Generaloberst* Ferdinand Schörner.[1] After the reorganization of the East Front in late January, Schörner became commander of *H.Gr. Mitte*. His exposure to the combat capabilities of *'Großdeutschland'* soldiers during this period served to save some division members from summary execution by court-martial during the following months of fighting. On October 5th a new offensive was launched by the First Baltic Front toward Memel using the 5th Guards Tank Army that reached the Baltic Coast by the 23rd. *H.Gr. Nord* and *H.Gr. Mitte* were now split, with the former army group holding a defensive line within Courland. A substantial number of troops, to include *Panzergrenadier-Division 'GD'* were trapped in a small pocket in the East Prussian town of Memel (Klaipėda).

By early October the frontline stabilized somewhat, mainly due to Soviet regrouping. The pocket of Memel formed around *Panzergrenadier-Division 'GD'*, *Grenadier-Regiment 220* from the *58.Infanterie-Division*, and *Panzer-Füsilier-Regiment 'GD'*, which formed the right flank; in the center was the *7.Panzer-Division*, and on the left flank was the *58.Infanterie-Division* with *Grenadier-Regiment 209*, and *Panzergrenadier-Regiment 'GD'*. On October 11th the Soviets launched a major attack to breach the German defenses and reach Memel, but failed in their objective. Two German cruisers the *Lützen* (formerly the *Deutschland*) and *Prinz Eugen* arrived off the coast to assist in the defense by using their gun batteries to strike Soviet units.

By the end of November the division began its transfer from Memel to its new assembly area in Sensburg, East Prussia where it fell under command of the new *Panzer-Korps 'GD'*. Between November 22nd-23rd elements of the division were sea lifted to Königsberg. The *I.(gep)/Pz.Rgt. 'GD'* departed Memel on the 6,000 GRT *Cometa* on November 27th, with two ships and an armed freighter for escort. On November 28th elements of *Pz.Art.Rgt. 'GD'* embarked on the 7,800 GRT *Wolta*, followed by other elements of the division two days later. *Major* Fabich, former Director of the *'Großdeutschland'* communication's center in Rastenburg, the location of Hitler's *Wolfsschanze*

---

1   Schörner was a World War I war hero. He received the Pour le Mérite, Germany's highest military decoration, in October 1917 at the battle of Caporetto masterminded by a then young Erwin Rommel. He later joined the *Reichswehr*. Schörner gave his early support to the nascent Nazi movement when he participated in the 1923 Beer Hall *Putsch*. He earned the Diamonds to his Knight's Cross for the defense of Kurland in late 1944. His successful defense of Kurland was rooted in his draconian leadership measures that included the execution of numerous soldiers for cowardice. He established roving squads of police to hang anyone caught in the rear areas that should not be there. He sacked *Korps* and *Division* commanders not considered tough enough. His mantra was "fear of their commander should be greater than fear of the enemy." Schörner's battlefield reliance on draconian punishment and belief that a strong "will" could overcome adverse physical conditions resonated with Hitler. It is no coincidence that Schörner benefited from a close relationship with the *Führer* and was selected as the last *Oberbefehlshabers des Heeres* in Hitler's last Will and Testament.

(Wolf's Lair)[2], had begun the preparations to receive the troops in the area and prepare them for reconstitution. The division's strength on December 1st numbered 17,955 but in the last 5 months the division had suffered 5,997 casualties and received only 2,441 replacements.

The division was ordered to reorganize as a *Panzer-Division 44*. The reorganization was complete by January 8th. The division consisted of the following units with exceptions noted below: *Stab/Pz.Gren. Div. 'GD'*, *Panzer-Regiment 'GD'*, *Panzergrenadier- Regiment 'GD'* (*I., II., III.Bataillon*-unofficially reformed), *Panzerfüsilier-Regiment 'GD'* (*I., II., III., IV.Bataillon*), *Panzer-Artillerie-Regiment 'GD'* (*I., II., III.Abteilung*), *Heeres-Flak-Artillerie-Abteilung 'GD'*, *Panzerjäger-Abteilung 'GD'*, *Panzer-Aufklärungs-Abteilung 'GD'*, *Panzer-Pionier-Bataillon 'GD'*, *Panzer-Nachrichten-Abteilung 'GD'*. Most of the supply units were converted into *Korps* troops.

During the four weeks of the reorganization the following units were either disbanded, removed, or converted:

-*I.Btl./Pz.Rgt. 'GD'* was transferred back from the *6.Panzer-Division*.

-*II.Btl./Pz.Rgt. 'GD'*, which had been assigned to the *5.Panzer-Division*, was rebuilt and assigned to the *Führer-Begleit-Brigade*.

-Disbanded were: *I.(gep)/Füs.Rgt. 'GD', 16.(Flak.Kp.)/Pz.Gren.Rgt. 'GD', 15.(Pz.Jg.Kp.), 16.(Flak. Kp.)/Pz. Füs.Rgt. 'GD', 3.* and *5.Kp./H.Flak.Art.Abt. 'GD'*, and the *3.(gep)/Pz.Pi.Btl. 'GD'*.

The following units were converted to *Korps Truppen* (Troops) to form *Pz.Korps 'GD'*:

-*s.KB-Zug 'GD'* (of *Stab/Pz.Gren.Div. 'GD'*), *III.(s)/Pz.Rgt. 'GD', III.Btl./Pz.Gren.Rgt. 'GD', 6.Kp./Pz.Art.Rgt. 'GD', IV./Pz.Art.Rgt. 'GD', lePz.Brücke-Kol. 'GD'* (of *Pz.Pi.Btl. 'GD'*), *FE.Btl. 'GD'* and the supply troops (*Kdr.Div.Nach.Tr. 'GD', Kf.Pk.Tr. 'GD', Verw.Tr.Abt. 'GD'* and part of *San.Tr. 'GD'*.

Sturmgeschütz-Abteilung 'Großdeutschland' was intended to be incorporated into *Panzergrenadier-Division 'BR'* as *II.Btl./Pz.Rgt. 'BR'*. Instead the *Abteilung* was converted into a *Heeres-Truppe* and re-designated *Sturmgeschütz-Brigade 'GD'*, but it was tactically attached to *Panzergrenadier-Division 'BR'*. This left the *'Großdeutschland'* division without considerable combat power so it was decided to reform the previously disbanded *Pz.Jg.Abt. 'GD'*. The division also decided to unofficially form the *III. Btl./Pz.Gr.Rgt. 'GD'* and the *III.Btl./Pz.Füs.Rgt. 'GD'* by cross-leveling replacement personnel from regimental training units.

Panzergrenadier-Division 'GD' never again enjoyed the high level of strength or combat powered it did in 1943-44. As it reorganized it found its armored sub-units cross-leveled into other divisions across the *Wehrmacht* and *'Brandenburg'*. Other elements were converted into *Korps* units. Experienced officers and senior enlisted soldiers were individually transferred to the forming *Panzergrenadier-Division 'BR'* to help provide the requisite cadre leadership and skills in conventional combat tactics required to convert a disparate light infantry force into a new cohesive *Panzergrenadier-Division*.

---

2   On November 20th Hitler left the Wolf's Lair for the last time and headed to the *Führerbunker* in Berlin where he would spend the rest of the war. He issued orders for the demolition of the Wolf's Lair that were carried out at the end of January, days before the Soviets occupied the former command center of the *Führer*.

6

Formation of *Panzergrenadier-Division* *'Brandenburg'*, December 1944-January 1945

The regimental remnants and support units of *Division 'Brandenburg'* were out of combat by early December. They began to arrive by train in Mauerwald, East Prussia (to the north of Rastenburg (Ketrzyn) and move into quarters between Angerburg (Węgorzewo) and Lötzen (Gizycko) for their long awaited reorganization into a *Panzergrenadier-Division*.[1] Not long after their arrival the Division was split up. Some elements remained in Lötzen while others were quartered 75 kilometers to the southwest in Ortelsburg (Szczytno). The regiments of *zbv Division 'Brandenburg'* were not in good shape. Several were decimated after the fighting around Belgrade in October. Most had lost key leaders, experienced NCOs and soldiers. Serviceable equipment lacked among the survivors. Not everyone who debarked into their new assembly areas completely understood the 'deal' that Erasmus made between *OKW* and the *SS* in order to maintain their integrity. It seems apparent that at that time, no effort was made to explain the rationale to the actual soldiers of the *Division*. Many viewed their change in status from a *Sonder* to a regular *Heer* unit as being "sold out". Morale among the survivors of *'Brandenburg'* was likely at the lowest point experienced by its collective membership since the war began.

Oberleutnant iG Hamburg Bröker, the new *IIb* (Assistant Division Adjutant) recounts the early formation of the new *Panzergrenadier-Division*:

In a Top Secret order dated September 13th, 1944 from *OKW/WFST*, the *Division 'Brandenburg'* was reorganized into the *Panzergrenadier-Division 'Brandenburg'* as part of *Panzer-Korps 'Großdeutschland'* with some of the special use personnel being turned over to *Sonderkommando Skorzeny*. (At that time, the command post was in Oranienburg near Berlin.)

The orders required for the reorganization were arranged by *Oberstleutnant iG* Erasmus through the operations department of *OKH* and *WFST*.

So the reorganization of the troops continually being dissolved/newly entering units being deployed as such was undertaken with the headquarters move to Baden near Vienna (Weilburg) starting in mid-September commanded by *Hauptmann* Witauschek—who at the time was the *IIb* of the division—and *Leutnant* Biske, among other people.

In particular, *Regiment 4 'BR'*, which later became *Jägerregiment 1 'BR'*, and the *Panzer-Sturm-Pionier-Bataillon 'BR'*, were put together early.

From *Regiment 2 'BR'*, the majority were lost during the [Soviet] penetration at Belgrade and the remainder of the regiment was able to join *Regiment 1 'BR'* at Esseg, Hungary and form a *Kampfgruppe 'Brandenburg'* that was initially commanded by *Generalleutnant* Kühlwein, and then under *Oberst* Schulte-Heuthaus. *Panzer-Artillerie-Abteilung 'BR'* was set up in Wildflecken.

Panzer-Artillerie-Regiment 'BR' started from, among other things, an *Artillerie-Abteilung* of the *1.Panzer-Division* and, as far as I know, was immediately taken to the Angerburg-Lötzen

---

1   Mauerwald was the site of the *OKH* field headquarters. It represented the largest of the bunker complexes associated with Adolf Hitler's "Wolf's Lair".

Image 1. A new cuff band was authorized to commemorate the establishment of
Panzergrenadier-Division 'Brandenburg' and distinguish it from its sister *Panzergrenadier-
Division 'Großdeutschland'* when they formed the new *Korps* in December 1944. In the
World War II collector's market original *'Brandenburg'* cuff bands are often incorrectly
associated with the *Sonderkommando Division 'Brandenburg'*. Author's collection.

deployment area, which received all the parts of the division until late December 1944 and for a
short period served as a training area (with *'GD'* demonstrations and joint midwinter exercises)
with the participation of units of all *'GD'/'BR'* units in the vicinity of Lötzen).

The area of Wiener Neustadt and Baden near Vienna was supposed to serve as a reception
area for all the units of the former *Division 'Brandenburg'* from all parts of Europe (primarily the
southeast and the east). Unfortunately nearly the entire *Regiment 3 'BR'* had most recently been
deployed against partisans in the Fiume-Trieste-Oberkrain area since (about) March 1944 and
later fought as *Gebirgsjäger*, sometimes in the Italian/French Alps, and sometimes further south
in Italy. After it was reorganized into a division, the commander in chief, *Generalfeldmarschall*
Kesselring did not take them out of Italy; he split them up into *Gebirgsjäger-Divisions* and *MG-
Bataillon 'Kesselring'*. However, individual officers and enlisted personnel managed to get to the
Panzergrenadier-Division 'Brandenburg' in the *zbV* manner (vacation, ostensible official trips, etc.).
There were strenuous complaints made because of this affair at *OKW*, but they were unsuccessful.
The reorganization, which began about late December 1944, was initially a very bold venture
because of the situation with the individual units distributed among all sorts of theaters of war
and the unusually placed former use and equipment, the many new individuals added, and units
transferred from other divisions, thanks to the continued ideas of the division commander, *Oberst*
Schulte-Heuthaus. At this time, the entire division, including the armored units, was in the area
of Lötzen and Angerburg as it concerned the *KAN* and *KStN*.[2]

The plan was to deploy into the frontline in East Prussia under the *Panzer-Korps
'Großdeutschland'*. The situation gave rise to its own orders!

OKH recognized the effect of recent combat on the subunits of *'Brandenburg'*. They ordered
a complete restructuring of the *Division* as part of the general reorganization of *Panzer-Korps* and
Panzergrenadier-Division 'GD'. While it maintain the name of a *Panzergrenadier-Division* its original
organization was as a *Panzer-Division 44* with six *Panzergrenadier* battalions and other extra combat
support formations, the new *Division* was altered to a *Panzergrenadier-Division 44* around the core of
two regiments with two *Panzergrenadier* battalions each.

Regiment 4 'BR' (without the *I.Bataillon*) was the first unit to arrive at the assembly area in
Baden and fell under the *Division's* new *Arbeit-Stab* that had operational control of forming the new
Panzergrenadier-Division. Soon the remains of the other units of *'Brandenburg'* began to assemble
temporarily at Mielau (Mlawa) and Wildflecken then boarded trains east. They were followed by the
men of *III.Btl./Pz.Art.Rgt. 73* currently assigned to the *1.Panzer-Division*. Other non-*'Brandenburg'*

---

2   *Kriegsausrüstungsnachweisung (KAN)* Tables of Organization and *Kriegsstärkenachweisung (KsTN)* Unit Composition.

also arrived. These included the *s.Art.Abt. 843 (Heer)* assigned to *IV.(s)/Pz.Art.Rgt. 'BR'* and the remnants of *Sturm-Division 'Rhodos'* as per order *OKW/WFSt/Op (H)Südost Nr. 0012164/44*, though in the latter case these soldiers were ordered transferred to *'Brandenburg'* as early as October 10th.[3]

As previously noted the *Division* was issued two separate *Gliederung*. The first one called for a *Panzer-Division 44* on September 13th, but this never occurred as the *Division* was spread out across the Balkans and engaged in heavy fighting. That *Gliederung* was altered to a *Panzergrenadier-Division 44* due to the *Division's* heavy losses when the reorganization order was issued to *Panzer-Korps 'GD'* on December 13th, which is reflected in the organizational structure below. *Panzergrenadier-Division 'Brandenburg'* was organized as follows by the eve of the Soviet winter offensive on January 12th. Note that every attempt was made to accurately reflect the names of veterans who served in each of the below units based on the actual assignments they held in the new *Panzergrenadier-Division*. Many of these assignments are derived from a careful review of the names mentioned in the veteran's accounts and not by an official list as no such document was found in the archives.

Panzergrenadier-Division 'Brandenburg'

Div.Kdo. [Division Staff]
Commander: *Oberst* Hermann Schulte-Heuthaus (promoted to *Generalmajor* on March 1st, 1945)

Ia (Chief of Operations): *Oberstleutnant iG* Erasmus

Ib (Quartermaster): *Major iG* Uhl (KIA or MIA)

Major iG Volkmar

Major iG Helmuth Spaeter (1943 Knight's Cross recipient)

IIa (Adjutant): *Hauptmann* Werner Lau (1942 Knight's Cross recipient); promoted to *Major* in April

IIb (Assistant Adjutant): *Oberleutnant iG* Hamburg Bröker

Begleit-Kompanie (mot) 'BR' [Division Escort Company]:
Fully operational.
Commander: *Oberleutnant* Mischkeres

Division-Kartograph-Stab (mot) 'BR' [Division Cartography Staff]

Feldgendarmerie-Truppen (mot) 'BR' [Military Police Company]:
Commander: *Leutnant* Feldmüller

---

3   The *Sturm-Division 'Rhodos'* was organized in 1943. It consisted of: *Sturm-Regiment 'Rhodos'*, *Panzer-Aufklärungs-Abteilung 999*, *Panzer-Abteilung 'Rhodos'*, *IV./Artillerie-Regiment 999*, *Flak-Kompanie 'Rhodos'*, *Pionier-Kompanie 999*, *Panzer-Nachrichten-Kompanie 'Rhodos'*, *Versorgungs-Einheiten 999*. In May of 1943 the division consisted of soldiers garrisoning the military fortresses located on the Aegean Islands and remnants of the *999.leichten-Afrika-Division*. By October 1944 parts of the division were sent to the *17.Division* in Belgrade and *Panzergrenadier-Division 'Brandenburg'*. The senior staff was sent to form the *IV.Panzer-Korps*. However, given the extent of fighting in Belgrade and the Balkans in general, it is not clear how may men from *'Rhodos'* actually transferred into the ranks of *'Brandenburg'*. See NARA T78/533/276.

Schwere-KB-Zug (mot) 'BR' (this sub component likely only existed on paper)

Jägerregiment 1 'Brandenburg'
Formed from personnel from the *Rgt. 1* and *Rgt. 4* of *Division 'Brandenburg'* as well as new replacements. The *III.Bataillon* was detached from the division in the December 13th reorganization and it was re-designated *II.Btl./K.Pz.Füs.Rgt. 'GD'* and assigned to the *Panzer-Korps 'GD'*. The *I.Bataillon* was equipped exclusively with *Schützenpanzerwagen* (*SPW*), which refers to the *Gepanzert* (*gep*) or "armored" designation. On January 10th it was reported that both its *Bataillons* had not completed their reorganization.

Stab [Regimental Staff]
Commander: *Oberst* Erich von Brückner (transferred to *OKH* reserve on 8 Feb); *Major* Wandrey (KIA around February 24th); *Major* Bansen
O1 (1st Assistant Adjutant for Operations): *Leutnant* Grosser
Adjutant: *Leutnant* von Bremen

Stab-Kompanie (gep) [Regimental Staff Company (Armored Halftrack)]
Commander: *Oberleutnant* Frömmel

10.Kompanie sIG (mot Z) [Company with a Heavy Infantry Gun Platoon]

11.Kompanie

I.(gep)Bataillon [*Panzergrenadier* Battalion (Armored Halftrack)]
On January 10th only the armored command vehicles were reported as still missing.
Commanders: *Oberleutnant* Hebler; *Hauptmann* Froböse through March; *Hauptmann* Schuster starting on April 16th

1.Panzergrenadier-Kompanie (gep) [*Panzergrenadier* Company (Armored Halftrack)]

2.Panzergrenadier-Kompanie (gep)

3.Panzergrenadier-Kompanie (gep)

schwere 4.Panzergrenadier-Kompanie (gep) [Heavy *Panzergrenadier* Company (Armored Halftrack)]
Commander: *Hauptmann* Schäfer; with 2x Sd.Kfz. 251/2 medium mortar carriers and 4x Sd.Kfz 251/9 7,5cm KwK 37 L/24

Versorgung-Kompanie (mot) [Supply Company (Motorized)]

II.Bataillon
Commanders: *Hauptmann* Hunhold through April 27th when he was severely wounded in a friendly fire incident; *Rittmeister* Sandmeyer (from *Panzer-Aufklärungs-Abteilung 'BR'*) took over command on April 28th; *O1 Leutnant* Drenger, and Administrative Officer *Leutnant* Hasse

5.Panzergrenadier-Kompanie (mot) [*Panzergrenadier* Company (Motorized)]
Commander: *Oberleutnant* Zülch

6.Panzergrenadier-Kompanie (mot)
Commander: *Oberleutnant* Röseke until early February; *O1 Leutnant* Krosch; 2x Officers, 16x NCOs, 144x Soldiers (2x MG42 and 36x *Sturmgewehr* assault rifles)

7.Panzergrenadier-Kompanie (mot)
Commander: *Oberleutnant* Geisenberger; O1 *Leutnant* Bürk

8.Machinengewehr-Kompanie (mot) [Machinegun Company (Motorized)]
Commanders: *Oberleutnant* (later *Hauptmann*) Grabert; *Leutnant* Prohaska

9.Granatwerfer-Kompanie (mot) [Mortar Company (Motorized)]

Versorgung-Kompanie (mot) [Supply Company (Motorized)]

Jägerregiment 2 'Brandenburg'
I.Bataillon NCOs and enlisted personnel were formed in part from the remnants of *I.Btl./Rgt. 2* of *Division 'Brandenburg'*, *Fsch.Jg.Btl. 'BR'*, and new replacements. The *III.Bataillon* was ordered disbanded in the December 13th reorganization and it was re-designated *I.Bataillon* due to the lack of manpower. *II.Bataillon* was formed from elements of the *II.Btl./3.Rgt.* that arrived from Italy and *III.Btl./Rgt. 2* of *Division 'Brandenburg'*. It was reported in January that both *Bataillons* were still forming, though it had received all required combat replacements. Its combat personnel, the report noted, lacked tactical training. There was a shortage of specialists noted, likely communications personnel.

Stab
Commander: *Oberstleutnant* (later promoted to *Oberst*) Karl Heinz Oesterwitz
Adjutant: *Hauptmann* Vincenz
Medical Officer: *Stabsarzt* Dr. Backhausen

Stab-Kompanie (mot) [Regimental Staff Company (motorized)]

11.Kompanie sIG (mot Z) [Company with a Heavy Infantry Gun Platoon]
Prime movers for its guns had still not arrived.

12.Kompanie

I.Bataillon
Commander: *Hauptmann* Kurt Steidl (1944 Knight's Cross recipient); later promoted to *Major* on May 5th 1945

1.Panzergrenadier-Kompanie (mot) [Panzergrenadier Company (Motorized)]
Commander: *Oberleutnant* Wirth; *Leutnant* Esser; with 1x Assault Platoon (3x Squads with *Sturmgewehr*), 1x Machinegun Platoon (2x MG42), 1x Sniper Squad, 1x Anti-Tank Squad (*Panzerschreck*)

2.Panzergrenadier-Kompanie (mot)
Commanders: *Oberleutnant* Kieffer; *Oberleutnant* Gutweniger

3.*Panzergrenadier-Kompanie (mot)*
Commander: *Oberleutnant* Schmalbruch

4.*Machinengewehr-Kompanie (mot)* [Machinegun Company (Motorized)]
Commanders: *Oberleutnant* Gabel; with 1x heavy Machinegun Platoon, 1x Platoon 7.5cm Pak, 1xZug 2cm Flak (self-propelled)

5.*Granatwerfer-Kompanie (mot)* [Mortar Company (Motorized)]
Commander: *Oberleutnant* Gabi; with 2x Platoons 8cm Mortars, and 1x Platoon 12cm Mortars

Versorgung-Kompanie (mot) [Supply Company (Motorized)]
Commander: *Oberzahlmeister* Treu was reassigned and command passed to an unknown *Zahlmeister*)

II.Bataillon
Commander: *Major* Renner i.V, *Oberleutnant* Eckart Afheldt through February 1st until relieved by a senior officer because of a dispute; *Hauptmann* Zinkel took over on February 1st; *Major* Renner rejoined the unit and took command on February 15th

6.*Panzergrenadier-Kompanie (mot)*
Commander: *Oberleutnant* Sauter; *Leutnant* Maier; with 1x Assault Platoon (3x Squads with *Sturmgewehr*), 1x Machinegun Platoon (2x MG42), 1x Sniper Squad, 1x Anti-Tank Squad (*Panzerschreck*)

7.*Panzergrenadier-Kompanie (mot)*
Commander: *Leutnant* Stalf; *Schützen-Kpn.*

8.*Panzergrenadier-Kompanie (mot)*
Commander: *Oberstleutnant* Krieger; *Schützen-Kpn.*

9.*Machinengewehr-Kompanie (mot)* [Machinegun Company (Motorized)]
Commander: *Oberleutnant* Planer (KIA on 2 Feb); with 1x heavy Machinegun Platoon, 1x Platoon 7.5cm Pak, 1xZug 2cm Flak (self-propelled)

10.*Granatwerfer-Kompanie (mot)* [Mortar Company (Motorized)]

2x Platoons 8cm Mortars, and 1x Platoon 12cm Mortars

Versorgung-Kompanie (mot) [Supply Company (Motorized)]

Panzer-Artillerie-Regiment 'Brandenburg'
Most of the artillery units formed between the last week of October and the last week of November ahead of the main regiments. Existing elements of *Division 'Brandenburg'* were incorporated with some exceptions. *4.Kp./II.Abt.* was formed from the *7.Kp./Pz.Art.Rgt. 73* of *1.Pz.Div,* the *III.Abt.* was formed from the *III.Abt./Pz.Art.Rgt. 73* of the *1.Pz.Div.,* and *IV.Abt.* was formed from the re-designated *s.Art.Abt. 843 (Heer).* The original *III.Abt.* was re-designated *II.Abt./Pz.Art.Rgt. 500* and assigned to *Pz.Korps 'GD'* in the December 13th re-organization, and the *IV.Abt.* was simultaneously re-designated *III.Abt.* Only the *III.s.Abteilung* and a single *Batterie* of

II. Abteilung were ready of combat operations. All batteries of *I. Abteilung* were immobile due to a lack of prime movers.

Stab (mot)

I. Abteilung

Stab

Stabs-Batterie (mot)

1. Batterie leFH (mot Z) [Light Field Howitzer Battery with a Motorized Platoon]

2. Batterie leFH (mot Z)

3. Batterie sFH (mot Z) [Heavy Field Howitzer Battery with a Motorized Platoon]

II. Abteilung

Stab

Stab-Batterie (mot)

4. Batterie leFH (mot Z)

5. Batterie leFH (mot Z)

III. schwere-Abteilung
Commander: *Hauptmann* Spievogel

Stab

Stabsbatterie (mot)

8. Batterie 10.5cm sK (mot Z)

9. Batterie sFH (mot Z)

10. Batterie sFH (mot Z)

Heeres-Flak-Artillerie-Abteilung 'Brandenburg'
Formed from the re-designated *H. Flak-Art. Abt. 280 (Heer)* and still forming in southern Hungary. This unit would not join its division until February. This unit had no previous organizational affiliation with *Division 'Brandenburg'*. *Oberarzt* Dr. Braune, who documented his time in the *Abteilung*, was formerly from the *Kriegsmarine*.

Stab
Commander: *Major* Voshage

Stab Batterie

1.sFlak-Batterie (mot Z) [Heavy *Flak* Battery with a Motorized Platoon]

2.sFlak-Batterie (mot Z)

3.mFlak-Batterie (mot Z) [Medium *Flak* Battery with a Motorized Platoon]
Commander: *Leutnant* Heyer
3,7cm Flak Motorized Platoon and 2cm *Flak-Vierling* Platoon (quadruple self-propelled gun mount)

Panzerjäger-Abteilung 'Brandenburg'
The December 13th re-organization detached the *3.Kp.*, re-designated it *1.Kp./Pz.Jg.Abt. 'GD'* and assigned it to *Panzergrenadier-Division 'GD'*. This was done in part to supplement *Panzergrenadier-Division 'GD'* for the loss of its *Stug.Abt. 'GD'*. The *4.Kompanie* was simultaneously ordered to be re-designated as *3.Pz.Jg.Kp. (mot Z)*. By mid-January it was combat ready with all authorized strength and a full complement of 21x StuG IVs. This unit formed at the Mielau training grounds and did not train with other units of *'Brandenburg'* in December and January before it deployed straight to battle in mid-January. By mid-February the *1.Kompanie* and *2.Kompanie* consisted of both *Sturmgeschütz III* and *Sturmgeschütz IV* due to the increasingly difficult supply situation across the Reich. This unit had no previous organizational affiliation with *Division 'Brandenburg'*. Much of the activity of this unit is based on the diary kept by *Leutnant* Kass who served as a company commander until wounded by a Soviet mortar. His diary entries did not cover the fighting from March-May, suggesting that he may have transferred out of the unit. After April 16th there are only a few direct mentions of the *Abteilung* in the various veteran accounts.

Stab
Commander: *Hauptmann* Fritz Königstein (died of wounds on April 26th after driving over a mine); *Hauptmann* Plange took command and was killed in the defense of Olmütz (Olomouc)

Stab Batterie

1.Panzerjäger-Kompanie (StuG IV) [*Sturmgeschütz* Assault Gun Company]
Commander: *Oberleutnant* Hoppe and senior non-commissioned officer *Hauptfeldwebel* Kottutz

2.Panzerjäger-Kompanie (StuG IV)
Commander: *Leutnant* Kass until wounded in February by a Soviet mortar; replaced by unknown officer who was killed during an armor engagement at Olmütz in early May

3.Panzerjäger-Kompanie (mot Z) [Anti-tank Company (Motorized)]
Commander: *Oberleutnant* Meier (known as monocle Meier who went missing at the end of April)

Versorgung-Kompanie (mot) [Supply Company (Motorized)]

Panzer-Aufklärungs-Abteilung 'Brandenburg' [Armored Reconnaissance Battalion]
Formed at Wildflecken using personnel from across all original regiments of *Division 'Brandenburg'*. Based on the available accounts it appears that a single platoon was attached to *Panzer-Sturm-Pionier-Bataillon 'BR'* most of the time. It also appears that reconnaissance platoons were supplied

to other battalions intermittently based on the references of *"Erkundungszug"* at various times. There are only a few references to the *Abteilung* operating as a single unit as it likely found itself supporting many different elements of the *Division* in an ad hoc fashion.

Stab
Commander: *Major* Pansen (KIA or transferred out by the end of March); *Rittmeister* Frey

Stab Kompanie

1.Panzerspäh-Kompanie 'c' [Armored Car Company]
Commander: Unknown.

2.lePanzer-Aufklärungs-Kompanie (gep) [Light Armored Reconnaissance Company (Armored Halftrack)]
Commander: Unknown.

3.Panzer-Aufklärungs-Kompanie (gep) [Armored Reconnaissance Company (Armored Halftrack)]
Commander: *Rittmeister* Sandmeyer (took over command of *II.Bataillon/Jäg.Rgt 1 'BR'* on April 28th)

4.schwere-Panzer-Aufklärungs-Kompanie (gep) [Heavy Armored Reconnaissance Company (Armored Halftrack)]

Versorgung-Kompanie (mot) [Supply Company (Motorized)]

Panzer-Sturm-Pionier-Bataillon 'Brandenburg'
It is not entirely certain if elements of *Division 'Brandenburg'* were used in this unit's formation. One account cites that personnel from *Küstenjäger-Abteilung 'BR'* (Costal Command Detachment) of *Division 'Brandenburg'* were incorporated with members of the *78.Sturm-Division*. It is possible that the inclusion of *Küstenjäger-Abteilung 'BR'* into this unit was likely based on a paper proposal that never actually occurred. If the *Küstenjäger* were not assigned, where they went is unknown, but it could be surmised they were sent to form the new *Aufklärungs* unit. The *Pz.Stu. Pi.Btl.* commander *Hauptmann* Friedrich Müller-Rochholz provides an account of the battalion's formation that does not mention the inclusion of any *'Brandenburgers'*. He states that this unit was formed in September 1944 around the remnants of *Sturm-Pionier-Bataillon 178* of the *78.Sturm-Division* destroyed in the fighting around Orscha, Soviet Union as part of the *4.Armee* earlier in 1944. Only 40% of the men in the battalion were veterans from the *78.Sturm-Division* and the other 60% were young well trained volunteers. While the unit reformed in the Karlsruhe-Knielingen area it was reinforced by *Pionier-Ersatz-Bataillon 35* and served to assist in a variety of construction efforts when required. For example, during September a major Allied bombing run against the Daimler-Benz Factory destroyed a bridge over the Murg River. The battalion deployed and quickly built a Bailey-Bridge within hours. At the start of October Müller-Rochholz received word from *OKH* that his unit was to be incorporated into the forming *Panzergrenadier-Division 'BR'*. He met with the *Division* staff of *'Brandenburg'* on October 10th to determine what was needed to bring the battalion up to full strength. In the initial conversation with *General* Kühlwein, it was suggested that the battalion was to be outfitted with bicycles. This did not sit well with Müller-Rochholz and by the evening the situation was clarified by Erasmus who

promised to obtain armored halftracks. Additional personnel requirements were filled by *Panzer-Pionier-Ersatz-Bataillon 6*. The entire battalion then moved to Wiener Neustadt in Austria where it continued with its training "day and night" in all light weapons and the MG42. Particular attention was given to *Panzerfaust* training. By the end of December the battalion was considered exceptionally trained when it was sent to East Prussia to join its parent *Division*. The battalion had a total strength of 400 men and was considered fully replenished by mid-January. Only the *3.Pionier-Kompanie* was still missing its compliment of *SPWs* upon deployment. The Light Bridging Column was likely disbanded in March after the retreat across Poland. A Construction Company was unofficially assigned to the battalion during March. This unit had no previous organizational affiliation with *Division 'Brandenburg'* and none of its personnel served with the original *Sonderkommandos* prior to its formation.

Stab
Commander: *Hauptmann* Friedrich Müller-Rochholz
Adjutant: *Leutnant* Clemeur

1.Pionier-Kompanie (mot) [Pioneer Company (Motorized)]
This company was reformed as an armored company (*gep*) with *SPWs* from the *3.Pi.Kp.* around April 22nd.
Commanders: *Oberleutnant* Bank (KIA on April 22nd or 23rd at Uhsmannsdorf); *Hauptmann* Michaelis; with 3x Platoons and 1x Heavy Machinegun Platoon

2.Pionier-Kompanie (mot) [Pioneer Company (Motorized)]
Commanders: *Oberleutnant* Schlosser (KIA around April 17th or 18th at Ober Wehrkirch); *Leutnant* Koch; with 3x Platoons and 1x Heavy Machinegun Platoon

3.Pionier-Kompanie (gep) [Pioneer Company (Armored Halftrack)]
Commanders: *Leutnant* Puls with 3x Platoons and 1x Heavy Mortar Platoon (Sd.Kfz.250/7)
This company's remnants were sent to reform the *1.Kompanie* and *2.Kompanie* at the end of April.

lePanzer-Brücke-Kolonne [Light Armored Bridging Column]
Commander: *Oberleutnant* Hasper; with Sd.Kfz.251/7)
This company was disbanned at the end of April.

Versorgung-Kompanie (mot) [Supply Company (Motorized)]
Commander: *Hauptmann* Michaelis (took command of *1.Pi.Kp.* after the death of Bank)
This company fell under the *Ib* Section at the end of April.

Panzer-Nachrichten-Abteilung 'Brandenburg'
Formed using the *Na.Abt.* of *Division 'Brandenburg'*. It was fully operational with the exception of six *SPWs* that were still missing. These were likely Sd.Kfz.250/3 *Funk-Panzers*, though the report did not mention the specific model.

Stab

1.Panzer-Fernsprech-Kompanie [Armored Telephone Company]

2.Panzer-Funk-Kompanie [Armored Radio Company]

Versorgung-Staffel [Supply Section]

Feldersatz-Bataillon 'Brandenburg'
Formed using one battalion of *Lehr-Rgt. 'BR'* of *Division 'Brandenburg'*. The entire battalion was re-designated *II.Btl./FER 500 (Feld-Ersatz Regiment)* of *Panzer-Korps 'GD'* and removed from the division as part of the December 13th re-organization. However, this battalion was unofficially reformed in early February after the withdrawal of the *Division* to the Oder River. Its composition at that time cannot be accurately detailed.

Sanitäts-Truppen 'Brandenburg'
The *San.Kp.* was formed in part by using medical personnel from *Pz.Gren.Div 'GD'* and the *Kr.Kw. Kp.* was re-designated from *Kr.Kw.-Zug 258* of the *258.Inf.Div.*

Sanitäts-Kompanie (mot) [Medical Company (Motorized)]

Kranken-Kraftwagen-Kompanie (mot) [Ambulance Truck Company]

Feldpostamt 'Brandenburg'
Formed by re-designating *FPa zbV 794 (Heer)*.

Other Supply and Maintenance Units
Based on the December 13th re-organization order, *Kommandeur-Division-Nachschub Truppen 'Brandenburg'*, *Kraftfahrpark Truppen 'Brandenburg'* (*Werk.Kp. 1. 'BR'*, and *2. 'BR'*), and *Verwaltungs-Truppen Abteilung 'Brandenburg'* were re-designated *Nach.Rgt. 500, 4.Kp.* and *5.Kp./ Pz.Inst.Abt. 500*, and *Verw.Abt. 500* of *Pz.Korps 'GD'* respectively and detached from the *Division*. This was based on the need to consolidate supply and maintenance units under the *Korps* to better support both assigned divisions. By March all three units were unofficially re-formed by *Panzergrenadier-Division 'BR'* using ad hoc personnel.

Sturmgeschütz-Brigade 'Großdeutschland'
The brigade was in Lübben waiting for a replenishment of vehicles. They received their full complement of 35 *Sturmgeschütze* (StuG III and StuH) on January 15th and deployed immediately toward Litzmannstadt without the benefit of training on their vehicles or even with the soldiers of *'Brandenburg'*. The unit was originally subordinated temporarily until the *II.Btl./ Pz.Rgt. 'Brandenburg'* was to arrive (see below section for an overview of *Pz.Rgt. 'Brandenburg'*.) That never happened. This unit was renamed *Sturmgeschütz-Artillerie-Brigade 'GD'* on March 13th. All of its *Sturmgeschütze* except a single command vehicle were turned over to the *Panzerjäger-Abteilung 'Brandenburg'* at this time as they were replaced with 31 *Jagdpanzer IV/70s*. *Sturmgeschütz-Artillerie-Brigade 'GD'* remained with the *Division* until the end of the war.

Stab Batterie
Commander: *Hauptmann* Metzger
1.Zug (Platoon)
Commander: *Leutnant* Keller (?)
2.Zug
3.Zug
Panzer-Werkstatt-Zug (Tank Maintenance Platoon)

Fahrschwadron 'BR'

The Horse-Drawn Squadron was established on February 8th, 1945. Each Squadron consisted of 10 teams of horses and Hf1 wagons (60x horses x 40 men). It does not appear that a third Squadron was actually formed.

Commander: *Leutnant* Gruber; *SS-Sturmbannführer* Graf von Egloffstein

1st Sergeant: *Hauptwachtmeister* Böhnke

1.Schwadron

2.Schwadron

3.Schwadron

During actual combat deployment the *Division* typically employed its sub-units as follows: *I.Bataillon* of *Jägerregiment 1 'BR'* as a frontline unit, while the *I.(gep)Bataillon* of *Jägerregiment 1 'BR'* was employed as an independent reserve battalion often reacting to the tactical situation. *Jägerregiment 2 'BR'* typically operated with both battalions together, supported by the *Sturmgeschütze* of *Panzerjäger-Battalion 'BR'*. *Panzer-Sturm-Pionier-Bataillon 'BR'* could be found operating independently with the *Sturmgeschütz-Brigade 'GD'*.

The new *Division* was expected to receive its own *Panzer-Regiment* but this never happened as noted above in the *Introduction*. *Panzer-Regiment 'Brandenburg'* never served under *Panzergrenadier-Division 'BR'* and its deployment is worth further discussion given the often confused treatment the unit has received in postwar histories. *I.Bat./Pz.Rgt. 26* was formerly part of the *26.Panzer-Division* serving in Hungary during the fall of 1944. On January 15th it was ordered to Guben, south of Frankfurt/Oder, where it was redesignated *I.Bat./Pz.Rgt. 'Brandenburg'* and scheduled to be incorporated as a Panther battalion into *Panzergrenadier-Division 'BR'*. Originally the regiment was to move to Breslau where it would receive its compliment of Panthers, but the Soviet winter offensive prevented that movement. The regiment soon received its compliment of 45 Panzer Vs (Panthers). Its order to deploy to Litzmannstadt and join the division was cancelled because of the pace of Soviet operations. Instead, it was tactically subordinated to the *Panzergrenadier-Division 'Kurmark'*. Two companies, the *3.Pz.Kp.* and *4.Pz.Kp* immediately went into action south of Seelow Heights. The battalion's *Stab, Stab.Kp.* and the remaining *Panzer-Kompanien* were ordered to Fürstenwalde to complete their reorganization. Based on documentary evidence it is not clear if this happened, or if these elements rejoined the deployed two companies serving with *Panzergrenadier-Division 'Kurmark'*. *I.Bat./Pz.Rgt. 'BR'* continued to fight with *Panzergrenadier-Division 'Kurmark'* and the *9.Armee* for the remainder of the war.

II.Bat./Pz.Rgt. 'Brandenburg' also never served with *Panzergrenadier-Division 'BR'*. On January 17th, 1945 *OKH* issued an order to establish *II.Bat./Pz.Rgt. 'Brandenburg'*. This unit was intended to be fully operational by February 28th and sent to *Panzergrenadier-Division 'BR'*. The personnel for this unit was to come from *Pz.Abt. zbV 12*, which had previously served with *Division 'BR'* in the Balkans. The unit was formed at Grafenwöhr training ground. *Pz.Abt. zbV 12* left all of its vehicles in Hungary requiring a complete replenishment of vehicles. A combination of the Soviet winter offensive and the long replenishment prevented the unit from ever deploying to its parent division.

After three months of forming the *II.Bat./Pz.Rgt. 'Brandenburg'* finally reported on March 30th that it was 100% replenished with personnel, and 30 % with materiel (with another 5 % of the required materiel in transit) and 25% with motor vehicles. However, it still had not received any *Panzers*. The battalion remained behind the frontline and was stationed in the Alps at Hohentauen, Austria through the end of the war. It did not participate in further combat action after its deployment south from Grafenwöhr. *II.Bat./Pz.Rgt. 'Brandenburg'* consisted of the following organization:

Stab
Commander: *Major* Waldeck
O1 (Adjutant): *Hauptmann* Noeres
Nachrichten Offiziere: *Oberleutnant* Schilken

Abteilung V/Kfz.
Commander: *Hauptmann* Broy

Abteilung IV A.
Commander: *Oberzahlmeister* Wulff

Stabs-Kompanie:
Commander: *Hauptmann* von Kardorff

4.Kompanie:
Commander: *Oberleutnant* Albrecht

5.Kompanie:
Commander: *Oberleutnant* Möllmann

6.Kompanie:
Commander: *Hauptmann* Fischer

Werkstatt-Kompanie:
Commander: *Leutnant* Hayn

The unit's *Adjutant, Hauptmann* Herbert Noeres provides some background to this unit:

This *Abteilung* as a *Pz.Abt. zbV* was known as the "Balkan Fire Brigade" (its tactical symbol was a devil on a tank barrel). The *Abteilung* could not do anything else because it was the only *Panzer-Abteilung* in the *OB Armee Serbien*. Until July 1944, it bore the name of *Pz.Abt.zbV 12* and according to the *OKH*, it was renamed *II.Bat./Pz.Rgt. 'Brandenburg'* starting in August 1944. Supposedly it was sent to the *Division* in September. The *Division 'Brandenburg'* then took it over in November 1944, but only on paper. In the meantime, the *Abteilung* was rolled over by time in the truest sense of the word. All the armored vehicles were destroyed. The reason was the way they fought in the Balkans at the time. In spite of multiple protests by the Commander, Waldeck, the *Abteilung* was, and had to be, deployed in anti-partisan fighting a company at a time in the unmanageable terrain. The result was that the individual *Kompanien* were completely annihilated on their way back. The headquarters and the Stabskompanie were in Belgrade the entire time. The *Kompanien* were deployed over large areas exclusively by radio. In the meantime, the headquarters and the *Stabs-Kompanie* were deployed as well. As the Russian Front moved back, what was the *Abteilung* headquarters at the time was tasked by *Major* Metzler, the garrison commander for Belgrade, with developing the tank defense plan for Belgrade. This plan was illusory in that the unit in Belgrade only had three vehicles (Skoda type). The rest had to be deployed as infantry. During the attack on Belgrade, an attempt was made to at least avail themselves of their three vehicles to do a thrust using the remainder of *II.Bat./Pz.Rgt. 'Brandenburg'* along with the alert units quickly set up in the chaos and startled headquarters units. Some movement was made and then there was no more ammunition available and the vehicles had to be blown up. During the movement (about October 10th, 1944) and the entry into the downtown area about 6:00 p.m., one of the vehicles was almost knocked-out by an alert unit using a Flak gun. (Thank God, the courageous crew of the gun fled in a hurry as the *Panzer* rolled in.)

While the majority of the alert units retreated to the Kalemegdan, the *Abteilung* formed a loose receiving line in the vicinity of the transmitter. *Hauptmann* Noeres and *Oberleutnant* Schilken then killed two arriving T-34 Soviet tanks and seriously damaged three more. Then the Russians retreated and that made it possible to build a defensive position on the bridge over the Danube during the night. There the *Abteilung* fought for 5 more days in extremely restricted space. The retreat was completed as infantry until the reorganization order came in late 1944. The *Abteilung* was moved to Grafenwöhr. After the reorganization, the *Abteilung* was then supposed to be moved to the *Division 'Brandenburg'* in late February, 1945.

Again, the quickly-approaching front thwarted this order. In vain, *Major* Waldeck and his adjutant, *Hauptmann* Noeres, tried to push the order through. The deployment was as part of a newly-established *Kampfgruppe* in southern Germany. These *'Brandenburger'*, who were within the framework of the *Division 'Brandenburg'* but had never seen it, spent the end of the war in the High Tauern (Alps).

The following were additional notes regarding its planned reorganization at Grafenwöhr from *Hauptmann* Noeres:
The unit's equipment was as follows:

<u>Stabs-Kompanie</u> : 3x *Skoda* Panzer (Pz. 35t), 1x *Panzerspähwagen*. The *Panzerspähwagen* was an escort vehicle for the Commander in Chief (Weichs).
1x Self-Propelled Gun Mount with a 2cm cannon.

The *3.Kompanie* had:
An M-15 armored vehicle (Italian)
A Hotchkiss " (French)
5cm main gun. Very hard to supply with ammunition. However, it was ideal for the mountainous terrain in the vicinity.

Reorganization in Grafenwöhr/during acceptance into *'Brandenburg'*. (The *Division* refused this equipment and promised to lobby for Tigers. Discussion between *Major* Waldeck—the *Division* commander, *Hauptmann* Noeres – the adjutant, and *Oberst* Milldebrath—Inspector of Panzer Troops at *OKH* at the time (now in Dortmund) but were then allocated Panthers (through *Oberst* Koppenburger of the reorganization staff in Grafenwöhr).

At the Grafenwöhr Troop Training Area, the *Kompanie* was then trained on:

Panzer IV: (2)
Panther: (8)

No units of *Panzer-Regiment 'Brandenburg'* ever served with *Panzergrenadier-Division 'BR'*. To replace the lost *Panzer* strength the *Sturmgeschütz-Brigade 'GD'* was tactically assigned to *Panzergrenadier-Division 'BR'*. It remained with its new division for the rest of the war.

Division 'Brandenburg' went through a rapid, but incomplete reorganization into a *Panzergrenadier-Division 44* organizational structure between December 13th, 1944 and January 12th, 1945. Somewhat unrealistically, the reorganization was planned to be completed in 30 days by

January 15th. As the regiments assembled in East Prussia the combat strength of what was *Division 'Brandenburg'* was low after the Balkan fighting. We know from Erasmus' August letter to Jodl that he noted the entire *Division* totaled 14,000 men. His number represented what the *Division* looked like on paper fully staffed and was chosen to convince Himmler that acquiring *'Brandenburg'* was not worth the resource intensive effort. We know the regiments that arrived in East Prussia had suffered grievous losses and the *III.Regiment* was never released to return to its parent *Division*. There is no report that shows the *Division's* combat strength at the time of its reorganization, but a conservative estimate places its strength between 3,500-5,500 men in total. A rapid infusion of personnel was required. Because of the forward thinking of the *General* von Pfuhlstein in early 1944, two replacement and training units were established.

There was the *Lehr-Regiment 'Brandenburg'* and *Ausbildungs-Bataillon 'Brandenburg'* where the *Division* initially drew any remaining recruits that had not elected to join Skorzeny's *SS*-Commandos, though the number that remained is not known. Disband units of the old *Division 'Brandenburg'* provided additional personnel to fill the depleted ranks, as well as both official and unofficial transfers of personnel from a variety of other burnt out units. A number of new recruits were former *Luftwaffe* and *Kriegsmarine* men being retrained as infantry. Basic infantry training for raw recruits typically lasted months, but in this case, weeks or even days had to suffice. Transfers of officers between *'Großdeutschland'* and *'Brandenburg'* also occurred. The new commander of *Panzergrenadier-Division 'BR'*, *Generalmajor* Schulte-Heuthaus, was the former commander of *Panzergrenadier-Ersatz-Brigade 'GD'* and former regimental commander of the *Panzer-Füsilier-Regiment 'GD'*. Some of the *'Brandenburg'* soldiers were sent to fill in the ranks *of 'Großdeutschland'* while two experienced junior officers of *'Brandenburg'*, *Oberleutnant* Säuberlich and *Major* Plitt, now commanded the *Korps-Begleit-Kompanie* and *II.Btl./Pz.Korps-Füs.Rgt. 'GD'*, respectively. There were likely a number of unofficial transfers of NCOs and soldiers between the two units.

How many men of the new *Division* were part of the original, elite *Sonderkommandos*, is not clear. A conservative estimate is that about 30%-35% of the unit was carried over from the original *Sonderkommandos*. Entire units of *'Brandenburg'* like *Panzer-Sturm-Pionier-Bataillon 'BR'*, *Panzer-Jäger-Abteilung 'BR'*, *Panzer-Artillerie-Regiment 'BR'* and *Heeres-Flak-Artillerie-Abteilung 'BR'* were formed by incorporating units of other shattered divisions. More than a half-dozen units came from military formations outside *'Großdeutschland'* or *'Brandenburg'* replacement system to form the new *Division*. Some of the regimental companies might have retained an earlier esprit de corps as officers and enlisted men from the *Sonderkommando* days stayed together, but *Panzergrenadier-Division 'BR'* as a whole was not an elite unit. It might have shared the same name as the earlier *Sonderkommandos*, and even some personnel from *'Großdeutschland'*, but not its earlier élan.

The overall strength of the rebuilt *Division* at this time is not precisely known. A good estimate based on the calculation of personnel totals derived from the various first person accounts place the division's total available strength in January between 8,000-9,500 men with its combat strength at around 3,600 men. Spaeter himself states that the *Division's* overall strength in December was "extremely low" and that he estimated its strength in January had reached 10,000.[4]

Hauptmann Steidl, commander of *I.Btl./Jäg.Rgt. 2 'BR'* provides the following overview of his time in the *Panzer-Korps 'Großdeutschland'* assembly area. He comments on the new officers and new men that made up his battalion, and the training that needed to be done:

> I met my new officers. *Hauptmann* Kieffer was already in Hungary before us due to illness and I hoped to meet him soon. The new officers made a good impression on me. *Oberleutnant* Wirth was back from his field hospital and was commanding the *1.Kompanie*, the *2.Kompanie* had *Oberleutnant* Gutweniger from South Tyrol, the *3.Kompanie* had *Leutnant* Schmalbruch, and

---

4   Spaeter, *The History of Panzerkorps Großdeutschland*, p. 5-6.

the *4.schwere-Kompanie* had *Oberleutnant* Gabel. Another supply company was also formed, which *Oberzahlmeister* Treu turned over to the new *Zahlmeister* because he was reassigned. I was very sorry about him.

The young *Leutnants* were there fresh out of Officer School. *Leutnant* Lany, had a talent particularly worth talking about, *Oberfeldwebel* Albers, a southwestern man, tall as a tree, and a few others as well. The new organization led to a lot of work. My hand hurt a lot from the extreme cold and I had to go to the field hospital every day to be bandaged up. The *Division* was on the Mauer See in the barracks of what had been the command headquarters. There were a few other units and there were lots of lively goings-on in Angerburg.

The former *Fallschirmjäger* units were there as well. Franz Selgard also made it there with his *Feldersatz-Bataillon* and we joyfully embraced each other. That's how I met some old friends again. Säuberlich, who was commanding the *Korps-Begleit-Kompanie*, also called me. Unfortunately the state of my wounds forced me into bed; an inflammation occurred because of the cold. Kurt Bauer and his wife often visited me, as did Oesterwitz, who was promoted to *Oberstleutnant*, and even *Korps-General* von Saucken, who was now commanding the *Panzer-Korps 'Großdeutschland'*, was in my sick bay.

I moved Kurt Bauer onto my staff. He moved onto the first floor next to the two girls from the Rominter-Heide and frequently joked with Hilde and Edith. Günther Schmalbruch as well lived over there with his trusty sidekick Niederer.

I was out of bed again, but I couldn't move my hand anymore.

We celebrated New Year's Eve and *Leutnant* Simons' birthday. All of the officers, including Franz Selgard, came to visit me. Around midnight, there were some wild fireworks in the city. Ziegeler also visited me on New Year's Eve. With lots to eat and drink, in the best of spirits, we celebrated the last New Year's Eve of the war. The days went by putting the new troops through rigorous training.

There was an eerie calm before the storm.

One interesting item of note is that that the extreme cold clearly had an adverse impact on training. There is no record of the training regimen that the new *Division* followed during these days other than Steidl's comment that it was "rigorous", but the extreme cold likely had a limiting factor on how long the men could train each day. There were significant issues with equipment as well. Many of the vehicles sent to the *Division* were not factory new. They were repaired vehicles or older models used for training. This presented significant difficulties as the soldiers of *II.Btl./Jäg.Rgt. 2 'BR'* found out when half of their assigned vehicles arrived in an unserviceable condition.

Training new recruits brought its challenges, but so did re-training the veterans of *Division 'Brandenburg'*. Their collective experience was forged during the last eight months of fighting lightly armed partisans. Now, amidst an extensive reorganization, these former *Sonderkommandos* were expected to become proficient at division level mechanized warfare and all the standard infantry tactics required like building fixed positions and integrating fires from artillery and armor.

The men had no time to conduct training beyond the platoon and company level. There was no battalion, regimental, or division level training. Weapons familiarization and basic combat tactics were likely the best that could be achieved in the few short weeks. Many of the members in the combat battalions likely never conducted battlefield training with *Panzers* or *Sturmgeschütze* before. The assigned *Sturmgeschütz-Brigade 'Großdeutschland'* was still in Lübben awaiting the arrival of their vehicles. The brigade would not even have the benefit of training with their own vehicles before deploying to the frontline as their full complement of *Sturmgeschütze* was received only on January 15th. They deployed into battle without conducting a single training exercise with the soldiers of their assigned *Division*. New soldiers assigned to the brigade had to learn by experience.

Korps HQ vehicles adopted a tactical symbol of a black steel helmet on a yellow background. To identify both units tactically, *Panzergrenadier-Division 'BR'* adopted a tactical symbol of a white steel helmet with a red Brandenburg Eagle. The *Panzergrenadiers* were awarded a new *'Brandenburg'* cuff band, but retained a *'Großdeutschland'* insignia on their shoulder board straps. This new cuff band is often erroneously linked with the earlier *Sonderkommandos* but it was actually not authorized until after the *OKH* re-designated *'Brandenburg'* as a *Panzergrenadier-Division* in September.

A series of efficiency reports issued at both the *Korps* and *Division* level on January 6th, 7th, 10th, and 13th provide a final overview of the *Panzergrenadier-Division 'BR'* readiness before its first combat deployment. In summarizing the reports, the *Division* was rated a *Kampfwert II* on January 10th by the *Korps* Staff, meaning that it was capable of only "limited offensive action" as a *Kampfgruppe*. There were significant personnel, maintenance and equipment issues still being addressed. The *Begleit-Kompanie* was fully operational. *Jägerregiment 1 'BR'* and *Jägerregiment 2 'BR'* were still understrength due to a shortage of replacements. It was stated that both regiments were still "severely burnt out" from the recent heavy fighting. *Jägerregiment 1 'BR'* was noted as still "forming" on January 10th. *I.(gep)Btl./Jäg.Rgt. 1 'BR'* was short the armored command vehicles. It did receive 21 medium *SPWs* sometime between January 6th-10th that the battalion had to outfit, make ready for operations, and conduct familiarization training with the soldiers. *Jägerregiment 1 'BR'* reported that while it was fully outfitted with authorized weapons, its soldiers lacked the training to operate and employ them tactically. It lacked specialists in the battalion. It was still awaiting delivery of 25 trucks and the prime movers of *11.(sIG)Kompanie* were still missing on January 6th, but a subsequent report suggests that they arrived before the 13th. In the *Panzer-Artillerie-Regiment 'BR'* only *III.(s)Abteilung* and a single battery of *II.Abteilung* were combat operational. All three batteries of *I.Abteilung* were immobile due to a lack of prime movers. *Panzerjäger-Abteilung 'BR'* was at full strength and fully combat capable with 21 operational *Sturmgeschütz IVs*. *Panzer-Sturm-Pionier-Bataillon 'BR'* was at full personnel and equipment strength with the exception of all of its *SPWs*. Only *1.Kompanie* and *2.Kompanie* had all their *SPWs*. The *3.Kompanie* was missing all of its *SPWs* and could not fight as a completely motorized unit. *Panzer-Nachrichten-Abteilung 'BR'* was fully operational, but short six *SPWs*. *Heeres-Flak-Artillerie-Abteilung 'BR'* was still in Hungary and had not arrived. As previously noted, the *Panzer-Regiment 'BR'* also did not arrive and was eventually redirected to *Panzergrenadier-Division 'Kurmark'*. Overall, the division still lacked trained signals specialists, and was still missing 43 light *SPWs*, and 130 medium *SPWs* that were apparently in transit. Erasmus concluded that he believed the *Division's* missing tractors, armored vehicles and trucks would arrive by January 15th, but that it would take another 10 days of training to integrate the vehicles successfully.[5]

On the eve of one of the largest Soviet offensives of the war, *Panzergrenadier-Division 'BR'* was far from a fully capable combat division. It was not ready for the combat tasks the force was about to face in the coming weeks. *Hauptmann* Helmuth Spaeter noted at that time that "the entire reorganization of the divisions and the *Panzer-Korps* took place under considerable time constraints, consequently the older, badly battered units were unable to grow together again" and that "all in all, the time was much too short to weld both units together."[6] When the time came to deploy, *Panzergrenadier-Division 'BR'* did not even go into battle with its sister *Panzergrenadier-Division 'GD'*. It deployed with *Fallschirm-Panzer-Division 1 'Hermann Göring'*. Neither division spent a single day training together in the prior

---

5   Reports are as follows from BAMA RH10-114: *OpAbtIM Nr.197/45 g.Kdos. 6.1.45 "Stand der Aufstellung der Pz.Gren. Div.Brandenburg."*, and *Arbeitsstab (Pz.Jäger) Ref.Ia/Az.11 Nr.2/45 g.Kdos. Hirschberg, den 7,Jan.1945 "Aufstellung über den Stand der personellen u.materiellen Ausstatung der von Arbeitsstab (Pz.Jäger) in Mielau, Milowitz, Burg, beneschan, u.Neuhammer umzugliedernden, aufzufrischenden usw. Abt. u. Kp. Nach dem Stichtag vom 6.1.45, 24.00 Uhr."*; and RH10-121 *Freyer Oberst des Genst, des Generalinspekteurs der Panzertruppen Nr. 989/45 geh. H.Qu.OKH., 13.1.45 "Ergebnisse der Besprechung am 8.1.1945 beim Gen.Kdo.Pz.Korps "G.D.",* and *OKH/Chef H Rüst u BdE/AHA/Stab Ia (1) Nr. 10 111/44 g.K.v.20.12.1944 "Stand der Aufstellung und Umgliederung".*

6   Spaeter, *The History of Panzerkorps Großdeutschland*, p. 13.

month. There was no rapport established between the officers and soldiers of the two divisions that were expected to go into battle together, or with the command staff of *Panzer-Korps 'GD'*. The initial deployment of the *'Brandenburg'* served as their final training evaluation. The men had no choice but to quickly became proficient in their craft and establish their bonds of camaraderie in the crucible of battle.

7

Vistula-Oder Strategic Offensive, January 12th-17th

(Reference Maps 4, 5, 6, 7,8, 9, 10, 11, 12 and 13)

The Red Army amassed 2.1 million soldiers as well as 6,400 tanks and assault guns opposite German formations by early January 1945. *Wehrmacht* forces amounted to 520,000 soldiers as well as 800 *Panzers* and *Sturmgeschütze*.[1] *OKH* predications of the overall Soviet strength were off by as much as 60%. Two weeks prior to the Soviet Winter offensive, Guderian's chief of Foreign Armies East, *Oberst* Reinhard Gehlen wrote in a January 5th memorandum that due to the long preparation time the Red Army had it must be expected that Soviet leadership "intends to decisively destroy the German Eastern Army in the next offensive." He was right. The Soviets prepared well over the last four-five months for the coming offensive. The Red Army also benefitted from the withdrawal of many key German units to the west in preparation for Operation *Wacht am Rhein* that started in December 1944. German defensive strength in the east was weak. There were few operational reserves. Guderian prudently worked to build a series of defensive lines. In theory, combat formations would fall back and occupy them through a series of withdrawals in order to slow down a Soviet advance. On paper there was the Hubertus Line running about 30-60 kilometers behind the *Hauptkampflinie* (*HKL*: main combat line), followed next by the A-1/A-2 Line 30-70 kilometers behind along the Pilica-Riegel Rivers, and lastly the B-1/B-2 Line, along the Warthe River, west of Litzmannstadt, yet another 60-70 kilometers behind the A-1/A-2 Line. These lines were little more than geographic designations across a relatively flat, open landscape. They were not developed, fixed positions with bunkers and interlocking trench systems, though trenches and anti-tank ditches may have dotted the outskirts of certain key towns and villages. Even if these defensive positions were relatively developed Guderian lacked forces to man any defense-in-depth. According to one calculation there were no more than 72 German soldiers per kilometer of frontline. Hitler's direct interference with the defense in the East contributed to its overall weakening. Refusing to believe that a Soviet offensive was imminent or that available forces as large as Gehlen predicted, Hitler ordered available reinforcements in the form of the *11.Infanterie-Division, 61.Infanterie-Division, 121.Infanterie-Division, 1.Panzer-Division*, and *4.Panzer-Division* sent to *Heeresgruppe Mitte* and not to *Heeresgruppe A* where the main Soviet attack occurred. He ordered operational reserves, which were few, to be placed in the 10 kilometer zone extending west from the *HKL*. This zone was still within reach of the initial Soviet artillery barrage. Finally, Hitler refused to allow a second main defensive line created outside the *HKL* and out of reach of Soviet artillery. Overshadowing all these decisions was a general lack of concern for the Baranov Bridgehead at the southern end of *Heeresgruppe A*.

The Soviet Vistula-Oder Strategic Offensive was one the largest offensives of the war with the highest superiority in force levels ever achieved by the Red Army up to that time. Two powerful Soviet Fronts were arrayed against *Heeresgruppe A*. Each commanded by the Red Army's top military

---

1   David Glantz, *1986 Art of War Symposium: From the Vistula to the Oder: Soviet Offensive Operations, October 1944-March 1945* (Center for Land Warfare: U.S. Army War College, 19-23 May 1986) p. 516.

commanders. In the north was Marshal Georgy Zhukov, commander of the 1st Belorussian Front. To the south was Marshal Ivan Koniev, commander of the 1st Ukrainian Front. While Zhukov was Koniev's senior (Koniev had served under Zhukov earlier in the war), Koniev had risen to an equal rank and become a bitter rival of Zhukov. This rivalry played out on the battlefield and arguably contributed to the survival of *Panzer-Korps 'Großdeutschland'* after the start of offensive. Koniev's offensive was to start on January 12th, followed two days later by Zhukov on the 14th. There ended their overall coordination.

Zhukov planned a 25 minute artillery barrage followed by a strong reconnaissance in force. Soviet rifle divisions were expected to break the German frontlines identified by the reconnaissance troops, followed by a release of two tank armies into the breach to exploit the breakthrough. Koniev, to the south, decided to launch a one hour artillery barrage, followed by a massive attack that included his three tanks corps in order to breach German defenses immediately.[2] Both Fronts were expected to advance in the first stage to achieve the capture of Warsaw, followed by a line running from Bromberg-Poznan-Breslau. Depending upon the success of the operation to that point, Soviet forces were to continue their advance.

Planning for the offensive across Poland began in November 1944. Koniev recalled the planning sessions in Moscow and the importance of his Front's objectives in a postwar context.

> In those days, being called to Moscow, I carried there the operational plan, developed by the command of the front, and personally reported about it at the Headquarters of the Supreme Command to I.V. Stalin, in the presence of members of the State Defense Committee.
>
> I remember well how I.V. Stalin discussed the plan of the operation in detail, and he paid special attention to the Silesian industrial region, which was represented on the map in relief. According to our plan, the attacks of the troops were to by-pass this region, to the north and south of it, as in itself this industrial region was an enormous cluster of industrial enterprises, constructed of reinforced-concrete, as a rule, of mines with powerful equipment located inside. All this, taken together, represented very great obstacles for maneuvering actions of the troops in an assault on this industrial region from the front.
>
> Even on the map, the scales of the Silesian region and its power were given quite expressively. Stalin—as I understood perfectly—specially calling my attention to this circumstance, indicated the map with his finger, outlined this industrial region, and said: : "Gold".
>
> This was said in such ways that, in essence, no further commentaries were required.
>
> ....we must take measures to preserve the industrial potential as much as possible all the more so in that after the liberation, these age-old Polish territories must be returned to Poland.[3]

For Koniev, his objective was clear. Isolate Silesia and preserve it for the eventual shift of postwar borders that would see the transfer of this region to Poland, while the millions of Germans living there were forced out.

Once the operation started on January 12th, the momentum of the attack completely shattered the thin German defensive line, allowing the Soviets to achieve their greatest advance in terms of operational depth than at any other point in the war.[4] Zhukov's attack launched from two bridgeheads north of a German salient that ran along the Weichsel River. The smaller of the two attacks launched from the Pulawy Bridgehead while the main attack launched from the Warka/Magnushev (Magnuszew) Bridgehead farther north, just south of Warsaw. This attack took place almost two days after Koniev's

---

2   Ibid., pp. 514-521.
3   Cornelius Ryan Collection, Section: Soviet Forces. Koniev Memoir (Box 72/Folder 3), pp. 1-2.
4   While Guderian did plan to withdraw his frontline soldiers prior to the Soviet artillery barrage, it does not appear that any of his commanders attempted to execute this complex pre-attack operation.

attack began. Marshal Koniev's attack was launched from the Baranov Bridgehead (known to the Soviets as Sandomierz). As mentioned above, all German reserves, with the exception of *Panzer-Korps 'Großdeutschland'*, were placed directly behind the frontline.[5] The Soviet planners knew this and they conducted their operations accordingly. First they denied these reserves freedom of movement through air and artillery strikes, then they either by-passed them or defeated them in detail. The Soviet 1st Belorussian Front struck the left flank of the *Heeresgruppe Mitte's 2.Armee*. Over the course of the next several weeks it drove northwest, generally following the course of the lower Weichsel River. The 1st Belorussian Front also struck *Heeresgruppe A's 9.Armee* and *4.Panzer-Armee*, splitting the two armies in the process. The 1st Ukrainian Front's attack pierced the right flank of the *4.Panzer-Armee* and the northern flank of the *17.Armee* as it drove southwest toward Breslau, Silesia, and the upper Neisse River. Once the German frontline was breached Soviet tank armies raced 600 kilometers across Poland to reach the Oder River, achieving a daily advance rate of 35 kilometers per day. Their advance was aided by the flat terrain of Poland and the low temperatures that froze the ground hard and the rivers solid. There were few natural obstacles to slow down the Soviet armored advance across the generally hard, frozen ground. Between the 1st Belorussian and 1st Ukrainian Fronts ran an inter-front boundary running from south of the Pulawy Bridgehead in a northwesterly direction to just south of Litzmannstadt (Lodz). As this was the extreme left wing of Zhukov's Front, and extreme right wing of Koniev's Front, their main axis of advance happened to coincide with the inter-front boundary of the German *9.Armee* and *4.Panzer-Armee*. This proved a benefit to German forces that were caught between the two advancing Soviet commanders, giving them room to maneuver and withdraw west. Another added benefit was the inherent rivalry between Zhukov and Koniev. This rivalry prevented any operational coordination that might have prevented a large mass of German combat formations to escape west and reform behind the Oder and Neisse Rivers in February. Instead of coordinating their operations to surround and defeat the bulk of the *4.Panzer-Armee*, both rivals focused on advancing west as fast as possible—arguably recklessly—leaving *Wehrmacht* formations behind that were able to fight their way back to German lines and offer continued resistance in the coming months.

By the end of the offensive the German Eastern Front in central Poland ceased to exist. By the beginning of February the Soviets had reached the Oder River and were just sixty kilometers from Berlin. Many of the *Wehrmacht* formations were shattered and required months to rebuild. Despite the advantage in men and firepower, the Soviets suffered a total of 383,000 casualties (8,400 per day of operation), and 1,267 tanks and assault guns (55 per day of operation).[6]

Koniev's Attack, January 12th-16th

Koniev's attack started at 8:00 a.m. (10 a.m. Moscow time) on January 12th with a 67 minute heavy artillery barrage that racked across the thinly held German positions. 45 minutes into the barrage, there was a brief pause as reinforced platoons advanced to capture key tactical strongpoints before the barrage resumed and prior to the main attack. The 1st Ukrainian Front had crammed some 90% of its infantry divisions and armor units inside the Baranov Bridgehead. The sheer force ratio of attacker-to-defender was so overwhelming that Koniev's motorized infantry divisions breached the German frontline easily, advancing some 20-25 kilometers by the end of the first day. Both the 3rd Guards Tank Army under the command of Colonel-General P.S. Rybalko and 4th Guards Tank Army under the command of Colonel-General D.D. Lelyushenko were introduced into the breach along with the 31st, 25th, and 4th Guards Tank Corps. The Germans were surprised by the ferocity and size of Koniev's attack, as all *Fremde Heeres Ost* predications had placed emphasis on the Soviet

---

5   Glantz, p. 511-12.
6   Krivosheev, pp.153, 263. According to a report located in NARA T311/167/440, dated 5 February 1945, the Germans reported that the number of Soviet tanks destroyed from the period of January 14th-31st was 996. The number is fairly close to the Soviet assessment.

bridgehead to the north and not the one to the south. Koniev's force conducted a reconnaissance artillery firing at 3:00 a.m. (5 a.m. Moscow) followed by an advance of Penal Battalions to identify and clear minefields. This move, coupled with the bad weather, convinced German commanders in the area that this was not the prelude to a major offensive. They were wrong. As per the operational plan, Koniev left 150 meter wide corridors open in his artillery barrage that allowed his T-34s and Su-76M platoons to advance and strike the forward elements of the *XXXXVIII.Panzer-Korps.* The German reaction was to fire their own artillery at the Soviet formations, and release ground units to engage them. This caused the German units to reveal their positions, allowing Koniev's artillery to more accurately pinpoint German formations and strike them with the weight of his barrage. In this manner, elements of the reserve *17.Panzer-Division* were immediately caught in the opening artillery barrage while the *68.Infanterie-Division* and *168.Infanterie-Division* bore the brunt of Koniev's ground assault and shattered within the first several hours of battle. The German divisions splintered down to the *Kompanie* level as command-and-control fell apart. Survivors withdrew west without orders, ear drums shattered, noses bleeding, shocked and stunned looks in the eyes. Koniev's commentary on the state of captured German soldiers during his initial advance captures their state of shock under the weight of unprecedented Soviet bombardment:

> Commanding officers of German units captured in the first hours of the breakthrough indicated that their soldiers and officers, as a result of our artillery barrage, lost their self-control. They wilfully abandoned their positions, and for the Germans this, we must say directly, is not characteristic. The German soldier, as a rule—and this rule was confirmed throughout the extent of the entire war—stays where he is told, as long as he has not received permission to retreat. But on this day—12 January—the power of the fire was so pitiless that the German soldiers who remained alive wilfully abandoned their position and hurried back into the depths of their defenses.[7]

The *4.Panzer-Armee* immediately ordered the *72.Infanterie-Division* to advance in regimental groups toward the gap that opened up between the *68.Infanterie-Division* and *168.Infanterie-Division.* As they advanced, the *72.Infanterie-Division* regimental elements ran into the attacking Soviet 59th Army and were also overwhelmed and forced to retreat west.

Infanterie-Regiment 575 of the *304.Infanterie-Division* initially maintained a staunch defense of Stopnica along the left flank of Koniev's breakthrough until 2:00 p.m. against repeated attacks of the 9th Guards Rifle Division, 14th Guards Rifle Division, and 273rd Tank Brigade. It subsequently withdrew before it could be surrounded. Soviet artillery fire did not prove effective in destroying German combat power in the *69.Infanterie-Division* sector. The Soviet assault bogged down after 3-5 kilometers in the first several hours, primarily due to the minefields that were still intact. The 150th Tank Brigade maneuvered around the minefields and advanced to a depth of 15 kilometers to an area near Kielce where it was attacked by elements of *General* Dietrich von Müller's *16.Panzer-Division.* This division, already positioned too close to the frontline, was now identified by the Soviet artillery and targeted. Its counterattack, apparently launched on its own authority, robbed the *XXXXVIII. Panzer-Korps* of its only real reserve, which was now growing heavily engaged in a tank battle south of Kielce.

Soviet artillery destroyed German field communications, meaning that orders via landline were impossible. While wireless radio worked locally, orders typically needed to be sent via courier. This caused a significant lag in orders being generated and received. German formations were not able to react fast enough to the Soviet attack. It was not until the afternoon that the commander of *Heeresgruppe A, General* Josef Harpe, began to issue orders out to subunits. Among them was the release of the *s.Panzer-Abteilung 424* to counterattack. Soon the *17.Panzer-Division* was also on the

---

move toward Kielce.

As German resistance increased, Koniev released his 3rd and 4th Guards Tank Armies into the frontline to attack German positions before the infantry had forced a breakthrough. In effect, Koniev focused the combat power of seven various armies, and two independent corps against the *XXXXVIII.Panzer-Korps* during the afternoon of the 13th. Koniev ordered his forces to aggressively attack through the night. He was in a race to achieve a wide and deep breakthrough before Zhukov was expected to start his offensive. Speed was of the essence and according to Koniev a special focus of training before the offensive.

> Incidentally, in the tank troops special attention was paid to training the tank men to fire their weapons, firing when moving, and also in fast actions, mobility, and maneuverability.
> As one of the examples of such training, which was going on everywhere, I remember the special training sessions organized at the bridgehead by the commander of the 4th Guards Tank Army, Colonel-General Lelyushenko. The military Council of the Front was present at this training, at which they learned how to fire from moving tanks and how to destroy enemy tanks with their own tanks. They did not fire at dummies, but at real "Tigers" and "King Tigers" captured by us in previous battles here, at the Sandomierz Bridgehead.[8]

A particular objective was the capture of Litzmannstadt, which was at the inter-front boundary between the two Soviet Fronts. On January 13th Koniev's tank armies had begun their exploitation. A reinforced tank brigade was sent to each tank corps to lead the advance. They were the equivalent of a small task force with attached infantry riding on tanks or in trucks (the Soviet infantry enjoyed no mechanized protection like their German counterparts), combat engineer elements, anti-tank elements, multiple rocket elements, and other necessary components that the corps commander determined was necessary for the operation. In this exploitation phase it was common for the forward tank brigades to operate 60 kilometers ahead of the main forces, with the other tank brigades of the tank corps operating 40 kilometers apart (either abreast or in line depending on the situation) and the tank armies themselves operated some 120 kilometers apart. This separation of space was on one hand extremely disruptive to German lines-of-communication, forcing them to often withdraw to avoid encirclement. Soviet supply of these forward elements was limited during the advance. The most important commodity was fuel, and in order to maintain their advance the Soviets would mix oil with captured German kerosene and add that to their armored vehicles and trucks. According to one Soviet veteran, the engines ran hot with this mixture, but they still ran, allowing the Soviet forces to continue their advance. Operating at this depth also brought issues as by-passed German formations often attacked weaker Soviet infantry formations in their attempt to make their way west, and advancing Soviet tank brigades occasionally ran into superior German forces that dealt them heavy losses.

The Soviet 4th Guards Tank Army became embroiled in a series of flank battles at Kielce, while elements of the 6th Guards Mechanized Corps and the 10th Guards Tank Corps began to outflank the area and head north. The forward elements of the 3rd Guards Tank Army advanced west on Czestochowa, while the 59th Army under the command of Lieutenant-General I. T. Korovnikov, led by the 4th Guards Tank Corps, advanced toward Krackow. Koniev's tank armies were no more than 40 kilometers from the *Heeresgruppe A* headquarters located at Tschenstochau.

On the morning of January 13th the 34th Corps of the 5th Guards Army under the command of Colonel-General A.S. Zhadov and elements of the 4th Guards Tank Corps reached the A-1 position along the Nida River. The Germans had destroyed the bridges. The thin ice in this area prevented any crossing without pontoon bridges, delaying the Soviets a few hours. Elements of the shattered *68.Infanterie-Division* and *17.Panzer-Division* managed to put up weak resistance at Chmielnik

---

8   Ibid., pp. 11-12.

into the late morning. Between this point and Kielce to the north was the *XXIV.Panzer-Korps* of *General der Panzertruppen* Walther Nehring. The forces located here were the headquarters of the *17.Panzer-Division*, which was already fighting as separate units, the *s.Panzer-Bataillon 424*, the *16.Panzer-Division* that was already engaged in combat, the *20.Panzergrenadier-Division* making its way southwest toward the front and a *Kampfgruppe* of the *10.Panzergrenadier-Division*. The terrain was ill suited for tank warfare across the forested, soggy, stream crossed ground. Maneuverability was limited on both sides.

At the start of the Soviet attack the *17.Panzer-Division* was placed 20 kilometers (still within range of Soviet artillery) from the Soviet frontline between the proposed A-1 position and the unfinished Hubertus line. The division was in an unfavorable position directly in front of a tributary of the Weichsel that required bridges to cross. On several occasions the division commander, *Oberst* Brux, requested that the *XXIV.Panzer-Korps* move the division's current position further back. Not even requests by *General* Harpe, the *Heeresgruppe* commander, could affect a change in any of his unit's deployments. The *17.Panzer-Division* had about 210 operational *Panzers* at the start of the operation. Many of their crews were untrained, which contributed to the near immediate loss of some 25% of its *Panzers* at the start of the battle according to *Oberst* Liebisch, who commanded the *I.Bataillon* of *Panzergrenadier-Regiment 40* of the division. On January 12th the Soviet artillery fire opened up. *Oberst* Liebisch observed from his command post that "between 3:00 and 5:00 a.m. on 12 January, there was a continuous barrage of artillery units firing all calibers in an extent that had hitherto been unknown to us. The horizon was as bright as daylight. Between 8:00 and 10:00 a.m. this firestorm was repeated and I would like to say that out impression was like heavens falling down on earth."[9] By midday the frontline of *Infanterie-Division 68*, directly in front of the *17.Panzer-Division* was breached and Soviet tank columns of the 3rd Guards Tank Army and the 53rd Guards Army were now visible advancing around and through the positions of the *17.Panzer-Division*. At the headquarters of the division there was no communication with the *XXIV.Panzer-Korps*. Communications had been interrupted by the artillery barrage. For nearly eight hours *Oberst* Brux waited in vain for orders. Finally by late afternoon an order arrived to "ready" the *Panzers* for operations but communications were interrupted again. Before they could be reestablished several Soviet tank brigade surrounded the division headquarters by evening.

Oberst Liebisch received his first order by radio for the day that requested his *Panzergrenadier-Bataillon* to head to Lugi and relieve the surrounded division headquarters. During the night the first and only organized counterattack of the *17.Panzer-Division* took place. Two battalions of *Panzergrenadier-Regiment 40* and the *Panzer-Regiment 39* launched a night attack in the direction of Chmielnik but were unsuccessful due to the number of Soviet forces already present. The division headquarters, surrounded and outnumbered, surrendered to the Soviets.

The following day the remaining *Kampfgruppe* of the *17.Panzer-Division* found itself not in contact with any other elements of the division or higher headquarters. It was now operating on its own and it attempted to breakout west by Podlesie but the roads were under Soviet fire and the attack was halted. The next day on January 14th the *Kampfgruppe* consolidated its forces south of Lugi. The skies cleared enough to allow Soviet aircraft to operate and they quickly began attacking German forces in the open terrain. Direct fire from ground forces forced the Soviet aircraft to ultimately decide to find easier targets by the afternoon. Soviet infantry formations, following on the heels of Koniev's tank forces, moved into the area all around the cut off German units.

The *Kampfgruppe* launched a breakthrough attack on the night of January 14th/15th along the Chmielnik-Celiny-Moraywicke road, but were confronted with blown bridges across the various streams that impeded movement and prevented many of the soft-skin vehicles from continuing. Communication, even among the battalions of the *Kampfgruppe* was limited to non-existent.

9   Glantz, p. 617.

Coordination was all but impossible. During the night advance the *Kampfgruppe* ran into a Soviet blocking position southeast of Morawicka. Heavy Soviet defensive fire from anti-tank and anti-air guns poured on the lead elements of the *Kampfgruppe,* forcing them to swing east. By the light of the morning on January 15th the lead elements reached the Nida River and located a river crossing near Morawicka still held by the rearguard of the *16.Panzer-Division.* The *Kampfgruppe* crossed into German lines. *Oberst* Liebisch noted that at this time "no uniform command and control had existed in the operations. The will to breakthrough had induced us to joint action."[10] A new *Kampfgruppe* was formed under the command of *General* von Müller that combined the surviving elements of both *Panzer-Divisions.*

Under the command of the *17.Panzer-Division* was the *s.Panzer-Abteilung 424* (formerly 501) with 51 operational Pz.Kpw. VI Tiger IIs assigned. This Tiger II battalion was assigned to the *XXIV. Panzer-Korps* and positioned in unfavorable terrain too close to the Soviet frontline like other *Panzer* formations. During the course of January 12th no orders came to the unit until the evening. Then the *3.Kompanie* was ordered to entrain at Sandomierz and transported to the south of Kielce. Once it detrained it received orders to relive the encircled headquarters of the *17.Panzer-Division.* The attack, however, did not begin that night as other elements of the unit were expected to arrive by the morning on the 13th. Soon additional elements of the *Abteilung* in the form of the *1.Kompanie* and *2.Kompanie* detrained and the *Abteilung* was ordered to attack in the direction of Lisow.

The attack began with the King Tigers of *1.Kompanie* on the left, *3.Kompanie* on the right, and *2.Kompanie* trailing. The attack immediately bogged down due to the soft terrain. The local bridges that crossed the numerous streams proved incapable of bearing the weight of the sixty-eight ton *Panzers* inhibiting movement, and even causing one to collapse into the stream along with the traversing King Tiger. By midday the Soviets were engaged in battle and the *Abteilung* claimed 27 Soviet tanks knocked out, but the King Tigers were soon ambushed by heavy Soviet Joseph Stalin (JS-2) tanks from the 13th Heavy Tank Regiment. A number of King Tigers were themselves knocked out to include the command Tiger. As many as another 30 Soviet tanks were hit by the desperate *Panzer* crews struggling from being overrun, many with immobilized King Tigers. The remnants of the *Abteilung* withdrew during the night toward Kielce and fell under command of the forming German pocket under *General* Nehring.

Along with the attack of the *s.Pz.Abt.424*, elements of both the *20.Panzergrenadier-Division* and the *16.Panzer-Division* attacked south in an ad hoc manner. Approximately 50 *Panzers* advanced southeast into a Soviet ambush. Soviet anti-tank guns knocked out the lead German company led by *Hauptmann* Caprivi of the *16.Panzer-Division,* forcing the rest to withdraw northeast. The Soviet 16th Mechanized Brigade pushed northwest of the Germans, and bounced the Czarna Nida River to the left of Morawicka, where it established a bridgehead on the other side. Soviet infantry of the 13th Army followed. To the east, the *16.Panzer-Division* regrouped and launched another counterattack against the flank of the Soviet 6th Mechanized Corps. The flanking Soviet infantry divisions bore the brunt of the attack and were unable to launch an effective counterattack. Unknown to von Müller or *General* Nehring, commander of the *XXIV.Panzer-Korps,* was that the remnants of the *17.Panzer-Division* attacked north to regain German lines. At that point the danger to the flank of Koniev's offensive grew acute and he ordered the 10th Tank Corps turned around to attack eastward against the German formations.

By January 14th the fierce fighting subsided temporarily. Confusion and the fog-of-war dominated the battlefield. Many German and Soviet formations were comingled. Unlike the Soviets, the German formations had little command-and-control and were fighting to survive. Most units cut off by the initial assault now moved north toward Kielce. The pause in the fighting altered Koniev's thinking. He ordered his formations to resume their attack west, looking toward his second and third

10   Ibid. p. 619.

echelon formations to deal with the still resisting German formations. This decision by Koniev proved detrimental to his further advance east and was later criticized by Stavka at the end of the offensive.

The *XXIV.Panzer-Korps* formed the southern edge of a pocket than ran along the forests to the east and south of Kielce. By January 15th the *20.Panzergrenadier-Division* and remnants of the *16.Panzer-Division* were positioned there and still resisting. It was during this day that the withdrawing remnants of the *17.Panzer-Division* reached, then crossed the Czarna Nida River, while the survivors of the *168. Infanterie-Division* withdrew over the Lubrzanka River. The bridgehead established on the 13th by the Soviets, was now exploited as the combined forces of the Soviet 13th Army's 76th and 120th Rifle Corps advanced behind the *XXIV.Panzer-Korps* and captured Kielce with the 389th Rifle Division and 150th Tank Brigade. Orders finally reached Nehring from the *Heeresgruppe* to hold the Czarna Nida River line and protect Kielce, but the orders were already overcome by the operational realities on the ground. The only option left to Nehring was to withdraw northwest toward German lines.

Nehring quickly reorganized his forces and ordered an attack on the morning of January 16th to the northwest, through Soviet occupied Kielce. The Soviets, following Koniev's orders to maintain momentum west, left only two weak Soviet divisions, the 172nd and 121st, to hold the area. The attack was successful and Nehring recaptured the town and established blocking positions along the bend of the Weichsel. This allowed the cut off *XXXXII.Armee-Korps* to withdraw to German lines. The 4th Guards Tank Army continued its attack northwest toward Litzmannstadt. Koniev attempted, somewhat half-heartedly, to form a pocket around the German formations moving northwest by employing the 25th Tank Corps, but failed.

Koniev downplayed the ability of Nehring to extract himself from the potential encirclement unfolding around Kielce. He mentions the fighting in his postwar memoir, but dismisses Nehring's escape as a solid Soviet victory.

> Having concentrated in the approaches to the city of Kielce, the Germans fought stubbornly, and this at first slowed down the rate of advance of Gordov's 3rd Guards Army and Pukhov's 13th Army.
>
> Having received a report of this, we, without losing time, turned the 4th Guards Tank Army of Lelyushenko that was in motion, directing it to by-pass the city of Kielce from the southwest. As a result of this maneuver of the fourth day of the offensive, 15 January, the city of Kielce was taken, and a great part of the German troops resisting in the approaches to it were defeated, and their survivors were pushed into the forests north of Kielce.[11]

By the end of the January 17th, Koniev's forces reached a depth of 160 kilometers. The German frontline was shattered, but the German formations operating on his northern flank were still generally intact and had begun to form a roving pocket behind Koniev's lines.

Zhukov's Attack, January 14th-17th

Zhukov's attack began at 6:30 a.m. (8:30 a.m. Moscow time) on January 14th. He opened his offensive with a 25 minute heavy artillery barrage across the German frontline. When the barrage concluded he sent 22 reinforced infantry battalions to conduct a reconnaissance in force of the German positions. If they ran into resistance, the attack would halt, and a second artillery barrage would occur, followed by the main assault. Due to the lack of German strength, poor placement of frontline positions, and a lack of reserves, the Soviet reconnaissance in force breached two defensive belts clearing the way for the main attack force with the second artillery barrage. With the attack by the 1st Ukrainian Front already underway, *Heeresgruppe A* was expecting the coming attack from the Magnushev and Pulawy Bridgeheads. The day before on January 13th, the *9.Armee* released the *25.Panzer-Division*

---

to support the *VIII.Armee-Korps* defending opposite the Magnushev (Magnuszew) Bridgehead and the *19.Panzer-Division* to support the *LVI.Panzer-Korps* opposite the Pulawy Bridgehead. A *Kampfgruppe* of the *10.Panzergrenadier-Division* was released to support the *LVI.Panzer-Korps* as well. The weather was cold and snowy on January 14th when Zhukov's attack began. He had planned for extensive use of air support during the opening phase of the attack but no aircraft could take off.

Zhukov's artillery preparation began on schedule. He achieved a concentration of about 250 guns (8,700 artillery, rockets, and mortar tubes) per kilometer of front. At his command were 1.1 million men, 1,900 tanks and 1,200 self-propelled assault guns. The artillery hit their mark tearing up German defensive positions. Guderian wanted German forward units to extract themselves prior to the initial Soviet barrage and withdraw to a rearward position in order to avoid their destruction. German *Bataillon* and *Kompanie* level commanders apparently expressed concern in conducting such a complex maneuver that would cause them to evacuate well established defensive positions for less developed ones further back. There apparently was little support at the *Armee* or *Heeresgruppe* level to force the issue on behalf of Guderian. Unfortunately this position cost them dearly. With the advantage of thick fog, Soviet advanced battalions in the Magnushev Bridgehead from the 61st, 5th Shock, and 8th Guards Armies assaulted the stunned German frontline positions promptly after the first 30 minute barrage as Zhukov planned. To the south in the Pulawy Bridgehead, Soviet soldiers from the 69th and 33rd Armies' assault battalions did the same. While there was some resistance by German defenders at several tactical strongpoints, an operational breakthrough by the Soviets occurred within hours. German communication networks were shattered. A lack of manpower and effective supporting fires by Soviet artillery and mortars prevented any meaningful resistance. In the Magnushev Bridgehead the Soviets drove deep wedges through the shattered *251.Infanterie-Division* and the left flank of the *6.Volksgrenadier-Division*. Zhukov recognized the momentum he achieved with his initial assault and moved to the second phase of his operation. He introduced the 9th Guards Tank Corps to exploit the opening. By noon his attack reached a depth of about 9 kilometers where German regimental headquarters were located. About an hour after the initial Soviet attack began the commander of the *XXXX.Panzer-Korps*, *General der Panzertruppen* Siegfried Henrici ordered the *19.Panzer-Division* and *25.Panzer-Division* to launch immediate counterattacks. Both divisions moved into their assembly areas at around 10:30 a.m. and the *19.Panzer-Division* was immediately attacked by supporting tank elements of the Soviet 28th and 29th Guards Rifle Corps. Likewise to the north, the *25.Panzer-Division* was also unable to initially develop a counterattack due to the pace of Soviet operations. By the end of the day in the Magnushev Bridgehead sector, the tenuous German defensive line established along the Pilica River was already breached by Soviet infantry. Bridgeheads across this last tactical obstacle were established by day's end and complete operational maneuverability was gained. Into these bridgeheads were pouring the advance tank units of the 9th Guards Tank Corps of the 2nd Guards Tank Army and the 11th Guards Tank Corps of the 1st Guards Tank Army.

Developments in the Pulawy Bridgehead were even more spectacular for the Soviets. The breach made against the German *214.Infanterie-Division* by the elements of the Soviet 16th and 38th Rifle Corps achieved a 10 kilometer breakthrough. This allowed immediate exploitation by the 9th Tank Corps that drove another 4 kilometers breaking through the German defensive zone and capturing Ciepielow. A *Kampfgruppe* of the *10.Panzergrenadier-Division* launched an immediate counterattack but was unable to reach Ciepielow before it was itself engaged in heavy combat and splintered. It began a withdrawal along with the left wing of the *214.Infanterie-Division* back toward Radom. The 61st and 25th Rifle Corps of the 69th Army also achieved a major breakthrough that day against the *17.Infanterie-Division*. The breakout of the 11th Tank Corps through this breach was spectacular. Against almost no opposition Soviet tank formations drove into the *LVI.Panzer-Korps* rear area reaching the outskirts of Radom by evening—some 30 kilometers from the Soviet frontline.

By the evening of the 14th German combat units, especially at the regimental level and below were focused on survival in the wake of the initial Soviet attack. They were in no position to put up cohesive resistance. The reserves introduced into the fight were often caught in their assembly areas and subjected to immediate, withering Soviet artillery fire. No further reserves were available to the *9.Armee* to introduce into the fight. The *45.Volksgrenadier-Division* and the bulk of the *17.Infanterie-Division* were still holding positions on the Weichsel River and found themselves in real danger of being surrounded. The *LVI.Panzer-Korps* headquarters was under direct threat and was in no position to conduct an effective defense with what remained of the German units on hand. The *Kampfgruppe* of the *10.Panzergrenadier-Division* was now in full retreat and no longer a cohesive force.

The German defense opposite Zhukov was non-existent by the evening of the 14th. Zhukov specifically ordered a halt to the attack for the evening. This was done specifically to rest, replenish, and move up artillery forces. It appears that Zhukov was aware of the movement of the two *Panzer-Divisions* and decided to ensure their immediate destruction before resuming his advance. When dawn broke an equally powerful 40 minute artillery barrage hit the German defensive line including the two *Panzer-Divisions*. According to Colonel Illarion A. Tolkanyuk, who served as Chief of the Operations Department and Department Chief of Staff, 8th Guards Tank Army recalled how the *19.Panzer-Division* "fell under our morning raid and was shattered. . . . The *25.Panzer-Division* suffered the identical horror a bit later."[12] When Tolkanyuk travelled through the area he recalled seeing "vehicles, tanks, [artillery] pieces, and people mixed up with the ground." The 8th Guards Army soon continued its advance.

On the 15th the Soviets began to advance from their small bridgeheads over the Pilica. The main force now had to cross the frozen river. The ice was capable of handling the infantry, but not tanks. The Soviets broke the ice, placed pontoons then began to move tanks across the river. Soon elements of the 40th Guards Tank Brigade of the 11th Guards Tank Corps pierced the German lines directly between the *19.Panzer-Division* and *25.Panzer-Division* and were on their way southwest toward Litzmannstadt. The 11th and 9th Tank Corps than advanced another 10 kilometers from their positions and enveloped the city of Radom securing its capture on the 16th along with a substantial number of German prisoners.

During January 16th orders were issued allowing both the *45.Volksgrenadier-Division* and *17.Infanterie-Division* to withdraw west from their positions on the Weichsel between the two advancing spearheads of Zhukov's forces. Up to this date poor weather had grounded Soviet aircraft and given the Germans some freedom of movement. By the 17th the weather cleared and Soviet aircraft finally took to the skies in support of the advancing Soviet forces. The *Feldgrau* of German soldiers and vehicles was easily detectable against the background of the recent snows making them easy targets for Soviet aviators. By the end of the day the forward elements of Zhukov's 8th Guards Army and Koniev's 69th Army met at Litzmannstadt cutting off Nehring's forces to the east.

Between the Bridgeheads

Oberst Hans von Ahlfen was in command of the defensive line between the *9.Armee* and *4.Panzer-Armee*, nearly dead center between the Pulawy and Baranov Bridgeheads. He was in command of *Heeres-Pionier-Brigade 70* that became the core of *Sperrverband von Ahlfen*. His units withdrew west and joined the *XXIV.Panzer-Korps*. This combined group of withdrawing German units under the command of Walther Nehring, now became known as *Gruppe Nehring*. Von Ahlfen's daily account offers an excellent operational overview of the situation and the conditions faced by the German forces at that time. Upon reaching German lines, von Ahlfen was promoted to the rank of *Generalmajor* on January 30th, and assigned the responsibility of Fortress Commander Breslau.[13]

---

12   Colonel David M. Glantz, *Red Army Officers Speak! Interviews with veterans of the Vistula-Oder Operation (January-February 1945)* (David M. Glantz, 1997), p. 12.
13   Von Ahlfen soon began arguments with the city's *Gauleiter* Karl Hanke over military operations of the defending

January 13th (afternoon)
Artillerie-Regiment Stab z.b.V under the command of *Oberst* Korcianczyk, *le. F.H. Abteilung (mot.), s.Mot. Abteilung (2x 10 cm K, 1x s.F.H.), Pionier-Brigade 70 (Pi. 48* and *70)* were ordered subordinated to *Panzer-Armeeoberkommando 4* and sent to Kamienna.

January 13th (evening)
Strength of the *von Ahlfen Sperrverband* as of the evening of January 13th: *M.G. Btl. 442, Radfahrer-Sicherungs-Bataillon 232, Sicherungs-Bataillon 955, Sicherungsbataillon 956,* le.F.H. *Abteilung (mot.),* Cossack battalion made up of 4 squadrons, mixed radio and telephone Company, and a medical company. <u>Combat</u> strength: about 3,000 men, formerly 4,800 men [AN: before the departure of the above mentioned units].

January 14th
4:30 a.m.: Beginning of sustained fire on our neighbors to the left (*214.Infanterie-Division*), Pulawy Bridgehead. In addition, at about 1:00 a.m. strong assault troops conducted attacks against our right sector on our front to tie up our troops (*Sicherungs-Bataillon 956*). The enemy, which had penetrated until it was just to the east of Tarlow, was repelled or pushed out by 2:00 p.m. in a counterattack across the Weichsel, which had frozen solid.

   5:30 p.m.: The left flank (*M.G. Btl. 442*) was pulled back from Solec to 4 km north of Lipsk because of an attack on the left neighbor. There, there was a tenuous link with the *214. Infanterie-Division.*

January 15th
9:30 a.m.: Order from the *XXXXII.Armee-Korps*: "Immediately abandon the Weichsel Front. Defend a rear position on both sides of Sienno and defend Ilza. The troops at Ilza, a *Feldersatz-Abteilung* and a *Mörser-Abteilung* [heavy mortar battalion], are subordinated to you."

   Starting at 1:00 p.m.: Evacuation of the Weichsel position and retreat to the position ordered. The enemy followed carefully with reconnaissance troops. With the exception of the left flank, where the enemy was taking Lipsk from the north, movements on the afternoon of January 16th and the night from January 16th-17th were successful, delayed merely by artillery attacks on Tarlow.

January 16th (morning)
New *Korps* order: "Enemy penetration near the *XXXXVIII.Panzer-Korps* and the right flank of the *XXXXII.Armee-Korps* and the *LVI.Panzer-Korps* (left neighbor is *9.Armee*) completely successful. The *Sperrverband* is to speed up its retreat west while defending the road junction at Ilza until reaching the Hubertus position (a general line west of Skarzysko and Szydlowiec). Defend it. While moving there, defend the left flank of the *Korps.*"

   This order was the last long-distance communication with the Commanding General and Corps Commander.

   A radio order to that effect was acknowledged by all radio stations for all friendly troops. Radio stations for the *955.Sicherungs-Bataillon* and *956.Sicherungs-Bataillon* used the acknowledgment to report the positions of their support units (there at the order of their commanders). Because the position of our units was not known, it is doubtful whether the order reached the battalion commanders in a timely fashion. The command section did not have any other communications.

   It is thus to be assumed that the *955.Sicherungs-Bataillon* and *956.Sicherungs-Bataillon* (not

---

troops in the city and was removed as commander on March 8th, 1945. He was replaced by *General der Infanterie* Hermann Niehoff.

including the support troops) were no longer getting this order and that those in the area of Sienno had been pushed out and taken prisoner.

11:00 a.m. thru 2:00 p.m.: There was a successful defense of Ilza in close combat against enemy forces attacking in superior strength from Ilza (infantry regiments reinforced with tanks) with the personal deployment of the command section with a SPW and parts of a *Feldersatz-Bataillon* until friendly units (including portions of the *214.Infanterie-Division*) moved through south of Ilza and the *Mörser-Abteilung* and our *l. F.H. Abteilung* changed places. Enemy movement against the left *Korps* flank was prevented. The movement out toward the west was successful.

8:00 p.m.: Last *Korps* order (radio): "1. Enemy tanks have pushed through from Szydlowiec to Kamienna. 2. Do not defend the Hubertus position. 3. Immediately break through Kamienna south to Ruski Brod, going to the general headquarters." (Ruski Brod is in the area west of Przysucha).

This order cannot be implemented. Reason: all the paths and roads from the east of Kamienna are blocked by big parts of the *XXXXII.Armee-Korps* and Kamienna and the surrounding roads are under continual bombing attacks. So the decision was made: move at night through the expansive forests between Kamienna and Szydlowiec. Troops: In addition to our own, units of the *214.Infanterie-Division*, Army Artillery and Anti-Aircraft.

January 16th-17th (evening)
The night movement through the woods was successful. There was enemy activity southwest of Szydlowiec. The enemy limited itself to scattered artillery fire and did not make any thrusts into the forests. On two north-south roads that were crossed on the way west, there were traces of enemy tanks and our shot-up support units from the *XXXXII.Armee-Korps* and the *214. Infanterie-Division*.

Sperrverband von Ahlfen was indeed lucky. Spared the opening Soviet attack, its successful withdrawal west through the woods prevented early destruction by the main Soviet attack force that was directed along the main road arteries.

The German Eastern Front was shattered by the Soviet offensive. As Colonel Alexander F. Smirnov, Chief of Staff of the 100th Tank Brigade, 31st Tank Corps of Koniev's 1st Ukrainian Front noted after the war ". . . we considered that [the Germans] had made a gross operational error. They placed their tank reserves within the tactical defense, in the second zone and even closer . . . and during the artillery preparation and the aviation strike, they suffered losses and their [command and] control went to pieces as a result."[14] *Oberstleutnant* H. von Humbolt who served on Guderian's operation staff made the same observation ". . . on the explicit order of Hitler, [the operational reserves] had been moved so close to the frontline that they were hit by the Russians preparatory artillery fire, and they were weakened even before joining battle."[15] New operational reserves to counter the Soviet advance were immediately ordered to the area by the *OKH* operations staff.

---

14   Glantz, *Red Army Officers Speak!*, p. 31.
15   Ibid., p. 88.

8

Panzer-Korps 'Großdeutschland' Deploys South, January 16th–19th

(Reference Maps 14, 15, 16, 17, 18, 19, 20, 21, 22, 23, 24 and 25)

After the first 24 hours of the attack the reports sent back to *OKH* made Guderian realize that the Soviets had in fact launched their expected winter offensive. As the Soviet attack developed against the *LVI.Panzer-Korps* of the *9.Armee* and the *XXIV.Panzer-Korps* of the *4.Panzer-Armee*, Guderian recognized the threat to the inter-army boundary. On January 13th *Heeresgruppe Mitte* released *Panzer-Korps 'Großdeutschland'* to *OKH* for operation use in order *Okdo.H.Gr.Mitte, Ia Nr. T151/45 g.Kdos.*[1] At the time *Panzergrenadier-Division 'Großdeutschland'* was in a staging area at Krasnosiele while *Panzergrenadier-Division 'Brandenburg'* was ordered to move at midnight the evening of January 13th/14th to assemble at Chorzele in preparation for rail movement.

Guderian was desperate to prevent his armies from being split by the Soviet offensive. He drew up recommendations to Hitler in a January 15th *OKH/Genstab/Op.Abt (Ia) No. 450 011/45 g.Kdos.Chefs* report. Among them was the immediate release of *Panzer-Korps 'GD'* from East Prussia to halt the Soviet attack out of the Baranov Bridgehead and reestablish a solid frontline. He stated Specifically:

Holding the Pilica front and maintaining the solidarity between the *4.Panzer-Armee* and the *9.Armee* is particularly important because that is the only way that it will be possible to maintain the conditions under which we can perform countermeasures against the enemy forces operating in the big bend of the Weichsel.

I have therefore decided to assign the *Panzerkorps 'Großdeutschland'* (*Panzergrenadier-Division 'Brandenburg'* and the *Fallschirm-Panzer-Division 1 'Hermann Göring'*), which is currently en route, to clean up the enemy penetration on the northern bank of the Pilica and then to attack to the south across the Pilica. No clear overview is available today as to the extent that this intention can be realized, given the assembly of the corps in the area east of Tomascew that won't end until 19 January and the possibility that the situation could quickly develop unfavorably in the *9.Armee* sector. I ask you, my *Führer*, to authorize my decision concerning the use of the *Panzer-Korps 'Großdeutschland'*.

The overall situation in the middle of the eastern front will not be decisively improved through the use of the *Panzer-Korps 'Großdeutschland'* that has been reported or by the infantry divisions coming in to defend the Upper Silesian industrial region. The major Russian offensive from the great bend in the Weichsel that requires a solution, can only be brought to a standstill if additional strong armored and infantry units are immediately brought to *Heeresgruppe A*.[2]

The decision to deploy *Panzer-Korps 'GD'* into the breach was disastrous. Its deployment could not make a difference given both the pace of Soviet operations and the *Korps'* limited combat power.

---

1   NARA T78/645/0368.
2   NARA T78/305/6256016-18.

8

As an experienced strategist and former *Panzer-Group* commander, Guderian should have realized this. Perhaps this is why after the war he placed the blame for this particular debacle on the shoulders of Adolf Hitler, stating in his apologetic memoir *Panzer Leader* that "On January 15th Hitler interfered for the first time in the defensive battle, by issuing an order, despite my protests, for the transfer of the *Panzer-Korps 'GD'* from East Prussia to Kielce where it was to block the break-through . . ."[3] A review of the records of *OKH* reveal that Hitler played no part in the decision to deploy the *Panzer-Korps*. The burden of this decision was Guderian's alone.

The following day Guderian sent a Top Secret "flash" message *OKH/Genstab/Op Abt (Ia) no. 450 013/45 g.Kdos.Chefs* to the officers of *Heeresgruppe Mitte* and *Heeresgruppe A* that provided *OKH* guidance on the current Soviet winter offensive. It appears that Guderian received permission from Hitler to authorize his earlier recommendation to release *Panzer-Korps 'GD'*:

> 1) The major Russian offensive from the large bend in the Weichsel is to be brought permanently to a halt no farther than in the general line:
>> Weichsel east of Krakau-b-1 position to west of Radomsko-along the Pilica to Rzeczyza-Mszczonow-*Festung* Warsaw inclusive-Weichsel to Modlin.
>
> This line is to be defended absolutely, and any enemy that has already broken through it or will break through in the next few days is to be attacked and pushed back immediately. The order to defend the entire line is a minimum requirement. *Heeresgruppe A* must make efforts to bring the enemy assault to a halt at Line a-2 in order to secure an appropriate forward area in the east for the Upper Silesian industrial region.
>
> 2) Within the framework of the guidelines issued in 1 above, *Heeresgruppe A* has a free hand. The main point is to maintain the connections among the northern parts of the *17.Armee*, the *4.Panzer-Armee*, and the *9.Armee* and to bring the existing units into the new defensive front still able to fight. *OKH* reserves for itself only the decision about the deployment of von Saucken's *Panzer-Korps [Großdeutschland]*, which is currently in transit. The *Korps* is expected to leave the Tomaschow/Litzmannstadt area and be deployed directly north of the Pilica between the flank and the rear of the enemy forces operating between the Pilica and the Weichsel. Preparations are to be made accordingly.
>
> 3) ...

Panzergrenadier-Division 'BR' continued to assemble at Chorzele as per *Okdo.H.Gr.Mitte, Ia Nr. 168/45 g.Kdos.*[4] Later that day *OKH* issued order *OKH/GenStd H/Op.Abt. Ia, Nr. 553/45 g.Kdos.* that stated *Panzer-Korps 'GD'* including *Panzergrenadier-Division 'BR'* and *Fallschirm-Panzer-Division 1 'HG'* along with the required supply troops to embark by train to *Heeresgruppe A* for immediate deployment to Litzmannstadt, and from there occupy positions along the line Konskie-Tschenstochau if possible.[5] At some point during the 15th a decision was made to deploy the *Panzer-Korps* without *Panzergrenadier-Division 'GD'* and instead replace it with another new, unproven division *Fallschirm-Panzer-Division 1 'HG'*. No documents have been uncovered to explain what factors contributed to Guderian's decision. Not only was he sending a new *Korps* command into a disastrous operational situation that it could not reverse, but he sent two new divisions that had never trained together. Both divisions also operated under two separate command structures, as one was *Heer* and the other

---

3   Heinz Guderian, *Panzer Leader* (Da Capo Press: Cambridge, 2002), p. 392. This is one of many fabrications Guderian penned to whitewash his role in various disastrous strategic and operational decisions during World War II.

4   NARA T78/645/0355.

5   NARA T78/645/0352.

Luftwaffe. At least *Panzergrenadier-Division 'GD'* was a combat proven division that shared both common training and personnel with *'Brandenburg'*. Instead, *Panzergrenadier-Division 'GD'* was separated from the *Korps* and ordered to remain in East Prussia and attack and restore the situation in the area of the *129.Infanterie-Division*. Never again did the two divisions operate together during the rest of the war.

The situation in the area of *Heeresgruppe A* was shaping into a complete disaster. The immediate failures were blamed on its commander, *Generaloberst* Josef Harpe and his subordinate commanders. Harpe was replaced by *Generaloberst* Ferdinand Schörner on January 16th. *General der Panzertruppen* Smilo Freiherr von Lüttwitz was replaced as commander of the *9.Armee* by *General der Infanterie* Theodor Busse on January 19th. While *General der Panzertruppen* Fritz-Hubert Gräser's command of the *4.Panzer-Armee* remained intact, his Chief of Staff *Oberst i.G.* Christian Müller was replaced by *Generalmajor* Wilhelm Knüppel on January 25th. A complete reshuffling of commands occurred along the Eastern Front near simultaneously with the replacement of key commanders. On January 24th the new *Heeresgruppe Weichsel* was established and combined forces of both the existing *Heeresgruppe A* and *Heeresgruppe Mitte*. On January 25th *Heeresgruppe Nord* was renamed to *Heeresgruppe Kurland*, the existing *Heeresgruppe Mitte* in East Prussia became *Heeresgruppe Nord*, and *Heeresgruppe A* ceased to exist and became *Heeresgruppe Mitte*. Within this turmoil of changing senior leadership and shifting command responsibilities, *Panzer-Korps 'GD'* deployed.

Panzer-Korps 'GD' was not prepared for deployment. Its staff was still new. Its subordinate units were still forming and organizing. For example, the sub-units of the division that were formally detached in the December 13th *Korps* reorganization that consisted of *Begleit-Kompanie 500*, *II.Btl./Korps-Panzer-Füsilier-Regiment 'GD'*, *II./Panzer-Artillerie-Regiment 500* and *II.Btl./FER 500* were still tactically subordinated to the division, but had not completed their reorganizing and were considered "not combat ready." A month was not enough time to forge the *Panzer-Korps* into a cohesive fighting force. The men of *'Brandenburg'* had little time to train beyond the company and battalion level as previously noted, their reorganization was far from complete. Unlike its sister division, *Panzergrenadier-Division 'GD'*, *'Brandenburg'* had not fought together as a single unit in the past and had no experience in operating as a conventional force.

The first trains with *'Brandenburg'* rolled out of Angerburg, East Prussia on January 15th taking the route Allenstein-Gnesen-Wreschen-Garotschin, arriving in the area of Kutno-Litzmannstadt-Petrikau during the evening of January 16th/17th. Some took a route through Thorn. Many were designated "high speed" trains and given priority over other locomotives. Not all of *Panzergrenadier-Division 'BR'* units were located in East Prussia. The *Sturmgeschütz-Brigade 'Großdeutschland'* was still replenishing in Lübben. They immediately received their full complement of 18x *Sturmgeschütze*, loaded them onto trains with ammunition and fuel, then rolled east. The following account by *Fahnenjunker-Unteroffizier* Held-Kleingründlach, *Sturmgeschütz* commander in *Sturmgeschütz-Brigade 'GD'* attached to *'Brandenburg'*, offers a view into the chaotic situation:

> We were barely done mounting the machine guns [to the newly received vehicles] when *Leutnant* Keller informed us that we had to go to Czenstochau immediately by rapid transport. Loading went very quickly, so quickly that we then had to wait for hours for the locomotive.
>
> We were finally ready. From Lübben, we went to Cottbus. There we experienced an aerial attack on the railway station by fighter bombers. The individual enemy aircraft circled around and shots from cannons and MGs rained down. We sat in our fighting vehicles and watched the play. The machinegun with the periscope did a marvelous job and our tracer rounds got right to their target. Unfortunately we didn't shoot anything down, but the guys were warned and they got out of there as quickly as they could.
>
> After a while, our transport train started moving and we went to Litzmannstadt via Sorau,

Glogau and Lissa (Leszno).

The staff of *Panzer-Korps 'GD'* and the men *of Panzergrenadier-Division 'BR'* were ordered to confront a massive Soviet offensive with the men of *Fallschirm-Panzer-Division 1 'HG'* who they never trained with before and were completely unfamiliar with the *Luftwaffe* organization. Back in East Prussia, *Panzergrenadier-Division 'GD'* remained behind with *Fallschirm-Panzergrenadier-Division 2 'Hermann Göring'* under the command of the newly formed *Fallschirm-Panzer-Korps 'Hermann Göring'* that was headquartered in Lancellenstädt.

Fallschirm-Panzer-Division 1 'Hermann Göring'

Fallschirm-Panzer-Division 1 'Hermann Göring' formed with its sister division *Fallschirm-Panzergrenadier-Division 2 'Hermann Göring'* under the command of *Fallschirm-Panzer-Korps 'Hermann Göring'*. The *Fallschirm-Panzer-Korps 'Hermann Göring'* was ordered formed on September 24th, 1944 under order *OdL 11b12.16 Nr. 13266/44 g.Kdos.*, only a few days after *Panzer-Korps 'Großdeutschland'*. The commander of the new *Luftwaffe Korps* was *Generalleutnant* Wilhelm Schmalz who was the 882 recipient of the Knight's Cross of the Iron Cross with Oak Leaves. Schmalz was the former commander of the veteran division *Fallschirm-Panzer-Division 'Hermann Göring'* that was established in October 1942 and became the nucleus of the two new *Luftwaffe Panzer-Divisions*.

Fallschirm-Panzer-Division 1 'Hermann Göring' was originally commanded by veteran Knight's Cross winner *Generalmajor* Hanns-Horst von Necker who had commanded the *9.Panzer-Division* for nine months in 1942 before becoming the *Ia* of the *16.Armee*. By February 9th, command changed to *Generalmajor* Max Lemke whose only prior experience commanding a division was during his temporary command of the *7.Panzer-Division* from January 5th-22nd of 1945. The division consisted of the following units: *Divisionsstab, Fallschirm-Panzer-Regiment 'HG' (2 Abteilung), Fallschirm-Panzergrenadier-Regiment 1 'HG' (2 battalions), Fallschirm-Panzergrenadier-Regiment 2 'HG' (2 battalions), Fallschirm-Panzer-Füsilier-Bataillon 1 'HG', Fallschirm-Panzer-Aufklärungs-Abteilung 1 'HG', Fallschirm-Panzer-Pionier-Bataillon 1 'HG', Fallschirm-Panzer-Artillerie-Regiment 1 'HG' (3 battalions), Fallschirm-Panzer-Nachrichten-Abteilung 1 'HG', Feldersatz-Bataillon 1 'HG', Sanitäts-Abteilung 1 'HG',* and *Feldpostamt 1 'HG'*. The main combat power of the division was its Panzer Regiment that was organized into two battalions. The *I.Bataillon* consisted of four companies totaling 40x Pz.Kpw. V Panthers, while the *II.Bataillon*, also of four companies consisted of 35x Pz.Kpw. IVs.

Like *Panzergrenadier-Division 'BR'* its reorganization during the fall of 1944 was hampered by a lack of personnel, equipment, training, and motorized vehicles. But unlike *'Brandenburg'*, which would not receive most of its personnel until December, *Fallschirm-Panzer-Division 1 'Hermann Göring'* was combat capable in October and participated in a series of battles along the East Prussian border against the Soviets. During October 19th-21st it participated along with the *5.Panzer-Division* in the counterattacks at Gumbinnen, then Großwaltersdorf. The division maintained the defense in the area of Gumbinnen through November, before moving slightly west to Insterburg. The *Fallschirm-Panzer-Korps 'HG'* remained headquartered around Gut Austinshof.

After its brief combat operations in October the division continued its reorganization as part of the *Korps*. However, elements of the division went back into combat even in the days before it deployed south. For example, the *Aufklärung-Abteilung* was used in a counterattack east of Gumbinnen in support of the *5.Panzer-Division, 549.Volksgrenadier-Division* and *61.Infanterie-Division* when elements of the Soviet 28th Army broke through the German defensive line at Eydtkuhnen. The reorganization was still ongoing by mid-January. Due to a lack of motorized vehicles, horse drawn carts were required to take the place of missing motor vehicles. It had no organic *Flak-Abteilung* or supply troops. *I.Btl./Flak-Regiment 'HG'* with six batteries were transferred from *Korps* troops along with some supply units. Its strength remained in its Panzer-Regiments that contained 32x Panzer IVs

(2 in short term repair), 39x Panzer V Panthers (6 in short term repair), and 13x Sturmgeschütze (4 in short term repair).[6] The division was detached from *Panzer-Korps 'Hermann Göring'* on January 13th. At midnight on January 15th it boarded rail cars in East Prussia, and then headed south for Litzmannstadt where it fell under command of *Panzer-Korps 'Großdeutschland'* based on order *OKH/ GenStdH H/OPAbt (Ia) Nr. 553/45 g.Kdos.v.15.1.45.*

Fallschirm-Panzer-Division 1 'Hermann Göring' deployed by rail toward Tomaschow, southwest of Litzmannstadt, northeast of Petrikau. As the division was still unloading they were attacked by advancing Soviet forces and immediately thrown onto the defensive.[7] The division immediately began to withdraw west, south of Litzmannstadt. They had no direct communications with the HQ of *Panzer-Korps 'GD'*. The division's deployment was disastrous and was forced to retreat almost immediately. Elements of the division, acting independently, had to conduct repeated counterattacks to keep the Soviets off balance as the division tried to reach *Panzer-Korps 'GD'* and reform. The division withdrew to Pabianitz on January 18th. The next day it was withdrawing west, south of Lask. Then it headed north after linking up with *Panzer-Korps 'GD'*. Finally on January 21st the division was able to reassemble and organize after its deployment.

Deployment of *Panzergrenadier-Division 'Brandenburg'* south of Litzmannstadt

The rail cars moving southwest were packed not only with soldiers, but refugees fleeing ahead of the Soviet advance. The mood on board the trains could not have been anything other than foreboding for the coming drama unfolding between the Weichsel and Oder Rivers. The debarkation stations for the two regiments were located across a 60 kilometer arc running from Kutno in the north to Petrikau in the south, both suburbs of Litzmannstadt.

Among the first units to arrive was *8.Kompanie* of the *II.Bat./Jäg.Rgt 2 'BR'* under command of *Oberleutnant* Krieger. The company debarked north of Litzmannstadt in the evening of the 15th. As it advanced toward its planned deployment south of the city it was caught by Soviet reconnaissance units and scattered almost immediately. On the night of January 16th/17th the rest of *II.Bat./Jäg. Rgt. 2 'BR'* (except the *7.Kompanie*) under the command of *Oberleutnant* Afheldt arrived and quickly occupied defensive positions in the dark as the ominous sounds of battle could be heard to the south. The *I.Btl./Jäg.Rgt. 2 'BR'* under the command of *Hauptmann* Steidl arrived shortly after. Afheldt's men quickly moved into quarters in the village of Sulejów on the Pilica River, southeast of Petrikau. His men were obviously tired from their rail movement, and unsure of the tactical situation as they deployed into unfamiliar territory. That night they failed to post security or any screening elements outside the village. This poor tactical decision cost the *II.Btl./Jäg.Rgt. 2 'BR'* dearly as bearing down on Litzmannstadt were advance elements of the 7th Guards Cavalry Corps and 10th Guards Tank Corps.

Advancing from the Baranov Bridgehead, the Soviets had split the *9.Armee* and *4.Panzer-Armee*. Their advance was rapid so far, meeting little German resistance. As Soviet units advanced into the village of Sulejów in the pre-dawn hours of the 17th they likely did not expect to find German units occupying the homes there. Their surprise was perhaps as great as that as Afheldt's soldiers who were caught sleeping. Despite the mutual surprise, the Soviets were ready for a fight, and the *Panzergrenadiers* of the *II./Jäg.Rgt. 2 'BR'* were not. Afheldt's entire battalion was routed in the surprise attack. Unable to mount a defense, the men scattered on foot with the equipment they could carry as heavy weapons and vehicles were abandoned in their flight. Each company took cover in the surrounding woods until the daylight hours. Cut off from any communications to their regiment, and unable to effectively reorganize, Afheldt gave the order to withdraw northwest toward Lask.

The next elements of *'Brandenburg'* that arrived were the *7.Kompanie* of *II.Btl./Jäg.Rgt.2 'BR'*

6   RG 242 German Armed Forces Operations and Situation Maps, 1939-1945. H.Gr. Mitte. Box 351. *HGr. Mitte GenStdH Op.Abt. IIIb Prüf Nr. 57235 Stand: 13.1.45 Abends.*
7   Account by Wolfgang Hartlet, Platoon Commander in *I.Btl./Pz.Rgt. 'HG1'.* Glantz, 1986 p. 631.

followed by *Pz.Stu.Pi.Btl.* The *7.Kompanie* received orders on January 17th to move 60 kilometers west to Lask, where it would provide security for the forming headquarters of *H.Gr. Mitte* under the command of Ferdinand Schörner, who would soon be ordered by Hitler to take command of the defeated armies of *Heeresgruppe A*. *Panzer-Sturm-Pionier-Bataillon 'BR'* left East Prussia on three trains on January 15th. The HQ and *1.Pionier-Kompanie* were on one train, followed by the *2.Pionier.- Kompanie* and Supply Company on the second, and finally the *3.Pionier-Kompanie (gep)* on a third train. They left the bridging personnel in Drenfurth, presumably to await another train, though their vehicles were loaded onto the third train. During the night the trains made a stop. The HQ and *1.Pionier-Kompanie* unloaded, then realized that their destination had not been reached. The train was reloaded and continued on its southern route with several hours of valuable time wasted due to the confusion. As the first two trains passed through Kutno and continued on toward Litzmannstadt, the third train halted. The *3.Pionier-Kompanie (gep)* unloaded and became subordinated to *Oberst* von Brückner's *Jägerregiment 1 'BR'* that had arrived on the 16th (see below). It was now January 17th.

The two remaining trains of *Panzer-Sturm-Pionier-Bataillon 'BR'* continued south. The first train arrived in Petrikau where the HQ and *1.Pionier-Kompanie* unloaded. Along the way they had picked up *Oberstleutnant i.G.* Erasmus who recognized the division, when it made its earlier stop farther north, and boarded. He now rejoined the division from his assignment in Berlin. The second train with *2.Pionier-Kompanie* and the Supply Company unloaded slightly north of Petrikau at Baby. Soviet aircraft strafed the disembarkation point as they were unloading during the daylight hours and destroyed several vehicles.

Meanwhile the *9.Armee* struggled to determine the extent of the Soviet assault across its southern front. It clearly did not realize that the Soviets had penetrated through the *4.Panzer-Armee's* northern flank and issued orders to the arriving *Panzergrenadier-Division 'BR'* to assemble in the forest east of Petrikau and south of Tomaschow. *Oberstleutnant i.G.* Erasmus, the division *Ia*, received this order by radio. He knew little of the tactical situation. Oesterwitz's *I.Btl./Jäg.Rgt. 2 'BR'* under Steidl quickly took command of the immediate area of Petrikau around midday on the 17th. It was noted that communication with Afheldt's battalion was lost and their whereabouts unknown. Oesterwitz deployed the arriving *Panzer-Sturm-Pionier-Bataillon 'BR' (-)* to the southeast along with the two batteries of *Pz.Art.Rgt. 'BR'* that also just arrived. Stragglers of Afheldt's defeated battalion likely stumbled into the forward German observation posts along the road leading to Sulejów, as well as those along the Pilica River. Their reports informed Oesterwitz of the presence of Soviet tank formations. Alerted, Oesterwitz had little choice but to order a withdrawal of his weak screening line to the northwest of Petrikau, then finally toward Litzmannstadt during the early evening as Soviet tanks finally appeared on the road to the east. His informed reaction prevented an unorganized rout to Litzmannstadt, which soon became a rallying point for arriving elements of *'Brandenburg'*. No communication initially existed between any parts of the division, or with the division headquarters. Only Erasmus finally established communications with the commander via wireless radio.

Among the withdrawing elements of *'Brandenburg'*, *Hauptmann* Metzger's *Sturmgeschütz-Brigade 'GD'* arrived by train midday in Litzmannstadt. They completed their detraining by 2:00 p.m. Metzger's eighteen *Sturmgeschütze* were given verbal orders to advance south to the suburb of Pabianice (Pabianitz), which it did while under harassing fire from Soviet aircraft. The column arrived without damage. New orders were quickly issued to join with the *2.Kompanie* of *I.Btl./Jäg.Rgt. 2 'BR'* and advance south to secure the village of Pawlikowice where it setup defense along the division's southern flank. The small group occupied the village and held it through January 18th without any enemy contact. Held-Kleingründlach's account provides detail on the initial deployment of the unit:

> [Litzmannstadt] was bombed by Russian pilots the previous day and the railway station showed major damage. We had a long stay in Pabianitz. There were rumors running around that the

Russians were already in Tomaschow. The railway workers therefore wanted to unload there, but our headquarters was against it. We were supposed to get as far from the enemy as possible and not unload until then. In the meantime, it was night and we waited until our locomotive had filled up with water. But it never came back. Now that was a dodgy situation. According to the latest news, the Russians had already gotten to within 20 kilometers of us. That caused us to set up a temporary unloading ramp made out of bales of straw so that we could move the *Sturmgeschütze* down them. After three *Geschütz* were unloaded that way, a locomotive came suddenly anyway and pushed the transport train into the railway station at Litzmannstadt. In the early morning, we started unloading on a normal loading ramp. I got a "sledge" [*Sturmgeschütz*] different than the one I had set up. The *Geschütz* I took over from *Unteroffizier* Bliem did not have ammunition loaded or armored skirts installed. It took a lot of effort for us to attach the skirts as quickly as possible. Finally it was done and we reported that we were ready to move. Coincidentally I found an ammunition train on the adjoining track that had tank ammunition, among other things. I determined to my great joy that it fit our *Geschütz* and with another man, whom we had picked up from the *19.Panzer-Division* shortly before, took it box by box to the *Geschütz* until we had about 100 rounds for the *Geschütz*. This man was basically a panzergrenadier and did not have the slightest idea about armored vehicles. I also was lacking a fire direction NCO, so I was both the fighting vehicle commander and fire direction NCO all in one.

So off we went through the Litzmannstadt morning where the inhabitants were scurrying along the streets, stirred up like an anthill. The sights we saw were miserable. I particularly noticed that the *Volkssturm* was marching and occupying the prepared defensive positions outside the city. We stopped in the dairy at Pabianitz. This dairy had wonderful whole milk and we were able to take it by the can. Next to it was a slaughterhouse, and every three men were able to get a piece of meat. Unfortunately, we were missing the kitchen equipment we were used to. What a marvelous set of stuff we had to give up with the old *Geschütz* to the unit that relieved us in Memel! So we made ourselves spit-roasted meat in a rather primitive fashion. The crews for the individual *Geschütz* were divided up again. Our panzergrenadier left us and I got *Gefreiter* Becker on my *Geschütz*. He was already quite familiar to me from Guben. As the fire direction NCO, I got *Stabsgefreiter* Wiechers from the *Stabsbatterie*.

At 2:30 p.m., we were ordered to get ready to move and 18 *Sturmgeschütze* were reported as clear. Then the commander showed up and watched the armored vehicles that were now to be thrown into the defensive slaughter move out. Along the road out of the city, we ran into the enemy. On the way, we were frequently surprised by Russian aerial attacks. I had to find out that the airspace was ruled by Ivan to an extent I had never known before. During an attack of this sort, we were fired on by a vehicle in an oncoming column. It tore off an armored skirt and sent it flying over the head of the loader. It could have gone in his eye and been what is known as a smiling death! As night broke, we went into position at the edge of a forest. However, shortly after that we were ordered to change position and we went on until we met some units of the *Division 'Brandenburg'*. We were supposed to be deployed with this division. All 18 *Sturmgeschütze* were on security duty until the next morning [January 18th]. Then we got the deployment order. A *Kompanie* of *Jäger* were sitting split up among the individual *Geschütz* and off we went. We rolled into the area of Pawlikowice. Here we took up a security position and the village was occupied according to plan. With two groups from the *Jäger-Kompanie*, we moved into a little house and make ourselves comfortable there. In the evening, Russian cavalry was reported and it was already in the next village. For this reason, the guard forces were reinforced and one man in each crew had to remain in the *Geschütz*.

The Soviet cavalry unit that occupied the nearby village was likely from the 7th Guards

Cavalry Corps.

During January 18th the *Pz.Jäg.Abt. 'BR'* unloaded at Görnau, to the north of Lodz. *Leutnant* Kass, a company commander in the unit, was present and recorded those moments in his diary: "We were supposed to be unloaded in Görnau (a suburb of Litzmannstadt) in order to be deployed in the vicinity of Petrikau, where there were already parts of our artillery and a *Jäger-Bataillon*. While we were unloading, four Russian tanks moved in. After we had killed two of them with *Panzerfausts*, it was calm." Soviet tanks of the Soviet 1st Guards Tank Army's 8th Guards Mechanized Corps had simultaneously reached the train station and surprised the *Panzerjägers*, many of whom were likely young recruits seeing action for the first time. Two of the *Panzerjägers*' *Panzerfausts* found their mark knocking out an equal number of Soviet T-34s (likely model 85s) and forcing the others to withdraw. *Pz.Jäg.Abt. 'BR'* was able to complete unloading in the ensuing calm, assemble, and then head south toward Petrikau to locate other elements of the division. It was minus the *3.Kompanie* that arrived earlier and detrained at Kutno to the north (see below). The *3.Kompanie* was surprised by elements the advancing 1st Guards Tank Army and scattered. Once the *Pz.Jäg.Abt. 'BR'* arrived in Pabianice they were assigned to a security mission to the south along the edge of Waldau. The news soon reached them that the Soviets were already advancing on Petrikau. According to *Leutnant* Kass "We killed another three tanks there" along the Waldau-Petrikau road.

The *Division Adjutant, Oberleutnant iG* Bröker, recounts those first few days of the division's deployment south and the "fog of war" present among the deployment of *Jägerregiment 2 'BR'*. He went to Petrikau with a transport of *II.Btl./Jäg.Rgt. 2 'BR'*, the regiment's HQ and the *1.Batterie* and *2.Batterie* of the division's *Pz.Art.Rgt. 'BR'*.

Mid-January 1945: The penetration of the Russians occurred at the bridgehead near Baranov, with a focal direction toward the Oder and central Silesia, thereby confounding the East Prussia deployment of the *Panzer-Korps 'GD'* as a unit because the Russian units moving north might cut off East Prussia.

Around January 17th, quickly assembled *Kampfgruppen 'BR'* was taken toward Poland by rail and some of them ran right into the Russian forward tank units. The following order of the *9.Armee* command was already there:

"*Panzergrenadier-Division 'Brandenburg'* will assemble in Walfe right to the east of Petrikau."

This was a completely counterproductive order because of the situation—units retreating, Russian tanks south and north of Petrikau, some of them even visible at the edge of the city.

Oberstleutnant Oesterwitz, the commander of *Jägerregiment 2 'BR'*, however, had some of the unloaded troops taken to the eastern edge of Petrikau as ordered, took over the defense of Petrikau from the retreating local commander, and put up security on all edges of the city on an emergency basis.

As evening approached, the situation became unpleasant because of the appearance of the first Russian tanks and units in the western part of the city. The commander of *Jägerregiment 2 'BR'* then had the security on the northwestern edge of Petrikau, with the big highway to Litzmannstadt in his rear. The situation was anything but transparent!

By coincidence, we managed to talk long distance to the division headquarters, which had in the meantime arrived, and the commander of *Jägerregiment 2 'BR'* got in contact. A big "hello" on both sides that there was a connection to the division again. *Jägerregiment 2 'BR'* received the order to move toward Litzmannstadt the next day and to take up security near Shieratz.

Also in Petrikau were elements *Panzer-Sturm-Pionier-Bataillon 'BR'* that had just arrived by rail. By the following day the HQ and *1.Pi.Kompanie* were forced to conduct a disorderly retreat back through Petrikau to the north. The commander, *Hauptmann* Müller-Rochholz, quickly assembled his companies, minus the *3.Pionier-Kompanie (gep)*, and set up a defensive perimeter at Moszczenica, south of Baby. A Soviet armored reconnaissance unit advanced west from Tomaschow on *Hauptmann* Müller-Rochholz's position, but was quickly forced back after his men put up some resistance. The first stragglers of *Gruppe Nehring* now emerged from the frozen swamps along the defensive perimeter of 'Brandenburg' like ghosts. Their appearance from out of the gloom undoubtedly unnerved some of the newer recruits as the haggard survivors told shell shocked stories of previously unknown Soviet firepower and massive tank attack. The Soviets, they informed the *Jäger* of 'Brandenburg', were right behind them.

Deployment of *Panzergrenadier-Division 'Brandenburg'* north of Litzmannstadt

So far the deployment of 'Brandenburg' to the south of Litzmannstadt was confused and un-coordinated. The deployment north of the city was arguably no better, and was about to turn disastrous. At around 1:00 p.m. the first trains carrying the lead elements of *Jägerregiment 1 'BR'* under the command of *Oberst* von Brückner reached Kutno to the north of Litzmannstadt on January 16th. Both the *6.Kompanie* and *7.Kompanie* had to turn over most of their vehicles, including drivers, to *Jägerregiment 2 'BR'* and *Pz.Art.Rgt. 'BR'* a few days before their departure from East Prussia. All the vehicles that were left were a single commander's vehicle and a field kitchen.

Due to reports regarding the proximity of Soviet forces, it was decided to detrain without moving further south. The refugees fleeing along the road from Warsaw brought news of the Soviet advance to the east, as well as tales of misery and destruction, which certainly put some of the new recruits at ill ease. *Oberst* von Brückner decided to set up the regimental headquarters on the spot. He deployed the *6.Kompanie* and *7.Kompanie* immediately to the east and south of Kutno, setting up a makeshift defense. Supporting forces at the disposal of von Brückner were a local *Transport-Sicherungs-Bataillon 318* and four *Sturmgeschütze* of the *2.Kompanie* of *Pz.Jäg.Abt. 'BR'*, and the *3.Pionier-Kompanie* of *Pz.Pi.Btl. 'BR'*.

The *6.Kompanie* deployed along the road facing east toward Warsaw, while the *7.Kompanie* faced south toward Litzmannstadt. Each company contained about 140 men, 12x MG42s, and some *Gewehr 43* semi-automatic assault rifles. Most were armed with the KAR98K bolt action rifle. They were lightly armed and had no heavy support weapons. *Oberleutnant* Röseke, who commanded the *6.Kompanie* and was an experienced 'Brandenburger', deployed his platoons as follows: 1st Platoon under *Leutnant* Krosch 5 kilometers east of Kutno to Stara Wies, approximately 300 meters east of the rail-road crossing, A *Panzerjäger* squad was attached for support; 2nd Platoon under *Feldwebel* Lämmerhirt near the Malina Estate, approximately 5 kilometers northeast of Kutno along both sides of Zychlin-Kutno road; 3rd Platoon under the command of *Oberjäger* Haacke was placed in tactical reserve at a farm at the Stara Wies rail road crossing, 5 kilometers east of Kutno. The *Kompanie* HQ was placed in the Railroad line hut at the Stara Wies railroad crossing. A platoon of *Transport-Sicherungs-Bataillon 318* under the command of *Leutnant* Holzinger deployed into open terrain between Stara Wies and the Malina Estate. The only movement to the east was a steady stream of refugees.

The *7.Kompanie* under *Leutnant* Bürk sent out a patrol down the road toward Litzmannstadt in the hope to establish contact with the other units of 'Brandenburg', but it never returned. At this point in the day the Soviets were already infiltrating between Kutno and Litzmannstadt so it was likely that the patrol was ambushed and scattered. *Oberleutnant* Röseke, commander of *6.Kompanie*, wrote of his experiences in an official report he gave his command on February 8th. Below are his initial experiences of deployment and combat around Kutno:

Tuesday, January 16th
The *Kompanie* was loaded onto the railway starting at 8:00 p.m. in Angerburg, East Prussia.
    Combat strength: 2 officers / 16 NCOs / 144 soldiers

Weapons and light ammunition supply: Full compliment.

There were 12x light MG 42s and 36x *Gewehr 43* on hand.

The majority of the combat vehicles and the drivers had been detached to *Jägerregiment 2* during the previous few days and to the artillery regiment of the division for an unspecified time. There were still the commander's vehicle, one B-Krad, two support trucks, and the field kitchen detached from the *Versorgungs-Kompanie* on hand.

Along with the *6.Kompanie*, the *7.Kompanie* commanded by *Oberleutnant* Geisenberger and the Regiment's *Stabskompanie* commanded by *Oberleutnant* Frömmel, were loaded on the same transport. The Regimental Commander, *Oberst* von Brückner, was also on the transport.

At 9:00 p.m., I reported to *Hauptmann* Hunhold, the Bataillon Commander, that the *Kompanie* had been loaded.

Wednesday, January 17th

Shortly after midnight, we moved out of Angerburg. Our goal was the Kalisch area in Poland. We went straight to the southwest. In the late afternoon, Thorn was passed.

Thursday, January 18th

At 1:00 a.m., the transport was at the Kutno railway station.

Alarm! Unload immediately! The heads of the *6.Kompanie* and *7.Kompanie* went to the garrison headquarters. The situation: the Russian offensive had begun in the Warsaw area, in the southeast, enemy tanks had already penetrated to Litzmannstadt and were soon expected in Kutno as well.

The city was to be defended with all available weapons. Those were our two *Jäger-Kompanien*, a few units of *Transport-Sicherung-bataillon 318*, and four *Sturmgeschütz* as our only heavy weapons.

The *6.Kompanie* was placed on the road to Warsaw, and the *7.Kompanie* on the road to Litzmannstadt.

The companies made themselves ready for combat immediately. Strong reconnaissance with combat forward posts was sent out. In a building in the vicinity of the railway station, I set up a supply strongpoint for the *Kompanie* under the command of *Hauptfeldwebel* Schacht. The field kitchen, most of the kit and a reserve of ammunition remained there. The *Kompanie* was ordered to use assault kit.

While it was still night, *Leutnant* Krosch and I reconnoitered planned positions on the eastern edge of Kutno. In the meantime, the *Kompanie* was given warm food and was able to rest for a few hours.

While it was getting light, the platoons were sent to their positions and the main battle line was set.

I deployed them as follows:

1st Platoon: eastern edge of Stara Wies, 5 km east of Kutno, both sides of the road from Warsaw to Kutno, 300 meters east of the railway crossing. The *Panzer-Jägers* was placed under the 1st Platoon. Sector commandant: *Leutnant* Krosch.

2nd Platoon: near the Malina estate 5 km northeast of Kutno on both sides of the road from Zychlin to Kutno. Sector commandant: *Feldwebel* Lämmerhirt.

3rd Platoon: as a deployment reserve (motorized with one truck) in the farmstead near the Stara Wies railway crossing 5 km east of Kutno. Commander: *Oberjäger* Haacke.

Kompanie command post in the railway superintendent house at the Stara Wies railway crossing 5 km east of Kutno.

At 7:00 a.m., *Oberst* von Brückner showed up at the position and was informed about the measures taken.

Four *Sturmgeschütz* were subordinated to the *Kompanie*. Of these, two were placed in the 2nd Platoon sector, and two took up long-term positions at the railway crossing.

One platoon of *Transport-Sicherung-Bataillon 318* under the command of *Leutnant* Holzinger was subordinated to the *Kompanie* and deployed to the open area between Stara Wies and the Malina estate.

One platoon of the division's *Pionier-Kompanie*, which had in the meantime arrived in Kutno as well, got the order to prepare the road bridge 200 meters east of the railway crossing for demolition and to mine the road to there.

During the mornings, motorized reconnaissance penetrated far to the east. *Leutnant* Krosch on the road to Warsaw went on the road to Zychlin himself. No enemy activity. The roads were clogged with columns of refugees, mostly ethnic German civilians, but with some dispersed soldiers and *Reichsarbeitsdienst* units among them.

During the entire day, the positions were aggressively built up and many stand-by positions were identified to fight tanks. In a windmill right outside the main battle line, an observation post was set up; it had about a 4 km field of vision to the east.

The sector commandants got clear battle orders.

In the afternoon, I visited the supply point. *Hauptfeldwebel* Schacht received extensive power to act on his own, because it was feared that once the battle began, contact would be cut off.

Then I reported to the regimental commander to get oriented about the situation. I found out that a platoon from the *7.Kompanie* went south on the road to Litzmannstadt for reconnaissance under the command of *Leutnant* Bürk had all been dispersed and some of them had been captured.

More motorized recon to the east and the northeast, which I started in the late afternoon, had not run into any more enemy activity. According to refugees, however, the Russians were advancing along the road from Warsaw.

Before darkness fell, I went out with the sector commandants to their positions once more. The *Sturmgeschütz* received expanded combat taskings.

The work of the engineer platoon was sped up. Electrical and directional fuses were prepared to blow up the road bridge.

Shortly after 8:00 p.m., a foot patrol (with a B-Krad), commanded by *Obergefreiter* Eckardt, stopped at a fork in the road 4 km east of Stara Wies and reported by using light signals that the enemy was approaching.

At about 11:00 [8:30] p.m., the first Russian tanks hit the positions of the 1st Platoon. They were initially brought to a halt with heavy defensive fire.[8]

No radio contact could be made with the regiment, but *Oberst* von Brückner showed up at the position at 8:45 p.m. The combat noise fell silent again.

At 9:10 p.m., there was another Russian attack. A Sherman tank was shot by *Oberjäger* Hahmann and *Obergefreiter* Tröger using the "tank horror"; [*Panzerfaust*] it burned up within a few minutes. Three additional tanks broke through and were standing right next to the road bridge. The bridge was then blown up. At the same time, one of the tanks hit a mine and turned over into the ditch at the side of the road with damage to its tracks. The crew got out, but was killed because they put up resistance. The third tank retreated.

At about 10:00 p.m., the Russians tried to overrun our positions for the third time. However, they did not move down from the road. *Gefreiter* Kofler handled the first tank with a *Panzerfaust*. Right next to my covered hole to protect me from tanks, which wasn't even very deep because the ground had frozen hard, a T-34 came to a stop. The distance was too short for the *Panzerfaust*,

8   The time of "2300" hours is listed in the original report but it does not make sense sequentially with the rest of the recorded action and is likely an error. I have inserted 8:30 p.m. as the likely time of the first Soviet attack.

but I was able to calmly put some hand grenades I had in the hole into the tracks and set them off. However, there wasn't an awful lot of effect. Nevertheless, the hatch was opened and I was able to use my pistol to shoot the emerging commander. In the same moment, one of my men on the other side of the road jumped in and threw a hand grenade into the open hatch. The detonation destroyed the crew, but the tank was now in flames, the gun and machine gun ammunition was detonating, and I couldn't leave my covered hole for about a quarter of an hour. In the meantime, an additional T-34 hit a mine and was handled by *Leutnant* Krosch using a *Panzerfaust*. The other tanks had again retreated. Two comrades were slightly wounded by shrapnel, but they stayed in the position.

Both the *6.Kompanie* and *7.Kompanie* started to withdraw from their positions the following day, first by choice, then based on the situation to the south. The *3.Pionier-Kompanie* of *Pz.Pi.Btl. 'BR'* was not immediately notified of the withdrawal and caught in a race against Soviet forces to reach the crossings at Warthbrücken.

I.(gep)Bataillon/Jäg.Rgt. 1 'BR' armored personnel carriers deployed south of Litzmannstadt. It is not clear in the historical record if they detrained north or south of the city. It is clear that they deployed south of Litzmannstadt and operated as an independent support battalion for *Jägerregiment 2 'BR'* and the main elements of the division withdrawing west.

General von Saucken arrived in Litzmannstadt on January 18th where he set up a temporary *Panzer-Korps 'GD'* HQ in a cloth mill on the outskirts of town. There was almost no organization around Litzmannstadt. His divisions were spread out over a 100 kilometer arc around the city. *'Brandenburg'* was to the north and south of Litzmannstadt, while *'Hermann Göring'* deployed farther southeast. Little to nothing was known of their locations. A detached section of the *19.Panzer-Division* was reportedly in the area, having withdrawn west on its own or been cut off after the Soviet offensive began. They fell under von Saucken's command but there is no record of how they were employed. There was little control over local units. One such unit, *Volkssturm-Bataillon 'Warthbrücken'* was subordinated to *'Brandenburg'*. Its O1 was *Oberleutnant* Martens from *'Brandenburg'* was assigned as commander. This unit went missing on January 19th along with others. The fate of von Saucken's defensive line was decided before he reached Litzmannstadt by the rapid advance of Soviet forces. His units needed to withdraw back to the Warthe River or face imminent destruction.

Gruppe Nehring **Retreats West**

Oberst Ahlfen's account continues with his goal of escaping Soviet encirclement and reaching what would become *Gruppe Nehring*. This pocket grew to number an untold number of soldiers, though estimates by veterans who were among the men surrounded report a total of more than 100,000. The SPWs of the *17.Panzer-Division* alone carried between 8-10 divisional commanders.[9]

January 17th (most of the day)
Continuation of movement toward Konskie on bad mountain side roads, because the road from Kamienna to Wolow was blocked and being bombed.

Multiple hours of attempts to get any sort of communications using a 100 watt radio station. Success: a response from a radio station from the area of the *9.Armee*: "Break out to the west through Opoczno."

Our own higher echelons and neighbors were silent.

5:00 p.m.: The area north of Wolow was reached. Enemy news: Heavy enemy at Konski, lots of noise from firing.

---

9   Glantz, p. 620.

January 17th-18th (evening)
Night movement passed east of Gowarczow on blocked roads.

January 18th
8:00 a.m.: Although we intended to continue movement toward Ruski Brod, we got news that there was lots of noise from firing in that direction in the early morning. So we decided: Move west. Then came news that *General der Infanterie* Recknagel, the commanding general of the *XXXXII.Armee-Korps*, and *Oberst* von Drabich-Waechter, General Staff, the head of the *Korps*, had been killed in action.

1:00 a.m.: We reached Bialaczow. *Generalleutnant* Heinrich Nickel [commander of the *342. Infanterie-Division*], *Generalleutnant* Dr. Hermann Hohn [commander of the *72.Infanterie-Division*] and the liaison officer for *General der Panzertruppen* Nehring, the commanding general of the *XXIV.Panzer-Korps* were there.

This was the first time we had the capability again for coordinated command and for joining forces.

In and around Bialaczow were portions of: Nickel's division, the *72.Infanterie-Division*, the *88.Infanterie-Division*, Finger's division [unknown] and the *168.Infanterie-Division* as well as the *von Ahlfen Sperrverband*. Most of the intact units were from the Nickel division, which was not attacked outside of Baranov. There was nothing from the headquarters of the *XXXXII. Armee-Korps*.

There was a lack of artillery and gasoline.

The enemy made feints from Opoczno and Konski and was repelled.

Enemy news: Paradyz occupied by the enemy. In addition, the enemy that had penetrated did not appear to have deviated from its westerly attack direction and did not appear to have directed any serious forces against us.

Therefore a decision was made: Move under the command of *Generalleutnant* Nickel to Paradyz at night and break through to Sulejów. *General* Nehring would then break through to Sulejów via Bialaczow and Paradyz with the remainder of his *Korps* starting at noon on January 19th.

When formations of Koniev's 3rd Guards Army and 6th Army met during the night of January 17th/16th near Kielce, they found no German formations. Nehring had already ordered a withdrawal west. Two entire German *Korps*, the *XXXIV.Panzer-Korps* and *XXXXII.Armee-Korps* and other assorted formations were gone. Nehring received a radio message from the *9.Armee* that *Panzer-Korps 'GD'* had arrived in the area of Litzmannstadt and that was now his destination. His motley group of formations now became known as *Gruppe Nehring* across the command of *Heeresgruppe A*, soon to be renamed *Heeresgruppe Mitte* on January 21st.

Eliminating German formations was not Koniev's or even Zhukov's priority. Driving ever westward was. Koniev makes this point clear in his memoirs:

Later on the remains of these troops, [Nehring] having joined other groupings [von Saucken], retreating under pressure from the First Belorussian Front, combined into one quite large grouping, consisting of several divisions. This grouping remained deep in our rear, pressed between the flanks of the First Ukrainian and First Belorussian Fronts. A characteristic feature of the war in general, was noted in this. We already were not worried about creating a double front—inner and outer—around each surrounded enemy grouping in spite of everything. We considered—and considered correctly—that if the advance in depth was developed at an adequate fast rate, these groupings of the enemy remaining in our rear were of no danger to us. They would be defeated and destroyed in some way or other by the second echelons of our troops.[10]

Contrary to Koniev's claim, the second echelons did not destroy the developing pocket of German forces. His lack of coordination with Zhukov allowed them to slip through their lines. If both commanders decided to coordinate their efforts to the east of Tomaschow and focused on destroying *Gruppe Nehring* they would likely have achieved a far greater victory than either man expected by their drive west toward the Oder. The capture of more than 100,000 German soldiers, dozens of field commanders and generals, not to mention the tens-of-thousands of serviceable weapons and equipment would have been a devastating blow to the *Wehrmacht* and the *Ersatzheer* at this point of the war. This force was reconstituted into the *4.Panzer-Armee* that later delivered the final operational defeat of Soviet forces during the war in late April. What fueled the continued drive west by Zhukov and Koniev? That question's answer is likely found in the fact that in less than four weeks Stalin was going to meet with President Franklin D. Roosevelt and Prime Minister Winston Churchill in Crimea at the Yalta Conference (February 4th-11th). The top agenda item was the future of Poland. Clearly Stalin's position at the negotiating table would be ironclad if Poland was already occupied by the Red Army.

While *Gruppe Nehring* slipped west along the inter-front boundary of both Zhukov and Koniev, their advanced forces were racing hundreds of kilometers west of Litzmannstadt, which was essentially encircled by Soviet forces on January 19th. Zhukov's 1st Guards Tank Army soon bypassed Poznan, which was ordered to be defended as a Fortress. The Soviets occupied the city of Konin on January 20th against little resistance. Kalisch fell on the 23rd without a fight. Soviet tanks continued west capturing Ostrowo on the move. By January 23rd Soviet forces reached the Oder River between Oppeln and Ohlau. Krakow had fallen. Koniev's 4th Guards Tank Army continued its drive west toward the Oder River north of Breslau. The 3rd Guards Tank Army was ordered south on January 20th. With the German frontline non-existent, Koniev's priority shifted to the control of the German and Polish industrial regions in Silesia as per Stalin's previous guidance. Main soviet forces continued to maneuver west, to the north and south of *Panzer-Korps 'GD'*, which was growing more isolated by the day.

Von Saucken Decides

Gruppe Nehring was withdrawing from the Baranov Bridgehead where it fought its way toward Kielce with a string of shattered formations following closely behind. Von Saucken was not immediately aware of Nehring's decision to reach his lines at Litzmannstadt. This was due to a lack of wireless communication. He had to make a choice to either attempt an attack southeast and join with Nehring's main body, or withdraw and establish a solid blocking position along the Warthe River where he could wait for their arrival. His decision was soon made for him when reports came in that an advancing Soviet force from either the 6th Guards Mechanized Corps or 25th Guards Tank Corps, attempted to eliminate the German bridgehead near Shieratz held by units of *'Brandenburg'*. Given the emergency on his southern flank, *General* von Saucken decided that events on the ground dictated he withdrawal west to establish a blocking position on both sides of Shieratz with both *'Brandenburg'* and *'Hermann Göring'*.

Now everyone began moving west. Most of *'Brandenburg'* was not in direct contact with the headquarters of *Panzer-Korps 'GD'* or even each other. Many learned of the order to withdraw to Shieratz while on the move as each regiment, battalion, and company fought as an individual unit to survive. To the north of Litzmannstadt *II.Bataillon* of *Jägerregiment 1 'BR'* withdrew west from Kutno to Kroschwitz (Krozniewice). Upon reaching the crossroads Soviet vehicles were identified on the road ahead so the regiment headed south, around the town, toward Warthbrücken. Arriving at the

---

10   Koniev, p. 25.

town, *I.Bat./Jäg.Rgt. 1 'BR'* took command of assorted *Alarm* and *Volkssturm* units and established a blocking position along the river crossing. Withdrawing German units reached the bridge and crossed in duress as low flying Soviet aircraft strafed the column and attempted to bomb the bridge to destroy the crossing site. Panic ensued among the German defenders on the eastern bank causing many to withdraw without orders across the frozen ice.

The elements of *'Brandenburg'* holding from Litzmannstadt to Petrikau headed west to the direction of Grebitz. Elements of *I.Btl./Jäg.Rgt. 2 'BR'* and *Stu.Gesch.Brig. 'GD'* fought through Soviet lines and conducted rear guard actions through the forests south of Pabianitz. Soon the combined force of *Sturmgeschütze* and *Panzergrenadiers*, many riding on the vehicles, appeared at Karzcmy (Kcrczmy) meeting up with the *Pz.Stu.Pi.Btl 'BR'*. Once they crossed the Gabria stream, they continued northwest on the road toward Lask, before they turned west toward Shieratz and the Warthe River. All bridges along the road were wired for demolition to slow down the advancing Soviets. Elements of the 8th Guards Mechanized Corps of the 69th Army were now on the heels of the retreating German formations. The *1.Pionier-Kompanie* of *Panzer-Sturm-Pionier-Bataillon 'BR'* set the charges and stood by ready to detonate the stone bridge at Lask when *General* von Saucken arrived. He knew that Nehring's forces were somewhere behind him working their way northwest, and subsequently ordered the demolitions removed. In the evening two Soviet tanks approached the bridge, including a JS-2 heavy tank, but both were knocked out by an anti-tank gun. With the immediate danger of the Soviets capturing the crossing, von Saucken changed his mind and gave the orders to blow the bridge.

Hauptmann Müller-Rochholz, the *Pionier-Bataillon* commander, and twelve men raced to the bridge in three *Schwimmwagen* to set the demolitions. However, the decision came too late. The Soviet infantry had crossed in force and could not be dislodged. The *Sturmgeschütz* nearby were out of petrol and low on ammo. An effective counterattack could not be undertaken. *Leutnant* Bätzing was wounded along with two other *Pioniers*. The Soviets realized how important this crossing was and fought hard to force the *'Brandenburgers'* back.

The situation for *I.Bataillon* under *Hauptmann* Steidl became a catastrophe. With the *Sturmgeschütze* immobilized due to a lack of petrol, his *Panzergrenadiers* took to the woods to make their way west. The Soviets pursued them and dispersed the German forces under withering fire. The *1.Kompanie* under *Oberleutnant* Wirth and *2.Kompanie* under *Oberleutnant* Gutweniger went missing on January 20th, as their soldiers worked their way west in small groups. A day later on January 21st the survivors rejoined their regiment.

On the 20th von Saucken established the *Panzer-Korps 'GD'* headquarters in Shieratz. For the first time since he deployed he began to build a picture of the debacle that occurred when the *Korps* reached Litzmannstadt. Von Saucken's first priority was to reestablish command of its forces. The second was to conduct reconnaissance of the bridges and crossing sites in the marsh and bogs around Marcenin, southwest of Lask, in order to identify crossing points for Nehring's withdrawing forces. The task fell to the *Schwimmwagen* of *Panzer-Sturm-Pionier-Bataillon 'BR'* scout platoon and the battalion's *2.Pionier-Kompanie*. All available fuel was gathered from units to supply this small force. They traveled southeast through the snow and ice reaching Marcenin in the morning of January 22nd. *Hauptmann* Müller-Rochholz personally led the force, as he typically did, and they soon encountered the advance elements of *Gruppe Nehring* at 11:00 am.

For the last two days heavy fighting for control of the Warthe Bridges raged after the *Kampfgruppe* of the *6.Kompanie* and *7.Kompanie* of *Jägerregiment 1 'BR'* reached the city of Warthbrücken. Under the leadership of the 17 year old *Jäger* Hähnlein the *6.Kompanie* crossed the river ice, followed by the *7.Kompanie*, and they attempted to hold a blocking position. The *3.Pionier-Kompanie* of *Panzer-Sturm-Pionier-Bataillon 'BR'* that detrained north of Litzmannstadt with the lead elements of *Jägerregiment 1 'BR'* was nearly wiped out by Soviet forces that attacked its flank. The company did not receive the orders to withdraw west in time. The unit withdrew west well behind the companies of *Jägerregiment 1 'BR'* from Kutno toward Warthbrücken. It conducted a series of defensive battles to stall the Soviets and prevent themselves from being surrounded. Its commander, *Oberleutnant* Laurentz, was hit twice in the chest but saved by his technical sergeant. Another member of the company, *Leutnant* Hertkon, was killed.

The men of *Jägerregiment 1 'BR'* could not establish a solid defensive line along the Warthe before the Soviets arrived. The Soviet's fought their way into Warthbrücken ahead of the *3.Pionier-Kompanie*, crossing the bridge into town with some tanks and infantry. As the *Pioneers* reached the Warta Bridge it was blown in front of them to prevent anymore Soviets from crossing. The *Pioneers* attempted to make repairs but the German vehicles backed up, blocking the road and panic ensued. The members of the unit tried crossing the drifting ice, which was now broken by Soviet shelling. Only a few made it to the western bank. Hundreds perished in the freezing water. Soldiers who were holding the west bank cracked under the Soviet pressure and withdrew west without orders. Surviving members of the *3.Pionier-Kompanie* on the eastern bank climbed aboard several remaining vehicles and headed north on their own.

The area south and west of Litzmannstadt was a jumble of German and Soviet military units. Most were operating off general movement orders and not executing any planned tactical maneuvers. *Gruppe Nehring* withdrew northwest from the direction of Kielce to reach the area south of Litzmannstadt where they believed the recently deployed German forces had established a defensive line and were waiting for their arrival. *Panzer-Korps 'GD'* deployed into an unknown situation and was immediately placed on the defensive. The command was confused, overwhelmed by the pace of events and ordered their forces to withdraw to the Warthe River line while awaiting the arrival of *Gruppe Nehring*. Both Zhukov and Koniev continued their race west with their main forces ignoring both their flanks and the German forces caught between them.

9

Retreat to the Oder River,
January 19th–February 1st

(Reference Maps 26, 27, 28, 29, 30, 31, 32, 33, 34 and 35)

A temporary defensive line was ordered setup in Schieratz to await the advance of *Gruppe Nehring* along the Warthe River. *Gruppe Nehring* was to the west of the Pilica River fighting for survival between the flanks of Zhukov and Koniev. While Nehring's force was not the main objective of either Soviet commander's movements, second echelon forces were on the move west and constantly harassing the withdrawing Germans. No one in the roving pocket knew the tactical situation. There was the constant threat of the advancing Soviet spearheads swinging north or south to trap the pocket in place and destroy the German forces inside. Nehring's soldiers were without any resupply. No food, ammunition, or petrol had reached them since the start of the Soviet offensive nearly a week ago. The mood in the pocket grew desperate by the day. Between January 19th/20th the withdrawing elements of *Gruppe Nehring* held a bridgehead long enough for their battered units to cross between Tomaschow and Sulejów. They passed south of Litzmannstadt heading west between the 21st/22nd. Their avenue of withdrawal was generally between Pabianitz and Petrikau, running along the line Lask-Freihaus-Schieratz. Once *Gruppe Nehring* rejoined the main German frontline at Schieratz on January 23rd, this force, combined with the disorganized command of *Panzer-Korps 'GD'*, conducted a fighting withdrawal west some 235 kilometers to the upper Oder River over the course of the remainder of the month. The trek to the Oder was one of survival as Soviet units, primarily Zhukov's 11th Tank, 9th Tank, and 7th Guards Cavalry Corps in the north and Koniev's 10th Guards Tank, 6th Mechanized and 9th Mechanized Corps to the south flanked and continually harassed the withdrawing German units.

Due to a lack of coordination between Zhukov and Koniev neither joined efforts with the other to encircle and defeat the withdrawing German force. Advanced elements of Zhukov 1st Belorussian Front actually reached the lower Oder River near Küstrin on January 23rd, nearly five days before the combined units of *Panzer-Korps 'GD'* and *Gruppe Nehring* did. Once *Gruppe Nehring* combined with *Panzer-Korps 'GD'* a nearly month long race west ensued. The first goal was the Oder River. This was the next major natural barrier past the Warthe River. A delay in reaching the Oder meant that the Soviets might be able to cut off, surround and destroy the retreating German force. Once the Oder was reached, and if there was still no stable German frontline, then the entire roving pocket faced the prospect of yet another withdrawal to the Neisse River. Ammunition, petrol, food and water became diminishing commodities while desperation grew in abundance. The withdrawing force was on its own with limited knowledge of the tactical or operational situation. They knew little about exactly where the Soviet forces were, or what their next objective might be. They did not know the situation behind their own German lines, or what to expect when they reached them.

Friday, January 19th

To the north of Litzmannstadt the elements of *Jägerregiment 1 'BR'* began to withdraw west under pressure from Zhukov's 1st Guards Tank Army's 11th Tank Corps, 28th and 29th Guards Rifle Corps. Their goal became the west bank of the Warthe River at Warthbrücken. The *II.Bataillon* took the brunt of the Soviet attack near Kutno with the result that the *6.Kompanie* and *7.Kompanie* were scatted about 15 kilometers southwest of Slupca (Grenzhausen) by Soviet tanks, along with the *8.Kompanie* farther south. The *9.Kompanie* went to Lissa and suffered heavy losses, while the *10.Kompanie* went missing in the vicinity of Posen. To the south of Litzmannstadt *Jägerregiment 2 'BR'* and *Panzer-Sturm-Pionier-Bataillon 'BR'* attempted to hold a solid frontline under increasing Soviet pressure from Koniev's 6th Guards Mechanized and 102nd Rifle Corps in order to wait for *Gruppe Nehring* approaching from the east.

We now begin with Röseke's fight for survival during the flight west of the *6.Kompanie* and *7.Kompanie* of *Jägerregiment 1 'BR'*. This account will be referred to as *Kampfgruppe Röseke*.

Shortly after midnight, the Russians again attacked, this time from the front on both sides of the road, using tanks and advancing infantry in between them. A heavy night battle broke out. The windmill in the 1st Platoon's sector was set on fire to light up the battlefield. Four additional tanks were taken out of combat by the *Sturmgeschütze* right on the main battle line and in close combat. In support of this tank wreckage, there was a penetration by Russian infantrymen near the *Gruppe Mosig*; however a decisive attack by my command troop leader, *Feldwebel* Ebermann, was able to clean that up. Some prisoners were taken and interrogated immediately. They said that about 40-50 tanks of various types, including T-70 (which is an armored vehicle) were about to attack to clear up the road to Kutno. The battalion commander had already led during the first attack. At about 2:30 a.m., it was quiet again. The Russians had had to retreat for the fourth time. There were only a few firefights with dispersed personnel between then and dawn.

Things were calm in the 2nd Platoon sector. The stream of refugees continued on the road from Zychlin.

Four Russians in German uniforms with German identification and German money were taken prisoner there and taken to the regiment.

The commander's vehicle with *Obergefreiter* Votteler and some wounded was set in motion as a supply point. It had an accident en route, but it remained capable of movement.

At 6:00 a.m., *Leutnant* Holzinger reported that some of his people had left the positions during the night and gone back to Kutno on their own. This platoon of *Transport-Sicherung-Bataillon 318* now consisted primarily of NCOs and had not had any combat all night in its sector, with the exception of minor tank firing. I ordered *Leutnant* Holzinger to bring the manning of his sector up to full strength.

In the morning, there was heavy observation to the east. From the 2nd Platoon, there were combat posts placed toward the northeast, which the 1st Platoon could support on the flanks if needed.

A clear and cold winter morning started, fortunately without any fog.

The 1st Platoon noted that Russian infantry was setting up/assembling in a farmstead 800 meters east of our positions. The *Sturmgeschütze* recognized Russian antitank guns that had dug in on an open field southeast of the railway crossing during the night.

At about 7:30 a.m., without any further preparation with heavy weapons, there was another Russian attack, this time in the 2nd Platoon sector as well. *Leutnant* Holzinger had not managed to get his positions re-manned. I therefore had to bring this sector between the 1st and the 2nd Platoon into my fire plan. For this sector, we were especially missing steep angle indirect fire capability.

Fire activity grew on both sides. Our *Sturmgeschütze* fired well, but they had to save ammunition.

At 8:30 a.m., a *Hauptmann* from the regimental headquarters showed up with an order that we should start to deploy to the edge of Kutno starting at 9:00 a.m. Although I was convinced I could hold off the Russians in my position, provided that they hadn't yet deployed heavy weapons, it did not appear to me to be advisable to let it wait to the last minute and it would have been better if the movement could be done while we still had the cover of darkness.

Right at 9:00 a.m. in response to the "green flare of light" sign, the forward-deployed platoons, leapfrogging with the 3rd Platoon, which was still standing by as a deployment reserve, started to move. It was high time: on the entire breadth of the front, we could see masses of Russian infantry spread out and going forward in formation. There were perceptible tank noises from the south. These clearly were supposed to hit us in the flanks or in the rear. So the point was to get to the city of Kutno as quickly as possible.

At 9:15 a.m., the 1st Platoon was at the railway embankment near the company command post. From there, the enemy could still have incurred substantial losses had we used all our *Sturmgewehre* in massed fire, which led to its attack coming to a standstill again. Under the protection of this standstill, the platoon could quickly move on a good piece. I myself remained with a light machine gun crew and *Sanitätsunteroffizier* Molzahn as the last people next to the enemy. The Russians immediately pushed on and from a north-south elevated path had the capability of interfering with and reducing our movements by firing individual shots. There were a few wounded, all of which, however, could be brought with us.

In the meantime, the *Sturmgeschütze* had shot off all their ammunition and had retreated in a group to the edge of Kutno.

At about 11:11 a.m., the *Kompanie* also reached the northern edge of the city and took up positions that had been found well built up. There were trenches to move through that took us to behind the first buildings with full cover.

The *Kompanie* got the order to assemble in the square near the church in the eastern part of the city. I myself remained with a group of the 2nd Platoon with three light machine guns still in position. I was able to use traces of light from my rifles to assign targets and hold off the Russians still to some extent. At 11:30 a.m., we suddenly got out of position.

Through an errant shell (the Russians were firing up the city with artillery harassing fire), the remainder of the *Panzerjäger* force was put out of combat and there were some wounded. That meant that the force had ceased to exist and had acted outstandingly under the command of *Oberjäger* Hahmann during its first, and simultaneously its last, deployment.

With strong security to the rear, the *Kompanie* moved off toward the railway station. A few buildings in the city were already burning. Polish civilians were beginning to loot. One of my groups was still able to secure some cartons of cigarettes for the *Kompanie*.

In the vicinity of the railway station, I came across the 7.*Kompanie*. *Oberleutnant* Geisenberger and his men had shortly before retreated from the positions on the road to Litzmannstadt. He had lost about 1/3 of the *Kompanie* the previous day during the reconnaissance. His night had been calm. However, he had observed our combat activity and had a motorized reserve ready for us.

The regimental headquarters and the regiment's *Stabskompanie* had already moved off to the west. The two *Kompanien* were given the order through a motorcycle messenger who remained behind to first reach Kroßwitz, 15 km west of Kutno, and to fight their way through to there. The *Sturmgeschütze*, which had ammunition again but nowhere near enough, remained subordinated. Some vehicles standing around were made ready to move and the wounded were placed in them. They immediately moved out.

The last engineer to leave the city was supposed to blow up the railway station based on the order of the garrison commandant, who, however, had already left the city the evening before. (*Oberst* von Brückner had been the battle commandant at the time.) There were several tons of stockpiled ammunition, explosives and aircraft bombs there. I undertook the mission and set off the load with two long explosive cap fuses after the two companies had already left the city going in a westerly direction. I got under cover with the B Krad and waited for it to go off. A large part of the railway facilities and the railway station building itself were heavily destroyed.

The Russians must have already reached the eastern edge of the city. However, they initially delayed penetrating into the city. So we still found time to get away from there as quickly as possible. The *7.Kompanie*, which had calmed down a bit, had taken on security using the *Sturmgeschütze* for a rear guard. Moving on the icy road was extremely difficult; it was repeatedly impeded by low-flying Russian aircraft that, although they were flying at an altitude of about 50 meters along the road, for some unfathomable reason did not open fire. If they had, there would have been heavy losses.

Shortly before we reached the road crossing 3 km east of Kroßwitz, we suddenly heard battle noise to our rear. The Russians had left Kutno for a further attack toward the west and were fighting our rear guard. The *Sturmgeschütze* were able to knockout an additional 2-3 enemy tanks.

At the same moment, I noticed a long line of Russian tanks moving toward the head of the two *Kompanien* on the road running from the north toward Kroßwitz at a distance of about 80 meters from us. So we were in a pincer that the Russians must not have intended.

A look at the map indicated that the only possibility was to divert to the south through open farmland to a forest about 2 km from there. That was what was decided and the order was given.

In a situation like that, one can see whether a group is disciplined and whether their commander can keep his cool.

The *6.Kompanie* and *7.Kompanie*, as well as the men from the regimental *Pionier-Kompanie* that had lost its command and had been picked up in Kutno, had provided the evidence for that and mastered the situation. We crossed the farmland, well spread out and in formation. Fortunately, the Russians restricted themselves to scattered fire from their armored guns and did not pursue us. They apparently had orders to push through to the west as quickly as possible and not get themselves stopped.

Oberleutnant Geisenberger and I decided to move to a nearby farmstead to defend ourselves if need be. Maybe we could keep hidden there until it became dark and then try to get further west.

The group was completely exhausted, and in addition there hadn't been any hot food for 24 hours. We never found our supply vehicles with the field kitchen in Kutno; they went with the regimental headquarters.

Using the map and some personal reconnaissance, we determined that the railway line from Warsaw to Posen, which meant that it went in a straight line west, passed extremely close by. We decided to move along this railway line, assuming that the Russians would initially keep to the main roads in their movement forward.

Shortly before darkness fell, we left the farmstead and first reached the railway yard at Kroßwitz, which was completely abandoned. Behind the railway station, we rested in one railway sector for an hour. A *Sturmgeschütz* experienced damage to its tracks when it crossed the tracks. After the fuel and the ammunition were removed, it was blown up.

The NCOs in the two companies were given a detailed briefing on the situation by *Oberleutnant* Geisenberger and I. Our next goal was Warthbrücken, about 35-40 km east of Kroßwitz. We had to get there before dawn in order to initially get to the other side of the Warthe. So we had an extremely difficult slog before us and the NCOs were taught to fight sleep with anything they could and to keep their groups and platoons together.

Some slightly wounded persons and people with movement problems were able to sit on the remaining three *Sturmgeschütze* and also tried to get to the west along the railway.

At 7:15 p.m., we moved out. A light snowfall hindered visibility on all sides, but we did not have to deal with enemy contact initially. Security for the movement was ordered anyway. The movement was very difficult. Some of it was on the iced-over railway bed and some of it on the adjoining land. The railway stations and the railway linemen's buildings were empty but not destroyed. Increasing battle noise was perceptible from the northwest. The Russians had clearly already pushed further on through Kroßwitz and were also fighting our rear guards on the road to Warthbrücken. Would they beat us?

We were exhausted to the max. We had to rest more and more often, and in the end it was at least five minutes every quarter hour. The men fell down in the snow and fell asleep immediately. *Oberleutnant* Geisenberger and I, along with some NCOs, unceasingly encouraged them and pushed them, although we were at the end of our rope ourselves.

My *Kompanie* and I were at the front; a security group commanded by *Leutnant* Krosch was about 200 meters in front.

There was also battle noise audible toward the south. All over everywhere to the east, north and south one could see the flames of burning buildings and other things.

A decision to find a place where the two *Kompanien* might move to until dawn was shown to be incapable of implementation. The towns were too far away from the railway line and to some extent might have already been occupied by the Russians. At one of the roads crossing the railway line from north to south, we determined that there were fresh tank tracks in the snow.

To the south the *II.Bataillon* of *Jägerregiment 2 'BR'* held off a Soviet attack during the night near its *6.Kompanie* sector. The *Kompanie* held a bridge open at Schieratz over the Warthe. One T-34 was knocked-out. The regiment moved out in thick fog during the early morning hours. Ominous noise of advancing tanks could be heard to the north. Farther to the east was *Panzer-Sturm-Pionier-Bataillon 'BR'. Unteroffizier* Hans Stübling recounts the actions of his *Pioniers*:

The *Panzer-Sturm-Pionier-Bataillon 'BR'* withdrew back from the area of Moszczenica—securing the north flank of our moving pocket through Grabica to the west toward Lask.

However, the *Panzer-Korps 'GD'* had the mission of extending a hand to *Gruppe Nehring*, which was further east fighting its way to the west. That led to one of the most famous difficult situations at the bridge over the Grabowka near Karczmy, a new concrete bridge along the main road from Petrikau to Lask.

According to a division order, the bridge was supposed to be prepared to be blown up after the last friendly forces had passed (*Panzer-Aufklärungs-Abteilung 'BR'*), or blown up if a large enemy force approached. Two wooden bridges (3 and 8 km northwest of Karczmy) were accordingly prepared and secured by the *1.Pionier-Kompanie*. While the [*Division*] commander was at the *1.Pionier-Kompanie*, the [*Korps*] commanding general showed up at Karczmy and ordered the ordnance officer, *Leutnant* Bätzing, who had prepared the concrete bridge for demolition using all his available ammunition, and was specifically designated for this focal point, to remove the charge because the bridge absolutely had to remain intact for *Gruppe Nehring*.[1] When the commander arrived at the bridge shortly thereafter, the Reconnaissance Platoon was sent toward Petrikau and a Pak was placed at the bridge. Shortly before dawn, first three, and then more and more Russian tanks showed up. Two of them were knocked-out. A JS-2 was knocked-out right in the middle of the bridge. When the Reconnaissance Platoon reported the Russian tanks, Müller-Rochholz went to the division to clear up the issue of "to blow up or not to blow up." *General* von Saucken showed up in the discussion. The new situation led to an order: "Blow it up at any cost!"

In the meantime, it became dark. The Russians were on the bridge. The farmstead next to

---

1   It is not clear if by "commanding general" it was of *'Brandenburg'* or *Panzer-Korps 'GD'*. It is the author's opinion that it was the commanding general of *'Brandenburg'*.

it was burning brightly. The road on this side was under enemy tank fire. (*Leutnant* Bätzing was wounded. *Hauptmann* Müller-Rochholz attempted to reach the river valley south of the bridge using three amphibious vehicles to cross plowed and hard-frozen fields. He made it under fire. Twelve men worked while climbing—each with two Teller mines (as demolition ammunition) on the river bank toward the bridge. If the farmstead was not lit by fire, it could have worked, but everything was brightly lit and there were Russian infantry standing in droves behind their tanks, right next to the bridge. One made it safely under the bridge, but then the Russians saw us and a nice bunch of fireworks made it impossible to carry it out. The tanks that were making the retreat really steely appeared to only have armored piercing shells. So we got out of there with only two casualties. However, we placed an additional layer of mines on the bridge.

The wooden bridges were blown up by the *1.Pionier-Kompanie* according to plan. During the night, the Russians did not proceed any further near Karczmy. If Metzger had had fuel, the collection of tanks east of the bridge would have been eaten up; his *Sturmgeschütz* were right in the vicinity.

Gruppe Nehring continued their westward march during the evening of January 18th/19th. *Sperrverband* units under the command of *Oberst* von Ahlfen reached the outskirts of Paradyz at 3:00 a.m. Soviet forces were already in the eastern part of the village. Paradyz was of tactical importance as it sat astride a key secondary road that led to Sulejów and the bridge over the Pilica. An attack was quickly organized. With the help of five *Sturmgeschütze* the Soviets were surprised and fell back as the small German force occupied the eastern part of the village. Further progress was hampered as the Soviets, who were now alerted, sent reinforcements from the area of Zarnow to the south that consisted of motorized infantry and some 20 tanks. By 9:00 a.m. the German attacking force went on the defensive ending further westward movement. As the crisis developed, von Ahlfen's forces withdrew back east. Then, just at the right time, *General* Nehring arrived with units of the *XXIV. Panzer-Korps* that included elements of the *16.Panzer-Division, 20.Panzergrenadier-Division*, and a *Kampfgruppe* of the *17.Panzer-Division*. The now larger German force knocked-out the Soviet tanks and forced back their accompanying motorized infantry. Paradyz quickly fell, and the combined force continued their northwest advance on Sulejów. By 11:30 p.m. the eastern bank of the Pilica north of Sulejów was reached, but the Soviets were already there.

Saturday, January 20th
Kampfgruppe Röseke separated from the rest of their battalion near Kutno and attempted to withdraw west with elements of the regimental *Pionier-Kompanie* from Kroßwitz toward Warthbrücken, which was about 40 kilometers to the west. The town of Warthbrücken was the objective of both retreating German units and advancing Soviet forces due to its available road and rail network, and as a crossing point across the Warthe River. During the night the *Volkssturm-Bataillon 'Warthbrücken'*, which was subordinate to *Panzergrenadier-Division 'BR'*, left their defensive positions without orders as the Soviets reached the eastern bank. Warthbrücken, however, was still held by German troops as *Oberst* von Brückner's regimental command post for *Jägerregiment 1 'BR'* was established in the town. They planned to wait a few hours for the arrival of Röseke's *6.Kompanie* and *Oberleutnant* Geisenberger's *7.Kompanie*, then if they had arrived, the regiment would move west. Fighting was already raging on the eastern approaches. *Oberleutnant* Röseke's account of the retreat toward Warthbrücken of *Kampfgruppe Röseke* follows:

At about 1:00 a.m., we ran into an unexpected obstacle: a railway bridge across a river, steel construction, had been blown up. The ice in the river appeared too unsafe to me. So crossing the obstacle took nearly 2 hours because of the dangerous crawling over the iced-up steel girders. The

Sturmgeschütze didn't go any further. They had to seek another way to cross the river. They turned to the south and since then, all of the 20-30 people in them went missing. [AN: this was likely the bridge over the Agitówka stream at Tonningen, a crossing that has long since disappeared, along with the stream.]

In the dawn, Warthbrücken, on a cliff on the edge of the Warthe, was visible in the distance. With this goal in sight, the movement onward went more smoothly and without incident. At about 9:30 a.m., we were still 5-6 km from the city. The *Kompanien* moved further on and secured on a stretch of railway. *Oberleutnant* Geisenberger and I took a few men to go about 2 km ahead to scope out our subsequent route. Suddenly we recognized a number of Russian tanks heading toward Warthbrücken on a road parallel to the railway line and about 300 meters south of it. Now all that needed to happen was that the Russians that had been expecting us on the road from Kroßwitz would get there before us, and they would have us in their grip again. So the greatest of haste was called for. Using the map and the terrain, a road was set up using the field glasses that should be usable for getting into the city from the northwest, but the road from Kroßwitz would have to be crossed in the process.

It was a risk, but it worked. Russian tanks were already firing their guns into the city when we, under good cover crossing heavily broken-up terrain reached the northern portion of it.

In Warthbrücken, there were friendly troops under the command of an *Oberst* as the battle commandant. Our regimental headquarters with *Oberst* von Brückner, especially our support train with the field kitchen, was still in the city. The two *Kompanien* had already been given up on, so our arrival was overall a pleasant surprise.

The *Kompanien* were supposed to initially rest in order to be put to defending the city later. I immediately got a temporary battle mission and immediately started to scope out possible positions. In the meantime, the *Kompanie* moved into residential buildings in the downtown area. In spite of the every stronger enemy fire (including artillery fire), people slept. A shell that landed in the quarters of the 3rd Platoon killed *Gefreiter* Bunzl; *Gefreiter* Weber was severely wounded.

At 2:30 p.m., there were orders issued by *Oberst* von Brückner. I got an order to take up position with my *Kompanie* at a place where three roads came together in the southern part of the city that had already been set up and was supposedly occupied at the time by reliable *Volkssturm* personnel.

I had just got there to carry out this order when it was superseded by another new one. Get ready to move out immediately! I hurried to the regimental command post again to find out more. However, all I found out there was that a decision had been made to evacuate the city at dusk without fighting. Maybe the Russians were already to our west, so our further retreat was again into the unknown.

At least there was still time to give the *Kompanie* something hot to eat. Then the support train had to try to get over the bridges over the Warthe, which were already under enemy fire, as quickly as possible. My driver, *Obergefreiter* Votteler, who was going back with the command vehicle again to collect the wounded, showed himself to be particularly courageous.

The bridge was affected so much by the enemy that no one could walk on it. Then one of the youngest soldiers in the *Kompanie*, 17-year-old *Jäger* Hähnlein, on a messenger trip to take up communications with the *7.Kompanie* reconnoitered a path across the frozen Warthe on his own. We crossed the city under heavy artillery fire, reached the other bank of the river, which we crossed all together, and met the *7.Kompanie* at the northern exit from the city.

The remainder of the regimental *3.Pionier-Kompanie* got in their vehicles and moved toward the north. They have been missing in action since then.

The *6.Kompanie* and *7.Kompanie* were now together again and relying on each other. It was clear to *Oberleutnant* Geisenberger and me that additional battles would have to be avoided under any circumstances; the troops were simply no longer combat-capable and besides, there was only a little ammunition on hand. Since the night of January 17-18, when we were unloaded in Kutno, we had hardly been able to rest. The movement performance since then, which was partly accomplished while fighting, was about 50 km, and at the moment no one could even say how long we still had to move before we would be safe behind a German front.

We decided to move north, toward Hohensalza, and we stayed on a side road. After we had moved a few kilometers, we ran into some refugees who told us that the Russians had already pushed their way through to there and were now going further to the south and west. When darkness came after an unusually colorful sunset, we moved into a village along our movement route. Security was set up. We wanted to spend the night there, move out the next day, and in the meantime reconnoiter the area as well and widely as we could. The village was called Luczywno.

A reconnaissance patrol under the command of *Oberjäger* Augst, who spoke Polish, left the village at 7:30 p.m. in civilian clothing in a horse-drawn cart toward the north so that he could get to Deutscheneck, about 9 km away, if he could.

The *Kompanien* had fallen asleep like logs.

Before it was even midnight, the patrol was back, reporting that the Russians had been seen in a forest bivouac even before they got to Deutscheneck. There were a number of fires observed, but no tanks were recognized in the darkness. Instead, the neighing of horses led to the conclusion that it was a horse-drawn troop. So we must have already been well in the rear of the attacking Red Army.

To the south *Jägerregiment 2 'BR'* and other units of *'Brandenburg'* continued to hold for *Gruppe Nehring*, despite the Soviet pressure on their flanks.

A platoon of the *1.Kp./I.Btl./Jäg.Rgt. 2 'BR'* was engaged in heavy fighting during the morning as the vanguard of *Jägerregiment 2 'BR'*, and then it withdrew west to Waldau on *Sturmgeschütz* by midday. The rest of the *I.Bataillon* followed. As they reached Kcrczmy (or possibly Teadory) a platoon of the *1.Kompanie* was fired on by Soviet antitank guns and tanks. The *1.Kompanie* and accompanying *2.Kompanie* dismounted. A light truck with German wounded was set on fire by a Soviet shot, and the wounded could not be saved. They burned alive. The five *Sturmgeschütze* of *Sturmgeschütz-Brigade 'GD'* moved out to the left over a bald hill to work their way around the Soviet positions, but apparently became confused in the ensuing battle after losing contact with the infantry and headed west on their own.

The town's buildings were situated mostly on one side. A sunken road ran through the farming town, and there was forest at both ends. In the hopeless confusion of the initial Soviet attack the two German companies that deployed—*1.Kompanie* under command of *Oberleutnant* Wirth and *2.Kompanie* under command of *Oberleutnant* Gutweniger—fled back into the forest. A Soviet tank moved alongside a farmstead 300 to 400 meters away from the *'Brandenburg'* infantry firing from its gun while they withdrew. In the meantime, the Soviets set up a heavy machine gun on the road at the end of the forest and conducted suppressing firing on both German companies. Some of the German infantry reached the forest jumping in groups. When they re-assembled, there were still 76 men of the *1.Kompanie* and 50 men from the *2.Kompanie*. Both company commanders were missing. *Oberfeldwebel* Ascher of the *2.Kompanie* and *Feldwebel* Resch of the *1.Kompanie* took point. The remaining soldiers fought their way west through the forests. Many soldiers became separated, lost, or killed by the pursuing Soviets. The remnants crossed the highway at Lask and soon reached the *Bataillon* HQ at 10:00 a.m. the next day. Only 10 men remained.

The *II.Btl./Jäg.Rgt. 2 'BR'* conducted security in the area of Freihaus, west of Lask. In the afternoon, it withdrew through Schieratz as the Soviets advanced. One village that *II.Btl./Jäg.Rgt. 2 'BR'* passed through had to be freed from a platoon of Soviet reconnaissance troops equipped with a few anti-tank guns. The Soviets were advancing across the forests and marshland to reach tactically important road junctions ahead of the Germans. All along the road noted one *'Brandenburger'* that "German troop units were fleeing everywhere" one looked.

Panzerjäger-Abteilung 'BR' also set off west for Karczmy. During the night, they knocked-out two Soviet tanks, but were soon surrounded. They fought their way out toward the west during the morning dawn. Using secondary roads the *Abteilung* pushed west along with elements of the *Panzer-Sturm-Pionier-Bataillon 'BR'* that were encountered along the way. Soon new orders reached the *Abteilung*. They were to advance 30 kilometers southwest of Lask and cross the Warthe at Schieratz.

Sturmgeschütz-Brigade 'GD' was deployed farther southeast than most units of *'Brandenburg'*. Like the rest of the division, they fought their way west. They also encountered elements of *Fallschirm-Panzer-Division 1 'HG'* along the way. *Fahnenjunker-Unteroffizier* Held-Kleingründlach account continues:

I was just coming back from guard, that is, I was just intending to wake up my successor, a little before 3:00 a.m., when suddenly some wild shooting started. No doubt about it, the Russians were attacking! I had to determine that in no time at all, everyone had been alerted and the building was evacuated. Forward we went to the counterattack. I went by the building with my *Geschütz* to the exit to the village. Wild antitank fire met me, and in between them, the hits of mortar fire were in the direct vicinity. The target couldn't be seen in this darkness; only the fire from enemy machine guns and artillery pieces gave me the general direction. I fired a couple of shots in that direction, but I stopped because of course one can't be successful. Behind the entrance to the village, I got the first hit directly on the baffle, and one of my optical squares was shot off. That was only a 4.5cm antitank gun, as I discovered when I calmed down. When I wanted to get my bearings to see how far it was form the neighboring *Geschütz*, that is, when I was leaning my upper body out of the turret, the second shot came. I only saw a red glint and then nothing else. I was blind. Those are feelings! The *Geschütz* was practically no longer deployable and we had to stop. I also had that reported by radio. *Leutnant* Wegener drove over to take a look at me. To my great joy, I was able to determine that I was again seeing a glimmer before my eyes. It was the burning house at the edge of the village. My sight slowly came back, but it didn't return in its entirety within the next few days. (It wasn't until about a week later that I could see normally again.) I felt considerably improved and could run the deployment again. Using explosive shells, I put the crew of the antitank gun, which I could finally make out, out of commission. Then I blew up two machine guns with their crews. I drove by the machine gun nests, got out and determined that there was nothing more to destroy for the two Maxim machine guns. Suddenly Russian machine guns rang out to my right and the first hits from grenades were about 20 meters away from my *Geschütz*. So I went back into the *Geschütz* really quickly! If only my eyes weren't so teary and hurting so much! I was pushing the sleeve of my winter overalls over my eyes all the time to make out the exact place where the enemy weapons were.

The *Geschütz* to my left let out a salvo like I hadn't seen for a long time. It was amusing that they were concentrating their fire on the extreme left flank; I was firing to the right. We then moved further on in a straight line and suddenly I saw lots of Russians retreating under constant fire about 30-50 meters in front of me during the trembling flashes of detonations. Where the blue flames just bubbling out of the darkness are, that's where the machine guns must be! Now they found us and the fire was hitting our armor. It wasn't a nice feeling, but we felt safe. I commanded, "5 percussion fuses!" and aimed the gun myself, because I was the one who had found the target most accurately. The very first shot landed right in the middle. But one machine gun was still firing. Further shots silenced it as well. We stopped both machine guns in the meantime and suddenly the enemy fire was at its end. There were some more sporadic shots crackling around the village and then it was generally quiet. This enemy night attack was repelled! Now a word about our infantry escort, the *Jäger* of our sister *Division 'Brandenburg,'* that along with the *Division 'Hermann Göring 1'* formed the *Panzer-Korps*. They attacked in an exemplary fashion and hit the enemy with alacrity. I particularly noticed one platoon leader. Tall, blond with noticeable features and an overwhelming Bavarian calm. He was also a southern German and was probably from the vicinity of Nuremberg. The group making up my infantry protection acted as if we had been conducting attacks day in and day out for years. While smoking a cigarette, we discussed the course of the fighting and I was glad to hear that our fire had landed so well that they basically did not have a lot more to do.

Then we went back into our initial position. That was shortly before daybreak. It had just barely become actually light when we got a whole bunch of heavy machine gun and mortar fire in the village. Our guys from the *Jäger* had to get out of the warm houses and find cover in the cold. The shit was hitting the fan here in this backwater town! The Russians were involved in air operations as never before. But after a long time, I finally saw large numbers of German *Jäger*. But what was this swelling and droning to our left that is pushing its way into our ears in waves?! We heard it in front of us, and then we heard it well behind us. We couldn't find an explanation until a messenger arrived about 2:00 p.m. and, in addition to giving us the order to move, explained the eerie noise. It was hundreds of Russian tanks on their way to the west. And we were in the middle of two moving tank columns. That wasn't encouraging news, but morale didn't sink for that reason. So we got ready to change position. The wounded were loaded onto a truck, and a *Mannschaftstransportwagen* (*MTW*=troop carrying transport) from the *Fallschirm-Panzer-Division 1 'Hermann-Göring'* took over protecting them. The *MTW* quickly had engine damage and couldn't go any further. *Unteroffizier* von Kamptz's *Geschütz* took it in tow. Our destination was Karczmy. The road went through a pine forest that in its winter splendor reminded me of home. But I was abruptly startled out of my mind. I saw that there was suddenly movement in front of us. *Leutnant* Wegener, who was riding point in front of me, signaled, "Warning!" I noticed why. A Russian with an injured foot was limping in front of us without seeing us, going to his unit, which had come back to within our sight range. We attacked, moving forward in a broad wedge formation. In the process, we came upon a group of houses to our right. We were able to spread out over the fields behind them and put the enemy, which was along the road at the edge of the forest, under fire. It was a horse-drawn antitank unit and it returned fire in a thrice. I called a short halt and had about 10 percussion fuse rounds fired at the target recognized.

The first shots were too short, but the rebound effect wasn't bad. Then an antitank gun tumbled and a horse and a man hit our machine gun fire in the craziness that followed. In the midst of this inferno, we got a blow that made the *Geschütz* shudder. It was a hit from an antitank gun – from behind and it shattered our skirt. I immediately determined that there was massed antitank fire coming from the houses behind us as well. Now we were in the crossfire, and I saw the *Geschütz* next to us being hit as well. I then determined that the others had gone much further in the meantime and I was the last fighting vehicle. The *Jäger* had already jumped out of our *Geschütz* when the battle began. Some of them had reached the protective forest that we were all trying to get to. Now we were out of the witches' cauldron and saw the hits we had gotten. *Leutnant* Wegener's *Geschütz* had been hit once in the tank skirt and once in the chain. *Unteroffizier* Hawle's guide roller had been hit, while *Unteroffizier* Walter had taken a hit to the chain cover and the steel cable. My *Geschütz* got one at an angle from behind on the left, and it shattered on the skirt. The skirt had a hole the size of a child's head, but otherwise it was all intact. Unfortunately the attaching pieces had failed and we had to take the torso completely off because it was only hanging on loosely. There was only one last armored plate hanging, almost like an in memoriam sign. I determined that if it weren't it would have gone into our eye. The stragglers from among the *Jäger* who had pushed their way through by roundabout routes then reported to us that the village was heavily occupied by Russians and that *Unteroffizier* von Kamptz's *Geschütz*, the *MTW* and the truck with the wounded were blown up by shots that hit them dead on. That was simply terrible! However, this tragedy was all the greater because in *Unteroffizier* Kamptz, who like me was a *Fahnenjunker*, I lost a good comrade whose humor and unforced joy was something I always valued. This smiling fresh face is no longer the same as that of calm *Obergefreiter* Kamm, who also died in action. To my left, I suddenly saw Russian cavalry, which hadn't seen us while they were moving in a gully but were suddenly striving to get into the village. Some machine gun fire got various brown faces and their horses to tumble all over themselves. I took out an Ivan looking at us with binoculars using my rifle sight to aim at him. I could not tell whether it hit or not, at any rate he disappeared. Now the *Jäger* sat down again and we continued our movement to Karczmy. After a short time, I noted that the engine on my *Geschütz* wasn't turning over anymore. I fell back and involuntarily brought up the rear. The *Jäger* got off and divided themselves among the other *Geschütz*. "The dog bites the one in the back," comes to mind, but the column can't wait for me. Those were unpleasant trains of thought moving me in this situation, particularly because Paul (*Unteroffizier* Czichowski), our driver, was really nervous. Then *Unteroffizier* Kallweit voluntarily came to my aid with his *Geschütz*. He went behind me at reduced speed and provided escort protection to me. It was typical of Kallweit, the taciturn East Prussian, who was always supporting his people. Finally the town showed up. We had to cross a bridge that had been prepared for demolition by the engineers. We stopped in a farmhouse behind it. Paul immediately started repairing the damage to the engine, and we helped him with it as best we could. After a half hour, he managed to fix it and I went off to find my bearings. I couldn't find the desperately needed fuel anywhere. However, I did meet a wounded *Jäger* from my home town and gave him a few more cigarettes before he was transported away. Back at the *Geschütz*, I used the Scissor Scope to take a look at the area from which we had just come. My heart almost came to a stop!

On the same route that we had been traveling a mere hour before, there were about 20 Russian tanks with infantry on them, led by a captured German *Krad*. I saw a Russian on the *Krad* giving hand signals, apparently the leader of this column, probably a Commissar. They came in our general direction and the Russian infantry swarmed out, calm and cocky, as if they were going out to hunt rabbits. I had never seen Ivan coming toward us this way. I went to radio contact, but there was no order to attack. So I fired two shots right in the middle of the infantry, in response to which the tanks immediately stopped and then moved slightly to the left. Why weren't all the *Geschütz* opening fire now?! Why weren't we attacking?! Instead, we got an order to retreat about 800 meters. Now I knew why we weren't allowed to send radio transmissions in between! A lack of ammunition and fuel! Unfortunately the latter was really bad; I didn't believe I even had enough fuel in the tank for 3 km. Under these circumstances, one can really not make much progress. Now it was evening and uncomfortably cold. The bridge had not yet been blown up. What were people still waiting for? When it was fully dark, we finally got the order to get fuel and ammunition. I personally made the effort to go to the issue point with canisters to get the fuel. My God, four canisters = 80 liters was the entire yield! With very mixed feelings, the loader and I took the precious contents to the *Geschütz*. It worked better with ammunition. 30 rounds of percussion fuse and 21 rounds of tank ammunition. But it was high time, because we had shot it all off; at the end, there were still four boxes of ammunition for our two MG 42 and one box of hand grenades. For my Beretta, an Italian-made machine pistol with which all the fighting vehicle crews in Krugau had been armed, there was nothing. But we still had two captured Russian machine pistols with four 72-round drums!

Suddenly light signals went off in the darkness. It was green balls, certainly not German manufacture. There was the muffled sound of rolling tanks that could not be very far away. Men from the assault platoon that were just returning reported that the Russians were going over the bridge to the right. In response, we dug in with our guns pointing toward the engine noise. *Unteroffizier* Walter was the first to fire into the Egyptian darkness. When the grenades went off, we noticed that the Russians were trying to get to a farmstead about 500 meters in front of us. A Russian tank was also firing at us, but the shells were landing behind us on the roof of a shed. Now the other *Geschütze* were firing as well. Now I told my fire direction NCO that we would try to fire by the light of a flare. I let loose and while the light was slowly sinking, we had our eyes peering into the darkness. There was nothing visible. On the third try, we saw the outline of a tank. Three antitank shells were fired in that direction. The last one must have hit it – we recognized the muffled metallic crash when a shot hits an armored vehicle. The grinding and chain noise stopped, but the tank must have still been there. Now a green beam climbed from its place. Suddenly it turned foggy and we lost all sight. Tank noises were only audible again through the thick fumes. Okay, our friend was being towed! I was being congratulated without envy for the hit under these circumstances, but I would have preferred a shot of Schnapps because it had turned even colder. Then we got food. Cheese in tubes, crispy bread, cigarettes and drops. I wouldn't have found this "Chayka" stuff tasty otherwise, but today I was scarfing them down one after another. We were trying to get a bit of shuteye. One of the four of us was always on guard. We were out in a flash. Then I was awakened. It was terribly cold. I got out and did a couple of movement exercises. Then I saw the field guards and infantry security positions being withdrawn and heard that we would move again at daybreak.

A couple of *Landser* couldn't suppress the urge to curse us out. "Cowardly pigs" and "skedaddle" was the tame version. I tried to explain to them that without any fuel, we could only defend [and] couldn't undertake any gutsy attacks. It rankled me a lot, because I thought they were being unfair. Besides I had personally always had a soft spot for infantrymen and had loaded up many wounded who had already been given up on, usually under heavy fire, because an armored vehicle draws it like a magnet. After all, I had been assigned as infantry often enough, even though I am definitely an artillery man. When I think of Rosslawl, Jelnja, Karatschew, Tula or Bolchow, it is hot and cold for me at the same time, even after the fact. I woke up my relief and tried to take advantage of every minute of sleep. Things went back to normal when day broke. The *Sturmgeschütz* were again moving along in column. The movement took us to Schieratz, where there was apparently an armored troop training area. It was sad that we had to find out that the stopped training tanks had wood gas propulsion. So our fuel situation had become so bad that our full-track vehicles had to be fitted with these shapeless steel containers in order to keep training going at all! From there, we went on to Chojne. [AN: Chojne is south of Schieratz, along the Warthe River].

Gruppe Nehring crossed the Pilica on a weak wooden bridge in the early morning. Nehring now exerted command of all German units withdrawing west across the bridgehead. The crossing was efficiently organized as follows: people, horses, horse-drawn vehicles, cars and light trucks crossed the ice, and trucks up to 12 tons crossed the wooden bridge, which had undergone makeshift reinforcement. *Panzers* tried to cross the frozen Pilica first. A Panther and a Tiger went through the ice, which was too thin for their weight. Since no ford could be found, the remaining six *Panzers* waited for everyone else to cross the wooden bridge, and then they tried. Two *Panzers* broke through the bridge. A makeshift crossing was established over these *Panzers* that had broken through, so the last four finally reached the western bank.

During the crossing, the Soviets used Ratas (Polikarpov I-16 airplanes) and T-34s to push against the narrow bridgehead. After an airplane was shot out of the sky and a tank knocked-out, the Soviets stopped their reconnaissance activity and also did not undertake a further attack. By 5:00 p.m. the forward units reached the area northeast of Petrikau.

Sunday, January 21st

Zhukov and Koniev now tried, though halfheartedly, to seal up the gap between their two Fronts. From the north came elements of the 9th Tank Corps. From the south came the 13th Army. While these Soviet forces began to converge on Schieratz and the withdrawing *Gruppe Nehring*, Zhukov's 1st Guards Tank Army was only two days away (40 kilometers) from Posen, and Koniev's forces were three days (60 kilometers) from reaching Breslau. Meanwhile, *Panzer-Korps 'GD'* and *Gruppe Nehring* were some 70-80 kilometers away from the German main battle line in the west.

To the north of Litzmannstadt, the regimental staff of *Jägerregiment 1 'BR'* including the *9.Kompanie* and *10.Kompanie*, as well as attached elements were withdrawing west independent of the command of *Panzergrenadier-Division 'BR'*. The withdrawal of *Kampfgruppe Röseke* continues:

3:30 a.m., wake up, get ready to move on. The body doesn't want to cooperate, but it has to be forced by hard will.

We had decided not to go any further north, but rather to retreat to the railway line running north of Warthbrücken and go along it further west toward Posen.

At 4:00 a.m., we moved out. At 6:00 a.m., we reached the rail line. There was some more exhausting movement across the railway ties or across the frozen gravel on the railway beds. The area alongside was impassible because it was heavily guarded by shrubbery. Fortunately, the thick fog, which we wanted today, favored our movement forward and back.

Frequent resting was required. Ammunition and weapons were split equally as loads so that the physically weaker could be spared.

The *6.Kompanie* was again moving at the front, with *Leutnant* Krosch and a security group in front of them. A Polish civilian whom we ran into was forced to come along as an ammo bearer and also to prevent him from betraying us.

At a rest stop at about 10:00 a.m., three men, including *Obergefreiter* Harald Heinz and *Obergefreiter-Offizieranwärter* Werner Lubke from the 1st Platoon were reported as missing. They had apparently remained behind to get some rest. Some comrades went back along the railway line to look for them, but unfortunately in vain. We had to go on, however, because the point was to take most of the *Kompanien* to safety, and the time for doing so was extremely limited and valuable.

At about noon, we reached the area of the city of Konin. [AN: this is on one of the main east-west routes to Posen] Shortly before we got to a main north-south road, we stopped and did some recon. Two civilians were found and interrogated. They said that Konin had already been occupied by the Russians days before, as had the railway station north of the city and an airfield directly to the north of this railway station. So in any event we had to leave the railway line and there were four ways left to go further. We could go around the city to the south (but there were swamps on the map), go between the city and the railway station, go between the railway station and the airfield, or go around the airfield to the north. The extensive reconnaissance that would have been necessary would take too long. It was hard to make the right decision, but it was made easier because we could suddenly hear the noise of battle coming from the north. We wanted to try to go on the nearest paths between the railway station and the airfield. The thick fog was favoring our plans now more than ever. We carefully went out of the forest onto the open land, with a platoon of the *7.Kompanie* in formation under the command of *Leutnant* Bürk. Suddenly a Russian tank with infantry on it emerged from the fog. The lead platoon was involved in a battle, and the majority of the companies retreated back into the forest. Only part of the lead platoon followed them; the remainder either managed to push their way through or they wound up prisoners. Fortunately, there weren't any losses. How could we supply such people, let alone take them with us?

An additional attempt to go around the airfield on the north was also unsuccessful because the Russians had become vigilant there as well. After a wild firefight in and out of the fog, we moved back into the forest. There we found a few dispersed soldiers from other units, who joined us.

Our last decision was to wait for nightfall and under cover of night, attempt to go to precisely worked out movement goals between the railway station and the city. With a messenger, I reconnoitered a good portion of this route.

At 6:00 p.m., the companies broke out. Unfortunately, the fog had in the meantime lifted and the night was lit by a half moon. At the head was *Leutnant* Krosch again with a group; he was simultaneously responsible for keeping track of the number of people moving, which I checked continually. The group went initially through a deep gorge and a quarry. Multiple wire fences had to be cut without making any noise. Now we had reached the open terrain between the city and the railway station. From a building that was well lit, about 300 to 400 meters away, we heard screams and hooting, apparently drunk Ivans [raping] women.[2] We carefully sneaked by. I looked back repeatedly at the long line of moving companies, but we were lucky; the Russians had not noticed anything in their drunken state.

Our movement initially went in a southwesterly direction. We crossed the loops of the frozen Warthe more than once. The ice cracked under our feet, but it held. The faces in the white camouflage suits showed black in the moonlight. It was not until shortly before midnight that we were able to rest for half an hour in the vicinity of a blown-up bridge. From there, we wanted to attempt to reach the railway line by going further north. So far we had had fabulous luck. But what would happen next?

To the south, the mood in Schieratz was panic. "Everything was going back to the west!" according to the accounts of veterans who were there. *Panzergrenadier-Division 'BR'* received orders from *Panzer-Korps 'GD'* to hold out a bit longer at Schieratz and pick up the survivors of the *XXIV.Panzer-Korps* and *General* Nehring's forces. Reconnaissance by force with elements of *'Brandenburg'* toward Petrikau ran into Soviet infantry and support trains moving up. Soviet tank units had already rolled on west. *Panzergrenadier-Division 'BR'* was practically encircled. The time of what their veterans called the "wandering pocket" was now beginning.

Elements of *Jägerregiment 2 'BR'* continued to hold a defensive line at the bridgehead around Schieratz, but they could do little more as their own losses mounted. According to a veteran, one of the well-known *"Führer* orders" of the time read *"Panzer-Korps 'Großdeutschland'* will relieve encircled *Gruppe Nehring* in the area of Petrikau!" As the veteran remarked after the war "that was dumb. We had just enough gas to get there. The commanding general, *General der Panzertruppen* von Saucken, refused to carry out the order." It is interesting how the unnamed veteran seemed to suggest Hitler was behind such apparently reckless orders. In the decades after the end of the war a general attitude developed among the German veteran community that placed the blame for every conceivable military misfortune on the shoulders of their once revered *Führer*. As already discussed in Chapter 8, it was Guderian and not Hitler that issued the order to deploy the *Panzer-Korps* into its current tactical situation.

The *Panzer-Sturm-Pionier-Bataillon 'BR'* received the order to reconnoiter across the Warthe, south of Schieratz and prepare a favorable crossing for *Gruppe Nehring*. A heavy auxiliary bridge, not shown on the map, was found in the vicinity of Chojne. The bridge was prepared for demolition. The big bridge near Schieratz was also still intact and was not in Soviet hands, as had been suspected. The *Bataillon* reached Schieratz amidst the chaos. Its *2.Pionier-Kompanie* was sent to Chojne to the south.

---

2   While the ethnicity of the women is not known, this town was well within Poland's 1939 borders making the victims likely Polish.

Gruppe Nehring continued to withdraw to the area southwest of Lask through the night of January 21st/22nd. Multiple Soviet tanks were knocked-out in close quarter combat during the early morning. Through the limited wireless radio communication that existed between *Gruppe Nehring* and *Panzer-Korps 'GD'* it was relayed that units of *Panzergrenadier-Division 'BR'* were awaiting the arrival of *General Nehring* and his forces in the area of Schieratz where they were to maintain a bridgehead over the Warthe open. Thick fog permeated the farm fields south of Lask. Visibility was down to 50 meters at 8:00 a.m. Soviet messengers on bicycles, cars, and individual trucks were observed with alarming frequency on the north-south roads between Petrikau-Lask-Litzmannstadt. *Gruppe Nehring* fired on any, and all, that were in weapons range. By noon, the forward elements of *Gruppe Nehring* encountered a Soviet infantry battalion holding the road junction south of Pabianitz in Waldau. The remaining German *Panzers* were deployed to repel the Soviet tanks that were moving between Pabianice and Belchental until it got dark, thus keeping the road junction open for German units to get through toward the west.

Monday, January 22nd

By the end of the day most of *Jägerregiment 1 'BR'* was hopelessly split into a number of smaller *Kampfgruppen* withdrawing west between the advancing columns of Soviet forces. Like the rest of *'Brandenburg'*, main roads were used sparingly, and many units kept to the secondary dirt tracks, forests and swamps to cover their movement. Exact information on the deployment of the rest of *Jägerregiment 1 'BR'* at this time is limited. It is known that the *8.Kompanie* deployed at Litzmannstadt and was quickly scattered by a Soviet attack. Both the *9.Kompanie* and *10.Kompanie* withdrew with the Headquarters Staff of *Jägerregiment 1 'BR'* west. The *9.Kompanie* reached German lines at Glogau with the Regimental Headquarters at the end of January, but it suffered heavy losses in the process. The *10.Kompanie* became separated. It withdrew farther north, was cut off, and went missing in the vicinity of Posen. Unfortunately no accounts have been identified for these latter two companies that may shed light on their activities during the following days. According to Spaeter's notes he wrote of this time: "Retreat. Details unknown." The *I.(gep)Bataillon/Jäg.Rgt. 1 'BR'*, equipped with *Schützenpanzer* armored personnel carriers, deployed south of Litzmannstadt and operated as an independent support battalion for *Jägerregiment 2 'BR'* and the main elements of the division withdrawing west. Farther north, the remnants of *Kampfgruppe Röseke* were on their own trying to survive and reach German lines to the west. The account of *Kampfgruppe Röseke* for the 22nd picks up after passing to the south of the Soviet occupied city of Konin:

> At about 1:30 a.m., we reached the main highway to Posen, right to the west of Gohlen (Golina)! There were individual Russian vehicles and tanks going in both directions. *Oberleutnant* Geisenberger and I attempted to find out more about the general situation by asking the residents of an isolated house. We still hoped to finally see the fire of a front, hear combat noise from afar, or run against friendly troops, but unfortunately that hope was in vain. Our two companies were already well in the rear of the Red Army.
>
> We decided to stop one or more Russian vehicles so that we could capture something to eat. After security for this enterprise was set up on both sides of the road, a small truck column, about 5-6 vehicles, was stopped; fortunately it wasn't a troop transport, just drivers and assistant drivers. They were taken a bit off the road and the trucks were searched. They had loaded ammunition and combat engineer equipment, but there were also a few bags of dry Russian bread, a few cartons of canned meat and a jar of sunflower-seed oil. It was all immediately divided among the companies lying under cover. We left some passing Russian vehicles in peace—and they did the same with us. We wanted to set the stopped trucks on fire, but we considered it better to let them go further on after the companies had crossed the highway and had gone a good bit further north to keep the

Russian prisoners from, say, putting some unit that just happened to be passing by on our trail. It all worked without further incident.

At about 3:00 a.m., we had reached the railway line again. We then looked for a place to stay the rest of the night. After all, we had again spent 24 hours without sleeping. We found a few isolated farmsteads. There was heat, rest, and especially food. When going to the widely scattered places to stay, I had the misfortune of getting lost in the thick fog, which in the meantime had lifted, and I needed more than an hour to get my bearings because I didn't have a compass at that time.

At dawn, we moved out quickly. It was high time. According to the local residents, most of whom, by the way, thought we were Russians, the surrounding towns were already in the hands of the Russians.

Our movement along the railway line continued on, again favored by the thick fog. There weren't any people anywhere. A few towns right on the railway line were bypassed in big arcs. Unfortunately, the only 1:300,000 map we still had come to an end right to the west of Konin; we were missing the map that adjoined it to the west, which caused an unpleasant feeling of insecurity.

About midnight, we reached the area of the city of Grenzhausen (Polnische Slupca). An attempt to bypass the city to the north turned out to be impossible because heavy vehicle traffic could be seen on the roads heading north and east from there.

The companies rested in the shelter of the railway embankment. *Oberleutnant* Geisenberger and I carefully went a bit further west and were able to get to right next to the main highway from Warsaw to Posen that re-crossed the railway line there. It was heavily occupied by vehicles of all sorts, especially columns of horse-drawn vehicles. The roar of drivers pushing their horses on was clearly audible. In the ditches by the road, there were toppled horse-drawn wagons with dead horses everywhere, probably from refugees. So it wasn't possible to cross this highway during the day and we decided to first wait for night.

We managed to get to the terrain beyond the railway embankment, which offered better cover, by going through an underpass for a field road. The two companies moved into a small farmstead, tightly squeezed, and at least found some warmth and rest for a few hours. The food was again at its end. However we were able to kill two piglets, we found a sack of potatoes and we were able to have some soup cooked for the companies in all the containers we could find.

With my company troop leader, *Feldwebel* Ebermann, I determined our combat strength. We were now 2 officers, 10 NCOs and 88 enlisted, so exactly 100 men. We had weapons! Eight light MG 42s with two full boxes of ammunition each, 27 *Sturmgewehre*, 8 *Panzerfäuste* and a sufficient number of hand grenades, plus six compasses for movement.[3] We were already missing 11 men since Warthbrücken. The *7.Kompanie* had become even a bit weaker because of the losses it had had near Kutno and later near Konin.

Oberleutnant Geisenberger and I had a thorough discussion with our most-experienced men about our situation. We came to the conclusion that it would not be possible in the long run to make it through with most of the companies. The closer we got to a front, the thicker the concentrations of troops would be, so the more difficult it would be to remain unnoticed. Consideration was therefore given to having the companies broken down into small units and having these units move off separately under the command of officers and the best NCOs. These groups would then be better able to feed themselves off the land and were better prepared to deal with surprises, particularly because of their mobility. However, it appeared advisable to us to cross the highway in front of us together, because a certain combat strength might still be needed to do that.

After darkness fell at about 6:00 p.m., we approached the highway along the northern side

3   The other nearly 70 men were armed with the bolt-action KAR 98K.

of the railway embankment. I took the front and *Oberleutnant* Geisenberger took the rear. The road was still occupied by vehicles of all sorts, but most of them were motorized. The Russians were, however, using lights to travel, which was very favorable to our plans. But we had to take the bright light of the moon into consideration, which made the farmland on both sides of the highway visible for a long distance.

At about 6:45 p.m., I reached the railway lineman's building at the railway crossing, and initially I was alone. It was not occupied. However, a Russian motorcycle rider suddenly veered from the road to the railway lineman's building. I just managed to disappear around a corner, but I think that the Russian recognized me and I took my pistol off safety . . . but all Ivan did was to light a cigarette in the lee of the building and go on.

At 7:00 p.m., I ferried the companies in groups across the highway, using the distance between the individual vehicles and the columns. Orders were given to assemble in a forested area 800 meters southwest of the railway crossing that we had seen the previous day. At about 10:00 p.m., the last parts of the companies fortunately had crossed the highway. A column of APCs that had just passed appeared to have noted something and was firing into the terrain from the road. But we were already safe.

Because the railway line ran parallel to the highway from Grenzhausen (Polnische Slupca) on, we now had to abandon it once and for all. We first wanted to go about 10-15 km to the southwest, then dissolve the companies there, and then have the groups go individually to the west, with movement goals of 12 to 20 km. After all, someone should be able to find a German main battle line out there somewhere. "And if it isn't until Portugal . . ." one of my men noted with grim humor.

In the patch of forest 800 m SW of the railway crossing, the entire *Kampfgruppe* assembled without any more losses. At 11:00 p.m., we broke out, the *6.Kompanie* in front again, with security in front of them. We bypassed a village that was apparently occupied by the enemy; one could see campfires and laughing and singing could be heard.

Panzerjäger-Abteilung 'BR' withdrew toward Schieratz knocking-out a Soviet KV-I along the way. Three *Geschütz* were set up as rear guard when they reached the crossing point over the Warthe. Once the river was crossed, *Leutnant* Kass and his men moved farther west.

Panzer-Sturm-Pionier-Bataillon 'BR' was supposed to hold the bridges in the Marcenin swamp open for *Gruppe Nehring* and conduct reconnaissance in force back east to find the withdrawing German units, in order to lead them to the crossing pints. However, the *Pioniers* had no petrol left. Under the orders of *General* von Saucken all of the fuel in the entire *Panzer-Korps 'GD'* was collected in order to provide a single *Pionier-Kompanie* with enough petrol to push its way east across the Warthe River and locate the forward units of *Gruppe Nehring*. If *Gruppe Nehring* could not be located, then *Panzer-Korps 'GD'* might have to withdraw, given their desperate situation.

The *Panzer-Sturm-Pionier-Bataillon 'BR's 2.Pionier-Kompanie* and a Reconnaissance Platoon from *Panzer-Aufklärungs-Abteilung 'BR'* performed the mission. The *2.Pionier-Kompanie* was equipped with mules as their main transport, while the Reconnaissance Platoon was equipped with its amphibious vehicles. At dawn, these units advanced east from Chojne—into the unknown and through blowing snow. As one veteran remarked "thank God there was no visibility". The small *Kampfgruppe* advanced toward the small village of Marcenin, fighting only slippery ice and snow banks along the way. They found the bridges intact, and then quickly secured them. At about 11:00 a.m. the *Pioniers* could make dark silhouette of a vehicle in the snow fall. Fingers tensed, then relaxed as the vehicle turned out to be the familiar shape of a German armored personnel carrier. *Hauptmann* Müller-Rochholz advanced by foot, hand extended, and met an *Oberst* with a wooden leg—the first soldier of *Gruppe Nehring*. Both men embraced each other. Then the *Pioniers* inquired about petrol and received a full complement from the cut off *Gruppe Nehring*. Apparently the *Pioniers* had used their last stocks to reach Marcenin in their rescue effort.

The bridge near Chojne was turned over to *Gruppe Nehring* who organized the crossing of their forces across the Warthe and into the frontline of *Panzer-Korps 'GD'*. Now the remnants of the *4.Panzer-Armee* moved to the troop training area south of Schieratz. By the evening the exhausted German troops spent their first night in a building in a week. Petrol remained a critical issue and was needed as a general retreat west was planned for the morning. The meeting between *Gruppe Nehring* and *Panzer-Korps 'GD'* was welcome by the soldiers who had just survived nearly two weeks of intensive fighting along the Weichsel River. The meeting soon brought unwelcome news. As *Oberst* Albert Brux, commander of the *17.Panzer-Division*, recalled ". . . we hoped that we would be able to penetrate the enemy lines; but we were grossly disappointed when we found out that the *'Brandenburgers'* also had no more fuel for their vehicles, and when they told us that the Russian elements were far to our west already."[4] On this day Nehring became the 124th recipient of the Swords to the Knight's Cross with Oak Leaves awarded for leading his men from the Weichsel River to the lines of *Panzer-Korps 'GD'*. The strongest units of Von Nehring's force to include the *Kampfgruppe 16.Panzer-Division*, *19.Panzer-Division*, and *20.Panzergrenadier-Division*, *Kampfgruppe 72.Infanterie-Division* and *342. Infanterie-Division* now fell under the direct command of von Saucken. The infantry divisions would detach in early February along with the *19.Panzer-Division* on February 6th and the *Kampfgruppe 16.Panzer-Division* by February 15th. The *20.Panzergrenadier-Division* remained subordinated through early March.

Tuesday, January 23rd

Elements of *Jägerregiment 1 'BR'* continued to withdraw west cut off from the main force of *Panzer-Korps 'GD'* by the northwest advance of Zhukov's forces heading toward Poznan. They have to fight their way southwest in individual groups as *Kampfgruppe Röseke* now did with disastrous consequences for the regiment. Röseke's account continues:

> After midnight, we reached a group of isolated farmsteads and moved into them. Fortunately food was found and immediately distributed. *Oberleutnant* Geisenberger and I agreed that the moveout would be at 6:45 a.m.
>
> I was in quarters with the 1st Platoon, whose commander, *Leutnant* Krosch, took care of his men in an exemplary manner. A piglet was slaughtered, roasted and eaten. In addition, there were steamed vegetables; there was no bread to be found anywhere. When the snack was over, I found out that the piglet had been the house dog. "Never mind," as the country folk say. The rest of the night was short and passed without incident. Security was set up.
>
> At 6:00 a.m., we woke up and had breakfast. At 6:30 a.m., *Leutnant* Krosch reported to me that the *Kompanie* was ready to move out. I was forced to say a couple of words to my men. I revealed the decision to them to dissolve the *Kompanie* that evening and form small groups that would be able to push their way through more easily. These groups were supposed to form within the platoons while it was still day because one couldn't simply issue orders about putting them together and leading them in such a situation; their personal relationships, friendships, etc. had to be taken into account. This plan was also recognized by the men as the best solution and an absolute necessity. Everyone was still infused with a spirit of getting through under any circumstances.
>
> At 6:45 a.m., we met the *7.Kompanie* and moved further on to the southwest with them at 7:00 a.m. The terrain was slightly hilly, covered with bushes to some extent. It was foggy. The movement sequence was as before; Krosch in front, *6.Kompanie*, dispersed people from other

---

4   Glantz, p. 622.

units, *7.Kompanie*, Bürk as the rear guard. Security from the sides was distributed among the platoons. I myself went with *Oberleutnant* Geisenberger at the head of my *Kompanie*, with a line of sight to *Leutnant* Krosch. We spoke about our situation; the responsibility for our *Kompanien* was pressing on us and we discussed in detail whether we had so far made the right decision and whether our further plans were doable. We also thought about the possibility/probability of becoming involved in combat again and were clear that any contact with the enemy had to be avoided at all costs. I also remember that we talked about the danger of becoming prisoners of the Russians. *Oberleutnant* Geisenberger thought that he would never survive such a fate alive. As a 'Brandenburger' officer, no one would have any chance of ever seeing his homeland in such circumstances.

At about 8:00 a.m., we crossed a road on which fresh tank tracks were visible. We sped up but suddenly the cry came from the last third of the *7.Kompanie*, "Tanks coming from the left!" After a paralyzing moment, *Oberleutnant* Geisenberger and I hurried back to the road and saw that there actually were a number of tanks coming out of the fog just about to leave the road and attack our flank—with infantry advancing in between them. The Russians immediately opened up random fire. There was a heavy battle, but we could no longer put up any organized resistance. The two companies had been moving in a line with a movement depth of about 500-700 meters. From this formation, there was a sudden change in the front and a formation of depth about 90 degrees to the left. *Kampfgruppen* under the leadership of the most dedicated *Unteroffizieren* were formed. The last order I could give my company was to yell out, "Get through individually! The goal is 'Brandenburg'!"

Right after that came a cry from the front as well, "Tanks coming from the right!" So the Russians had us in a vise. (Today I suspect that this assault wasn't coincidental; we were betrayed during the night by the residents and they were proceeding against us from a prepared position.)

The dispersed companies, sometimes a man at a time and sometimes in groups, attempted to gain ground to the southwest. There the edge of a forest was visible a few hundred meters away. I myself was with *Oberleutnant* Geisenberger at the end of the two companies, right in the vicinity of the road, so we were the furthest toward the enemy. We were separated from the majority of the companies by two or three tanks with infantry on them and chased across the open field. The next goal that offered itself was a farmstead about 300 meters away along the road. The tanks followed us and were clearly having fun repeatedly stopping right behind us and firing at the runners one after another. Finally, a group of about 10-12 men, including *Oberleutnant* Geisenberger, his company troop leader—*Feldwebel* Kratky, and me, reached the farmstead. A couple of civilians sitting there who wanted to stop us but didn't have any weapons were run over, a picket fence was jumped over, and behind we went right down into a stream bed. We broke through the ice down to our waists, got to the other bank while the Russians stopped first at the farmstead. But then they started chasing us again; the steep bank and the stream were not an obstacle to them. *Oberleutnant* Geisenberger called to me while running, "Hide in the bushes!" I called back, "That's way too small, they'll get us out of there! We have to go right, into the Russians' rear!" I don't know whether he heard that, but at any rate I ran on, in an arc to the right. After about 100 meters I looked around me; I was alone. To my left, there were still 3-4 men running across an open field with one of the tanks right behind them. *Oberleutnant* Geisenberger and a couple of men had gone into the small bushes. While I was running, I saw two tanks stop right in front of them and infantrymen getting out and going into the bushes. I heard shots and screams—and then it was quiet. At the same time, I got a shot in my back and through the left side of my chest. The impact pushed me to the ground; I recognized the shooter about 150 meters from me but he didn't get any closer. The crews of the two tanks at the bushes had gotten back in, but I couldn't recognize whether they had taken my comrades prisoner. In all likelihood, they along with *Oberleutnant* Ernst Geisenberger had lost their lives. I thought about my conversation with him—it was barely half an hour before.

When the tanks had left, I dared to get up a bit and was able to get myself a bit further away. I was still very close to the road and I could have been discovered at any moment. Not far away, there were still a few dead or wounded from the first firefight with the Russians. I had, after all, attempted to get into the Russians' rear.

I lay in a deep furrow and attempted to dig further down in the frozen ground with a light covering of snow, but my strength failed me. I must have been unconscious for a while. I could see that I had lost quite a bit of blood. At any rate, my white camouflage blouse was completely stained with blood. After a while, the fog lifted and the sun broke through. The shooting still hadn't gone silent. I heard it from the direction the forest in the southwest where at least one part of the *6.Kompanie* must have gotten. But I especially heard the fire of an individual light MG 42s and, as I later found out, that came from *Oberjäger* Mosig, who was giving fire support to the comrades following him, who continued to change position as they came out from the edge of the forest.

There were a lot of dead and wounded on the battlefield, including Russians. Suddenly engine noise could be heard on the road. I stayed lying down motionless; a few tanks and 2-3 trucks went by me and stopped at the farmstead, about 300-3400 meters from me. To my astonishment, I saw the Russians unloading a large number of prisoners, about 60 men from the two companies. They were placed at the wooden fence. Machine guns in front and hands up. Through my good 10 x 50 field glass, I could see them having to throw the contents of their pockets down on the ground some time later. They were then searched with a lot of roaring and shooting into the air. Unfortunately I couldn't recognize individual comrades among the prisoners. It was too far away for that and besides most of them were still wearing head coverings.

It must have been around noon (the sun was already high) when the Russians started doing a search of the battlefield. I saw a few wounded still capable of walking ferreted out; they were pushed to the farmstead with blows from weapon butts and bayonets. Suddenly I saw the Russians use pistol shots to kill the wounded who couldn't walk as they went by, and I think my blood must have run cold . . . . They took their own dead with them, but there weren't many of them. A group searching the battlefield was getting closer and closer to me. They reached the road. I was lying completely motionless but I could see through my almost fully closed eyelids that a Russian stepping out of the group was coming toward me with a rifle in front of him. I closed my eyes completely. I can no longer say today what I was thinking or imagining at that moment. I felt the Russian step on me with his boot and turn me half on my side. He must have thought I was dead, seeing me lying there covered with blood and dirt, pale and already almost frozen stiff. At any rate, I heard the steps going away again . . . .

I continued to lie down for a long time without moving. When I opened my eyes again and looked around very carefully, the prisoners were still standing at the fence of the farmstead with their hands up. Shortly thereafter, I must have been unconscious for a while. Heavy machine gun fire woke me up again suddenly and I now saw, it was so terrible, that talking about it now still overcomes me. A group of prisoners, about 20 men, was herded to a haystack on the other side of the farmstead and bowled down with machine guns and submachine guns at close range . . . . The cries of the unfortunate comrades made their way to me. Some of them attempted to get away, but it was in vain—the flashes of fire from the machine guns pushed them to the ground after a short run. Finally two tanks rolled up to the haystack and ran over the dead with their tracks, maybe including some who were only wounded.

(I add to this section of my report that I made this observation in full possession of my faculties. It was later confirmed by a comrade who was also there as someone believed to be dead who saw this terrible event.)

Right after that, the remaining prisoners, about 40 men, were loaded onto a truck. The Russians were probably only able to house these 40 men and they "simply" shot the other 20 men . . . .

The Russians moved out. All was quiet on the battlefield; it must have been after midnight by then. I tried to get up and I in fact managed to move myself on. My next goal was an open field barn, about 300 meters to the east. I got there and crawled into the warming straw. Then I heard a rustling beside me; I reached for my pistol that I had stuck at my belt, but to my happy surprise, I heard a voice, "It's me!" "Who's there? I asked back. "*Jäger* Michels from the *7.Kompanie*!" "Hey, how'd you get here?" And I saw a figure scrambling out of the straw, no less astonished than I was. The guy had run east at the very beginning of the battle and was able to hide in this barn the entire time; the Russians didn't find him either. Fortunately he was not wounded. I asked him whether more comrades had gotten out and he thought that about 15-20 men had run further east. They still had to be found. I told the guy to go off quickly to look for them. He should let me continue to lie there; I didn't have any hope of getting out anyway. Though I didn't have any more pain, I appeared to have a high fever. The guy still had some water in his field canteen and gave me something to drink. "I'll stay with you, *Oberleutnant*, I won't leave you alone!" the faithful guy said.

After I had warmed up a bit, we dug in together in the straw, looked around and determined that the coast was clear. We carefully peered further east. I wasn't able to stand up very well on my feet; the guy supported me. His name was Jonny; he was 17, from Hamburg and had not gotten to the *Bataillon* until Angerburg.

In fact, we found a few survivors from the *7.Kompanie* in the afternoon in a clump of bushes. They in turn had contact with additional comrades lying in a trench in the vicinity. In the end, there were 14 of us.

It was foggy again and we decided initially to go in an easterly direction along the path. An isolated house was spotted. We wanted to find it to warm up and get something to eat if possible. It belonged to a village that was already occupied by the Russians, maybe the same unit that had attacked us that morning, but it was so far away that we dared to move in there. The Polish residents were friendly, but they were forbidden from leaving the house because they couldn't be trusted. A two-person cordon was set up that was supposed to report any danger, approach of people or anything else that was important. I moved into the warm kitchen to take a look at my wounds. It was a straight through and through. The entry wound was right next to the spinal cord and the exit wound was on the left side of my chest. The bleeding had stopped. But I had initially lost quite a bit of blood. The pain had again become noticeable in the heat. The comrades bound me up with bandages and white stuff from the linen closet of our involuntary hosts and then, sitting next to the stove, I was able to get some sleep. We wanted to move on further at night. The 14 comrades treated me as their leader quite as a matter of course in spite of my wounds. I felt this responsibility and it also gave the power to continue to hold on.

As for weapons, we still had some *Karabiner*, *Maschinenpistolen* and pistols. The ammunition was split up equally. All excess equipment and stuff we didn't need at the moment was burned. I determined that we had only two movement compasses. So only two groups could be formed because without a compass, there was absolutely no way one could think about getting through. I split up these two groups the way they were. The comrades still included a young *Fahnenjunker-Unteroffizier*, Rudi Kruck from Landsberg on the Warthe, but I didn't want to entrust a group to him. On the other hand, there was an old experienced *Obergefreiter* who could lead a group. I took over the other group, including the *Fahnenjunker*. I wrote another report addressed to the regiment, saying something along the lines of the *6.Kompanie* and *7.Kompanie* had been completely dispersed on January 23, 1945 at 8:00 a.m. 15 km southwest of Slupca (Słupca) during a Russian tank attack and that I had been wounded myself. I gave it to the *Obergefreiter* to be used if he managed to get through, while I had little hope for myself.

At about 7:00 p.m.—we had so far not been disturbed at all, we had warmed up and had regained some strength – the group under the leadership of the *Obergefreiter* left the house to start moving on a compass heading of 18 degrees. A last handshake with my comrades and they disappeared into the dark of night. I don't know whether they made it through.

I myself left the house at 7:30 with my group toward goal 16. That led across the previous day's battlefield. We wanted to at least take the identification tags from a few dead. But there was nothing more to indicate the drama that had been playing out here a few hours before. The moon shone calmly on the white fields. Suddenly there was fire from the left! We took cover and heard cries from Russians, who were, however, still a bit far from us (though it was hard to tell at night). The terrain favored disappearing quickly to the north.

We went around villages and individual farmsteads in big arcs, initially single file, far enough away that we could see each other, and then in alternating twos and threes, hooked up firmly, because we were all completely exhausted and didn't know what stresses still awaited us. Traitorous dog barking continually forced us to spend a while being motionless as "bushes." Simply sitting or kneeling camouflages one well from a few steps away; then one looks like a shrub or a clump of dirt in the moonlight. I went myself with Jonny at the front. My Bézard compass showed me the movement direction, but today the stars were also nicely disposed to be an orientation aid. How often my gaze went to the "big bear" and the North Star, how often I computed in silence: Rising moon, eight twelfths, so subtract, it's now 11:00 p.m., less eight, that gives fifteen, so the moon is where the sun is at 3:00 p.m. and the sun at 3:00 p.m. is in the southwest . . . . In such a situation, one can see the uses of a good education.

Sometimes there was a big haystack along our way, and then we rested for 15 to 30 minutes. We still had a couple of cigarettes that we smoked bit by bit. The coffee in three canteens had frozen. The fever had in the meantime led to me shivering for periods of time and I had to take care not to have my teeth chattering loudly. But we went forward relatively quickly.

A highway had to be crossed, but everything was quiet. Fresh horse dung indicated that there were horse-drawn or horse-mounted troops in the vicinity.

To the south *Panzer-Sturm-Pionier-Bataillon 'BR'* moved out of Schieratz in two columns ahead of *Jägerregiment 2 'BR'*. *Oberarzt* Dr. Perkhoff led in the front with the field ambulance to turn over two more wounded at whatever field station he could locate. "It took some effort and often hard actions to keep the *Bataillon* together in the maelstrom of retreating support units, troops and refugees" according to *Hauptmann* Müller-Rochholz. The *Bataillon* advanced 5 kilometers toward the village of Wehrbg when they came under fire by Soviet forces that crossed the Warthe to the north of Schieratz during the night and were now trying to cut off the route of withdrawal between Schieratz to Kalisch. The two columns came to a halt on the clogged road and were in a tactically vulnerable position. An attack plan was drawn up that included a two phased assault.

The *1.Pionier-Kompanie* would advance through the snow covered fields south of Kościerzyn under the command of *Oberleutnant* Bank and provide covering fire for the joint attack of *2.Pionier-Kompanie* and elements of *Sturmgeschütz-Brigade 'GD'* that would advance and capture the village of Charlupia-Mala. Thirty-minutes after drawing up the attack plan, *'Brandenburgers'* and Soviet soldiers locked in combat. Charlupia-Mala had not been occupied yet by the Soviets and they ran into the advancing *2.Pionier-Kompanie* and *Sturmgeschütze* from the south. Combat flared among the village houses. A well placed MG42 on a haystack worked effectively against the Soviets, who attempted advancing across the frozen level surface. The Soviets quickly withdrew without their horse-drawn antitank gun and without their heavy machine gun into a sunken road to the north of the village.

The *2.Pionier-Kompanie* kept its village firmly in hand. The *1.Pionier-Kompanie* had supported this attack from 2 kilometers to the west. Soon the *1.Pionier-Kompanie* received effective antitank and machine gun fire from the northwest, directly into its flank, while maneuvering across a field with no cover, sloping slightly to the north. There was no place to hide on the hard frozen soil. The Soviets were well emplaced in a stream bed and killing the exposed men of the *1.Pionier-Kompanie* one-by-one. *Hauptmann* Müller-Rochholz watched the situation develop with increasing alarm as an armored reconnaissance vehicle from *Fallschirm-Panzer-Division 1 'Hermann Göring'* pulled up and "just wanted to look at the action". Incensed, Müller-Rochholz forcibly commandeered the vehicle. The ordnance officer, *Leutnant* Bätzing, jumped in the back and at breakneck speed—continued suppressive antitank fire—and off they went straight across the frozen field to the *1.Pionier-Kompanie*.

Hauptmann Müller-Rochholz directed the reconnaissance vehicle into the streambed where the two companies of Soviet soldiers were located. The anti-tank gun on the reconnaissance vehicle could not depress low enough to fire at the Soviets in the trench so instead all the men in the vehicle were ordered to open the boxes of grenades, and *'Brandenburger'* as well as *'Hermann Göring'* soldiers alike threw them into the trenches. *Leutnant* Bätzing daringly ran up the edge to the *1.Pionier-Kompanie* and threw the first hand grenades. The *1.Pionier-Kompanie* also got up and took the stream bed by storm. The Soviets left many dead and 80 prisoners were taken in the quick action. However, on the German side, *Leutnant* Linder was killed in action, "dying as an example to his men during an assault attack". The *1.Pionier-Kompanie* lost 11 dead and a number of others wounded that day.

In the meantime, *General* von Saucken arrived at the *2.Pionier-Kompanie* where he saw the entire battle and the Soviets withdrawing west past the regiment on the horizon. This was the first time that von Saucken saw his *Pionier-Bataillon Hauptmann* in action, and was arguably impressed. The *Korps* command post, which was in the vicinity of Wehrbg, found out what had happened. *General* von Saucken took *Hauptmann* Müller-Rochholz to the *Korps* HQ. There *Hauptmann* Müller-Rochholz provided a report and was assigned the *Korps-Pionier-Bataillon* for local defense.

Sturmgeschütz-Brigade 'GD' was located at Chojne to the south of Schieratz. There it prepared for a counterattack in the morning of the 23rd to the northwest to assist *Panzer-Sturm-Pionier-Bataillon 'BR'*. *Obergefreiter* Klingenschmid's account continues:

> Formation was at 7:30 a.m. The commander explained the situation to us and noted that we were forming up for a counterattack. I then updated my diary because I had not been able to do that during the previous few days. While I was doing that, I was disturbed by *Leutnant* Greiling, who grabbed me to type some goddamned lists. However, *Leutnant* Wegener saw to it that I was released because as a *Geschütz* commander who was supposed to go into battle with his vehicle, I really had other things to worry about! And however it was, I saw myself getting back with my crew. To my surprise, my former "fire direction", *Stabsgefreiter* Wiechers, went back to the *2.Batterie* and in exchange for him, I got a loader, who had in the bargain crushed his right arm on the full deflector. My former loader was therefore supposed to do fire direction, and Paul, my driver, was horrified at that and told me that he wouldn't deploy that way. He was really agitated overall, but it was easy to explain that; the *Wehrmacht* report indicated that the Russians were at Oppeln and Deutsch-Eylau and Paul was from Upper Silesia. For the entire day, more and more Landser came in fleeting to the rear. These men had hardly slept for 8-10 days and had had nothing to eat. It was a depressing sight. In addition, we had our continued worries about the wretched fuel situation.
>
> January 23rd. We took up night quarters in a school, where we slept warm and good. Shortly after we woke up, we were told that we would be moving out at 9:30 a.m. For this purpose, we were supposed to get 20 liters of Russian fuel per *Geschütz*. Unfortunately, there was nothing more

there. We were going against the streams of fleeing columns moving to the west; we were going toward the enemy for security. During a stop, Paul suddenly got terribly bad, and he couldn't go any further. He also appeared to be at the end of his rope. *Gefreiter* Diebig (*2.Battrie*), with whom I was already familiar from Guben as a recruit, took over from him. In addition, I got Gunner Knauder from Kolberg, who took over from the wounded loader. After we filled up with 50 liters from a fallen *Geschütz*, we followed *Leutnant* Wegener with four *Geschütz* into a village about 2 km away from the highway. The name was Charlupia-Mala, which could be translated as "little village of huts". We suddenly got antitank fire and *Leutnant* Wegener was hit three times on his front right away. It was a small caliber, so the shells bounced off. We moved apart from each other, going left and right, and went into position for an attack. Then came the *2.Pionier-Kompanie* of the *Pz.Stu.Pi.Btl.* 'BR' as infantry reinforcement, and we did a forward thrust with them. The antitank positions, well camouflaged behind snow fences, were quickly found using the fire from their barrels and handled in an instant. *Obergefreiter* Wolski, the good shot who was *Leutnant* Wegener's "fire direction," did the lion's share of it. The Russians were now attacking with infantry. In the background, there was a horse-drawn column coming along pleasantly, its silhouettes clear against the sky. The estimated distance was about 1,000 meters. I told my new "fire direction" that he could now show whether he understood the craft. I had him aim at the first team towing a gun and gave the command to fire. The first shot was way too short, but the second hit the target. Now I put the last team under fire and then all the ones in between. There was a nice shootout. This bunch of Ivans would never again be deployed! Now I saw the Russian infantry come out of a low spot in the ground o my left and then disappear into a side road. I took a look at the site myself and went with a high explosive shell in the meantime. Unfortunately, there were no more Russians to be seen there, but they were still moving forward because shortly thereafter, there was an exchange of hand grenades between a security group of engineers and them. The two groups of forces were unfortunately jammed up too much against each other, so I no longer dared to fire the cannons. I grabbed my *Zielfernrohrgewehre* (Scissor Scope) and picked out some Russians getting up to fire it at. Shortly thereafter, Ivan got out and moved back into a village in the background. Unfortunately, this battle cost us four more dead. In the evening, we took up a position at the exit to the town. Shortly thereafter, there was some more movement in front of us. The Russians moved forward again. About 50-100 meters in front of us, there were about 100 dark points in the snow. In spite of the darkness, they stood out clearly recognizable against the snow. Heavy grenade launchers went behind me into position and used individual shots to always take out the forward shapes. I then called to them in Russian to come over to us. One after another, they stood up and looked over until a commanding voice rang out with, "Down you . . . (typical Russian cuss word)," in response to which they lay down again and stayed lying down silent in the snow all night.

The battalions of *Jägerregiment 2 'BR'* around Schieratz evacuated their defensive positions with the arrival of *Gruppe Nehring* along the Warthe to the south. They now moved toward Ostrowo—almost peacefully—after being relieved. However, Soviet forces moved into the area along the main roadway running east-west. The Soviets crossed the Warthe at night to the north of the German positions, as previously noted, and attempted to cut the retreat path of *Panzer-Korps 'GD'* and *Gruppe Nehring*. Fighting occurred as elements of *Pz.Stu.Pi.-Btl. 'BR'* and *Sturmgeschütz-Brigade 'GD'* fought the Soviets to clear a section of the road blocked by Soviet forces. *Jägerregiment 2 'BR'* moved south of the area, then west, rejoining the main road and continuing the withdrawal. During the early afternoon, *1.Kompanie* of *Jägerregiment 2 'BR'* reached Stören (Zamaay). They soon found this village also occupied by the Soviets. Fighting broke out, and *Oberleutnant* Wirth, the company commander was seriously wounded and died the following night. The first attack was called off. Both the *1.Kompanie* and *2.Kompanie* of *Jägerregiment 2 'BR'* joined with strength of about 90 soldiers under the command of *Oberfähnrich* Albers to attack the Soviets a second time. Assistance came in the form of two *Sturmgeschütze* from *Pz.Jäg.Abt. 'BR'* under the command of *Leutnant* Kass, and *Leutnant* Stalf's *7.Kompanie* that led the assault. The late afternoon attack was successful. The town of Stören was taken from the Soviets and the road west reopened. The price was heavy as twelve other 'Brandenburgers' were wounded and *Leutnant* Langer and *Oberfähnrich* Albers were both killed.

A large part of *Panzergrenadier-Division 'BR'* now passed through Stören and moved into the large town of Kalisz or Schwarzau by early evening. Security was set up but everyone was exhausted and the sentries soon fell asleep. During the late night hours three Soviet reconnaissance armored personnel carriers drove straight into the town's marketplace without detecting any German forces along the way. Elements of *Jägerregiment 2 'BR'* were awoken by their noisy arrival in the night and understood what happened. The Soviet armored personnel carriers were knocked-out with *Panzerfausts*.

Gruppe Nehring spent most of the day recuperating and re-distributing fuel and ammunition. By late afternoon they set out west toward Ostrowo along the main road from Schieratz-Kalisz. With the on-going fighting between 'Brandenburg' and the Soviets for control of the main road underway, *Gruppe Nehring* took an alternative route south through Iwanowice, across the frozen marsh toward Olobok, then across the frozen Prosna. The early evening movement soon turned into an all-night withdrawal to the area south of Opatowek (Spatenfelde). There, *Generalmajor* von Necker's *Panzergrenadier-Regiment* of the *Fallschirm-Panzer-Division 1 'Hermann Göring'* met with officers of *Panzer-Korps 'GD'* met. This was the first time that elements of 'Hermann Göring' and the *Korps* met since the deployment to Litzmannstadt nearly two weeks ago. News was received that units of *Panzer-Korps 'GD'* and the *19.Panzer-Division* were south and southwest of Kalisch (Kalisz), which was occupied by the enemy. This information was likely incorrect, as accounts put the units of *Panzer-Korps 'GD'* farther north along the road to Kalisch. In the confused situation behind enemy lines, information on Soviet whereabouts was crucial, as incorrect information could quickly lead to a prisoner-of-war camp or even death.

Wednesday, January 24th

As the units of 'Brandenburg' withdrew west they noticed that throughout the towns and villages they passed were cheerful banners and garlands hung by the Polish residents for the advancing Red Army. These images certainly weighed heavy on the minds of the German soldiers who knew they were already well behind the Soviet forward lines. The prewar German border was their goal. Only after crossing the Oder then Neisse Rivers could they finally rest.

Some 90 kilometers north of the main body of 'Brandenburg' and *Gruppe Nehring* was *Kampfgruppe Röseke*. Cut off behind Soviet lines, and operating without any communication to higher HQ, the men were no longer a tactical military unit. They broke into small groups of survivalists working their way west in the hope to avoid Soviet capture and reach German lines. Röseke's account continues:

> Shortly before daybreak, we came to a canal with steep concrete banks. Crossing this obstacle cost us lots of strength and time.
>
> When it was light, we found an isolated house, very close to what appeared to be a large forest [AN: likely the hamlet of Linden]. If there weren't any Russians there, we wanted to spend the day there and especially have a couple of hours of sleep. It was not advisable to move during the day because there were more and more open spaces, roads and other dangerous places that had to be passed. It was also to be feared that Polish civilians and partisans were hunting dispersed German soldiers.
>
> The house was occupied by a Polish family that was willing to take us in. We moved into the

roomy living room and took all the necessary precautions. First of all, the Poles were forbidden to leave the house. In addition, a two-person guard force was assigned, but they couldn't set up in front of the house. Instead they looked through two windows to the east and the west.

We used hot coffee, sausage and bread to get strengthened. I had stabbing pains and a high fever again, but I was able to sleep a bit on a bed without unfastening anything. For noon, we had "ordered" chicken soup and the lady of the house already had it cooking but at about noon, the sentry looking to the east yelled out, "The Russians are coming!"

I went up to the window and saw about 15-20 riders, just about to move to the house from about 150 meters away. Only the side to the forest was still open. But before we managed to leave the house through the window on that side, we heard horse hooves and neighing on the front part. Some Russians got off and pushed their way through the door into the house. All seven of us stood in the living room with our weapons in our hands. We no longer had time to think about what to do; all we knew was that we had to defend ourselves to the end.

Faster than it can be described, the following happened; the living room door was kicked in, and a big guy, a white fur chapka with a red Soviet star on his head and a submachine gun at his waist, was standing in front of us; he saw us and fired immediately. I saw the fire coming out right in front of me and I got a blow against my right shoulder. At the same moment, however, I fired my pistol and hit the Russian, who was two meters away, in the belly. He fell forward to the floor with a roar, throwing his weapon away, and I was also thrown to the floor by the shot and now lay next to him. The people with him had left the house in a panic, jumped on their horses and ridden off, apparently not counting on our heavy opposition. In the meantime, my comrades, fortunately none of whom were wounded (my shot had hit the Russian at just the time he fired, so all he hit with his firing was me, while the remaining shots went upward into the ceiling), had torn out the back window with the strength that the danger of the moment lent them, taking the window frame out of the wall in the process, and left the building to reach the nearby forest—a bare 50 meters away. They considered me dead during the first moment.

In the meantime, while still lying next to the Russian, who was now moaning terribly, I attempted to reload my pistol because the cartridge had gotten stuck, but my right arm and my right hand weren't working at all. A nerve in my shoulder had been hit, my arm and my hand were completely stiff, and the pistol stayed put as if it were in a vise. I tried to undo it with the left hand, but that one as well was unusable because of my wounds from the previous day. Outside I heard more shooting and yelling. In this hopeless situation and in the feat that I would fall into Russian hands while wounded, the only possibility I saw for avoiding this fate was to shoot myself.

With my last strength, I took my small 7.65 mm pistol out of my camouflage blouse with my left hand, took it off safety, held it next to my temple and pulled the trigger. But the weapon failed. I pulled again, but no shot went off.

At this moment, I heard a voice calling from the window, "*Oberleutnant*, get going, get out!" and one of my comrades was back with me in the living room. He picked me up and took me to the window. At the edge of the forest, the other 5 men had gotten into position and were firing "out of all the keyholes" to keep the Russians, who wanted to get closer to the house again, back.

Things went dark before my eyes, but I was able to stand on my feet. I used all my strength to get to the edge of the forest—and I was saved!

But we couldn't stay long. The Russians were already moving under the cover of the house. Fortunately the forest had some thick underbrush. We moved back, up a cliff, going ever deeper into the forest. With their horses, the Russians couldn't follow us, but we didn't know how big the forest was and we had to count on them surrounding it. After half an hour of tiring movement through the brush, we took a rest.

We comrades silently shook hands and I am not ashamed to admit that I had tears in my eyes. The two wounds—my seventh and my eighth one—had rendered me almost incapable of fighting; to start with, I could not move either my right or my left arm. My hope of getting through was diminishing again and I told the men that they should leave my lying there because I didn't want to be a burden to them getting through further. But the brave guys didn't think about leaving me in the lurch.

When I investigated my small pistol, which had failed so, I determined that . . . it was missing a firing pin! It appeared that a *Kompanie* headquarters section messenger (probably *Gefreiter* Kagerer) who had had the pistol in Angerburg for cleaning had either lost it or forgotten to put it back in. This foolishness would have also had bad consequences if I had needed the weapon for defense, but in this case, this notable stroke of fate had saved my life. Even if I hadn't been repeatedly convinced in the previous years of the war that our fate lay in the hands of God and that this knowledge also gave upright soldiers the spiritual strength to hold on, this experience would have opened my eyes, because I am sure that it was not just a random coincidence.

We moved through the forest, which was now lighter, continuing on toward target 16. It was bitter cold on this January day. My right hand, which I could now move a bit and in which I held the compass, was getting stiffer; after all, it had second-degree frostbite. Our lips were chapped by the strong wind. Our external appearance was already shameful, but this wasn't the time to think about that.

We dared to leave the forest when it was still daylight. Right in the vicinity of a small palace occupied by the Russians, which with its baroque style stood out like a sore thumb in this landscape (I made such observations in jest while we were still in our terrible situation), we went across an open area with large distances between one man and the next.

In the late afternoon, however, we were in front of a wide north-south highway, heavily occupied by vehicles and pedestrians. There was clearly a fairly large city very close by. [AN: this was likely Liebenstädt]. Because we had no map, we had no idea as to where we were. All we knew was that movement goal no. 16 would have to take us somewhere on German soil.

We had to wait for night and we hid in a fir forest. Suddenly we heard steps and rustling right next to us. It was two German *Landser*, *Luftwaffe* soldiers, older men. They, like us, had made their way through from the area of Litzmannstadt and asked to join us. I really wasn't keen about granting this request because the fewer of us there were, the better our chances of making it. But because the two of them promised to stay with us and obey me, I took them in. First, however, they were "stripped." They had thick rucksacks with them with all sorts of things from their caserne in Litzmannstadt. I had to separate them from this stuff, because our further efforts required traveling light. They also had food still and I declared that one part of that was an "iron portion" for all of us.

At about 6:00 p.m., we left our hiding place and approached the highway. However, there was still a lot on it and we had to go back from our location on the edge of the forest across about 200 meters of open terrain to the road and from there a good bit further into the forest on the other side. I sent *Oberjäger* Kruch to scope out the terrain, and he returned after a short time with the news that there was a trench along the road in the vicinity and that it probably emptied into a canal undercrossing. We had to use this capability. We could crawl through it to a long distance away. For me this was unspeakably stressful; it was continually dark before my eyes and to my dismay I determined that I was coughing up blood. My right lung had apparently been hit at noon. I needed almost an hour to crawl the 200 meters to the road embankment. The trench did indeed feed into a canal pipe, but the pipe was blocked up. So we had to sprint across the road one at a time, always waiting until there was no vehicle to be heard. We went back through the piece of open terrain on the other side and reached a corner of the forest that way, where we were all together at about 9:00 p.m.

A forest road was going in the same direction as we were and we used it although fresh footprints and vehicle tracks were visible in the snow. After half an hour underway, we saw a light very close by but a bit to the side. It was an isolated house in the middle of the forest and from a huge set of antlers over the door, we saw that it must be a forester's dwelling. We knocked on the window from which the light was shining and waited with pistols with the safety off, always expecting to be greeted by Russians. But it was only the forester with his family in the house; however, as a precaution, I had everything carefully searched because you never know . . . . The people were friendly and glad that we were "only" Germans. They were afraid of the Russians. We again had a warm room, coffee, bread and potatoes. When the old man saw that I was wounded, he grabbed a bottle of schnapps. It raised our spirits again and it was nearly like having a round sitting around the round table in the Polish forester's house. Someone suddenly started with a song and soon we were singing quietly, "The road back to our homeland is far—so far. The old times are there with the stars over the edge of the forest. Every brave engineer secretly yearns for them, but the road back to the homeland is far." But a soldier's life is unique: blood, dirt, cold, hunger and lice threaten to bring you down – then you find a little warmth, a piece of bread and a swig of schnapps and then everything is good again and you continue to sing and smile . . . . Of course we set up a sentry, but everything was calm and the forester also thought that the house was so out of the way that no Russians could be expected tonight. Soon we lay down to sleep! The Forester even offered me his bed and there was nothing more for me to do than to lie down in it in my uniform and my boots. At 1:00 a.m., we wanted to move out again because I had seen on a map, which was, however, only 1:25,000, that the forester showed me that we would first have to cross a big open area of fields in the west before we were back in a large forest. We wanted to put this open area behind us while it was still night. However, it cost untold effort to get out of sleep again and it wasn't until 3:00 a.m. when we moved out. Besides, the forester wanted to keep me with him, pretend I was his son in law and nurse me back to health—but I wanted to stay with my comrades.

Due to losses and ineffective command-and-control it was decided that the *1.Kompanie* and *2.Kompanie* of *Jägerregiment 2 'BR'* be consolidated and taken over by *Oberleutnant* Gutweniger who was formerly from the *I.Bataillon*. At about 7:00 a.m., the units of *I.Btl./Jäg.Rgt. 2 'BR'* withdrew from Stören to Steinfelde, northwest of Schwarzau, where they turned west off the main road and follow the mass of withdrawing German forces toward Ostrowo.

Panzer-Sturm-Pionier-Bataillon 'BR' and the attached *Panzer-Pionier-Bataillon 500 'GD'* received fuel during the night while moving northwest. Soviets were again encountered on the main highway heading west toward Opatowek/Kalisch. As *Unteroffizier* Hans Stübling recalled: "Oesterwitz [*Jäg.Rgt. 2 'BR'*] and Metzger [*Stug-Brig. 'GD'*] fought their way free again, and off we went! The Reconnaissance Platoon reported that directly behind us there was one T-34 after another rolling down the highway toward Kalisch. We passed the *Sturmgeschütz-Brigade 'GD'*. We had contact again and felt better, in a union with our assault artillery personnel."

The now combined force of *Pioniers* and assault guns of the attached *Sturmgeschütz-Brigade 'GD'* left the main highway and took to the secondary roads, driving cross-country toward the city of Ostrowo. Along the way they advanced through the local hills reaching a large regional town of Chełmce. These units were now in the lead of *'Brandenburg'*, while other elements of *Gruppe Nehring* were already advancing along available routes west. *Hauptmann* Müller-Rochholz's account of the fighting continues:

Going via Chełmce, which with its church on the high mountains dominated the landscape for miles around, we went straight west. From Chełmce, we saw the Russian moving in long columns parallel to us to the north.

But there was also another threat from the south as well. Ostrowo was in Russian hands. Metzger and I received an order from *Oberstleutnant i.G.* Erasmus to cordon off Ostrowo from the north and west in order to secure the northern passage of *Panzer-Korps 'Großdeutschland'*.

The *1.Pionier-Kompanie* and the command staff got off at Metzger's location. We drove north to the western exit from Ostrowo. The Reconnaissance Platoon was out in front having a firefight with Soviet trucks. They were a rear guard for the enemy tanks that were already moving further west. The Reconnaissance Platoon was handling such minor matters by itself. We took the *Sturmgeschütze* to the western edge of Ostrowo without any further enemy contact. Metzger and I set up a command post in a small park. The *1.Pionier-Kompanie* and *2.Pionier-Kompanie* got the order to occupy the eastern edge of a suburb (according to the map). However, the suburb and the city of Ostrowo had already merged into each other. While the Soviets were looting German supply trains 1,500 meters to our south, the *2.Pionier-Kompanie* was occupying its position to the right. Bank suddenly sent a report from the railway station, where the Soviets were fueling up. Because we were much too weak to fight in a city and also wanted to use Metzger's *Sturmgeschütze*, the *1.Pionier-Kompanie* was withdrawn. There were a lot of problems with snipers; there were also Poles shooting from under the roofing tiles. Sometime about the afternoon, we had put up screening lines that were to some extent tactically sufficient, but thin, very thin. Too many houses and gardens. The Soviets continually fought with T-34s and JS-IIs. As far as I know, three T-34s were knocked-out, one with a *Panzerfaust*. One *Sturmgeschütze* was knocked-out by a JS-2, which could not be seen behind its house. The men were dead. However, my German shepherd bitch, who was my true comrade the entire war, remained.

A Russian armored reconnaissance vehicle buzzed us, coming from the west through friendly lines. It was traveling at full speed, firing out of all its openings. We were ashamed and ran away. The streets were blocked against this nonsense using gasoline containers lying around empty everywhere. Shortly before that, *Feldwebel* Gräter, the driver of the team command *SPW*, did a showpiece exhibition. From Ostrowo, two Studebakers broke through to the west at high speed. There were civilians in them. No one knew whether they were friendly or enemy cars. I went with Gräter on his B-Krad right up to the *1.Pionier-Kompanie* again. We saw the cars as well. Gräter looked at me questioningly; they were after all coming from the *1.Pionier-Kompanie*. I looked to the right and shots rang out. The B-Krad was no longer there; Gräter was shooting with his machine pistol. Two shots were fired. Two small holes in the windshield of the first Studebaker. We had seven prisoners, one car full of fuel, and one full of tank ammunition. The most important thing was that we had two drivable cars, certainly selected to be good, because they didn't go looking for old jalopies for this penetration. (These cars were later to perform another noble purpose. In Zietenfelde a wine cellar—a storage facility for the Reich Ministry of Foreign Affairs— awaited us and now we had transport facilities and fuel for this unusual situation!)

It was dark and dicey. Everywhere there was movement. There was shooting in front of us and behind us. Metzger and I looked at each other worried. The order read, "Stay put until 2:00 a.m." Neighboring villages in the north had been on fire for hours. To our south and in the rear, the Soviets were at the railway line. At about 1:30 a.m., we started moving, carefully. There was always a machine gun everywhere, a couple of men with a *Sturmgewehr* at every *Sturmgeschütze* and we regularly just oozed back and gathered in the park near the command post. Then suddenly all hell broke loose right where we were sitting. Red light signals more and more. The Russians, probably led by Poles, had infiltrated in multiple places. Five minutes of panic. Everyone was firing. But we got the last vehicles out, including the two that got stuck; we got in them about 1,000 meters west and off we went again to the west. *Sturmgeschütz-Brigade 'GD'* and *Panzer-Sturm-Pionier-Bataillon 'BR'*; we liked to fight together. And it always worked.

The following morning found this combined force of *'Brandenburgers'* on the main road between Ostrowo and Krotoschin.

The following account covers the experience from the perspective of the rear of the column observed by *Fahnenjunker-Unteroffizier* Held-Kleingründlach of *Sturmgeschütz-Brigade 'GD'*:

At 4:30 a.m., we changed our position without being noticed and got onto the highway as the last vehicle in the division. We slowly went back to it. On my own responsibility, I took a prime mover with *Flak-Geschütz* to the *Heeres-Flak-Artillerie-Abteilung*, which had remained behind all by itself. To do that, I had to go back into no man's land, which was not looked upon very favorably. But how happy the guys from the crew were when the engine turned over after 1 km and they could move on their own power! But now my engine was running worse again. The picture on the road was typical of a retreat. There were an awful lot of blown-up and intact vehicles in the ditches to our left and our right. That was a great misfortune for *Leutnant* Wegener! It started with the track breaking, and then he couldn't be pulled up onto the slippery iced road anymore. The *Geschütz* was hooked up for towing and after a short time went down the embankment and unfortunately hit a tree so hard that the left drive gear broke. It had to be blown up! That was a powerful blow to us. We passed the place where the Russians had occupied the highway and our fuel column didn't go any further. It looked great there. Dead Russians were lying with their machine guns and antitank guns as if they had been mown down. This included a lot burned to a crisp. "How did they get caught", I wondered? [AN: this was likely the work of the advancing *Pz.Jäg.Abt. 'BR'* or *Panzer-Sturm-Pionier-Bataillon 'BR'*]. At a place named Schwarzau, we settled in and went back into secure position. On this occasion, I met an old acquaintance whom I had served with back in the *2.Batterie I.Btl./Art.Rgt.'GD' (Le.F.H. 18)*. It was *Leutnant* Steidl from Bodenbach-Mittelgrund. The fact that the Russians were breathing down our neck was something we noticed immediately. I had barely checked the tracks and the ammunition when the shooting started again.

To the left and right of the road, they were continuing to attack with infantry, while in the background, they were getting into position with near big haystacks. I opened fire at 800 meters and killed two heavy machine guns that the Russians were dragging behind them. Then I handled an antitank gun before it could get set up. Our defensive fire was magnificently supported by a SPW *Leutnant* [from *I.(gep)Btl./Jäg.Rgt 1 'BR'*] who cleaned out enemy riflemen extremely effectively with his rapid cannon fire. The guy really had guts, because he, like the last three of us *Geschütz* were still on a wide stretch of ground and the first artillery shots were hitting the village.

When I was routinely looking through the scissor sight at the terrain, the highway was running through my field of view and then everything was really dicey for me. Specifically, there was one T-34 after another rolling towards us. I had a couple more shots fired at the lead tank and then we all got away from the enemy; at the same time I fired off an entire belt with the MG42 on the Russian infantry that had in the meantime gotten really close. As the last *Geschütz*, I was again bringing up the rear of the *Division*. Enroute, I ran into groups of released and wounded *Landser* who had lost their units. I had my people stop several times and took them with me. These looks from their eyes were something I couldn't forget and many of them thanked me with both hands before they said goodbye after we had hooked up with the big group. Although the crew grumbled because of the torsion bars being overloaded, everyone was full of joy and satisfaction afterwards. After stopping once again for security, we went into position in a town that was characterized by its mountain church. There was practically nothing left in the fuel container. I went off to division headquarters with a couple of canisters and ran into *Major* Spaeter there. He was the *Ib* for *General* von Schulte-Heuthaus. I explained the situation to him and how terrible our fuel situation was. With his approval, I was able to get five canisters and I felt decidedly better. While it was still night, about 1:00 a.m., we moved again without the enemy contact. While we were moving, there was a tragic accident. A *Sturmgeschütz* from *Pz.Abt. 7* and the infantry in it slid off a bridge [over the Prosna River] and flipped over into the water. *Leutnant* Wegener attempted to extract them using his vehicle. Five men from the infantry in it were retrieved alive. Right after that, we and additional *Sturmgeschütz* came. With our combined efforts, we managed first to get the *Geschütz* onto its tracks and drag it into shallow water. Two men in the crew were still alive.

The units of *Panzer-Korps 'GD'* and *Gruppe Nehring* advanced west across the frozen Prosna to the area of Altskalden (Skalmierzyce), halfway between Ostrowo and Kalisch. The standing orders from von Nehring were simple: head west toward the city of Lissa and avoid combat when possible. The Prosna bridge crossing south of Kalisch was kept open, defended, and later blown up by the *Panzer-Pioniere 19* of *Generalleutnant* Hans Källner's *19.Panzer-Division*.

Thursday, January 25th

Gruppe Nehring continued movement by foot and horse-drawn units under the command of *Generalleutnant* Hohn. All motorized vehicles and *Panzers* were now subordinated to *Panzer-Korps 'GD'* and placed under the command of von Saucken. *Panzer-Korps 'GD'* led the withdrawal west of the combined force sometimes referred to as *Gruppe Saucken*. Von Saucken's headquarters was in the vicinity of Raschkow (Raszkow). Among the units subordinated were *Panzergrenadier-Division 'BR'*, *Fallschirm-Panzer-Division 1 'Hermann Göring'*, *16.Panzer-Division*, *19.Panzer-Division*, *20.Panzergrenadier-Division* and the *Von Ahlfen Sperrverband*. Elements of *'Brandenburg'* led the vanguard, while other units operated in the rear of the main body of *Panzer-Korps 'GD'*. *Gruppe Nehring* followed. This loose organization did not mean that the main body of forces was conducting its withdrawal in any tactical sense reminiscent of an organized maneuver. Units were operating largely independent of each other at the battalion level or below. Communications was near non-existent. Information about Soviet troop movement or impassible roads were passed by motorcycle couriers, or more frequently through word of mouth as one unit passed another along the road. The situation changed kilometer-by-kilometer. A town that one unit passed through hours before could quickly became occupied and defended by a Soviet unit, forcing the following German units to divert around into the unknown. German combat formations routinely became lost or separated. Commanders had to make quick, often independent decisions to ensure their survival.

In one example *Fallschirm-Panzer-Division 1 'HG'* found itself under considerable Soviet pressure. *Generalmajor* von Necker ordered its remaining Panthers to conduct a rear guard action while the rest of the division continued its withdrawal west. *Oberfähnrich* Wolfgang Hartlet, a platoon leader in *Panzer-Regiment 1 'HG'* organized the defense with his remaining five Panthers of the battalion. He was attacked by an armored force of T-34s and in the process of his defense claimed to have knocked-out some 25 Soviet tanks. These were possibly from the Soviet 93rd Separate Tank Brigade of the 4th Guards Tank Army. More importantly, his rear guard action allowed the division to withdraw ahead of the advancing Soviets. This action earned him the Knight's Cross, which he received on February 23rd, 1945.[5] The westward withdrawal of *Panzer-Korps 'GD'* and *Gruppe Nehring* consisted of numerous small units actions like this. Desperate men fighting desperate battles, most of which have been lost to history.

To the north of the main force, *Kampfgruppe Röseke's* evasion and survival across the Polish farmland continues:

---

5   *Oberfähnrich* Hartlet's award citation read: "On 25 January 1945, *Oberfähnrich* Hartlet with 5 Panthers was forming the rear guard of the division, when the rear guard, while on the road march, was attacked by 25 enemy T-34s. On his own decision, the *Oberfähnrich* attacked the five-fold superior enemy and at the head of his company destroyed all attacking tanks. With this action the number of enemy tanks knocked out under his command increased to 59, of which he personally knocked out 17." Glantz, p. 636.

We moved on through the forest, which had a thick coat of snow here. The moon was bright and we used a road sketch that *Oberjäger* Kruch had made from the forester's measurement table sheet.

Suddenly I noticed—I was just thinking about how long we had already been traveling—that the previous day, January 24th, was my 24th birthday! Exactly the unfortunate day that just missed becoming my dying day by a hair's breadth. My comrades congratulated me when I told them that and we were all somehow impressed by this irony of fate.

However, we were soon so exhausted by the movement in the deep snow that we had to rest every 15 minutes. We threw ourselves into the snow dead tired and it always took a hard struggle with ourselves to get back on our feet. I myself was getting worse and worse; breathing the bitter cold air caused stabbing pains in my right lung, which had been shot. I also had not had any proper wound treatment yet, especially no tetanus shot, and I had to worry about getting tetanus cramps. But when I somehow felt from the statements and the behavior of some comrades that they did not want to give up their faith that we would make it through, I got new strength.

When I wonder now, right after these difficult days in Poland, what gave me the ability to hold on and what gave me physical strength that I would never have imagined I had, I must say that some of it was the fear of becoming a prisoner of the Russians, but especially it was the responsibility I had as the leader of this group of eight dispersed soldiers and the more doubts that arose from my comrades, the stronger my will was to see my homeland with them again.

Burning thirst tortured me and I started eating snow even though I knew that it would hurt me. An animal that was wounded, but not fatally, would also undoubtedly instinctively behave properly, but Homo sapiens loses all his sense when he's really "done." And we were "fucked."

We did not manage to put the open agricultural land I was talking about behind us. We were not at the edge of the forest until morning was breaking. A farmer's house right next to the forest into which we wanted to move turned out to be still occupied by the enemy at the last minute. At any rate, there were a couple of Russian baggage trucks in the yard. After we had looked through my good spyglass one after another to evaluate the terrain as to what to do next, we decided to press on immediately. In the distance we could already see the big forest that was supposed to take us in.

Walking two at a time out of the forest with 300 meters between groups, we ventured out into the open area. We crossed several paths, a single-track railway line and a canal. A few houses and three villages were visible in the vicinity. But we weren't noticed. We came closer and closer to the forest and then suddenly came across two bicyclists, apparently civilians, who stopped right in front of us, turned around and rode away toward the nearest village, about 1 km away. We had to assume that both of them had recognized us as Germans and now wanted to betray us to the Russians, who were undoubtedly in this village. So double time, as hard as it was! So we fortunately reached the forest, but before the last person could crawl into it, we could already see a troop of horsemen coming from the village. It was high time! Unfortunately the forest was initially very light, not an obstacle even for horsemen. Shots rang out over our heads into the trees. We ran for our lives! The patch of forest in which we were turned out to be very narrow; it was probably just an extension of the big forest that we saw on the map. So we had to turn north, which cost us valuable time. The horsemen had already arrived at the edge of the forest, but they stopped there. Fortunately we got to a sort of nursery planted with young trees. We found cover there and were able to catch our breath there. But we had to go on before the Russians took up the chase again. We tore through the forest like hunted game. Suddenly there was engine noise right next to us! A road crossed the forest here and we recognized while we were standing as if rooted to the spot that there was clearly a truck with Russians in it and a few riflemen on motorcycles— apparently also on the hunt for us! So this was the situation: the horsemen behind us, motorized enemy in front of us, the village to our right, and another stretch of open field to our left, about

300 meters to the next edge of a forest. So there was nothing more to do than to run there. But immediately after we left the forest, we were recognized by the motorized Russians. The truck approached us, the Russians jumped out and they took up the hunt by foot. But more and more of them remained behind, because we were already close to the edge of the forest on the other side. The runners couldn't shoot and those remaining behind would have hit their own comrades had they opened fire. In addition, we had split up into three groups spreading apart from each other. That was definitely the proper behavior, but unfortunately it dispersed us again. We all reached the forest and immediately attempted to get deep into it. I was alone when I ran into two comrades later and two other comrades, including *Oberjäger* Kruch, ran into us. We never saw the other comrades and I don't know whether they made it through.

When we were somewhat in safety and did not have to worry about being chased further, we initially had a bit of rest. I coughed up some more blood but otherwise I was sort of "in sorts". Fortunately, I was also able to raise my left arm halfway again and raise my right arm far enough that I could at least hold my pistol.

We had to cross a busy forest road again, but thanks to the thick underbrush on both sides of the road, that didn't pose a problem. In the afternoon, we reached an isolated farmstead in a clearing. We approached it cautiously, made shrewder by our experience so far. An ethnic German farmer and his family lived there. We were glad to be well treated but the people made us promised to leave their farm because they were afraid of being turned in by the neighbors. They had to expect to be chased out of there anyway. But we got some bread. In another nearby farmstead we attempted to warm up, but the Poles set their dogs on us. The curs were shot and we hurried to get back into the forest.

A beautiful broad forest road led in the direction we were moving. From time to time, we ran into individual vehicles or pedestrians and we preferred to hide on the other side of the road until they had passed.

When night fell, we found a small farmhouse at the edge of the forest, more a cottage, occupied by an old woman, her daughter and the daughter's infant. The people were friendly and put us up; they cooked some soup and gave us milk and bread. We wanted to treat ourselves to a couple of hours of rest. I got into one of the beds, not exactly white as snow. My wounds—two entry and two exit—were burning bad and the fever was making me shake. Jonny cooled my forehead with wet cloths so I was able to get to sleep. Suddenly however, the young woman with her infant came into my bed and that was the end of the rest.

We got out of there again before it was even midnight. It couldn't be far from here to the Warthe River, but we had to cross it again. We wanted to do that while it was still night.

Jägerregiment 2 'BR' advanced west with apparent little knowledge of the events unfolding to their front. They did not know that Ostrowo was occupied by Soviets and that *Panzer-Sturm-Pionier-Bataillon 'BR'* had already tried to cordon off the city, then simply moved around and headed west the day before. The *II.Bataillon* entered the city in the early morning hours to find it occupied by Soviets. The *Jägers* quickly fought their way out west on the move, apparently having surprised the Soviets who thought that there were no more Germans approaching from the east. Krotoschin was occupied by Soviets and *Jägerregiment 2 'BR'* moved south of the city, passing through Kobylin (Koppelstadt) and settling into Zietenfelde (Smolice) by the afternoon. *Pz.Jäg.Abt. 'BR'* passed to the north of Ostrowo heading west, intermittently on its own and at other times among the columns of withdrawing *Gruppe Nehring*. They also passed south of Krotoschin, moved through Kobylin and reached Zietenfelde soon after *Jägerregiment 2 'BR'*. The roads between Ostrowo and Kobylin were surprisingly free of Soviets, though they were present to the north and south.

Panzer-Sturm-Pionier-Bataillon 'BR' reached Zietenfelde in the late afternoon. Zietenfelde now became a stopping point for many units of *Panzer-Korps 'GD'*. The artillery of *Fallschirm-Panzer-Division 1 'HG'* settled into the southern part of the town while most of *Jägerregiment 2 'BR'* under *Oberstleutnant* Oesterwitz settled into the northern part. *Hauptmann* Müller-Rochholz forbade occupation of the palace that contained wonderful artistic treasures in marvelous condition. Only a few officers from *'Hermann Göring'* took up residence there. The Reconnaissance Platoon was given little time to rest. As the rest of the *Panzergrenadier-Division 'BR'* and *Panzer-Korps 'GD'* settled in for the evening, the Reconnaissance Platoon was ordered to screen to the south. The next day's withdrawal toward German lines was to be southwest. *Unteroffizier* Hans Stübling describes the events that unfolded in Zietenfelde:

As evening came, Dr. Perkhoff reported that there was an extremely good stock of alcoholic delicacies in the palace in Zietenfelde. In the estate's distillery, we had already filled up our tanks with 97% alcohol. Although it let the engines run hot, that was better than not having any more fuel.

Now the more noble gifts of Zietenfelde were visited. Right away, the stocks were confiscated in the name of the *Panzer-Korps 'GD'* for field hospitals. One full *Kübelwagon* went off to each of the *Sanitäts-Kompanien*, Oesterwitz, Metzger, etc. Then Müller-Rochholz went to the division and took them their share of the loot, but a prime selection was also taken to *General* von Saucken and I confessed that I had taken it upon myself to confiscate it in the name of the *Korps*. *General* von Saucken appeared initially to not be amused, but the vintages must have brought him around. Napoleon from 1811, Cognac and wine from 1894, 1904 and 1921. The units of the *Pionier-Bataillon* took their shares with a promise that they would order a 'drinking day' as soon as the situation allowed. We wrangled some as well. The stuff remaining was put on a Studebaker (Gräter's most important steps from Ostrowo!) because of the cold in the fertilizer. These were supplies that the Ministry of Foreign Affairs had stored there. Thanks a lot!

During the evening, five Soviet armored reconnaissance vehicles moved unrecognized along the main road from Kobylin into Zietenfelde. Most of the German soldiers were asleep—passed out from exhaustion or alcohol—and two of the Soviet vehicles drove through the town heading west. The *Jägers* of II.Btl./Jäg.Rgt. 2 'BR' soon realized what occurred and quickly closed in on the remaining three, destroying them with *Panzerfaust*.

The majority of *Sturmgeschütz-Brigade 'GD'* was northeast of Ostrowo in the early morning hours. A relief flight of JU-52s arrived, landing in a makeshift runway at Hirschweide (Jelitow). The historical record is not clear how this aerial relief was coordinated, but they brought both ammunition and desperately needed fuel as described by *Fahnenjunker-Unteroffizier* Held-Kleingründlach:

The crew was still alive. Through the masses of *Landser* streaming back, some of them very demoralized, we came upon a field airstrip, where we loaded up some Ju-52 transport aircraft with the wounded. In Hirschweide, we went into a secure posture again and moved into a Polish farmhouse. The family spoke good German and Stascha, the daughter of the house, took care to make everything as nice as possible for us. She helped us cook a warm meal that we had long done without and we devoured the roast pork with potatoes and cabbage with a great appetite. Unfortunately at 8:15 p.m., the order to move out came and we had to leave the warmth of the hospitable house. The family wasn't happy that we were leaving and Stascha told me that she was really worried about the Russians, particularly since she was employed in a German military plant. I cordially wished that the family would get out of it well, because they were really nice. Then we went on again.

Friday, January 26th

Gruppe Nehring halted their movement west due to a lack of fuel. The already rationed petrol was now allowed only for the most important combat movements, and even those could only be of limited extent. Soviet armored forces converging against the westward moving pocket from the south, east and north were being repelled "with loss of *Panzers*" according to von Ahlfen. They continued their movement slightly northwest of Kobylin toward Lissa, halting at the area northeast of Krobia.

Kampfgruppe Röseke passed south of Liebenstädt, due southwest during the afternoon of the day before. By morning, over a period of some 10-12 hours they made their way more than 40 kilometers across the frozen lakes north of Santomischel, then across the Warthe just north of Schrimm.

> The terrain was now becoming very hilly. We had to slow down. In addition, we had to move almost exclusively on paths and roads. There was thick underbrush all through the forest and there were fences and hedges all over the open terrain. We were lucky that at least the small and the large bodies of water were iced over and were thus passable without any difficulty.
>
> When morning broke, we were suddenly right outside a village, the surroundings of which seemed too difficult for us. We therefore wanted to get through the place once and for all. In spite of traitorous dog barking, we did that—almost. At a building in the middle of the village, there was a sentry who called to us "Stoy!" when we had gotten right next to him. There was nothing else to do except go up to him and kill him right away with my pistol—this is a self-defense requirement. So we still had some time to get out of there before the alarm was raised. For some reason, nothing happened and we weren't chased either. Apparently the Russians were used to having their sentries shot at night.
>
> At about 7:00 a.m., we were on the banks of the Warthe. We crossed the river without any effort. As I later determined, we were about 5 km north of the city of Schrimm. A building on the other bank, as we determined when we had our hands on the door handle, was occupied by the enemy. We hurried to cross the steep western part of the bank and found a big farmstead on the edge of it. Two women met us and we found out in response to our question about whether the Russians were there yet that they had captured a unit of 40 German soldiers right in the vicinity a few days before. It therefore appeared advisable to us to abandon this area.
>
> Because all that was in front of us was terrain with no cover, we followed the Warthe a bit south. At an edge of the forest, we stopped and suddenly heard voices behind us. It was armed civilians; Polish youth who were hunting German soldiers. There were a lot of them in those days all over Poland. We had to get to the next forest as quickly as possible, about 300 meters away, and we dared to sprint across open land while our pursuers' shots were whistling by our ears. From the right as well, where there was also a farmstead, there were some figures approaching us and there was some more running for our lives. But we reached the forest unscathed and disappeared immediately into its depths. Though we could hear our pursuers looking for us, we were safe there.
>
> The forest went further west and we could move on undisturbed until noon. But then we came to another big open area and it appeared too risky for us to cross it. We selected a small farmhouse right at the edge of forest to rest at. It was occupied by two women, apparently a mother and a grandmother, with multiple children. They gave us hot milk and bread with butter. For the first time since the railway transport from Angerburg, we took off our shoes and socks to warm up our banged-up feet at the stove. They were already badly swollen and we all had excoriated feet as well. Our stockings had holes all over and were torn, ice crusts from water from snow had formed at the threads and they tore our skin until it was bloody as we moved. I myself also had a bad feeling that a piece of shrapnel in the sole of my left foot—memories of Apatin/Batina in Hungary—that I had since left without observation in spite of the warning of our *Bataillon* physician was suddenly starting to rumble; a superlative focus had already started to form.

At about 5:00 p.m., the sentries, which I had set up as I always did, reported that a number of horse-drawn carts on the main road nearby had turned off it and were coming close on the road coming toward our house. A look through the glass showed me: Russians! They had apparently moved their allotted daily movement and wanted to rest there. Head over heels we left the building, shoes and stockings in our hand, back to the forest. It was high time; shots were being fired after us.

Fortunately it was already night; we were able to move right on. Crossing the main road was again very difficult. Horse-drawn columns were underway. [AN: this was the main road between Schrimm and Karlshsn].

It started snowing and our strength was disappearing more and more. A shining light beckoned us and we came to another forester's house. We were willingly invited in and hosted. I traded my table knife for a pair of the forester's old stockings. I didn't trust his son, a young guy age 17 or 18, and I told my comrades not to let him out of their sight. We lay down to sleep on the floor and the table when I was awakened at about 11:00 p.m. by one of my men. "The young man has gone!" We could imagine what was going on: the Russians were supposed to 'grab' us here. So we preferred to say goodbye as quickly as we could . . . and not a moment too soon: we could hear shouts very close to us. The forest welcomed us again, offering us the best protection any day we were in Poland.

The *II.Btl./Jäg.Rgt 2 'BR'* left Zietenfelde in the morning and soon crossed the old Reich boundary near Waffendorf some 45 kilometers to the west and moved into quarters. In the confusion of units and orders, *Leutnant* Kass and the rest of *Panzerjäger-Abteilung 'BR'* was ordered toward Görchen (Geischen) where *Oberleutnant* Gabel's *5.(schw.)Kompanie* was supposed to have moved. Instead of finding German forces there, *Leutnant* Kass ran into approximately three battalions of Soviets. According to Kass "I captured two of them and took them to the division command post." Still looking for *II.Btl./Jäg.Rgt. 2. 'BR'*, Kass went back to Görchen with *Oberleutnant* Gutweniger, Gabel's then commander, and "I again ran into a squadron of Russians that was attacking just then." They held off the Soviet attack.

Sturmgeschütz-Brigade 'GD' was operating some 40-50 kilometers behind the main body of *Panzer-Korps 'GD'* and was still north of Ostrowo in the late evening of January 25th, having just received valuable petrol from a relief flight of JU-52 transport aircraft. After a brief rest at a Polish farm the unit was given orders to make their way west at night in attempt to make better progress. *Fahnenjunker-Unteroffizier* Held-Kleingründlach account continues:

As we approached Radlau (Radlow), a great volume of shooting suddenly rang out. Some of the SPWs [from *I.(gep)Btl./Jäg.Rgt. 1 'BR'*]were in combat with a well-protected Russian supply column. But I couldn't do anything about it because I wasn't yet on the causeway that we had to go across. [AN: the main road between Ostrowo and Raschkow]. I was really amazed at how my driver, *Gefreiter* Diebig, moved the *Geschütz* over the extremely steep embankment with his Westphalian calm in spite of the fire. And immediately there was fire from tank guns. This column of Russians was driving in a tank convoy. One of them was already on fire and there was also a house burning. That gave us a good "target light-up". There was something black behind a barn and the light of fire was coming out of it again and again. With all the noise, it was impossible to tell outgoing shots from hits anymore. I had tank shells hiss towards this black something and a dark red flame went up for a moment. The thing wasn't shooting anymore, but something hit our track cover. Heavy machine gun fire hit Rieger's *Geschütz* and he had three dead among the infantry he was carrying. Two *SPWs* and a kitchen vehicle were lost. We went through the town and ran into the abandoned Russian vehicles of the blown-up column. They were all American

GMC trucks loaded with fuel. There was an oversized American machine gun above the cab of each vehicle. In the sweat of my brow, my gun loader and I took two full gas cans from one of the vehicles and put them on the back of the *Geschütz*. It's a pity that there isn't any more space there! But at any rate, I felt incomparably better at this point. Off we went to Kobylin (Koppelstadt)."

Once *Sturmgeschütz-Brigade 'GD'* cleared the main road they spent the rest of the day advancing west along the same route as most of the *Korps* keeping south of Krotoschin and finally reaching the area of Kobylin and Zietenfelde by the late afternoon.

The withdrawing units of *Gruppe Nehring* inexorably quickened their pace toward the Oder River and the perception of its security, now that the Reich Border was reached after weeks of continued withdrawal. The road arteries to the few river crossings became clogged with the assorted vehicles of the *20.Panzergrenadier-Division, 19.Panzergrenadier-Division, Fallschirm-Panzer-Division 1 'HG'*, and *Panzergrenadier-Division 'BR'*.

Saturday, January 27th

Back at the *Führerbunker* Hitler, Guderian, and *SS-Gruppenführer* Hans Georg Otto Hermann Fegelein, acting as *Reichsführer-SS* Heinrich Himmler's representative of the new *Heeresgruppe Weichsel* established on January 21st, were discussing the potential deployment options of *Panzer-Korps 'GD'* and *Gruppe Nehring*. Over a map, hundreds of kilometers away, these men discussed German formations, which were shattered, without any sense of the situation faced by the soldiers on the ground. The following transcript excerpt from the Nuremburg Trial Record (Document: 3786-PS Volume XXXIII) provides a stark contrast between the view from Berlin and the realities on the frontline. Twenty-four senior officers and administrative clerks attended the situation brief at 4:20 p.m. on January 27th, 1945 in Berlin. Many topics were discussed, to include the situation on the Eastern Front. While looking at the *Lage Ost* situation map produced the night before, Hitler pointed at the central front and asked the question *"Was ist das hier?"* (What is this here?). Guderian promptly launched off into a long explanation of the tactical situation. He then stated how *"Korps Saucken"* would be employed to attack south from the area of Schmueckert in order to destroy the dangerous bridgeheads of Koniev's 4th Guards Tank Army. He noted how the *Panzer-Korps* had just that day knocked out 16 Soviet tanks and that their northern flank was being successfully screened by the *19.Panzer-Division*. After some discussion about the defense of the Tirschtiegel defensive line, Guderian reinforced:

> Guderian: This is the *Gruppe Saucken* [*Panzer-Korps 'GD'*]. The *ReichMarshal's* division [*Hermann Göring*] and the *Division 'Brandenburg'* are here. They are supposed to conduct this attack in order to destroy the entire group that is in Steinauer-Oderbogen.

> *Führer*: That is good.[6]

---

6   Vol. XXXIII. Trial of the Major War Criminals before the International Military Tribunal. Nuremberg. 14 November 1945—1 October 1946, pp. 93-94. It was during this conference that discussion came up about 10,000 Allied Air Force Officers currently interned at Sagan. Göring interjected this fact into the briefing given by Guderian as Soviet forces were soon approaching the area. Hitler, stunned, said *"Warum transportiern sie die nicht frueher weg? Das ist eine Schlamperei sondergleichen"* (Why were they not transported away earlier? This is sloppiness beyond compare). Göring responded that all he could do was report the situation *(Ich kann das nur melden)*, as it was the responsibility of the *RF-SS* Heinrich Himmler who served as *"Befehlshaber des Ersatzheer"*. Hitler quickly ordered that these men should be marched out on foot under guard by *Volkssturm*. "Anyone who falls out," Hitler stated flatly, "would be shot." *(Wer aus resist, wird erschossen)*. Further discussion did continue about how best to transport the prisoners, and again, in front of the entire group Hitler said again that they have to be removed immediately by *Volkssturm* and that if anyone tried to escape, then they should be shot by firing squad *(Fluchtversuch wird mit Erschiessen geahndet)*, which was a modification to his earlier statement. No one in the conference raised any concern with his instructions. See pp. 101-05.

This exchange illustrates how much Guderian, more than Hitler, was driving the tactical decision making. If Hitler had actually been the one who ordered the *Panzer-Korps* to deploy south, he certainly would have had more tacit understanding of the situation. *Panzer-Korps 'GD'* was in no shape to launch any counterattack and neither was *Gruppe Nehring*. Guderian had no idea what was happening on the ground. Not once during the nearly 2½ hour conference recorded on 96 pages of transcript was there any reflection of the seriousness of the situation of the ground forces. Some relief did come in the form of petrol and ammunition columns that arrived from Glogau via Fraustadt (Wschowa). But the Soviets had reached Lissa first. The city was fortunately being staunchly defended by *Alarm-Bataillonen*. Also in the city was *Oberst* von Brückner along with the *10.Kompanie* and the headquarters staff of *Jägerregiment 1 'BR'*. This defense kept the Soviet forces tied down to a great extent, keeping the roads to south along the line Fraustadt-Krobia-Kobylin open. As the southern approaches were defended by elements of *'Brandenburg'* all of *Gruppe Nehring* reoriented themselves and moved away from Lissa, their objective for the last several weeks. During the evening of January 27th/28th a night movement was ordered southwest via Krobia to the Guhrau area, which was reached between 3:00 a.m. and 6:00 a.m. Unfortunately Brückner and the remnants of *Jägerregiment 1 'BR'* became pinned down in Lissa as Soviet division cut off their avenue of withdrawal.

As *Gruppe Nehring* shifted its movement southwest, *Kampfgruppe Röseke* did the same:

A snowstorm started and it hit us in the face from the west. You could hardly see your hand in front of your face. We relieved each other going in front and monitoring our movement. Now we were in close groups of two.

Surprisingly we were suddenly faced with a barbed wire obstacle that crossed our movement route. We had to go through it because of the danger that the terrain was mined, because we could hear screams from the right, apparently from a village. Naturally we didn't have any wire cutters, so we tore our trousers and blouses in our haste. There was a system of trenches behind the wire obstacle. It was apparently former unused and unoccupied German positions built by the *Volkssturm* and *Hitlerjugend* units that had been working on building the "eastern wall" for a year.

The shrapnel in my foot tortured me more and more. I already had to tilt my foot when walking in order to walk on it at all.

I went with Jonny as the very last group. We had pulled our snow hoods well over our faces and could only see to our fronts so as not to lose our connection to our comrades. Suddenly they went to the ground. Right in front of us, a searchlight ramped up. Our three comrades were hit by the cone of light. They immediately threw themselves to the ground. Now we could hear engine noise and I recognized from very close up, about 10-15 meters, a Russian wheeled armored vehicle, the simplest type, with a machine gun on the turret. The vehicle stopped. The three comrades did not dare to move. Jonny and I were still lying in the dark. I made a snap decision—it was actually more of an emotional act, and took out the last *Stiel* hand grenade that I had stuck in my belt, made a run to the tank, pulled the pin and threw it into the broad opening. Detonation! We could hear the Russians screaming. The vehicle burned, the ammunition went off, the searchlight went dark and we ran off, over the road and into another open field. The tanks following them wanted to take up the chase—apparently we had run right into a motorized patrol—but we had already disappeared into the dark and the Russian machine gunners missed their target. However, we were dispersed again; I was alone with one comrade, Richard. Our cries did not penetrate the heavy wind. But we had to find the comrades because they didn't have a compass, and without one, there was no way they could get through. We decided to go far enough west to get to the nearest forest. From there, we wanted to take up the search for our comrades the next morning.

First we had to get across a deep tank ditch; we needed nearly an hour to do that. Then we got into a forest that was like a park with huge trees and well-cared-for facilities. When daybreak came, we first hid in the bushes to take a look around. Suddenly we heard voices very close to us. We looked excitedly and it was our three dispersed comrades. What luck that we found each other again!

We moved a bit further to the west. When it was completely light, we reached a small piece of forest extending on a few hundred meters. Looks through the glass in all directions showed that there were enemy-occupied villages nearby. There was nothing else to do except spend the day in this piece of woods hidden. At about 10:00 a.m., we suddenly heard aircraft engine noise. Right after that, we heard the mounted weapons firing and bombs falling. German ground attack aircraft were attacking a concentration of Russian tanks in the next village. But our joy about that didn't last long; when the pilots had gone, the Russians hurried to leave the village with their tanks and to go right into our little forest to get cover from the aircraft. We quickly put out the small fire that we wanted to warm ourselves with and were able to disappear into thick brush. A bare 100 meters from us, there were Russian tanks. The Russians lit fires, drank schnapps and bellowed. We couldn't move and had to spend hours lying down in the snow. Jonny was right next to me. He wanted to chicken out, get up and run away—this stress was really unbearable. I had to keep the young man at my side by force. Our bodies got more and more stiff from the cold; we had almost no feeling in our extremities. We always had to fear being discovered and I don't think that we would have had any more strength to defend ourselves or to get away. It was not until it was about evening that we were saved; the Russians moved back into the village. As soon as it was dark, we carefully moved on, giving the enemy-occupied village a wide berth. We wanted to look for a place to stay as quickly as we could where we could warm up and get something to eat, but we had to put a lot of kilometers behind us without hitting a settlement. The moon was very bright and we continued to move on at big intervals. The terrain was alternating flat and hilly.

Most of *Panzergrenadier-Division 'BR'* now reached prewar German territory having survived a harrowing withdrawal across Poland. Many units went into quarters for the first time in nearly two weeks. *Sturmgeschütz-Brigade 'GD'* brought up the rear of the *Korps* and reached Kobylin in the morning. As most of the German units had left, the city was already celebrating its liberation as the *Sturmgeschütze* rolled into town making for an interesting spectacle for *Fahnenjunker-Unteroffizier* Held-Kleingründlach:

We arrived there in the morning. The Polish flag hung from the church steeple and on the houses. The population apparently no longer took us into account because we were operating in the enemy rear. The garlands over the house entrances had been woven a bit too early. But no one could be seen at all; it was all as if dead! The *Sturmgeschütze* first had to secure the northern exit to the town. Then we moved on to the Bergelsdorf estate! We *Geschütz* commanders went to a meeting in which we were informed about a new personnel subordination of the crews. The crew members that did not belong to the *Brigade* would all be replaced by *Brigade* members. I got two old buddies from the *3.Batterie. Obergefreiter* Funke-Kaiser and *Obergefreiter* Januschkowetz were great guys and stellar, also somewhat strong in body, definitely regulation 'GD' size. Karl-Heinz Becker became a loader again. At any rate, I had a first-class crew with me. We moved onto the estate and made ourselves comfortable. Unfortunately the nice period didn't last long; the Russians started making a racket again. That was it with calm, because we were immediately put on alert and sent to secure the town. The houses in the vicinity were overstuffed with *Landser*, so we could find no place to sleep for the night. The fire had now completely stopped. We slept in shifts in a stall, deeply buried in the straw, nice and warm. No one could talk about freezing.

Sunday, January 28th

Gruppe Nehring prepared for its final push west. *General* von Saucken's *Panzer-Korps 'GD'* headquarters established itself in Klein-Ellguth north of Guhrau during the early morning hours. Reconnaissance determined that there was one enemy infantry division between Guhrau and Glogau, and heavy street fighting in Lissa. The road from Glogau to Fraustadt and side roads from Fraustadt to Guhrau had no enemy on them. Based on the decisions at the *Führer* conference the previous day von Saucken received orders from *Heeresgruppe Mitte* under the command of *Generaloberst* Ferdinand Schörner to move south across the Bartsch River against the northern flank of the enemy advancing on the Oder. This order was clearly beyond the capacity of the weakened forces of von Saucken to accomplish. The units that did not belong to *Panzer-Korps 'GD'* (like von Ahlfen's *Sperrverband* and other units of *XXIV.Panzer-Korps*) were released back to von Nehring. *Gruppe Nehring* continued their movement northwest to Glogau. Von Saucken held the southern flank and rear during *Gruppe Nehring's* final withdrawal. Then the forces of *Panzer-Korps 'GD'* readied themselves for an advanced southwest toward Steinau in preparation for the ordered attack.

Kampfgruppe Röseke continued their evasion to the south and west. Their trials grew more harrowing as they lost their stamina. Interestingly, Röseke did not change into civilian clothes. Doing so might have made his evasion easier, and given that the old *'Brandenburger'* was trained in concealment and infiltration he made a conscious decision not to discard his German uniform.

At midnight, we reached an isolated house. It was, however, on a road heading north to south on which one could see fresh tracks of tanks and horse-drawn vehicles. There was no forest to be seen for miles around. Nevertheless we wanted to rest there because our exhaustion had reached the point that led us to fear that we would fall asleep during one of the next rest breaks in the snow and that we wouldn't wake up again from that.

We asked to get into the house; there were no enemy in it. The Polish farmer's family gave us milk and bread with liverwurst. Then we slept at the warm oven without posting a sentry this time.

Suddenly my shoulder was being shaken. "Watch out, Ruski are coming!" said the old farmer. I looked through the door jam and in fact in the meantime the road had become occupied. A horse-drawn column that couldn't be overlooked was going by outdoors. At the moment, we couldn't think of getting away. Hopefully no Russians would come into the house . . . I woke up my comrades; they were immediately wide awake. Our hearts beat wildly—we were, after all, in a terrible situation. And what we had feared did in fact happen. A horse-drawn wagon stopped in front of the house and some Russians came across the small garden to the door. The old farmer was shaking like aspen leaves. The women were crying—they knew that if the Ivans found Germans in their house it would be bad for them. I was just able to say, "Hey, get hidden!" One of my men grabbed the kerosene lantern on the table and threw it to the floor so that the room became very dark. Then there was a knock on the door with rifle butts. One of us had hidden in a corner in a bunch of clothing, another behind a cupboard, one got into bed with the old Mamushka and the fourth tried to get under the bed. Then the farmer opened the door and three Russians came in. I myself couldn't find a place to hide quickly; my wounds also made it hard for me to do that. So I stayed in the background of the room along the wall and took my pistol off safety. There was bright moonlight outside and it was pitch black in the room, so the Russians, who fortunately didn't have any pocket flashlights with them, needed a few minutes to get their eyes accustomed to the darkness. I heard them demand something to eat from the farmer. I was able to understand the words "khleb [bread]," "maslo [butter]" and "moloko [milk]." The farmer and his wife got them what they wanted, quaking with fear. Suddenly one of the Russians spied me and came to me. I was in my white camouflage blouse, my snow hood and my field cap were off, and I couldn't be recognized as a German soldier without some effort. Only my spyglass near my chest gave me away as a "military man." I thought it over super quick; I still remember what I was thinking. The Russian will recognize me as a German, but before he grabs his weapon, you'll shoot him at close range. Then the issue will be whether my comrades are "on the ball" and whether they can neutralize the other two comrades—otherwise we will not leave this house alive. Then the Russian talked to me. Of course I couldn't understand him, but I heard the word "Soldat," which is the same in Russian as it is in German, and I suspected—also super quick—that I was being asked whether I was a soldier. God knows how I found the answer but I said, "Da da, polskiy soldat!" [Yes, yes, a Polish soldier]—and something unbelievable happened. The Russian said, "Khorosho tovarishch – idi syuda, kuchat!" (Fine, comrade, come here, eat with us!) I cautiously let my pistol get into my pants pocket without letting go of it, and I followed the Russian to the table. I heard him say something to his companions about "polskiy partisan" and stuffed my mouth with bread so that I didn't have to say anything. Fortunately the Russians did not have much time and after a couple of minutes, they were on their way. All three of them shook my hand—I could have roared with pain—and then they were all outside. I heard the whips cracking and the horse-drawn wagon started moving. But the column was not yet at an end and we didn't want to risk such an adventure again. We therefore preferred to leave the house through a rear window and get out of there as quickly as possible.

After going a few more kilometers, we had to again cross a busy road and shortly thereafter a railway yard. Apparently we were again in the vicinity of a rather large city. We still didn't have a map. All we could find in our quarters were the kind that came from old school atlases in which the "Kingdom of Poland" reached to the Elbe!

As morning broke, we wound up in an enormous farmstead. One could see a few main buildings, the stables and big haystacks. We wanted to hide in one during the day. But first we were interested in finding out whether the farm was occupied by the Russians. We carefully sneaked around with our pistols in our hands off safety and ran into an old man who was coming with a dragging gait. We stopped him and asked him in German whether the Russians were there. He answered, also in German (most of the residents of this part of western Poland have mastered German) that there was no one on the farm except for the Polish staff although the Russians had been there to requisition straw and potatoes. We believed the old man and felt safe. There was light burning in a house so we went there to thaw out a bit in a warm room before getting into the straw. The room in which the light was burning was on the ground floor and could be reached through a narrow hallway. Jonny and I went in front. My comrades remained at the house door, naturally with their pistols in their hands, ready to shoot. I opened the door to the room and I saw a Russian officer sitting at a table and two women besides. We stared at each other for a second. The Russian recognized me as a German based on my field cap. He wanted to jump up. At that moment, Jonny pulled the trigger and the captain fell. We hurriedly left the house, taking our comrades waiting outside with us. Behind us, the women started to yell and windows and doors everywhere started to open; the farm was crawling with Russians and the old man had swindled us! We ran past the stables, found ourselves standing suddenly in front of a field kitchen where they were just making a fire but before the baffled Russians noticed what was going on, we were already further away, running along a path away from there. While I was running, I lost something metal that rattled, but I didn't pay any more attention to it. The path ran into a street about 100 meters later and there was a sentry at this intersection! He called from far off, "Stoy! Stoy!" I dashed away from him and pulled the trigger on my pistol—but the 08 left me in the lurch: I had just lost the magazine! So I was standing in front of the Russians with an unloaded pistol. He didn't dare move and my comrades were then able to run a bit further along the road. I went back carefully a step at a time, always pointing my empty pistol. After about 15 meters, I suddenly turned and ran as far as I could from there. The Russian, however, did not have his rifle in his hand; he had laid it in a horse-drawn cart a few meters away. By the time he had gotten it, taken it off safety, loaded it, aimed it and pulled the trigger, I had already disappeared into the darkness. He shot the entire contents of a magazine at us—but we got away. However we were separated again. I only had two comrades with me. The other two had run away to the left across an open field, which at the moment was the only right thing to do. We could already hear the cries of the pursuers; they were on horseback and we let them gallop by while we hid in a clump of bushes near the road.

It would soon be light. We had reached a forest and a happy coincidence brought us back together with our comrades. A village in the vicinity was occupied by the enemy; we went around it carefully. When a Russian bugler played the wakeup call, we were in terrain with heavy growth and cuts through it that offered good cover and favored our movement by day. But you always have to look out for surprises. However, we had to change our direction of movement and go southwest because a number of settlements and roads with lots of traffic were visible in the west. Based on our experiences up until that time, we preferred to stay away from them. Besides, we couldn't be all that far from the front; there were signs pointing to that everywhere.

Our outer appearance had suffered even more over the last few days. We had actually repeatedly had the opportunity to get civilian clothing. Why didn't we do that? An un-definable dread of this dangerous anonymity caused us to still present ourselves as German soldiers even in this situation.

Our physical status was also getting significantly worse. Hunger and cold as well as the continuing restlessness and being on edge gnawed on our strength. We all felt stabbing pains when breathing. Our body and stomach aches must have come from our habit (which we couldn't really give up) of eating snow to fight thirst. Our eyes were heavily inflamed and the skin on our faces had been tanned by the strong wind blowing through the snow and it was unbearably stretched. Our lips were completely crusted over and continually bled. Our ears and noses, but especially our extremities, showed signs of first and second-degree frostbite. I myself had to bite down hard to hold on. The pains in the wounds and the fever had indeed gone down, but they continually showed up and surprised us. I could now lift both arms again up to about my waist. The shrapnel in my left foot became ever more unpleasantly noticeable, and walking with my excoriated and swollen feet was torture.

I was always wondering about all the things that could keep us from moving. I myself would never have trusted myself to survive something of this sort, and wounded to boot. But our wartime experiences and stress so far were nothing to be sneezed at either. But as I said, my will to hold on was fueled by my fear of becoming a prisoner of the Russians and my responsibility for my comrades. I hope that I continue to have the strength to be their leader.

These days in Poland have brought home to me what comes with "being their leader." Throwing that phrase around is always distasteful to me anyway. In such conditions, however, it becomes clear whether it was possible to meet the demands of our professional duties: "extreme ability" and "untiring care." That's what it comes down to in the final analysis, and it's of no interest how many meters of lacing one has on one's uniform or how many stars or piping one has. The important thing is the sight of what is needed for what "the emergency requires;" that's what men's trust comes from and if one has it, one has all the capability of not being conquered by anything. I had learned that there were no "doubtful situations;" there were at most doubtful people that weren't handling these situations.

The evidence for that was provided by the small group of dispersed German soldiers, the remnants of two proud 'Brandenburger' Jäger-Kompanien. Our comradeship would have been blemished by the bad behavior of a single person, and there was never a "if or but" when it was time to implement a decision.

However, I had the bitterest thoughts during those days when it was quiet. One was about how my return to the division would be accepted, should it be successful, and what the commander would say when I stood in front of him, a company head without a company, while the majority of the men entrusted to me were killed in action, captured, missing in action and dispersed. However, when I look at the events since Kutno today, I didn't do or fail to do anything that could burden my conscience. Today, it appears improbable even to me that I had that type of luck while I was unlucky.

In addition, I was tortured by my concern about the "big picture." Where were the Russians now? How would this winter campaign in the east end; where would the Red Army finally be brought to a halt? I saw the masses of tanks and people of this army and I was afraid that our *Wehrmacht* bled dry would succumb if the promises of our leadership weren't kept . . . .

But the first thing for me and my comrades was to get back to Germany.

At about 8:00 a.m., we got to a group of large haystacks and decided to settle down there. We attempted to bundle into the freshly cut hay, but didn't get in very deep. There was no way we could think about sleep, so the cold moved us onward.

At 10:00 a.m., we moved on. On all the roads, including the secondary roads that we passed, there were fresh vehicle tracks visible. *Oberjäger* Kruch looked around with his spyglass without interruption.

Suddenly we had another unpleasant surprise: we were right on a long generally downward slope with a road going by at the lower edge. There a column of Russian tanks unexpectedly showed up. They apparently recognized us and the person at the front stopped at a distance of barely 300 meters. We stood motionless for some anxious minutes, but the tanks went on without firing a shot. Maybe they considered us one of their own reconnaissance patrols or a squad of Polish partisans.

Around noon, we reached a large forester's house. However, we didn't enter it; we initially stayed in a shed. These precautionary measures turned out to be the right ones, because right in the vicinity one could hear engine noise, a Russian passenger car (a looted Opel Kapitän) going by. However, only a civilian got out and the car went on. Finally I dared to go with Jonny into the house and then we had terrible hunger. I also hoped to find out something more about the vicinity of the front. In fact, there was a good map in the forester's office. However, I couldn't take it with me because if I did, the otherwise friendly civil servant would certainly raise hell. So I punched out our further path and Jonny made a sketch. We were still some 40 km to the border of the German Reich. We were on the Obra wetlands/right on the Obra Canal. [AN: north of Kriewen]. The far forward elements of the Russians were supposed to be about 20-30 km away. So extreme caution was now called for.

We moved on along the canal, now in a northwesterly direction. The bridges and catwalks over the canal had been blown up. A thick forest on both banks made it easier for us to go forward. When we came across pedestrians or vehicles, we hid and let them go on.

In the late afternoon, we reached a village that probably was not occupied by the enemy yet. We carefully crept up to it and fortunately we confirmed our suspicion. We moved up to one of the nearest houses. The people were friendly, or at least they acted that way. A young man occupied the house with his wife, two children and his mother in law. The husband of this mother-in-law was still a prisoner of the Germans as a Polish officer. We were therefore very cautious, because under such circumstances, one can't trust anyone.

However, we got soup, bread, coffee and cigarettes. We warmed our frozen feet at the stove, but that wasn't good because they soon swelled up even more and we had to cut our boots a bit in order to get into them at all. I now got the piece of shrapnel out of my left foot with a knife heated red hot and pressed out the pus. It was high time; there were already signs of blood poisoning in my leg. A bandage closed off the wound and now I could walk better again.

At about 7:00 p.m., we went on, initially a bit along the canal and then directly to the north across an open field. There were supposedly extensive forests there that reached to the Reich border. The terrain now became varied, but it was hilly mostly. We frequently had to rest, but the closeness of our goal wouldn't let us in peace any more. During such a rest, two men ran into us, also dispersed Germans: a customs inspector and a political officer (known to us soldiers as a "golden pheasant.") They came from a small town about 100 km south of there and had been hiding in the forests until then. During this night, they wanted to "cross-over" and so they asked whether they could join us. They must have assumed that they would have better luck with us soldiers than if they tried on their own. Unfortunately they didn't have a map either and Jonny's road sketch had shown itself to be useless. So we went on straight ahead and the two civilians followed us. It was a clear starry night.

II.Btl./Jäg.Rgt.2 'BR' conducted an attack on a village in the vicinity of Waffendorf (Saborroitz/ Zaborowice) that was infiltrated at night by Soviets cutting off the main westward route between Guhrau-Bojanowo. The Soviets operating near Lissa likely learned of *Gruppe Nehring's* approach to the south and attempted to harass their movement.

In the morning *Sturmgeschütz-Brigade 'GD'* was still at Bergelsdorf. *Fahnenjunker-Unteroffizier* Held-Kleingründlach account continues:

The morning brought me an unpleasant surprise. *Wachtmeister* Doskocil showed up and reported that at the commander's orders, I would have to help out as the adjutant at *Ia* effective immediately, primarily to handle all the written stuff. He would take over my *Geschütz* and I would go to the *Brigade* headquarters in order to report in there. At 1:00 p.m., a patrol group went to a patch of forest from which fire had been coming the previous day especially. It was determined that there was a JS-2 Stalin tank in there and that it had apparently settled in and was well protected by infantry.

Then one of our trucks loaded with fuel was stuck in the snow in front of our position and was dragged out by several *Sturmgeschütze*. They moved forward and were unexpectedly fired upon by the Stalin tank from the patch of forest. Before they could bring effective fire, both of them were knocked-out. The following were killed in action: *Unteroffizier* Albert Kallweit (the *Geschütz* commander), *Unteroffizier* Werner Peters (the driver). The following were severely wounded: *Unteroffizier* Heinz Blunck from Hamburg and *Obergefreiter* Heinz Melchart from Eferding near Linz. Both of the *Geschütz* had to be blown up. The two dead comrades were buried by us with full honors. Two of our old reliables were no more! I went to see the severely wounded people, who had been badly hurt. Blunck had had both legs shot through right above the ankle, though the skin had held together, and Melchart had deep wounds in the back and the hips. I took care of getting them taken immediately to the nearest house, which was occupied by infantry, and I called for a medic. Finally one showed up, but he made a befuddled impression as though he didn't know why he was dragging his bandaging stuff around. I had to be very blunt to get him to help bind up the wound. Blunck's legs were splinted and enough bandages were applied to Melchart that no more blood soaked through. Then I looked around for a way to transport them out of there. I found places for them both on a troop car and they were out of there shortly after that. Then we moved as well. At 3:15 p.m. we were supposed to move out and at 4:15 we actually did. But I was no longer the proud commander of a fighting vehicle in an armored column; I was driven in a Volkswagen. However, the difference was a bit blatant and I wasn't very enthusiastic, but orders are orders. We went via Waffendorf to the Klein and Gross-Kloden estate. The command *Geschütz* went in front of us and I following in the Volkswagen. Among other things, I had two large boxes with front fighter packages that had been entrusted to me. Suddenly a light signal went up and the firing immediately started again.

Russian antitank and grenade launchers covered us almost entirely and I noticed that there were an awful lot of phosphorus shots hitting in our direct vicinity. The Command *Geschütz* in front went into reverse gear and went back. My driver attempted to turn the Volkswagen around and we went into the snow-filled ditch in the process. The Volkswagen turned over and we wound up lying underneath the vehicle. The driver quickly freed himself from his unfortunate situation while I continued to wiggle around alone under the vehicle. Finally I managed and I tried to get out of the ditch. The Russians in the meantime got to the vehicle while I, no more than 20 meters away from there in snow up to my chest, was laboriously making my way away from there in the revelry of shell fire. In the process I lost my pistol, and given the darkness and the circumstances, I was no longer able to search for it. My gloves were also lost and I was freezing in the biting cold. I finally made it to the *Geschütz*, exhausted and half frozen. Now we reached the village on a broad front. We were proceeding forward efficiently and the enemy was retreating. *Oberwachtmeister* Lehrmann's *Geschütz* was hit in the track rollers. We captured two fully-intact Russian antitank guns and a few motor vehicles.

The rest of *Panzergrenadier-Division 'BR'* prepared for their final drive toward the Oder River.

Remnants of *II.Bataillon/Jägerregiment 1 'BR'* and *Gruppe Nehring* reach Glogau, Monday, January 29th through Thursday, February 1st

Gruppe Nehring finally reached Glogau at 3:30 a.m. The *4.Panzer-Armee* headquarters staff received von Nehring's motorized units and *Generalleutnant* Hohn and the foot units that marched there under his command. Von Ahlfen's command arrived with one armored personnel carrier with the commander and a command section, the *MG Btl. 442* with about 150 men, and small parts of the *Radfahrersicherungs-Bataillon 232*, and the *lFH Abteilung (mot.)* under *Major* Alex with two tubes ready to fire. Von Ahlfen was now promoted to *Generalmajor* and ordered to take on a new role, that of *Festung Kommandeur* of Breslau. Dozens of German units began their refit and rebuild process under the efficient *Ersatzheer*. In just two months this motley group of survivors would defend against the final Soviet offensive against Germany.

Forty kilometers north of Glogau, the men of *Kampfgruppe Röseke* were at the end of their strength.

In a thick forest that could only be passed through on bad paths, we got lost. That is, we suddenly discovered that we had been going around in circles in spite of the compass. We were, however, back in open terrain again soon. During the next rest, the two new arrivals stepped aside and smoked cigarettes. They apparently didn't want to give us anything: they really weren't comrades! Richard went up to them and asked them to share with us because that was the custom of soldiers. But they didn't want to do that although they surely had all sorts of thing in their thick knapsacks. Then Richard took out his pistol and said, "Get the heck out of here, you pigs, and don't let us see you again!" They hesitated and wanted to turn to me, but Richard took his weapon off safety and counted, "One, two . . ." and then they toddled off. We were "in our own space" again and that was for the best.

We crossed a highway and a canal once again—everything was calm and nothing was moving around us—and now we must be back on German soil. Now extreme caution was called for. . . .

From the edge of a forest, we saw a burning village not too far away. So the front had to be right in the vicinity. We left the forest and carefully approached the burning houses. I sent *Oberjäger* Kruch and another comrade to do reconnaissance. In the meantime, dawn came. Suddenly something was whistling over our heads: light artillery! The impacts were in the middle of the village. So there was no doubt; this village was still occupied by German soldiers. We were still hesitant—things were lively in the forest behind us and Russian infantry was coming out of it in three waves to attack! Now it was high time. We ran as fast as we could, and then out two comrades came up to us and called to use, "Hey come on, it's a German strongpoint!" German defensive fire immediately started. They joined direct and indirect fire with mortars and sub-machineguns and initially brought the Russian attack to a standstill. So we were able to reach the village under good cover.

We managed it—we were back in Germany!

The strongpoint—it was the village of Schwenten (Świętno)—was about 5 km in front of the actual main battle line. The strongpoint commandant was an old *Oberst*. It was "WBK type" [AN: *Wehrbezirkskommando*—military recruiting district headquarters]; he had 400 men there but only a few heavy weapons. I reported to him and he wanted to use us immediately. When I explained to him what we had gone through and that I had been wounded twice myself, he shouted to me, "You coward! We fight to the last man here!" So I turned around speechless and went away. He sent his adjutant, a *Hauptmann*, after me. The *Hauptmann* was supposed to take my spyglass away from me but I of course brushed him off.

In the meantime, the Russian artillery fire had started again and soon the attack waves would start again. There was the danger that the strongpoint would be surrounded and we hurried to get out of it as quickly as we could. At the home of an old Silesian farm woman who had not fled, we got bread and coffee. She showed us the way toward Konitz, where the German main battle line supposedly was.

For the first time in many days we could move openly on the road without being caught by surprise. In abandoned buildings along the way, we found food, mostly stewed stuff. Jonny brought us an entire box of candy from a gourmet food shop. A carriage came up behind us suddenly, apparently the last refugees. They let us sit down and we reached the small town of Konitz before it was even noon. There was a *Waffen-SS* unit there. We reported to the commandant, a *SS-Hauptsturmführer*. He sent us into a warm room and took care of food. In the evening, there was going to be a wounded transport leaving and we could join it.

The transport left in the late afternoon. Mostly it was people with minor wounds and they sat or lay in a bus. Everything had caught up that day and people said that they were glad they would get out of the witch's kettle that way. Besides, the strongpoint of Schwenten, I found out, had been occupied by the Russians that morning and none of the people manning it had made their way to the main battle line. A young *SS Leutnant* told jokes and cheered people up. We five 'Brandenburgers' lay in a corner and slept.

In the evening we came to a main medical station. Some of the wounded were unloaded and the "difficult cases"—including us—were transported further. At night we were in a field hospital in Grünberg, Silesia. We spent the night there.

The few survivors of *Jägerregiment 1 'BR'* continued to filter back toward German lines during January 30th/31st at Glogau with the other elements of *Gruppe Nehring. Kampfgruppe Röseke*, representing many of his comrades' fate cut off behind advancing Soviet lines, concludes his account as follows:

The transport went on to the war hospital in Sagan (Zagan) (boarding school). We were taken in there. We got physician care. Now after I had survived everything and my mental energy had dwindled, I was "bushed." The physician had an expression of concern. I lay apathetically in bed and didn't want to eat or drink anything—just sleep. My comrades were in this hospital as well. Richard had acquired a dangerous pulmonary infection and the others had especially frostbite and were completely exhausted besides.

Wednesday, January 31st
I found out that the *Werkstatt-Kompanie* of the *Division 'Brandenburg'* was right in this town! So the big part of the division couldn't be far away! Our will to live came back immediately. I called up the division engineer and found out from him the location of our division's *Aufklärungs-Abteilung 'BR'*. There I was given the location of *Jägerregiment 1 'BR'* and that of the *Versorgungs-Kompanie* of the *II.Btl./Rgt. 1*.

I wanted to get to the regiment at any cost in order to report there about what had happened to the *6.Kompanie* and *7.Kompanie*. But since the physician wasn't letting me go, there was nothing else for me to do but to break out of the hospital.

I told my comrades and they wanted to accompany me. However, I didn't allow them to do that because first they had to recover properly. I would send them leave vouchers the quickest way I could.

So we said goodbye to each other during the evening. The five of us would undoubtedly never forget this time in our lives!

Oberst von Brückner, his headquarters staff and the *10.Kompanie* had spent 5 days cut off in Lissa as the rest of the *Division* withdrew across the Oder. Brückner proposed to the Fortress Commander a breakout with the remaining forces that consisted mainly of *Alarm* and *Volkssturm* units. The plan was approved and during the evening of February 2nd Brückner led some 2,000 soldiers out of the Lissa and reached Glogau the following day with a single loss. For this accomplishment he received the Knight's Cross on March 11th.

The *II.Bataillon* of *Jägerregiment 1 'BR'* began to reform near Gruenberg (Zielona Gora), to the north of Sagan where the regiment was headquartered. The *I.(gep)Bataillon* was still operating with the main body of *'Brandenburg'* to the south.

On Thursday, February 1st Röseke left the hospital on his own without being noticed.

I could hardly stay on my feet, but I reached the arterial road going out of the city toward Glogau. There I found a truck recognizable as one of our division's trucks by the red Brandenburg eagle on a white helmet and so I managed to get to Glogau by noon. On the way, one could see that the roads were full of columns of refugees, a picture of misery, mostly old men, women and children with carts full of stuff, carefully pushing them on, continually pushed into the ditches by *Wehrmacht* vehicles.

A truck from *Panzer-Sturm-Pionier-Bataillon 'Brandenburg'* took me to the division's message center and from there a vehicle belonging to the *Versorgungs-Kompanie* of *II.Btl./Regt. 1 'BR'* picked me up.

I was back home at my *Bataillon*.

From February 2nd–6th the comrades of the *Versorgungs-Kompanie*, which was in and around Töppendorf, fed and took care of me lovingly. I hoped I could get healed from my wounds here, but the physicians were decidedly against that.

A room with all the comforts had been set up for me in the castle of the former German crown prince: a wonderful bed, an armchair and a radio.

I began writing this report.

Röseke, while leading many of his men, spent nearly two weeks behind enemy lines completing an arduous 230 kilometer journey behind enemy lines. He was wounded multiple times and attempted suicide once. For his efforts he was awarded the Knight's Cross on April 14th.

10

Counterattack at Steinau

(Reference Maps 36, 37, 38, 39, 40, 41, 42, 43, 44, 45, 46, 47, 48, 49, 50 and 51)

E lements of the Soviet 4th Guards Tank Army reached the Oder River in the vicinity of Steinau around January 24th. East of Steinau was the city of Lüben that contained a major road and rail network. The Berlin-Breslau *Autobahn*, ran through the city, and this major transportation artery was a main objective for Koniev's forces looking to encircle Breslau to the south. There were no German combat divisions immediately located in the area for defense.

In its continuing feat of organizational efficiency the *Ersatzheer* quickly deployed the special staff (*zbV*) *Division Nr. 408* out of *Wehrkreis VIII* that was currently based in Liegnitz. *Division Nr. 408* was responsible for supplying trained replacements to *Wehrmacht* combat units through four geographically located regimental staffs. Now this training cadre was transformed almost overnight into a combat division, at least on paper, and sent into battle. The authority to mobilize training staffs fell under a prewar plan known as *Gneisenau*. The plan was highly effective. If during a war enemy forces reached a *Wehrkreis*, the *Wehrkreis* had the authority to mobilize and deploy local training and replacement units under the local training division staff. Without this contingency plan established in the 1930s, resistance along the East Front might well have collapsed under the pace of the Soviet winter offensive. The plan bordered on brilliance in terms of simplicity and effectiveness in application. The nascent divisions fielded by the *Wehrkreis* served to slow down Soviet forces enough to often allow other, more fully capable units to deploy in defense of the area. Time and again during the period January-April 1945 the *Ersatzheer* and *Wehrkreis* system did more to stave off final defeat than any single organization in Germany.

The new *Division Nr. 408.* mobilized as a *Gneisenau Alarm-und-Volkssturm Einheiten* division of around 4,800 men around January 21st/22nd. It consisted of *Volkssturm* who were typically ill-equipped and lightly armed, as well as enlisted soldiers from the NCO Academies located at Steinau, Tetschen-Bodenbach and Jauer. This combined force deployed to Steinau armed with bolt-action rifles, light machineguns and *Panzerfaust*. On the evening of January 23rd the Soviet 10th Guards Tank Corps conducted a direct attack south of Steinau and were able to capture the rail bridge across the Oder intact, despite losing 24 tanks in the process to *Panzerfausts*.[1] The Soviets wheeled north and advanced into the town reaching the Rathaus on January 24th but were stopped from advancing further. The town quickly was in flames, and hundreds, if not thousands of refugees were caught waiting for trains west that would never come. The Soviets were merciless, opening fire on mass of unarmed civilians, killing and wounding indiscriminately. Rapes followed. Soon word of the terror unleashed by the advancing Soviets reached the soldiers defending further west.[2]

The soldiers of *Volkssturm* and training battalions did stabilize their defense and establish a perimeter in Steinau. The Soviet 10th Guards Tank Corps was joined by the 6th Guards Mechanized Corps to the north of the town, and both units continued to slowly expand their bridgehead while

---

1   RG 242 German Armed Forces Operations and Situation Maps, 1939-1945. H.Gr. A. Box 507. *HGr. A GenStdH Op.Abt. IIIb Prüf Nr. 53759 Stand: 23.1.45 Abends*.
2   Rolf Hinze, *To the Bitter End* (Helion: West Midlands, 2005.), p. 118.

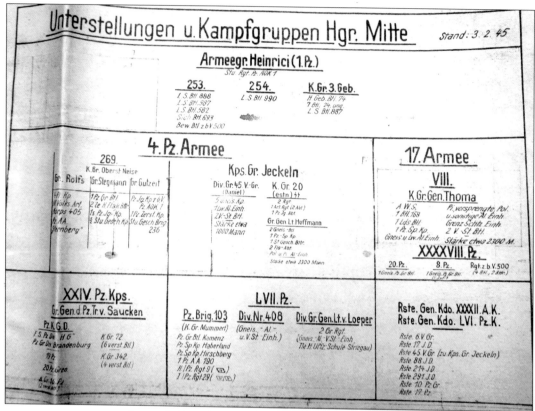

Image 2. Organization of *Heeresgruppe Mitte*, 3 February.

completing their encirclement of the town. Another newly mobilized unit by the *Ersatzheer* was deployed to lead the southern attack on what was now known as the Steinau Bridgehead. The *Panzer-Brigade 103* under command of *Oberst* Werner Mummert was sent by a "Blitz train" from its training home at Grafenwöhr to Liegnitz at the end of January. *Panzer-Brigade 103* was formed under order *Op.Abt. (III) 1077/45 geh.v.20.1.45* and consisted of *I.Btl./Pz.Rgt. 39* (Panthers), *II.Btl./Pz.Rgt. 9*, *I.Btl./Pz.Rgt. 29* (Panthers), and *Panzergrenadier-Regiments 'Neuhammer'* and *'Kamenz'*. When the unit deployed, however, only the *II.Btl./Pz.Rgt. 9* consisting of Jagdpanzer IV/70s, and *I.Btl./Pz.Rgt. 29* consisting of a company of Pz. IVGs, and Panthers along with the *Panzergrenadier-regiments* arrived and formed *Kampfgruppe 'Mummert'*. The *I.Btl./Pz.Rgt. 39* did not deploy with the *Brigade*.[3]

Generaloberst Schörner ordered an immediate counterattack to relieve the town and destroy the Soviet bridgehead from the north and south. On the southern end of the Steinau Bridgehead *Kampfgruppe 'Mummert'* went into combat first on January 29th knocking out some 15 Soviet tanks that had tried to advance across the *Autobahn* between Lüben and Porschwitz. It then prepared for its attack on the following day. Among the units selected for the attack from the north were the withdrawing elements of *Panzergrenadier-Division 'Brandenburg'* and *Fallschirm-Panzer-Division 'Hermann Göring 1'*. The attack was scheduled for February 3rd, but the assigned divisions had to get across the Bartsch River first.

The *I.Bataillon* and *II.Bataillon* of *Jägerregiment 2 'BR'* received orders to move toward Steinau and prepare for an immediate counterattack. Orders were issued to retake the town and eliminate the

Soviet bridgehead. *Jägerregiment 2 'BR'*, however, still had to cross the Bartsch River.

Jägerregiment 2 'BR' began a series of combat actions designed to open the way for a further withdrawal west. The *1.Kompanie* reached the Schlaube estate in the vicinity of Schätz astride the main road from Guhrau to Rawitsch and fought off a Soviet force that was located there. *II.Bataillon* secured a small town in the vicinity of Waffendorf (Saborroitz/Zaborowice). *'Brandenburg'* was now moving southwest to cross the Bartsch River.

In the evening of January 28th *Panzer-Sturm-Pionier-Bataillon 'BR'* reached the vicinity of Waffendorf-Geischen. *Hauptmann* Müller-Rochholz went to the division HQ and received orders that a crossing of the Bartsch River was to be undertaken during the night. The *Panzer-Sturm-Pionier-Bataillon 'BR'*, *Stu.Gesch.Brig. 'GD'* and the *I.(gep)Btl./Jäg.Rgt 1 'BR'* prepared for the new mission. Because there was supposed to be a bridge at Rützen, *Hauptmann* Müller-Rochholz went forward in the *General's* Kübelwagen to evaluate if it had the capacity to support the division's vehicles. What he learned from his reconnaissance was that the bridge was lightly guarded and that most of the Soviet troops decided to occupy the large Manor House. As a coincidence of war, the Manor House belonged to *Oberleutnant* Count Carmer who served as the *Panzer-Korps 'GD' O1* and later the *O1* of *H.Gr. Mitte*. A plan was developed to take the bridge before it could be blown, then attack the Soviets while they were still in their quarters. The plan called for 12 men from the *Begleit-Kompanie* under the command of *Oberleutnant* Mischkeres, disguised in Soviet Army uniforms, to infiltrate through the town and take the bridge by surprise. An immediate attack by *I.(gep)Btl./Jäg.Rgt 1 'BR'* and *Panzer-Sturm-Pionier-Bataillon 'BR'* on the Soviets occupying the Manor House would follow. The rest of the vehicles of the division would then cross the wooden bridge to the west bank of the Bartsch.

Oberleutnant Mischkeres' men made it through the town, soon reaching the bridge. As they neared their objective an alert Soviet sentry challenged the team of *'Brandenburgers'* who immediately opened fire. The sound of battle was heard outside the town. With the element of surprise evaporating every passing minute, *Hauptmann* Müller-Rochholz ordered the main assault on Rützen to commence. *Unteroffizier* Hans Stübling recounts the fighting:

> With light from the shining moon, in the shiny snow on a hard surface, we went cross country to Rützen.
>
> Everything was calm without any enemy contact. The village of Rützen with its big field barns on the northeastern edge was peaceful at night and there was nothing to suggest how we would get bitten here.
>
> About 1,000 meters outside the town, the Gun-Platoon (4th Platoon's Sd.Kfz. 251/9s) of the *I.(gep)Bataillon* opened fire. That was the big wakeup call for the Russians who, it turned out, were all in the Manor House in Rützen, surely felt safe and maybe when we moved in without shooting acted like scared rabbits, or at least could have been more surprised. When we broke into the town from the northeast, all of the fire was coming from the Manor House. In particular, the street going down to the marketplace and the bridge was under heavy fire from infantry weapons. The *Sturmgeschütze* drove through. The wooden bridge had very weathered boards, but with caution, i.e., moving directly on the travel boards, they could hold for *Sturmgeschütze*. The second or third *Sturmgeschütz* rolled right of the travel boards, broke through, turned over and lay upside down in the water. The crew did not make it out. People worked feverishly. The *Geschütz* was pulled out. Two of Metzger's comrades drowned.
>
> If the *Division* was supposed to make it through, we had to take the Manor House. Besides, it belonged to the head of the *Heeresgruppe*, *General* von Natzmer, or Count *Conrad* and so on, people said. The Russians—with the courtyard covered in full horse-drawn carts mostly with captured items—almost gave the impression that it was a support unit. But they furiously defended themselves. Although we could approach from the east and get to within 50 meters,

we were unsuccessful in getting into the Manor House. The entrance was in the middle of the courtyard. However, well-aimed rifle fire was coming out of the basement openings and windows from all over everywhere. Every attempt cost us dead, and there were multiple wounded. *Leutnant* Bätzing, who was accompanying me, also got a shot to his upper thigh. He lay on a bed in the command post—a house on the eastern edge—and was bandaged. Now we left him behind as well, a man who in the best sense of the words was my right hand during these weeks.

It was a hard blow for me personally and no less so for the *Bataillon*. *Hauptmann* Schäfer from *I.(gep)Bataillon* was also severely wounded.

Our *General*, who was running this deployment himself, had to leave. We tried some more to capture this damned palace. From the south, it was on a cliff; there was no way to get in there. In the morning, we gave up on a chance. Part of the Russian occupation force left and tried to go north cross country. We followed them in the SPW and unfortunately shot up most of them! If we had let them go, the others would also have left and we would have had the route open.

The General was back and a 10.5cm [gun] was set up directly in front of the broad side of the Manor House. We fired into the windows. There was still fierce resistance. It seemed almost laughable to us that we couldn't overcome these 50 meters. Then we systematically fired a breach into the right wing (from the north) and finally managed to jump in with some men into the Manor House. Now we moved systematically left from one window to the next. Inside, we took one room after another with *Panzerfausts*. When we reached the upper floor, some individual Russians were holed up in sacks of straw. This must have been a labor service camp or something like that. At this penetration, our *General* was with the first soldiers at the Manor House.

Hauptmann Müller-Rochholz was wounded, but it was only a grazing wound in the shoulder.

During this situation Erasmus radioed, "Crossing at Wiersewitz!" In any event, a crossing southeast of Rützen was now in our hands. The battle was stopped. The Russians acted like scared rabbits. The *2.Pionier-Kompanie* of *Panzer-Sturm-Pionier-Bataillon 'BR'* was ordered through the woods south of Rützen to secure the route.

Sturmgeschütz-Brigade 'GD' was situated at Klein Kloden, southeast of Guhrau when its movement began. *Fahnenjunker-Unteroffizier* Held-Kleingründlach provides his view of the fighting for Rützen:

At about 3:30 a.m., we moved into a Manor House that resembled a palace. [AN: possibly at Schätz]. Here I had the opportunity to see how many people lived up until recent times. There was nothing noticeable about the war as concerned food. Here we ate good and hearty from the ample supplies of the well-filled larders. Now I took the time to yet again take a warm bath after a long time. When I was taking off my clothes, I determined that everything was full of dried blood under my winter suit. The shirt was just a single crust of blood. I touched the place I was hit, and my finger must have been frozen because I couldn't stand the pain anymore. At the *Brigade* command post, I had to write various orders, which became torture for me because I could hardly type or answer the telephone because of the pain. But I didn't forget to take care of bodily comforts and made a proper mulled wine for the headquarters. The atmosphere was overall pleasant and no differences in rank were noticeable here. They treated me as if I were already an officer. Unfortunately this harmony was soon disturbed when there was suddenly an alarm. After a while, everything calmed down again. A Russian truck was captured with Russian communication personnel who were supposed to set up a communications circuit between two Russian tank corps. I looked at the prisoners, who so far had not said much at all. When I talked to them in Russian, they visibly thawed and a cigarette from me got them to start talking. I found out the number of their unit and where they were most recently deployed. In addition, they told me that they thought they would be immediately shot because they were also wearing one German *Luftwaffe* and one infantry uniform each for camouflage purposes. They had so far had a lot of luck until today. But some of our German soldiers spoke better Russian than they did and didn't fall for their tricks, even though the trucks had a "WH" painted on them [AN: the Russians encountered members of *'Brandenburg'* with that symbol painted on their vehicles, which stood for "*Wehrmacht Heer*", and most of the old veterans of *'Brandenburg'* knew at least one foreign language, to include Russian]. Then I went back to doing my business at the headquarters. The commander, *Hauptmann* Metzger, had to go to the *Division*. It was not until a long time later that he came back with the news that an undertaking would be started that very day. It concerned a bridge occupied by Ivan, about 8 km [in Rützen]. From there a group of *'Brandenburg'* under the command of an officer in Russian uniform was supposed to occupy it in a surprise attack and the *I.(gep)Btl./Jäg.Rgt 1 'BR'* was supposed to take the village behind it. Finally we managed it and the *I.(gep)Bataillon* was off with us behind it.

Right after that, the *Panzer-Sturm-Pionier-Bataillon 'BR'* had enemy contact and there was heavy shooting. In the course of the battle, an *SPW* was hit and it flew into the air. We had many dead. The center of enemy resistance was the Manor House on the Rützen estate. There were a large number of heavy artillery-shell launchers about 250 meters away from me under good cover, and they were throwing things all over the place. But when it became too motley for me, I moved back into a building because the shrapnel were buzzing wildly about in the immediate vicinity. It was occupied by the *Division* headquarters.

Here, in addition to *Major* Spaeter, I met *General* von Schulte-Heuthaus—the *'Brandenburg' Division* commander—and this was the first time I came in contact with him. (After successfully defending the division command post in the Litzmannstadt area, he shook my hand in recognition.) Now I had the opportunity for a short chat with him. This one-armed General was a person in whom one could immediately have confidence. He was a gentleman in uniform and had a sort of fatherly quality about him, which made him very nice. In a room near the entrance, there was a severely wounded man who had just been retrieved from a rain of shrapnel of Russian shells. I determined that there was injury to the liver and I bandaged the open wound as best I could with my bandaging kit. There were no medical personnel in the vicinity. Then I was taken back into the rooms of the division staff where I was asked to bandage another wounded officer [AN: this was *Oberleutnant* Bätzing of *Panzer-Sturm-Pionier-Bataillon 'BR'*]. He appeared to be a higher class of person. He didn't forget to thank me very graciously in spite of the pain. It became light slowly and I could now get a picture of the entire area. I ran into *Leutnant* Greiling, who told me that my service at the brigade staff had ended for the time being because I had to replace a missing loader in *Wachtmeister* Will's *Geschütz*. I swore like a trooper, but orders are orders! Yesterday a *Geschütz* commander, today a loader and maybe tomorrow an orderly for the *General*, I thought I had a terrible fury in my belly. I got into *Wachtmeister* Will's *Geschütz*, but not as a loader. At his request, I was there as a "fire direction", which I much preferred, because as the one firing, from a psychological point of view, one has more of a contribution to the success than does the *Geschütz* commander. In the *Geschütz*, I heard that in our "bridge" mission, one of our *Sturmgeschütz* broke through and two men drowned in the incident. We appear to be persecuted by bad luck!"

II.Btl./Jäg.Rgt.2 'BR' now under command of *Oberleutnant* Afheldt continued to provide security at Schlaube along the Guhrau-Hernstadt road. While fighting at Rützen continued to the west, *Oberleutnant* Afheldt ordered his forces withdrawn in the afternoon as their staging area came under Soviet artillery and rocket fire causing light casualties. They moved southeast toward Gross-Wiersewitz on the Bartsch River where they were ordered to take the small town. A late night attack was planned. The challenges of preparing for a night attack on the march played out. The artillery and mortar preparatory fire was not well planned hitting the battalion's own heavy infantry gun position. The attack began at 11:00 p.m. on Gross-Wiersewitz with the *8.Kompanie* taking up a screening position along the left flank, south of the town. The main attack on Wiersewitz was conducted by the *6.Kompanie* along an anti-tank ditch. The *7.Kompanie*, initially in reserve, advanced behind four subordinate *Sturmgeschütze* from *Panzerjäger-Abteilung 'BR'*. The attack was planned by *Oberleutnant* Afheldt, however *Leutnant* Stalf led the main assault.

The attack initially went as planned as the *6.Kompanie* under *Oberleutnant* Sauter destroyed the dug-in JS-2 Stalin tanks at the entrance to the town using *Panzerfausts*. Additional tanks were knocked-out by the *Sturmgeschütze*. The burning town was occupied by the *6.Kompanie* and later by the *7.Kompanie* by 5:00 a.m. Eight to ten Soviet tanks withdrew back to the edge of a piece of forest about 200 meters south and fired on the town from there. Because all the officers of the *6.Kompanie* were wounded during the attack, *Feldwebel* Hasenschwanz took command. The *6.Kompanie* then moved to the right (west) bypassing the Soviet tanks, and then pushed from behind (from the south) into the forest in order to strike at the tanks that no longer had infantry protection. Unfortunately, there were too few *Panzerfausts* on hand to knock-out all the Soviet tanks at one time so the *6.Kompanie* waited for the *7.Kompanie* under *Leutnant* Stalf. While they waited, they received an order to withdraw. *Feldwebel* Hasenschwanz brought out the *6.Kompanie* along the same attack route. Then the battalion moved through the anti-tank trenches, while it received harassing fire from both artillery shells and the Soviet tanks. The battalion assembled and secured itself in the vicinity of the original staging area. *Oberleutnant* Afheldt was promoted to *Hauptmann* on February 1st for this attack and subsequently received the Knight's Cross on March 17th.

Once the Soviets were pushed out of the town, the bridge crossing to the west became available to the *Division*. *Oberleutnant* Afheldt was given orders in the evening of January 31st to lead a night movement across the Bartsch, then find a way across the Oder River. He immediately began the movement as the spearhead of the *Division*. It was at this point that von Saucken made the decision not to support the order by Schörner to attack south. The available *Lage Ost* maps for January 29th depict what appears to be a counterattack south between the Bartsch and Oder Rivers toward Steinau.[4] Based on the available accounts there was no southern attack. Both *'Brandenburg'* and *'Hermann Göring'* moved in the opposite direction to cross the Oder near Glogau reaching the western bank on the night of January 31st into February 1st.

Fighting continued at Rützen while efforts to cross the Bartsch continued. *Sturmgeschütz-Brigade 'GD'* actions continued as recounted by *Fahnenjunker-Unteroffizier* Held-Kleingründlach:

> In addition to two wagons, we took two Russian trucks from the vicinity of the Manor House in which the Russians had barricaded themselves. That was our private war, because we didn't have any orders to pursue it. It was also dangerous to go to the steel side of vehicles of American origin (General Motors) under fire. But maybe we could capture some fuel in the process, and that continued to be our most basic issue. Back in our old hole, we searched the vehicles. They were practically still intact, but without any fuel. However, they had all sorts of delicious stuff. I found pieces of bacon of a diameter I had never seen stamped "Made in Uruguay", American goulash and corned beef cans, Danish ham in large cans, Russian crackers, Russian tobacco and white bread and glass jars with homemade stuff that clearly came from German houses. We first had a hearty breakfast and exchanged our captured items for vodka that the *Jäger* had acquired in large quantities. It was "endless summer" and we were soon in a very upbeat mood. Then we accompanied an assault troops NCO several times onto the estate, which, we found out,

---

4   RG 242 German Armed Forces Operations and Situation Maps, 1939-1945. H.Gr. A. Box 352: *HGr. Mitte GenStdH Op.Abt. IIIb Prüf Nr. 55458 Stand: 29.1.45 Abends.*

belonged to a general-staff officer [AN: Count Carmer]. A couple of times there was suspicious clanging in our boxes—*Panzerbüchsen*! [AN: Soviet anti-tank rifle fire against the hulls of the *Sturmgeschütze*] Unfortunately, we had to give up the attempt to take the estate although it was being hit heavily by our artillery, which had gotten very close. I was silently amazed at the Russians with their bullheaded bitterness because there was no doubt that we were in the majority and still couldn't attain anything. Every movement outside of cover brought heavy shell fire with it. They must have had bunches of ammunition! In the meantime, it became dark again and we moved into a group of houses for the night. At 10:00 p.m., there was an order to tank up and we finally filled up the fuel tanks completely.

Thursday, February 1st

On January 28th *Kampfgruppe 'Mummert'* went on the offensive through the lines of the 10th Tank Corps, breaching the Soviet encirclement of Steinau. *Oberst* Mummert's *Panzergrenadiers* joined forces with the soldiers of the NCO Academy and *Volkssturm* that had held out for the last several days, cut off behind Soviet lines. The combined force quickly formed a solid defense. The Soviets immediately counterattack with tanks the following day losing a half dozen, but the land corridor held. Mummert's *Panzers* maintained a land corridor between the *LVII.Panzer-Korps* and the town until January 31st.[5] On the same day the Soviet counterattack managed to force Kampfgruppe Mummert back to its start lines, though they lost some dozen T-34s in the process.[6] Schörner was obviously not pleased with the development. He likely saw the potential to cut off the bulk of the Soviet combat formation of both the 6th Guards Mechanized Corps and 10th Guards Tank Corps, achieving an important victory that might offer *H.Gr. Mitte* additional breathing room to establish a solid defense. He certainly put pressure on von Saucken to get *Panzer-Korps 'GD'* into action from the north.

Oberleutnant Afheldt's night movement brought him southwest to Lübchen, then northwest to Herrnlauersitz, followed by a turn west through Oderbeltsch and finally across the Oder River by ferry to Niederfähreichen. *Jägerregiment 2 'BR'* was next, followed by the rest of the division with *Sturmgeschütz-Brigade 'GD'* following as the rearguard. *Division 'Brandenburg'* finally crossed the Oder River.

Sturmgeschütz-Brigade 'GD' continued to fight rearguard actions against the advancing Soviets in the area of Neu-Wiersewitz as described by Held-Kleingründlach:

> The battle lasted until the morning. Then we went back to Heidendorf where the command post was. Underway, we loaded up fighters from *'Brandenburg'* who were still wounded and were again gutsy in battle and they kept the enemy infantry off our backs. This last aspect was particularly important during night attacks because no one has any chance against enemy tank-fighting troops as a combat vehicle crew member. At the command post, I met *Leutnant* Greiling, who greeted me as though I had risen from the dead and in the same breath complained to me because I had

5 Mummert's force had engaged a Motorized Rifle Battalion of the 62nd Guards Tank Brigade, 1st Company, 3rd Battalion, 4th Guards Rifle Regiment of the 6th Guards Rifle Division and the 112th Rifle Division. It was noted by intelligence officers of *FHO* that based on the reports it received from the frontline the 60th Guards Tank Brigade suffered light casualties in the Rifle Battalion totaling 3 dead and 10 wounded but that some 46 Soviet tanks were lost. While nothing more is noted, this seems to suggest that this Soviet unit did not put up a particularly effective defense. In the 1st Company of the 4th Guards Rifle Regiment's 3rd Battalion almost half of the 65 Soviet soldiers exhibited a complete loss of morale (*gesunken*) during the fighting. This is likely a reference to their outright surrender or defection. A prisoner of the 112th Rifle Division told his interrogators that all German soldiers captured were being shot: "*Alle deutschen Kriegsgefangener werden erschossen.*" RG 242 German Armed Forces Operations and Situation Maps, 1939-1945. H.Gr. A. Box 353: *HGr. Mitte GenStdH Op.Abt. IIIb Prüf Nr. 55999 Stand: 31.1.45 Abends.*

6 RG 242 German Armed Forces Operations and Situation Maps, 1939-1945. H.Gr. A. Box 352: *HGr. Mitte GenStdH Op.Abt. IIIb Prüf Nr. 55185 Stand: 28.1.45 Abends, Prüf Nr. 55458 Stand: 29.1.45 Abends, Prüf Nr. 55731 Stand: 30.1.45 Abends,* and *Prüf Nr. 55999 Stand: 31.1.45 Abends.*

stopped reporting to him. I made it clear to him that he had himself given me the order to take over for *Wachtmeister* Will without taking care of a replacement for my duties at headquarters. Now I was on a *Geschütz* and felt more at home. The command post was left behind and the infantry went back to the edge of the forest as well. Here a friendly anti-tank gun finally got into position. We spent the entire day here securing it. We continued to hear the noise of tracks and engines of Russian tanks in the forest, but there was no combat activity. The Russians fired mortars regularly only in a group of buildings to our left. Then the sound of T-34 tracks grew in the forest and we became really nervous again. At about 5:00 p.m., we got an order to move and find a way to join the battalion. We went back to a highway and then we waited until the regiment had filtered in. Here we came upon the *20.Panzergrenadier-Division*, whose infantry we put on our *Geschützen* and carried for some distance. Then there were longer pauses in which we could always hear battle noise, primarily shots and hits from Russian tank guns.

The *Sturmgeschütz-Brigade 'GD'* withdrew west through the Rützener Wald in the direction of Herrnlauersitz.

We reached the Oder at the crack of dawn. The *Pioniers* had set up a ferry service and we used it to get to the other bank. In the process, we reached the town of Niederfähreichen and moved into the Kanitz farmstead [to the south]. The Russians were already at the bank where we were and were laying artillery fire on all the roads and the walking paths. Our farmstead and its buildings were heavily covered. Some hits were damned close and I chose to stop my meat-roasting efforts so I could devote my efforts to the *Geschütz*. It was just about 3 seconds later that half the roof came down, right at the place where there was still a spark flickering. Lucky again! Then our *Geschütz* got the order to get three barrels of gas and 11 boxes of ammunition from Niederfähreichen. We obtained a heavy farm wagon and hooked it up behind the *Geschütz*. During the supply run, though people called us dumb and made fun of us because of our modern vehicle, we did solve the transport problem as best we could. We filled up and secured the ammunition allocated to us after we returned to our old hole. During our absence, two artillery rounds landed directly where we had been standing and it is doubtful whether we would still have been alive. Good luck saved us from the worst. The artillery fire let up a bit, but the food didn't taste quite right today. From 10:00 p.m. to midnight, I was on guard. It was thawing and even raining a bit, so almost all the snow was going away.

At 4:00 a.m., there was suddenly an alert to be ready to move out in 8 minutes. We then moved to Niederfähreichen again and reported to the *Korps*. There we met *Hauptmann* Plange, our battery commander, whom we had not seen since Rössel (East Prussia). After a hearty greeting, he told us that the *Sturmgeschütz-Brigade 'GD'* was to be moved to Guben to be reconstituted. In the meantime, we would have to wait until there were enough *'Brandenburger'* personnel to relieve us. I had to get out once again for a change and was ordered to act as a strongpoint leader for a supply company, where I have served without a break. A small consolation for me was the report from an *Obergefreiter* at headquarters whom I know that my promotion to *Wachtmeister* went through on January 1st, 1945. Then I reported to the orderly room of the *'BR'* unit, which was in Altwasser. Then *Obergefreiter* Friedrichs, who was the driver for our brigade commander, brought me supplies that I was supposed to take to our forward *Geschütz* crews. Unfortunately, it was almost dark and besides, I couldn't go forward at all, because I couldn't get through. There were urgent fighting alarms coming from the main battle line, which actually wasn't far away at all. That night, I slept in a luxurious bed with a mattress. Unfortunately, the unaccustomed softness was so harmful to good sleep that I woke up repeatedly.

Friday, February 2nd

As *Panzergrenadier-Division 'BR'* began to reassemble itself after its rapid ferry crossing of the Oder, *Generaloberst* Schörner called again for an immediate counterattack of the Soviet bridgehead at Steinau to the south. This was the *Heeresgruppe* commander's second call for *Panzer-Korps 'GD'* to attack. The *Korps* was not in good shape. According to available reports *'Brandenburg'* had only 20 operational *Sturmgeschütze*. By comparison, *'Hermann Göring 1'* was noted as having only 5 operational Panzer IVs and 22 operational Panzer V Panthers.[7] Thought these numbers were little more than estimates given that the *Korps* had still not officially reached German lines and begun regular reporting back to Heeresgruppe headquarters. The actual *Panzer* strength was likely much lower. Without the benefit of remaining documents or orders, it is not clear what Schörner actually intended as a concept of operation. It appears from surviving accounts that *Panzer-Korps 'GD'* was to strike due southeast along the Oder River, cutting-off the Soviet crossings from the eastern bank near the town of Steinau. The attack order was desperate, if not reckless, and does not appear to have been carried out as intended given the repercussions that followed for *General der Panzertruppen* von Saucken.

The men of *'Brandenburg'* were now operating beyond their capacity to conduct an effective offensive. Men were exhausted physically and mentally. Equipment, weapons, and ammunition were all in short supply. Despite the state of the *Division*, *Oberst* Schulte-Heuthaus ordered the attack. He had little choice as the orders came down from the *Korps* HQ, and they were issued in turn by *Generaloberst* Schörner who was on his way to the operational area. *Jägerregiment 2 'BR'* readied itself for the new task. *Oberst* Oesterwitz met with *Oberleutnant* Afheldt and issued him new attack orders. A reconnaissance in-force was to take place immediately to the south. The meeting did not go well. What was said between the two men has gone unrecorded. Whether *Oberleutnant* Afheldt disagreed with his objectives in the coming attack or just the idea that the division had to conduct an attack at all, is not known. At the end of the meeting, Afheldt was dismissed from command and immediately replaced by *Hauptmann* Zinkel. *Hauptmann* Zinkel took over command of the *II.Bataillon* and ordered his men and a company from the *Panzer-Aufklärung-Abteilung 'BR'* to lead the vanguard of the division south by taking Pilgramsdorf. The *Panzergrenadiers* headed south, likely along the route Ehrenfeld-Hochkirch, reaching their objective by the afternoon. They immediately set up a defensive perimeter in time to fight off a Soviet patrol that approached from the direction of the Steinau bridgehead to the southeast. The company from *Panzer-Aufklärung-Abteilung 'BR'* was then directed to advance toward Raudten to the east and determine the strength of the Soviets in the large town. As the Reconnaissance Platoon advanced across the open, rolling hills toward Raudten, the unit was caught in the open by the Soviets and was all but wiped out in the ambush. A handful of survivors made their way back to Pilgramsdorf and informed the *II.Bataillon*.

Generalmajor Schulte-Heuthaus ordered the *Division* to attack Raudten the next day and eliminate the Soviet force there. Raudten sat astride both a key north-south road junction and rail line and had to be secured if an attack toward Steinau was going to be successful. *Jägerregiment 2 'BR'* was given the orders to attack toward Raudten and eliminate the Soviet forces there. Both battalions were to launch simultaneous attacks, with the *I.Bataillon* advancing from Polach due east toward the Raudten brickworks, and the *II.Bataillon* from Pilgramsdorf, to the southern part of the town. *Sturmgeschütz-Brigade 'GD'* was to advance east between both *Bataillons*, ready to provide support to either if required. Further south of *II.Bataillon*, the *Panzerjäger-Abteilung 'BR'* along with *I.(gep) Bataillon* of *Jägerregiment 1 'BR'* was ordered to screen toward Mlitsch and cut off the north-south road to Raudten. Participating in the attack was a *Kampfgruppe* of *Fallschirm-Panzer-Division 1 'HG'* that had the objective to attack east and cut the north-south road from Raudten, to the south of *II.Btl./ Jäg.Rgt. 2 'BR'*. The attack began in the early morning hours.

---

7   RG 242 German Armed Forces Operations and Situation Maps, 1939-1945. H.Gr. A. Box 353: *HGr. Mitte GenStdH Op.Abt. IIIb Prüf Nr. 56879 Stand: 3.2.45 Abends.*

The *I.Btl./Jäg.Rgt. 2 'BR'* assembled under cover of the forest west of Polach, then advanced east over open ground. The *1.Kompanie* soon reached the Raudten brickworks and engaged in close-quarter fighting with the somewhat surprised Soviets. *Feldwebel* E. Peintner, who was the Platoon Leader for the 3rd Platoon, was killed in the action, and the attack soon stalled among the buildings of the brickworks. *Sturmgeschütz-Brigade 'GD'* moved out at dawn after the *panzergrenadiers* began their attack, as not to alert the Soviets by their engine noise. Along the right flank the *II.Btl./Jäg.Rgt. 2 'BR'* was spotted further to the south advancing east, unfortunately their movement was noticed by the Soviets. In the early morning, *II.Btl./Jäg.Rgt 2 'BR'* assembled in the forest just south of Pilgramsdorf for their attack. The Soviets, who were already altered to the presence of German forces in the area from the previous day, hit the *Panzergrenadiers'* assembly area with indirect mortar and artillery fire. As it became light with the rising sun, the men of the battalion launched their attack against the Soviets who were in fortified forest positions near the rail line. The *II.Bataillon* then advanced north over open terrain, across marshy meadows, toward the line of hills on both sides of Hill 141 (east of Pilgramsdorf) in the direction of Polach. From here, they turned east and reached an area just south of the Raudten brickworks. *Hauptmann* Zinkel's men reached a hill that was separated from Soviet positions by a gorge. It was recognized that "any further friendly attack appeared to be suicide because we were downhill and again in the clear sights of the enemy." The losses among the *'Brandenburgers'* had already mounted during the course of the fighting with the *6.Kompanie* suffering 10 wounded, and even higher losses from the others. *Oberleutnant* Plaser, the commander of the *9.Kompanie* was killed in action and the *7.Kompanie* lost 3/4s of its strength in an attack against a Soviet heavy machine gun position. Soon fighting ensued at Hill 141 where *Obergefreiter* S. Rainer and *Gefreiter* Kuhn were killed in action. *Hauptmann* Zinkel withdrew his battalion back west at 2:00 p.m., following the retreat path of the *Kampfgruppe* of *Fallschirm-Panzer-Division 1 'HG'* through a valley that sheltered them from Soviet fire. The men of *'Hermann Göring'* apparently shared a similar fate to that of the *II.Bataillon*, and recognized they could not advance further east under the withering Soviet fire. The main assault on Raudten was now over. The overall attack confirmed the concerns raised by *Oberleutnant* Afheldt that cost him his command.

Farther to the southeast the armored personnel carriers of *I.(gep)Btl./Jag.Rgt.1 'BR'* under the command of *Hauptmann* Froböse advanced along with *Hauptmann* Königstein's *Sturmgeschütze* of *Panzerjäger-Abteilung 'BR'* in support. This combined force succeeded in advancing to the crossroads just north of Mlitsch, where they took up a defensive position as originally ordered. An immediate reconnaissance was ordered to the east and south, which quickly identified almost 20 T-34s mounted with infantry near the cross-roads. The *Panzergrenadiers* held their position through the day and into the night without incident. After midnight the Soviet regiment launched a surprise attack and overran the defensive position. *Leutnant* Kass recounts the day's events:

> We attacked in the south via Pilgramsdorf, Jauschwitz and Militsch headed east and passed Raudten to the south. *Sturmgeschütze* with Königstein and Froböse, along with an *SPW Bataillon* [*I.(gep)Btl.*] bored into the bridgehead. However, the attack came to a halt at their neighbors to the left and right. I was at what must have been the most thinly occupied place, a road junction 1 kilometer east of Jauschwitz, and made a hedgehog with four *Geschütz*. I used a couple of men to do a night patrol and found 20 T-34s with infantry on them. I subsequently got a group from the *Aufklärungs-Abteilung* for support. At 12:30 a.m., we were attacked by this regiment. We killed seven tanks, six rolled through and the rest turned around. Two *Geschütze* were lost and I was wounded. With the medic and an infantryman, I captured a 7.62 self-propelled gun that we had initially thought was one of our armored artillery pieces.

On the afternoon of the following day *Leutnant* Kass moved back toward Pilgramsdorf and set up a defense there.

The staunch defense of the 6th Guards Mechanized Corps proved too hard for the weakened units of *Panzergrenadier-Division 'BR'* to breach. The 16th and 17th Guards Tank Brigades, backed by the 49th Mechanized Brigade fought tenaciously to block any further advance. Meanwhile the situation at Steinau had grown critical for *Kampfgruppe 'Mummert'*. Units of the 10th Guards Tank Corps renewed their attacks to dislodge the German force and finally capture the town after the garrison broke out.[8]

Saturday/Sunday, February 3rd-4th

Despite the losses of the previous day, the *Division* was ordered to renew its attack as desperation grew in Steinau and Schörner saw possible victory, no matter how unrealistic it was, slipping from his grasp. *Jägerregiment 2 'BR'* extracted itself from the outskirts of Raudten and shifted southeast toward the position established by the *I.(gep)Bataillon* of *Jägerregiment 1 'BR'* the previous day. *Jägerregiment 2 'BR'* launched a new attack west, but further south of Raudten. The *II.Bataillon* attacked from Jauschwitz in the afternoon, toward the Sternberg (a forested area southeast of Alt-Raudten), along the left flank of the *I.Bataillon*. The *Panzergrenadiers* advanced across the rail line (their objective from the previous day) and soon reached a position between Hills 130 and 132. Here they established a defensive position along the main road running from Raudten east toward the Oder. They ambushed and destroyed several Soviet supply columns heading toward Raudten along the road. By the evening, the *II.Bataillon* advanced up the opposite side of the road to Hill 161, effectively cutting off the Soviet force in Raudten from resupply. The Soviets counterattacked twice with infantry supported by mortars and anti-tank guns but failed to dislodge the men of *'Brandenburg'*.

The *I.Bataillon*, operating on the right, attacked toward Töschwitz from positions north of Mlitsch. There were heavy losses on both sides. It was noted that *Jäger* Stadler of the *1.Kompanie* was killed in the fighting while taking the town. In Töschwitz, the commanding general of the *Division*, *Oberst* Schulte-Heuthaus, had advanced into the town with the first attack wave, and soon found himself pinned down under Soviet tank fire. *Sturmgeschütz-Brigade 'GD'* renewed its attack toward the Oder along with a *Kampfgruppe* of *Fallschirmjäger-Panzer-Division 1 'HG'*. They started in the vicinity of Mlitsch and attacked due east, just south of the positions of *Jägerregiment 2 'BR'*.

Wachtmeister Held-Kleingründlach of *Sturmgeschütz-Brigade 'GD'* was detailed to work a resupply mission for *'Brandenburg'* in the wake of the second attack on the Steinau bridgehead. The account of his meeting with *Generaloberst* Schörner related below may appear incredible to some, but is indeed true and corroborated by a number of other accounts that reflect Schörner's draconian actions behind his frontline, which received the highest praise from Minister of Propaganda Joseph Goebbels (see below section Attack at Lauban (Lubań), March 3rd).

> Early in the morning, supply company vehicles moved forward with fuel and ammunition. The field kitchen was there as well. I used this opportunity to take the supplies that had been entrusted to me with me. We went through Hochkirch, Barschau, Pilgramsdorf and Mlitsch. All of these were towns that were still in Russian hands yesterday and which the *Division* had freed through fighting in the meantime. It must have been heavy fighting because there were a bunch of dead Russians around and there must have been antitank artillery, vehicles and other artillery all around. It extended all the way to the front lines.
>
> When we were right on the village road, a heavy shell landed in the yard right next to us. We took the vehicles among the buildings a bit away from the road, which was clogged with vehicles. Here I saw the first units of the *'Hermann Göring' Division*. In the basement of the building, we

---

8   RG 242 German Armed Forces Operations and Situation Maps, 1939-1945. H.Gr. A. Box 352: *HGr. Mitte GenStdH Op.Abt. IIIb Prüf Nr. 56879 Stand: 2.2.45 Abends.*

felt a bit safer, particularly since the fire had strengthened us. Heavy and heavier shells whistled and detonated with hellish crashes.

Then we moved out and went left into the terrain where our *Sturmgeschütz* went through a farm. This was where the front line was, and it could still be seen by the enemy. We and our vehicles were moving onto the gently sloping hill as though we were on a serving platter. This was where we tanked up [with petrol]. Personally, I considered it an idea coming from a drunken mind to bring wheeled vehicles next to the *Geschütze* to tank up under these circumstances. In addition, we still had to load ammunition from the trucks onto the *Geschütze*. And it was borne out in a real rain of shrapnel and shots. The Stalin organs especially roared every moment and their "blessing" was distributed throughout the area. It is really amazing that nothing else happened. But we all helped to get rid of this serious load as soon as we could! I ran into *Hauptmann* Königstein, the commander of *Panzerjäger-Abteilung 'BR'*, and met *Hauptmann* Walter. I asked *Hauptmann* Walter to take over the supplies for the *'GD'* crew under *Leutnant* Baer. He refused to do that, indicating that he did not want to take the responsibility and then I turned it over to *Feldwebel* Granser's *Geschütz*. *Unteroffizier* Sacher took the things and the responsibility for them.

There was a lot of air activity in this sector and it was often impossible to distinguish what was friend and what was foe. Then we withdrew. I noticed a *Sturmgeschütz* in the terrain that was hard to move through because of the trenches and the holes and I had my truck stop. It was a *Geschütz* without a commander or a fire direction officer. I heard that both of them were killed in action and that the *Geschütz* and the wheeled units had gone back to get two men for the crew. We were the wheeled units. So I told my driver and I got into the *Geschütz*. I put my voice microphone on around my neck and briefed the driver. After a while, we had reached the road. We had been driving on it about 200 meters when we were stopped by "Chain Dogs" [AN: Military Field Police] in which there was a high-ranking officer standing. Signaling disks were used to indicate "stop" and we stopped the *Sturmgeschütz*. I didn't trust my eyes when suddenly the figure of *Generaloberst* Schörner moved forward. The following conversation took place, "Get out! What are you doing with the *Geschütz*?" I answered, "As far as I know, two men on the crew died in action and the *Geschütz* is on the way back to get two replacements." "What do you mean back? You have all forfeited your lives and I will have you shot. Right here and now. Anyone in the tank, get out right now!"

The two of us stood up trembling in front of the *Generaloberst*. "You and that guy there," he pointed at me, "will be shot immediately because of cowardice in the face of the enemy!" I really felt queasy at this point because I had already survived six years of war to some extent and now I might be shot for something that I didn't feel guilty for in the least. Desperately, I told Schörner, "If I'm going to be shot, then I ask to say my last words!"

"Well," he said, and I continued, "There are only two crewmen on this *Geschütz*; I'm not one of them. I was taking ammunition, fuel and supplies forward and I just dug the driver out of un-trafficable terrain. In addition, I am a member of the *'Großdeutschland'* Division and detached to *'Brandenburg'.*" I took out my pay book and he processed what I said.

He studied the page with orders and awards especially carefully and said, "O, you're a *'GD'* man and an old hand already, so let's temper justice with mercy right now." He turned to the two men in the *Geschütz*: "Both of you get in immediately and go forward again for right now! When the Russians see a single armored vehicle of ours, they'll start running. Only special courage can save you from execution!" And then he said to me, "And you, get back to where you belong!" I made the effort to make a brisk bow and got out slightly befuddled. Thank God the column had seen what was going on from some distance away and was waiting for me, because otherwise I would have had to trek 15 kilometers or so by foot. The more time passed since this unfortunate incident, the calmer I was. It's supposed to serve as an example to me that as a supervisor, one should first clinically and properly check every opportunity before letting one's hectic impulse have free rein. I can accept the lack of self-control of this *Heer* Commander only because the fighting spirit of German Eastern Front soldiers was to some extent already very bad.

The men of the *II.Bataillon, Jägerregiment 2 'BR'* held their ground through the day. In the early evening, the Soviets launched a counterattack along the open left flank of the *II.Bataillon* that forced the *Jäger* to retreat back to Polach along the route they had advanced into the Sternberg Forest or become cut off. The Soviets also launched a southern counterattack along the right flank of the *I.Bataillon*. The *I.Bataillon* began to fall back, unfortunately leaving *Oberst* Schulte-Heuthaus and other members of the *Divisional* staff cut off in Töschwitz. A rescue mission was quickly ordered.

As *'Brandenburg'* again found itself being cut off, *Kampfgruppe 'Mummert'* could no longer hold off the increasing Soviet attacks. The Soviet cut off their land route between Steinau and the main German line to the west. Running low on ammunition and supplies, *Oberst* Mummert quickly ordered a breakout for the evening of February 4th. The attempt was successful and the remaining defenders of Steinau reached the lines of *LVII.Panzer-Korps*.

Panzer-Sturm-Pionier-Bataillon 'BR' arrived in the vicinity of *I.(gep)Bataillon*, which was still holding their positions at Mlitsch from the previous days' attack. *Hauptmann* Müller-Rochholz arrived at the division command post established at Jauschwitz and received his orders. The *Panzer-Sturm-Pionier-Bataillon 'BR'* deployed in a defensive line between Jauschwitz and Mlitsch. After arriving at the command post, *Hauptmann* Müller-Rochholz received interesting news and takes up the account:

> The battalion was deployed to Mlitsch. Mlitsch was booby-trapped when we moved out. Even though it was clearly marked, a unit—I no longer know which one—moved a pump rod and was injured by our hidden charges [AN: this was likely a unit of *Fallschirmjäger-Panzer-Division 1 'Hermann Göring'*]. (At that time we were still mining the toilet seats—now I know that the Russians certainly aren't using them!)
>
> In very heavy battles near Alt-Raudten, our *General*, as was so often the case, was in the front lines and was cut off by the Russian thrust to Mlitsch toward the south. North of Töschwitz, several of our *Sturmgeschütze* were knocked-out and, among other things, Königstein had to be abandoned. Under these conditions, Erasmus and I had to push our way through from Mlitsch to Töschwitz with an 8-wheeled *Achtrad-SPW* loaned from the *Panzer-Aufklärung-Abteilung 'BR'*. to get the *General* out of there. We had just gotten to the meadows north of Mlitsch and then we had a brisk trip on a good road under Russian tank fire. We made it! Then we got out of Töschwitz and Königstein after we had gotten there with a tracked motorcycle, then we found our *General* after we pushed our way forward to find him behind the *Sturmgeschütze*. We made it back.

The entire division now began a withdrawal west. *Panzer-Sturm-Pionier-Bataillon 'BR'* established a defensive position close to the rail line east of Gross Rinnersdorf as the other units withdrew and reoccupied many of the start positions before the attack, running from Pilgramsdorf-Gross-Rinnersdorf. Once this frontline was established, the *Pioniers* withdrew as ordered through the forest during the night to the vicinity of Dammer to establish a second defensive line. The counterattack at Steinau was over.

Defensive Actions, February 5th-10th

The next five days found the scattered elements of the *Panzergrenadier-Division 'BR'* fighting to maintain a defensive perimeter in the between Polkwitz-Raudten. The weakened battalions of *'Brandenburg'* fought with the overextended Soviets. See saw skirmishes continued as villages changed hand and neither side was able to mass enough force tactically to hold terrain for long. The Soviet 6th Guards Mechanized Corps, and the 10th Guards Tank Corps were now joined by infantry divisions of the 3rd Guards and 13th Army preparing for a renewed offensive west. The fighting took a toll on *Panzer-Korps 'GD'*. According to reports issued on February 5th, *'Brandenburg'* had only 7 operational *Sturmgeschütze* with 11 in short-term repair. *'Hermann Göring 1'* was noted as having only 2 operational Panzer IVs and 1 operational Panzer V Panther with 9 and 22 in short-term repair respectively.[9] These losses were likely not all related to combat damage but reflected a combination of losses and lack of routine maintenance as both divisions were now in constant combat for nearly a month.

In anticipation of a Soviet attack out of the Steinau Bridgehead *'Brandenburg'* was ordered to advance east and block the northward approaches of the expected advance. The *I.Btl./Jäg.Rgt. 2 'BR'* advanced and reoccupied Alt-Raudten while *II.Btl./Jäg.Rgt 2 'BR'* entered Polach and set up a defense, building positions through the 7th. After several hours of heavy bombardment against the battalions of *Jägerregiment 2 'BR'* the Soviets launched an expected attack west from Raudten in the early morning hours. The *I.Btl./Jäg.Rgt. 2 'BR'* defensive positions, particularly those established in the by the *1.Kompanie* and *2.Kompanie* in the forested terrain, proved effective. Both companies were able to halt a Soviet infantry attack accompanied by two heavy assault guns just 100 meters from their position. The *II.Btl./Jäg.Rgt. 2 'BR'* was hit hard and the *6.Kompanie* attempted to withdraw from the Soviet attack force that was supported by heavy ISU assault guns. The *6.Kompanie*, fighting its way back house-to-house, withdrew to the *Bataillon* command post at a Manor House where a new defensive position was established. A captured Soviet assault gun brought in for reinforcement by *Leutnant* Maier knocked-out two Soviet assault guns stuck in the swamp. One Soviet armored reconnaissance vehicle was shot off the road. Around noon, the *6.Kompanie* position was re-occupied and reinforced with the *7.Kompanie*.

The *'Brandenburgers'* continued to hold their position in spite of increasing Soviet attacks of battalion and regimental strength that were supported by mortars, antitank guns and tanks. German casualties mounted. As evening approached, Polach was captured by the Soviets on the left flank, and the forest position was then attacked from two sides. According to *Oberleutnant iG* Bröker who was soon cut off: "When I started breaking through to the *I.Bataillon* (our neighbor to the right), I was followed by six more men, including one with severe injuries. All of the others were killed in action. During the night, some more released personnel from the *II.Bataillon* made their way into the *I.Bataillon*. Two *Kampfgruppen* with 25-30 men each were formed with the *6.Kompanie* and *7.Kompanie* under *Leutnant* Stalf, the *8.Kompanie* through *10.Kompanie* and Battalion Staff under *Hauptmann* Zinkel." They setup security on a hill near Pilgramsdorf to await further orders.

Held-Kleingründlach offers a picture of the activity around Pilgramsdorf, where the command post of *Panzergrenadier-Division 'BR'* was established:

The order to move came at about midnight. It was to move to Pilgramsdorf, where the command post was. The entire village was full of miscellaneous vehicles and artillery. A 21-cm *Nebelwerfer* was right in front of the building. It was very interesting for me to learn about this weapon that I previously had not known was made by Germans. The sound when it fired was about that of an lFH 18 and, as I found out through binoculars, the effect it had when it hit the edge of a forest occupied by enemy about 2 kilometers from here wasn't bad. At any rate, there was kindling wood all over everywhere. There were continually new fire commands and there was breaking and crashing over there where our *Artillerie-Abteilung* was massing fire. Housing, as you might imagine, was bad. I slept in a tiny kitchen with an additional three men. The only thing that redeemed it for me at all was the good food. After a long time, there was another fighting vehicle

9   RG 242 German Armed Forces Operations and Situation Maps, 1939-1945. H.Gr. A. Box 353: *HGr. Mitte GenStdH Op.Abt. IIIb Prüf Nr. 5x751 Stand: 10.2.45 Abends.*

package and a packet of Schöna-Kola. The night was quiet and while I was on guard duty, I could let my thoughts move a bit to my far-off homeland.

Commander of *II.Btl./Jäg.Rgt 1 'BR'*, *Hauptmann* Hunhold, occupied a village southeast of the Töppendorf Wald, which was likely Hochkirch, as his battalion reformed. Röseke provides a final account of his unit in this area on February 6th through the 7th:

On the evening of February 6th, I reported to the regimental commander, *Oberst* von Brückner, in a village southeast of Töppendorf. I told him about my experiences since Warthbrücken with *Oberleutnant* Frömmel and *Stabsarzt* Dr. Fischer present. Now the time that I had dreaded so much had come. I was waiting for the question, "So where are your men?" But the *Oberst* and the two comrades silently shook my hand and the commander told me when I was alone that he wanted to recommend me for award of the Knight's Cross.

I took a vehicle of the *Versorgungs-Kompanie* to the command post of *II.Btl./Rgt. 1 'BR'* and reported to *Hauptmann* Hunhold. *Major* Wandrey had not yet returned to the *Bataillon*.

There was "trouble brewing" and we had to expect that the Russians would dare to break into our positions. My old *Kompanie* officer, *Leutnant* Klaus, showed up, unshaved as always with a club in his hand, which caused his men to give him the nickname "Rübezahl."

I also found a number of old comrades from the former *III.Btl./Jäg.Rgt. 1 'BR'*, including my *Hauptfeldwebel* Schacht, *Unteroffizier* Nitschner and *Unteroffizier* Wickl—the clerks—and a few drivers who had managed to get to Silesia from Kutno via Warthbrücken and Posen with the regimental headquarters and other motorized units without enemy contact. Most of those found with the *Bataillon* were, however, new.

The *8.Jäger-Kompanie* suffered a similar fate to the *6.Kompanie* and *7.Kompanies* near Litzmannstadt, and they have been irreparably dispersed since then. The *9.Kompanie* (heavy weapons) got to Lissa without any major losses, but has had a lot of casualties since then. The *10.Kompanie* (mortars) went missing in the vicinity of Posen.

I spent the evening with my old comrades to say goodbye to them. It wasn't easy for me to do that, but I could see myself that I finally had to go to the hospital.

Despite the heavy fighting some normalcy returned. As the *Panzergrenadiers* finally settled in after weeks of retreating across Poland, many got their first taste of a bath and hot food in German villages. Many relished the taste of American coffee and other foods, captured from the Soviets who were well supplied by the copious amounts of Allied lend lease material. As many walked into German homes, they experienced running water and electricity. Luxuries not felt for a long time by some. As one veteran recalled: "The electric light was still on even though it was a military operation area. It was a funny feeling to know that Ivan in the neighboring village could also turn on the lights and play the radio like we were doing." On February 8th, the Regimental Commander of *Jägerregiment 1 'BR'*, *Oberst* von Brückner, was transferred to the *Führer* Reserve of *OKW*. *Major* Wandrey now took over command.

As the end of the war approached, providing the troops with petrol became ever more critical, so motorized units were forced to go "hot" and run on a blend based on alcohol. Not even *Panzer-Korps 'GD'* was spared from that. For this reason, Spaeter assembled miscellaneous stocks of petrol and equipment from a dissolving infantry regiment that was to form the basis for a cobbled-together *Fahrschwadron*. On February 8th the Senior Veterinarian, Dr. Hein, and *Leutnant* Gruber were sent to the Primkenau area to take over setting up the *Fahrschwadron 'BR'*. That was where the remainder of the infantry's miscellaneous vehicles were located. However, the proximity of Soviet forces, forced the further withdrawal of *'Brandenburg'* HQ to prepare the creation of an initial *Fahrschwadron*. This place was between Spreefurt and Milkel. Amazingly, it was determined by the *Division's* staff that the new unit was the second one that had been quartered there during the war. So the location was well suited for its establishment. Within a week, the affairs of the old infantry unit were wrapped up and the first *Fahrschwadron 'BR'* came into existence. It was commanded by *Leutnant* Gruber, who's First Sergeant was *Hauptwachtmeister* Böhnke. It had two groups of 10 teams, plus the miscellaneous vehicles, all Hf 1 wagons. Horse strength was about 120 and personnel about 80. Because a large portion of the men were not trained to deal with horses, they first had to be retrained and "Thanks to *Hauptwachtmeister* Böhnke that was managed marvelously in a short time." This first transport troop was ready for operations in two weeks and placed under the command of *Major* Spaeter as the *Ib* for supply purposes.

The Soviets finally launched a breakout from their bridgehead at Steinau starting on the evening of February 7th/8th. Their attack began the start of Koniev's Lower Silesian Operation. The attack began with a fifty-minute artillery bombardment followed by a ground assault at 6:00 a.m., just before dawn. The advance west was hampered somewhat by the thawing ground, as mud soon replaced the hard permafrost that had aided the Soviet advance across Poland the month before. The Soviets shifted their main thrusts north and south of Raudten against the weaker units defending along the flanks of *Panzer-Korps 'GD'* after experiencing too much resistance against the *'Brandenburg'* frontline and began moving west with "endless armored columns."

11

The Retreat to the Queis River, February 9th-11th

(Reference Maps 52, 53 and 54)

For the next three days *'Brandenburg'* continued to hold an exposed salient as the Soviets continued their Lower Silesian Operation offensive across the Oder River from the Steinau Bridgehead. The Soviets advanced northwest to Glogau where house-to-house fighting raged. The small garrison had to breakout through Soviet lines in order to reach the main German defensive line farther back. Elements of the Soviet 4th Guards Tank Army conducted a westward strike toward the city of Lüben, while the 13th Army pushed southeast along the *Autobahn* to cut-off Breslau. To the north of the *Panzer-Korps* advanced the spearheads of the now familiar 4th Guards Tank Army's 6th Guards Mechanized Corps that reached Primkenau by February 9th after quickly driving through the thin screening lines of *Kampfgruppe 16.Panzer-Division*. Behind the 4th Guards Tank Army came the 3rd Guards Tank Army leveraging the established bridgehead over the Oder. The 6th Guards Tank Corps of the 3rd Guards Tank Army defeated the newly deployed training and replacement units of *Division Nr. 408* on the southern flank of *Panzer-Korps 'GD'*, reaching Kotzenau also on the 9th. *Panzer-Korps 'GD'* was again stuck holding an exposed position and could quickly become cut off behind Soviet lines. *Panzergrenadier-Division 'BR', Fallschirm-Panzer-Division 1 'HG'*, and the *20.Panzergrenadier-Division* were now being outflanked and in danger of being encircled. *General* von Saucken radioed the *4.Panzer-Armee* and notified them of the situation and requested a withdrawal. The answer was "no".

On February 8th, for reasons of his own, *Luftwaffe Generalmajor* von Necker resigned his command of *Fallschirm-Panzer-Division 1 'HG'* and his *Luftwaffe* commission that he received on January 1st, 1945. He was placed into the *Führerreserve* and later regained his *Heer* commission. He was replaced as commander by *Generalmajor* Max Lemke. It is likely that von Necker was tired of the situation or perhaps he received a dressing down by Schörner himself over the progress to reach Steinau. Alternatively, he might have been upset with von Saucken's handling of the situation during the crossing of the Oder River. In any event, the change of command during the current tactical situation did little to help the soldiers looking for senior leadership to guide them through the current crisis.

The *Panzergrenadiers* of *'Brandenburg'* began a withdrawal west from their positions around Pilgramsdorf, to Dammer, followed by Herbersdorf then to Heerwegen. The withdrawal was one of necessity and it was not authorized by the *4.Panzer-Armee*. On February 10th the *Korps* HQ was located outside the forming pocket in the village of Herbersdorf. The commanders of both *Fallschirm-Panzer-Division 1 'HG'* and the *20.Panzergrenadier-Division* were apparently at the *Korps* HQ consulting with von Saucken. Only *Oberst* Schulte-Heuthaus was inside the pocket with *'Brandenburg'*. Finally, the request was approved to withdraw the *Korps* but precious time had been lost. By the time the order to withdraw was received from the *4.Panzer-Armee* headquarters, it was already too late for the troops as they were now encircled by the Soviets between Heerwegen and Raudten. On the evening of the 10th von Saucken stepped into an armored car and drive through the Soviet lines into the pocket to personally take command.

During the night between February 8th-9th, the *I.Btl./Jäg.Rgt. 2 'BR'* moved back to Pilgramsdorf from the forward positions around Raudten. At noon it withdrew again. In the evening it came into contact with Soviet forces as it made its way through a nearby forest. Heavy combat erupted among the fir trees. During this combat, *Panzerfausts* were used against Soviet infantry, sometimes 20 to 30 meters away, which proved very effective according to accounts. The Soviets continued to infiltrate behind the lines of the *'Brandenburgers'* with the intent to cut off their line of march west. During the night the Soviets succeeded in their efforts, cutting off the westward withdrawal route. Three *Sturmgeschütze* of *Panzerjäger-Abteilung 'BR'* led the breakout west with *Leutnant* Stalf's platoons from the *7.Kompanie* of *II.Btl./Jäg.Rgt. 2 'BR'*. The rest of *Panzerjäger-Abteilung 'BR'* provided a rear guard along with *II.(gep)Btl./Jäg.Rgt. 1 'BR'*, under the command of *Hauptmann* Hunhold. New withdrawal plans were discussed among the key leaders at Herbersdorf. The withdrawal got underway through the final part of the forest, then the column of vehicles moved through open fields for several kilometers, having to abandon several precious vehicles that became stuck in swampy ground. About 20 kilometers outside of Sprottisch-Waldau, a Soviet tank obstacle impeded the withdrawal. Led by *Leutnant* Stalf without any orders or further support, twelve men from the *6.Kompanie* and some men from the *7.Kompanie* attacked. With a *Panzerfaust* and lots of shouts of "Hurra", the first Soviet anti-tank gun was taken and turned around. The *'Brandenburgers'* shot off what ammunition they had, then acquired three German 7.5cm and six Soviet 7.62cm antitank guns with trucks, attacking each Soviet defensive position in turn. About 30 Soviets were killed in exchange for only a single wounded *'Brandenburger'*. The *Geschütz* of *Leutnant* Kass received a long-range hit by a Soviet anti-tank gun, but managed to keep moving and soon reached a road. He wrote that "now I was supposed to cover movement for Roßmann's *Panzer-Regiment 'Hermann Göring 1'*, but I refused. Stalf and 12 men attacked a Russian antitank cluster and captured them. We took a couple of those things with us." With the Soviet anti-tank defensive line defeated in detail, the withdrawing column made it through. The captured Soviet material was blown up, and everyone was back on vehicles heading west. By the evening the column reached 5 kilometers outside of Sprottau and set up security.

Sturmgeschütz-Brigade 'GD' also began their withdrawal after a Soviet attack:

> The next morning was ushered in at about 7:00 a.m. with Russian extended fire that included everything. In the first fifteen minutes, it was impossible to distinguish outgoing and incoming at all. Everything was a powerful simmering and buzzing. Some hits landed directly on the building and the air pressure, combined with the shrapnel, shredded the front windows. During the morning, the fire continued to diminish until finally there were only a couple of strikes now and then remaining. Around evening, I moved from the 2nd floor to the ground floor where *Wachtmeister* Eberlein, a clerk and two sick people from the *Jägerregiment* were lying down. I was assigned to guard duty and was checking the guard posts when Eberlein and the clerk came to see me with the news that we would move this very day. At about 11:30, it was time; I put my baggage on a gasoline-powered vehicle and was coincidentally able to go along in a passenger car. The trip was terrible. The column stopped at every moment. We had an especially long stay at a hill the enemy could see. Finally we went on toward Dornbusch, and settled into a big estate with a Manor House similar to a palace.

There was no uniform command initially among the withdrawing elements of *Panzer-Korps 'GD'*. Von Saucken's presence was soon felt once he exerted command, and he personally organized the breakthrough of the Soviet encirclement. *Division 'Brandenburg'* assembled in the vicinity of Sprottau. In among them were parts of *Fallschirm-Panzer-Division 1 'HG'* and many other units. "It was rather chaotic" according to a member of *II.Btl./Jäg.Rgt. 2 'BR'*. He recalled that "at about noon, enemy fire (artillery, mortars, tanks and infantry weapons) sent the stalled masses into a panicked flight to the west. We ourselves went back in an orderly fashion. In the forested areas that followed, there was some measure of order in the entire cluster. The remainder of *Jägerregiment 2 'BR'* took over point in the upcoming battles to break through to the west."

The movement of both *Panzer-Sturm-Pionier-Bataillon 'BR'* and *Sturmgeschütz-Brigade 'GD'* became intertwined along the secondary roads running between Polkwitz and Lübben. *Fahnenjunker-Unteroffizier* Hans Stübling's account covers the entire division and adds additional information to the fighting of *Jägerregiment 2 'BR'* as well as the *Panzerjäger-Abteilung*:

> In the morning, right when the *Sturmgeschütz-Brigade 'GD'* was returning from Dornbusch (and thus from the north) to Dammer, we were moving through Dammer to the southwest on forest trails. In the forest between Dammer and Frei-Friedrichswalde, we were dammed narrowly squeezed between the Russians. Behind us (to the northeast), they were firing from Dammer and in front of us (to the west-southwest) on the road from Heerwegen (Polkwitz) to Lübben. There was one T-34 after another with infantry riding on them. We acted like scared rabbits. Full of pride, we pointed it out to our commanders, who with their radio-equipped *SPW* were in the middle of a pocket with us, as always. It would have been suicide to leave the forest at this point to cross the road at Friedrichswalde. Men and vehicles from all sorts of units in our division hid in the forest here and excitedly watched the Russians commandeering the farm buildings directly in front of us—they were followed by many tanks and troops. We had to act like rabbits, damn it!
>
> As night fell, the Russian traffic on the road died down as well, thank God. We sent out a Reconnaissance Platoon in front and behind us was an unending line of vehicles from our division, army equipment and other places. When we left the forest on a narrow swampy field road south of Heerwegen (Polkwitz), we saw Soviet tanks among the buildings in the southern part of the town. As calmly and quickly as we could, we tried to go forward, but soon the tracks of the trucks were so deep in the soft road that ordinary passenger vehicles could no longer make it through, and the exit from the field road to the main road between Heerwegen and Herbersdorf (on the sharp switchback) was so steep and made such a sharp turn to the right that trucks slid off and had to be put back upright. On the road east-northeast of Herbersdorf, the *Pioniers* had put mines 500 meters to the west. The Russians were also in Herbersdorf. Anything that hadn't disappeared over the causeway from the eastern exit from Herbersdorf in the forest northeast of Parchau would come under fire from two sides and one could hardly expect vehicles to make it through. Under these circumstances, the Reconnaissance Platoon and I went and turned over all the vehicles that were stopping movement on the field path. An astonishing amount of Schokakola went into the swamp and a paymaster supposedly broke his arm because he remained seated in the vehicle, but every minute counted. Most of the division was behind us and the night was fast approaching! The *1.Pionier-Kompanie* was still missing as well. When we were finally able to go further, it became clear that we would not come out unscathed on this site between Heerwegen and Herbersdorf.
>
> The *1.Pionier-Kompanie* ran into us again without a vehicle. What had to happen, happened. On the causeway between Heerwegen and Herbersdorf, there were still endless amounts of vehicles, including those of our *1.Pionier-Kompanie*, but the men were almost all there. They were split up on trucks belonging to the *2.Pionier-Kompanie* and the headquarters, and we moved further west, depressed by this unnecessary loss of our tracked vehicles.
>
> Probably this day, but it is impossible to indicate the place at this time, we reached the *Division* headquarters in a village oriented north-south [AN: this village was Parchau]. On the western side, Russian foot soldiers, mostly ash and trash, moved by and the southern part of the village was occupied by Russians. In a short house-to-house combat with hand grenades through holes in the roof, we got enough respect that the Russians left us in peace until things proceeded further.

The *Division*, along with units of *Fallschirm-Panzer-Division 1 'HG'*, was in the Primkenau Forest. The Reconnaissance Platoon was moving without interruption. *Unteroffizieren* Benedikt and Bernhardt were moving west, northwest and southwest, one task after another, to find routes that were free of enemy and also (because of small bridges) usable. On many occasions, the entire column stopped for hours because there was simply no basis for making a decision. Once I was underway for an hour with Erasmus on foot in order to finally clear up the situation with the enemy and the roads.

Then the decision was made. *Major* Roßmann from *Panzer-Regiment 'HG'* was there with a few Panthers [and would lead the final breakthrough]. In Sprottisch-Waldau, some of us were in a fight going east (the road to Primkenau). (I think it was Lau with the *Feldersatz-Bataillon*). We wanted to push our way north out of the woods to Sprottisch-Waldau. The Russians were extremely strong. Antitank artillery and lots of infantry. Two attacks (by *Jägerregiment 2 'BR'*, I think) were unsuccessful. On the left flank the *Panzer-Sturm-Pionier-Bataillon 'BR'* reached the edge of the forest with the *Panzerjäger-Abteilung* of *Leutnant* Kass, but they didn't make it out. Then it became dark and we broke through to Sprottisch-Waldau in one multiple places under direct fire from tank and machine guns. We immediately went on to Sprottau. Finally back home and some sleep.

Unteroffizier Hans Stübling did not realize that *Jägerregiment 2 'BR'* and *Panzerjäger-Abteilung 'BR'* did in fact make it out, but in the confusion of the final attack, they were separated from the rest of the *Division*.

Meanwhile *Wachtmeister* Held-Kleingründlach offers his view of the chaotic withdrawal from Pilgramsdorf to Sprottau:

At about 4:00 a.m., I finally got to sleep and was still in an area to be set up for a unit. At 8:00 a.m., I was woken up by the Russians' great fire. I went into the kitchen and made some milk from powder. When I came back, I met *Unteroffizier* Martin Johlig, one of the old wizened tank drivers who, along with his *Geschütz*, was fired on early this morning. He had shrapnel in his right shoulder and his lung. *Wachtmeister* Voss was killed in action. The Russians fired antitank guns and heavy artillery into this Manor House, which apparently belongs to someone in the Kaiser's family because pictures, books and coats of arms in the library point that out. Now, however, the fire is quite uncomfortable. The Russians push harder and harder. Supposedly, T-34s have been seen on the road to Heerwegen. We moved back to Dammer, while the wheeled units were supposed to travel through the forest to the highway. We set off with 10 vehicles. Shortly thereafter, we ran into the Russians. They fired on the *SPW* in front.

Through the evening into the 11th …

A tree was hit and was lying right across the roadway, cutting off the return trip for the *SPW* so that the occupants had to leave it behind. However, it was later recovered by a reinforced assault force. We turned around and turned right. In the process, we came upon the Senior Staff Physician's column. In front of us was the division headquarters. The movement speed was laughable because of the bad road conditions. We were just creeping there. It was a pitch black night, lit up in a ghastly fashion by burning buildings on the horizon. We spent half the night in a forest of fir trees in uncomfortable cold. While this was going on, I was thinking that today was my 26th birthday. You couldn't even smoke a cigarette! What would the coming year bring? After we suddenly broke out onto the highway, we moved into a group of buildings. The residents had not yet fled or been evacuated. For the first time, we could talk with the local population. The people were very friendly and treated us to pork cracklings, bread and homemade preserves. We had barely eaten when the machine guns and the tank shells let loose again, this time to our rear. The fire was coming closer and closer and I would have felt decidedly safer had I been sitting in my *Geschütz*. In the next few minutes, fire was covering us such that we had to go into a covered position. I saw the column in front of us going off and anything on foot running right away from the fire. Then there was a powerful hit and I saw one bright red light, and I don't know anything else. After a while, I came to again and determined that I was lying under the ruins of the barn where I had sought shelter. I was trapped and could not use my right elbow anymore. I was bleeding really profusely from the right wrist. I had no time to examine anything closely because there were still a couple of figures in my vicinity getting out of there as hurriedly as they could. I joined them as best I could, even though my right shoulder was very painful; I was running for my life. And the Russians were shooting all their tubes behind us. After a kilometer or two, I reached the main concentration and got myself onto a "mule" [truck] belonging to the *Panzer-Sturm-Pionier-Bataillon 'BR'*, on which I traveled until I got to the main road, where the entire vehicle column was. Unfortunately, the radiator busted, so we had to get out and transfer the wounded. I found a place in the commo *Leutnant's* vehicle, which was offered to us first. He himself was nowhere to be seen. A salvo of Russian tanks let loose again in the forest, and the size of the salvo grew by the minute. In addition, the latest Russian fighter planes fired down on the column and tore it apart with their guns, and there were machine guns in between. The front of the column was involved in heavy combat. Then came an order from the front, "Anyone who isn't a driver or wounded, report to security!" I grabbed my .38 pistol with my left hand and went to secure the flank. I spent some time with *Wachtmeister* Eberlein and then I lost sight of him. I went with a group of about 10 men through the forest to a village.

We were supposed to scout the way to determine whether the *SPW* and the remainder of the column could go back on the road. While doing that, we again lost sight of a large number of people. Only a small group stuck around me. When we saw the outline of a *Fernsprechkraftwagen 23* (Kfz 23 = telephone motor vehicle) approaching as darkness fell, I stood in the middle of the road and shouted, "Stop!" When the vehicle stopped, I recognized the approximately 10 people in it as Russians. Not a second too soon, I jumped in the ditch at the side of the road because a bunch of submachine guns were already rattling over me. As quickly as we could, we moved into the darkness. With a light rain, we moved further west. On one road, we moved into a shack to look at the map and smoke a cigarette. Two Volkswagens drove by on the road outside; we could not stop them to warn them. They ran into the Russians and promptly fell into their hands. We heard a couple of shots and then the engine noise abruptly stopped. So we couldn't stay in the hut any longer and we got out of there as quickly as we could and away from the road. We jumped over a ditch and we were just consulting each other in a damp meadow when the Russians came down the road toward us. We immediately got onto our stomachs. There was about a company of them and the moving columns stood out clearly against the horizon in spite of the darkness. Marching in a staggered column, they were carrying three antitank weapons, grenade launchers and heavy machine guns. The wooden shack must have also drawn their interest because they also entered it to smoke a cigarette. The two Volkswagens were now driving behind the formation. We were lying with racing pulses a bare 20 meters away from them and waiting and trembling until they all went into the building one after another. What if they had found us there! We finally moved on and were able to get on our way. We slogged across terribly muddy terrain covered with large puddles of water. In a short time, our feet were completely soaked, and we all lay down on a spot together to sleep. Unfortunately, I woke up again almost immediately later because of the wet feet and the penetrating cold. The front cannot be far away at all. One could clearly hear a German MG 42 crackling, but the noise slowly and steadily moved away in a generally westerly direction. So we were in the enemy rear area. In the morning, we moved on. After a short trip, the commander of our group decided to find a place to hide so that we could rest all day there and go further on during the night. I didn't like the idea because I wanted to gain as much ground as possible. A young member of 'Brandenburg' joined me. We tiptoed a good way through some woods. We nearly ran suddenly into the Russians, who crossed our paths twice. The first time I noticed big red spots in the forest that perplexed me. We took a closer look at the location and determined that it was Russians covered in quilts sleeping on the ground in the woods. Suddenly there was movement in the forms. They got up and got out of the blankets. Their gaze went in our direction and I think they must have seen us. One of them picked up his rifle and we slowly got down on the ground with our pistol safeties off. But he let it down again and the whole group broke up and disappeared into the forest. We continued our movement and crossed a road going through the forest. When my gaze fell to the left, I saw two guns with corresponding crews in position. Before the Russians were properly aware of us, we had gone past them and disappeared into the brush. We retreated further into the brush and found a protected site where we set up a place to wait for the evening. It was frightfully cold and there was no way we were going to get our wet feet dry. We took the last *Möve* cigarettes, which had had a bit of a trip with us, out of our winter jacket pockets. The battered stumps were smoked with real craving. In the process, we got to know each other better. He was barely 17, while I was already 26. We exchanged home addresses just in case something happened. Finally, it was night. We moved out and changed our direction of movement several times, using the far-off battle noise as an orientation feature. The Russians moved in front of us on the highway in long columns. If they ran into any obstacles, you could hear the people in charge screaming and cursing loudly in the night. After we moved a long distance through a forest, we wanted to get our bearings, but everything suddenly became deathly quiet and the sky had also gotten covered in the meantime. At my suggestion, we lay down and waited for the cloud cover to clear. That happened at about 3:00 a.m. and I was able to make out the North Star well and determine where the west was. My young comrade suddenly doubted the direction I had pointed out and said the opposite direction was the right one. I found that really nerve-racking. Every minute was precious and we were arguing about celestial navigation. I told him in a short decisive fashion that I was going my way and he could find his own way. After half a minute, he was with me again, full of remorse. We crossed the highway on which the Russian columns were moving briskly. In the meantime, we went to the other side. I thought to myself, now there are 30 assault guns, then the first enemy vehicle revs up, and then the last one and then all the ones in between are on all cylinders! I could not understand Ivan being comfortable traveling with the light on at all. He seemed to be feeling very safe. We came to a road embankment and suddenly heard sounds in front of us. We quickly got on our bellies and observed the terrain in front of us. I couldn't make anything out. When I lay down, I hit my wounded right shoulder so hard again that I had to hold my pistol in my left hand. While our eyes were boring into the darkness, I suddenly heard muffled steps in my ear. I turned my head and saw the silhouettes of about 10 figures standing out against the sky. At the same time, the barrels of their weapons were aimed at us. I asked breathlessly, "Germans?" The answer came, "Yes! But you were really lucky, because we considered you Russkis and wanted to kill you right away!" We joined their staggered formation. They were released soldiers from a *Luftwaffen-Feld-Division* who also wanted to make their way through the lines. Each of them had a *Sturmgewehr 44* with enough ammunition and I felt decidedly better with them than I had before, because, after all, they represented more firepower than we did with our pistols. In addition, my right hand hurt, and my elbows and my shoulder were simply unbearable, but there was no time to examine them now. After a long silent march with me in the rear, a "Stop" came from the front. We stopped moving for a short time. When I tried to sit down on a supposed bunch of rocks, it suddenly moved and a cloud of alcohol-infused mist confronted me. It was a Russian who apparently had not grasped the situation. Now, however, he started to take out his submachine gun, which was hanging right across his chest. This movement caused me to act with lightning speed, because he couldn't go into the forest.

What happened next in this account was not found in any of archival files of *'Brandenburg'*, but what is known is that *Wachtmeister* Held-Kleingründlach finally reached the *Korps* HQ near Sprottau.

Gefreiter Siebert-Göttingen, a member of a 51 man strong *Fahnenjunker-Kompanie* named *Kampfgruppe Spornring*, provides an interesting account of his unit's formation and fighting in the Primkenau area at this time. His *Kompanie* was dispatched as field replacements for *'Brandenburg'*.

After the first ones were promoted to *Gefreiter* effective December 24th, 1944 (including the senior *Abteilung* member), we were called back from building defensive positions, promoted to *Fahnenjunker-Unteroffizier*, and distributed among the individual divisions belonging to *Panzer-Korps 'Großdeutschland'*. The members of the *3.Abteilung/2.Inspektion* went back to the *Führer-Begleit-Brigade* or the *Führer-Grenadier-Regiment* in the Stettin area, while many members of the former *4.Abteilung/2.Inspektion* went with me to *Division 'Brandenburg'*.

On February 10th, 1945 we were being escorted from Cottbus by a *Leutnant* Spornring, supposedly to Glogau. At Ottendorf, however, we had to leave the train and went to Primkenau. The Russians were right outside the town with multiple tanks and we were supposed to secure the retreat. There were about 51 *Fahnenjunker* who went with me to Primkenau (from Ottendorf). About noon, we engaged in the first close combat and received our first tank fire in Primkenau. Only volunteers from the fleeing troop units and the *'GD' Fahnenjunker* were taking part in the defense of the town. Because we had set off from Cottbus to the front without any weapons (including side arms!), our equipment, after we had augmented it with the weapons lying in the street trenches, made a rather haphazard impression.

Primkenau could not be held and we withdrew. For the defense of Petersdorf (about 7km from Primkenau toward Sprottau), there were only 13 of us *Fahnenjunker* moved from Cottbus that morning; the remainder were already missing about this time, some of them killed in action or wounded. *Leutnant* Spornring was with the 13 of us and led our deployment. The battles with the Russian T-34s that had moved up and the infantry remaining in Petersdorf lasted until the evening. Then this town had to be surrendered as well. As I recall, five or seven T-34 were knocked-out in Petersdorf and on the next day, seven of us, including myself, received the Tank Destruction Badge for our actions. An officer, called *"Panzer* Meyer," gave us the awards based on a witness statement from *Leutnant* Spornring, which under the conditions of the time only bore his signature. The Tank Destruction Badges were then given to us the next day in Sprottisch-Waldau by the *Division Ib*.

On February 12th, we remaining 13 *Fahnenjunker*, still consolidated as the *Kampfgruppe Spornring*, were finally able to report to *Panzergrenadier-Division 'Brandenburg'* sometime about [noon]. The headquarters that day was right in a large estate in Schadendorf. On the evening of that day, we withdrew with the remaining *SPW* from the pocket to Mallmitz along with the *Division* HQ.

Jägerregiment 1 'BR' was operating in mixed groups with other withdrawing units during the fighting. Its commander, *Major* Wandrey reportedly took command of a *Kampfmarsch-Bataillon* on the spot and led a counterattack to rescue the *Feldersatz-Bataillon 'BR'* that had been surrounded by Soviet forces. Confusion reigned inside the pocket among the members of the three divisions. Again they found themselves behind enemy lines, low on supplies. The men of *'Brandenburg'* formed the vanguard of the pocket's forces and began a breakout west with the *Jägerregiment 2 'BR'* in the lead. The elements of the *20.Panzergrenadier-Division* and *Fallschirm-Panzer 1 'HG'* in the pocket were placed under command of *Luftwaffe* officer *Oberst* Stremmer-Johann. The long column trekked through marshy forests, along unimproved roads, which helped them as the Soviets found little maneuverable terrain to attack from in the area. The column passed Weissig in the Primkenau forest, and advanced toward the Weissig-Wolfersdorf-Primkenau road, forcing a Soviet defensive line in the process. The *II.Btl./Jäg.Rgt. 2 'BR'* set up a defensive circle that allowed the rest of the column to pass through within six hours, followed by the rear guard of the *6.Kompanie* and *7.Kompanie* that rode on the top of the Panthers of *Panzer-Regiment 'HG'* of *Major* Roßmann.

Within the Primkenauer Forest a series of sharp, independent battles were fought between the hastily deployed *Volkssturm-Bataillon Primkenau* armed with *Panzerfausts* and the anti-tank detachments of *Heeres-Panzerjäger-Verband 'GD'*. The hand-to-hand fighting against Soviet tanks took its toll on the *Volkssturm-Bataillon Primkenau* as they lost 38 killed, or missing out of 51. Only 13 survivors made their way back to Primkenau, with the claim of nearly a dozen Soviet tanks knocked-out. *Oberleutnant* Herbig's *Heeres-Panzerjäger-Verband 'GD'* was met with overwhelming Soviet firepower in the forest and fell back further north to Waltersdorf, then back along the line Sprottau-Sagan, and eventually across the Queis River.

Advancing from the west was a combination of *Feld-Ersatz-Bataillon 'BR'* that took up positions around Sprottauer Forest northeast of Primkenau under the command of the *Division Adjutant Hauptmann* Lau. *Hauptmann* Lau prevented the Soviet advance along the main road between Primkenau and Sprottau and provided a way for the pocket to reach the main German lines through the forest to the north.

Also advancing was a supply column led by *Major* Spaeter. During his movement into the forest south of Heerwegen, Spaeter's supply column was briefly encircled by the Soviets. He carried petrol, food, and ammunition for the forces inside the pocket. For some twenty-four hours between February 10th and 11th Spaeter's column endured heavy Soviet attacks and lost precious vehicles and supplies in the process. *Oberstleutnant* Oesterwitz led a rescue effort that reached the supply column and allowed Spaeter to link up with *Hauptmann* Lau's position. Ultimately the desperately needed supply was delivered to the withdrawing elements of *'Brandenburg'*. Oesterwitz's actions later earned him the 734 Oak Leaf to his Knight's Cross for this combat action.

12

Battles between the Queis and Neisse Rivers, February 12th-15th

(Reference Maps 55, 56, 57, and 58)

Few reinforcements arrived to the Queis sector between Naumburg and Bunzlau. *Polizei-Brigade Wirth* and *Volkssturm-Bataillons* arrived for the defense of Naumburg directly. A *Feldersatz-Bataillon* came from Konstanz, along with an infantry battalion with six light field howitzers to defend between Naumburg and Freystadt where the *XXIV.Panzer-Korps* now became exposed along its southern flank. South of Sagan was the vast Neuhammer Troops Training Grounds under command of *Generalleutnant* Bordihn. He quickly mobilized and deployed his trainees into battle, blocking the Berlin-Breslau *Autobahn*. The only other units available for the immediate defense of the Queis River were the battered units of *Panzer-Korps 'GD'* that just escaped from the second Soviet encirclement in a month and were low on ammunition, supplies, and petrol. Each of the divisions of the *Korps* was now listed as a *Kampfgruppe*. Almost all their heavy weapons were lost. *Fallschirm-Panzer-Division 1 'HG'* had no operational *Panzers*; *'Brandenburg'* reported three Panthers and three *Sturmgeschütze* as operational (the Panthers were likely temporarily attached from *'Hermann Göring'* after the breakout); the *Kampfgruppe 16.Panzer-Division* reported two Pz.IVs, two Panthers, and four assault guns operational; *Kampfgruppe 17.Panzer-Division* reported only seven assault guns operational; *Kampfgruppe 25.Panzer-Division* had no operational armor; and *Kampfgruppe 20.Panzergrenadier-Division* reported one operational assault gun. On February 12th the *Sturmgeschütz-Brigade 'GD'* was ordered to reorganize. It was ordered to send the remaining StuG IIIs and Stu.Hs over to *Panzerjäger-Abteilung 'BR'*. In return it received 31 *Jagdpanzer IV/L70* from the Central Ordnance Department. The *Brigade* had to train on the new system and quickly become familiar with their new vehicles. When this transition took place is not recorded in the available documents. It can be reasoned that the *Brigade* was temporarily withdrawn from the frontline likely to Hermsdorf where the *Korps* Headquarters was located. If the vehicles were already ordered, they could have arrived by train before February 15th. In any event the transition of assault gun models was completed by the end of February. Its name also changed. The unit was now redesignated *Sturmgeschütz-Artillerie-Brigade 'GD'* a month later on March 13th. Not counting the reforming *Sturmgeschütz-Brigade 'GD'*, there was a total of a about a company size worth of armor between six combat division available for defense.[1] The danger was recognized by *OKH* and the *21.Panzer-Division* was redeployed from the Küstrin sector of *H.Gr. Weichsel* to the southern flank of *Panzer-Korps 'GD'* along the Queis where it took up positions next to *'Brandenburg'*.

The *21.Panzer-Division* arrived understrength, but it was far better than any of its neighbors. Its condition report for February 1st listed the *Panzer-Regiment 22* as consisting of 18 operational Pz. IVs and 29 Panthers, but lacked any command *Panzers*. The *Panzerjäger-Abteilung 200* had 15 operational *Jagdpanzers*. The *I.Bataillon* of *Panzergrenadier-Regiment 125* was at 65% authorized strength while

---

1 RG 242 German Armed Forces Operations and Situation Maps, 1939-1945. H.Gr. A. Box 353: *HGr. Mitte GenStdH Op.Abt. IIIb Prüf Nr. 60992 Stand: 18.2.45 Abends.*

4.Pz. Armee	16.Pz K.Gr	17.Pz K.Gr	21.Pz K.Gr	25.Pz K.Gr	20. Pz.Gr.	H.G. Brdbg	Pol.Pol K.Gr	35.44 K.Gr 72.J.D	1072 72.J.D	1342 542.J.D	Div.Stb 608 "M"	Div.Stb wanga	44-Div Dirle- Hoffmann	Rgt.Gr 3121 (G.D.)	Pz.Jgd Abt.4 (G.D.)	Pz.Abt 681 1	Pz.Abt 2	Pz.Jg Stu.Geschs.44 183	Pz.Jg "G.D" Abt 669	Summe	Summe H.Gr Mitte
Pz.III, IV, Art.&.Pz., Pz.Bef.Wg	2(4)			20(41) 0(2)		0(6)													20(26)		
Panther, Panther Bef.Wg	2(3)		13(32)			0(6) 3(3)										17(17)					
Tiger, Tiger Bef.Wg						0(1)															
St.B.III, IV, St.Haub, Jgd.Pz.IV, Jgd.Pz.38	4(12)	7(12)	1(2)	0(2)	1(2)		3(8)								15/20 8(23)		31(31) 28(28) 4(8)				
Sturmpanzer																					
Jagdpanther																					
Jagdtiger																					
Nashorn, Elefant																			72(12)		
Gesamtsumme:	8(19)	7(12)	34(73) 0(4)	1(2)	0(13) 6(16)										15,20 8(23)	31(31) 45(45) 4(8)	20(26) 72(12)			191/300 411/910
Summe der leichten Haubitze	16(27) 24(20)																				92(147) 374(650)
7,5 cm Pak mot Z u.Sf	2(3)	15(18) 7(17) 1(1)	1(1)		3(3) 7(7) 8(9) 7(9) 3(5) 5(9)										25(25)						60(77) 311/460
8,8 cm Pak mot Z		3(8)						2(2)								16(16)					21(24) 151/350

Image 3. *Panzer* and *Sturmgeschütze* returns for the *4.Panzer-Armee* as of 15
February. The fighting over the last month took its toll on the divisions.

the *II.Bataillon* was at 76%. *Panzergrenadier-Regiment 192* was weaker with the *I.Bataillon* reporting
46% of authorized strength and the *II.Bataillon* 41%. The *Panzer-Aufklärungs-Abteilung 21* was fully
capable at 91% of authorized strength. *Panzerartillerie-Regiment 155* reported the *I.Abteilung* was
at 79%, *II.Abteilung* 92%, and *III.Abteilung* 93% respectively. The division received orders at 5:45
p.m. on February 9th to deploy south. By midnight they arrived in Müncheberg and had boarded
"Blitz-Trains". By 6:00 a.m on the 10th their rail cars were rolling south to Silesia where they arrived in
their new area of deployment by February 12th. Besides a new combat assignment the division also
received a new commander. *Generalleutnant* Werne Marcks assumed command on February 10th.
An experienced *Panzer*-Commander from Erwin Rommel's *Afrika-Korps* and Knight's Cross winner,
Marcks was considered a "hard, ruthless" commander "feared" by his troops.[2] Their arrival along the
Queis was welcome by the *4.Panzer-Armee*.

Von Saucken was relieved that his forces escaped yet another pocket. Upon reaching Sprottau
General von Saucken was ordered to report to the Commanding-General of the *4.Panzer-
Armee* where he received thanks from *General der Panzertruppen* Fritz-Hubert Gräser and new
deployment orders.

Panzergrenadier-Division 'Brandenburg' was immediately assigned to defend the Queis River
south of Sagan along the rail line running south through Tschiebsdorf-Dober. *II.Btl./Jäg.Rgt. 1 'BR'*
was already at Tschiebsdorf but the rest of the *Division* was still in Sprottau. *Jägerregiment 2 'BR'*
reached Sprottau at dawn on February 13th after a long evening march. It immediately received orders
to secure the flank for the retreat between Sprottau and Tschiebsdorf. After darkness fell, *II.Btl./Jäg.
Rgt. 2 'BR'* moved to Tschiebsdorf. It was at this time that *Major* Renner was reassigned and now
took over command of the *II.Bataillon* again. The *I.Btl./Jägerregiment 2 'BR'* was ordered to deploy
to Dober. *Panzerjäger-Abteilung 'BR'* was still in Sprottau and joined by the *Feldersatz-Bataillon 'BR'*
under *Hauptmann* Lau. Both were soon sent south of Sprottisch-Waldau with *Panzer-Sturm-Pionier-
Bataillon 'BR'* under *Hauptmann* Müller-Rochholz. While discussing the deployment of troops,
Leutnant Kass received a direct hit from a Soviet mortar and was wounded. While available records
are not clear on what happened to *Leutnant* Kass, there are no further accounts that follow after this
incident. He was likely transferred to another unit after completing a period of convalescence.

Fahnenjunker-Unteroffizier Stübling's account of *Panzer-Sturm-Pionier-Bataillon 'BR'* provides
more detail on the withdrawal across the Queis south of Sprottau:

The division command post for the *'Mallmitz' Bataillon* moved out of Sprottau in the early

---

2   Werner Kortenhaus, *The Combat History of the 21.Panzer-Division* (Helion: West Midlands, 2014), pp. 397, 400.

Image 4. Four Panzer 38T Hetzers sit abandoned in Sagan, spring 1945. One appears to be damaged while the others suggest they might have been left after running out of fuel, which was a common occurrence during the winter 1945 retreat. *Panzer-Korps 'GD'* defended Sagan in mid-February and these Hetzers likely belonged to the attached *20.Panzergrenadier-Division*, which was equipped with these vehicles in February 1945. Author's collection.

morning. Terrifying scenes. Women holding small children by the hand were begging to be taken along. Unforgettable.

We took a quick trip and reached Tschiebsdorf. The command post was in a gravel pit west of Tschiebsdorf.

The new road bridge (concrete) over the Queis was prepared so that engineers (*Landesschützen-Verbände* or something similar) could blow it up. (The *Panzer-Pionier-Bataillon 500 'GD'* under Gehrke was, as far as I know, in Eisendorf.) Oesterwitz [*Jägerregiment 1 'BR'*] had the Tschiebsdorf sector. In the afternoon, the Russians were already thick on the other shore. Explosions—the bridges were now being blown up by the *Landesschützen* engineers. The demolition was insufficient. The main supports were only destroyed on one side. The Russians could easily overcome this small gap. Because the Russians were already in position with machine guns on the south edge of the bridge and the road could be controlled from the bridge, a *Goliath*[3] had to be brought in for subsequent demolition. (I no longer remember exactly, but I think that we got the *Goliath* in there and also did the demolition, but as far as I know, the bridge was still passable by infantry.)

In the late afternoon and throughout the night, a heavy battle broke out. It was over a building in which the Russians had settled in. South of Tschiebsdorf, the *Panzer-Sturm-Pionier-*

---

3   Known in German as *Leichter Ladungsträger Goliath (Sd.Kfz. 302/303a/303b)*, this was a remote controlled demolition vehicle packed with explosives and used to destroy tanks, buildings, or bridges.

Bataillon 'BR' was deployed. The Russians were already in the forest southwest of Tschiebsdorf. The Reconnaissance Platoon and a *Pionier-Kompanie* spent the entire night pushing their way through in the forest and a construction site (or motor pool). I was also there in the dark night.

Leutnant Grosser, a member of *I.Btl./Jäg.Rgt. 1 'BR'* recounts his harrowing experience during the fighting:

On the evening of February 13th, 1945, the unit was in Tschiebsdorf on the Queis. After the Russians had repaired the bridge over the Queis south of Tschiebsdorf, they attacked and came into an attack that we had started at the same time. When an assault force attacked an isolated building that dominated the road with its fire (demolition ammunition!), five of us were simultaneously wounded by a burst from a submachine gun, right nearby. I had previously fired one of our remaining *Panzerfausts* into the building. The wounded (of which I was one) were collected in a thick concrete bunker (it belonged to a big industrial facility, a gravel quarry?). From there, we were taken out of the pocket on an *SPW*. (I had one shot through the throat, which had broken the 1st rib and the collarbone, causing a pneumothorax, and exited through the armpit.)

Reports now filtered back to the *Division* that behind them, to the northwest, in Sorau the District Seat, was already burning as Soviet tank units advanced into the city. The reports were correct. The 7th Guards Mechanized Corps easily sliced through the still forming defensive line along the Queis south of Naumburg ordered established by the *Kampfgruppe* of the *16.Panzer, 17.Panzer,* and *21.Panzer-Divisions*. Into the breach followed the 10th Guards Tank Corps. *Fallschirm-Panzer-Division 1 'HG'* held onto Sagan to the right of *'Brandenburg'*, while directly to the west two *Bataillons* of the *16.Panzer-Division* and *20.Panzergrenadier-Division* were forced out of Sorau and were fighting to prevent yet another encirclement from the north. To the south of *'Brandenburg'* the *21.Panzer-Division* was holding its front, but to its right flank, the recently arrived and weak *6.Volksgrenadier-Division* under the command of *Generalleutnant* Friedrich was starting to give under Soviet pressure. The *Kampfgruppe 17.Panzer-Division* was quickly rushed to the area to bolster the defense. An attack by elements of the 7th Guards Tank Corps on February 16th from Heiligensee west, cut the road between Rauscha and Klitschdorf encircling the bulk of *Panzer-Regiment 22* operating under *Gruppe Hauptmann Herr*. An immediate counterattack by elements of *Kampfgruppe 17.Panzer-Division* from Tiefenfurt freed the unit, but a general Soviet offensive now opened up along the frontline of the *21.Panzer-Division*. The following day the division was ordered to withdraw west across the Lausitzer Neisse River.[4]

II.Btl./Jäg.Rgt. 2 'BR' arrived at Tschiebsdorf on Wednesday, February 14th and took over the defensive sector there. In addition, a *Sicherungs-Bataillon* was subordinated to it. As evening approached on the 14th, ever stronger Soviet artillery and mortar fire began to rain down on the town. During the night the Soviets managed to get across the Dober Bridge to the south, which had only been partially demolished, and penetrated into the eastern part of the town, while advancing north to Tschiebsdorf. The *Sicherungs-Bataillon* disintegrated as its members fled west.

I.Btl./Jäg.Rgt 2 'BR' became pinned down by the Soviets in Dober. Mortars and heavy weapons were brought across the Queis during the night, and their presence on the western bank made the *'Brandenburgers'* position difficult. The Soviets successfully infiltrated Tschiebsdorf to the north and the *II.Btl./Jäg.Rgt. 2 'BR'* spent the entire night in house-to-house fighting there. The *II.Bataillon* launched a successful counterattack with units of the *Panzer-Aufklärungs-Abteilung 'BR'* under *Major* Bansen, supported by several *Sturmgeschütze* of *Hauptmann* Königstein *Panzerjäger-Abteilung 'BR'*.

---

4   Kortenhaus, pp. 403-04.

The attack dislodged the Soviets from the town and allowed the *'Brandenburgers'* to reoccupy their positions held in the morning. Further Soviet attacks were repelled throughout the day.

At dawn on February 15th, *II.Btl./Jäg.Rgt. 2 'BR'* withdrew from Tschiebsdorf without being noticed by Soviet forces. New orders were received to withdraw about 10 kilometers west by foot to Hermsdorf. There the *Bataillon* set up a new defense along the Tschirne. The Soviets advanced west slowly in the following days, probably due to the lack of fuel and supplies they suffered after their long drive across Poland. A few days later, the *II.Bataillon* withdrew further behind the Neisse River south of Muskau. They stayed there about a week, received replacements, conducted patrols on the other side of the Neisse, and generally relaxed for the first time in a month.

As the *II.Bataillon* prepared to withdraw, there was a Soviet attack along the right flank of *I.Btl./ Jäg.Rgt. 2 'BR'* in Dober at about 3:30 a.m. The Soviet attack was repelled by Resch's platoon after it advanced to the command post. The *I.Bataillon* under *Hauptmann* Steidl soon withdrew west to Hermsdorf, then south to Pechern. It reached its new positions by the 20th, where it immediately began building defensive positions along the Neisse River.

Hauptmann Müller-Rochholz offers a view of the withdrawal of *'Brandenburg'* from the dual villages along the Queis. *Panzer-Sturm-Pionier-Bataillon 'BR'* was maintaining the rearguard and responsible for bridge detonation:

> The Russians were exerting powerful pressure in Tschiebsdorf. The command post was in the forester's office west of Tschiebsdorf.
>
> Oesterwitz [commander of *II.Btl./Jäg.Rgt. 2 'BR'*] and we had gone our separate ways in the early morning and now it all boiled down to getting the bridges over the Hammerbach [AN: actual maps refer to this stream as the Tschirne] near Hermsdorf blown up before the Russians got there, because it had already been shown that the engineers in the *Sicherheits-Bataillon* were not proficient enough to do that.
>
> The road bridge right to the east of Hermsdorf was a brickwork arch bridge. (Something like that lasts a damned long time, as even the Etruscans knew.) The charges we had were laughable! Radio message to Michaelis: "Demolition munitions, demolition munitions forward!!" North of that in the forest, there was still a wooden bridge. The charges on it were reinforced with pots of hand grenades. All of the bridges still had to remain open for our last units.
>
> We blew up a catwalk south of the road bridge when the last of Oesterwitz's forces were on the other side. The Reconnaissance Platoon did reconnaissance against Sagan to the north and reported "There are still 2 (or 3?) of our *Sturmgeschütze* coming. There are Russian tanks right on their heels!"
>
> "Good Lord, demolition munitions!" "Hooking up the electrical and the fire fuse, everything is ready." Now if we had munitions. Then the *Sturmgeschütze* came. The last one was still shooting behind it. At the last minute, a Studebaker came from the west around the curve in Hermsdorf moving fast. Yes, it was from one of our supply companies. Bravo Michaelis! The ammunition boxes were flying onto the bridge. Four large ammunition crates. Now we weren't scrimping. The last *Sturmgeschütz* drove through. The first Russian T-34 showed up. This time, we could not let it travel across the bridge. Our fuses were on the bridge. "Ignition!" It was really thoroughly destroyed!
>
> I let my breath out and went into the village. Oesterwitz's command post was on the northeast edge. He greeted me with two cases of Wilhelm II [wine]. Somewhere in Hermsdorf, a "precious storage location, just right for us" had been found.
>
> The *Panzer-Sturm-Pionier-Bataillon 'BR'* withdrew to Wolfsdorf.

The following day ...

The *Panzer-Sturm-Pionier-Bataillon 'BR'* was in the sector to the southwest and south of Wolfsdorf. In order to have lines of communication with *Jägerregiment 2 'BR'* on the left and *Panzer-Aufklärungs-Abteilung 'BR'* on the right, we had to let our front run through the woods, so we were in fact soon formed on a forest lane 50 and 20 meters away from the Russians in the sector of the *2.Pionier-Kompanie* (*Leutnant* Koch), which was deployed to our left. On a stretch of about 400 meters, we were in a large stand of fir trees and the Russians were in a thicket of fir trees!! Oesterwitz could also not extend anything to the right, which would have made it possible for me to at least get out of the forest. Bad news! The *1.Pionier-Kompanie* (Bank) at least had a clearing in front of it for half its sector; it could set up machine guns there and keep the men somewhat deeper in the forest further to the right. Bank was looking for long lines of communication to *Panzer-Aufklärungs-Abteilung 'BR'*. We had received a lone Pz. V Panther (just one and in the forest to boot!). Greiling came later with some wagons. There was proven trust there. But before he came, the shit hit the fan. That was my 31st birthday. The *1.Pionier-Kompanie* (good old Bank!) had sent me a cake and a bouquet of flowers with a beautiful card (how could the brothers in this situation bake cakes?)

Unusually strong shooting with Koch, *2.Pionier-Kompanie*. With three Schwimmwagen, the Reconnaissance Platoon—our reliable fire brigade and catchall—made it through. Naturally, the Russians broke through where the thicket of firs was. Koch was wounded; he had a shot to his ankle.

With a roar and our good *Sturmgewehre*, we got in immediately at just the right time. The men to the right and left of the penetration site were, of course, soft; we had pushed the Russians back/handled them in an instant but there was no way of getting back out of the tank trap pits that the men of the *2.Pionier-Kompanie* had dug in deep enough in front of the fir clearing. There was uninterrupted noise, and there were still the cap bombs that made everyone nervous.

Then the Russians could clearly be heard getting ready with a lot of "Davay" and "Skoro." We were only one line and our gaps were always at least 30 meters apart. The artillery forward observers in a hole 20 meters behind me could no longer intended to fire. No ammunition. Our calling connection turned into a yelling connection. "Hey, if you don't break up their prepared positions, the Russians will get my kitchen! We can't hold them back, not hordes like that!"

Shortly after the penetration, Bank was there with an additional couple of men. Now even he had had enough pressure. I went over to the *Wachtmeister* from the artillery. "Connect me to Spielvogel!" "Karl-Heinz (was that his name?), release some ammunition!" "I changed my location, you can't ask for anything more." "Then things are messed up here!" "The best I can do is to try for the 8.8cm battery." "So get started!" The good *Wachtmeister* fired quickly and well, but the shells still went too far. The Russians were, after all, right in front of us. "Stop! Stop even more!" He refused and he was right in doing so. "They aren't crossing our high fir trees anymore. We'll handle it ourselves!" I ordered that another 50 be stopped! There was crashing in the treetops above us. A reporter behind the tree got hurt. He heard everything and knew that it was from me, but there was a lot of wailing with the Russians. They landed right. The *Wachtmeister* repeated the recipe. Thank God. They won't attack so quickly. It became calmer, still isolated shots that didn't worry us much. Then someone from the neighboring hole motioned to me. I followed his arm—the *General*! Our *General* was walking behind us among the firs. I jumped out of the hold and asked him to come a bit more into the "shadows". I got a birthday package. A coat and a sweater from the abandoned English officer Prisoner-of-War camp in Sagan and a good bottle. I won't ever forget that, *General*, nor will the men who were there. Not because of the clothes, but because they still wanted to move a bit forward, forward to our holes, and that with an arm missing!!

The *Division* commander agreed to my proposal and we were able to move our position back a bit. We were able to deploy the machine gun better and Oesterwitz's right flank worked with us.

Hauptmann Königstein's *Sturmgeschütze* conducted a counterattack with *Feldwebel* Breitkreuz in order to break through Soviet lines at the Anna Forestry House as they were surrounded and "written off". After reaching *Oberstleutnant* Oesterwitz's *II.Btl./Jg.Rgt. 2 'BR'* at Wolfsdorf, his men deployed to the gap in the line and supported *Oberleutnant* Gabel's *I.Btl./Jg.Rgt. 2 'BR'*. The Soviets continued to mount harassing fire on their positions.

During the next few days it was quiet south of Wolfsdorf. Even though both Soviet and *'Brandenburger'* positions were located close to each other, especially in the forest, neither side had the energy for much fighting. Amazingly the *3.Pionier-Kompanie* that had been missing since it headed north along the Warthe River in mid-January finally arrived after its own harrowing journey. The survivors simply appeared at the Neisse River crossings at Lichtenberg near Pechern. The men of *3.Pionier-Kompanie* had little time to rest or celebrate their reunion.[5] At time when every unit was needed they were deployed east of Muskau, securing the bridges for any *'Brandenburger'* units still fighting to the west. They soon welcomed the arriving *Panzer-Aufklärungs-Abteilung 'BR'* as support.

On February 19th, the *Pz.Stu.Pi.Btl 'BR'* received new orders to withdraw toward Priebus and occupy a reception line for the German units still fighting east of the Neisse. In the fluid frontline along the Neisse, the situation changed minute-by-minute as the Soviets were still pushing west wherever they could find an opening. As *Hauptmann* Müller-Rochholz stated:

> We had barely reached Priebus when we got a new order: The *Pz.Stu.Pi.Btl 'BR'* is to defend Priebus. The *Kompanies* were deployed and the bridges near Priebus were prepared for demolition. The charge was reinforced and the fuse was checked.
>
> A few hours later came a new order: The Neisse is the main battle line; the *Pz.Stu.Pi.Btl 'BR'* will use engineer measures to reinforce the division's sector from Sagar (north) to Steinbach (south). That is about 32 kilometers!

The entire *4.Panzer-Armee* frontline was broken through along the Queis. *Panzergrenadier-Division 'BR'*, *Fallschirm-Panzer-Division 1 'HG'* and the *20.Panzergrenadier-Division* were forced back along the lower Queis River, where the Soviets pushed further west and crossed the Oder near Beuthen and Crossen, south of Guben on the 18th. This forced the *4.Panzer-Armee* to withdraw its frontline west of Löwenberg, north-west of Lauban-Rothenburg to the Neisse River west of Sorau, Sommerfeld and Guben, then back along the Lausitzer Neisse to the confluence of the Oder and Neisse Rivers. Between February 18th and the 21st the *XXIV.Panzer-Korps* withdrew west toward the Neisse while already outflanked by the Soviet 25th Tank Corps to its north and 6th Guards Mechanized Corps to its south. To the south of the 6th Guards Mechanized Corps was *Panzer-Korps 'GD'* that was also moving west, but the *21.Panzer-Division* on its right was doing an admirable job of keeping the Soviets from conducting any threatening flanking maneuver. The Neisse line was occupied by the withdrawing *4.Panzer-Armee* on February 21st.

Hauptmann Müller-Rochholz established his command post at Pechern on February 23rd while the *Division* command post was established at Heide. Finally, the frontline began to stabilize along the Neisse River line. The *Pioniers* became especially busy with establishing defensive zones from February 20th-25th:

> Several very large tree roadblocks were constructed on the road from Birkfähre to Priebus. T-mines were laid on roads and paths. S-mines were laid in meadowlands near Lichtenberg Jamnitz.
>
> Preparations were made for demolition and then the bridges were blown up near Sagar, Pechern and Priebus. (The ammunition for demolition consisted of the filling for 8.8 shells that

---

5   No record of the units' route or experiences during the month behind Soviet lines was identified. They likely followed a similar route as the men of *6.Kompanie* and *7.Kompanie* from *Jägerregiment 1 'BR'*.

was brought from the ammunition factory at Pattag.)

Blowing up the bridge and the dam near Pechern at the same time was a special problem. The bridge, which adjoined the dam, had to be permanently destroyed. The dam had to remain in place enough for the water level in the Neisse upstream of Pechern to be high enough not to let the Russians wade through it at night. After all, it had been shown way back in March that the Neisse could be crossed by foot in multiple places, particularly north of Pechern. The electric plant at Pechern (further on) was completely destroyed. Hidden charges were used in this plant and in the buildings in Lichtenberg and Jamnitz.

The regiments were given construction teams for building up positions.

The most difficult task was removing mines in the friendly area of Sagar, Kaupenhäuser, Pechern and Neudorf. Engineers from the security units had mined the forest roads in this area and had not prepared laid down any maps of the mines. *Major* Wandrey [Commander of *Jägerregiment 1 'BR'*] lost his life north of Pechern because of this stupidity.

After his death, *Major* Wandrey was posthumously recommend for the Oak Leaves to his Knight's Cross. The recommendation was approved and he became the 787th recipient on March 16th. Command of *Jägerregiment 1 'BR'* passed to *Major* Bansen.

During these days and nights, the *Pioniers* were employed to the last man, including the supply company, without a break. They continued to emplace minefields, even in front of Soviet positions on the eastern bank of the Neisse River. They had to be very careful in their movements because of the existing mines and hidden charges, particularly in the vicinity of Pechern, that were previously placed by local units.

This position was generally static until the start of the Soviet attack on April 16th as Koniev's Front took a strategic pause to reorganize its forces and prepare for the final attack west. To his north, Zhukov also paused along the Oder River. His focus now shifted north to reducing the "Pomeranian Balcony" along his exposed right flank. Between the third and fourth weeks of February, active combat operations finally transitioned to defensive operations along the frontline. The Soviets continued to launch local attacks in local sectors with the intent to establish bridgeheads across the Neisse, but major combat operations were now over.

13

Defense on the Neisse River,
February 21st-March 31st

(Reference Map 59, 60, 61, 62, 63 and 64)

The westward withdrawal of defending German units from the upper Oder River exposed the town of Lauban to Soviet attack during the opening phase of the Lower Silesian Operation. The town became part of the frontline and ad hoc formations were rushed in to defend it from Soviet attack. A *Flak-Sturm-Regiment* under the command of *Oberst* Lyncker arrived and was ordered to the northern outskirts of the town. Soviet infantry penetrated inside the town itself and fighting raged along the cemetery defended by an unknown *Sturm-Bataillon* rushed into the defense. The frontline settled across the center of the town, along the Lauban-Görlitz road, and into the hills to the south.[1] Guderian grew concerned about this area and issued instructions to both *H.Gr. Weichsel* and *H.Gr. Mitte* to work together and close the gap. In *OKH/GenStdH/OpAbt.I Nr. 450138/45 g.K.Chefs* dated February 21st, he specifically ordered *H.Gr. Weichsel* to shift forces from its ill-fated Operation *Sonnenwende* to the army group's right flank with *H.Gr. Mitte*.[2] By February 24th the Lower Silesian Operation against the *4.Panzer-Armee* was official ended on order of Koniev. All Soviet bridgeheads, which in reality were actually very small toeholds across the Lausitzer Neisse, were abandoned. The exception was a hotly contested bridgehead between Forst and Guben along the left flank of the *4.Panzer-Armee*.

Panzer-Korps 'GD' was placed some 60 kilometers south of Guben in the middle of the *4.Panzer-Armee* frontline. This sector of the front was commanded by *SS-Sturmbannführer* Graf von Egloffstein who was the battle commandant of Muskau[3], but soon *Panzer-Korps 'GD'* took over that responsibility starting on February 28th as the Neisse became the frontline. The headquarters of *Panzer-Korps 'GD'* initially set up to the north of Weisswasser in Lieskau, then continued to re-deploy south to Spreefurt and finally to Niesky around mid-April. Both the *Sturmgeschütz-Brigade 'GD'* and *Panzerjagd-Abteilung 4* were assigned as the *Korps* operational reserve and located with the headquarters. The *Korps* now commanded five divisions. *Kampfgruppe 20.Panzergrenadier-Division* was on the left flank manning the line just south of the Berlin-Breslau *Autobahn* to the north of Muskau. *Kampfgruppe Fallschirm-Panzer-Division 1 'HG'* took up a defensive line around Muskau. Its frontline was considerably smaller than its neighbors', a function of both its lack of strength and tactical capability at that time. *Kampfgruppe 'Brandenburg'* occupied its right flank from Sagan down to Priebus. On its right was the *21.Panzer-Division*, which was subordinated to the *Korps* HQ, but would soon be redeployed. To the right of this division was the *Division zbV 615* that was also subordinated to the *Korps* that occupied a line down to Penzig that also marked the boundary with the *17.Armee*.

I.Btl./Jäg.Rgt. 2 'BR' was initially given responsibility to secure and prepare defensive positions along the Neisse near Pechern. Assigned to the battalion were the newly arrived *Pioniers* of *3.Kp/*

---

1   Hinze, p. 120.
2   NARA T78/305/6255851.
3   Graf von Egloffstein was promoted to *SS-Sturmbannführer* on February 21st by *Generalleutnant* Scherer.

Panzer-Sturm-Pionier-Bataillon 'BR'. As early as February 21st these men were ordered to guard the bridge crossing sites across the Neisse near Pechern as the rest of the division withdrew across the river. On February 22nd, they fought off a Soviet surprise attack and kept the crossing sites open.

SS-Sturmbannführer Graf von Egloffstein reported to *Oberst i.G.* Bleicken, who was the Chief of Staff for *Panzer-Korps 'GD'* on February 23rd. Von Egloffstein was given new responsibility as the Battle Commandant for Weisswasser now that the *Korps* occupied this part of the Neisse. He was directly subordinate to *Panzergrenadier-Division 'Brandenburg'*, which took over command in Muskau.

Weisswasser was an industrial city of about 15,000 inhabitants. It was the biggest glass industry city in Europe with Osram-Werke, Vereinigte Lausitzer Hohlglas, bituminous coal, sawmills, porcelain, brickworks, and ironworks. The area around it was known as the Lausitzer Heide and was an area situated in a large industrial zone of Silesia. Hitler's attention was drawn to the defense of this area in the weeks and days before the final Soviet attack west in April. The area was a "bowl" shape with a rim 134 meters above sea level to the east, in the north up to 160 meters above sea level, in the south up to 150 meters above sea level. Along the northern end were open-pit bituminous coal mines full of water. It was a key transportation hub with a railway junction for the E-Bahn from Berlin to Görlitz, with the line single-tracked from Muskau to Teplitz and Forst to Guben. The road from Bautzen-Weisswasser-Muskau, and the road from Weisswasser-Gross Düben (Schleife)-Spremberg crossed the area.

The *Ia* (Operations) staff of the *Panzergrenadier-Division 'BR'* set up in Heide south of Muskau along with the rest of the command staff, and the *Ib* (Quartermaster) staff went to Weisskeissel farther north. On March 1st, *Oberst* Schulte-Heuthaus was promoted to *Generalmajor*. The *Panzer-Sturm-Pionier-Bataillon 'BR'* deployed along the Neisse to the area east of the customs house in Heide to build defensive positions. The *Panzer-Artillerie-Regiment 'BR'* deployed to the forested area south of Heide. In Weisswasser, other units of *'Brandenburg'* deployed along with *Volkssturm-Kompanie 'Weisswasser'* under the command of *Oberleutnant* Jilski. This *Volkssturm-Kompanie* was surprisingly well equipped and trained. This was likely due to its location, being in the center of a major transportation-industrial hub. This unit reportedly fought well. *Feldgendarmerie 'BR'* under command of *Leutnant* Feldmüller and some 10 motorcycle messengers of the *Division*, including *Gefreiter* Franzeln from the South Tyrol, were also situated in Weisswasser to provide quick dispatch communication.

Some of the population of Weisswasser was evacuated, but to the surprise of *'Brandenburg'* the factories were fully functional. After months of constant combat and deprivation across a largely rural Poland, the sights and sounds of a functioning city largely left alone by the destruction of war surprised the men of *'Brandenburg'*. This fact translated into problems with defensive planning between *'Brandenburg'* and Mayor Wenderoth of Weisswasser as well as the leadership in Niesky Kreis with regard to the *Volkssturm*. The civilian authorities still did not comprehend the defeat that had befallen the *Wehrmacht* in the east that winter, or the realities that the frontline demanded in regards to proper command relationships. Many civilian leaders refused to be directed by the military and continued to take their orders from the Nazi political hierarchy.

Under the orders of the *Ia, Oberstleutnant i.G.* Erasmus of *'Brandenburg'*, *SS-Sturmbannführer* Graf von Egloffstein deployed foreign slave-laborers and prisoners-of-war to build defensive positions all around Weisswasser. Egloffstein provides a brief description of the task:

> . . . west of the forestry office in Weisswasser, then north to the open-pit coal mines, then west towards Janhstrasse, Jahnteich, Braunsteich Park, the Schützenhaus water tower, the Grüner Weg pit, and the Weisswasser forestry office. Strongpoints were built forward to north of the Elt-Werk charcoal factory and the "Green Firs", to the turnoff along the Gablenz *Autobahn* from the road from Weisswasser to Muskau about 2 km northeast of Weisswasser.

These defensive positions were set up under the supervision of the *'Brandenburg'* Pioniers based on our most recent experience. These strongpoints were connected to the battle commandant's staff in the Weisswasser city hall using trenches and field telephones.

.... Demolitions were set on the railway bridge over which there were always arguments with *Panzer-Korps 'GD'*, because I thought that there was no point in blowing it up because 100 meters to the left and right of this road bridge, it was possible to cross the railway line at grade with all the vehicles. But there was still an order from *General* Schörner.

Reinforcements began to arrive, to include the rebuilt *Fahrschwadron 'BR'* on February 23rd. *Major* Spaeter offers a description of the new transportation units he utilized for resupply missions:

Now the squadron was combat-ready and the order came to move up into the division area. At 6:00 p.m., the *Hauptwachtmeister* reported that the unit was ready to move out and we moved at night about 50 km via Spreefurt, Nochten and Weisswasser to Weisskeissel (Route 115, 1 1/2 km before Rietschen), where we arrived at 2:00 a.m. on the morning of February 24th.

In the meantime, the *2.Schwadron* was also set up in Weisswasser. Unlike the *1.Schwadron*, it consisted of farm horses and vehicles normally found in rural areas; its horse stock consisted of 120 horses. The commander of this unit was *Leutnant* Göpfert.

We went off on deployment with these two units. Under the command of *Leutnant* Gruber, it was possible to retrieve valuable materiel from the main battle line on the Neisse while under fire.

The squadrons were also well supplied as concerned veterinarians. Medicine and shoeing material were made available by the Police Veterinary School in Cottbus. It was used to set up Office IVe of *Panzergrenadier-Division 'Brandenburg'*, per *Division* order. The head veterinary officer was Senior Veterinarian Dr. Hein. In addition to the aforementioned *Division* horse stock (an average 500-600 horses with assigned units), he was responsible for the butchering platoon and food monitoring and hygiene for *Division* units.

Soon a *3.Schwadron* was added and in that process the *'Brandenburg'* Transportation Battalion was officially established as part of the *Division*. Numbering some 352 horses and with a capacity of 90 tons, it was used extensively to help resupply the *Division* spread out across dense forest that ran parallel to the Neisse River.

Panzer-Korps 'GD' headquarters moved back to Lohsa. *Fallschirm-Panzer-Division 1 'HG'* deployed on the left flank in the area of Muskau and *Panzergrenadier-Division 'BR'* to its right flank near Niesky.

Attack at Lauban (Lubań), March 3rd

The *17.Armee* under the command of *General* Friedrich Schulz was forced back out of the industrial basin of Upper Silesia around Katovice toward the Neisse River line by Koniev's 3rd Guards Tank Army in the course of their Silesian Offensive Operation in February. During that operation the Soviets launched out of their bridgehead at Steinau reaching as far as Lauban to the west as noted above. Lauban was important due to the rail line that ran northwest and southeast. It could be used by *H.Gr. Mitte* to maintain supply through the entire front. On February 27th Guderian issued a set of orders to *H.Gr. Mitte*. Among the specific instructions found in *OKH/GenStdH/OPAbtl. Nr. 450 158/45 g.K. Chefs* was the following:

It is the responsibility of *H.Gr. Mitte* to use *Panzer* forces in flexible, limited offensives, to crush the enemy and impact his deployment schedule for a major attack. To accomplish this, the *Führer* has agreed to an attack by *H.Gr. Mitte* on both sides of Lauban during the first days of March.[4]

---

4   NARA T78/305/6255828-29.

The order also directed that after the completion of the Lauban operation, *H.Gr. Mitte* had to use their forces to relieve the surrounded city of Breslau. The attack on Lauban was directed by *OKH*, and not Schörner.

Command of the attack was given to *Panzergruppe Nehring*. The *LVII.Panzer-Korps* led the main effort from the south with the *Führer-Begleit-Division*, *8.Panzer-Division*, and elements of *Panzer-Brigade 103* situated in Lauban itself. Assisting from the north was the *XXXIX.Panzer-Korps* that commanded the *Führer-Grenadier-Division*, *Kampfgruppe 17.Panzer-Division*, *Kampfgruppe 6.Volksgrenadier-Division* (both these divisions were weak from the prior months fighting and labeled as *Kampfgruppe* by *H.Gr. Mitte*) that were placed under command of *Führungs-stab Oberst von Luck* that was temporarily detached from the *21.Panzer-Division*. The operational plan called for a single envelopment of the town, as it was decided not to commit forces into the costly, on-going street fighting. The attack began at 1900 in the evening on March 3rd. Initial German progress was slow. As the Soviets became aware of the impending envelopment to their rear, they attempted to withdraw their forces out of the salient down the Queis valley. They were too late. Soon, the *8.Panzer-Division* attacking from the south and the *17.Panzer-Division* attacking from the north, cut off Lauban from the west. In order to ensure complete success, the *Führer-Grenadier-Division* was committed to cut the valley off to the east in a double envelopment. Tank and anti-tank fire alike rocked the Queis valley. The German divisions captured the high ground to the north and drove deep into Soviet positions pushing the frontline along the north wing of the *17.Armee* forward some 5 kilometers. During the battle hundreds of Soviet tanks were knocked-out, several batteries of guns captured, and thousands killed. In terms of armor engagements, it was one of the sharpest this late in the war. The Soviet 54th Guards Tank Brigade, 22nd Guards Motorized Rifle Brigade and the 214th Rifle Division were caught in the pocket and destroyed. The 69th Mechanized Brigade and 71st Mechanized Brigade also suffered losses under the weight of the counterattack. The *17.Armee* claimed some 80 T-34s knocked out the first day, and the *8.Panzer-Division* claimed another 150 total. Few prisoners were taken. The fighting was particularly bitter as no quarter was drawn. The surrounded Soviet soldiers typically fought to the death, probably because they knew their actions in Lauban would draw harsh retribution. The German soldiers who entered the city noted numerous atrocities committed against refugees and women, and unleashed their anger upon any Soviet soldier that fell into their hands.[5] The interrogation of a Soviet soldier from the 22nd Guards Motorized Rifle Brigade revealed that while "attacks against civilians were prohibited, they constantly occurred."[6] The successful attack was used as a propaganda piece as *Generaloberst* Schörner ordered a contingent of a hundred '*Großdeutschland*' from *Wacht-Regiment 'GD'* in Berlin to Lauban to participate in a ceremonial propaganda event with Minister for Propaganda Joseph Goebbels. Goebbels wrote favorably of the experience and lauded Schörner in his diary as a general who showed the correct 'political'—meaning National Socialist— attitude and was just not a "map general". Goebbels was particularly supportive of the way Schörner dealt with defeatist soldiers, noting how they were hung from the nearest tree and around their neck was placed a sign that read "I am a deserter and have declined to defend German women and children."[7] This latter observation of Schörner's command style was echoed by many of the veterans that served in his *Heeresgruppe*.

---

5   Hans von Ahlfen, *Der Kampf um Schlesien, 1944-1945* (Stuttgart: Motorbuch Verlag, 1963), pp. 159-69 and Hugh Trevor-Roper, ed., *Final Entries 1945* (U.K. Pen & Sword: Barnsley, 2007) pp. 81-82.

6   "*Übergriffe gegenüber Zivilbevölkerung zwar verboten, kommen aber ständig vor.*" Marked on RG 242 German Armed Forces Operations and Situation Maps, 1939-1945. H.Gr. A. Box 354: *HGr. Mitte GenStdH Op.Abt. IIIb Prüf Nr. 64887 Stand: 3.3.45 Abends.* This highlights a lack of discipline and control over Soviet soldiers by their officers that proved a constant issue for the Red Army as it advanced into Germany.

7   Trevor-Roper, p. 80.

Activities of *Panzer-Sturm-Pionier-Bataillon 'BR'* in Defense, February–March

The boundary of *Panzergrenadier-Division 'BR'* was extended further south toward Niesky, where the division redeployed in the coming weeks. *Panzer-Sturm-Pionier-Bataillon 'BR'* was kept busy from the end of February through early March building fortification and coordinating on defensive positions. The following overview of the deployment of the unit by *Hauptmann* Müller-Rochholz provides a sense of the rear-area activity during that time:

> Transfer of the division to the southern sector forward of Niesky.
>
> *1.Pionier-Kompanie* went into foxholes in the middle of the forest near Neudorf. (The first sergeant of the *1.Pionier-Kp.* was Bruno Möller.) In March, the Russians had thrown out a woman's corpse bloody below the waist—and naked—on the edge of their trench north of Sänitz. Here we sacrificed our last multiple rocket launchers, explosiveness and petrol. The mission was carried out by the *1.Pionier-Kp.* They attacked, and the pigs had to leave some dead behind for that.
>
> *2.Pionier-Kompanie* went into barracks near Tränke. *2.Pionier-Kompanie* was put back completely into motorized status with 17 Steyr trucks. In Rietschen, the vehicles were rebuilt to their new purpose and set up. (*Panzerfausts*!) [AN: this reference is not entirely clear. It could very well mean that the trucks were modified to fire *Panzerfaust* mounted somewhere on their chassis.]
>
> The remnants of the *3.Pionier-Kompanie* initially went to Inselheide (Laurentz). Then the *Ersatz-Pionier-Kompanie* was brought up from Forst, which had trained in Cottbus and then deployed to Forst. Training!! In late March, *Leutnant* Hermann of the *3.Pionier-Kompanie* arrived north of Muskau via the Neisse River. He was behind the Russian lines for 5 weeks and still managed to make it back!
>
> The *Versorgungs-Kompanie* went to Weisswasser with the motor-pool and armor workshop staff. Some *Feldwebel* and *Unteroffizieren* were sent for temporary duty to see *SS-Sturmbannführer* Graf von Egloffstein, the Commandant at Weisswasser, to provide assistance in setting up the defenses all around. Best of coordination.
>
> Headquarters and Reconnaissance Platoon and signal platoon deployed in the forest near Brand.
>
> In late February, a big slaughterhouse was set up in Weisskeissel that put the battalion back on its feet after the hard weeks without any meat or sausage.

Significant events from this time:

A model fortification was placed at the Zigeunerbergen (Görlitzer Hospitalforst), and gradually all the officers and NCOs of the division were taught about building fortifications there.

The *1.Pionier-Kompanie* and *2.Pionier-Kompanie* took turns—one company on deployment with engineering work in the *Division* sector, and one company going to training in Rietschen.

A *5.Pionier-Kompanie* of engineering construction troops was set up and the bunkers were produced on the assembly line. The sawmills being administered by Count Arnim were put into use and being used. The narrow-gauge railway was put into use and supplied because half the division deployed parallel to the Neisse. Supplies were moved along this route even from Weisswasser.

A corduroy road was built by the kilometer from Weisskeissel to Weisswasser. The same thing happened near Heidehäuser. *Volkssturm* personnel and a Cossack convalescent battalion distinguished themselves doing this.

All of the foresters in Count Arnim's administration were made into soldiers. They got green uniform coats and formed the forestry platoon in the *Panzer-Sturm-Pionier-Bataillon 'BR'*. With their thorough knowledge of the terrain, they found a network of roads and marked them clearly with letters and numbers. Supply routes, access routes for reservists, *Panzer* highways. Maps of them went to all division units marked 'Not for Dissemination'.

As the days grew warmer, the danger of a forest fire grew. An observation and reporting service was set up using the existing fire watchtowers for the entire division area and occupied by signal troops. Firefighting teams were assigned to all units with specified areas of responsibility because we were afraid that the Russians could easily get us into a fatal situation by firing phosphorus rounds.

From the *Feldersatz-Bataillon* under *Hauptmann* Breda that arrived in Heideanger, a *Pionier-Ersatz-Kompanie* was set up with volunteers and trained at Heideanger. All young volunteers! Shop Steward Weckert put all the vehicles in Weisswasser back in the best of condition. Retreating *Luftwaffe* personnel in Weisswasser were relieved of a wood-gas vehicle, given more fuel and that helped a lot in saving fuel. *Hauptmann* Voss from the *Feldgendarmerie* continued to bring us vehicles from 'Schörner stuff'. (He was one of my *Leutnanten* in 1941.) [AN: It is not known exactly what 'Schörner stuff' referred to, though it can be surmised that the general's staff stockpiled weapons and vehicles from a variety of sources in his area of operations.]

From Dessau-Rosslau (the *Pionier* School), a freight train with engineering equipment of all sorts was brought in on the sly, including a completely-equipped workshop trailer!

Concerning the defenses all around, foreign laborers had connected the open bituminous coal pits, which were full of water and quite deep, north of Weisswasser by pushing through slag heaps, thus making this terrain useless for tanks. Mrs. von Gelsdorf, a *Wehrmacht* auxiliary, distinguished herself by reorienting the organization's work and later by her brave endurance.

The relationship between the *Wehrmacht* and the Party at the time may be illuminated by the following episode: The *Volkssturm* commander for Rothenburg, *Oberlausitz* Kreis at the office of the *Kreis* leader in Niesky, was insistent on getting the *Kompanie* in Weisswasser sent to Niesky although there were already about 2,000 men in the *Volkssturm* there, and Weisswasser had no troops except for the *4.Volkssturm-Kompanie*; even though the *Volkssturm-Kompanie* in Weisswasser was already subordinate to the battle commandant, and thus to the *Wehrmacht*. Negotiations with the commander in Niesky were fruitless; the *Panzer-Korps 'GD'* called on him to give up so that it wouldn't lead to discord with the Party. Because the *Kompanie* in Weisswasser, including its commander, only wanted to fight in Weisswasser, I informed the *Volkssturm* commander in Niesky by long distance that his order to move to Niesky would be carried out by the *Kompanie* in Weisswasser, but that I would prevent an additional battalion from going there, using force of arms if necessary. Then he would be made fully liable for the consequences and I would make certain that he would be called to account appropriately. Then I made myself unreachable by long distance for half a day. Everything remained as it was, and I never saw or heard from him again.

At the end of March, Weisswasser was subordinated for a time to *Fallschirm-Panzer-Division 1 'HG'*, which was in Muskau, and then to back to *Panzergrenadier-Division 'BR'* again. In March, I again had to see *General* Jauer in the exhibit hall of the Osram-Werke in response to an order and prepare for *Wehrmacht* Day, and when the event began, I got an order to give a presentation or a talk to the commanders of the *Panzer-Korps 'GD'* about reinforcing or defending a strongpoint based on documents from the city of Weisswasser. Thank God, it went well. With the assistance from our division, a front movie theater was set up in Weisswasser and the newest films were shown there.

This account offers an interesting view of the routine of the frontline in Silesia and along the Eastern Front in the spring of 1945. It highlights that overall lack of strategic defensive planning, and the tension between Party officials and the *Wehrmacht* at the operational level.

General der Panzertruppen von Saucken is Replaced

On March 12th *General der Panzertruppen* Dietrich von Saucken was ordered to report to *Generaloberst* Schörner's headquarters in Prague. Von Saucken and his aide *Oberstleutnant* Kohl arrived after a long, but picturesque drive through the mountains. Upon reporting, von Saucken was told that he would be called when the commander was ready for him. This was a sign that something was not right as Schörner kept him waiting for four hours. After a long wait, both von Saucken and Kohl were ushered onto Schörner's command train, but only von Saucken went to see Schörner. *Oberleutnant* Kohl recalled what happened next: "Two minutes later, he came out highly incensed. Now we were both going to see the *Führer*." They immediately traveled to Berlin via Dresden. Schörner had made it clear to von Saucken that he was displeased with the handling of the unsuccessful attack on the Steinau Bridgehead. Once they arrived in Berlin *Generalleutnant* Wilhelm Burgdorf, who served as Chief of the Army Personnel Office and Chief Adjutant to Adolf Hitler, arranged the meeting in the *Führerbunker*. After the brief meeting with Hitler, Von Saucken was placed in the *Führerreserve* for a brief time then was ordered to take command of German forces of the *2.Armee* in Danzig on March 23rd. His replacement to command *Panzer-Korps 'GD'* was *Generalleutnant* Georg Jauer, who simultaneously was promoted to *General der Panzertruppe*. The new commander, *General* Jauer, had been the first commander of the *Artillerie-Regiment 'GD'* in the *Infanterie-Division 'GD'* during the first half of 1942. His background allowed him to assume command without being considered an outsider during a difficult transition.

Fallschirm-Panzer-Division 1 'Hermann Göring' Defends Muskau, March 9th-12th

The remnants of *Fallschirm-Panzer-Division 1 'Hermann Göring'* reached the area of Muskau at the end of February and early March after its retreat across the Oder. It was immediately ordered into defense on the eastern bank as the Soviets tried to expand their bridgehead in that area. Starting on the evening of March 9th, the Soviet 112th Rifle Division supported by the heavy self-propelled guns (either ISU-122s or ISU-152s) of the 327th Guards Self-Propelled Artillery Regiment under the veteran command of Lieutenant-Colonel Andrei Mikhailovich Simonenko, attacked the frontline of both *Fallschirm-Panzer-Division 1 'Hermann Göring'* and its neighbor to the left flank, the 545. *Volksgrenadier-Division*. *Generalmajor* Lemke's *Panzers* held their ground against the Soviet heavy self-propelled guns and accompanying JS-2s. During the following three days of fighting the division successfully fought off all Soviet attempts to eliminate the German bridgehead or expand their own opposite the *545.Volksgrenadier-Division*.

General Jauer read a proclamation to the soldiers of *Fallschirm-Panzer-Division 1 'HG'* on March 13th that stated among other things:

> You achieved great defensive success on March 10th and 11th, 1945 in the bridgehead at Muskau. The forces of a Bolshevik rifle division reinforced with tanks were shattered by your steadfast defense, courage, and massed fire from all types of weapons. You proved to your Fatherland that you are the solid defensive wall that they have faithfully trusted.
>
> *Obergefreiter* Willi Ritsege and *Gefreiter* Fritz Blien of the *5.Kp./Fsch.Pz.Gren.Rgt. 1 'HG'* achieved 29 sniper kills during those days, along with seven knocked-out tanks that included two Josef Stalins with close combat weapons. This is for me the best evidence of your desire to fight and win.
>
> I give the highest recognition to your commander, *Generalmajor* Lemke, for his overall leadership that he has kept solidly in his hands at all times and to all of you for your exemplary deployment.
>
> Our solution is and remains: Not a single step more of German motherland to the savage, murdering Bolsheviks and deploy everything to destroy them!

On March 13th *Fallschirm-Panzer-Division 1 'Hermann Göring'* evacuated the Muskau bridgehead it held and withdrew into a reserve position under the *4.Panzer-Armee* around Görlitz. The *545.Volksgrenadier-Division*, which was in reality little more than a *Kampfgruppe*, took over the vacated position.

Lessons Learned from the Attack on Striegau (Strzegom), March 9th-13th

On the morning of March 2nd the Soviet 118th Rifle Division breached the thin German defensive line that ran north-south along the rail embankment and stormed in the city of Striegau (Strzegom). *Generaloberst* Schörner ordered an immediate counterattack to retake the city. The city of Striegau contained an important rail station and road hub that would help improve the movement of reinforcements and supplies through Upper Silesia. The *17.Armee's XXXXVIII.Panzer-Korps* commanded the operation. The *208.Infanterie-Division* arrived near Striegau in early March and replaced the *Polizei-Regiment 'Schön'* of the *31.SS-Freiwilligen-Infanterie-Division 'Böhmen und Mähren'* that shifted to the division's right flank. The *208.Infanterie-Division* quickly counterattacked in the early morning of March 9th with *Infanterie-Regiment 337, Infanterie-Regiment 338, Füsilier-Bataillon 208* and *Pionier-Bataillon 208*. A *Kampfgruppe* of the *31.SS-Freiwilligen-Infanterie Division* provided support to the south. The attack was launched at 3:00 a.m. Berlin time. *Infanterie-Regiment 338* jumped off first to capture the village of Streit and the hills to the northeast, which was completed at 4:06 a.m. and 6:15 a.m. respectively. The *Füsilier-Bataillon 208* attacked next recapturing the rail line to the east at 4:20 a.m., followed by the hill to the east at 6:00 a.m. and finally the village of Muhrau at 1:50 p.m. *Infanterie-Regiment 337* supported by *Pionier-Bataillon 208* conducted the main assault. The men of the regiment reached the north and east of Striegau between 3:45 a.m. and 6:40 a.m., while a blocking force from the south, likely from the *31.SS-Freiwilligen-Infanterie Division*, set up a screening line. The Soviet infantry had not prepared a defense of the city or the surrounding area. They were surprised by the immediate counterattack and likely under the heavy influence of looted alcohol as they demonstrated a lack of combat discipline. Once they noticed German soldiers entering the city from the north they attempted to flee east in their vehicles, headlight blazing in the dark. The men of *Infanterie-Regiment 337* had easy targets who were more interested in escaping then fighting, and they were quickly shot down in the early morning hours. It was estimated that two Soviet battalions were destroyed in the fighting. Any Soviet who managed to make it out of Striegau ran headlong into the positions of either *Infanterie-Regiment 338* or the *Füsilier-Bataillon*. Few, if any, made it out of Striegau alive and if any did surrender, they might not have been spared. Once the soldiers of *Infanterie-Regiment 337* re-occupied Striegau it quickly became obvious why the Soviets did not want to be caught by the Germans in the town. The liberation revealed atrocities against the civilian population everywhere as discussed in the Introduction. Von Ahlfen recorded in his history of the fighting in Silesia, "the enemy had cruelly treated the population that remained in Striegau. A large part of the population had been bestially murdered." One German soldier who participated in the fighting reportedly said to his commander that "after what we saw and experienced in Striegau, you can't ask us to take prisoners!"[8]

There were five Soviet counterattacks launched on March 10th against the new lines of the *208.Infanterie-Division*. Twelve Soviet tanks were knocked out during the attacks. On March 11th the 118th Rifle Division was reinforced with the 226th Tank Regiment and another counterattack launched. Again the Soviet attack failed. On the 12th the Soviets brought in the 14th Guards Rifle Division as it too joined the attack to recapture Striegau. In this attack they captured the hills to the north of Muhrau, but were thrown off in desperate fighting the following day. The front subsequently stabilized in the area until the end pf April.[9]

---

8   Von Ahlfen, pp. 159-69.
9   RG 242 German Armed Forces Operations and Situation Maps, 1939-1945. H.Gr. A. Box 355: *HGr. Mitte GenStdH*

The fighting at Striegau generated an interesting classified "lessons learned" report on the tactics employed in the attack titled *Bemerkung für die taktische Führung, die zur Vorbereitung gegeben wurden, mit Skizze und Erläuterungen* (Comments on tactical leadership prepared with map and notes) subtitled *So entstand der Erfolg von Striegau (Kleine Anleitung, wie man es machen soll)* (How the success at Striegau originated (Small tutorial on how to accomplish this). This document was issued by Schörner's headquarters and sent to *OKH*. This document was added as an attachment to *OKH GenStdH/Ausb.Abt.(II) Nr. 0388/45 geh.* and issued out to front commanders on March 19th under the title *Kampferfahrungen der Heeresgruppe Mitte* (Combat Experiences of *H.Gr. Mitte*).[10] The report noted that the attack was launched by primarily infantry companies. They advanced silently during the night without any preparatory fire to gain the element of surprise. It was noted that there was generally a lack of quality in the Soviet infantry, who were not trained in night fighting. Interestingly, the lessons learned pointed out that "orders must be checked by higher commands" and that Staff Officers must deploy Signals Officers with the frontline troops. These suggest that from Schörner's perspective there was a chronic breakdown in communications that required reinforcement. He stated this in another way by exclaiming "the value of personal influence and leadership" still matters and that "combat progress always must be checked" and the troops "must be exerted forward." This statement suggests that reports up the chain-of-command may have been falsified in some cases. Another aspect pointed out was the complete lack of combined arms training, and the overreliance by the frontline German infantry on artillery to stop a Soviet attack. Schörner's report decried the use of artillery, stating how it must be "radically sparred" in order to force the infantry to fight with their weapons and stop an assault. From this "we will only then again learn combined weapons training" and "if this does not work, the responsible officer must be replaced on the spot or punished."

Additional remarks about the fighting were noted in the document as follows:

- Organize artillery by ammunition type for better effectiveness.
- Ensure that the *Panzers* and *Sturmgeschütz* fire on Soviet positions even if they cannot take part in the attack directly: "All combat vehicles take part in the fighting day and night somehow."
- The infantry must attack right after the first artillery strike, and advance in depth and not "bunch up". They were reminded to use their automatic weapons. Immediately after a successful attack they were expected to organize a defense in depth. "Entrench, immediately despite fatigue."

This last point is common sense to any infantryman, but the fact that a *Heeresgruppe* commander has to remind his soldiers of this shows just how low training standards had fallen in the *Wehrmacht*, due to the rapid fielding of replacements to the frontline in the spring of 1945. Infantry were recommended to push further beyond their initial attack targets and find suitable terrain for anti-tank troops.

These instructions were directed to be passed down to each battalion, but they should not fall into the hands of the Soviets. There were clear issues with leadership, integration of weapon systems, and tactical procedures among the units. We also see Schörner's need to reinforce discipline through draconian measures.

Op.Abt. IIIb Prüf Nr. 66647 Stand: 9.3.45 Abends, Prüf Nr. 66948 Stand: 10.3.45 Abends, Prüf Nr. 67236 Stand: 11.3.45 Abends, Prüf Nr. 67594 Stand: 12.3.45 Abends, and Prüf Nr. 67883 Stand: 13.3.45 Abends.
10   This document was found within the *Heeresgruppe Weichsel KTB* in NARA T311/168.

Deployment of *I.Bataillon/Jägerregiment 2 'BR'*, March 5th-31st

Hauptmann Steidl's *I.Bataillon* of *Jägerregiment 2* deployed along the Neisse River to Steinbach on March 3rd. It immediately set up a small bridgehead on the eastern bank on the Neisse using the 2nd Platoon of the *1.Kompanie*. It was situated not too far from the town of Penzig located on a nearby hill. The church tower was clearly recognizable. The small bridgehead was held at night by sending over the 2nd Platoon in rubber boats supplied by the *Pioniers*. During the day it was evacuated, and at night heavy weapons and mortar fire were employed from the west bank to keep the Soviets from entrenching themselves in the German positions. On March 5th there were three Soviet attempts to eliminate the bridgehead at night, but they were kept in check by the 2nd Platoon during a fierce close quarter defense with hand grenades. Fighting occurred for several more then days, then died down through March 13th. *Hauptmann* Steidl describes how difficult manning a forward defensive position is under the gaze of a Soviet sniper's lens:

In the morning, I went through the positions on the left battalion sector with Kurt. *Oberleutnant* Franing's company was occupying the trenches. The trenches were shallow and the bunkers were hastily built. We crawled hidden through a small forest to the trenches furthest to the front and had to lie on our bellies to some extent. Individual sniper shots came over our heads from well-camouflaged positions on the other bank, the Russian one. We jumped into the most forward trenches and at the same time, the soldiers in the position carried a comrade with a shot to his neck by us. He was already dead. We looked at the enemy shore, about 50 meters away. There was nothing to see, nothing was moving. There was inertia flowing in the sunlight in the brown water of the Neisse a few meters in front of us. Kurt and I got out of the trenches in order to get to the next trench after crossing a piece of un-built position. Kurt was right behind me—a shot rang out and I threw myself flat on the ground. Kurt fell down right behind me and cried out. He was hit— the shot from a Bolshevik sharpshooter had hit him from behind through the chest and had made a fist-sized hole before exiting his front. I yelled out to some medics and called back to Kurt. He wandered painfully. I bandaged him up immediately; bullets whistled by a few centimeters over our heads; the Russians had put us in their sights. I lost my pistol. Some medics were wounded. With an effort, we got Kurt to the next trench. We had to crawl on the ground because we were under strong sniper fire. At Franing's command post, I had my tub fetched and used it to get Kurt over the bumpy road to the battalion aid station. Dr. Blut bandaged Kurt. He was very weak and told me to say hello to his wife. Then I brought him the things he needed for the field hospital and said goodbye to my comrade Kurt for the last time. Kurt died during the operation. That was at 1:45 p.m. in Daubitz near Rietschen. In Teichroda, Kurt went to his final resting place in the company of an honor guard of the *Verwaltungs-Kompanie*. I was very exhausted by this tragic loss. It was extremely difficult for me to tell Kurt's wife. Three days before, she had asked me with tears in her eyes to bring her husband back safe and sound. So fate is merciless and cruel. The best comrades are torn from our midst. When will we be next? But we have no time to be sentimental; only bits of time remain in our hearts and the oath to take revenge to our last breath, whatever it costs. And so my Kurt lives on as a bright example among the countless other heroes and gives us the strength to trust in humankind in spite of everything and now to put all our efforts into keeping the honor of the war until the last shot. Long live Kurt! We experienced so many adventures together in true comradeship; you'll always be in my memory!

During most of March the sector of *Jägerregiment 2 'BR'* was generally quiet. The building of trenches along the Neisse was interrupted with periods of rotation to the rear for training, followed by patrols. Mortar fire, snipers, and the occasional Soviet patrol kept the tension at the front high. According to Steidl, Saturday March 17th was particularly active. He recalled that "the activity of enemy snipers grew and there were multiple dead and severely wounded. Shots to the head. You couldn't raise your head over the trenches for a moment or it would roar out over there."

New recruits filtered in from a variety of replacement battalions supporting *Panzergrenadier-Division 'BR'*. These recruits were young and had no-combat experience. Steidl commented that "*Leutnant* Gahrmann's *Kompanie*, which was in a position in the middle of the battalion's sector, was relieved by another *Kompanie* for 14 days. It moved to the regimental command post for training. The young replacements still need to be polished."

On March 19th, *Generalmajor* Schulte-Heuthaus arrived at the HQ of *Jägerregiment 2 'BR'*. He met with both Steidl and *Oberleutnant* Oesterwitz to review their sector and be briefed on observed Soviet activity along the eastern bank of the Neisse. Of particular concern was a Soviet bunker recently constructed some 250-300 meters east of the *Bataillon's* eastern bridgehead's perimeter. The decision was made and the orders given: "launch a raid to destroy the Soviet bunker and capture several prisoners!" On March 20th the raid by Steidl's troops was executed. Steidl recounts the event:

The day went smoothly; I was with *Leutnant* Esser on the right sector of the battalion. In the palace on the main battle line, we discussed the upcoming assault force with *Feldwebel* Resch, my best platoon leader, with whom I had already fought in the Caucasus.

Leutnant Esser had his command post in the palace.

The interior rooms were ornate, but unfortunately looted. In the Knight's Room, there was a lovely grand piano on which I played rather often. The observer for the shell launcher was on the roof. The enemy trench system, laid out in multiple lines, was clearly visible; the Russians were ceaselessly digging in and expanding it. The "Red House", which was the target for the assault force's morning attack, was clearly visible. It had been built up into a small fortress. The plan was clear; Steffi Resch, the assault troop leader, had nerves of steel. Hopefully everything would be successful, because so far everything that had been undertaken in the division sector had failed; everything over there was mined and the enemy was vigilant. The last preparations were made during the evening. *Stukas* came in and 35cm smoke rounds were fired with destructive results. That was supposed to be the first thing to wake people up. The heavy machine guns were coupled and the artillery was guided to their targets.

I spent the night in the palace after *Generals* von Jauer and Schulte-Heuthaus had previously been with me in the bunker and were amazed at the status of the trench work on the main battlefield.

Oesterwitz came to see me at 2:00 a.m. We crawled into the trench that was the furthest forward at 4:00 a.m. In front of us, the water in the Neisse was rippling. It was dark and calm. Resch and his people had gone over during the night to the small bridgehead on the enemy shore. At 5:00 a.m., I gave the order to the supporting heavy weapons to open fire. With a terrible drone, the *Stukas* growled in the enemy village. The air pressure of the detonation pressed us to the wall of the trench, and the batteries shot short bursts of sustained fire; the machineguns hammered in the morning dawn. While this was going on, Resch stormed the first trenches, cleaned out the red building and blew it up; it all happened in a matter of minutes. The enemy was surprised. Resch had the mission of taking prisoners, which he accomplished quickly. During the retreat to the crossing site, Resch's soldiers wound up in a minefield with their prisoners and after a terrible explosion, the people could no longer be seen. So Resch had to come back without any prisoners and with his own painful losses. The Russians fired on our positions with all their tubes because they suspected something important was going on. Oesterwitz and I made our way to the palace basement under heavy fire and expressed our recognition to Resch for his courageous trip. Enemy losses were estimated at 80-100 men. Friendly casualties: 3 dead, 6 wounded.

Resch's platoon went to Teichroda for relaxation for a few days.

In the morning, I submitted the combat report for the assault troop and went through the positions in the afternoon. Enemy sniper activity began again.

The report was filed as follows:

1.Kp./I.Btl./Jäg.Rgt. 2 'BR'. Close combat day: Reich's assault troops went to Steinbach to attack the enemy bunker position near Sähnitz.

Killed in action during this undertaking:
Obergefreiter Hartmann (runner)
Oberjäger Flick (*Pionier*)
San.Sold. Brechtezanda (medic)
Gefreiter Wittasek (Deputy Assault Commander)
All attempted to recover wounded personnel wound up in a minefield and were killed in action. They all went voluntarily!

Implementation of the planned assault troop by Resch's platoon (*1.Kp./Jg.2*).
The building was reached without a sound and a Russian sentry was carried away wounded. A bunker was blown up. When they returned after accomplishing their mission (to bring in prisoners regardless of the circumstances), the troop bringing people in got into a minefield after it left the Russian position. There were wounded. The minefields were blown up by remote detonation. *Feldwebel* Resch's messengers and a medic died. It was impossible to retrieve the dead, because further casualties had to be avoided. Going back to our own bridgehead. Additional friendly [fire] accidents raised the number of casualties to five dead and five wounded. A sad result.

The following day, an unrelated, but interesting incident occurred. This afternoon, a four-engine U.S. bomber crashed here in the area near Klitten. Soldiers from *I.Bat/Jäg.Rgt. 1 'BR'* searched the woods for survivors. According to *Oberarzt* Dr. Braune, "the crew was taken prisoner after we took a little time to find them in a rather extensive forested region east of Klitten. Two of the Americans had sustained minor injuries parachuting into the tree branches. So I still had something to do as a physician. Then they were transported away in the *Korps* headquarters passenger vehicle." These were the first American military personnel encountered by the soldiers of *Panzergrenadier-Division 'BR'*, but not their last.

On Saturday, March 24th, Steidl decided to surprise the Soviets again.

Ivan is busy in the red building across from the palace. He is ceaselessly building bunkers and long trenches, masterfully camouflaging things and taking ammunition to it, and bringing guns into the position in huge quantities. We've scoped out the targets, but I'm missing the weapons I need to fight them. I'm getting *Sturmgeschütz* platoon from *Hauptmann* Königstein's *Panzerjäger-Abteilung 'BR'*. The commander and I scoped out positions for the assault personnel in the morning in *Leutnant* Esser's sector.

In the afternoon, I was at Franing's listening post. All of the [Soviet] conversations were intercepted. We know exactly when Ivan over there is going to take a bath, go to the movies, or has inspections.

Our excavation work is also proceeding well, because all of the rear units have been brought in to do it.

Monday, March 26th: The *Sturmgeschütze* rolled into the scoped-out positions and started firing on enemy machine gun nests at short range. They worked great. The answer from over there was rapid artillery fire to which I set up a response that was just as strong.

Training continued on March 27th. "In the afternoon came officer training for the entire *Korps*. We took vehicles until we were west of Rietschen. A lot of *Generals* were assembled. The subjects were 'building positions, obstacles and fighting in depth.' We old hands at the front just fooled around—it was just old fairy tales for us." This was the training that *Hauptmann* Müller-Rochholz was asked to prepare, as noted above.

Patrols, sniper activity, and aerial reconnaissance continued across the *Jägerregiment 2 'BR'* frontline. On Thursday, March 29th two additional Flak guns arrived. *Feldwebel* Zimmermann immediately set them up in covered positions on the western bank. Soviet reinforcements were observed moving into the positions on the opposite bank, a sure sign they were preparing for a renewed offensive.

Around this time *Generaloberst* Schörner dispatched one of his many reprimands to the troops. One such dispatch decrying the rear-area soldiers as "Bohemian rabble", struck a chord with *Oberarzt* Dr. Braune who spent much of his time among those Schörner decided to single out. Braune was so incensed by the dispatch that he did not even refer to Schörner using his military title:

We received some daily orders in the last few days from the *Heeresgruppe*. The following "blooper" was signed by Mr. Schörner:

When will these men get the courage to form an *Infanterie-Trupp* with their Motor Sergeants who have mostly become really too fat to work at night? How long will these people, some of whom only work 7-1/2 hours, and other metal workers who wear the forbidden sideburns, aka "Scheuerleisten" of our former [Bohemian] attic dwellers of the Grinzing neighborhood of Vienna and the Schwabing neighborhood of Munich?" or "Between these clear signs of shameless laziness and lack of will to fight, however, the underworld organization of the "Motor Sergeants," civil servants and supply troops still laze about in "their cars," usually without the knowledge or consent of their commanders.... The brave grenadier is astonished and is being sprayed by these drones with mud to boot.

One would actually expect a bit more from the commander-in-chief of a *Heeresgruppe*.

The rear-area "Bohemian rabble", as Schörner like to call them, were not immune to the frontline realities. The Soviets routinely attacked the Rietschen railway station with low-flying aircraft for example. Rietschen was an important supply hub and railway trains still arrived there, mostly at night, but sometimes during the day when it was calm. The "Motor Sergeants" and other supply troops were required to unload the trains and dispatch their cargoes to the frontline troops all the while "enemy IL-2 Sturmovics flew in a small circle and rather low" to attack indiscriminately as "no anti-aircraft guns disturbed them—and they were concentrated entirely on their target" as noted by Dr. Braune.

By the end of March everyone began to expect an imminent Soviet attack. According to Spaeter's notes *Panzergrenadier-Division 'BR'* was highly valued as a defense force, "both as concerned its spirit and its weapons and equipment, while it didn't look particularly rosy for the neighbors (such as the stomach battalions)." *Jägerregiment 2 'BR'* was moved to Kahle Meile because that was where the focus of the main Soviet attack was expected based on intelligence assessments. Soon the rest of the *Division* shifted south. The *Ia* (Operations) staff headquartered at Ödernitz near Niesky, while the *Ib* (Supply) staff moved to See, also near Niesky. Additional units were subordinated *Panzer-Korps 'GD'* for the defense that included *Verband Böhmen* and the *545.Volksgrenadier-Division*.

14

The Calm before the Storm, April 1st–15th

(Reference Maps 65, 66, and 67)

By early April the approximately 625 kilometer frontline of *Heeresgruppe Mitte* had stabilized. Its front ran south from the confluence of the Oder and Neisse Rivers, through Silesia, across the Carpathian Mountains, to the area south of the city of Rosenberg (Ružmberk), near the southern border of Czechoslovakia. This frontline was almost three times the size of *Heeresgruppe Weichsel* and contained twelve *Korps* commands to maintain the front compared to the seven *Korps* of its northern neighbor. The *4.Panzer-Armee* under the command of *General der Panzertruppen* Walther Nehring held the left flank of the *Heeresgruppe* from the area just north of Guben south to Löwenberg, an area approximately 150 kilometers in length. It was followed by *General der Infanterie* Wilhelm Hasse's *17.Armee* in the middle and the *1.Panzer-Armee* commanded by *General der Panzertruppen* Fritz-Hubert Gräser on the right flank. Geographically, *H.Gr. Mitte* was in a good defensive position, with its left flank running along the Neisse Rivers, and its right flank along the Carpathian Mountain range. Almost half of its combat divisions could be found with the *1.Panzer-Armee*. The *4.Panzer-Armee* contained the next highest division count, to include the majority of the *Heeresgruppe's Panzer* and *Panzergrenadier-Divisions*. Despite the relative stability of the frontline the *Heeresgruppe* claimed a large number of Soviet tanks and assault guns captured or destroyed. The total, calculated from March 10th through March 30th was an astounding 1,621.[1] The battles of Muskau and Striegau were likely included in those numbers, as well as other fighting in the areas of the *17.Armee* and *1.Panzer-Armee*.

   H.Gr. Mitte held prominence along the Eastern Front in the mind of Adolf Hitler. While *H.Gr. Weichsel* to the north was the last defensive line opposite the Reich Capital of Berlin, it was in *H.Gr. Mitte* where much of the remaining raw material as well as industrial and manufacturing capacity of the Reich remained by April 1945. In the area of *Panzer-Korps 'GD'* alone were six major coal and bauxite mines as well as a major iron and steel manufacturing facility. After the near disastrous fighting withdrawal across Poland all the various eastern commands suffered shortages of equipment and ammunition. Much of the responsibility to ensure the continued flow of military supplies not only to its own command, but those of its neighbors, specifically, *H.Gr. Weichsel*, fell to its limited capacity of motorized transportation. Compounding this problem was the high degree of centralization of Reich industry devised by Albert Speer in 1944. Raw material was sent to small manufacturing plants that were directed to build components for a particular weapon or ammunition type. Once complete, these components were transported to larger factories where they were assembled into a final product, that in-turn had to be sent to a specific command, then further on to the individual combat unit. Individual plants did not control the entire manufacturing of a product's life-cycle. Certain raw materials and military supplies had to be transported from as far away as Hamburg and Magdeburg, requiring the lengthy occupation of limited motorized assets. The *Heeresgruppe* was split into two geographic areas by the Carpathian Mountains. The manufacturing and raw materials that existed in what is known as the Moravian Gate area—the flatlands of Czechoslovakia between the Sudeten and Carpathian

---

1   RG 242 German Armed Forces Operations and Situation Maps, 1939-1945. H.Gr. A. Box 356: *HGr. Mitte GenStdH Op. Abt. IIIb Prüf Nr. 73390 Stand: 30.3.45 Abends.*

Mountains—required motorized transports to become canalized through the various mountain passes. This further reduced the ability to move required supplies quickly. Another drawback of this route was that it made the long motorized convoys easy targets for Soviet fighter-bombers that ranged across the front against little opposition by the *Luftwaffe*. Rail transport was out of the question due to its longer transport time caused by the frequent Allied bombing of marshalling yards that paralyzed the Reich's rail service by the spring of 1945. Each of *H.Gr. Mitte's* armies had a regional supply base established. The *4.Panzer-Armee* supply base was Bautzen. This was the terminus end for the completed weapons, equipment and ammunition to be distributed to the shattered divisions now rebuilding before the start of the final Soviet assault.

Replacements trickled into the *Heeresgruppe* area through several late war mobilizations of the Reich's remaining manpower. Fed into the *Ersatzheer*, these replacements were either young boys or older men. Many of the individual divisions also relied on their own replacement units to ensure their ranks were replenished. The new recruits arrived typically without training, basic filed kits, or weapons. The responsibility to equip these newcomers to the frontline fell to the individual *Heeresgruppe*. This taxed an extremely overburden supply system. Upon arrival new recruits were sent into a secondary defensive line near the front where they were equipped, trained, and readied to move forward into the frontline. This process served two purposes. First, it relied on the individual frontline combat units to conduct the training (reducing the need to maintain large cadres of trainees in the rear areas), and second it provided a quick reaction force to draw from in the case of an immediate Soviet attack or breakthrough. Vehicle replacements were also limited, and the *Heeresgruppe* had to fix as many as possible when they broke down or were damaged in combat to maintain readiness. Food was generally, plentiful.[2]

Hitler was convinced that the main thrust of the next Soviet attack expected to occur sometime mid-April would be directed south-southeast, and not toward Berlin, despite evidence to the contrary. During the April 4th military conference at the *Führerbunker* it was Hitler's opinion was that the Soviet 1st Ukrainian Front under Marshal Koniev would attack with the "strongest" forces from the area east of Görlitz, and west-northwest of Breslau in a south-southwest direction around Böhmisch-Mähr to capture the area.[3] Two days later he reiterated this position by stating that the main thrust of the future Soviet attack would come from the area Bunzlau toward Prague.[4] The area in question was a 40 kilometer stretch of frontline between Görlitz and Löwenberg on the far right wing of the *4.Panzer-Armee*. Hitler specifically ordered "all possible *Ausbildung*, *Alarm*, and *Volkssturm* units to be sent to the area eastward of Görlitz" on March 25th, 26th, 27th, and the 28th. He expressed concern that they not be deployed directly into the frontline (3-6 kilometers) opposite the Soviets, but between 8-10 kilometers, reiterating this again on March 29th.[5] So convinced was Hitler that the main Soviet offensive would develop from the area around Görlitz toward Prague that on March 29th he ordered the *Führer-Grenadier-Division* to deploy from *H.Gr. Weichsel* to the area around Görlitz, followed by the *10.SS-Panzer-Division 'Frundsberg'* on March 30th, and that these two divisions should be combined with the *21.Panzer-Division* into a special reserve force in the area effective April 1st.[6] These moves irrevocably weakened *H.Gr. Weichsel's* ability to defend the approaches to Berlin, where the final Soviet attack was indeed directed. What factors played into Hitler's perception that the final Soviet attack in April would be directed toward Prague is not revealed in any surviving documents and can only be guessed at. On April 6th Hitler voiced his opinion again that "the main thrust of the future Soviet attack would come from the area of Bunzlau toward Prague."[7] Three days later he

2   *ZA1-2759 Supply of H.Gr. Mitte and 4.Pz. Armee Jan-May 1945*
3   NARA T78/305/6256945-47.
4   NARA T78/305/6256877-78.
5   NARA T78/305/6256409-10, 6256310-11, 6256289-90, 6256257-58, and 6256231-32.
6   NARA T78/305/6256231-32, 6256217-18, and 6256336-37.
7   NARA T78/305/6256877-78.

still showed serious concern for *H.Gr. Mitte's* strength in the area around Görlitz and ordered that *Fallschirm-Panzer-Korps 'Hermann Göring'* and *Fallschirm-Panzergrenadier-Division 2 'Hermann Göring'* be sea-lifted across the Baltic from East Prussia then transported by rail to the *4.Panzer-Armee* and reconstituted.[8] The fact that this deployment did occur by April 23rd/24th and *Fallschirm-Panzer-Korps 'Hermann Göring'* entered combat with the *4.Panzer-Armee* was a miraculous feat of logistic support at this late stage of the war.

On April 5th *Generaloberst* Ferdinand Schörner was promoted to *Generalfeldmarschall* by Hitler. His counterattacks at Lauban and Striegau, draconian punishment of "defeatist" soldiers, and staunch support of the Nazi ethos won him his field promotion. Another factor that might have played to Schörner's favor was that his geographic command of southern Germany was a pre-occupation for Hitler in the final months of the war. In any case, Schörner was quick to please his master and reacted quickly to directives from the *Führerbunker*. He quickly took steps to place his defensive forces accordingly based on Hitler's concerns. He radioed the *Führerbunker* on April 10th to provide an update on his defensive planning and execution, echoing Hitler's predisposition that an attack would be launched south from his left wing. He also noted that he was suffering from shortages in ammunition and weapons to include *KwK-Panzer* ammunition, forcing him to request a special allotment. The entire memo stated:

Long distance conversation with the Commander in Chief, *Heeresgruppe Mitte*
No. 2160/45 dated 10 April 1945
transmitted at 2345

1) *Führer* and Commander in Chief of the *Wehrmacht*
2) Chief of the General Staff of the Army

Sir!
The fact that the enemy has advanced to the point of a major offensive against the left flank of my *Heeresgruppe* becomes clearer on a daily basis.

Three major issues have not yet been clearly determined:
1)   The extent of the enemy advance, i.e., the number and strength of enemy units,
2)   The direction of the attack and its boundaries and
3)   The time the attack will begin.

My specific judgments:
1.)   According to all the documents available today, we must count on at least two enemy tank armies (3rd Guards Tank Army and 4th Tank Army with multiple independent units, a total of about 1,500 to 2,000 tanks) and about 2-3 infantry armies. This does not solve the problem of the enemy's 5th Tank Army.
2.)   The focus of the enemy attack can be assumed to still be the area between Löwenberg and Görlitz. The boundaries of the attacks will be approximately between Goldberg and Muskau. There are no certain documents about the time the major attack will actually occur. We will have to wait a few days more for them. However, I can certainly assume that the Bolsheviks will launch attacks on multiple points on my front within the next few days to conceal their intentions and tie down our forces. I expect such enemy attacks at Ziegnhals, Striegau and Jauer, Golberg, Penzig, Priebus and Muskau.

You, Sir, are aware of my countermeasures.
3.)   Good *Panzer-Divisionen* (21.*Panzer-Division*, 10.SS-*Panzer-Division* and the *Führer-*

Begleit-Division) are standing ready behind the probable enemy foci. The *20.Panzer-Division* is being transported to an area behind the left flank of the *17.Armee*. In other words, everything has been done within our power that was at all possible. I have also become personally convinced on multiple occasions that the defensive organization at the *4.Panzer-Amee* has become beautifully well advanced. The fact that many parts of my front are now very thinly manned because the forces on the left flank have been consolidated and that there are weak spots in the probable foci is obvious but does not cause particular worry to me.

At my right flank, which will be extended tomorrow by the *XXIX.Armee-Korps*, the situation is somewhat difficult and not entirely clear. I hardly think that I can handle the mission with the forces available to the *XXIX.Armee-Korps*. It will be necessary to take additional forces there.

We will, and must, find help for the very palpable shortages of weapons, fuel and ammunition, as we have in the past. Only *KwK-Panzer* ammunition has become so scarce that I am asking for a special allocation here. The extraordinary severe fuel situation in the units of the *VIII.Flieger-Korps* as well leads me to fear that when the major enemy attack begins, the *Luftwaffe* will not be used nearly enough.

Every solider of my *Heeresgruppe* is completely on board with the very clear mission to hold the current main battle line under any circumstances. We see the development of the situation totally calmly and are awaiting it with full trust in you, Sir.

Long live my *Führer*!
signed Schörner
Generaloberst

Distribution list:
Adj Chef *GenStdH*
Chief of the *Führergruppe*
*Op Abt Chef/Ia**

Attesting accuracy
[signature]
Leutnant

*NARA T78/305/943-44.

As it turned out, Hitler and Schörner were both completely wrong in their assumptions of Soviet operational goals and intent. Muskau would form the extreme right flank of the Soviet main effort and not the left. The focus of the Soviet assault was north toward Berlin and not south toward Prague.

Organization of the *4.Panzer-Armee* on the eve of the Soviet Attack

By the eve of the Soviet attack, the *4.Panzer-Armee* HQ under the command of *General der Panzertruppen* Fritz-Hubert Gräser was situated a few kilometers northwest of Bautzen in Neschwitz, which was a hub for the regional road network and also contained a north-south rail line. In support of the HQ was 20 *Sturmgeschütze* of *Sturmgeschütz-Brigade 236*.

The *V.Armee-Korps* was located just to the east of Cottbus. Supporting were the Panthers and *Sturmgeschütze* of *Panzer-Abteilung 2*. From north to south were: *Kampfgruppe 35.SS-Polizei* with the attached *Ausbildung-Regiment 561*, *Korps-MG Bataillon 405*, *Alarm-Regiment 94* and *Alarm-Regiment 97*; *Heer-Pionier-Brigade 70* along with one regiment of the *275.Infanterie-Division*; *214. Infanterie-Division* with the attached *Alarm-Regiment 35*, *SS-Grenadier-Bataillon 6*, and elements of *Pionier-Brigade 70*; *Kampfgruppe 36.SS-Waffen-Grenadier-Division* (minus one bataillon); and the *342.Infanterie-Division* with an attached *Bataillon* of *Kampfgruppe 36.SS* and one regiment of the *275.Infanterie-Division*. In *OKH* reserve at Spremberg, 25 kilometers southwest of Forst, was the *21.Panzer-Division* along with an attached regiment of the *275.Infanterie-Division*.

Panzer-Korps 'Großdeutschland' headquarters was located in Spreefurt (Uhyst) along with the 15 *Jagdpanzers* and one command *Sturmgeschütz III* of *Sturmgeschütz-Artillerie-Brigade 'GD'*, *Panzerjagd-Abteilung 3* that consisted of 16 *Jagdpanzer 38s* and two *'Großdeutschland'* replacement battalions. From north to south were: *Kampfgruppe 545.Volksgrenadier-Division*; *Division Stab zbV 615*[9] with the attached *Heeres-Pionier-Brigade 687*, *Festung MG-Bataillons 3093, 3094, 3104*, *Festung Infanterie-Bataillon 1485*, and *Panzer-Pionier-Bataillon 500 'GD'*; and *Panzergrenadier-Division 'Brandenburg'* along with the *I.Bataillon/Fahnenjunker-Grenadier-Regiment 1244* and the attached *Sturm-Regiment-Panzer-Armee-Oberkommando 4* (also referred to as *Sturm-Regiment Pz.AOK4*.[10]

The *LVII.Armee-Korps* headquarters was located in Schönberg, southeast of Görlitz along with *Korps MG-Bataillon 457*, and *Panzer-Abteilung 1* (20 *Sturmgeschütz IIIs*) and *Panzerjagd-Abteilung 3* and *4 'GD'* (18 Pz. 38T Hetzers). From north to south were the *72.Infanterie-Division* with the attached *Festung Infanterie-Bataillon 1456* and *1460, 6.Infanterie-Division* with an attached *Alarm-Bataillon*, and within the city of Görlitz were the *Festung Infanterie-Bataillon 1459* and *1461*. In *Heeresgruppe* reserve to the west of Görlitz was the *Führer-Begleit-Division*, and to the south of the city near Schönberg was the *Fallschirm-Panzer-Division 1 'HG'*. The *10.SS-Panzer-Division* was in *OKH* reserve at Lauban directly behind the *6.Infanterie-Division* at the right wing of the *4.Panzer-Armee*.

In reserve behind the immediate *Panzer-Korps 'GD'* and the *LVII.Armee-Korps* frontline was a second screening line of replacement and training divisions under the command of *Korps-Gruppe General der Artillerie Moser*.[11] The *Korps* Headquarters was situated in the town of Löbau. From north to south were the *Panzer-Ausbildung-Verband 'Böhmen'* (behind the lines of *Kampfgruppe 545.Volks.Gren-Div.*), *Division Nr.464* (behind *'Brandenburg'*), *Division Nr. 404* (behind the *72.Infanterie-Division*), and *Division Nr. 193* (behind the *6.Infanterie-Division*). These divisions were particularly weak.

Along the rear area of the *4.Panzer-Armee* was *Sperrverband 'Reichenberger Senke'* that consisted of the *Stab Heeres-Pionier-Brigade 655*, with one *Pionier-Bataillon*, and two *Festung PAK-Kompanien*. The *4.Panzer-Armee* was also expecting the arrival of the *600.Infanterie-Division 'Vlassov'* (r) from *H.Gr. Weichsel* and *344.Infanterie-Division* on April 16th as reinforcements. The *Fallschirm-Panzer-Korps 'HG'* with the attached *Fallschirm-Panzergrenadier-Division 2 'HG'* were also expected to arrive to the *4.Panzer-Armee* at some point in late April.

On paper the *4.Panzer-Armee* totaled 189 operational *Panzers* and *Sturmgeschütze* (another 27 in short-term repair). This represented some 31% of the total operational *Panzers* and *Sturmgeschütze* (602) available to *H.Gr. Mitte* at that time (another 205 were in short-term repair as part of the *17.Armee* and *1.Panzer-Armee*). In looking at operational anti-tank guns, the *4.Panzer-Armee*

---

9   The *Division zbv 615* was an organic "special purpose" staff formed out of *Wehrkreis III* in early February that commanded a variety of composite *Heer* and *Alarm-Einheiten* units. During early March the decision was made to move newly recruited units close to the frontline where they would complete their combat training while simultaneously be able to respond to a Soviet attack. This worked in theory, but in practice, these units quickly shattered.

10   *Sturm-Regiment-Panzer-Armee-Oberkommando 4* was formed in May 1944 from the *Lehr-Bataillon* of the *Armee-Waffenschule* and consisted of *I.Bataillon (1.Kp., 2.Kp., 3Kp., and 4.Kp.), II.Bataillon (5.Kp., 6.Kp., 7.Kp., and 8.Kp.), 9.Kp., 10.Kp., 11.Pi.-Kp.* and *12.Wach-Kp.*

11   This unit was penciled onto the *HGr. Mitte GenStdH Op..Abt.IIIb Prüf.Nr. 78841 Stand: 14.4.45 abds*. Located in RG 242 German Armed Forces Operations and Situation Maps, 1939-1945. H.Gr. A. Box 357. It appears that four replacement and training divisions were placed under its planned command: *Panzer-Ausbildung-Verband 'Böhmen', Division Nr. 193, Division Nr. 404*, and *Division Nr. 464*. In the case of *Division Nr. 464*, elements of the division consisted of "Stomach Battalions". These were soldiers who had recovered sufficiently from an illness, like dysentery, or some other non-debilitating ailment, to be able to hold a rifle and fire at the enemy. Officially known in German as *'Magen'*, these men usually received a special diet for their aliments. There were also *'Ohren'* (ear), and *'Augen'* (eye) battalions deployed as well. The *404.Infanterie-Division* was apparently formed from *Schatten-Division 'Dresden'* (Shadow Division).

contained 128 (124 of 7.5cm and only four 8.8cm), which totaled 31% of the 7.5cm and only 8% of the deadly 8.8cm. The *4.Panzer-Armee* might have appeared a formidable force. But its divisions were weak and ill equipped. Many of its frontline infantry units were little more than recently mobilized replacements thrown together by the *Ersatzheer* and sent to the front line where they were expected to be equipped, trained, and ready for combat in weeks. Out of the 52 various combat formations under its command nearly 25% were labeled as a "*Kampfgruppe*", another 10-15% were formed in the last six months from various remnants of other divisions, and almost every other division, like *'Brandenburg'* had suffered significant losses in recent combat. The defensive positioning of the units was aligned with both Hitler's and Schörner's propensity to believe in a southern thrust by Koniev. It is unclear what might have occurred if the available reserves were positioned on the left flank of the *4.Panzer-Armee* given the fact that Schörner's defensive planning was uncoordinated with his northern neighbor and lacked any tactical flexibility. As it turned out nearly half of the *4.Panzer-Armee* was sheared off and caught in a pocket of forces that formed along with the *9.Armee* of *H.Gr. Weichsel* after the start of the Soviet offensive.

Panzergrenadier-Division 'Brandenburg' from April 1st-15th

Let us look at the known activities of *Panzergrenadier-Division 'BR'* during the first two weeks of April. The *Division* began the month holding a frontline along the Neisse from south of Muskau to Rothenburg. As units were repositioned based on Schörner's guidance reported to the *Führer* on April 10th, the *Division* shifted slightly to the south occupying a position from Steinbach to Penzig. Replacing *'Brandenburg'* in its old positions on its left flank was *Division zbv 615* under the command of Reserve Officer *Oberst* von Bülow that occupied the heavily forested area south of Muskau to Steinbach. Von Bülow took over the headquarters building that had been manned by Schulte-Heuthaus and his staff in the wooded estate at Heide. *Panzergrenadier-Division 'BR'* headquarters and the *Ia* (operations) section shifted further south. Its exact location before April 16th was not documented, but subsequent accounts strongly suggest that the area around Kodersdorf was the location. The *Ib* (quartermaster) section headquarters also remained at See, just to the west of Niesky. See was situated along the rail line that ran from the *4.Panzer-Armee* supply depot at Bautzen and allowed Spaeter and his staff to efficiently provide required logistic support to the combat battalions. *Jägerregiment 1 'BR'* occupied a position running along the Neisse from Steinbach to the north of Rothenburg, while *Jägerregiment 2 'BR'* occupied from south of Rothenburg to Penzig. *Jägerregiment 1 'BR'* placed its *II.Bataillon* into the frontline and kept *I.(gep)Bataillon* in reserve at Schlangenhauser. *Jägerregiment 2 'BR'* placed *I.Bataillon* into the frontline and kept the *II.Bataillon* in reserve at Kaltwasser. Manning the frontline between the two regiments of *'Brandenburg'* and centered in Rothenburg was the *I.Btl./Fhj.Gr.Rgt. 1244*, assorted *Alarm* units and a "Stomach and Ear Battalion" from *Division Nr. 464*. *Panzer-Sturm-Pionier-Bataillon 'BR'* under the command of *Hauptmann* Müller-Rochholz acted as a reserve force. In the beginning of April it secured a 500 meter stretch of the west bank of the Neisse between Klein Priebus and Rothenburg based on an anticipated Soviet attack that did not occur. Then *Panzer-Sturm-Pionier-Bataillon 'BR'* and a "stomach battalion" of convalescent soldiers shifted south to Geheege and placed temporarily under the command of *Jägerregiment 2 'BR'*. *Heeres-Flak-Artillerie-Abteilung*, under the command of *Major* Voshage, was situated along the main east-west road artery and north-south rail line in Wehrkirch. *Major* Voshage's headquarters was situated at the Castle (Manor House) in Nieder Wehrkirch. Several *Flak* guns were allocated north to the area of Steinbach in support of *Jägerregiment 1 'BR'*. The available guns of *Panzer-Artillerie-Regiment 'BR'* were also located just west of Wehrkirch along the line of pine trees that marked the start of the forest. *Panzer-Aufklärungs-Abteilung 'BR'* now under command of *Rittmeister* Frey was located on the southern end of the *Division's* deployment, likely as a reserve force. It is not clear where *Panzerjäger-Abteilung 'BR'* was deployed as no records mention the unit at this time. In keeping with general tactical practices, this unit likely was kept in reserve at the *Division* headquarters near Kodersdorf.

On April 6th the *Fahrschwadron 'BR'* arrived at See and fell under Spaeter's *Ib* section. It was expanded since its original formation back on February 8th. *Leutnant* Gruber was replaced as commander by a *Major* von O.[12] Gruber assumed command of the *1.Schwadron*. *Major* von O. was replaced almost immediately after arrival by *SS-Sturmbannführer* Graf von Egloffstein, who commanded the battalion until the end of the war. The unit was expanded and drew its leadership cadre from new NCO recruits still being trained. Gaps in personnel were filled by Hiwis "who acquitted themselves very well" as noted by one member of the unit.[13] The *1.Schwadron* was housed on an estate while the *2.Schwadron* was housed in the town of See itself. The unit was not motorized but consisted of 350 horses. It was noted that "their horses were in top condition for this time in the war." The overall composition of the unit was as follows:

Commander: *SS-Sturmbannführer* Graf von Egloffstein
Adjutant: *Oberleutnant* Schnier
IVa: Headquarters paymaster (?)
IVb: Assistant Physician, Dr. J.
IVe: Senior Veterinarian Dr. Hein (who also served simultaneously as head veterinary officer for
    the *Division 'BR'*)
1.Schwadron Leutnant Gruber
2.Schwadron Leutnant Göpfert
3.Schwadron Leutnant Schmidt

After the start of the Soviet offensive on April 16th the *Fahrschwadron 'BR'* was transferred to the Dresden area. The headquarters and the *1.Schwadron* with elements of the *3.Schwadron* went to Grünberg, while the *2.Schwadron* and the remainder of the *3.Schwadron* went to Ottendorf-Okrilla.

The early days of April brought a sense of calm across the *'Brandenburger'* frontline for the first time since its disastrous deployment to Poland in January. Only Soviet sniper activity was prevalent across the Neisse. In return, *'Brandenburger'* snipers were deployed. They were granted leave for each confirmed Soviet soldier killed. This was a coveted reward as the frontline was now back on German soil and many soldiers could easily acquire a pass home to see loved ones.

Life in early April generally took on a garrison routine. New units arrived. Medical appointments and training continued. Given the state of Nazi Germany at that time, the *Wehrmacht Ersatzheer* continued to send recruits to the front despite all strategic setbacks it experienced in the last twelve months. Strategically, the collapse of the Reich was near as the Western Allies raced across western Germany at a ferocious pace. They reached the Elbe River in a mere seven days—rapidly collapsing *OB West* and the Western Front in the process. On April 7th *Oberarzt* Dr. Braune, one of the *Division's* physician who was located at See with the *Ib*, was in the process of setting up a local dispensary in Klitten at the *Verwaltungs-Kompanie* (Administrative Company) located in a bicycle shop. He recorded in his diary his impressions on that day, revealing the mood and routine at the front:

Rapid allied movement forward to the east and increased [Soviet] preparations for attack. A *Gefreiter*, who was not completely healed, reported to me today. He had come from a field hospital in the west, had been released from there because of the advance by the western allies and sent home for convalescence. His home was in Klitten. Immunization has been underway for a week

---

12   No full name was identified in any of the available documents.
13   *"Hiwi"* refers to *Hilfsfreiwillige* or Auxiliary Volunteers. These were typically former Soviet POWs who volunteered to support the German combat divisions in varying capacities. In rare cases they were provided weapons and participated in combat, especially toward the end of the war.

with the supply units. Contrary to the regulations, I have been following the advice of Professor Nauck in Hamburg and administering immunizations in the long lumbar muscles. But even so, there are complaints about immunizations. Some of the guys claim that they can't properly move the arm in question the next day. I have not had any complaints myself.

The pleasant ordered life is slowly coming to an end. Tank obstacles are being built everywhere. There was a tank alert in Klitten at noon. The commander in chief of the *Armee* [Schörner] ordered it ... . *General* Jauer was also there. An exercise was played with a scenario of Russian tanks breaking through ... .

Five days later on April 12th, Dr. Braune recorded how the news of Germany's continued losses on the battlefield was received at the frontline and the growing concern of the upcoming Soviet assault. Of particular concern was how fast the Western Allies reached the Elbe River, just behind *H.Gr. Mitte's* rear area.

... something happened in the remaining part of Germany. The *Wehrmacht* report indicates today, 'Königsberg has fallen!' Attack on Magdeburg from the west! Advance in the west along the entire line: Hanover lost, battles for Bremen. (So the Nazis didn't have any reliable way out, if it had actually come to that.) News from *Division 'BR'* said that in the area facing us, there had been a Russian group/tank corps deployed. Overall, a Russian Army was supposed to be deployed across from us in the *Division* sector.

Another alert at 11:30 p.m.! This time it must have been serious because highest readiness was ordered, and in the next 24 hours, heavy Russian attacks could be expected. There was not yet any evacuation order for the civilian population, although everything was already quite turbulent.

The next few days saw increased Soviet activity across the Neisse River as they prepared for the final attack west.

The men of *Panzer-Sturm-Pionier-Bataillon 'BR'* kept busy preparing defensive positions after it was transferred to the area south of Rothenburg. It set up its headquarters in Wehrkirch at the Church.[14] The Church was a perfect location for its headquarters, not because of the prominent tower with its onion-domed steeple, but because of its high stone medieval defensive wall that surrounded the grounds. Between 800-900 years old, the defensive wall is an impressive measuring some six meters (20 feet) high and 1.5 meters (5 feet) thick. The *1.Pionier-Kompanie* deployed to Uhsmannsdorf, *2.Pionier-Kompanie* to Ober-Wehrkirch, the *3.Pionier-Kompanie* to Ober-Spreehammer and the *Versorgungs-Kompanie* to Kossel. Soon after two companies of *Pioniers* were sent forward south of Rothenburg and for 2-3 nights thereafter, mines were laid in front of the main battle line. Orders then arrived to dig a second system of positions behind the first. Additional units were subordinated to the *Panzer-Sturm-Pionier-Bataillon 'BR'* that included a *Volkssturm-Bataillon* (mainly convalescent soldiers), one Cossack Battalion and *Hitlerjugend* units *Fahnenjunker-Unteroffizier* Hans Stübling offers his recollections of this time period:

Across the *Division's* entire rear area, there was construction of tank obstacles—tree trunks, laid in twos right across the road, guarded by individual *Volkssturm* personnel for whom the *Panzerfaust* was as new and weird as the Russians. There were *Panzerjagdkommandos* everywhere in the rear, mostly highly-decorated NCOs and *Hitlerjugend*. In the Neuhof School, the *Kreisleiter* for

---

14   "Horka", an old Slavic term meaning "on the hill" was the name given to the original settlement around the 1200s. By the 14th Century the settlements developed from the original church in the north, or Nieder meaning lower, along the Weiss Schöpes (stream) to the south, or Ober meaning upper. Between the two was Mitte or middle. In 1936 the Slavic term was replaced by the Nazis with "Wehrkirch". In 1949 the name reverted back to Horka.

Niesky *Kreis* assembled about 120 *Hitlerjugend* for weapons training. The *Panzer-Sturm-Pionier-Bataillon 'BR'* had to send trainers for that. After a lot of bluffing, I persuaded the *Kreisleiter* to give me 60 young men. (In order not to fall victim to his own heroic courage; after [the Soviet attack on April 16th] started, the *Kreisleiter* could not be found anymore in Niesky). These young men were put in the *Versorgungs-Kompanie* as a *Hitlerjugend* platoon and served well there.

Every rear unit (ash and trash) had to be set up for defense. Put up positions, do alerts.

During the period of April 12th-15th, when the enemy intent and the imminent beginning of the attack must have been recognized, all the mines we had or could get were still being laid. Night by night, the *Kompanien* were moved forward a platoon at a time to lay mines in front of the main battle line. Scut work. First lay the mines at night and measure them, and second, draw the maps of the mine fields.

Even on the eve of the Soviet attack defensive work continued. During the night of April 14th/15th the *3.Pionier-Kompanie* on the left flank as well as the *1.Pionier-Kompanie* and two platoons of the *2.Pionier-Kompanie* on the right were ordered forward to lay mines.

Steidl's diary entries for the beginning of April highlight the monotony of the frontline duty among the soldiers of *Jägerregiment 2 'BR'* as everyone waited for the final Soviet attack.

Sunday, April 1st
I was invited to see Dr. Seeberger, our nice small assistant physician. The Russians were south of Wiener Neustadt! We were playing April Fools jokes. Oesterwitz sent me a "forest fire bomb". I fell for it and sent it on to Renner.

Monday, April 2nd
Oesterwitz was with me in the bunker. It was raining. The Russians were moving further into my homeland. I was thinking of the men—but, how did that help. The *Werwolf* had been alerted; the homeland was making its final efforts!

Tuesday, April 3rd
We were relieved of our positions to our surprise. The transfer took place quickly. At midnight, I reported to Oesterwitz in Kaltwasser that we had withdrawn. We spent a few more hours having champagne. During the morning, I was in Teichroda and sleeping with the support people. The *Kompanien* got to Teichroda by foot and moved to the new positions.

Wednesday, April 4th
On to Kaltwasser. I took over the new sector that is with the right flank 13 km north of Görlitz. In Kaltwasser, were we had recently been housed for a short time for deployment, we fired pistols at model airplanes. But we sat in humble unexpanded bunkers.

Thursday, April 5th
I went down to Gahrmann's positions. There was still a lot to do; the forward trenches were to some extent collapsed and the main battlefield was not built up much, while the Russian on the other side had trenches in depth and were dug in an extremely large number. Setting up strongpoints, where we were, but for the time being, it's still the "calm before the storm."

Friday, April 6th
I went to see the positions for *Leutnant* Esser and *Leutnant* Kuhner. Kuhner just arrived and is making a very good impression. The *General* went with me through the positions of the

1.Kompanie on the left flank of the battalion sector.

Saturday, April 7th
During the night, the Russians picked up a man from *Leutnant* Kuhner's *Kompanie*. The patrol was able to get across the Neisse unnoticed during the dark night. It was clear that we were furious, but we would have our revenge.

Sunday, April 8th
A wonderful, beautiful day. I left the positions. In the afternoon, *Leutnant* Hüsker and I were at the silver fox farm and the forest house. Enemy reconnaissance activity in the air was noticeable.

Monday, April 9th
The *General* is in front with *Leutnant* Whasmer, a platoon leader in *Leutnant* Kuhner's *2.Kompanie*. Strong sniper activity is noted. My snipers are on the lookout as well, and make a lot of kills. During the night, Kuhner took an assault force over the Neisse. A few nests were taken out, but no prisoners were brought back.

Tuesday, April 10th
Kuhner repeated his assault force and was successful in bringing a dead Russian back with them. All we know is that we are being faced with fresh Siberian troops. In the evening, a "combat geologist" came to see me in the command post. We had our fun with him and I sent him to see Gahrmann. He's supposed to check there about whether building positions below the river [line] makes sense! At night, the ash and trash do a lot of excavation out in front, but it unfortunately costs losses at night, because there is quite a bit of firing going on.

Wednesday, April 11th
Extensive firing by enemy heavy weapons. We could clearly see the [Soviet] forward observers setting up with their troops and firing heavy artillery over there as planned. When going through the positions, I wound up under heavy fire; there was crashing and dust next to me. *Leutnant* Esser shot a Russian officer and the discussions of deployment came to an end. Enemy columns rolled day and night; aerial imagery showed the enemy bringing in powerful artillery. Just opposite my battalion sector, there were 1200 tubes of artillery, not including the innumerable antitank guns. There was no doubt that we were about to have a major enemy attack. We were all nerves until the hurricane hit. We also knew that we didn't have any firepower like that. We hoped we would withstand the heavy fire, because it would not be easy for the Russians to get across the river. In the afternoon, I was at the *Versorgungs-Kompanie*, which was further to the rear on some factory grounds.

Thursday, April 12th
Long-range fire from enemy artillery has stopped; it can't be long now. Königsberg has fallen. I went to Kaltwasser to see the ash and trash, get my affairs in order and exchange my laundry. I am expecting a great battle soon. The *Ib* headquarters is in See. People have a very pessimistic outlook there; there is only a little heavy ammunition on hand.
   An enemy thrust (recon!!!) at Muskau was repelled during the night (April 12th/13th).
   (There was news that Roosevelt was dead. The *Wehrmacht* report indicated, "British troops in Wittenberge; American troops in Jena; American troops advancing on Dresden with tanks!")
   The alert issued on April 12th remained in effect!

Friday, April 13th

We heard about the death of Roosevelt, one of the people with the most hatred towards our people. May God let him rest in peace. American troops have already crossed the Elbe. We know that the last desperate struggle awaits us and we are prepared to shoot up to the last bullet and not surrender without honor

This day, I had been married for one year. But the events left me no time to think about it or to reflect on it. During the night, the Russians were crossing with heavy forces between Esser's *Kompanie* and Kuhner's and getting settled in some positions in the destroyed road bridge. I was in front in the platoon command post. There was fog on the river; one could clearly hear the thuds of pilings being laid. There was no doubt that the enemy was building a crossing. I sent out an assault force. *Leutnant* Hüsker was killed in action during this undertaking. We were unsuccessful in penetrating the enemy bridgehead; the enemy was too strong in our front and dominated our positions from the other side, simultaneously providing protective fire for their people. In the evening, heavy artillery fire started on our positions, the enemy crossed the river in the darkness with heavy forces and captured *Leutnant* Esser's first trenches in heated close combat. While it was still night, we attempted to at least surround the penetration site with the regiment's assault reserve. After a short discussion in my bunker, off we went into the raging night. My telephone and radio communications with the companies had been disrupted. There was heavy enemy fire on the positions. Renner attacked with his *Bataillon* and pushed his way forward to Esser's *Kompanie*, while I with my weak battalion reserve fell victim to the enemy bridgehead hitting my flank from the south. It was not possible to carry out our attack without heavy losses. *Leutnant* Stolf, one of our most courageous officers, was killed in action. *Leutnant* Esser was severely wounded. I spent the remaining hours of the night in *Leutnant* Kuhner's bunker. Heavy fire raged through the remainder of the night. There was no doubt that a strong enemy attack was imminent.

Saturday, April 14th

During the morning, *Leutnant* Hüsker and I shot a buck. It tasted good. Rupp brought me a Leica with film that he had purchased for me in the Sudetenland. I left the *Kompanien* positions. A defector swam across the Neisse to see us. He reported large enemy troop massing and large amounts of guns and ammunition. Some observations indicated continued enemy advances. Columns rolled night and day.

Units of *Panzer-Sturm-Pionier-Bataillon 'BR'* under *Hauptmann* Müller-Rochholz mined the shore (west bank) of the Neisse in the area south of Rothenburg to Neuendorf an der Neisse.

The alert remained in effect! Increased enemy fighter-bomber activity. Everything pointed to the Russian great offensive starting soon!! It was cold in the evening again!

During the weeks of March and early April the *Division* was reconstituted from the losses incurred during the prior months' heavy fighting.

The *Division's* replacements came from the trainees of *Panzergrenadier-Ersatz-und-Ausbildung-Brigade 'GD'* and *Lehr-Regiment 'BR'*. By April 15th *Panzergrenadier-Division 'BR'* overall strength was approximately 9,000 men. Its overall combat strength was likely not greater than 3-4,000 men if both *Jägerregiments* and *Pionier-Bataillon* are counted. No period document was located that offered a breakdown of the *Division's* ration strength and combat strength (*Kampfstärke*), which typically constituted about a third of its overall manpower. Based on an evaluation of its weapons inventory dated March 9th, the *Division* was equipped with the following hand-held infantry weapons:[15]

Sturmgewehre 44 (assault rifle)	501

---

15   NARA T78/529/923.

Maschinenpistolen (MP 38 or 40 submachine guns)	550
Karabiner 41/43 (Gewehr/semi-automatic rifle)	153
Karabiner 98k (bolt-action rifle)	5,130
Zielfernrohrgewehre (sniper rifle)	57
Gewehrgranatgerät (rifle grenade)	126
Leuchtpistolen	(flare pistol) 255

What this reveals is that the majority of the *Division's* combat platoons were armed with standard 5 round clip bolt action rifles. The submachine guns and semi-automatic rifles were likely dispersed across key squad positions and heavy companies. From existing accounts we know that the majority of the *Sturmgewehre 44*s were assigned the *Panzer-Sturm-Pionier-Bataillon 'BR'*. A late war Soviet Guards Rifle Division that contained approximately 9,619 men on paper was equipped with 5,426 rifle and carbines, typically the M.44 Mosin with standard 5 round clip and 2,398 PPsh-41 submachine guns.[16] This was nearly double the number of submachine guns available to a standard *Panzergrenadier-Division* at the time, let alone a standard late war German *Infanterie-Division*. The Soviets also enjoyed more ammunition and better serviced weapons. For example, a shortage of brass forced German manufacturers to adopt steel cartridges that had to have a lacquer applied to prevent rust. These steel cartridges often jammed in the weapons at the most inopportune times. Man for man, German infantry battalions in 1945 were outgunned by their Soviet counterparts. This is an important fact as some historians have, in a very unqualified way, attempted to credit the effective resistance of the *Wehrmacht* on the field of battle in the late war to a preponderance of "better" weapon systems.[17] Petrol was limited. Ammunition was limited, especially among *Panzer*, artillery and anti-gun weapon systems. Small-arms ammunition was general available.

Period documents state that on April 10th *Panzergrenadier-Division 'BR'* had operational two command Panzer IIIs, ten Sturmgeschütze IIIs (1 short term repair), five Sturmgeschütze IVs (2 short term repair), and 16 7.5cm Pak (Mot Z).[18] The *Sturmgeschütz-Brigade 'GD'* was renamed *Sturmgeschütz-Artillerie-Brigade 'GD'* on March 13th. It reported 15 operational *Jagdpanzer IV L/70 (lg)* and one Sturmgeschütze H on April 10th.[19]

Tactical training remained high by all accounts. Training continued as companies rotated in and out of the frontline, but unlike in East Prussia, training occurred beyond the battalion level. Even the command staff had the opportunity to conduct exercises. *'Brandenburg'* enjoyed about seven weeks of uninterrupted training, which was two or even three times the amount of time many of its battalions enjoyed before their first deployment back in January. Training in the *Wehrmacht* was often intense and realistic. This period of uninterrupted training was critical in forging both primary groups and cohesion and effective discussed in Chapter 4. German junior officer and non-commissioned officer leadership remained strong as noted by members of the *Division*. However, there were limited exercises with *Panzers* or artillery. The time and resources could not be spared with the Soviets just a few kilometers away and the *Reich's* industrial output and logistic network operating in an increasingly

---

16   The Rifle Divisions achieved a 2-1 or better ratio between rifles and submachine guns by 1945 at the regimental level. See *Handbook on USSR Military Forces, TM 30-430* (Washington, D.C.: U.S. War Department, November 1945) and Charles C. Sharp, *"Red Swarm", Soviet Rifle Division Formed from 1942 to 1945* (George F. Nafziger, 1996), p. 143.

17   For example, Professor Stephen Fritz writes in his recent work *Ostkrieg: Hitler's War of Extermination in the East* (Lexington, Kentucky: The University Press of Kentucky, 2011), p. 459 that the soldiers serving on the Eastern Front at the end of the war were "... generally well equipped with small arms, including large numbers of Panzerfaust..." This assessment is based on no primary documents and any serious research would prove this assertion false. Most German combat divisions were under equipped, and their "small arms" were primarily bolt-action rifles and limited stocks of ammunition. Man-to-man the German soldier was outgunned by their Red Army infantry counterpart by the spring of 1945.

18   NARA T78/R621/000493.

19   NARA T78/R621/000494.

diminished capacity. Joint training at the division level was non-existent. This proved problematic during combat operations where a lack of basic coordination resulted in at least one documented case of friendly fire with *'Hermann Göring'* (Chapter 18). Overall, this period of intense training was a critical factor in the combat performance and survivability of *'Brandenburg'* during the weeks to come.

On April 15th, the eve of the Soviet attack, Adolf Hitler issued the following proclamation:

Soldiers of the Eastern Front!

For the last time our deadly enemies, the Jewish Bolsheviks, have rallied their massive forces for an attack.

They intend to destroy Germany and to exterminate our people. Many of you eastern soldiers know well the fate that awaits above all German women and children; the old men and children will be murdered, the women and girls turned into barrack room whores, and the rest marched off to Siberia.

We have been expecting this attack, and since January this year have done everything possible to build up a strong front. The enemy will be received with massive artillery fire. Gaps in our infantry have been filled by countless new units. Our front is being strengthened with emergency units, newly-raised units and Volkssturm.

This time the Bolsheviks will meet the ancient fate of Asia, which means that they will bleed to death before the capital of the German Reich. Whoever fails in his duty now behaves as a traitor to our people. Any regiment or division that abandons its position will be acting so disgracefully that they will be shamed by the women and children braving the terror bombing in our cities.

Above all, be on your guard against those treacherous officers and soldiers [Seydlitz Troops], who, in order to preserve their pitiful lives, fight against us in Russian pay, perhaps even wearing German uniform. Anyone ordering you to retreat, unless personally known to you, will be immediately arrested and, if necessary killed on the spot, no matter what rank he may hold.

If everyone on the Eastern Front does his duty in these coming days and weeks, the last assault of Asia will crumble, just as the invasion by our enemies in the west will fail in the end, despite everything.

Berlin stays German, Vienna will be German again and Europe will never be Russian.

Form yourselves into sworn brotherhoods to defend, not just the empty concept of a Fatherland, but your homes, your wives, your children, and with them our future.

In these hours the whole German nation looks to you, my eastern warriors, and only hopes that by your resolution, your fanaticism, your weapons, and under your leadership, the Bolshevik assault will be drowned in a bloodbath.

In this moment, in which fate has removed from the earth the greatest war criminal of all time [Roosevelt], will the turning point of the war be decided.

Adolf Hitler

The final Soviet assault on Germany was now at hand.

15

The Final Soviet Assault Begins, April 15th-17th

(Reference Maps 68, 69, 70, 71, 72 and 73)

Soviet activity increased along the frontline on April 15th. *Luftwaffe* aerial reconnaissance images received at *Generalfeldmarschall* Schörner's HQ revealed that the Soviets were bringing in more and more soldiers and equipment into their staging areas. It was noted that they were openly moving up artillery to within 10 kilometers from the frontline along the Neisse River. As early as the 14th, artillery and mortar fire increased as Soviet guns began zeroing against intended targets through geographic aiming points. Reconnaissance in force operations proceeded Soviet bridge building across the Neisse along the main avenues of advance. *Fremde Heeres Ost* was aware of the expected axes of attack. On the evening of April 14th they marked their *Lage Ost* map for *H.Gr. Mitte* as they did for every army group across the Eastern Front each day. In this case, they drew a series of red lines. The most pronounced Soviet line of advance was marked "Tank Group" with a red line stretching from Rothenburg to Bautzen. The next longest line of predicted Soviet advance was between Cottbus and Spremberg. Several shorter lines noted secondary attacks, but it is clear that *FHO* did not know that Koniev's main thrust was between Cottbus-Spremberg and not Rothenburg-Bautzen, though this was the secondary effort. *FHO's* inability to correctly predict the Soviet main assault with certainty was driven by Koniev's ability to mask the final staging area of the 3rd Guards Tank Army. German intelligence officers had identified this tank army to the east of Görlitz on the 14th noting with a dotted line its movement north to the area of Forst. In reality it was staged in this area already, but it would take until April 17th before *FHO* noted this on the evening *Lage Ost* map. It was made clear on the April 14th *Lage Ost* map that the right flank of *Panzergrenadier-Division 'Brandenburg'* could expect a major attack in the next 24-36 hours.[1] In response to this intelligence assessment *Fallschirm-Panzer-Division 1 'HG'* was released from its reserve commitment and moved by rail to Görlitz, where it went into the frontline between *'Brandenburg'* and the *72.Infanterie-Division* by the morning of the 16th. It was obvious by looking at the map that *Panzer-Korps 'GD'* would not be spared from the opening attack of Koniev's forces. .

Koniev's main attack was directed at the frontline between the *V.Armee-Korps* and *Panzer-Korps 'Großdeutschland'*. This area south of Forst and north of Muskau was important terrain wise, as it was north of the dense Muskau Forest, dotted with a series of impassible open iron-ore and coal mines. The *Autobahns* between Breslau-Berlin and Dresden-Berlin also offered Koniev the ability to shift his forces north or south once he crossed both the Neisse and Spree River lines. Hitler recognized this and ordered *H.Gr. Mitte* to destroy the *Autobahn* overpasses running from Berlin-Forst on April 15th, but he ordered the east-west crossings to remain intact.[2] Defending this area was the *342.Infanterie-Division*, a *Kampfgruppe* of the *545.Volksgrenadier-Division*. The *21.Panzer-Division* remained in *OKH* reserve in the vicinity of Spremberg. The rest of the mobile divisions were in reserve further south on the right wing of the *4.Panzer-Armee* where Schörner expected that the Soviet thrust would

---

1   RG 242 German Armed Forces Operations and Situation Maps, 1939-1945. H.Gr. A. Box 357: *H.Gr. Mitte, GenStdH Op.Abt.IIIb Prüf Nr. 78246, Stand: 14.4.45 abds.*

2   NARA T78/305/6256572-73.

likely be directed. The secondary attack down the Rothenburg-Bautzen corridor placed his forces in a position to cut through the southern end of the *4.Panzer-Armee*, surrounding the bulk of *H.Gr. Mitte's* mobile forces and isolating them in difficult terrain.

The night before the attack, on April 15th, *Generalleutnant* Jauer radioed Schörner's headquarters with a question: "Based on the pressing enemy situation, I request permission to move back 8 kilometers in order not to provide a target for the artillery." "Don't go back a single meter or you will report to me tomorrow!" was the reply from Schörner. Jauer complied with the suicidal inflexibility but did move back his troops that consisted of the "stomach and ear battalions" that were armed with only "three pistols and four rifles for 40 to 50 men." Far to the north around the Seelow Heights in the *H.Gr. Weichsel* sector of the Front, *Generaloberst* Gotthard Heinrici executed a withdrawal westward of his frontline forces the 8 kilometers that *General* Jauer requested from *General* Schörner. Heinrici's defensive plan was predicated on such a maneuver. He spared his force thousands of casualties and preserved significant quantities of weapon systems, ammunition, and equipment in the first six-eight hours of battle. Heinrici's economy of force blunted Zhukov's offensive and allowed him to maintain some operational freedom for nearly three days until Hitler refused to allow the *9.Armee* to withdraw from the Oder River line and sealed the fate of *H.Gr. Weichsel*. Schörner's lack of a flexible defense, while keeping with his personality and established Nazi ethos that a soldier's "will" could win the day on the field of battle, left the *4.Panzer-Armee* with no tactical options and sealed its fate instantaneously.

Marshal Ivan Koniev launched his attack across the Neisse on April 16th at 0610 Moscow time. His operational plan was to suppress the German forces on the far bank with his artillery and air forces while laying a thick smokescreen for his assault crossing that consisted of his 3rd Guards, 13th and 5th Guards Armies. The Soviet engineers worked tirelessly to provide crossing points. In the area of the main assault of the 3rd Guards and 13th Army there were twenty bridges, nine ferries, twelve assault landing points, and seventeen assault bridges.[3] The 3rd Guards Tank and 4th Guards Tank Armies began their crossing operations as soon as the lead infantry echelons cleared the west bank. Koniev prepared his forces to drive toward Berlin before the battle, though it was not until after the battle began that he received the authorization from Stalin directly to wheel northwest toward the city after Zhukov proved incapable of breaking *Generaloberst* Gotthard Heinrici's defense of the Seelow Heights in the first 48 hours. He issued an addendum to the Stavka order that read "Bear in mind that part of the forces of the right wing of the front will aid the troops of the 1st Belorussian Front in capturing the city of Berlin."[4] In particular he singled the 3rd Guards Tank Army for this effort by issuing a specific order to "have in mind attacking Berlin from the south with a tank corps, reinforced with a rifle division from the 3rd Guards Army."[5]

The Soviet assault devastated the two German divisions defending in the area. The *545. Volksgrenadier-Division* was split in two with the bulk pushed south. The *342.Infanterie-Division's* front was "torn apart" despite "brave resistance" by its grenadiers and the remnants forced north across the Berlin-Breslau *Autobahn*. Attacked from the rear, it was reduced to fighting as a *Kampfgruppe*.[6] His tank forces quickly overwhelmed the weakly manned and lightly armed frontline positions, pushing inland quickly. In the first twenty-four hours of the operation, Koniev's forces reached the Spree River where the 3rd Guards Tank Army proceeded to conduct an assault crossing using shallow water fords.[7] Koniev was now over both major water obstacles and in a position to strike north toward his ultimate goal. The pace of Soviet operations was supported by 1,500 sorties of the Red Air Force that struck any moving target in sight. His 5th Guards Army attacked due west from the area of Muskau with the intent to screen the southern flank of main armored thrust.

---

3   Koniev, p. 71.
4   Ibid., p. 66.
5   Ibid.
6   NARA T78/304/6255426.
7   Koniev, pp. 81-82.

A secondary assault began further south along the axis Rothenburg-Bautzen by the newly established 2nd Polish Army and 7th Guards Mechanized Corps of the 52nd Army. This combined force was ordered to advance westwards in the direction of Dresden, but its primary objective was to provide support to the 5th Guards Army's screening effort and prevent any German counterattacks to the north.[8] Soviet pre-battle map reconnaissance was good. They knew that south of Muskau the rail and road lines running east-west from Rothenburg were their quickest route through the heavily forested area. The combined Polish-Soviet attack struck the middle of the *Panzergrenadier-Division 'BR'* at Rothenburg, hitting the lines of *I.Btl./Fhj.Gr.Rgt. 1244* and the *I.Bataillon* of *Jägerregiment 2 'BR'*. At the time the German forces on the frontline were not aware of the new Polish Army.

A report went up to *OKH* on the day's events. It was relayed that after a two hour artillery barrage followed by heavy aircraft attacks the first wave of Soviet soldiers launched their ground assault. The Soviet main effort was identified as being between Penzig and Rothenburg and between Muskau and Forst. It was estimated that the attack consisted of four Soviet Armies and two Tank Armies. By the end of the day secondary attacks struck the frontline of *'Brandenburg'*. The *545.Volksgrenadier-Division* was split by the Soviet assault. *Fallschirm-Panzer-Division 1 'HG'* that deployed into the frontline during the early morning hours remained in heavy fighting by Zodel, 8 kilometers south of Görlitz.[9] It was noted that during the day's fighting 31 Soviet tanks were destroyed.[10]

Feldmarschall Schörner wasted little time in reacting to the Soviet assault. Orders were issued releasing the *21.Panzer-Division*, *Führer-Begleit-Division* and the *10.SS-Panzer-Division* from *OKH* Reserve. He immediately directed them north toward the unfolding breach at Spremberg. In addition the *344.Infanterie-Division* was expected to arrive in the area shortly.

Sunday, April 16th

The Soviet attack was no surprise for the soldiers of *Jägerregiment 2 'BR'*. Already reports of losses were being received by *Oberstleutnant* Oesterwitz at the regimental command post in Kaltwasser. On the frontline was *Hauptmann* Steidl's *I.Bataillon*. *Major* Renner's *II.Bataillon* was in reserve at Kaltwasser and prepared for Oesterwitz to give the order to reinforce Steidl, if necessary. Renner's men had aided Steidl the day before, and he did not need to wait long before his men were once again ordered into the breach.

In the *I.Bataillon* sector, the Neisse was no real obstacle to the Soviets. The river was only about 15 meters wide, with the depth in many places no more than a meter. In *Leutnant* Esser's *1.Kompanie* sector the Soviets established a bridgehead on April 13th. On April 15th they attempted to build a footbridge, but a counterattack by *Leutnant* Körte's second platoon threw them back. The Soviets attempted this maneuver again in the afternoon and succeeded, in part due to the general lack of artillery ammunition available to *'Brandenburg'*. *Hauptmann* Kurt Steidl offers the following account of this Soviet activity prior to the main offensive in the area of *Jägerregiment 2 'BR'*:

> During the afternoon of this first warm and sunny Sunday, a report came in that the expected big Russian attack would take place on Monday in the early morning. One after another, the various buzzwords for upcoming major enemy attacks were invoked. The regimental command post all at once became a swarming anthill. Messengers, ordnance officers and adjutants were coming and going. Almost everything had to be handled orally. There was strong monitoring of the long distance communications and radio networks. A careless word or a poorly camouflaged utterance

---

8   Seidel states the Dresden was the objective of the Polish 2nd Army at the start of the attack, see pg. 261, fn. 3. However, Grzelak, et all state that the Polish 2nd Army was not ordered to capture Dresden at the start of the attack but only to screen Koniev's left flank, see p. 271. Given the known facts, it is the author's conclusion that the Polish 2nd Army was ordered to capture Dresden by its commander without first consulting Koniev.

9   NARA T78/304/6255425.

10   NARA T78/304/6255422.

Image 5. An aerial view of the city of Rothenburg looking west toward Wehrkirch (Horka) and Niesky. Rothenburg was the first objective of the Soviet 52nd Army on 16 April and it was captured in 24 hours. The 52nd Army's 7th Guards Mechanized Corps wheeled left along the rail-road line and headed in the direction of Weißenberg, while the attached 2nd Polish Army advanced down the main road toward Wehrkirch. In defense on the right and left of the city were *Jägerregiment 1* and *Jägerregiment 2* of *'Brandenburg'* respectively. Defending in the city was a mix of *Volkssturm* and *Fahnenjunker* battalions. Author's collection.

could betray our readiness to the enemy.

On the afternoon of April 15th, the Russians attempted to push a small bridge across the Neisse in the sector of *Leutnant* Körte's 3rd Platoon in order to establish a bridgehead of their own on the west bank. The Russians had attempted to do the same thing in the early morning. During the afternoon and evening, the Russians hit the *Kompanie* sector with continued shell fire, which pointed to something. The Russians then started putting up the bridge, and that could not be stopped because of the fire. The bridge was ready by the time it was dark. The *1.Kompanie* was put on alert.

The alert was barely out in the early evening, when the Russians overcame us with fire and crossed the bridge they had built. An immediate counterthrust by the 1st Platoon of the *1.Kompanie* was unsuccessful; instead, the Russians pushed as far as the gaps in the 3rd Platoon and split it into two pieces.

Slowly the entire company sector was rolled up, although the *1.Kompanie* continued to launch counterthrusts, which, however, were unsuccessful. Other parts of the company (particularly Ascher's platoon) continued to hold their position. The Russians made their way into the first buildings in Kahle Meile.

A company in Renner's reserve *II.Bataillon* was brought in from Kaltwasser and deployed with the parts of the *I.Kompanie* that was at the edge of the forest to defend along the road.

11:00 p.m. came. The night leading to April 16th was proceeding quietly.

In the early morning hours of April 16th the Soviets launched their main assault. The Soviet attack first struck *Jägerregiment 2 'BR'* positions in the forest southeast of Kahle Meile near the rail line running from Zentendorf to Biehain. The *I.Btl./Jäg.Rgt.2 'BR'* was hit hard, along with the supporting *I.Btl./Fhj.Gr.Rgt. 1244* to its left flank near Rothenburg. At about 5:00 a.m., *Leutnant* Esser, the *I.Kp./Jäg.Rgt. 2 'BR'* commander, attempted to assemble the remainder of his company but was no longer able to do so because the Soviets started their artillery barrage at about 5:15 a.m. The sustained fire lasted until approximately 7:45 a.m. The Soviet fire was particularly heavier in the sector that extended to the rear of the *1.Kompanie* to the positions of the *5.(schw.)Kompanie* of the *I.Bataillon*. The Soviets continued to move more soldiers across the Neisse, as well as antitank guns and various other equipment. At about 8:00 a.m., *Leutnant* Esser attempted to reassemble his company after the heavy fire because heavy losses had seriously reduced its strength. *Leutnant* Esser was himself severely wounded in the foot.

The Soviets managed to encircle parts of the *I.Btl./Jäg.Rgt. 2*, particularly the *1.Kompanie* and the *5.(schw.)Kompanie*. Those *Panzergrenadier* that did not withdraw, became prisoners. Even the command post of the *I.Bataillon* was attacked and had to move itself and parts of Renner's reserve battalion back toward Kaltwasser where the regimental command post was. By the afternoon of April 16th the command post of *I.Btl./Jäg.Rgt. 2* withdrew again, back to the Kodersdorf railway station. Here it established a new reception line in the hope to stop the withdrawing troops. *Hauptmann* Kurt Steidl relates the opening of the Soviet assault among his *Panzergrenadier* that fateful Monday morning, April 16th, 1945:

Shortly before 5:00 a.m., the earth moved. From thousands of gorges, shells of all calibers were chasing our positions at a depth of up to 15 kilometers. Heavy fire in amounts never before experienced raged. We flew from one corner of the bunker to another. Sticky smoke pushed its way through the air shaft. It never came to an end.

   Minutes turned into hours. We hoped it would stop at any minute because we would be buried under the roof of the bunker. But it continued. After a few hours, the sustained fire let up, but there were still shells going over our heads without interruption. Breitkeitz and I fell out of the bunker into a crater the size of a house in order to get an overview of the situation. The tall forest was mowed down, and craters were lined up one after another. About 100 meters from us, enemy tank columns were moving west and enemy infantry was moving along the railway. My battalion was torn to pieces except for a few men. We made our way back from one crater to another through the large open area to my battalion bunker in the forest. The *General* was there and gave me an order to move with the rest of my people to the partially occupied reception position at Kaltwasser. So we went back to Kaltwasser, again under heavy fire. Support and alert units were already hunkering down in the well-constructed trenches. It was a clear sunny day. For a few hours, we had relative calm and then the Russians were back and breaking through in the forest to our right with their tanks. They were even attacking us; we hit them with a few rounds. Even the enemy air force was showing its guns. We stopped in the afternoon, and then it was time for us to evacuate the positions because the enemy was too far to our rear. We went by foot to Mückenhain through forest that was thick in some places. The *General* was with us. We took up position in the railway station at Kodersdorf. We managed to knock-out 15 T-34 tanks during the night. But we were already the forward strongpoint in the general front line that had become disconnected. We moved into Mückenhain (battalion staff and *1.Kompanie*). In the early dawn, the Russians broke into the town with their tanks.

Obergefreiter J. Klingenschmid who served with the 3rd Platoon, *1.Kompanie* of *I.Btl./Jäg.Rgt.2* 'BR' offers his first-hand account of the Soviet assault and the first few days of fighting:

Even on the afternoon of April 15th, 1945, it was observed in the sector of our 3rd Platoon (*Leutnant* Körte) that Ivan was attempting to set up a bridgehead on this side of the Neisse, the bank occupied by our troops, by starting to put up a small bridge over the Neisse. Even during the early morning, Ivan had attempted to get across the Neisse, but his attempt was thwarted by an immediate counterthrust from the 3rd Platoon. But because Ivan continued to lay rather heavy shell fire on the 3rd Platoon sector during the afternoon and evening, it was impossible to prevent this bridge from being laid, because neither our artillery nor our grenade launchers had any ammunition for our own fire. So Ivan was able to set the entire bridge up successfully by the time darkness fell.

Because all the predictions were that an imminent attack could be expected, our entire *Kompanie* sector was put on alert when darkness fell. However, the attack came even sooner than anyone had expected. The alert order had scarcely been given, when one heavy fire attack after another fell on our entire position sector, so everything had to be put into the holes as quickly as possible. Protected by this fire attack, the Russians calmly crossed the bridge in the 3rd Platoon's sector and moved up to that platoon's positions. When the heavy fire calmed down a bit, the 3rd Platoon immediately launched a counterthrust, and Ivan was pushed back almost to the bank. Then Ivan attempted to push through at another spot in the rather poorly manned position system of the 3rd Platoon, and was successful in doing so. Here Ivan broke the comrades of the 3rd Platoon into two portions—one that immediately had to retreat to the company command post and one that retreated to Körte's platoon command post and then along the road until it also got to about the company command post.

So in a very short time, Ivan came into possession of the positions of the entire 3rd Platoon and then pushed our people, who were retreating to the company command post, along the trench. A bit of a distance away from the company command post, however, the 3rd Platoon personnel managed together again and held the Russians off for a little while, and in the meantime, we cleared out the command post and retreated into the 2nd Platoon's command post. The comrades of the 3rd Platoon then moved back slowly as well, some of them to the 2nd Platoon command post, and some of them setting up contact with their comrades in 2nd Platoon in that platoon's positions. Ivan then continued to advance along the positions and thus wound up in 2nd Platoon's sector, and he then got some of them out of their positions, so part of the 2nd Platoon also had to go back to their command post.

Here the parts of the 2nd and the 3rd Platoon and the company troops set up a pretty good defense and continued to push their way back in counterthrusts to the positions of the 2nd Platoon, intending to get back everything if possible, provided that there was a prospect of reinforcements from the reserve battalion in Kaltwasser. However, as soon as we made it a bit forward, the increasing numbers of Russians pushed us back even further. So in the end, the Russians were in front of the command post of the 2nd Platoon and would have kept us permanently surrounded in there had we not managed to jump out of the command post window facing the street at the last minute while the first Russians were pushing their way through the door into the building and had surrounded the command post from three sides, leaving out the side facing the street.

In the meantime, the other comrades had to leave the area around the command post and then moved to the other side of the street into the forest that began there, where we joined them again. Part of the 2nd Platoon and the entire platoon of our comrade Franz Ascher, however, maintained their positions firmly in hand. However, for some reason, the Russians did not make a serious attempt to get a foothold in these sectors.

We immediately moved security forces up to the forward edge of the road against what had formerly been the 2nd Platoon command post and set up a security line to our comrades in 2nd Platoon, which still had the position in their possession, while most of our 3rd Platoon set up for defense on the rear edge of the road in the forest. In the meantime, a company of our reserve battalion was brought from Kaltwasser, and they also set up for defense with the 3rd Platoon in the forest in order to resist any further attacks. In the meantime, it was now about 11:00 p.m. and the remainder of the night was relatively quiet until the early morning.

However, the high point of the battle didn't come until the early morning of April 16th, 1945. Shortly after 5:00 a.m., *Leutnant* Esser attempted to reassemble the people of the company, after we had become scattered all over everywhere during the darkness at night. But, there was no one in the entire company to be found except for the two radio operators and me. So *Leutnant* Esser and I retreated a bit into the forest in order to set up a temporary command post in the form of a hole with a roof. We had barely dug in about a half meter together, when a bunch of heavy fire made up entirely of smoke grenades burst out over us, and we really lost our hearing and our sight. Anyone who has not experienced it himself can really hardly imagine it. It lasted from 5:15 a.m. to 7:45 a.m. in the morning, and after just a quarter hour we were surrounded by so much smoke that we had severe breathing difficulties because none of us had a gas mask. It was impossible to see more than two steps away. We were later able to determine, and in fact we did, that the exclusion zone created by this sustained fire went left from the beginning of comrade Ascher's platoon sector across the 2nd Platoon's sector to the right of the former company command post and back to the shell firing positions of our 5.(schw.)Kompanie on the railway line en route to the bataillon command post and, to a lesser extent, even back all the way to the regimental command post in Kaltwasser. It is easy to imagine the impact of this long heavy sustained fire on the relatively small stretches. Nothing specific could be determined about the size of our enormous losses; all that was possible was to use the number of survivors to get an approximate picture of our great losses. Comrade Ascher, who in his deployments had already experienced lots of heavy sustained fire, told me that this was the longest and heaviest fire that he had ever experienced. Even today, it is a mystery to me how it was possible to survive these 2 1/2 hours with their indescribable dangers that felt like days. Here we had all come to terms with our lives when one shell after another howled past our ears, the air was hardly breathable and we were all just praying for the final shell. But fate still had something good in mind for some of us. We will never forget these hours, which demoralized even the strongest of us down to the core.

The end of the heavy sustained fire, *Leutnant* Esser, driven by his exemplary concern for the people of his company, left our covered hole to see to our comrades and our heavy losses after I had unsuccessfully attempted to persuade him to wait for the end of the fire, given that nothing could be retrieved from the entire situation at the moment. So it didn't take long for a messenger from *Major* Renner, who had come with a company of our reserve battalion from Kaltwasser and was in a hole not far from us, to come running up to get me because *Leutnant* Esser was severely wounded. So I made my way to *Major* Renner's hole were some comrades had just taken *Leutnant* Esser, who was severely wounded by a piece of shrapnel in his foot. Now I got a mission from *Major* Renner that by coincidence got me out of the encirclement in which half an hour later the remnants of our unit found themselves without us suspecting anything.

Specifically, I had to go back to the battalion command post with two urgent reports because no other messenger was available and none of the messengers from the other companies knew the exact route. I was supposed to come back as quickly as possible with the answers because the fate of the entire unit depended on that. So I and another man, who would be available to me as an escort in any case, set off about the time the heavy sustained fire ended, even though it was still especially heavy. The dangers we had to overcome to get through are almost indescribable. We worked our way through to the railway line where there was a group of 10-15 Russian men waiting for us on the right side of the route to the battalion command post, and they also followed us as they should have. Even so, we managed to get away from them in a piece of new-growth forest on the left, where they finally gave up on pursuing us. We had barely gone a bit further, when a group of Russians with an antitank gun in position passed us about 100 meters away. However, in their zeal they must not have noticed us, because we were able to get away from them almost unseen, and when they did catch sight of us, we already had gone a good bit further, thank God. Now we wanted to go on the road a bit further right, where to our astonishment, there was already an entire platoon of Russians moving completely undisturbed on the path to the battalion command post. So we had to continue to keep to the left in order to at least reach the battalion command post before the Russians and warn them in a timely manner.

We reached the battalion command post at the same time as *Oberleutnant* Gabi of the *5.(schw.)Kompanie*—he had fought back from the mortar positions to the Russians' right—and stirred up the battalion command post quite a bit with our reports. Everything was immediately set up for evacuation immediately because not a moment could be lost in getting back to the reception positions in Kaltwasser if people didn't want to immediately become prisoners of the Russians. The Russians had gotten well into our rear to the right and left of the barrage belt while the heavy sustained fire was still in progress and had encircled us entirely without our notice, because, after all, we couldn't see anything due to the smoke. My job then became to attempt to get back to our comrades with a message as quickly as possible so that they at least could made an attempt to break through the encirclement ring, because they probably had still not noticed anything about the encirclement. However, because *Hauptmann* Steidl had explicitly prohibited doing anything because it showed no prospect of success, the battalion staff, etc., and I had to retreat to Kaltwasser.

Our unit's remnants were now informed of their fate in the forest before them and none of the comrades of the 3rd or the 2nd Platoons, who had to get out of their positions, could make their way through. In the best of cases, the few that had still survived the heavy sustained fire became prisoners of the Russians if they had not met an even sadder fate.

The men of the *5.(schw.)Kompanie* that were cut off did find a way to survive and they continued to avoid captivity while withdrawing southward on their own, behind the advancing Soviet frontline. Steidl's *I.Bataillon* was shattered in the first barrage, even before the Soviet infantry attacked from the bridgehead they won the evening before. The men of the battalion were cut off and had to choose between a withdrawal through Soviet lines or surrender to the Soviets. According to Spaeter, whose comments are typically sympathetic to the soldiers he served with, "only small groups were able to make their way to the west, but they were overtaken and picked up by the Soviets. Others cowered in their holes and waited for rescue—but those who can should help themselves."[11] Spaeter's words suggest that discipline might have broken down, particularly among the new recruits of the battalion.

Jägerregiment 1 'BR' was not attacked by ground forces during the opening Soviet assault. Heavy Soviet air attacks did range across their front. Hähnichen, where the *Jägerregiment 1 'BR'* supply cache supply was located, was bombed by Soviet aircraft. Orders were soon issued by *Division* headquarters. The *I.(gep)/Jäg.Rgt.1 'BR'* under *Hauptmann* Schuster was ordered to assist *Jägerregiment 2 'BR'* once its desperate position was realized. *Leutnant* Grosser, the regiment's *O1* offers an amazingly detailed account of the first day's attack, and the enormous stress that weighed on *Major* Bansen's mind regarding the decisions he had to make:

---

11   Spaeter, *The History of Panzerkorps Großdeutschland, Volume 3*, p. 389.

It was not until after midnight that it became calmer in the command post. All of the preparations were made, the tense nerves did not allow any sleep, and the cigarette butts piled up in the ashtray.

But even before the dawn actually broke, it started becoming turbulent in front of us. Tank noises started coming from the right flank, and shortly thereafter the first enemy attempts to cross were reported, though not very extensive. Then at about 6:00 a.m., we got a report from the regiment on our right that there was a deep penetration by the Russians. We could not find out anything more specific. Apparently, our neighboring regiment was not completely clear about the situation.

In the meantime, our right flank reported that it had lost communications with its right. A *Pionier* platoon was order to the right flank for reinforcement and *Leutnant* Pietsch from the regiment was sent there as well. At the same time, the *I.(gep)Bataillon* went reconnoitering deep into the right flank to determine how deep the penetration area was.

7:00 a.m. arrived, and it started to get light. We still could not find out anything more specific about the situation of our neighbors to the right. It appeared that some sort of free-for-all was going on there. Calming news and alarming news canceled each other out.

This is how the picture was rounded out for us: Enemy attack on a limited front (2 to 3 km). No major attack or penetration attack. Enemy forces were not disproportionately large. Heavy weapons and artillery were present only in very limited quantities. There were some isolated tanks. Our reserves had not yet been deployed. After the situation in the area in question had been clarified, it shouldn't have been difficult to get rid of the enemy penetration.

However, based on the results of the reconnaissance done in the previous days, the situation appeared to be weird. Extremely great reinforcements with troops, armored forces and addition of a great deal of artillery had been noted. So far, none of this was noticeable."

At 7:30 a.m., the puzzle of the beginning of the massive sustained fire was solved. The earth quaked and moved. I had never yet experienced anything so enormous. I immediately attempted to determine the limits of the barrage area. The last conversation we had long-distance with *I.Btl./Fhj.Gr.Rgt. 1244*, and also the only one, ended with the words of *Oberleutnant* Schnier, the adjutant, "All hell has broken out with us, our bunker is dancing, and we hope that nothing hits us directly because it wouldn't survive that." The connection was broken and we were unable to reestablish it.

The sustained fire lasted for two hours. It was estimated at 2,000 tubes and 200,000 rounds of ammunition. The furthest forward positions of *I.Btl./Fhj.Gr.Rgt. 1244* were completely torn up and leveled by the shells. However, it was completely calm in our *II.Bataillon* sector.

The enemy was working with a lot of smoke, so for us as well, everything was covered in a thick screen of smoke and it became impossible to see anything.

One or two radio transmissions from *I.Btl./Fhj.Gr.Rgt. 1244*, the only reports that we got from there, indicated that the enemy was already on the high positions at the edge with tanks. Three tanks were killed in front of the battalion command post in close combat.

Because it was impossible to get any orientation about the situation from the battalion to our right and because communications had been lost with the armored battalion as well, my commander decided to get some clarity by himself.

After a few short orders, the *Krad* messengers and the *SPW* were ready. We stepped out of our bunker into the daylight. In other words, one couldn't believe that it was daylight without further confirmation because there was only a hazy dawn due to the heavy smoke. The enemy artillery fire had died down to scattered fire on the rear area and our vicinity. We had barely arrived when a *Krad* showed up in the fog in front of us: *Leutnant* Pietsch [Paetsch?]. The short blonde *Leutnant* with the German Cross in Gold quickly got off the *Krad*. His steel helmet was askew on his head and the camouflage netting was hanging down. The faces of the *Krad* crew were sweaty, and they were sprayed over and over with dirt. All the tires on the *Krad* were flat.

Leutnant Pietsch climbed up to the *SPW* and reported what he knew about the situation. He was just underway to the right flank when the murderous barrage started. The way he told it, all hell must have broken loose and he saw it as miraculous that he made it safely out of there. As far as he could determine, the troops in the forward positions were bombarded so much that no resistance worth noting could be expected from them. Most of the heavy weapons built into the hill positions must have been lost. Any that remained would be unable to see anything because of the fog. The communications within the battalion sector must have been completely disabled.

Leutnant Pietsch was released to the regimental command post. We moved on to the *I.(gep)Bataillon* in order to get into the rear area of *I.Btl./Fhj.Gr.Rgt. 1244* that way. We passed Dunkelhäuser, which was at a road intersection. The few buildings had been overwhelmed by a salvo from Stalin organs. Typical direct impact points. Tops of trees, roofing tiles and dirt lay all over the road. The asphalt was torn up from the impact. The town had fortunately been evacuated a few days before by troops, so there were no losses.

Here as well, there was a smoky haze over the area that did not allow one to see very far. At the edge of the town, we found some "fault seekers" restoring the destroyed [phone] lines to the *I.(gep)Bataillon*. The guys were in a good mood although they were continually harassed by low-flying aircraft, which continually strafed the roads. Because the lines were on poles, they had to climb down the telegraph poles each time an airplane came by in order to take cover in the ditches at the edge of the road. They had not yet seen any enemy infantry or tanks.

We went further into the haze, always expecting to run into the enemy at any time, but we did not know anything about the situation in the area where we were because the communications were down.

We went into Schlangenhauser, where the command post of the *I.(gep)Bataillon* had most recently been. There was relatively little destruction in the town itself. The command post was abandoned. The windowpanes were destroyed and the windows were barricaded with a sofa, a table and a wardrobe. There were impacts all around. A very warlike scene. After we had scratched our heads for a while about where we might find the battalion, we discovered a few men dug in behind the building. Soon the commander, *Hauptmann* Schuster, and his adjutant, *Leutnant* von Bremen, were on site. They had also lost contact with the battalion in front of them. They had set up a few forward command posts. A few wounded and released personnel had been brought back, and they described the same situation as *Leutnant* Pietsch had. There were individual bunches of tanks seen in the high edge position. Several tanks were killed in close combat. There were no communications within the battalion anymore. A group of about 30 tanks was reported in the forested area in front of the *I.(gep)Bataillon*.

A look out the window showed an 8.8cm *Batterie* from the *Heeres-Flak-Artillerie-Abteilung*. That provided some security, because the words "enemy tanks" have a very unpleasant connotation for infantrymen.

Assessment of the situation: The enemy was already in our positions with tanks. The forward positions were very heavily influenced by destructive fire. There was no more communication with the forward battalion. Uniform command of the battalion along the main battle line could no longer be ensured. (The command posts had been lost and nearly all the communications lines had been broken.)

My commander decided to occupy the second position behind the *I.Btl./Fhj.Gr.Rgt. 1244* with all the free forces available at the moment. Part of the second position had been torn down. The orders went directly to the commander of the *I.(gep)Bataillon* and by telephone or radio to the other reserve units. The line that was built this way was really thin, but it could be expected that it would be reinforced in a timely manner by released personnel and returning units.

We left the *I.(gep)Bataillon* in order to go to the new main battle line and then find the *II.Bataillon*. En route, we ran into some troops from the *I.Btl./Fhj.Gr.Rgt. 1244*, which we immediately stopped in order to have them integrated into the new main battle line.

When we went to the regimental command post and called up the *I.(gep)Bataillon* on the restored lines that was precisely when an order came from the division that the battalion was supposed to go to the neighboring regiment's sector. We had barely patched up the lines on an emergency basis, and now it was necessary to tear everything down again. That's something to despair about. After many telephone calls, the division ordered that part of the *I.(gep)Bataillon* sector be taken over by the *Pionier-Bataillon*. Finally, I had communication with the *Panzer-Sturm-Pionier-Bataillon 'BR'*. Take over the sector, sure; it's been ordered. But there was no way we could be in the sector in an hour.

We moved on to the *II.Bataillon*. We passed the regimental engineer platoon in Bremenhain. So far, the platoon had one casualty from artillery fire. Otherwise, everything in Bremenhain was in order. We moved on further to the *6.Kompanie* command post. In the meantime, the sun was beating down from the heavens. There was a peaceful mood in the forest. Everything was calm at the company command post. The accountant was in the process of handing out money. When you've come out of chaos, this peaceful scene appears extremely unreal.

Soon *Hauptmann* Hunhold, the battalion commander, a man from Southwest Africa, came in dressed in a short black leather vest. He described the situation in his sector to my commander. Multiple weaker attempts to cross were repelled. Otherwise, there was still nothing detectible in the sector since the major attack began. After the commander, *Hauptmann* Hunhold, had explained the big picture, we went back to Bremenhain in order to take a severely wounded man there back to the physician at the regimental command post.

We stopped at the farm. The poor guy was taken out of the basement on a stretcher and placed right across the *SPW*. His face was waxy white. He was fully conscious but contorted his eyes from time to time, so people suspected that he would soon be unconscious. As far as we could determine, he had a shot to his abdomen. We moved very slowly so that the wounded man did not experience unnecessary pain through the rocking of the *SPW*. I held his head, which he was moving in various directions due to his pain. He also repeatedly attempted to sit up, which I stopped him from doing, and I talked to him in a calming manner so that he would remain calm. He then rolled his eyes, fell back, rattled, stretched out and then stayed very weirdly calm on his back. I let out, "It seems to be over; I think he's dead!" Then the young man suddenly got up convulsively and looked around very appalled and doubtful. He was now sunk into exhaustion. Now he looked at me exhausted with his eyes wide open. He must have heard my words. It became clear immediately to him how terrible and hopeless his situation was. In embarrassment, my face turned red; what had I done? I could have bitten off my tongue because of my incautious and premature words. I didn't know what I should say and turned my face away. However, a new loss of consciousness caused the wounded man to sink lower, and there was foam on his lips. Shortly after his arrival at the command post, he died. The *Oberintendant*, *Leutnant* Schmidt, buried him with a few men not far from our bunker at the edge of the forest.

There were reports of low-flying aircraft and bomb attacks from Hähnichen and Spree, the villages in which the *Versorgungs-Kompanien* and the *Stabs-Kompanie* were located, and the *Stabs-Kompanie* had losses. (Shortly thereafter, the supply units were put under the command of *Ib* and were ordered to move. We lost contact with them.)

Shortly after that, the Russians passed us, pushing forward with tank forward elements to our rear, and were next to Spree. That definitively broke off our communications with the right regimental sector. A messenger from the left flank company of the *I.Btl./Fhj.Gr.Rgt. 1244* showed up from Rothenburg. He reported that parts of his *Kompanie* were in Rothenburg awaiting further orders.

At the same time, the company on the right flank of the *II.Bataillon* was attacked from Rothenburg and overwhelmed on its flank. It had to withdraw. Our front moved south. Shortly thereafter, there was a firefight on the southern edge of Rothenburg Russian artillery and tank columns were reported on the routes from Rothenburg toward Schlangenhauser.

Nothing was noted from either our tank defense or our artillery. The enemy columns were able to move further west without opposition. Schlangenhauser was evacuated after a short period of heavy street fighting, even before the *Panzer-Sturm-Pionier-Bataillon 'BR'* was able to properly set up for defense in the new sector. A short time later, the *Panzer-Sturm-Pionier-Bataillon 'BR'* was fighting on the eastern edge of Niesky. The Russians had broken through deep into our positions.

In the evening, as night fell, six *Sturmgeschütze* under *Oberleutnant* von Dunker were brought to us.[12] Because of lack of fuel, they could not initially be deployed. When they were fueled up, darkness had already started. The *Sturmgeschütze* remained on our flank near the second position as security.

This was the situation during the evening:

The Russians had broken into our positions with heavy tank forces and pushed deep (15 km) on a front of about 8 km. In our own sector, *I.Btl./Fhj.Rgt. 1244* had been broken up and scattered. The *I.(gep)/Bataillon* was taken from the division and moved to the sector of the neighboring regiment. *II.Btl./Jäg.Rgt. 1 'BR'* had been under attack from Rothenburg since the afternoon, starting on its flank. It became necessary to take the company on the right flank and a part of the *6.Kompanie* out of their positions and to move the front to the west. During the evening, Bremenhain also had to be surrendered in order to shorten the front line and prevent being surrounded. Right to the west of the regimental command post (about 1,000 meters), the enemy had pushed through. In the rear of the command post, it was at Spree (1.5 km away) in the afternoon, but it was pushed back. However, Spree had been evacuated by the supply units in the meantime and was now unoccupied, so the enemy could push through behind our rear without opposition.

Wire communications with the *Division* were broken. The *Division* radio net was silent. We were alone.

The radio operators were at their devices and continued to call the *Division*. We were desperately waiting to hear orders from the division or at least find something out about the situation. But the hours ticked by without us hearing anything from the outside world.

At about 9:00 p.m., the weak security lying scattered around the edge of our forest was recalled and consolidated with the *Sturmgeschütze* at the regimental command post. I set up a defensive perimeter as close to the bunker of the battalion command post as I could. The *Sturmgeschütze* were set up. Patrol and signal reconnaissance were set up in all four directions in order to detect any approach by the enemy or its installations. However, the forest was so wide and impossible to see that we could expect the command post to be overrun at any moment.

The commander was sitting with me in the bunker, and we were brooding about the situation that was showing up on the map with thick red blots and arrows, thin blue dashes and circles, and lots of big question marks. All of the blue spots on the map were surrounded by red. Open on the flanks, flanks up in the air and enemy in our rear are the hallmarks of our situation. When

---

12   Available research has not identified what unit von Dunker served. The available account by Grosser makes a clear distinction between the *Sturmgeschütze* of von Dunker and those of *Hauptmann* Metzger's *Sturmgeschütz-Artillerie-Abteilung 'GD'*. Grosser never mentions *Panzerjäger-Abteilung 'BR'* and notes that the last time he sees von Dunker is at the *Panzer-Korps 'GD'* headquarters, but we know that *Panzerjäger-Abteilung 'BR'* fought with *Jägerregiment 1 'BR'* in the coming battles around Bautzen, eliminating this unit as a possibility. Von Dunker likely was a member of one of the other *Sturmgeschütz-Brigades* supporting the *4.Panzer-Armee* at that time.

dawn breaks, we will be in a pocket or the Russians will cream us. How are we to act? How is this situation to be mastered? Who will relieve us and where are the reserves? Can we count on help or support at all? Those were the questions that repeatedly came up. And over all these questions was the *Führer's* order given to the troops 24 hours before: "There will not be a single step backwards. This battle will decide the war." And from an order by Schörner to the commanders: "I do not know concepts such as 'break off', 'fighting one's way back' or 'folding up'...."

How should we act? To leave our positions and fold up the southern front was in violation of the order. Staying in place and awaiting the enemy meant destruction, senseless loss of blood and useless loss of human life if we did not have reserves on site on time that had the power to grab the enemy penetration and close the gap in the front.

But could one count on such reserves? Didn't the *Führer's* order also say something about a monstrous artillery addition to our side? Did we notice any of that as today progressed? I thought we were abandoned, as we could now see clearly.

What decision could be made? The commander held in his hands the lives of several hundred men under his command. However, he also held in his hands the responsibility for the front sector entrusted to him; perhaps he had even more in his hands, specifically, whether it might be possible to use merciless holding of positions for a few hours to close gaps in the front with strong reserves. On the other hand, prematurely breaking off contact could end this possibility once and for all. Who could point out the proper path here? What did we know about the big picture? And the division still wasn't coming in!

The mood in the bunker was uncomfortable. Everything, particularly the time, was waiting on a decision. Although we were completely overextended by the stressful day, it was approaching midnight, and we repeatedly wanted to nod off due to lack of sleep, we also repeatedly woke each other up because of the agonizing feeling of responsibility that placed us in trembling unease. Our nerves were on edge, while our bodies repeatedly tried to fall off into sleep. And the clock face implacably moved forward. A decision had to be made if nerves were not to be torn apart. We could no longer hold our old position; of that we were fully aware. But the order remained in effect: hold on to the end; this battle will decide how the war will turn out. The *Division* still wasn't coming in. So no one could free us from this order; we could only follow our own intuition.

The commander's words came hard: "We will move south and set up a proper line. At this position, we are of no use to anyone. Common sense offers this solution. The regimental headquarters will remain here until dawn and if necessary will cover the setup of the new defense line. We should not be accused of lack of personal courage," he thought.

The extraordinary stress over us that threatened to push us over the edge let up. For a moment, the commander collapsed and remained lying on the couch exhausted. His eyes stared at the ceiling, but sleep still escaped him. His brain began to work again and the thoughts about further battles became a solid plan that pushed aside his disquietude over the consequences of the decision he had just made.

I left the commander and immediately started preparing orders for moving to the new positions. The messengers showed up again.

The commander's decision was sent off blindly to the *Division* in a radio message because the other radio station had still not come in. Feverish activity again erupted in our bunker after the paralysis among us of the last few hours.

To the north of *Jägerregiment 1 'BR'* the *Division zbV 615* failed to hold back an attack on its left flank by elements of the 5th Guards Army launched from a bridgehead they had gained around Muskau during the night of April 15th. The Soviets crossed both sides of the Sagar isthmus and subsequently forced aside the *Kampfgruppe 545.Volksgrenadier-Division.* A *Kampfgruppe* of the

Panzer-Pionier-Bataillon 500 'GD' from the *Korps* troops launched an immediate counterattack in the area with the orders to maintain a solid defensive line. The Soviets, however, were not interested in wheeling south behind the lines of *Panzer-Korps 'GD'*. True to Soviet operational form at the time, the forces of the 5th Guards Army received orders even before the offensive began to attack west and continue in that direction until the Elbe River was reached.[13] There was no anticipated coordination between the 5th Guards Army and Soviet units to the right or left. It is interesting to note that there were no German units on the Elbe River, just U.S. Forces that had reached the opposite bank nearly a week earlier. Soviet operational doctrine again cost Koniev dearly in the coming weeks as *Panzer-Korps 'GD'* extracted itself from a third pocket in as many months only to achieve the last operational battlefield victory of the *Wehrmacht* against the Soviets during the war.

The *Panzer-Sturm-Pionier-Bataillon 'BR'* under command of *Hauptmann* Müller-Rochholz was hit by advancing Soviet forces in the forest east of Geheege, between Rothenburg and Nieder Neundorf. This was where the *3.Pionier-Kompanie* was ordered to reinforce the left flank of *Jägerregiment 2 'BR'*. Müller-Rochholz attempted to deploy his *1.Pionier-Kompanie* and *2.Pionier-Kompanie* into the line to provide additional support, but a second battle began among the vineyards of Hill 199 where Soviet T-34s had just advanced. The *2.Pionier-Kompanie* along with other administrative staff and the Reconnaissance Platoon were forced to quickly set up a defensive perimeter. Orders were issued to avoid being surrounded if the Soviets attempted to bypass their positions. The *Pioniers* were to fall back to Ober-Wehrkirch that was defended by *Major* Voshage's 8.8cm guns of the *Heeres-Flak-Artillerie-Abteilung 'BR'*. *Hauptmann* Müller-Rochholz recounts the initial 24 hours of the Soviet assault:

Major attack!

The *3.Pionier-Kompanie* was deployed in the early morning in the vicinity of Ndr. Neundorf and immediately suffered heavy losses. A young *Pionier* knocked out a T-34.

The *1.Pionier-Kompanie* and parts of the *2.Pionier-Kompanie* were in the *Division's* northern sector moving back to their garrisons. That is how the battalion was broken down at the beginning of the major attack.

Because there was still no order from the *Division* and the company was forward of the command post, I went forward with the *Krad* in order to pull the company together and, if possible, bring the *1.Pionier-Kompanie* out of its movement immediately to get the *3.Pionier-Kompanie* out of there. I reached the *1.Pionier-Kompanie* and went with it into the forest west of Geheege. We deployed parts of the *3.Pionier-Kompanie* and men from *Jägerregiment 2 'BR'*. The Russians attacked in large groups. A T-34 was knocked-out by the courageous young men of the *3.Pionier-Kompanie*.

Through the *2.Pionier-Kompanie's* radio station (west of Geheege, at the edge of the forest), I ordered that my communications halftrack be sent forward. It made it through and reported that T-34s and large groups of Russian infantry coming from Biehain were already on the Weinberg hill (188). *Oberleutnant* Schlosser and the Reconnaissance Platoon and everything that used to be part of the headquarters as well as the *2.Pionier-Kompanie* in Ober Wehrkirch had occupied the hill. *General* Schulte-Heuthaus was there. An *SPW* was moving down the road from the Wehrkirch railway station toward Geheege and was fired upon from the right, that is, from the direction of Biehain.

So we had already been bypassed by the Russians from the south. Two platoons of the *2.Pionier-Kompanie* were deployed near Geheege to pick us up when we were retreating from the forest. So we went back to Geheege with the *1.Pionier-Kompanie* and the remnants of the *3.Pionier-Kompanie* while we continued counterattacks against the Russians and conducted fast withdrawals. Geheege and the edge of the forest south-southeast of Geheege, along with units of

---

13   Koniev, p. 122.

the *Heeres-Flakabteilung 'Voshage'* were held until the afternoon.

In front of the *1.Pionier-Kompanie* sector (the edge of the forest south of Geheege), were three T-34s circling in front of the accompanying Russian infantry, which was unable to get away from the edge of the forest east of Geheege. However, the tanks remained respectfully at *Panzerfaust* distance.

Then Bank [*1.Pi.Kp.*] was attacked in the forest from the southwest. The Russians wanted to roll us up from the flank. Bank had to turn and now was sitting with his front facing south, somewhere about the southern exit from Geheege in the forest. In the north, the Russians were going in columns toward Uhsmannsdorf along the road from Rothenburg to Dunkelhäuser. Geheege was under heavy tank fire. We had to retreat, because Bank was already being attacked again in the flank and the Russians would otherwise make our semi-fortified position into a pocket. Among the engineers there were men from both regiments all over everywhere, including a "stomach battalion". We went back to the northern side of the road from Geheege to Wehrkirch. The Russians were in there again immediately and we must have been about 1 hour apart, divided only by the road. Command was made very difficult due to the number of soldiers from other units; there was no clear structure. The people from the "stomach" units were moving about; the wounded were getting moved back.

Order: "Pass it on! *Pioniers* stand fast; everyone else withdraws to Nieder Wehrkirch, where the *Heeres-Flak-Artillerie-Abteilung 'BR'* is. From the bend in the road 1 kilometer southwest of Geheege, we dominated the road with machine guns and the Russians, first of all, couldn't go through and also couldn't go around us. Then, however, it came from the north on our side. But now we had a clear structure. The *1.Pionier-Kompanie* stayed put; the *2.Pionier-Kompanie* launched a fake attack to the north and moved, forming a place for the *1.Pionier-Kompanie* to be picked up. The maneuver was conducted three times and Ivan fell into the trap. Heavy losses slowed him and we were finally able to catch our breath. I could see us moving over the open area to Nieder Wehrkirch.

The Russians were sitting in the south on the railway track between the railway station and the edge of the forest. When we went across the meadows, we were flanked by their fire! Voshage's 2cm weapons were firing to our left and our right into the edge of the forest. That was also where the Russians were.

Old haystacks in the meadows were set on fire with smoke grenades; that meant that they started smoldering and the smoke went towards our forest. White tracer rounds told the *Flak* personnel that these were our troops; then *Feldwebel* Gräter took his *SPW* (our radio vehicle) full speed across the meadow, crossed the bridge and made it through to Voshage. It worked. Then he had Voshage fire smoke and we had to move. The sun was starting to come up when that worked. Assemble in the Nieder Wehrkirch estate manor (the palace) park.[14]

Voshage was practically in the estate's park and, I think, it had three 8.8cm guns among the buildings right to the south of it. If we wanted to withdraw them, the Russians first had to be removed from there. We went in and recaptured Nieder Wehrkirch to the railway station, putting the area back in our hands.

So that's the way the night passed; the Russians in the north in Uhsmannsdorf, where they moved in unbroken columns to the west with tanks and in the south at the railway station; we were at the estate wall and in the buildings south of the palace. The 8.8cm were taken out in the night and went back. Voshage let me keep the 2cm. Two Russian armored reconnaissance vehicles were destroyed with *Panzerfausts* near the wall at the entrance to the estate. At the gate, the crew that had been forced out into the sewage pipe under the entrance was put down with hand

---

14 The Palace in Nieder-Horka was built in 1908 in the Art Noveau style. Miraculously this beautiful and historic building survived the fighting and remains one of the few intact architectural examples of the period.

grenades. During the hard night battles lasting until about midnight, we must have knocked-out a dozen T-34s using *Panzerfausts*.

The wounded went back with the 8.8cm guns.

We had communications with the *Division*. In Ober Wehrkirch, *Oberleutnant* Schlosser and several men from the *2.Pionier-Kompanie* and the headquarters were killed in action!

The following experience was told by *Unteroffizier* Stübling who was in the Headquarters of *Panzer-Sturm-Pionier-Bataillon 'BR'* at the start of the offensive.

After heavy sustained fire lasting about two hours from all the tubes, Ivan attacked the entire front between Rothenburg an der Neisse and Neundorf. The battalion remained the last one at the front and it was in the nature of things that we were also the last to leave the trenches. Our commander, *Hauptmann* Müller-Rochholz, had a hard time making the decision to take this step, but in order not to be cut off, we had to dig ourselves into the ground.

At this moment, a young *Landser*, a fresh *'Brandenburger'*, came breathless into our small headquarters house. He appeared without a pistol belt or steel helmet on and a pistol in his hand, "I'm an NCO, give me a *Panzerfaust*, I got a Russian tank but it's still moving." He took my answer of no with disdain, turned around and disappeared to the place he came from. "Papa" Müller, the communications officer and I had already moved behind the road and moved back towards the enemy when a killed T-34 showed up about 50 meters sort of to our right front. However, before we had properly seen it, it suddenly went up in the air somehow—a thunderclap—and the remnants of the tank were in the pile of rubble that resulted. While we were wondering about the sudden appearance of the *Panzerfaust*, a few meters beside us appeared the grinning face of the *Landser* who had shortly before demanded a *Panzerfaust* from us. "Papa" Müller nodded at him in recognition without saying a word.

About 2:00 p.m., the battalion came for a short breathing break in a dense patch of forest. *Hauptmann* Müller told me while smoking a cigarette that he wanted to go see the *Landsern* to give them some more courage and comfort; I should put some cigarettes into it and in itself that was one of our own. For the Chief, that was an obvious matter; he did that almost every day. After we had also gone among the people, I determined that someone was looking for him and that person had found his victim. It was the young *Landser* from this morning... . "Papa Müller" indicated by winking that he did not want any reports and put his own Iron Cross I on the 17-year-old's jacket without a word. He gave him a few cigarettes and a case of Scharakola and said goodbye, saying, "You've done well, young man. You'll get an award after the fact."

At about 6:00 p.m., withdrawing *Pioniers* arrived in Wehrkirch, and held the town during the night leading into April 17th. Parts of *Infanterie-Bataillon 88* were subsequently subordinated to *Panzer-Sturm-Pionier-Bataillon 'BR'*.

The following account from Dr. Braune who was located with the *Heeres-Flak-Artillerie-Abteilung 'BR'* provides the view from the rear area on the day of the Soviet attack:

The alert remained in effect. It froze at night, and it was also cold during the morning. I went with Poratz to do immunizations in See. We froze miserably. We didn't do immunizations because everyone was standing sentry or "doing war." At the *Ib* headquarters, it had been expected that I would immediately take over as troop physician at the *Heeres-Flak-Artillerie-Abteilung 'BR'*. For me, the physician who was the newest arrival at the division and the youngest one by several years, that was a high honor because I would be quite independent as the *Abteilung* physician. *Flak* was also a weighty unit and had an outstanding commander. But even so, I was beyond surprised, because I know that I, as the young newbie, had to first fight my way into such a wizened unit. The old people know that already ... .

In See, I heard that the Russians had started their great attack in the area of Küstrin and Frankfurt. Defense wasn't that successful. In our sector, the Russians formed a bridgehead across the Neisse 1,000 meters wide and 400 meters deep yesterday evening, and we have so far been unable to make an impression on it because of lack of ammunition. So tomorrow morning things will probably get started for us as well.

At 4:30 p.m., I wound up at the *Flak* headquarters in Wehrkirch with my baggage and report to *Major* Voshage—the expected critical overview. The adjutant was *Oberleutnant* Schilling. My predecessor, *Stabsarzt* Dr. Grossmann, a loudmouthed Berliner, escorted me in. It is good that I learned to hold my liquor so well in the *Kriegsmarine*; besides, there are large amounts of alcohol and the supplies are being emptied here as well.

At 5:15 a.m., the Russians began their artillery preparation. We were rather firmly removed from our beds and the beds themselves were even taken. The headquarters was in a palace in the middle of a park. The park was bound on the east by a massive wall. Though the palace was in the middle of Wehrkirch, the nearest buildings were a bit further away. We were initially not reached by the preparatory fire. It was not until about 11:00 a.m. that the Russians fired heavy artillery into the village. Lots of air activity. A railway line right behind the palace park was soon broken.

By about 10:30 a.m., the *Abteilung* was only doing security against air attacks, nothing shot down, two personnel slightly wounded. Unfortunately, Grossmann never made it out of the *Abteilung*. He got an order to remain there temporarily. That made me over strength. We moved into the basement of the palace and prepared meeting space, storage space, etc.

In the afternoon, the *Division* was pushed back from the front. It then became uncomfortable very quickly for us. Apparently, the palace was recognized as a command center because starting at 4:00 p.m., we got uninterrupted heavy artillery fire right on us. The upper floors had to be evacuated. The *Abteilung* was now in a ground battle with all the units. There was only a temporary connection. For a long time, it was completely impossible to reach the *3.Batterie*. There was still no wounded coming. Since I had nothing to do, I made myself useful as a 2nd Ordnance Officer. At about 5:00 p.m., our situation suddenly became much worse. A few minutes later, there was a very severe bombardment and then there were Russian tanks in front of the wall around the park. There were a total of 18 of us in the Palace with two machine guns and an antitank gun of Russian origin. Nevertheless, with the combined forces of all the people, we managed to push the Russians back. The tanks were destroyed in close combat by firing over the wall, and the commander killed two armored personnel carriers using *Panzerfausts*. After the first advance, the men had broken through the wall around the park on the basis of firing charts in many places and dug trenches under the holes so they could no longer be hit by the ever-stronger artillery fire. The wall had previously stood up to hits from the highest caliber everywhere. A half hour later, Ivan moved back into the surrounding buildings. It appeared that the remainder of the village was Russian, that their rear was still uncovered, but that it was in flanking Russian fire. Apparently, the Russians were not strong and there were no more tanks to be seen.

By 6:00 p.m., it was possible to set up the *1.* and the *2.Batterie* behind the village such that they could give us flanking fire; in addition, the division had placed the *Panzer-Sturm-Pionier-Bataillon 'BR'* under the *Abteilung*, and by 6:00 p.m., about 40 men had jumped out to get into our palace and the park. In addition, it had started to get dark. Additional *Pioniers* managed to filter in; there were, however, a few casualties and we had some things to do. At about 7:00 p.m., *Hauptmann* Müller-Rochholz arrived. By 8:00 p.m., Wehrkirch was basically back in our hands in a counterattack. The losses were small.

A bit later, the *3.Batterie* was back and moved forward into the village. Then the defense of the town was reorganized. The *Division* named Voshage as the strongpoint commander. Subordinate to it were the *Heeres-Flak-Artillerie-Abteilung 'BR'* with all its units, the *Panzer-Sturm-Pionier-Bataillon 'BR'* except for the *1.Pionier-Kompanie*, stragglers of the two *Jägerregiments* (which were increasing in number all the time), and two *Batterien* of the *Panzer-Artillerie-Regiment 'BR'*—so it was a very striking bunch with which not a lot could happen. However, there was no longer a clear road to the rear; Ivan had it all or the roads had been made impassable by blowing up the bridges.

The situation in the *Division* sector, as far as we knew: loss of terrain to our front and about 7 km to our right. To our right, continued solid front. No connections to our left. Battle noise left to the rear, getting further away, increasing. There the Russians had apparently made it through. Patrols found neither friend nor foe in that direction. There was not much Russian fire activity in front of us. We ourselves were not firing anymore, because we could not have any targets in the dark after the village was retaken. There was no fighting to our right.

At about 9:00 p.m., I got the mission to recon a retreat route for the reinforced *Abteilung*. It was easy to handle this mission. About 300 meters beyond the town of Wehrkirch on the road there was a stretch of woods; from the palace, there was a field path going there with deep ditches on both sides. The *Panzer-Sturm-Pionier-Bataillon 'BR'* had gotten through to us in the evening along this route. The field path went east-west to the forest. Behind the forested area, the path veered to the south and continued to follow the edge of the forest, which the enemy continued to avoid. At the southern end of the woods, the path again veered to the west, crossed a swampy stream bed on a light bridge and then went through a larger piece of woods about 800 meters west of Wehrkirch to Niesky. The path was dry and solid and trafficable by all the vehicles we had if the bridge could be reinforced sufficiently. The *Panzer-Sturm-Pionier-Bataillon 'BR'* did that during the night. While we were scoping it out, there was direct Russian untargeted fire. From the east southeast, one could hear a steam pile driver at work; apparently the Russians were putting the demolished bridges back into operation.

The situation during the evening of April 16th/17th was chaotic. Much of *Panzergrenadier-Division 'BR'* was cut-off from *Panzer-Korps 'GD'* and the *4.Panzer-Armee*.

Each battalion of both *Jägerregiments* was on their own, often with no contact back to their respective regiments. The defensive battle along the Neisse River was over as soldiers of the *Division* sought to survive the Soviet onslaught. The *I.Bataillon* of *Jägerregiment 2 'BR'* was decimated with the survivors trying to reach German lines and reform, while the *II.Bataillon* was holding in the Kodersdorf-Mückenhain area with remnants of the *I.Btl./Fhj.Gr.Rgt. 1244*. The *II.Bataillon* of *Jägerregiment 1 'BR'* was in the forest east of Hähnichen withdrawing north where they began to meet elements of *Division zbV 615* withdrawing south. The *I.(gep)Bataillon* was cut off trying to reinforce the *I.Bataillon* of *Jägerregiment 2 'BR'*. It now found itself south of Wehrkirch. *Kampfgruppe Voshage* formed a defensive bastion in Wehrkirch with elements of the *Panzer-Artillerie-Regiment 'BR'*, *Heeres-Flak-Artillerie-Abteilung 'BR'* and the *Panzer-Sturm-Pionier-Bataillon 'BR'* in Wehrkirch. *Panzer-Pionier-Bataillon 500 'GD'* from the *Korps* deployed near Sagar. Located between Spreefurt and Weisswasser was *Sturmgeschütz-Artillerie-Brigade 'GD'* that arrived to support the *Division's* defense. The supply elements under *Ib, Major i.G.* Spaeter were still in their positions, ready to deploy west. On the right flank there was tenuous contact with the *Fallschirm-Panzer-Division 1 'HG'*.

Monday, April 17th

Panzer-Korps 'GD' HQ in Spreefurt was a cacophony of ringing phones and wireless sets. The curt chatter—when a connection to a higher or subordinate unit was made—was drowned out by the pounding of Soviet artillery and the drone of aircraft engines. From the start of the attack the

Kirche mit alter Wehrmauer

Gruß aus Wehrkirch, O.-L.

Kriegerdenkmal

Bahnhofs-Empfangsgebäude

Schloß Nieder-Wehrkirch

Image 6. The town of Wehrkirch (Horka) saw brief but intense fighting from 16-18 April. From left to right: Church that served as the headquarters for *Hauptmann* Müller-Rochholz's *Panzer-Sturm-Pionier-Bataillon 'BR'*; a First World War Memorial; train station (Bahnhof) where fighting occurred between *Pioniers* and Soviet T-34s; and the Castle that served as *Major* Voshage's headquarters for the *Heeres-Flak-Artillerie-Abteilung 'BR'.* Author's collection.

Wehrkirche Horka O/L

Image 7. A close up view of the medieval fortress-like Wehrkirch (Horka) Church where *Panzer-Sturm-Pionier-Bataillon 'BR'* established its temporary headquarters during the fighting on 17-18 April. Note the massive 20 foot wall that surrounded the church. This particular postcard is undated but was likely taken shortly after the end of the war as damage from direct fire weapons (likely tanks or assault guns) can be seen on the east facing façade. Author's collection.

Korps headquarters had lost all but the most tenuous control over *Panzergrenadier-Division 'BR'*. *Generalleutnant* Jauer had little information about the situation of his men, nor could he be expected too given the brutal pace of the Soviet attack. Soviet armor of battalion strength from the 7th Guards Mechanized Corps advanced through the breach between the lines of *Jägerregiment 1 'BR'* and *Jägerregiment 2 'BR'* and it was reported that at least 10 Soviet tanks had reached the town of Spree, behind the *'Brandenburgers'* main line.[15] The deployment of the 2nd Polish Army was still unknown to the *Korps* staff. Other elements of the Soviet mechanized corps and breached the left flank of *Jägerregiment 2 'BR'* and had reached Ullersdorf. The 2nd Polish Army soon entered the breach and developed its own parallel axis of advance west along the forest lanes between Reitschen and Niesky. *Panzer-Korps 'GD'* was being surrounded in a developing pocket. The only divisions available to reestablish defense on the *Panzer-Korps'* right flank were the *20.Panzer-Division* and *Fallschirm-Panzer-Division 1 'HG'* stationed just to the south near Görlitz. Both divisions were already ordered north to help seal the widening breech on the frontline. Further north on the *Panzer-Korps'* left flank the *10.SS-Panzer-Division 'Frundsberg'* was released from the *4.Panzer-Armee* reserve to counterattack where Koniev's main thrust threatened to split the *21.Panzer-Division* between Cottbus and Spremberg.

On April 17th Soviet forces of the 5th Army captured Weisswasser. The *Jägerregiment 1 'BR'* command post withdrew to Heidehauser. *Division zbV 615*, *II.Bataillon* of *Jägerregiment 1 'BR'* and the *Panzer-Pionier-Bataillon 500 'GD'* were now cut off from the rest of *'Brandenburg'* farther to the south. *Major* Benson subordinated his elements to the *Division zbV 615* commander *Oberst* von Bülow.

Jägerregiment 1 'BR' reconfigured its remnants. As related by *Leutnant* Grosser:

Movements and deployments had begun. The patrols were coming back and reporting that Bremenhain was occupied by the enemy. On the other hand, Spree was reported to be free of enemy. The Russians did not appear to be trusting in our forest during the night; at any rate, none of the patrols came across any enemy in the forests.

At the regimental command post, about 200 men and a number officers had assembled from released personnel of *I.Btl./Fhj.Rgt.1244*, other released personnel and the remnants of *Volkssturm-Bataillon Lorenz*. Under *Oberleutnant* Kappel, these splinter groups [to include *II.Bat./Jäg.Rgt 1 'BR'*] were brought together into a *Kampfgruppe*. This *Kampfgruppe* got the mission of occupying and holding Spree, the cornerstone of the new main battle line.

At 2:00 a.m., a radio operator popped in and reported that radio communications had been set up with division; the other station had acknowledged our transmission from midnight and was now sending a transmission to us. Thunderstorms. A heartfelt groan of relief came from my chest. That was because the attempt to set up land-line communication with the division was unsuccessful. At just the time that I had the *IIb*, *Oberleutnant* Bröker, in the loop, the connection was broken again and it could not be reestablished despite all our efforts.

The minutes until the transmission was received and decoded became an eternity. What would the general have to say about our decision? And the question came up again: Did we act properly or not?

We finally received a wireless radio message from the *General*:

Full recognition of our decision. Agree with course of action. Keep Spree at all costs. *20.Panzer-Division* and *Fallschirm-Panzer-Division 1 'Hermann Göring'* attacking from the south. *Sturmgeschütz-Artillerie-Brigade 'GD'* will be sent to Hähnichen to support the regiment. Signed Schulte-Heuthaus.

---

15   NARA T78/304/6255378.

An extraordinary relief came over us. The trace of bitterness that had held him since midnight disappeared from my commander's face. His eyes looked at me again with thanks. "Well, Good God, big guy," they said to me. However, the commander's mouth remained dumb. He stood up and when into his bedroom, fell down on the couch and a moment later was fast asleep. His breathing was calm and relaxed.

At 5:00 a.m., *Kampfgruppe Kappel* moved out. We went alone to the command post with a few men. The first light of the dawn came at 6:00 a.m. We climbed into the vehicles, the engines were turned on and were running warm with a soft buzz. The commander's right hand went up in the air. "Let's get going!" The *Pionier* roared, the *Kräder* pressed forward and the *SPW* and the *Sturmgeschütze* started moving with rattling chains. The early morning calm was filled with this noise.

The *Sturmgeschütze* immediately moved out to *Kampfgruppe Kappel* in Spree. We moved directly through Bremenhain to the new main battle line, which had been set up in the still of the night directly through the forest. We followed the route on the map with our fingers. Everyone's eyes look out attentively into the terrain. After a short trip, we met the first forward sentries for the new main battle line. The trip went further behind the main battle line to Hähnichen.

There we met some officers from the *Ausbildungs-Division* [AN: likely *Division Nr. 464*] and the commander of the *Sturmgeschütz-Artillerie-Brigade 'GD'*, a *Hauptmann* [Metzger]. The sectors for the *Ausbildungs-Division* companies were established. The [*Jagdpanzers*][16] were expected to be there in about an hour. First eight vehicles, then the other nine. That along with our *Sturmgeschütze* formed a proper fighting force. However, there was a shortage of ammunition for the *Geschütze*. But there was an ammunition train at the Hähnichen railway station with *Panzer* and mortar ammunition. That was a happy find. The *II.Bataillon* was immediately informed that it could again be supplied with ammunition.

At about 9:00 a.m., one could hear clear battle noise coming from Spree, infantry fire and tank shots. The *Jagdpanzers* of the *Sturmgeschütz-Artillerie-Brigade 'GD'* had already been moved to Spree, so there could not be an acute danger for the defense of the town. The Russians moved into the forested area east of Spree with tanks, going further north and attempted to go through Spree. No enemy activity was reported by the other units on the front.

There, at about 10:00 a.m., a messenger came from Spree and reported that the *Jagdpanzers* had left Spree without informing anyone. The *Kampfgruppe* now, robbed of its tank protection and its heavy weapons, had wound up in a very uncomfortable position, while the Russians had moved heavier tank forces in and had moved by the town on both sides. The danger of being encircled was very high.

The commander and I were completely floored. A *Jagdpanzer* was just going by on the road. I jumped onto the road and brought the *Geschütz* to a halt. That was the first time we learned that the entire brigade had been ordered to go somewhere else. Nevertheless, the sudden move out without taking the time to do a planned breakdown or at least sign out was digested after some worry and chickening out. Well it doesn't matter; the end result is, in any event, that we have all been left in the lurch.

Of Dunker's six *Sturmgeschütze*, four were in Hähnichen at this point, where they were just loading up with ammunition. Two *Sturmgeschütze* had been moved back for repair. There was a direct threat to Hähnichen posed by the enemy moving by Spree, and in addition the enemy could roll up our entire defensive system from the rear and the flank by taking Hähnichen. All of

---

16   The accounts by veterans provided to Spaeter are often not very specific to vehicle types. For example, we know as fact that *Sturmgeschütz-Artillerie-Brigade 'GD'* was equipped with *Jagdpanzers* and not *Sturmgeschütze* by April 16th. However, the infantry veterans simply referred to any turret-less gun carriage as "*Sturmgeschütze*" or simply "*Geschütze*". In order to be as specific as possible, "*Sturmgeschütz*" was replaced with "*Jagdpanzer*" when the specific account reference was known to be for *Stug.Art.Abt. 'GD'* during this time.

the men available in Hähnichen (*Volkssturm* and released personnel) were jammed together. The *Sturmgeschütze* moved to defend the town. There were *Pionier* demolition teams on two bridges in the town. They got the order to prepare the bridges for demolition.

The regimental command post was moved to Heidehaus. I myself remained in the forward command post in Hähnichen with the *SPW* and the *Krad* messengers. I had initially set up in a building near the bridge. Now I moved into the warehouse because it was really turbulent in the air and Ivan was also getting into the town with small-caliber weapons.

I had the *SPW* go to the back of the building where there was a vault-type area in the flat earth where one could make telephone calls and work in peace. The engine noise of the Russian pilots, who were pushing by our hideout continually for about 3/4 hour, the shots from their on-board weapons and the bombs dropping made a disgusting noise. Apparently they recognized the *Sturmgeschütze* and wanted to make them ineffective. However, no damage worthy of note occurred.

In order to determine what men had been found, I walked through the town. There were really not many of them. Maybe 50 men, mostly *Volkssturm*, who had their bicycles with small escape packs right by them. It later turned out that they had a good idea as to how to use the bicycles. The *Volksmänner's* weapons consisted of a French carbine with 10 to 15 rounds of ammunition, a type of ammunition that we could not get at all. Some of them had no weapons at all.

At the end of the town on the Spree side, I met *Oberleutnant* von Dunker. Spree had asked for support or relief. I discussed a plan for that with Dunker. Three *Sturmgeschütze* would be taken into Spree. Most of the *Kampfgruppe Kappel* immediately moved out to Hähnichen. Dunker held the town an additional 10 minutes with his *Sturmgeschütze* and as many men as could sit on them and then Ivan, properly spitting, back to Hähnichen.

An appropriate commander transmission that also provided the time for the beginning was set up. But again, the connection didn't want to work at the decisive time. The time had to be postponed and the transmission was finally canceled.

About 10 minutes before we started, there was murder running around in the town. I looked at the street in order to see what was going on again, and then *Krad* messenger Götz drove up quickly, reporting from Spree. At the same time, the *Kampfgruppe* managed to get out of the loop around Spree and move to Hähnichen before Spree was completely surrounded.

Götz and his copilot stood with beaming faces and eyes wide open with excitement in front of me. Their hair was plastered together with sweat. I didn't need to ask them any questions about their experiences. In his excitement, Götz blurted out,

Suddenly Ivan was at the edge of the town among the first buildings. I jumped out when the shots were fired to the corner of a building in order to get to my Krad. On the other side, a Russian was also running toward the vehicle. From a full-speed run, we both stopped and stared at each other for a moment. I was thinking, 'You won't get my mill, you dog.' I had a *Panzerfaust* in my hand. I raised it up, aimed it quickly and pressed the trigger. Ten steps from me, the Russian was pushed to the ground and at that moment, the *Panzerfaust* croaked. The air pressure put me out, and Ivan was blown up into a thousand pieces. Getting up, jumping on the vehicle and getting it going was done all at once. Right after that, I was safely on it.

In the meantime, everyone else moved out of the town. The two of us appeared to be the last ones. So we got on the *Krad* and moved down the road to Hähnichen full tilt. The shortest and the best road would be the fastest and the safest one. At breakneck speed, we got out of the town on the open rural road and we were soon met by Ivan with his rifle and machine gun fire. I hunkered down on the vehicle like an ape and floored the gas pedal. I had so many tears that even now it's blurry. Then there was a terrible blow, must have been a pothole, and I lost control of the vehicle. The next minute we were in the ditch. I looked around; nothing had happened to Hans. The plucky vehicle was still running although it was on its belly. I also still had all my bones. So we were really lucky. Ivan was firing from damned close so it was advisable to get out of there quickly. Crawl some more through the ditches at the side of the road? No! We wouldn't leave the *Krad* in the lurch. So on to it. We got the basket out of the dirt, got it up on the road and up on it. Geared up, full throttle and off we went. It was about time, because Ivan was starting to bang like crazy. Well, *Oberleutnant*, people have to be lucky sometimes.

I immediately got on a *Krad* and moved to the edge of the town. At the first buildings, Kappel's people were lying exhausted in the yards. Shortly thereafter, I found Kappel himself. We immediately set up the defense of the town of Hähnichen. Haste was called for so that the enemy couldn't force its way into our nest unexpectedly. It took all sorts of effort to put the men into their positions, because they were completely tuckered out. But there was nothing to be done; otherwise the Russians would set up a terrible chaos.

Fortunately, Ivan gave us some time, so the defense was up a half hour later.

The next thing for us to worry about was the ammunition train that was still in the railway station. How were we to get it away? There were no locomotives to be found far and wide, so the best one could do was to have the cars moved individually by horse. But even if the Devil wanted it, there was not a nag to be had anywhere. Though I had radioed everyone I could to have them come and get ammunition out of the train, no one had come so far.

From the other parts of the main battle line, the first enemy contact was reported. In the *Ausbildungs-Kompanie* sector, which was right next to Hähnichen, it became really turbulent in the early afternoon. Infantry and grenade-launcher fire. The noise was substantially increased through the forest, so a beginner might think that a big battle was in progress. The commander radioed me that I should take a look at the training people on the right, because they were continually sending crazy reports to him about extremely heavy battles.

On the *Krad*, I went over to the training people in order to take a look at what was going on. When I first met the officers, it was clear at first sight that they weren't 'Brandenburgers' or 'Großdeutschland'. The commander of the whole mess gave me the impression of a village schoolmaster; at any rate, the pince-nez made one suspect that was his profession. Our conversation was often interrupted because the "commander" was busy building a bulletproof shelter for himself. With a bit of discomfort, I said goodbye after some time; hopefully the Russians would not seriously attempt to get through because I would then have a bad feeling.

I wasn't in Hähnichen for much longer before it came to a head. Some bad firing broke out in the forest near the training people and not long after that, I had my first report that the Russians had broken through. With a groan, I got myself into the sidecar and off I went into the forest to see for myself what had actually occurred. After running around for a while in the area in which the Russians had supposedly broken through in huge numbers, I managed to determine more precisely what was going on.

In fact, about a platoon of Russians had filtered through our thin line in one place. What made the matter doubtful was that some of the Russians had disguised themselves in German uniforms shown by white armbands. That confused our people initially and they did not immediately behave properly among the brothers.

It got to be 4:00 p.m. The people from the *Ausbildungs-Division* appeared to be no longer reliable. At any rate, the Russians were continually filtering through their lines.

In Hähnichen, we got fire from the forest on the flanks where the training people really should have been. But their reports became ever more muddled, so I couldn't make heads or tails out of them anymore. Messengers and a *Sturmgeschütz* crew reported that shots had been fired on the road 500 meters behind the main battle line of the *Ausbildungs-Kompanien*.

There were no reserves at all that could get through to the terrain in question. All of the available men were deployed forward. So I decided to go to the terrain behind the *Ausbildungs-Kompanien* companies with my *SPW* so that there would at least be a pair of watchful eyes, even if there weren't any rifles. The thought that there might be a storm brewing in the rear of our defensive lines was very unpleasant, given our weakness.

I stopped my vehicle at a farmstead with a residential building, a stable and a barn. An observer from our *1.Artillerie-Abteilung* had make himself at home on the roof of the residential building. In addition, there were two men as forward sentries for the *Ausbildungs-Division* a short distance from the farmstead. However, I already had had enough of these pompous people and had no desire to deal with them anymore. These "combat forward sentries" came across to me as if they wert just a field exercise. The plucky guards knew nothing about the fact that they were in the rear of our defensive line; they said that they had nothing in front of them except for enemy. I just shook my head and moved on.

I took the *Krad* further on to the command post in Heidehäuser. It was a bad road between open ponds. In addition, I was plagued by a vile hunger. At the command post, people were busily setting up communications with as many units as they could in the vicinity. So far, efforts to set up a uniform command structure or a joint command post for all the units had been in vain. But another enemy awaited me. At the command post, I met a *Hauptmann*, the commander of the *1.Batterie* of *Panzer-Artillerie-Regiment 'Brandenburg'*. Like us, they were up in the air and wanted to join us. With a firm handshake, the subordination was confirmed. That was the birth of our *Kampfgruppe, Kampfgruppe Bansen* that the enemy would learn to fear within the next few days.

From Hähnichen, there was alarming news that my *SPW* passed on. The enemy did not appear to be totally united in conducting battle there. There was stronger pressure on the town. On the *Krad* again. At the farmstead, I found my *SPW* again. We went into Quolsdorf. When I got out of the *SPW* and into the *Krad*, *Leutnant* Niemeyer, the weapons officer for the regiment, ran up and grabbed me. Finally, the long-awaited man was there who was to get the ammunition off the train in Hähnichen that was so near and dear to our hearts.

We got on the vehicle and off we went. In the meantime, the enemy had surrounded Hähnichen on all sides. You could still get into the town on the rural road, but you had to go through enemy infantry fire for the last 500 meters. We clung to our vehicles for dear life and when the first bullets flew by our ears, we automatically crouched onto the seat.

We stopped at the warehouse. I ran through the park. Ivan was fiddling around with mortars in the town. Shot-off tops of trees littered the area. An unpleasant sight. A *Sturmgeschütz* was sitting in the middle of the town, shot up with its tube bent. Dark smoke in the air over my head, turning into serious whistling. I dived into a trench headfirst, dirt flying up behind me and shrapnel flying over me.

The training people had sent a *Hauptmann* who was supposed to join Hähnichen with his company. But not to the south; to the east. That gave the impression that we had already been written off and he was setting up a front on his own. Or were the guys really adhering so stubbornly to the old positions?

The discrepancies in waging battle were quickly put aside. It is truly no small matter to wage war with such a thrown-together group when one hardly knows the people by sight or name. In addition, there was already a lack of weapons, ammunition, medical treatment material and batteries for the radios. The *Volkssturm* people had mostly shot off all their ammunition. We had no ammunition for their French rifles and there was nowhere to get it from either. So the shotguns weren't good for anything except as a walking stick.

I took the same unpleasant path out of Hähnichen with a long wish list. Ivan was sending us his best whistling regards. But we were faster. While on the road, we ran into two *Sturmgeschütze* going to Hähnichen.

There was feverish activity in Heidehäuser; the noose was closing. Two telephones were constantly ringing.

Heidehäuser—that is the name on the map—is on a narrow stretch between two large ponds. The whole area has ponds lined up so that we could talk about a lake district on a small scale. You could also consider the area as the habitat of wood sprites and such with all the water, the damp meadows, small pieces of forest and lots of clumps of bushes.

The building itself in forester's house style appeared to no longer be suited for this original purpose. I considered it more likely to be a summer house that must have been inhabited during the war. But I could rather imagine a writer living here in quiet isolation. The living room was set up to be wonderfully cozy and very stylish. A thick hand-woven carpet covered the floor. Heavy furniture made the room homey. A comfortable couch and deep armchairs. I had particular joy in the library, in which all the classics, such as Rilke and Binding were represented. Such a wonderfully unreal and friendly feeling lay over the entire residence. It really wasn't lacking any fixtures. The residents must have left the house in a hurry.

All night there was stuff going on in the building so I couldn't get to sleep. My eyes kept closing while I was sitting in the armchair. I kept myself somewhat awake with cigarettes. So it was no wonder that fatigue threatened to overwhelm everyone. I hadn't slept for 48 hours.

Most of the work at night was for getting supplies. It was very difficult to set up communications with our supply units. But we managed to get the necessary weapons, ammunition and food in the early morning.

The reserve *II.Bat./Jäg.Rgt. 2 'BR'* found itself in the frontline without ever having to deploy. The Soviets had reached its positon during the first day's attack. The battalion, along with the regimental staff, put up a defense in the rail station at Kodersdorf, then withdrew to Mückenhain the day before. The Soviet renewed their attack along the left flank of *Jägerregiment 2 'BR'* as the 7th Guards Mechanized Corps pushed west. The remnants of Steidl's *II.Bat./Jäg.Rgt. 2 'BR'* withdraw southwest during the morning, to the town of Kodersdorf where a new defense was attempted. *Hauptmann* Steidl reported:

A bitter battle for the town against forces several times our size was raging in the streets. Gabel still had some units in Kodersdorf at the railway station and was cut off. I moved one town further south in order to secure my people's rear. In the meantime, Oesterwitz was thrown out of Mückenhain with the *II.Bataillon* units. Our good staff physician, Wolf Backhausen, was a casualty. He remained lying down severely wounded in the town after he had given his orderly the order to save himself.

The entire *Jägerregiment 2 'BR'* was about to be surrounded as Soviet armor maneuvered toward Rengersdorf. The situation was stabilized through an attack north by *Fallschirm-Panzer-Division 1 'HG'*. Panzer elements of the division launched a counterattack east of Kodersdorf where it won a pitched tank battle, against what was likely the 2nd Guards Tank Brigade, described by its division commander, *Generalmajor* von Lemke.[17] The division advanced to Kodersdorf where "from the edge of the woods, about 2 kilometers east of Kodersdorf, a large Soviet armored unit appeared, which we

---

17   Research suggests that this "Soviet" unit was actually a Polish Tank Brigade of the 1st Polish Tank Corps likely operating as a reserve force. However, this remains unconfirmed. It does not appear to belong to the 7th Guards Mechanized Corps as its single tank brigade was operating at Bautzen and it was not known to have been equipped with any JS-2 heavy tanks.

were alerted to by both ground and air reconnaissance." The 17 Panthers of *Oberstleutnant* Roßmann's *Panzer-Regiment* advanced in tight formation and remained well camouflaged in the town. The Soviet tank unit was caught advancing along a secondary road along the Schwarzer Schöps River as if it was in a peacetime exercise without any tactical discipline. Once the Soviet tanks advanced to within meters of the town, the Panthers of *Fallschirm-Panzer-Division 1 'Hermann Göring'* opened fire knocking out 43 Soviet tanks in 20 minutes. The remainder of the Soviet tanks surrendered and Roßmann's men captured 12 intact tanks, to include 3 or 4 of the JS-2, which according to *Generalmajor* Lemke were taken over by German panzer crews and employed a few hours later after being painted with a *Balkenkreuz*.[18] With the attack completed, Lemke's men were quickly pulled out of the line and transiting west fur further attacks, as the *17.Infanterie-Division* and *72.Infanterie-Division* shifted west into his positions.

An interesting facet of the fighting during this period is the fact that both sides captured and employed the other side's armored vehicles and equipment during the fighting between Rothenburg and Dresden. This was done for a combination of reasons that included expediency of use and a general shortage of equipment on both sides. The *4.Panzer-Armee* captured significant quantities of Soviet manufactured and U.S. Lend-Lease vehicles during the fighting in April as attested in both the above and following accounts. The Germans, for their part, painted a *Balkenkreuz* and put them to use against their prior owners for as long as petrol and ammunition held out. This went the same for the Soviets, who also employed functioning German armored vehicles whenever they could. This made for interesting scenarios as German columns operating behind Soviet lines were ignored by Soviet soldiers who took them for "friendly" units until they were opened fire upon—so used they were to seeing Soviet soldiers operating German vehicles. While rare, it is entirely possible that some tactical engagements occurred between Soviet manufactured tanks operated by German soldiers and German manufactured *Panzers* operated by Soviet soldiers.

Northwest of Kodersdorf the battles for Wehrkirch, Niesky, and See were underway. *Kampfgruppe Voshage* was hit by a major Soviet attack in the early morning hours of the 17th and was forced to withdraw by late afternoon. As reported by Dr. Braune:

At about 3:00 a.m., a strong Russian attack with tank support broke through the well-prepared defenses a few meters from our lines. We saw it from the upper, rather shot-out stories, of the palace. Firing was almost entirely with tracer ammunition; a nice picture. The assault forces knocked-out over 40 Russian tanks in close combat in the dark. It was then completely calm well into morning. It was not until about 9:00 a.m. that heavy preparatory fire began. At 11:00 a.m., I started moving the wounded into a tract of forest 300 meters west of Wehrkirch. Starting at 1:00 p.m., Wehrkirch was evacuated at division orders, and the reception position was the tract of forest. The two batteries of the *Artillerie-Regiment* had, in the meantime, been taken away. They no longer had any ammunition. At 1:30 p.m., Wehrkirch was evacuated; the losses were now growing rapidly. The dead had to be left lying. The tract of forest was held until 3:30 p.m. The Russians suffered heavy tank losses from anti-aircraft fire [8.8cm Flak guns]. Our losses from heavy Russian artillery and mortar fire were high.

At 3:43 p.m., the heavy weapons were moved to a larger tract of forest 800 meters west of Wehrkirch and covered the retreat of the last units from there. All of the wounded were collected in a timely manner and brought back. Thanks to the heavy weapons, the second withdrawal occurred without heavy losses. I set up a new aid station in a gorge in the large piece of forest and quickly had over 50 wounded there, some of them quite severe. All of the units were mixed up. The Russians were only slowly pushing their way into our sector. There was a battle alert to the left rear. There was a battle alert to the right; the Russians were advancing quickly there. At 4:08 p.m., the reinforced *Abteilung* got the order to break off fighting and retreat to the main battle line on either side of Niesky.

Major Voshage got a piece of shrapnel in the right arm when moving out of the patch of forest 300 meters west of Wehrkirch. He was running around with his arm in a sling. At 3:30 p.m., I got an order from him to set up transportation of the wounded. This was done using all the available vehicles without any problems. I was to accompany the column; on the way I expended a lot of effort to stop someone's bleeding. A piece of shrapnel had ruptured the external carotid artery of a *Landser* anterior to the right or the left ear. The bleeding did not happen until I put in an arterial clamp and wrapped it up in the bandage.

In the afternoon, we were no longer being deployed. We went to See, where there was marvelous quiet. The population had fled. I ordered milk and enjoyed the quiet.

We got reports that Spremberg and Cottbus were in the hands of the Russians. At about 8:00 p.m., the *Abteilung* moved to Quitzdorf.

Cottbus and Spremberg were still in German hands on April 17th, but the rumors were spreading about the dire situation to the north where Koniev's 3rd and 4th Guards Tank Armies had opened a 30 kilometer wide breech in the front opposite the *21.Panzer-Division* and were driving between those two cities on the northern flank of the *4.Panzer-Armee*. In fact the 17th was last day that a continuous front existed between the two German cities. Both the *21.Panzer-Division* to the north and the *Führer-Begleit-Division* had maintained a continuous front since arriving into position on the 16th. The *21.Panzer-Division* launched a counterattack in the morning but by the evening of the 17th had to return to its start positions due to attacks by fresh Soviet units, in this case the reinforced 23rd Guards Motorized Infantry Brigade. By the evening the connection between the two German divisions was broken and a gap began to open ever wider. On April 18th *Feldmarschall* Schörner ordered the *10.SS-Panzer-Division 'Frundsberg'* to close the breach.[19]

In the *Jägerregiment 1 'BR'* sector of the front light and heavy anti-aircraft guns played a decisive role in the defense, along with the explosives and *Panzerfaust* used by the *Pioniers* in close combat among the rubble of burning buildings. By midday the *Panzer-Sturm-Pionier-Bataillon 'BR'* withdrew to Niesky according to the account by *Hauptmann* Müller-Rochholz:

At dawn, the battle immediately started to be heavy. It went at hand grenade distance or closer for a long time around the buildings, in the yards and along the wall around the estate, where the Russians were separated from us only by the road. There was heavy fighting around the gaps in the walls that we had blown up to have firing ports, because the Russians were attempting to break through there. We would have moved, but that wouldn't work; in a minute the Russians would have been in the park and we and our few men would have been lost with no cover. So fighting was going on to the bitter end in the true sense of the word. At about noon it became calmer.

The movement began in the early afternoon. Between the estate park and the Neu Graben stream, there was a slight rise in the ground with a thin stand of pine trees. Voshage moved there so he could use his 2cm and machine guns to secure time for us to quickly move behind the rise when we left the estate for good. In order to make it difficult for the Russians to observe the second defense line—rise in the land to the end of the forest—the transformer station southwest of the park was prepared for demolition with a delay fuse and then the fuse was set off.[20]

19   Kortenhaus, p. 47. RG 242 German Armed Forces Operations and Situation Maps, 1939-1945. H.Gr. A. Box 357: *H.Gr. Mitte, GenStdH Op.Abt. IIIb Prüf Nr. 79140, Stand 17.4.45 abends.*

20   During the interview conducted by Spaeter he relayed to Müller-Rochholz that Dr. Braune stated to him separately that the *Division* Commander ordered Wehrkirch [Horka] vacated. Müller-Rochholz replied to Spaeter that he did not recall the *Division* Commander being the one to issue the order. Müller-Rochholz informed Spaeter that it was on his own authority that he ordered his men to withdraw to save them from encirclement. The minor point illustrates the confused

While the *Pioniers* were taking the rise, the 2cm were moving to the edge of the forest. During this movement, the bridges, which consisted only of four double T-beams, were still covered with boards that had to take Voshage's trucks out of the estate. It worked.

However, I was lying down with the last men in the Neu Graben. The Russians were already covering us with machine guns and grenade launchers. It wasn't even 100 meters to the edge of the forest. In order to make it difficult for the Russians to bring in vehicles, I ordered a young *Pionier* (tall with dark hair) to blow up the bridge supports, the boards for which we threw into the water, using a *Panzerfaust*. He was wounded when he did that and bled terribly from a wound in his head and his shoulder. We dragged him and the severely wounded *Leutnant* (Birkholz or Stier?) into the forest under fire. There were many wounded, and each had really given his all. The Russians also didn't dare to go into the forest immediately. Ammunition was in very short supply. Eat? Sleep?

Although we had no communications in the forest, a supply run from the *Versorgungs-Kompanie* arrived with ammunition, food and a truck for the wounded. *Division* radio order: The *Panzer-Sturm-Pionier-Bataillon 'BR'* is moved to Niesky to defend Niesky and is subordinated to the *Sturm-Regiment* of the 4.*Panzerarmee*."

At about 3:00 p.m., *Pionier* companies of the *Panzer-Sturm-Pionier-Bataillon 'BR'* moving separately arrived at the edge of Niesky. The *Bataillon* assembled at the Niesky railway station. The 3.*Pionier-Kompanie* under the command of *Leutnant* Puls never arrived. According to one officer of the battalion staff "the 3.*Pionier-Kompanie* was never heard from again!" This was now the second time during a Soviet offensive that the men of the 3.*Pionier-Kompanie* were considered lost during battle. In the twilight Soviet T-34s rumbled out of the forest to the east and attacked, but they were repelled by the *Pioniers* at the edge of Niesky.

In the late afternoon, the remnants of the *Panzer-Sturm-Pionier-Bataillon 'BR'* moved west from the edge of the forest near Nieder Wehrkirch. The commander went forward to the command post of the *Sturm-Regiment-Panzer AOK4* that was released by the 4.*Panzer-Armee* for immediate support, located in a building on the eastern exit from Niesky on the road to See.

Instructions were given by an unknown *Major* who was the commander of the *Sturm-Regiment-Panzer AOK4*. *Hauptmann* Müller-Rochholz recounts the event:

Immediately after they arrive at the Niesky railway station, the *Pionier-Kompanien* will be put en route to their sectors. Anything left over from the 3.*Pionier-Kompanie*, will join the 2.*Pionier-Kompanie*. *Battalion* strength is 180-200 men. The battalion command post is at the movie theater at the eastern edge of Niesky on the road to Neu-Särichen [Neu-Särichen was incorporated in Niesky after the war].

When I attempted to find the companies in the twilight hours (using a *B-Krad* driven by *Obergefreiter* Lipinski), we saw a Russian T-34 opposite us on the road to Neu-Särichen about 5,400 meters from the movie theater. Because we were right on a curve, we assumed that two T-34 had been knocked-out with *Panzerfausts* right next to the movie theater.

While on foot going to the companies, the 1.*Pionier-Kompanie* was in a night battle with Russian infantry in front to the east and the south. Bank had thought the sector was empty and, when he attempted to set up communications to the right, he ran into Russians looting. Shortly thereafter, he was attacked by about two companies of infantry between the buildings. The 1.*Pionier-Kompanie* held their sector but could not prevent being bypassed on the south. I later found the troops of the *Sturm-Regiment-Panzer AOK4* as a neighbor on the right to the south of

---

nature of the fighting and how little central command existed over the individual sub-units of *'Brandenburg'*. Each unit was fighting on its own.

the movie theater. They had not gone further forward than that!

The *2.Pionier-Kompanie* sector was in Neuhof on both sides of the railway embankment. On the right there was a connection to Bank with the same picture: the left flank was up in the air. North of the railway station on *Reichsstraße 115*, our *Sturmgeschütze* had a shootout with T-34s. From this position, I took the battalion independently back to the eastern and northern edges of Niesky. The *2.Pionier-Kompanie* took over the *1.Pionier-Kompanie* position on both sides of the movie theater (about half the front to the left as far as the railway station). One additional T-34 was knocked-out. Bank then moved north and took up a new position left of the *2.Pionier-Kompanie* via the railway station, *Reichsstrasse 115*, and the northern edge of the Christoph and Unmack plant. Now we had a good field of fire – except near the movie theater through the houses and at Christoph and Unmack through the northern forest. The men were really hard to keep awake, but we had to man the parapets. The radio *SPW* had communications with division— Mission: Defend Niesky!

I angrily went to the command post for the *Sturm-Regiment-Panzer AOK4* and asked the commander whether he had seen the western edge of Niesky. He asked me to move my command post to his place. That was done on April 18th after it was clear that the various units in Niesky were doing whatever they wanted and that the mission wasn't being carried out.

After the T-34 was knocked-out in the *2.Pionier-Kompanie* area about 10:00 p.m., the entire night remained calm. Our patrols reported that the Russians were also sleeping or eating!

'Brandenburg' demonstrated a strong tactical resilience after nearly two days of overwhelming firepower concentrated across parts of its frontline. Its soldiers knew little of the overall operational situation around them. Communications was infrequent, and when connections were established, the exchange of information was often incomplete or incorrect. As Soviet and Polish units sliced through the frontline and continued to drive west ignoring the pockets of resistance, the *Division* was able to briefly catch its breath and refocus its energy from a defense that no longer mattered to survival.

16

Survival, April 18th-23rd

(Reference maps 74, 75, 76, 77, 78, 79, 80, 81, 82, 83 and 84)

Schörner reported to *OKH* that on this third day of battle he had directed his reserves north, to the area south of Cottbus, across the Spree, in order to destroy the Soviet tank forces of Koniev that were now pushing to the northwest. The *10.SS-Panzer-Division 'Frundsberg'* and *344.Infanterie-Division* reached Spremberg to the south of the widening breach. He noted his own high losses and inability to conduct an effective counterattack due to a lack of petrol and ammunition.[1]

Koniev's 3rd Guards Tank Army wheeled northwest toward Berlin after capturing Spremberg and Cottbus on the 19th, cutting off the *V.Armee-Korps*, to include the *21.Panzer-Division*, from the *4.Panzer-Armee*. The 4th Guards Tank Army along with the 5th Guards Army attacked due west isolating the *344.Infanterie-Division*, *Führer-Begleit-Division*, and the *10.SS-Panzer-Division 'Frundsberg'* that deployed piecemeal into the frontline. By the fourth day of battle more than half of the *4.Panzer-Armee* strength was torn away, leaving some of the strongest formations in *H.Gr. Mitte* cut off with the *H.Gr. Weichsel's 9.Armee*.

While the bulk of the *21.Panzer-Division* was forced north into the southern flank of the *9.Armee* along with the bulk of the *V.Armee-Korps*, the *Führer-Begleit-Division* found itself temporarily surrounded in an exposed position to the east of Spremberg on the 19th. The advance elements of *10.SS-Panzer-Aufklärungs-Abteilung* reached the west bank of the Spree on the evening of the 17th, but the bulk of the division did not arrive for another 24-36 hours due to petrol shortages. By the time it assembled for an attack on the 19th, it was already too late to mount an effective counterattack. The *Führer-Begleit-Division* was able to extract itself from its temporary encirclement and link up with the right flank of *'Frundsberg'* while the *344.Infanterie-Division* arrived on its left flank. As a defense of Spremberg formed around these three divisions, the Soviet 4th Guards Tank Corps opened a breach between Spremberg and Weisswasser. By the 19th there was no connection between the *Führer-Begleit-Division* and the *Kampfgruppe* of the *545.Infanterie-Division* on its right as a pocket now formed around the three divisions defending Spremberg.

Panzer-Korps 'GD' was cut off from the *4.Panzer-Armee*. The Soviet 5th Guards Army was driving due west along its left flank while elements of the 2nd Polish Army and 7th Guards Mechanized Corps drove toward Klitten and Bautzen on its right. In the forming packet were the *Korps* headquarters, *Kampfgruppe 545.Volksgrenadier-Division*, *Division Nr. 464*, *Division zbV 615*, and elements of *Jägerregiment 1 'BR'*. General der Panzertruppen Jauer had three options. Attack north toward the widening breech near Cottbus-Spremberg where the main Soviet attack was developing, withdraw west toward the Elbe River where there were no *Wehrmacht* formations and run the risk of being overrun, or launch a counterattack south and rejoin the remnants of the *4.Panzer-Armee*. His choice was simple. An attack south was now planned and likely ordered by Schörner, though without the benefit of any available orders or telephone logs it cannot be ascertained with certainty who prompted the order. Jauer's attack south, coupled with the attack north of the remaining *Panzer-Divisions* of the *4.Panzer-Armee* located around Görlitz brought devastating consequences to the Polish and Soviet

---

1   NARA T78/304/6255329, 6255332.

Image 8. *Kampfgruppe Voshage* held off repeated Soviet and Polish attacks from 18-20 April in Niesky before breaking out south to German lines. Numerous T-34s were knocked along the town's streets. Author's collection.

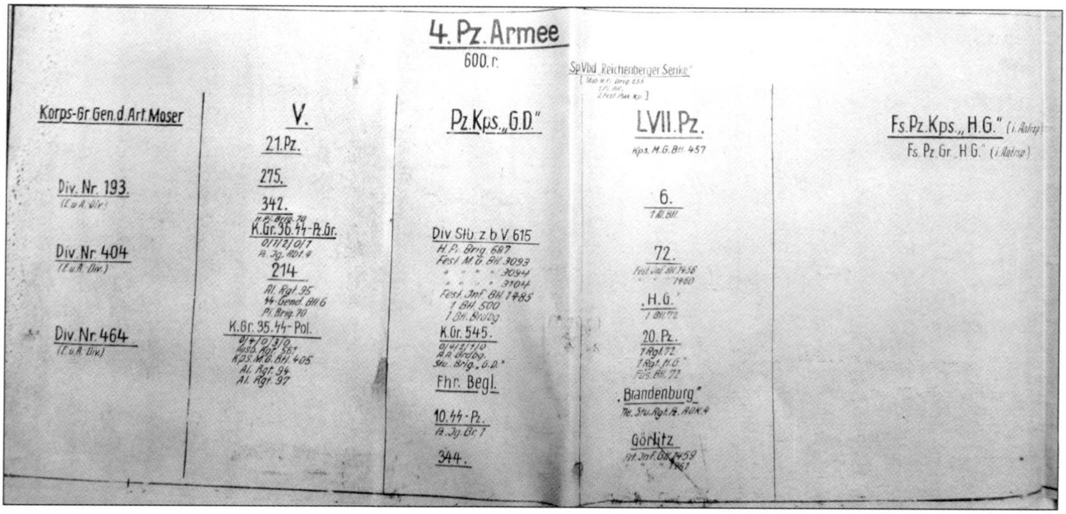

Image 9. Organization of the *4.Panzer-Armee*, 18 April.

Jänkendorf

Verlag von C. G. Hoberg, Niesky.

Image 10. The town of Jänkendorf was captured by the *I.Bat./Jäg.Rgt. 2 'BR'* after heavy fighting against elements of the Soviet 254th Rifle Division on 22 April. The losses in the *I.Bataillon* were so high that the attack became known as the "Black Day" of Jänkendorf. Author's collection.

forces operating between these two groups in the coming week.

Brief descriptions of the 2nd Polish Army and 7th Guards Mechanized Corps are warranted given their prominent role in the fighting opposite *Panzer-Korps 'GD'* and *'Brandenburg'* in particular. The 2nd Polish Army was formed under the watchful eye of the Soviet Red Army between August and December 1944. This paralleled the establishment of *Panzer-Korps 'GD'* to a great extent. There was a significant shortage of trained manpower to draw from in Poland after five years of Nazi occupation. The recruits that joined the ranks of this new unit were disproportionately young, inexperienced and lacked sufficient training for the tactical tasks they were assigned during the fighting in April.[2] Most were not enthusiastic supports of Communism or the Red Army that had just "liberated" Poland. Memories of the Soviet occupation of eastern Poland in 1939 were still fresh in some minds. Many Poles were motivated by a nascent sense of nationalism and joined "for Poland" and not "for Stalin and Communism".[3] While 85%-90% of the ethnic makeup of the new Polish Army was Polish, there were Russians, Jews, Ukrainians and Byelorussians that also filled their ranks.[4] Many officer positions from battalion up through the corps level were filled by Soviet Russians who did not treat their Polish officers or soldiers as equals. Because of a generally acrimonious relationship between Pole and Soviet Russian, Soviet officers could exert only limited influence over Polish soldiers. What little influence they had was often based on fear. Polish officers and soldiers alike often felt humiliated or degraded by their Soviet counterparts during classroom sessions and field training during the early formation of the

2   Seidel, p. 24 and Koniev, p. 123.
3   Grzelak et all, p. 91.
4   Ibid.

new Polish Army in the latter half of 1944. Desertions were common.[5] In the early days of formation the Soviets provided a Red Army General by the name of Stanislav Poplavsky to organize the new army. There were serious struggles of control and influence within the forming units. Soviet officers dominated the command structures of the 5th and 6th Polish Infantry Divisions. The relationship between Soviet and Pole was exacerbated by the outward belief of Soviet officers that they were not dealing with a "sovereign nation" but rather a conquered people. There was particular resistance by Polish soldiers against the instruction of Soviet Commissars.[6] Beyond the tension between Russian and Polish officers, the overall tactical training of the 2nd Polish Army lacked considerably. Polish infantry received 1.5 months of training totaling some 504 hours, which included 24 hours of political education (this was still more training than the new *Panzer-Korps 'GD'* conducted). They never conducted exercises above regimental level, and they lacked joint training with their tank units. No urban combat training occurred. When the 2nd Polish Army was officially mobilized on December 1st, 1944 some 40,824 (62.4%) of its 65,349 soldiers had never received any formal military training.[7] By December 1944 the Soviet General Poplavsky was replaced by a Polish commander, General Karol Świerczewski.

Karol Świerczewski was a Polish born communist who fought in the Russian Civil War on the side of the Red Army and subsequently rose through the ranks, seeing service in the Russo-Polish War in the 1920s, and in Spain during the Spanish Civil War. His combat experience to that point was only tactical, as he had never served as a staff officer or received professional military education. He was promoted to General in the Red Army and given command of the 248th Rifle Division after the German invasion of the Soviet Union in 1941. His division was encircled in October of that year, and he managed to extract himself from the pocket along with only five soldiers. The Soviet General Staff lost confidence in him and through 1943 relegated Świerczewski to training the reserves due to his ineptitude.[8] Now at the age of 47 he was given command of this new Polish Army just before the start of the final Soviet offensive against Germany. The training of the 2nd Polish Army improved little under his command. Shortcomings in tactics and combined arms fire continued. The focus shifted to coordination at the launch of an attack, in preparation for the final offensive expected in the spring. Deficiencies were noted in both the 7th Polish and 10th Polish Infantry Divisions. Lack of uniforms and supplies were also a limiting factor as in the case of the 9th Polish Infantry Division where nearly 25% of the soldiers could not train during half the month of January 1945 due to a lack of boots, or any comparable footwear.[9] Barracks were limited. Polish uniforms did not exist. Many recruits wore tattered civilian clothes or Russian uniforms. Disease ran rampant through the training camps during the winter months. Artillerymen received generally good training on their individual weapon systems. Tactical coordination with infantry during attacks was covered, but not tactical movement, which cost them dearly during the upcoming fighting. Polish tankers received training primarily in their crew related duties. Some training in infantry support at the company and platoon level occurred, but the majority of time was spent focusing on the employment of speed in aggressive attacks. This proved to be another weakness in the 2nd Polish Army's limited training regimen that played out disastrously on the battlefield.[10]

The 2nd Polish Army consisted of the 5th, 7th, 8th, 9th, and 10th Polish Infantry Divisions. It contained the 1st Polish Tank Corps with the 2nd, 3rd, 4th Polish Tank Brigades, the 16th Polish Tank Brigade, 1st Polish Motorized Rifle Brigade, several supporting Self-Propelled Artillery Regiments.

---

5   Ibid., pg. 91-92.
6   Ibid., p. 93.
7   Ibid., p. 194.
8   Ibid., p. 270. There is some suggestion that he was a heavy drinker. His constant inebriation, even during actual military operations, likely impaired his decision making.
9   Ibid., p. 195.
10   Ibid.

Total number of officers, non-commissioned officers and enlisted personnel totaled 69,945. It was equipped with 521 tanks, assault guns, and armored personnel carriers, 1,736 artillery and mortars, 8 observation aircraft, 2,219 assorted vehicles, and 8,185 horses.[11] The equipment was of Soviet manufacture and their tank and self-propelled tank brigades consisted of T-34/85s, Joseph Stalin IIs, and both medium and heavy assault guns like the SU-85s and ISU-152s. The 2nd Polish Army appeared formidable on paper. The army, however, deployed into the frontline at the end of February with insufficient training, no combat experience, and a questionable commander. As discussed in the Introduction, some of the officers and enlisted men—if not many—of the 2nd Polish Army were likely motivated by revenge as they entered Reich territory. They were responsible for a number of documented atrocities in their operating area that included rapes, looting, outright murder, and the shooting of unarmed German prisoners-of-war. The enthusiasm to share in the final conquest of Nazi Germany by the soldiers of this unit was unfortunately soon squandered in bloody fighting under their incompetent commander and his staff.

The 2nd Polish Army moved into its intended area of operations between April 11th and 12th. It was given a zone of attack that bordered Sagar in the north and Rothenburg in the south. During its actual attack, its forces concentrated in the area just to the north of Rothenburg. Świerczewski knew little about the enemy in front of him. It appears that when the Polish infantry divisions crossed the Neisse River on April 16th they knew about 70% of the German combat formations they might face but had little knowledge of their overall defenses.[12] The main attack was conducted by the 8th, 9th, and 5th Polish Infantry Divisions, the 1st Polish Tank Corps and 16th Polish Tank Brigade, supported by nearly all their artillery. Their first objective was Niesky. A reserve grouping of the 10th and 7th Polish Infantry Divisions was to secure the army's right flank. To the south of Rotenberg the 7th Guards Mechanized Corps of the 52nd Army, under the command of Lieutenant-General Ivan Petrovich Korchagin had the responsibility to advance due west toward Bautzen.

The 47 year old Lieutenant-General Korchagin was an experienced Soviet tank officer. A career member of the Red Army, he was arrested in 1937 during Stalin's purges and released three years later in 1940. He served as commander of a number of tank units, ascending to the command of the 7th Guards Mechanized Corps in May of 1943. His unit fought at Kursk as a mobile reserve behind the Bryansk Front, where he gained experience in attacking fixed German defensive positions. The 7th Guards Mechanized Corps, however, did not achieve any breakthrough, and suffered significant losses during the fighting. It was subsequently withdrawn and placed into a reserve status from October 1943-44 where it was rebuilt. In October 1944 the corps went back into the frontline of the 3rd Belorussian Front where it fought along the border of East Prussia. By December the 7th Guards Mechanized Corps was reassigned to 1st Ukrainian Front in preparation for the Vistula-Oder Strategic Offensive Operation. It remained with Koniev's Front through the end of the war. At the start of the final assault on Germany, Korchagin's forces consisted of the 24th Mechanized Brigade (with attached 13th Tank Regiment), 25th Mechanized Brigade (with attached 12th Tank Regiment), 26th Mechanized Brigade (with the 215th Tank Regiment), 57th Guards Tank Brigade and a variety of supporting elements. Each mechanized brigade contained between 2,100-2,200 men and 17 T-34/85s. The 57th Tank Brigade had 976 men and 34 T-34/85s. The entire corps totaled 10,910 men, 92 tanks (T-34/85s) and 52 self-propelled guns (ISU-122s and SU-76s) at the time of the attack and was short over 5,000 men, 90 T-34/85s, nearly a dozen self-propelled guns and over 140 anti-tank guns and mortars.[13]

The start of the 2nd Polish Army's attack on the morning of April 16th began with a poorly

11   Ibid., p. 123.
12   Ibid., p. 272.
13   Organization of the 7th Guards Mechanized Corps on April 16th, 1945 cited in cited in Eberhard Berndt, *Band 5. Spurensuche. Die Kämpfe um Weißenberg und Bautzen im April 1945* (Dörfler Verlag GmbH: Eggolsheim), p. 12.

executed artillery fire plan that led to diffuse use of its firepower and missed opportunities to acquire new targets. As a result the 8th Polish Infantry Division advanced only seven kilometers by the end of the first day and the 9th Polish Infantry achieved a penetration of only six kilometers. Their forces reached Nieder Wehrkirch, Uhsmannsdorf, and Spree. Over the course of the next several days the 2nd Polish Army's attack began to develop momentum as the units of *Panzer-Korps 'GD'* located north of the breech at Rothenburg awaited orders. Lulled into a false sense of security about his situation, Świerczewski overrode the objectives assigned to him by Koniev and gave his units the order to capture the city of Dresden.[14] He issued the order without informing the 1st Ukrainian Front or the 5th and 52nd Soviet Armies on his flanks.

As Świerczewski's vanguard, the 1st Polish Tank Corps furthered its attack west through the forest tracks between Kossel-Niesky toward Klitten and on to Neschwitz, and Kamenz. Elements of the 7th Guards Mechanized Corps along with the assigned 294th and 254th Rifle Divisions of the 78th Rifle Corps advanced along Ullersdorf- Weißenberg-Bautzen and soon reached a position 10 kilometers east of the city. Stretched out along a 50 kilometer line between these two armored forces were the advancing 8th and 9th Polish Infantry Divisions, along with two regiments of the 5th Polish Infantry Division and all the army's artillery assets. Back east between the Spree and Schwarzer Schöps Rivers, was the reserve 16th Tank Regiment, and further back at the Neisse River was the 10th and 7th Polish Infantry Divisions wheeled northwest against the frontline of the *zbV 615 Division*.

The *Panzer-Korps 'GD'* command staff prepared to withdraw from their location in the Spreeforth Castle as the Polish infantry approached from the east. The tactical situation facing *Generalleutnant* Jauer was stark, but no worse than the *Korps* staff had found itself in recent engagements during the winter. Meanwhile *Panzergrenadier-Division 'BR'* was split into three parts. *II.Bataillon/Jägerregiment 1 'BR'* was located northeast in the forming pocket of *Panzer-Korps 'GD'*. *Panzer-Sturm-Pionier-Bataillon 'BR'* and the *Heeres-Flak-Artillerie-Abteilung* were surrounded at Niesky where fighting continued throughout the day. *Jägerregiment 2 'BR', I.(gep)Bat./Jägerregiment 1 'BR'*, and the *Division* command staff were pushed south to Kodersdorf. The Polish and Soviets forces bypassed pockets of German resistance true to their operational training. It was expected that follow on forces would reduce any enemy forces that remained behind the main battle line. On the right flank of *'Brandenburg'* were *Fallschirm-Panzer-Division 1 'HG'* and the *20.Panzer-Division*. Both divisions were preparing for a counterattack north.

At this time the *4.Panzer-Armee* had to temporarily reorganize to accommodate the fluid battlefield it faced. *Panzer-Korps 'GD'* was assigned command of *Division zbV 615, Kampfgruppe 545, Panzer-Ausbildung-Verband 'Böhmen'* of the *Division Nr. 464, Führer-Begleit-Division* and the *10.SS-Panzer-Division 'Frundsberg'*. The latter three units were subordinated only briefly as they moved north and were cut off completely along with the *344.Infanterie-Division* by April 20th. The *LVII.Panzer-Korps* now commanded the *6.Panzer-Division, 72.Infanterie-Division, Fallschirm-Panzer-Division 1 'HG', 20.Panzer-Division, Festung Görlitz*, and *Panzergrenadier-Division 'BR'*.[15] While this transition occurred on paper, it is not clear how this was implemented during the actual fighting. One fact is clear, *'Brandenburg'* was split into a variety of groups, each of which fell under other combat formations for at least several days. Only the command staff was free of the forming encirclement of *Panzer-Korps 'GD'* and directly assigned to the *LVII.Panzer-Korps*. This grouping of divisions under the latter *Korps* commands reflected the immediate tactical situation of a widening Soviet-Polish breech between *Panzer-Korps 'GD'* in the north and the *LVII.Panzer-Korps* in the south.

Jägerregiment 1 'BR' (minus the *I.(gep)Bataillon*) and *Division zbV 615* were still in the Weisswasser area moving southwest. It was joined by the *Sturmgeschütz-Artillerie-Brigade 'GD'* and

---

14   Grzelak et all, p. 271.

15   RG 242 German Armed Forces Operations and Situation Maps, 1939-1945. H.Gr. A. Box 357: *H.Gr. Mitte, GenStdH Op.Abt. IIIb Prüf Nr. 79140 Stand: 17.4.45 abends.*

the *Panzer-Pionier-Bataillon 500 'GD'*, both of which led the evacuation from Weisswasser to Boxberg with the Soviets of the 52nd Army to their front and the 2nd Polish Army to the rear. There was only sporadic wireless radio contact between *Jägerregiment 1 'BR'* and the *Division* headquarters forcing the Hunhold's *II.Bataillon* to subordinate themselves temporarily to *Division zbv 615*. Confusion and apathy began to take hold among many of the co-mingled soldiers trapped behind the lines. Few had the will to maintain their positions against overwhelming Soviet firepower. While most men continued to withdraw west others, perhaps in frustration or desperation, turned toward the enemy. *Major* Theo Bethke from the *Korps* staff was one such man. He attempted to form a small *Kampfgruppe* of soldiers from a mix of units and advance toward the Soviet lines at nearby Spreefurt. He yelled orders, waved his arms in the direction of the enemy. No one paid him attention. He charged the enemy alone and was cut down by Soviet fire. Wounded, his body was recovered but died later at a field hospital. Soon the combined force moved from Daubitz-Rietschen through Forst Muskau and arrived in Boxberg on April 21st. Soviet T-34s of the 2nd Polish Army appeared in the Boxberg area. From here the combined *Jägerregiment 1 'BR'* and other *Divisional* elements began an attack southwest toward Spreefurt, which soon became a combined attack with other forces from the south to recapture Klitten.

Two companies of *Panzer-Sturm-Pionier-Bataillon 'BR'* defended itself in Niesky with about 200 men, a few *Sturmgeschützes* from *Panzerjäger-Abteilung 'BR'* and an assortment of stragglers. They had quickly become surrounded by April 18th. Part of the support units for the battalion managed to get out of the encirclement. Plans were made for a breakout south in the early morning hours of April 20th. During the night (ending on April 19th), all the preparations were finalized. These included collecting all the wounded and destroying all the immobile vehicles. The attack south was combined with a counterattack north by the new *Kampfgruppe Wiethersheim* of the *20.Panzer-Division* and units of *'Brandenburg'* that included Steidl's *I.Bataillon*.

Hauptman Hunhold's *II.Bataillon* of *Jägerregiment 1 'BR'* held its positions northwest of Hähnichen for another day along with *Division zbV 615*. *Kampfgruppe Kappel* became cut off in Hähnichen as Polish forces moved further west around the German strongpoint. *Leutnant* Grosser picks up the action and the new orders to advance south-southwest toward Weißenberg as part of a larger counterattack underway:

Early morning of April 18th. Kappel and his people, who are now sitting in the middle of the Russians in Hähnichen, are heavy on our minds. In our situation, we cannot arrange for any more help for them. But Hähnichen, according to our *Division's* orders that we got this morning, must be held at all costs. In the meantime, the situation has gotten even worse. Communications with the *Division* are almost always cut off because of the great distance. So our *General* cannot overlook our situation either. With a heavy heart, we decided to subordinate ourselves to *Division zbV 615* in order to ensure a uniform command structure in the front sector. After all, we are already in this division's sector. Hähnichen can be evacuated by order of *Division zbV 615* because it can no longer be included in the main battle line. There are also no forces to relieve it. Radio communication is permanently cut off. So Kappel had to work on his own decisions because the administrative officer (*Leutnant* Schmidt) that we sent to him could hardly get to Hähnichen.

The night proceeded calmly, so the men in the position could get a bit of rest. Only in the area around Hähnichen was the night something less than calm; the enemy attempted to get into the town under cover of darkness. The Reconnaissance Platoon under *Leutnant* Mende was deployed to do reconnaissance between the town and the edge of the forest. A short and heavy firefight resulted.

In the early morning hours, however, it was very turbulent from the get go. The Russians were attempting to get through everywhere. However, because they were not attacking in concentrations, they did not manage to get through anywhere.

At about 10:00 a.m., a message spread like wildfire in our area: The Training Company [from *Division zbV 615*?] had been ordered back to their regiment and had evacuated their position. We stared at each other for a moment without speaking. Would these abominable surprises never end? What now?

We were spared further deliberations because the telephone rang. *Hauptmann* Hunhold was at the other end of the line. The enemy had pushed its way through with about 30 tanks and infantry with them into the *7.Kompanie* (*Leutnant* Spornring) sector. The first tanks were already in our town; we had to evacuate the command post.

It was no use; we had to go back. It was grueling, this having to avoid the enemy. No one knew whether the enemy would leave us any time to reestablish ourselves. How easily a withdrawal can turn into a panicked flight if the enemy is right on your heels. How many killed-in-action, and especially wounded, comrades have to be allowed to fall into the hands of the enemy because they cannot be moved back anymore.

The first released personnel came in. They were collected by me and sent to close off the strait in the lake. A *Feldwebel* got the order. A field howitzer was provided for defense against tanks. The regimental headquarters was sent southwest under the command of the administrative officer, *Leutnant* Schmidt. The commander and I took the *SPW* and a *Krad* messenger to see *Hauptmann* Hunhold, who was somewhere between the ponds and had reported his location. On the way there, we only got fired upon once across a pond. However, there was firing everywhere in front of and behind us. The enemy must have remained right nearby and had clearly already advanced quite far to our positions.

The road was swampy. We got on the *Krad* and left the *SPW*. We also were successful in finding *Hauptmann* Hunhold. He and his staff were sitting in the swamp between the ponds. Ivan jumped out from in front and came out one at a time over the terrain to our rear. So we were in the middle of everything here. After the battalion commander had reported once again about the latest events, a discussion was held about what to do next.

Because the area with its abundance of water and its swamps could be seen as safe against tanks and a defensive line could save a lot of forces due to the many lakes, a new main defense line could be set up here with a view to lasting for some time.

In the middle of the conversation, our *SPW* sent out an SOS. Enemy in the forest 50 meters away from the vehicle, no shots heard, so the guys appear to have been scared to death. But we did not want to have the vehicle with its loads of radio equipment be up for grabs. The commander was therefore given permission to move.

Behind us, the Ivans started to move through the terrain again and they even started to fire. Tanks were firing further to our rear. Damn it, how far away are these guys!—We're holding the map; where can that be? Oh! The narrow strip of land we know about. It must be there. Well, we can still be calm because the heavy *Kompanie* got settled in there and set up a few nice problems [for the Soviets]. Besides, there's a 2cm there. Right, you can clearly hear the stuttering fire of the gun above everything else.

The commander and I moved out in order to regroup the *Kampfgruppe*. The vehicle was choking because the path was swampy. I had laid my machine gun with the safety off on my knees because it was probable that we would meet the enemy. But nothing happened. We passed the place where we had parked the *SPW* without any problem. There were no Russians to be seen.

We found the regimental headquarters on a forest route with deep sand. Multiple vehicles had moved there, and the column had moved so the vehicles were standing around hither and yon. Right behind it, there was a battery of our artillery battalion waiting. It wanted to get into the new position. Damn it, if only the Russians weren't in the way. But the people were all wonderfully calm and prudent, so with our joint efforts we managed to get the vehicle working again.

The commander and I went back to the front on two *Kräder* to the other wing. On the way, we found the support units for our neighboring division, *Division zbV 615*. Once we came upon a very lonely motor pool. There was only one old *Landser* there. What's going on, I asked the commander. The man answered that the others had gone with the horses and the light wagons. He was supposed to take care of the other vehicles. But now there was shooting going on everywhere and he thought that the Russians would be here any minute.

We met the commander of the *Heer-Pionier-Brigade 70*, our neighbor to the left, to discuss the new situation with him.

The headquarters had, in the meantime, moved. There was even hot food arriving. The nearest building was declared to be a command post and immediately dedicated with lunch.

In the evening, we had gotten the new defensive line between the ponds in order. But who knew what the night would be like. If Ivan paddled through the water and got behind our lines, there could be a great hullaballoo again. So when night fell, we had mixed feelings. The commander decided to spend the night out in front of *Hauptmann* Hunhold's command post so that he would be there if anything happened.

It had already become pitch black when I went to the division. The trip was over roads I knew well. The division [*zbv 615*] headquarters was at what had been our *Division's* command post before the change in sector.

I reported in to the *Ia*. He was hunched over the maps with the division commander by candle light. I was given a hearty welcome and had the impression that people were proud to get a bunch of '*Brandenburgers'* close at hand. I was immediately invited to a glass of red wine. In broad strokes, I reported on our situation, strength, and weaponry and asked to have the *Kampfgruppe* made subordinate to the division. We spent about an hour together. Then I set off on my way back to the command with a roll of maps under my arm and hope in my heart that there would be an end to this retreat.

After losing my way a few times in the devilish darkness, I found the commander at *Hauptmann* Hunhold's command post. It was an isolated building at the edge of the forest in which the entire battalion headquarters was crammed together like sardines in its two rooms. After I had reported back and made a report, I stumbled into a corner and fell immediately into a deep sleep.

Morning of April 19th. The administrative officer who had been sent out during the night came back and reported that Kappel and his *Kampfgruppe* had broken out of Hähnichen during the night. He had taken all the men out well and he and his groups were now to the side of and behind our sector. Kappel's *Kampfgruppe* was deployed with us in the sector, so our line became stronger.

The forward part of the front in which we now found ourselves because the Russians had also broken through to our rear near Muskau was now evacuated as ordered.

Oberleutnant von Dunker and his *Sturmgeschütze* had moved out to fuel up and get ammunition. He had been gone for 3 hours and had not reported back. Four of the *Sturmgeschütze* had been taken back from Hähnichen safe and sound. One *Sturmgeschütz* had damage to its tracks and was therefore incapable of moving. It had to be blown up in Hähnichen. One *Sturmgeschütz* crashed into a bridge while being moved and also had to be blown up.

During the morning, it was determined that von Dunker had left in violation of Kappel's orders. In addition, he had taken the men, about a platoon size, sitting on the *Sturmgeschütze*, with him. There was no trace of the *Sturmgeschütze* or the accompanying crews to be found anywhere. They were only seen once in the *Korps* command post in Spreefurt. Nor did they ever return to us during this part of the battle.[16]

---

16   It is possible that this platoon size element of *Sturmgeschütze* from what is likely *Panzerjäger-Abteilung 'BR'* became

Kappel's *Kampfgruppe* was here and was moved to the sector, so our line became stronger. The ponds saved us a lot of forces so we could become substantially denser in the new lines. However, there were initially some problems because some of the ponds on the map had dried up in the meantime and therefore were not an obstacle anymore, at least not for enemy infantry.

The day was spent setting up defensive positions and communications. In addition, the companies that had been split up in the chaos of the previous evening were sorted out again; we believed that we could hold this position.

In the afternoon, the division called to tell me to go there immediately. I got on a *Krad*.

Things were running smoothly at the division command post. The Russians had also broken through at Muskau, so the division and its neighboring division and their positions were well behind enemy lines. In the rear as well, there was still a narrow passage open that the Russians, however, could have closed at any time.

Starting in the evening, the division was supposed to evacuate the forward part of the front and concentrate its forces further west in order to effectively counter the threatened encirclement. Our *Kampfgruppe's* sector was moved just east of Spreefurt in the process. It was about a 20 kilometer front. Being that wide, the sector could only be held with strongpoints and with mobile motorized battles. There was an additional Cossack Squadron subordinate to us. We were initially quite skeptical toward them, but they maintained themselves in quite an exemplary manner during the next few days. We were allowed to start moving back into the new sector starting at midnight.

At this point in the battle *Generalleutnant* Jauer appears to have understood the broader operational picture. The Soviet 5th Army to his north was driving west and not going to risk diverting forces south through the heavy industrial zone of Weisswasser into the dense Muskau Forest. Whether he knew at this point he was facing mainly Polish army units to his east and south is not known, but an attack south would have appeared as his best option even without orders from the *4.Panzer-Armee* to attack in that direction. *Division zbv 615* along with its attached 'Brandenburgers' now prepared to lead the main attack south designed to reestablish a new frontline between *Panzer-Korps 'GD'* and the *LVII.Panzer-Korps* farther south.

Back to the regiment where feverish activity started immediately. The two commanders were summoned at the same time; the fuel and the vehicles were put together and split up among them. Then the sequence for withdrawal and moveout was discussed and the orders were given. We were still responsible for the old sector until 6:00 a.m., so not all of the forces could be withdrawn at the same time. At the same time, however, the units furthest forward had to be in the new sector when dawn broke in order to occupy the towns that were still being reported as free of enemy before the Russians were there. Although difficulties were compounding, because we still had our mission before us, things went more smoothly than anyone dared to hope.

It had already been light out for a long time when I woke up again. The night had been calm to our front. I shaved in front of the building and washed with cold water. So I saw the events that the new day would bring rested and freshened up to some extent.

One hour after midnight [on the 20th], the regimental staff and I set out. The Reconnaissance Platoon and the *Pioniers* had already gone out in advance to do reconnaissance. *Hauptmann* Hunhold took command and the responsibility for the sector until it was finally cleared out at about 6:00 p.m. The Reconnaissance Platoon had pointed out a really good route, so we initially made good progress. Then then there were sandy roads and the streets got clogged. When dawn broke, we arrived in Boxberg, our new command post. The Cossacks were already there waiting for us.

---

attached to the *Korps* HQ until the *Korps* reached the *4.Pz.Armee* lines on April 22nd. As noted previously, there is a lack of data on what happened to the *Abteilung* after the start of the final Soviet offensive.

Downtown Boxberg was cut by a rather broad and deep river, the Black Schöps. The bridge over the river was prepared for demolition with gravity bombs. The way for the enemy to get out of Boxberg was immediately blocked.

The reports from the two platoons quickly came in. The points ordered were occupied. No enemy. Both of them were sent further on. The *8.Kompanie* under *Leutnant* Klaus was there a short time later and occupied the left portion of the sector so that the *Pionier* Platoon could be taken out.

Our communications officer was very agile and soon had the wires up. I called our neighbors to the right in Spreefurt to introduce ourselves. It turned out that *Panzer-Pionier-Bataillon 500 'GD'* was our neighbor. I had a nice chat with the adjutant. The *Pioniers* had just spotted an enemy command post in front of their sector, just outside of Spreefurt. I took over the matter right away, because it was easy to get to the point in question from the rear. When the Reconnaissance Platoon arrived there, the position was already empty. *Leutnant* Mende was barely able to pull the ignition cable out before it blew up.

At noon, I was called to the *Division zbv 615* in Wochten (?). The *Ia* was highly upset and very surly. In addition, he was in a terrible hurry. He told me in haste that we definitely had to keep our position under all circumstances. That was of decisive importance. Besides, we had to be in possession of Klitten today. There was an attack coming from the south and we had to hold back the counter pressure from the moving enemy. Shaking my head about how much hot air was put out about such obvious matters, I went back to my regiment. There, our *Ia* had a very different clear set of orders!

In the early afternoon, *Hauptmann* Hunhold and the remainder of the *Kampfgruppe* arrived and moved into the sector. The *Ia* called impatiently, asking why our attack had not yet begun. Attack, attack, he repeated again and again. His annoyance was incomprehensible. I went to see the division again in order to familiarize myself again with the division's intentions. In addition, I made it clear that our people were much too valuable to take them on a shot in the dark into an unprepared attack under these circumstances. In addition, the entire *Kampfgruppe* had to be there in order to exploit the success of the attack and keep the ground. If we were given the order to attack and take a place, one could be certain that we would follow the order if it were humanly possible. But we were accustomed to having the execution of an order left to us. But in spite of everything, I couldn't figure out what was happening overall. I had the impression that the *Ia* wasn't totally up to speed when he got the order and so he didn't actually know what it was all about. Instead, the gentlemen were dealing with another problem. The *Division zbV 615* commander, *Oberst* Gerd von Below, had been promoted to *Generalmajor* [of the Reserves on April 20th]. How was he to get his new insignia in such a hurry?

In the late afternoon, the regimental command post was moved to Fonthaus. In Wilhelmsfeld, I myself put the company commanders in a situation so that the attack would proceed smoothly. The attack proceeded pincer fashion. The two assault units moved in the forest very close to the town in order to get to the Russians at the agreed-upon time like a whirlwind.

To my deep chagrin, I had to remain at the command post, while the *Major* went forward with *Leutnant* Schmidt.

The forester's house was hidden deep in the woods on the Schloßsee [AN: a small lake north of Klitten now just marsh]. A comfortable little house, a very narrow living room, but with a carpet, armchairs and oak furniture. Antlers on the walls. Soon there was a comfy hot fire in the fireplace. I had wire communications going forward to the *Major*. A telephone crew was setting up the connection, following the attack. So I was always up to speed about what was going on.

It had already started getting dark when the attack began. After a short heavy battle, the enemy was overwhelmed. Three tanks were knocked-out in close combat.

There was nothing to do at the command post, so I could get a little shuteye. The commander was still at the battalion command post. Not a lot of time had passed when I was shaken to wake me up. *Oberleutnant*, tanks! I jumped out in front of the door. In fact, there was tank noise not far from there at the flanks. That must be about where the *Pioneer* Platoon was staying for security. After listening for a long time, it could be determined that there were two tanks that had clearly gotten lost and were now wandering through the terrain. They were running around on our flanks and in our rear. After a while, they stopped more and more often and turned off their engines. I sent the Cossacks that I had available to the command post to secure it with *Panzerfaust*. I sent a troop of the *Panzerjagd-Kommando* off to go hunting them. But the enemy tanks quickly turned around and it finally became quite.

At midnight, the commander came back. The night remained quiet, so we could all get some more sleep.

Koniev had wheeled his forces right instead of left toward Dresden and southern Germany as Hitler and Schörner had expected. His attack northwest toward Berlin continued unabated on the 20th. The *Führer's* earlier deployment of powerful *Panzer-Divisions* from *H.Gr. Weichsel* to the *4.Panzer-Armee* in early April did little to blunt Koniev's 3rd and 4th Guards Tank Armies.

The below message was sent to the *Führerbunker* from *Feldmarschall* Schörner on April 20th. He lauded the combat prowess of his divisions and predicted that either today or the following day would be the "decisive" one. In fact, that decisive point was already reached the day before, though it wasn't realized. After Koniev's forces bounced two rivers—the Oder and the Spree—the *4.Panzer-Armee* had no natural barriers to assist in their defense and Koniev had none to slow him down. The *V.Korps* was cut off and forced north to join the *9.Armee*. The only force still available to possibly block Koniev's armored spearheads driving northwest was the *12.Armee* that did receive orders three days later on April 23rd from *OKW* to join with the *9.Armee* in a counterattack toward Berlin. That attack never materialized because *Generaloberst* Heinrici countermanded it and focused the remaining strength of *H.Gr. Weichsel* in rescuing as many soldiers and civilians as he could by conducting an unauthorized staged withdrawal west to the Elbe River. Such independent, if not traitorous action, against the *Führer's* orders was unthinkable for Schörner.

Operational Department *Ia*   20 April 1945
Copy
Long distance conversation of the Commander in Chief of *Heeresgruppe Mitte*
Ia no. 2363/45 g.K.
To
1) *Führer* and Commander in Chief of the *Wehrmacht*
2) Chief of the Army General Staff
Sir!
Concerning the situation, I report:
I.   The crises of the great defensive battle in the three areas of the *4.Panzer-Armee* have become a lot more serious this evening.

1)   I hope to grab the three Tank Corps with infantry that have broken through from the area of Rothenburg toward Bautzen and the area north of there by the root using a timely counterattack by the *20.Panzer-Division* [illegible] by units of the *Fallschirm-Panzer-Division 1 'Hermann Göring'* and the seasoned *Sturmgeschütz-Brigade 300* and make them harmless. Here I still have the hope that I can destroy the enemy that has broken through and thereby attain a measure of success.

2) On the other hand, the units of the enemy 4th Tank Army that have broken through from the area of Muskau and are now aimed against Neuerwerda and the area north of there are making me extremely worried.

The *Armee* has orders to fight its way to get the area of Spremberg back from the *10.SS-Panzer-Division* and the *Führer-Begleit-Division* and to cross the Spree, closing gaps in the defense.

I have no clear view of the situation there at the moment because all of my communications to there are currently damaged.

3) Counterattacks were launched from the north and the south west of the Spree against the 3rd Guards Tank Army, which was the most dangerous and had broken through north of Spremberg headed towards Kalau, in order to reclose our lines here. This is precisely where everything has to be tried in order to avoid a situation on the Spree between Spremberg and Cottbus that we cannot get a handle on.

I therefore consider the situation in this area to be extremely tense because it has continued to become more serious during the evening hours in that the enemy has penetrated into the northern part of Spremberg. Its efforts to expand the gaps there, especially the ones to the south, have been clear all day. Nevertheless, I hope that the local commanders there manage to throw this enemy out as ordered and to give a hand to our forces proceeding south along the highway by attacking to the north.

II. The troops have fought courageously. The severity of the battle and the enemy's numerical superiority (10 tank corps with Polish [noun missing], with an additional cavalry corps) have, among other things, posed a great challenge to the *Führer-Begleit-Division* and the *Panzergrenadier-Division 'Brandenburg'*, which have been behaving in an outstanding manner, as well as the infantry divisions. The lack of ammunition and fuel defines the tactical events in many cases.

Subsequently, I report:

The defensive and offensive accomplishments in many places should not overall hide the fact that the enemy has already brought in strong units, particularly in the northern and the southern breakthrough areas. Many tanks were killed and a number of trucks destroyed in the process. Overall, however, the defense in the rear area laboriously set up over a period of weeks, only complied with the promises that had to be made for it in a few places. When compared to the events at our *4.Panzer-Armee*, the fronts of my other armies are of lesser significance, with the exception of the area of Brünn.

At Brünn, the situation became more stable today. I had to decide, in spite of the heavy battles west of Mährisch Ostrau, to move the *Kampfgruppe 16.Panzer-Division* to the *8.Panzer-Division* in order to use a few other units brought from the *OKH* there within the next few days to aim for a complete solution in the attack.

At Mährisch Ostrau, the situation somehow has to be maintained with the remaining divisions.

The efforts against front-line units of the *17.Armee* are only significant as attacks to keep forces occupied.

April 20th and 21st, 1945 will be decisive days in the great defensive battle to the east of the Elbe.

I assure you, Sir, that we will use our last assets of tactical and mental leadership in order to carry out your tasking as much as humanly possible.

Attesting accuracy   Long live my Commander!
[signature]   signed Schörner, *Generalfeldmarschall*
Major, General Staff*

*NARA T78/305/6256453-54.

Because of the lack of *H.Gr. Mitte's* war diary, this update from Schörner is important because it sets the date of April 20th as to when both *Panzer-Korps 'GD'* and the *LVII.Panzer-Korps* received orders to launch a combined counterattack against the advancing Polish and Soviet forces along the Rothenburg-Bautzen corridor and destroy them. The attack is only referenced in the surviving daily report submitted by the *Heeresgruppe* to *OKH*.[17] The report cites that both the *20.Panzer-Division* and *Fallschirm-Panzer-Division 1 'HG'* were to attack north to Wehrkirch and re-establish a frontline with *Panzergrenadier-Division 'BR'*. It was not known at the time of the daily update that *'Brandenburg'* had already withdrawn from Wehrkirch to Niesky.

In the accounts of the men of *Panzergrenadier-Division 'BR'* below we can see that they had no knowledge of the larger operational picture. In most cases they were following local orders issued by a command other than their *Divisional* HQ while fighting to survive. *Generalleutnant* Jauer did receive some form of explicit counterattack instructions from Schörner's headquarters by wireless. While no document have been identified that outlines what the specific instructions were, we can draw a number of operational conclusions based on the surviving records. Inside the pocket a new temporary formation was formed known as *Gruppe Kohlsdorfen* that held the northern part of the pocket. *Division zbv 615* remained the strongest of the divisions under its command as it was assigned a number of attached combat formations that included *Heeres-Pionier-Brigade 687, Festung-MG-Bataillone 3093, 3094* and *3104, Festung-Infanterie-Bataillon 1485, Panzer-Pionier-Bataillon 500 'GD'*, and *Jägerregiment 1 'BR'* (minus *I.(gep)/Bataillon*). *Division zbv 615* held the eastern edge of the pocket. On the southern edge of the pocket were the mainly convalescent soldiers of *Division Nr. 464*. To the east was *Kampfgruppe 545* with the attached *Panzer-Aufklärungs-Abteilung 'BR'* and *Sturmgeschütz-Artillerie-Brigade 'GD'*.[18]

As an attack north toward Ullersdorf by armor elements of the *20.Panzer-Division* was directed by the *LVII.Panzer-Korps*, General Jauer issued orders for *Division zbv 615* and Kampfgruppe Kappel to attack south toward Förstgen. To the west *Kampfgruppe 545* was ordered to attack southwest behind the advancing 2nd Polish Army. During an early morning hours of April 21st *Panzer-Aufklärungs-Abteilung 'BR'* attacked from the east and captured Milkel, 13 kilometers north of Bautzen. A Polish force had unexpectedly occupied the town's castle-like manor house and could blocked a key road junction required for the *Panzer-Korps 'GD'* move south. *Leutnant* Hellmut von Leipzig, a Platoon Leader in the *Aufklärungs-Abteilung*, launched an immediate counterattack with his platoon that knocked-out a T-34 and drove the Polish force out of the manor house. Just to the north was the Kleine Spree, where the Polish remnants joined with reinforcements and were assembling for a counterattack to retake the manor house. Von Leipzig saw the threat development across the open field from an upper story window of the manor house. Despite the fact that his men had used up most of their ammunition in the first assault, he launched an immediate attack into the stream bed that turned into a hand-to-hand melee. At the cost of only three wounded men, the Polish force of 20-30 men was wiped out. A key road junction with Königswartha in the west and Bautzen to the south was now secured and *Panzer-Aufklärungs-Abteilung 'BR'* successful attack was reported to *OKH* that day.[19] Von

---

17   NARA T78/304/6255288.
18   BAMA Freiburg: Kart RH 2 *Ost Unterstellungen u. Kampfgruppen H.Gr. Mitte Stand : 21.4.45* cited in Eberhard Berndt, *Band 5. Spurensuche*, p. 26. For geographic dispositions see RG 242 German Armed Forces Operations and Situation Maps, 1939-1945. Box 358: *H.Gr. Mitte, GenStdH Op.Abt. IIIb Prüf Nr. 90340 Stand: 22.4.45 abends.*
19   NARA T78/304/6255256.

Leipzig was awarded the Knight's Cross on April 28th for his action. The elements of *Jägerregiment 1 'BR'* and *Panzer-Pionier-Bataillon 500 'GD'* were ordered to attack due south toward Weißenberg cutting all remaining links between the 2nd Polish Army and 7th Guards Mechanized Corps back to the 5th Army in the process. We know pick up the account of *Leutnant* Grosser beginning on April 21st. His account relates that by the 21st he became aware that the planned counterattack south was part of a larger operation designed to destroy the Polish-Soviets forces operating along the Rothenburg-Bautzen axis.

Being relatively well-rested, I finally did an extensive washing and shaved with gusto. An older *Hauptmann*, who wanted to talk to the adjutant, watched this holy treatment with growing impatience. However, because I wanted to get my outside in order, I didn't let him in on the fact that the person he wanted to talk to was right in front of him. His concern also didn't appear to us to be particularly important. Of course the old man wasn't particularly well-disposed when I finally introduced myself as the adjutant.

At about 8:00 a.m. the division commander from the *Division zbV 615* came, followed right by *Generalleutnant* Jauer, the general of *Panzer-Korps 'GD'*. Jauer requested the regiment to attack and take Weißenberg.

The enemy breakthrough axis to Bautzen was supposed to be broken, and if possible even surrounded. We were supposed to be the tip of the wedge. We were given an additional two *Batteries* of the *Sturmgeschütz-Artillerie-Abteilung 'GD'* to do that. In our rear, the enemy had pushed through from well back in Muskau and there were bitter battles in progress with vastly superior Russian artillery deployment at Weisswasser. There was no way we could get up there to the north with our own weak forces. On the contrary, we had to attack here today so that the front line in the north could be pulled back to the river sector near Boxberg.

General von Below suddenly opened his eyes because he hadn't known himself that the situation was like that. *Generalleutnant* Jauer also told us that he would subordinate us tactically directly to the *Korps* so that he would always have direct contact with the tip of the assault. Next to us, the *Panzer-Pionier-Bataillon 500 'GD'* was to lead the attack. Well, we thought, there is at least a proper bunch out in front.

Right after the generals had left, we and the staff went off to Klitten, where *Hauptmann* Hunhold's command post was.

There was still clear evidence of the battle visible in the town. The streets were strewn with roofing tiles; a shot-up tank was black as smoke in the middle of the town. There were dead Russians all over everywhere.

With the captured platoon leader, Klose and I went to the *Korps* in Spreefurt in a Volkswagen in order to deliver the prisoner there. On the way back, I dropped by the *Panzer-Pionier-Bataillon 500 'GD'* in order to set up personal contact. Then it was back to the regiment. The road and the forest on both sides of it were very desolate. There was a deep crater in the road at one place. Next to it there was the wreck of a T-34 in the meadow. It was blown up by the *Pioniers* in close combat.

In the afternoon, we again started off on the attack. The targets were Zimpel and Tauer (about 10 km southeast of Spreefurt). Hunhold and Kappel made a frontal attack. We took the seven *Jagdpanzers* into the flank of the lairs in order that the enemy might fall into our hands from there if they put up serious resistance.

The forward attacking units ran into stiff resistance from the Russians outside of Zimpel and soon they started doggedly fighting it out in the town. Five to seven Russian tanks made it hard to get to them and they were almost defenseless because they had no antitank weapons except for their *Panzerfausts*. We got deep into the enemy flanks without being affected by them and finally were at the edge of the forest about 300 meters outside of Tauer. With heavy friendly losses,

Hunhold and Kappel had managed to take Zimpel in the meantime. Several tanks were killed in close combat.

The assault on Tauer was beginning! The Russians were shooting out of every keyhole in order to save their skins. The *Jagdpanzers* were having a tough time staying in the town. There were lamps of fire shooting out of multiple buildings into the air and they lit up the picture of destruction in the eerie falling dusk. Our *Jägers* broke into the town. We moved up to take what was, from our perspective, the back part of the town. We had barely left into the open field when raging fire met us from the thick underbrush 200 meters away on our flank, machine gun and antitank fire. I turned the *SPW* around and properly stopped with the onboard gun between us and the fire. It wasn't easy at all, because the sighting mechanism was down. In addition, damned hesitation. But thank God, the antitank went silent; my first shots had made a real good landing. Next to me, the machine gun was shot off the radio *SPW*. But we were in the middle of the town. Everything was set up feverishly in order to defend against the expected counterattack. It became darker. There was heavy tank noise in front of us in the forest. From here, there was nothing to approach. A troop of *Panzerjagdkommandos* was sent into the forest. But even during the night, they did not manage to get to the gang of tanks because it was secured too strongly by infantry.

It was no longer possible to do another attack that day. So everything was set up to defend the town. A building in the middle of the town served as a command post. The residents came out of the basements anxiously. They shook our hands, "Thank God, German soldiers! The Russians did a lot of looting and drinking in the town. The girls were all raped."

The reports *Leutnant* Grosser received citing "Russians" as the source of the atrocities was likely committed by Polish soldiers (see Introduction). This is based on the fact that they were advancing south through the 2nd Polish Army's area of operation, and at that very moment, they were fighting elements of the 5th Polish Infantry Division.

The wounded were in the school. There was a terrible groaning. Dr. Fischer, the physician, was on site as always, but what could he do here out front? At the time, there was no way to transport anyone out because the Russians had closed off the gates behind us. The poor guys lying there so helpless and heaving in pain were terribly to be lamented. If they could only be helped!

But while the night was still in progress, we managed to open up the supply route again. This made it possible to give the wounded proper supplies as well.

As night went on the forward observers for several *Artillerie-Abteilungen* and a *Werfer-Abteilung* came to see us to offer their services for the next day. They all had plenty of ammunition, but they all lacked communications with their units. I had so much to do feverishly all night to prepare for the next day. The next day, the attack was supposed to go further toward Förstgen. In front of us, the road to Förstgen went on an isthmus between two lakes. That was the critical place for our move forward. Artillery and mortars were all allocated their areas of effect that were grouped around this isthmus.

But when morning came [on April 22nd], everything changed. All of the artillery and mortar personnel had again denied us their support. So we were unfortunately alone again and left to our own devices. Our original plan to make a direct assault on Förstgen could not be implemented with such weak forces without an extremely large risk that it might not work.

Our *Jagdpanzers* couldn't be properly used on the narrow street either. So it had to be done some other way. My commander had a great plan again. He would go around the lakes on the outside and thus automatically collapse the expected focus of the enemy defense, the isthmus.

Things started early in the morning. We moved through the forests making good progress around the lakes. Only a weak group remained at the edge of the town of Tauer in order to continue to tie the enemy down and deceive it about our actual intention as to an assault.

Without any resistance, we stalked through the forests. The Cossacks swarmed around us as our watchful eyes. Finally at about 10:00 a.m. from the forested hills, we looked at Förstgen lying at our feet in a valley pocket. Hunhold's battalion moved right outside of Förstgen. We moved deeper into the flanks with the *Jagdpanzers* in order to push into the town from right behind it. The *Infanteriegeschütze Kompanie* had also moved forward with us so that it could act on the town from a direction where it could deploy with a good field of vision.

The town was thick with Russians. There were a number of tanks recognizable and the noise of their engines and the rattling of their chains made their way to us. It was hard for the commander to decide what part of the town was the best place to dig in, because in any event, the slope going down to the enemy had to be overcome, and that could cost us a lot of blood.

The *Sturmgeschütz-Artillerie-Brigade 'GD'* commander, *Hauptmann* Metzger, and I went into a building right on the edge of the woods from which there was a good view of Förstgen and the surrounding terrain. There was a table with several chairs in front of a broad window. We could take a leisurely look at the town. Suddenly there was a terrible blow. The air pressure pushed me off the chair, bits of rock and household items flew around my ears, and chalk dust choked my throat and took my breath away. From the suffocating darkness, I heard the suffocated scream of my commander. A straight on hit—it went right to my brain. I jumped up and pushed my way through the sudden darkness to the door. I finally found it, tore it open and stood outside breathing in. Behind me, the commander and *Hauptmann* Metzger pushed through the door. We were looking at each other with smiles, when the next grenades hit the roof and the tiles flew around our ears. Then it was quiet. Golly, we were lucky. Nothing happened to anyone. Right next to the window at which we had been sitting, the wall of the building had a hole in it as big as a door. We hurriedly left the site of the disaster, because it is unpleasant to end one's life as a piece of a tank target.

The commander went back to see *Hauptmann* Hunhold to discuss the attack with him. He came back at 2:00 p.m. Hunhold was pushing for an attack. It was set for 3:00 p.m.

Time went on and at 2:30 p.m., there was a bunch of shooting at the other end of the town. There we could see our *Panzergrenadiers* storming down the slope. "Couldn't Hunhold wait?" my commander blurted out. The *Jagdpanzers* rolled into their firing positions and fired in front of the attack tip of the *Grenadiers*. The 2cm bellowed from over yonder.

We got on the *SPW* and went crawling into the town. I was glad when we were over the exposed slope without a scratch. And then into the town. Hunhold's people were already in the middle of it all. Right across the streets were Russian trucks and tanks. There were dead and wounded on the street and in the buildings. It was as though lightning had struck the Russians. On the other side of town, tanks and trucks were trying to get out. Our *Jagdpanzer* crews were also vigilant. One tank after another flew into the air or came to a halt; it was a killing field.

One company immediately thrust into the forest on the other side of the village. This is where the full picture of the Russian disaster first was unveiled. Squeezed between us and the *Panzer-Pionier-Bataillon 500 'GD'*, the Russians could no longer go forward or backward. There was a lot of shooting at them from both sides.

When it got dark, a day that was great and victorious for us came to an end. Fifty tanks were killed and captured, as were over 100 other motorized vehicles. Unmistakable captured items, food, ammunition, fuel and . . . beautiful, almost new vehicles made by the Americans!

In the evening, the Russians broke into the town using tanks. We changed positions and they were up on the top edge. All of the basic rules for defending the town were implemented. The *Jagdpanzers* as well were put at the entrances to the town for security. The crossing at the southern exits to the town was still under fire when I had to go across it. It is, however, an unpleasant feeling to go on a *Krad* between two barrages of this site from tanks.

   Night fell and the murderous struggle with sleep began anew. The commander lay down first and reacted badly to various attempt to wake him for calls around midnight, so I gave up and also resigned myself to lying down. But I had barely lain down when I was again brought out of sleep. Finally close to morning, I fell into a sleep that resembled death.

The attack south described by *Leutnant* Grosser was more devastating than he realized at the time. The combined force of *Panzer-Pionier-Bataillon 500 'GD'*, *Kampfgruppe Kappel*, and elements of *II.Btl./Jäg.Rgt. 1 'BR'* dealt a devastating, opening blow against the 2nd Polish Army. Elements of the 5th Polish Infantry Division's command staff, sappers likely from the 4th Polish Sapper Brigade, and other divisional support elements were in Tauer during the initial German attack south. Most of these units were destroyed on April 22nd. The division commander, Major General A.A. Vashkevich, was able to breakout of Tauer with part of his staff and a training battalion. They reached Förstgen were they joined with the reserve 16th Polish Tank Brigade and were subsequently destroyed with the continued attack of *Panzer-Korps 'GD'*.[20] Only 100 Polish survivors escaped to withdraw east.[21] The Polish tankers were surely alerted of the presence of German forces by the survivors of Tauer, yet this knowledge did not help them to organize a defense of Förstgen. The overall lack of training experience of the Polish forces clearly cost them on the battlefield. This defeat is a reflection of the inefficient formation and development of the 2nd Polish Army under their Soviet masters. The successful attack south closed off the Polish supply routes to the east and cut any command-and-control back to the 5th Army. Division zbv 615 now reestablished a solid line facing east with the left shoulder of the *17.Division* that was now redeploying to the positions of *Fallschirm-Panzer-Division 1 'HG'*. *Panzer-Korps 'GD'* broke out of its third encirclement and was free to rejoin the frontline of the *4.Panzer-Armee*.

   Outside of the main pocket to the south, *Kampfgruppe Voshage* had established a defense in Niesky and was subsequently bypassed by Polish units. Cut off and behind Soviet lines, *Hauptman* Müller-Rochholz provides his view of the defense of Niesky:

There was only insignificant shooting during the night and the morning. The Russians moved north in the forest via Moholz toward See and apparently let Niesky be. A patrol reported that the forest buildings in Jänkendorf were occupied by the Russians. No enemy activity from the south.

   During the night, the battalion was fed once more. Hepperle Korle, my orderly, came. This was the last time I saw him.

   The only vehicles we still had were the radio *SPW* and one *Krad*. Everything else was sent back.

   Even the vehicles from the *2.Pionier-Kompanie*, the Reconnaissance Platoon and the Signals Platoon appeared to have left Ober Wehrkirch on the 16th.

   No news from the *Versorgungs-Kompanie* (commanded by Kossel).

   The radio to the *Division* worked.

   We set up our position from the movie theater to the northern edge of the *Firma Christoph & Unmack* [C&U] plant. Cooking was done. Anyone who could went to sleep, naturally in the holes or the buildings that were set up for defense.

   There were still three *Sturmgeschütze* in Niesky [from the *Panzerjagd-Abteilung 'BR'*].

   In the afternoon, there were some more T-34s in front of the *2.Pionier-Kompanie* sector. They remained at *Panzerfaust* distance and could not be killed. Because we had a good field of fire, the infantry was separated from the T-34 and two attacks were conducted.

   For the *1.Pionier-Kompanie*, T-34 attacked without infantry. There, our *Sturmgeschütze*

20   Aleksander A. Maslov, *Fallen Soviet Generals: Soviet General Officers killed in battle, 1941-1945* (Frank Cass: Portland), p. 182.

21   Grzelak et all, p. 275. They also state that it was Brigadier General Alexander Waszkiewicz who was killed.

knocked-out several T-34. Two of them were moved away under our fire when it became dark. (*Reichstrasse 115*).

During the night ending on the 19th, there was constant battle noise, but no serious attacks. The Russians were now firing using mortars launchers. When morning came, we did not have any casualties.

At 7:00 a.m. on April 18th artillery and mortar fire struck along the entire eastern edge of Niesky and in the city without a break.

The main thrust (tanks and infantry) was on the road from Neu-Särichen. Here our machine guns (*2.Pionier-Kompanie*) had a decisive effect. The infantry didn't show up. A few T-34s broke through, shot up the log obstacle to the west of the movie theater and pushed their way into the city.

To the south of the movie theater, the Russians had made it through near our neighbors to the right. In Bank's area, there was no enemy attack from the north, just mortar fire.

At about noon, the *2.Pionier-Kompanie* was attacked from its right (south) and from behind and pushed towards the *1.Pionier-Kompanie* to its left. The commander of *Sturm-Regiment PzAOK4* summoned me to the command post several times. We were to be deployed around the regimental command post. Positions (which had been prepared before) had been set up there by the *Volkssturm*.

In the afternoon, I went back with the *2.Pionier-Kompanie* to the regimental command post. The *1.Pionier-Kompanie* remained in the position at the C&U plant oriented north-south.

We set up the command post through the yard west of *Reichstrasse 115*. From there, it was relatively easy to retake the 4 or 5 buildings east of the regimental command post using an assault force. The *Kreisleiter* office was occupied. There was no trace of the *Kreisleiter*, but in the basement of the *Kreisleiter* office, we found about 1,000 *Panzerfausts*. That was to be our salvation.

In the meantime, the Russians had filtered through into the forest between the guard tower and C&U to the west. We were cut off from Bank. Two attempts to set up communications among the buildings on *Reichstrasse 115* failed. The Russians were in the buildings in force. Continued attacks from the downtown area near the swimming pool toward the guard tower were repelled.

The *2.Pionier-Kompanie*, along with some men from the *1.Kompanie*, and some people from *Sturm-Regiment PzAOK 4* in between, occupied the positions set up near the guard tower. *Sturm-Regiment PzAOK 4*—with only a very few people remaining (I didn't actually see a complete unit) held the buildings right to the west of the command post.

An *Artillerie-Bataillon Trupp* had found itself with Bank (released personnel, I don't know which unit) using a *Dora* device (a small radio, worn on the belt). This happy coincidence was what the defense was built on for the next 48 hours. We had radio contact with Bank!!!

At the log obstacle on the road running from the marketplace toward the guard tower, there was a negotiator—a German *Feldwebel* with a white flag—who asked us to surrender. He said resistance was futile. He was shot and killed!

The *Feldwebel* was likely a "Seydlitz Troop" employed by the Soviets to weaken the resolve of defending German formations or sow discord behind their lines during the final months of the war.

In the late afternoon, two attacks from the pine forest to our north on our guard tower to swimming pool were defeated at close range. When the Russians attacked us, Bank in turn attacked them from the rear. If Bank were attacked, we struck the Russians in the rear from the guard tower. We were now well prepared. We had enough machine guns, enough ammunition and everyone had several *Panzerfausts* in the trench next to him. The fact that we could hold this small pocket was due to the prior combat experience of the *Sturm-Pioniere* from the battles near

Orscha [AN: in the Soviet Union] and our basic training—unusual at this point in the war—but mostly the spirit that we had loads of.

The opening of fire was awaited with discipline. We let the Russians come about 40 meters into the forest. That was the first shot we made with a *Panzerfaust*. The effect among the pine trees was outstanding. Then machine guns and *Sturmgewehre* immediately started working and were successful!

Some of the Russians ran back in panicked horror. The wounded screamed. A counterattack was launched with 5-6 men to win back a flank for the attackers. Excellent *Sturmgewehre*!!

With these attacks, my great worry was to keep the men in the trenches and only let out a small team for the counterattack. For reasons we could not discern, the Russians did not attack in a concentric fashion. Not a single time simultaneously from all sides (round about) during these days.

In the evening, we had already taken four heavy machine guns and several light machine guns from the Russians and put them in the command post and set them up as a last resort.

We continually had casualties due to mortar attacks landing in the trees. A lot of us stayed there. There were a lot of wounded in the basement of the command post. We were already short of things to bandage them with.

Today, Lipinski, our *Krad* driver, was killed in action.

It is interesting that both comments by the *Ia* of *Jägerregiment 1 'BR'* and the commander of the *Panzer-Sturm-Pionier-Batallion 'BR'* note a complete lack of cohesion in "Soviet" attacks. These forces were in fact Polish. The lack of "cohesion" was a combination of a lack of overall training in leadership and tactics. These "Russians" were likely soldiers of both the 116th Rifle Division of the 48th Rifle Corps, and the trailing 7th Polish Infantry Division. These German accounts highlight how the Soviets also struggled with key issues of fielding trained replacements and cohesive units just like the *Wehrmacht* at the end of the war. Discipline also became an issue among some of the Soviet combat formations that became caught up in the general looting, drinking, and raping that occurred throughout the conquered German territory.

Another report of experiences concerning the fight of *Panzer-Sturm-Pionier-Batallion 'BR'* in Niesky is provided *Unteroffizier* Hans Stübling whose account begins with events on April 17th:

Ivan only slowly managed to push his way through within the area of Rothenburg and Neuendorf. This sector was under our proud *Panzer-Sturm-Pionier-Abteilung 'BR'*. Its enormous fighting spirit caused Ivan lots of worry. Unfortunately, even this *Abteilung* by itself could not prevent the opposing force from continually moving forward, and the *Panzer-Sturm-Pionier-Batallion 'BR'* moved in the direction of Niesky in Lausitz, via Geheege and Wehrkirch, during April 17-18th. We set up our defense near the edge of the city sometime around 3:00 p.m. The three companies were separately sent to the city and were supposed to meet in the downtown area. When the headquarters, *Hauptmann* Müller-Rochholz, came in at the front at the railway station, the *1.Pionier-Kompanie* and the *2.Pionier-Kompanie* reported quickly, but we waited in vain for the "third." But there, about 500 meters away, it was moving on a railway crossing point. But the recognition signal had barely been set off, when we saw Russian figures, about an entire battalion.

The *3.Pionier-Kompanie* was subsequently attacked by the Soviets. Stübling's men moved machineguns into position on the rail embankment to aid support, but their effort was in vain as the *3.Pionier-Kompanie* had to withdraw from sight, pursued by the Soviets. When the *3.Pionier-Kompanie* did not arrive later, it was assumed by the command that "it had been torn apart."

We then moved into the downtown area and the western edge to defend it. Some T-34s that had made their way into the city in the meantime experienced such a terrible fate for tanks and then we had some quiet. Ivan appeared to be preparing for an extensive operation. The first sergeant of the *1.Pionier-Kompanie* once again brought us ammunition and food this evening and then kept some of the vehicles back with us. The night that came brought us the unexpected but well-deserved calm—before the storm.

The next morning, it was April 19th, at 7:00 a.m., all hell broke loose over us. Russian units had gone around us on the south and were now hitting us with one battalion of Cossacks.

The *Pioniers* quickly counterattacked, channeling the Cossacks into a constricted area of pine forest. "Men and horses quickly formed an inextricable crush that could no longer move. The whole thing lasted three minutes and only a few Ivans escaped this inferno."

But strong mortar fire started and it completely covered our small pine forested area north of the road. The shots that got into the tops of the trees had a grisly harvest among our comrades. The wounded pushed themselves with effort to the medics and our dying people could only be recognized with the greatest sacrifice of the last service as comrades. In the meantime, however, the continual enemy attacks on the flanks, which were now coming from all four directions, had to be repelled. To some extent, we answered them with counterthrusts, which gave us some air and even some captured weapons. Because of this situation, our "Papa Müller" had decided to ask the *Division* for relief, something that in turn required some waiting because our *Division* commander, *Generalmajor* Schulte-Heuthaus was already underway with his *Panzers* in order to get his *Pioniers* out of there. That was how the afternoon went and in the evening, our situation became ever more oppressive when an offer to surrender (brought by an officer of the Committee Free Deutschland) was answered by us in the negative. Attack waves came again and again from the flying Commissars of Ivan's forward elements against our small groups, and the forest of death remained ours. At about 11:00 p.m. at night, the attacks against our frontline gradually died down and we were able to prepare for our breakout, scheduled for about 2:00 a.m. The wounded got a bit of quiet but the vigilance of our sentries doubled. Our killed-in-action had already been buried during the day, so they had already found their eternal rest.

The breakout from Niesky was planned for the early morning hours of April 19th/20th. *Hauptmann* Müller-Rochholz's account picks up at this point in the morning of April 19th:

We couldn't get any rest the entire night; no one could. Everyone was in trenches, even the lightly wounded. The grenade launcher fire didn't let up. Getting is the wounded out of the trenches the 100 or 150 meters to the command post, where the wounded were practically lying on top of each other, usually cost more wounded. As morning came, it was calmer for about 2 hours. We soon knew why. The Russians were waiting for reserves. They came in big German cargo trucks. At least one battalion of infantry was unloaded on the road from Neu-Särichen near the movie theater. We immediately noticed that because from a forest lane near the guard town, we could see a road down the middle of the city. One of our three *Sturmgeschütze*, which had already killed a number of attackers in the scrub pine near the guard tower, was withdrawn about 250 meters and was then able to fire on the cargo trucks with direct fire. Using high-explosive fragmentation shells, it went directly in the middle of the column right in front of us. It worked. We had taken out the reserves permanently even before they were used. We were very glad.

Our radio *SPW* was now in a corner of a building at the command post; the antenna was installed on top of the building, but it had to be moved several times after grenade launcher attacks. However, we had communication with the division. I reported that I was taking over the team in Niesky. *Ic* reported that the Russians were cursing mightily about us in Niesky on their radio network and asking for more units.

In the morning, there was a report from the *Kreis* building: The Cossacks were attacking from the woods to the south. They were almost completely wiped out with machine guns from the windows.

The Russians had emptied too many mason jars and raped too many women. They didn't want to die anymore. When they were back at a position, we knew it 30-45 minutes in advance, because the officers were yelling about it so much.

It appeared that the Ivans didn't want to advance anymore. Our recipe: first *Panzerfaust* at short range, then shooting is very effective. Before they could see us, they were already tripping over their previous dead. The northern edge of the guard tower was full of Russian corpses.

At about noon, one of them lost his nerve. He ran down the southern slope and threw his rifle away. I jumped out immediately as well. I reached the fence about 80 meters in front of our position on the slope at the same time as him. I got through the fence a bit faster, thank God. He was dead. He had not reached the Russians, who were about 20 meters away from him in the fir trees. That was a matter of seconds; I thought about it for hours when I spent days in captivity. It was right; it was necessary! When I was in the trenches, I found out that he wasn't from the battalion. He didn't get there until it was light. He was saying again and again, "We have to desert; we're lost anyway!" Free Germany or nerves?

Müller-Rochholz shot who appeared to be a deserter from his ranks. His action clearly bothered him long after the incident. He questioned whether this straggler who joined his unit was a "Seydlitz Troop"—a member of what he termed the "Free Germany Committee". His musing on this point was not just a way of dealing with the psychological aftermath of draconian punishment. While the soldier may well have been a young recruit recently sent to the battlefield who found himself longing to seek safety from the war by surrendering to the enemy, he equally could have been a former German prisoner of the Soviets who was sent behind "enemy" lines to sow discord among the *Pioniers* putting up stiff resistance as related in the Introduction. No one will ever know for sure.

Afternoon: Attacks all the time, but never simultaneously on our entire front. Either from the north or the south or from the buildings on the east. At the guard tower, the five *Sturmgeschütze* (now what was this grand *Oberleutnant's* name?) were standing and waiting placidly until the Russians had robbed their way up the west face and when the tops of the scrub firs—about 1 meter high/maybe a bit more—started moving a lot, they moved up about 5-6 meters. The tubes were pointed all the way down—they had to be tilted a bit forward so that they could be kept down enough – and then there was noise in the fir trees and yelling and screaming, and we did not need to put out any riflemen to the west.

The *Wehrbezirk* commandant for Niesky, who was in the buildings right to the east of the command post with some people and civilians, came and asked whether we were breaking out, when we were breaking out and whether we would take them with us. I promised to let him know if we broke out.

From noon on, we had no more bandaging material. We used washrags from the buildings for bandages. Our trench manning became worse and worse. It was certain that we would not survive such a day. People looked on in fright if there was a minute without any cap bombs landing and there was a minute of peace.

The entire day, Bank didn't have a moment of peace in the C&U. plant either. Yesterday, the Russians had not understood at all how we were getting rid of them. Their strongest attacks were always coming from the north because the forest was there. When they came in, Bank shot them from behind. That's also why it was so weird for the Russian troops. However, starting on April 20th, today, Bank was attacked without ceasing and hesitantly jumped around the factory buildings with his couple of people. I radioed him to break through to us. In the twilight, Bank came with his last men.

The commander of *Sturm-Regiment PzAOK4* sat on the stairs to the basement where the wounded were and became more doubtful because of the screams of the wounded. In the evening, I told him: we're breaking out tonight! I think he was very much in agreement. The *Wehrbezirk* commandant—an *Oberstleutnant* of the *Luftwaffe*—came. It was a difficult conversation. He wanted to break out with us with about 200 civilians, women and children. I turned him down and remained silent. We had to fight and couldn't have women and children with us. Behind us, a long way behind us, he was saying, "Please!" He was very, very annoyed at me and I was terribly sorry. It's all about fighting. . . . But he made it out with his civilians a half hour behind us. Everything was going a lot better than we expected and it was also a bit miraculous.

I had a long talk with the *Oberleutnant* from the *Sturmgeschütz*. We agreed. A humdinger! We would hook up the shot-up trucks by their beds and move them on their rims fields and axles. The wounded would be on them; 80 wounded had to be on them! Under continued fire, we buried our dead when it became dark.

Everyone knew that now was the time. At 2:00 a.m. on the 20th, the breakout started. Nothing was to rattle, no one smoked, and no one shot without orders!

A small *Kampfgruppe* was supposed to go first, then the two companies under Bank, and then the *Sturmgeschütze* with the wounded with the *SPW* in front of them. With small Dora devices, the tip of the motorized units—four vehicles with truck chassis full of wounded—were supposed to move in spurts.

At about 1:00 a.m., we reconnoitered the route south of the breakout area. We reached the small road that ran about 400 meters to *Reichsstrasse 115* (Niesky bypass road) without running into enemy. It had become remarkably still since midnight. The opinion could be held that the Russians noticed what we had in mind and were glad to see us go. We started at 2:00 a.m. The last shots everywhere in the trenches. Then we were on the road. A row on each side of the road, so we moved one man after another without any noise. When we were going down *Reichsstrasse 115*, we heard the *Sturmgeschütze* approach. The axles and the rims were squeaking and screeching on the ground and the rocks.

Cigarettes were burning everywhere in the forest, to our right and to our left. It smelled just like Russians, like Machorka. As if they didn't see us. We all took our weapons off safety; everybody had their index fingers cocked. Nothing was moving. They considered us their own or preferred to let us go on. At any rate, we made it through, including the motorized units. So we made it through in the planned movement scenario to about 300 meters north of the big road intersection (*Reichsbahn 115* and Kodersdorf-See). The *Sturmgeschütze* closed ranks. Four men went into the crossing, they were called, they jumped into the ditches at the side of the road and, ha ha, Ivan fired shots. A machine gun set up to secure the road, an old story. We saw the fire from the mouth of the weapon. Now agitates the four people from the crossing started firing with their *Sturmgewehre*; the machine gun answered. We pushed our way through the forest to south and easily came up behind the firing machine gun and ... a *Panzerfaust*—our weapon those days! Two more shots. Radio transmission: March on, the crossing is free! We were in luck; no Russian units were coming at that moment and none came.

The *Sturmgeschütze* were barely 300 meters south of the crossing when Russian motorized vehicles were coming from behind. Our command vehicle with sparks flying on the cobblestone *Reichsstrasse* was coming from the right. The Russians went by. Right by the German *Sturmgeschütze*, right by the German *Landsern*, who were moving on the right and the left of the road. They had long been used to captured German vehicles and . . . had they been paying attention, we had our fingers crocked.

Unteroffizier Hans Stübling continues with his view of the breakout:

At about 1:00 a.m. on April 20th, the remainder of the *Bataillon* assembled without being noticed and moved near the regimental command post, sat on the five *Sturmgeschütze* we still had, and then our breakout towards the southwest in the direction of Rabental (Wiesa) began.

The groaning of the wounded loaded onto a captured truck did not stop, we broke through the Ivans, who were apparently taking a well-deserved sleep or when standing around with their hands in their pockets near their artillery and assumed it was their own tanks. It was not until they were put into a vice that Ivan appeared to wake up and fired infantry weapons at us, which, however, did not cause us any loss. Only the captured truck remained behind and our wounded comrades had to be retrieved by our *Division* comrades.

Two and a half hours later the scene changed, and after everyone involved behaved with discipline, we were able to get back into the open arms of our *Division* at about 4:30 a.m. However, we had hit Ivan a bit as only the German *Landers'* comradeship and willingness to sacrifice could pull off. We were so proud of our performance . . . .

The *Bataillon* had about 50% losses in wounded and killed-in-action.

The withdrawal southeast continued into April 21st. Once the combined force reached the split in the road at the edge of the forest south of Niesky that marked the continuation of *Reichsstraße 115* to Görlitz, it split into two columns. The combat elements proceeded further east and the civilians slightly west as they moved between the main road and the dual towns of Jänkendorf and Ullersdorf toward Rabental.

A new *Kampfgruppe* of the *20.Panzer-Division* under *Major* D. von Wiethersheim was formed to attack the Soviet and Polish units in their extended flank and to reform a continuous line for the withdrawing German units cut off in Niesky since the Soviet offensive began. *Kampfgruppe Wiethersheim* consisted of the Panthers, Panzer IVs, and *Jagdpanzers* of *Panzer-Regiment 21*, combined with other elements of the division like *Panzer-Aufklärungs-Abteilung 20*, *Panzerjäger-Abteilung 92* and the *Panzer-Artillerie-Regiment 92*, though the exact composition has not been presently identified in available primary documents. Joining the counterattack were reformed elements of *I.Bat./Jägerregiment 2 'BR'* that were subordinated to *Major* Wiethersheim after they reached the main lines of the *4.Panzer-Armee* on their own.

As *Fallschirm-Panzer-Division 1 'HG'* continued to fight along what was now the right shoulder of the *4.Panzer-Armee*, the *20.Panzer-Division* shifted to its left flank to launch the counterattack northwest. As it did, it cut across the frontline of *'Brandenburg'* separating the elements of *Jägerregiment 2 'BR'* in the Kodersdorf area and parts east from their *Division* headquarters and support units. What both forces did not realize was that the area south of Niesky was the main east-west attack corridor for the 7th Guards Mechanized Corps and its supporting elements of the 2nd Polish Army. The Soviet and Polish units had already occupied the towns of Jänkendorf and Ullersdorf and the surrounding area. Their main forces were operating well to the west near Weißenberg and even Bautzen as the second echelon troops began to move through the area. What is clear through the following accounts is that the communication among the fast moving Soviet forward units and the second echelon units was non-existent given the fact the German forces that crossed their route of advance appeared unexpected.

Unteroffizier Stübling continues with his account of the breakout southeast:

It was already getting dark when we came out of the forest west of Ödernitz. The Russian artillery was in position north of Ödernitz. We now took the units on foot off the road and went straight south. The motorized units went through. There was now nothing more than [to move forward], because south of Särichen near Wilhelminental, the units on foot recognized German troops beckoning to them. Radio transmission to the *SPW* and *Sturmgeschütz*: We made it! We made it! There are German troops in front of us. We can't believe it, but we're out of there. A half hour later, men from the *20.Panzer-Division* [*Kampfgruppe Wiethersheim*] greeted us.

At the *SPW*: When it was already getting dark, we were overtaken in the vicinity of Ödernitz by a German Opelblitz with 8.8's from our motorized units attached and it was moving, because the *SPW* was right next to the tubes, side by side with the *SPW* for quite a stretch. The truck was full of Russians. The two went into a bomb crater in the middle of the street during the hunt. However, the *SPW* moved in the truest sense of the word, specifically towards its rear. It made it. The truck slid into the *SPW*, it moved its flat nose down, and the Opelblitz flipped over. When the Russians figured out what had happened, the third *Sturmgeschütz* with its wounded behind it was going by.

Some 400 to 500 meters beyond our troops, the *20.Panzer-Division* with Panthers was going forward, a *Sturmgeschütz* again went into a bomb crater and didn't get out again. One Panther pulled it and all the wounded out. We made it through, all of us! Even the civilians, a bit further west, made it to the *20.Panzer-Division* through the meadows.

Hauptmann Müller-Rochholz was recommended for the Knight's Cross for his defense and breakout, though his award is considered contested today (see Appendix G). The remainder of his unit went immediately to Rabental for rest. His new HQ was established in the warehouse in Rabental.

The *Pioniers* were met by a counterattack of *Kampfgruppe Wiethersheim* and the *Panzergrenadiers* of *I.Btl./Jäg.Rgt. 2 'BR'*. Steidl's men of the *I.Bataillon* setup a defensive line to the east of Kodersdorf and repelled a number of Soviet tank attacks. Steidl's men were then placed under command of *Kampfgruppe Wiethersheim* and ordered to attack northwest as part of the relief attack. Below is his view of the events:

Very heavy battles with Polish units and the National Free Germany Committee [Seydlitz Troops], which provided fierce resistance. Very high losses.

Somewhat outside of Ullersdorf on the eastern edge of the town was a farmstead with surrounding walls, from which heavy Polish 8.8cm and German 12.6cm shell fire was coming. From our own side, there were only a couple of Panzer IVs in use.[22]

Steidl met with *Oberfeldwebel* Martl, discussed the situation and settled in for a calm but cold evening in their forest bivouac. Steidl's account continues:

In the morning, I headed north and set up communications with the *II.Bataillon* and with my platoon under *Feldwebel* Ascher. We moved into the small village of old Wiese (Rabental at the time). *Major* Wiethersheim put me and all my cut-off units under the division. We took on securing the town and over the night knocked-out nine enemy tanks that wanted to cut us down in the town.[23]

Parts of Ascher's platoon and the 3rd Platoon (*l.Kp./I.Btl./Jäg.Rgt 2 'BR'*) were able to make their way through and later joined the *I.Btl./Jäg.Rgt. 2 'BR'* near Ullersdorf. The *1.Kompanie* was

---

22   In some of the accounts of this period "*Panzer IV*" is actually a reference to "*Jagdpanzer IV*". In this particular case the reference is not entirely clear as both types of vehicles were operating in the area.

23   It appears from Steidl's account that his battalion was separated from the *Division* headquarters for the moment. The '*Brandenburg*' headquarters was likely west of Kodersdorf at the time and trying to exert control over the disparate combat units of the *Division*.

replenished here after its heavy losses, particularly personnel, and reorganized. Just after this was done, the Russians attacked with weak forces (forward forces) again. Then *I.Bataillon* started its own counterattack to push back the Russian forward elements. That made it possible to push our own security measures forward for the night.

Friday, April 20th. There was an increasing attack against Ullersdorf in front of us. The town was taken in a bitter struggle. *Oberleutnant* Gabel was wounded and went to the field hospital. The town burned and was totally destroyed. In the evening, I moved with my headquarters into the town. In the morning, the units of the *I.Btl./Jäg.Rgt 2 'BR'* were ready and in the afternoon, these units—with the support of *Panzerjäger-Abteilung 'BR'*—met for an attack against Ullersdorf. The Russians had, however, previously withdrawn because of the German advance, and some more enemy tanks had been knocked-out by our *Sturmgeschütze*. The town of Ullersdorf was taken back into our possession and secured. The Russians, however, were sitting on a hill in the vicinity, which had set up for temporary defense. The night went by calmly for *I.Btl./Jäg.Rgt 2 'BR'*. Ullersdorf was reached in spite of strong enemy resistance. In the restaurant at Ullersdorf, an enemy Polish mortar group was destroyed by our *Sturmgeschütze*.

Obergefreiter J. Klingenschmid who served with the 3rd Platoon, *1.Kompanie* of *I.Btl./Jäg.Rgt.2 'BR'* recounts what happened to the men since they were cut off during the initial Soviet attack back on the 16th:

The men of the *5.(schw.)Kompanie* that were cut off did find a way to survive and they continued to avoid captivity while withdrawing southward on their own, behind the Soviet frontline *Oberleutnant* Gabi of the *5.(schw.)Kompanie*

The majority of comrade Ascher's 3rd Platoon, however, and the portion of the 2nd Platoon that had maintained their position even during the heavy fire, was able to join the remnants of our battalion three days later, on April 19th, in a forest in the vicinity of Ullersdorf after making a long detour. Our joy about that can be considered great. Comrade Ascher, on his own initiative, had the morning came the order to assault the hill and take the town of Jänkendorf, which was behind the hill.

That was the morning of April 21st. We made good progress up to the hill, got onto the hill, but were immediately fired upon with extremely heavy shell fire, so our attack came to basically a standstill. Then there was also heavy rifle and machine gun fire, which also got me. I was severely wounded by an explosive round on the upper right arm; specifically, the bullet fractured it. That ended the deployment for me. I then had to get out from under the heavy shell fire over the hill and I nearly got a couple of other severe fractures in the process. Sanka and I went from the troop aid station in Ullersdorf to the main aid station and then to the Görlitz patient collection point.

With his battalion largely intact, Steidl received a further order from by *Major* Wiethersheim to attack further north and retake the adjoining town of Jänkendorf behind the hill occupied by the Soviets. Along with the *I.Bataillon*, elements of the now rescued *Panzer-Sturm-Pionier-Bataillon 'BR'* were assigned to the attack as well. This would open the way south for units of *'Brandenburg'* that were cut off at Niesky. Early in the morning of April 22nd his force moved out and attacked, taking the Soviet-occupied hill. When they got on the hill, the attacking *Panzergrenadiers* were met with heavy Soviet mortar, machine gun and rifle fire, so the attack came to a standstill. Despite the resistance Jänkendorf was retaken. *Hauptmann* Steidl's account continues:

In the early morning, there was a major attack by our strong forces against Jänkendorf. Armored units were put on standby. It was to push the well-forward units of the Soviets on our flanks and to cut off the important supply routes. The enemy had barricaded itself strongly behind every building. It was a few meters from us in the town. We got started. Strong defensive fire from all the tubes whipped over us. The enemy knew what it was about. Our losses were substantial; we only made a few steps forward. The attack stopped after hours of hard fighting. We attempted to go around over the right hilly terrain, which was, however, open. But we didn't manage to get into the town there either. Most of my people were killed in action or wounded. The *1.Pionier-Kompanie* was deployed. But that was in vain as well. The commander [*Oberleutnant* Bank] was killed in action. The Russians started a counterattack and it took some effort to claim that we still had Ullersdorf, which we had taken the day before. In the evening, the situation became dangerous. We assembled everyone to hold our positions. The losses were enormous. Streaming rain started but the position was held through the night with the pumped-up last *Landser*. The "black day" of Jänkendorf leaned toward its bloody earth. Tired and worn out, I crawled under a shot-out basement arch with my messengers.

Hauptmann Müller-Rochholz relates his view of the situation at the time of the attack on Jänkendorf:

> The battalion gathered behind the sector of the *Panzer-Pionier-Bataillon 20*. The wounded were picked up and cared for by the *20.Panzer-Division*. The commander of *Sturm-Regiment AOK4* reported in at *20.Panzer-Division*.
>
> The battalion moved through Schäferei Freischütz to Rabental, because supposedly there were '*Brandenburg*' units there.
>
> At 10:00 a.m., arrival in Rabental. *Major* von Wiethersheim was in the palace there. There was no contact with the division. The *Sturmpionier* grabbed a couple of buildings in southeastern Rabental and went to sleep. No feeling of hunger, just sleeping, sleeping. No thinking, so many were killed in action.
>
> Von Wiethersheim knew where the ['*Brandenburg*'] *Division* headquarters was; Bischdorf. I decided to go there, asked von Wiethersheim to let the men sleep and not to deploy them under any circumstances as long as I was away! Order to *Oberleutnant* Bank [of the *1.Pionier-Kompanie*]: "Don't let yourself be seduced!!"
>
> At the *Division*, people were very glad that we would make it out after all. Immediately quiet! (Either the *Division* command post was in Bischdorf or the *Panzer-Sturm-Pionier-Bataillon 'BR'* was moving to Bischdorf.)
>
> I went back immediately. Our support people had all found each other. Spaeter assembled them. From there, trucks were sent off to Rabental. The *Panzer-Sturm-Pionier-Bataillon 'BR'* was deployed to Rabental. Shot-up Russian tanks were on the road to Ullersdorf-Jänkendorf. Bank was killed in action in Ullersdorf. We sat apathetically in and around the last three buildings in Rabental. The *Pioniere* attacked with Steidl's *I.Bataillon*. Nothing went forward. Bank went forward! Like he always did! He was dead. We had not slept from April 16th to 21st, had hardly eaten, and our proud *Bataillon* had barely the strength of a *Kompanie*. But the Russians helped us; we didn't have time to think about it. They were attacking Ullersdorf again. We went forward with them. It became calmer about midnight. On the morning of the 22nd, we went off to rest, as we had already been ordered to do the day before, in the vicinity of Bischdorf.

During the combined counterattack of *Kampfgruppe Wiethersheim* north and the southern attack of the various '*Brandenburg*' elements, the rear area of the 7th Guards Mechanized Corps was overrun. The command-and-control between the Soviet 52nd Army and advancing elements of the 7th Guards Mechanized Corps and 2nd Polish Army. In addition the attack caught the headquarters element of the 52nd Army's 254th Rifle Division around Ullersdorf killing the division's commander Major General M.K. Puteiko.[24] Several regiments of the division were already farther west operating around the outskirts of Bautzen. Twelve kilometers southwest was the 294th Rifle Division that had just occupied Weißenberg. The 294th Rifle Division had no situational awareness with its command element wiped out. Cut off from the 52nd Army to the rear, this Soviet division likely had no idea that German formations were maneuvering to destroy it with a concentric attack.

The first echelon Soviet and Polish forces that bypassed Niesky moved through forest lanes to reach Quitzdorf where the support units that made up *Kampfgruppe Voshage* had withdrawn from Wehrkirch. The *Heeres-Flak-Abteilung 'BR'* was forced to withdraw again and soon join the *Ib* section. Dr. Braune's account continues:

After wonderful deep sleep, there was a good washing with lots of hot water in the morning. While we were doing that, we completely overlooked the fact that Ivan was suddenly right outside the village with some tanks at about 9:00 a.m. The *Abteilung* had not taken particular precautions to protect itself. Put into running at full speed by tank shells, we left Quitzdorf but were able to take everything with us.

We moved to Gross Radisch. It was sunny spring weather and we moved by fleeing and doubting German women and children under blooming fruit trees; a cruel contrast.

In Groß Radisch, I got an order to go to the *Ib* headquarters in Steinerlen. *Stabsarzt* Dr. Grossmann then was with the *Flak*. At about 11:00 a.m., I said goodbye to the *Flakabteilung*; I had experienced life much faster than I could ever have expected in my wildest dreams. *Major* Voshage said goodbye to me, saying, if the *Stabsarzt* becomes a casualty, you're welcome to come back, Doctor.

In Steinerlen, the *Ib* headquarters took part in defending the village, led by *Major* Hans Spaeter. I set up an aid station in the palace.

At about 4:00 p.m., the village was attacked by tanks and motorized troops. We moved into a forest. Our own *Stukas* kept us down, so any defense became impossible. We wondered whether they were actually our aircraft, but they were German models.

Stabsarzt Dr. Schultze-Pätzold had set up an ambulance on the edge of the forest, in which we moved the last returning *Landser* and moved ourselves on the worst side roads in a generally westerly direction with the *Ib* staff. The big roads were all occupied by the Russians; every now and then we were fired upon by tank shells.

At Gross Saubernitz, we got infantry fire and had to turn around. A Russian tank followed us. Because the field road we used had a lot of turns and often went through stretches of forest, we were initially able to evade them well. Unfortunately, the road led to a quarry in the middle of the forest. When we attempted to take the vehicle through the forest via a clear-cut area, we got stuck on a stump. During the attempt to make the vehicle speedy again, the tank following us killed it. Three severely injured personnel from another division, whom we had loaded on en route, died. We don't know their names. Missing! The tank caught us with well-placed machine gun fire from about 300 meters away. It took some effort to get away. No one was wounded. By foot, under fire to some extent, we moved further west. At about 8:00 p.m., we reached a town in the dead of night where the *Sanitäts-Kompanie* doctor was. I could not find out the name of the village. Big evening snack. During the night, we moved to Kaupa. I slept a bit there.

The *Stukas* referred to by Dr. Braune were none other than those of *Oberst* Hans Ulrich Rudel's

24 Maslov, pp. 179-80. Maslov states that is was here that the Deputy Commander Maximov of the 7th Guards Mechanized Corps lost his life. His account is incorrect. Maximov was captured wounded by the Germans days later and succumbed to his wounds after the war.

Schlachtgeschwader 2 'Immelmann' that were operating daily around Görlitz. Rudel's tank busting squadrons took a toll from the advancing Soviet and Polish armor that had little cover while traversing the open farm fields north and west of Bautzen. Rudel found the area around the *4.Panzer-Armee* so rich in Soviet targets that he turned down several attempts by Hitler to appoint him to another assignment just so he could continue his support to *H.Gr. Mitte*.[25]

With the successful counterattack south by elements of *'Brandenburg'* and the northward attack by *Kampfgruppe Wiethersheim* both *Panzer-Korps 'GD'* and the *LVII.Panzer-Korps* reestablished a solid frontline. A follow-on counterattack was now ordered at Weißenberg. It is likely this attack was ordered by *Generalfeldmarschall* Schörner himself, though no records exist that detail the planning for this next phase. The attack of the *20.Panzer-Division*, which had received support in the form of an attached regiment from both the *17.Infanterie-Division* reached the town of Ullersdorf, six kilometers south of Niesky, offering a bridge back to *4.Panzer-Armee* left wing line for both the *Panzer-Sturm-Pionier-Bataillon 'BR'* and other elements of the *Division* that were cut off.

This initial counterattack on the 20th-21st, drove into the rear of both the 2nd Polish Army and Soviet 7th Guards Mechanized Corps forces advancing along the axis Rothenburg-Niesky-Malschwitz-Weißenberg-Bautzen, and stabilized the left wing of *H.Gr. Mitte* (or the new right wing of the *4.Panzer-Armee* as it now pivoted to face north), achieving *Generalfeldmarschall* Schörner's initial goal. General Świerczewski did not grasp the operational disaster unfolding around his army. Instead of halting his forces and consolidating them, he again issued orders to take Dresden on April 22nd. He directed the 1st Polish Tank Corps to advance as fast as it could, followed by the 8th, 9th, and elements of the 5th Polish Infantry Divisions. Soon his tank corps outpaced his infantry leaving both forces extended and vulnerable.[26] Farther north Schörner likely had similar expectations that the divisions under the command of *Kampfgruppe Jolasse* might also be successful in a counterattack against the advancing tank armies of Koniev and re-establish a frontline with the cut off *V.Korps*. He likely did not realize that his reserve force of three divisions would themselves be cut off and form the Spremberg Pocket.

Spremberg Pocket, April 20th-May 1st

Koniev's 6th Guards Mechanized Corps and 4th Guards Tank Corps advanced passed Spremberg to the west and south leaving the *10.SS-Panzer-Division 'Frundsberg'* under the command of *SS-Brigadeführer* Heinz Harmel, the *Führer-Begleit-Division* under the command of *Generalmajor* Otto-Ernst Remer and the *344.Infanterie-Division* commanded by *Generalmajor* Johannes Erwin Jolasse in a pocket by April 19th. The situation reached a decisive point for the encircled divisions over the next 24 hours. On April 20th Jolasse was placed in command of the three divisions in what became known as *Kampfgruppe Jolasse*. Orders were received by both *OKW* and Schörner to attack north and close the gap opened by Koniev's forces between Spremberg and Cottbus. The order was contrary to all reality on the ground and could not be carried out. At best, all three divisions could only hope to reach German lines either to north or south of them, but every day they waited to take action meant that the breach between their *Kampfgruppe* and German battle lines widened. Schörner, true to his form ended the order with the statement "You must carry out the attack to victory or fall with your Division."[27]

Jolasse was promoted to *Generalleutnant* later in the day. Following his promotion all three division commanders met and discussed options. Both Harmel and Remer wanted to breakout while Jolasse

25   Rudel claimed that his squadron was responsible for slowing down the Soviet and Polish advance west of Görlitz and that they dealt a particular heavy blow to the 7th Guards Mechanized Corps around Bautzen. See Hans Ulrich Rudel, *Stuka Pilot* (Bantam Books: London, 1979), pp. 260-74.
26   Grzelak et all, p. 275.
27   Wilhelm Tieke, *In the Firestorm of the Last Years of the War: II.SS-Panzerkorps with the 9. And 10.SS-Divisions "Hohenstaufen" and "Frundsberg".* Translated by Frederick Steinhardt. (Winnipeg, Canada. J.J. Fedorowicz Publishing Inc. 1999.), p. 402.

was inclined to hold out given his recent promotion and the potential of a summary court-martial if he did. At the end of the conference he gave authorization to both Harmel and Remer to breakout on their own, but he decided to remain. The following morning on April 21st Koniev unleased a massive artillery bombardment against *Kampfgruppe Jolasse*. The withering fire changed Jolasse's mind that he had no hope of holding out on his own after the other two divisions departed. He prudently changed his mind and decided to join the breakout scheduled for later that night. Koniev's artillery bombardment was nothing more than a preparatory strike before he ordered the reduction of the pocket by elements of the 5th Guards Army on April 22nd.[28]

The breakout began toward the northwest, but soon split into separate groups as the men of the *344.Infanterie-Division* continued in that direction while both the *10.SS-Panzer-Division 'Frundsberg'* and *Führer-Begleit-Division* turned west than south. The breakout initially made progress but as soon as the Soviets realized what was happening they moved to cut the breakout off. At an open meadow near Neu Petershain the three divisions passed through a rain of anti-tank and machinegun fire that shredded the column of withdrawing Germans. An account by *Oberleutnant* Arnold of the *Führer-Begleit-Division* illustrates the chaos that ensued almost immediately:

> Before us several hundred grenadiers, armored troop carriers, and tanks had already set off across the meadow. Mortar shells fell among them and among the vehicles. Several tanks and armored troop carriers were already burning. On the left, a tank was stuck in a marshy spot. It was hit, caught fire, while the crew bailed out. From the east and west the tracers of the anti-tank and machine gun ammunition reached out for the grenadiers and vehicles like long, illuminated fingers.
>
> Dead lay strewn all around. Wounded staggered, screaming; more and more vehicles were knocked out, human bodies whirled through the air, shattered, burned.
>
> A frightful scene!
>
> And the breakout had only just begun!

The *344.Infanterie-Division* quickly split up into individual combat groups with the goal to reach the Western Allies. Over the course of the next several weeks Jolasse continued to head west with a small band of officers and soldiers, his command having been dissolved. He eventually reached the Elbe River near Torgau with 25 men and surrendered to the Western Allies.

The *10.SS-Panzer-Division 'Frundsberg'* suffered losses during the breakout but maintained unit cohesion and wheeled south after bypassing Radeburg. By April 26th the division rejoined the lines of the *4.Panzer-Armee* to the northwest of Dresden, its arrival aided by the counterattack underway around Bautzen that forced Koniev to redirect elements of the 4th Guards Tank and 52nd Armies to turn back east (see Chapters 17 and 18). While their added strength helped bolster the *4.Panzer-Armee's* defense, Schörner was not pleased and immediately sacked *SS-Brigadeführer* Harmel on April 28th. He was replaced him with *SS-Obersturmbannführer* Franz Roestel. The *10.SS-Panzer-Division 'Frundsberg'* was now reduced to the status of a *Kampfgruppe*. The division did participate in a local counterattack northwest of Dresden on April 29th/30th keeping elements of the Soviet 1st Guards Cavalry Corps at bay. *Kampfgruppe Frundsberg* withdrew south after the start of the Soviet Prague Offensive in early May and ended the war near the Ore Mountains along the Czechoslovakian border.

Remer's *Führer-Begleit-Division*, which was only a "division" on paper in terms of its strength at the start of the Soviet offensive on April 16th, was reduced to 400 men. They reached German lines to the west of Dresden and at this point in the fighting, likely escaped any notice of Schörner. *Kampfgruppe Remer*, as it was now called had rejoined German lines outside of the *4.Panzer-Armee's* operational control. Remer remained in command and his men also ended the war along the Ore Mountains.

---

28   Koniev, p. 106.

17

Battle for Weißenberg, April 22nd-25th

(Reference Maps 85 and 86)

Then initial Soviet attack by Koniev's first echelon forces on April 16th violently breeched the weak German defensive line. The armored and mechanized units of 52nd Army's Soviet and Polish formations followed their respective orders to drive aggressively westward towards Bautzen and screen the flank of the 5th Army further north. German units caught in the widening breakthrough that offered resistance were by-passed. Isolated and fighting for survival, these German formations were not defeated. Now, as the operational picture came into focus, the *4.Panzer-Armee* began to exploit the opportunities presented on the battlefield.

General der Panzertruppen Gräser lost an entire *Korps* and most of his *Panzer* reserves. A second *Korps*, *Panzer-Korps 'GD'*, was cut off and the entire left wing of *H.Gr. Mitte* torn open. Despite these setbacks the staff of the *4.Panzer-Armee* demonstrated an amazing operational resilience. After several days of defensive action they recognized that the Polish and Soviet forces driving west through the breech at Rothenburg were overextended. Gräser quickly pivoted his remaining *Panzer* units to conduct the first in a series of aggressive attacks against the rear and flank of Koniev's forces. Reliable infantry divisions were shifted from the inactive frontline further to the southeast and deployed into the recaptured areas where they established the new right flank of the army. New command elements and reinforcements also arrived into the area of the *4.Panzer-Armee* even as Germany was being split in two between the Western Allies and Soviet Union. It what can only be viewed as a miraculous feat of late war German logistics the *Fallschirm-Panzer-Korps 'HG'* along with *Fallschirm-Panzergrenadier-Division 2 'HG'* was moved by sea from their defensive position at Heiligenbeil, East Prussia straight into the battle occurring along the *4.Panzer-Armee* frontline. They arrived around April 21st by train from the north German coast and took over command of *Fallschirm-Panzer-Division 1 'HG'*.

The initial joint attack between elements of *Panzer-Korps 'GD'* and *LVII.Panzer-Korps* was successful. The two *Korps* that were separated for the last four days of battle established a tenuous frontline as the *4.Panzer-Armee* began to pivot from east to north. The attack on Ullersdorf and Kodersdorf cut off the main supply route for the forward Soviet and Polish units. This tactical victory had a major impact on the ongoing operations of the 2nd Polish Army and 7th Guards Mechanized Corps as the operational initiative shifted. The generally more experienced combat units of *Panzer-Korps 'GD'* now organized a series of aggressive, division level attacks, with devastating effect.

Panzergrenadier-Division 'BR' was fighting in two parts. The *Division* staff, and the *I. (gep)Bataillon* of *Jägerregiment 1 'BR'*, *Jägerregiment 2 'BR'*, *Panzer-Sturm-Pionier-Bataillon 'BR'*, *Panzerjäger-Abteilung 'BR'*, as well as the *Artillerie* and *Flak* units under *Kampfgruppe Voshage* had reached the lines of the *20.Panzer-Division*. They remained under operational control of the *LVII.Panzer-Korps*.[1] *II.Bataillon* of *Jägerregiment 1 'BR'*, *Sturmgeschütz-Artillerie-Brigade 'GD'*, and *Panzer-Aufklärungs-Abteilung 'BR'* were operating as part of *Panzer-Korps 'GD'* and assigned to the *Division zbv 615's Kampfgruppe Kappel* and *Kampfgruppe 545* respectively. Spaeter's *Ib* staff was south of Bautzen with elements of the *Korps* other supply units.

---

1   NARA T78/304/6255225.

Image 11. The town of Weißenberg looking northeast from the western bank of the Löbauer Stream. The town avoided significant damage during the war. The first Soviet artillery struck the Bahnhof on 17 April followed by a quick occupation by the 7th Guards Mechanized Corps the following day without significant resistance. The Soviets withdrew from Weißenberg on 24 April limiting fighting to the fields northeast of town. Author's collection.

Tactical German intelligence based on both captured prisoner interrogations and battlefield operations noted that the 1st Polish Tank Corps had the mission of capturing Görlitz, which was incorrect, then Dresden, which was correct. Each tank brigade had in addition to the normal allotment of 10 self-propelled 85mm guns, one Russian howitzer artillery regiment with 16x 122mm howitzers, and at Niesky it was noted an additional 10 "*Salvengeschütze*" (unknown automatic gun carriage) were present. Units of the corps were used alongside or attached to Russian battle groups. Also noted was that the Polish soldiers were "forcibly recruited", as almost all their officers were "liquidated". This was a reference to the Katyn Massacre by the Soviets of March 1940 where some 22,000 Polish Army Officers, Police Officers, and members of the intelligentsia were massacred by the NKVD and Red Army.[2] The intelligence assessment was accurate with the exception that Görlitz was not an objective for the Polish 2nd Army. It might have been on the list of potential targets of opportunity for the 7th Guards Mechanized Corps, but their focus remained on Bautzen, further west. The key element of this assessment was the view that Polish soldiers' morale was likely not strong.

General Jauer and the commander of the *LVII.Panzer-Korps*, *General der Panzertruppen* Friedrich Kirchner, received orders from the Headquarters of the *4.Panzer-Armee* located southwest of Bautzen in Neustadt in Sachsen on April 21st. Jauer received an overview of the recent counterattacks of the *20.Panzer-Division* and *Fallschirm-Panzer-Division 1 'HG'*.[3] Two new counterattacks were ordered to be carried out. The first objective was to recapture the town of Weißenberg occupied by the Soviets, followed by Bautzen where a siege was ongoing against a surrounded German garrison. Further attacks

2   Typewritten note located on RG 242 German Armed Forces Operations and Situation Maps, 1939-1945. H.Gr. A. Box 357: NARA *Lage Ost H.Gr. Mitte, GenStdH Op.Abt. IIIb Prüf Nr. 90362*. Evening of 23 April 1945.
3   NARA T78/304/6255288.

Image 12. A picturesque view of Dresden in the spring before its destruction in the Allied firebombing raids. Dresden was the self-directed objective of the 2nd Polish Army's commander General Karol Świerczewski. He saw personal, political, and perhaps even national glory in Dresden's capture ahead of the Soviet forces of Marshal Koniev. The counterattack of *Panzer-Korps 'GD'* devastated Świerczewski's army in the worst defeat suffered by Polish forces since 1939 and prevented him from achieving his objective. Świerczewski was relieved from command by Koniev. It would be Soviet and not Polish forces that occupied Dresden in early May without a fight. Author's collection.

against the flank of the 2nd Polish Army would follow. The primary goals were to re-establish a solid frontline and prevent the capture of Dresden. Tactical intelligence provided by a soldier, possibly from the *Heeres-Flak-Artillerie-Abteilung 'BR'*, noted some 80 T-34s moving into the woods toward Bautzen, accompanied with about 30 trucks loaded with infantry and towing heavy mortars behind them along the east-west rail-line.[4] Weißenberg was a key road junction for the Soviet forces. It provided a quick reinforcement and resupply route from the 52nd Army (that had already been cut-off at Kodersdorf) and also provided a key north-south route for any follow-on Soviet offensive. Once Weißenberg was captured, thereby cutting off the main east-west link for overextended Soviet formations, Bautzen was to be retaken, securing the northern shoulder of the *4.Panzer-Armee*. The recapture of Weißenberg was assigned to *Panzergrenadier-Division 'BR'*. Upon completion of this task *'Brandenburg'* would be assigned to support the *20.Panzer-Division* and *Fallschirm-Panzer-Division 1 'HG'* in their attack on Bautzen.[5]

Weißenberg was captured by the Soviet 7th Guards Mechanized Corps on April 18th. The 294th Rifle Division was left behind to garrison the town and maintain an open passage of its east-west road network as the rest of the corps advanced on Bautzen further west. The attack south of *Panzer-*

---

4   Type written note located on RG 242 German Armed Forces Operations and Situation Maps, 1939-1945. Box 358: *H.Gr. Mitte, GenStdH Op.Abt. IIIb Prüf Nr. 90362 Stand: 23.4.45 abends.*
5   Von Ahlfen, pp. 204-10.

Korps 'GD' and the stunning victories between Förstgen and Kodersdorf, to the extent that they were known to the Soviet command, alerted the 7th Guards Mechanized Corps to the growing threat around Weißenberg. During the mid-morning hours of April 22nd Lieutenant-General Korchagin ordered his on-going assault on Bautzen stopped. He directed the 57th Guards Tank Brigade and 25th Mechanized Brigade, a total of 2,043 men, 15 tanks, 17 self-propelled guns, 36 guns and nine armored vehicles to turn back east and reach Weißenberg. He sent his Deputy Commander, Major-General Maximov to lead the reinforcement column. Once they reached the lines of the 294th Rifle Division, Maximov would take command of the defense.[6] From the north came reserve elements of the 7th Polish Infantry Division as well.

The men of *'Brandenburg'* did not understand the larger operational picture or the goals of the upcoming attacks. They just knew they had to execute their orders. Steidl's battered *II.Bataillon* of *Jägerregiment 2 'BR'* withdrew from the destroyed village of Jänkendorf on April 22nd to another village southwest for some rest. Steidl himself "moved into the *Feldgendarmerie* building and had a peaceful day with my people. The town had been abandoned by its inhabitants. We even lay down in proper beds. Breitkeitz set it up. After a long time, I was again reading a book. *Die magischen Wälder* (*The Magic Forests*), stories from Siberia." As Steidl read the book he pondered "will this be our fate as well?" His day of rest came "mercilessly quickly to an end" and on the morning of the 23rd when orders were received to prepare his men to move out for yet another counterattack "further west".

On April 23rd the *II.Bataillon* of *Jägerregiment 1 'BR'* began its final movement back toward the left wing of the *4.Panzer-Armee*. Its orders were clear "Make for Gröditz", which was just to the northwest of Weißenberg along the Löbauer Wasser River. Their advance took them through towns and villages already occupied by advancing Polish troops. Scenes of atrocity awaited the *Panzergrenadiers*. *Leutnant* Grosser's account continues:

All the units worked feverishly to inspect the stuff we had captured and find things of value for us. That would make it possible for the entire *Kampfgruppe* to be motorized. Hunhold's battalion created its second motorized set of equipment using that. The original set, after all, was with the support units. The *Pioniers* [from *Panzer-Pionier-Bataillon 500 'GD'*] and the Reconnaissance Platoon were also motorized.

In the afternoon, the first people to greet us from the area were the *Stabskompanie* with food. It's nice when old friends run into each other in the living room. At the same time, they brought an order to move out that was supposed to get us together with the division. Today's moveout destination was Gröditz.

All of the moveout preparations were made and the moveout orders prepared. I went forward with the radio *SPW* and the *Pionier* platoon in order to scope out the movement route. The area through which our route went was apparently no man's land.

We had barely left Förstgen when we came upon a chaotic scene of smoking shot-up enemy vehicles, tanks and guns. Yet again, the picture of destruction rolled before my eyes. Russian combat aircraft strafed us out of the air, and once we escaped by a hair.

The trip went on. The first place we reached [Groß Radisch] was dead as a doornail. There was not a soul to be seen. Where could all the people be? There was a gruesome solution to the mystery. There were about 40 men, women and children in front of a building on the street. Shot to death . . . cut down. A gruesome paralysis overtook me. Could anyone believe something that appalling at all? Is anything that bestial possible?[7]

Like something spit out, this abominable sight went by and the trip went on. In one of the

---

6   Eberhard Berndt, *"Die Kämpfe um Bautzen 18. Bis 27. April 1945"* in *Kriegsschauplatz Sachsen 1945. Daten, Fakten, Hintergründe* (DZA Verlag für Kultur und Wissenschaft GmbH, 1995), pp. 62-63.
7   Confirmed in the research completed by Seidel, p. 67.

next villages, we met the first German residents again. They shook our hands while sobbing. German soldiers, finally some more Germans! They must have experienced something bad, poor people. When it was dark, we entered Gröditz [AN: along the Schwarzwasser west of Gebelzig]. A weird silence in the city streets. You'd think that there was an eye and a rifle barrel hiding behind every window and in every doorway. I stopped in front of the palace and let the *Pioneer* Platoon out. It got the order to prepare the command post and to take over local security until the regiment arrived.

I personally went on to the *Division*. It was pitch black, so I had to be very careful not to miss the right street. We had to go via Weißenberg. It was the next path. There was a *Sturmgeschütz* on the forward area, right next to the street, the first forward positions of the division. Onward we went. Figures raced in the field to our right. I leaned out of the vehicle and called over to ask from which unit they were. No answer; on we went. The first building, a two-story one, was in front of us. Suddenly we were met by fire. The vehicle stopped next to the building. I leaned out and yelled, "Stop doing it, stop, damn it again." The people over there weren't thinking about it at all. On the contrary, they were now firing at us from the building into our vehicle from above as well. Shit, we were now in a pickle. Turn around! Hell was breaking out now. A light antitank gun and mortars started to shoot from point blank range. The vehicle moved back and was now sitting with its rear deep in the ditch at the side of the road. The engine was stalled. Shit, Good God, has everything taken an oath against us!

Thank God, the vehicle then immediately started up again. Lying down low, we lay behind the armored walls of the vehicle. Don't drive it so hard or we will have our tracks jump off and then it might give up entirely, but at any rate, we got out of here again. Yay, we're out. Floor it and out! The hits from the antitank gun were bursting behind us. Too short, guys, you'll never get us now. The mortar was firing to our side, oh, yes, now the damned *Sturmgeschütz* was on the road in front of us. Now it's clear; that wasn't a German one, it was a Russian one. So floor it, whatever the thing can do, so that the brothers can't have any of us. We went hunting past the tanks from which the Russian servicing crew was just jumping out. I exhaled deeply. Did something happen? "Yes, *Leutnant*, someone caught me in the back," *Wachtmeister* Stolz answered. We stopped to bandage him up. But we couldn't get to him because space was so tight. He wasn't bleeding much. Clench your teeth, Stolz, we'll go to Gröditz fast and then we'll put things in order.

Grosser had taken a wrong turn into what he thought was Gröditz. It is possible that he entered Gebelzig to the northeast of Gröditz where he encountered members of the 7th Polish Infantry Division.

When we arrived in Gröditz, we took the *Wachtmeister* into the palace. The wound turned out not to be very bad; it wasn't bleeding much. It must have been a piece of shrapnel from an explosive round. Gentlemen, we lucked out.

I took a walk through the palace. It looked terrible. Everything thrown hither and yon, drawers pulled out. The garbage and a thousand little things were on the stairs. The library was strewn all the way to the front of the house.

My stay was short, and then I went to the regiment. I met the staff right before they were going to move out. I was given a hearty welcome. People had heard about my experiences already through a radio transmission. We were soon in Gröditz. After a few short exchanges of gunfire, it was calm. For the first time in a long time, I fell completely exhausted into an actual bed sometime around morning.

The *II.Bataillon* and *I.(gep)Bataillon* of *Jägerregiment 1 'BR'* were now reunited after a week of separation. *Kampfgruppe Kappel* was officially dissolved. The remaining *Sturmgeschütze* of *Panzerjäger-*

Abteilung 'BR' also deployed to Gröditz under the *Division* headquarters and readied themselves to support *Jägerregiment 1 'BR'* in the coming attack.

As both *Jägerregiments* advanced concentrically toward Weißenberg, *Panzer-Sturm-Pionier-Bataillon 'BR'* remained in Bischdorf for several days. Here, the *Pioniers* rested and received replacements—even this late in the war! The new *Pioniers* arrived from the *Feld-Ersatz-Bataillon*. *Hauptmann* Müller-Rochholz recalled "many new, young and trust-worthy faces filled the gaps punched by the uninterrupted battles that started on April 16th. We remember our dead." The replacements allowed the *Bataillon* to form two complete companies again. With the reorganization complete, the *1.Pionier-Kompanie (SPW)* was commanded by *Hauptmann* Michaelis and the *2.Pionier-Kompanie* (mot) by *Leutnant* Koch. The drivers for the *SPWs* were assigned from the *I.(gep) Bataillon* of *Jägerregiment 1 'BR'* and the *Versorgungs-Kompanie* that was formerly under the command of *Hauptmann* Michaelis and now subordinated to the *Division Ib* under command of Hans Spaeter.[8]

On April 23rd, *Hauptmann* Müller-Rochholz's *Pioniers* moved west to the area south of Bautzen. They briefly stopped in Löbau, where "storerooms for U-Boat submariners were cleared out. Almost all the members of the *Bataillon* now had leather items." The drivers now wore black U-Boat leathers, while the *Pioniers* donned grey. The new uniforms were credited to the crafty work of the *Bataillon* pay officer, Kieffer, who Müller noted, "was on the ball again". The following day the *Bataillon* moved to positions west of Bautzen to the town of Pietzschwitz. Müller-Rochholz's command post was established in nearby Sollschwitz (?). The *2.Pionier-Kompanie* occupied Storcha where it set up its command post in the town's white church. The elevation provided a commanding view, as the town was already on a hill that dominated the northeast, east and southeast. On the evening of April 25th the *1.Pionier-Kompanie* was ordered to prepare for an attack on Bautzen in support of the armored *Kampfgruppe* under command of *Major* von Wiethersheim expected to launch on the morning of the 26th.

On April 24th, *Jägerregiment 2 'BR'* prepared for battle. *Hauptmann* Steidl's *I.Bataillon* had the lead in the attack on Weißenberg. *Major* Renner's *II.Bataillon* provided support. Steidl recorded that "It makes sense to conduct a big attack. Haste is needed. In the town of Weißenberg, there are division-sized units" of the Soviets who maintained a thin defense. "We wanted to retake it. I raced to Krischa (Bucholz) on the southern flank", while *Jägerregiment 1 'BR'* approached from the north. In the west a blocking position was established, and all that was needed was to block the eastern withdrawal route. "When we arrived in Krischa, I took up a position on the northern edge of the town that the Russians had abandoned." Krischa, contrary to Steidl's recollection is almost 1 kilometer due east of Weißenberg opposite flat farmland. Weißenberg sits on the northern bank of the Löbauer Wasser and is little more than 500 meters long. The terrain on either side is generally broad, open farm fields with only a few small gently rolling hills and small patches of forest to break up the landscape. The town itself is a relatively indefensible place, unless you take advantage of the surrounding towns and terrain features. The Soviets, who were alerted to the approach of the *'Brandenburgers'*, did not prepare a solid defense. While Germen forces were expected from the south and even the east, the appearance of the *Hauptmann* Hunhold's *II.Bataillon* from the north in Gröditz was a surprise and a real threat. The Soviet force had gone days without any resupply and were low on petrol, ammunition, and food. Major-General Maximov did not want to become surrounded and ordered his combined force of infantry and armor out of the town through what he perceived to be a gap in the German lines to the northeast. His tactical decision seems to suggest that he did not realize that the *4.Panzer-Armee* had already reestablished a continuous front further east, making any attempt to reach the 52nd Army

---

8   While Müller-Rochholz originally wrote to Spaeter that the *SPW* drivers came from *Panzer-Aufklärungs-Abteilung 'BR'*, this is unlikely given that that unit was still operating well to the northwest as part of *Kampfgruppe 545.Volksgrenadier-Division*. His drivers were likely drawn from the *I.(gep)Bataillon* of *Jägerregiment 1 'BR'* that became cut-off to the south after the initial Soviet attack on April 16th.

highly unlikely. His desperate action brought destruction to the Soviet force.

Hauptman Steidl's *I.Bataillon* now seized the initiative. In two columns the Soviets streamed northeast from the town across the open farm fields with the goal of the dense Krischa pine forest.

I could clearly see columns of enemy breaking out in the dawn from Weißenberg with armored vehicles, tanks and trucks going east. He smelled a rat. But it made sense to avenge Jänkendorf! I set up all the guns from heavy *Sturmgeschütze* to *Vierling-Flak* and put in any [ammunition] the guns could fire. The enemy needed to move through a completely uncovered open area if it wanted to get out of the pocket. He wanted to do that, but was being torn up by my guns.

Steidl's men opened fire from their ambush positions with fury. All available German artillery and rockets were used. "Numerous tanks and vehicles were burning on the horizon, horses were trampling each other, and enemy infantry were mown down by the thousands. This drama lasted to the evening. I started the last blow."

On the same day to the east *Hauptmann* Hunhold's *II.Bataillon* positioned itself to join combat. *Leutnant* Grosser recalls:

In the morning, an administrative officer came from the *Division*.

"Make the regiment combat-ready immediately. The Russian division defending itself in Weißenberg is attempting to break out to the east!"

The messengers were sent out running as fast as they could. The town that has so far been so calm came to life. A bare half hour later, the *Sturmgeschütze* rolled in and the *1.Kompanie* left Gröditz on their mechanized vehicles. We drove by the forward-moving columns. *Sturmgeschütze* released from an unknown *Abteilung* were [also] taken with us immediately for the attack.

Subsequent events suggest that the "*Sturmgeschütze*" that arrived to pick up *1.Kompanie* were from *Panzerjäger-Abteilung 'BR'* that advanced with *Jägerregiment 1 'BR'*. The *Sturmgeschütze* released from an "unknown *Abteilung*" were likely from *Panzer-Abteilung 1* attached to the *4.Panzer-Armee*. Grosser's account continues:

An interim command post was set up in a railway superintendent's house and the regimental moveout was set up from there. The residents of the house were foreign workers.[9] They had to be removed. There was a terrible stink in the place. To top it off, *Major* Lau, the *Division* adjutant, came and wanted recommendations for promotions and iron crosses. An incessant coming and going of messengers and administrative officers.

Onward. We looked at Weißenberg from a hill. *General* [Schulte-Heuthaus] was there as well. The Russians were shooting with artillery and antitank guns. At the exits to the town, an unmistakable amount of enemy vehicles and tanks. Shot up, abandoned by their crews. Smoke, some from smoldering embers. Among it, flitting figures of fleeing enemy.

The command staff of the *II.Bataillon/Jäg.Rgt. 1 'BR'* was witnessing the results of *Hauptmann* Steidl's initial attack.

The *General* ordered impatiently, "Attack!" Messengers rushed off to the battalion. The *General* himself went with our administrative officers across an open flat field to a farmstead occupied

9   By "foreign workers" this meant forced or slave laborers that were increasingly used throughout the Reich in the latter war years to replace needed manpower in the industrial sector that were increasingly being sent to fill the gaps in frontline combat divisions.

by the enemy. He walked there standing up. It took my breath away. A couple of people pushed together and sent after the *General*. But it was already too late. A machine gun started bellowing dangerously from the flank.

A bullet pushed the *General* to the ground. His leather coat was torn right at the back. An explosive round![10] But only a few pieces of shrapnel got into his back. Our men were already in the farmstead in question. The Russians had left. The *General* had turned his *SPW* around and was back with us. The pains were strong at the time. The wound bled seriously. But he hadn't taken any time to have it bound up. Now, however, he had to go back to a physician.

The attack was moved forward. Now we were on a hill right outside of town. The bandages were put back in order and all was prepared for the second attack that was supposed to take us into the town.

I stood with the *SPW* at the mouth of a narrow road and I looked at the city. At the exit to the city, the Russians left the town bent over, sometimes creeping or jumping. Everything could be seen clearly through the glass. In front of us, there were two antitank guns positioned ready to fire. It could be clearly seen that one or two men were jumping out of the column and firing in spite of our firing on it. It was also clearly visible where the guns were aimed. So I also notice them looking at my vehicle and had it put under cover quickly, as I could see the shot going over our heads.

The *Sturmgeschütze* came up and the infantry jumped out to the assault. They were in the city like a whirlwind. *Jägerregiment 2 'BR'* attacked from the other side at the same time.

Hunhold's *Panzergrenadiers* and accompanying *Sturmgeschütze* advanced southeast from positions that ran along the line Weicha-Wuischke. Attacking on the move through a Soviet minefield, they struck the flank of the withdrawing Soviets. Anyone caught in the open could flee back to Weißenberg where they would be caught in a closing vice, stand and fight in the open where they were likely to be killed under the murderous fire, or attempt to flee to the safety of the woods. Many abandoned their equipment in the open and chose the latter option. Now turning back to Steidl's account of the *I.Bataillon*:

With a "hoorah," we charged out of our positions and took prisoners in great numbers. The captured stuff was uncountable. Alcohol, sugar, coffee, etc. 1,500 vehicles fell into my hands. Unfortunately, an order to move out to Nechern came in during the sorting. There was supposed to be a major movement. I took along on the captured vehicles what I could grab. They included good 3-axle Studebakers of American origin.

The Soviet 294th Rifle Division, 57th Guards Tank Brigade and 25th Guards Mechanized Brigade were utterly destroyed in the attack by 'Brandenburg'. It was an incredible victory for a German division at this stage in the war, and in particular one that conducted the attack after operating as separate groups who were fighting for survival during the past week. Maximov organized his men that escaped the carnage in the farm fields into small groups and reached the forest. He gave them orders to make their way back east in an attempt to reach Soviet lines of the 52nd Army. These small bands were hunted down in the pine forest where they were killed or captured. Several groups that emerged from the forest in the area of Jänkendorf-Ullersdorf were themselves caught by the German *17.Armee* on April 25th and eliminated. Also caught in the battle were some elements of the 7th Polish Infantry Division and the artillery and anti-tank units of the 2nd Polish Army that were likely operating to the northeast of Weißenberg and also caught unaware of the German counterattack. Many of the Polish artillerymen attempted to man their guns in the face of the oncoming attack of 'Brandenburg', but as

---

10   Explosive rounds were banned by the Geneva Convention but were used by the Soviet Union who never signed the convention.

previously noted they received no training on how to conduct a tactical defense. Despite a desperate defense the Polish artillery units soon lost cohesion and became scattered.[11] 3,000 Soviet and Polish soldiers were killed in the battle, with an unknown number of prisoners taken. Both Soviet brigade commanders were killed in battle. One of the prisoners captured was Maximov himself who was severely wounded by a German rocket while seeking cover in a nearby copse of woods. He was treated and brought to the headquarters of the *4.Panzer-Armee* and interrogated by German intelligence who produced a report of his statement. Maximov told his captors that the 7th Guards Mechanized Corps was "refreshed" in March. It received replacements and equipment to replace the losses from the prior months of combat. The corps was placed under the command of the 52nd Army in April, just before the attack, and given the orders to capture Weißenberg, Bautzen, then advance on Dresden, driving northeast of the city, where they were to linkup with the Anglo-American forces. His orders also included the caveat to avoid all cities and large towns. Maximov relayed how after the lines east were cut he was ordered to restore a link with the 294th Rifle Division and the 52nd Army via Weißenberg and Altmarkt (Diesha just to the west of Jänkendorf). Maximov could have been shot by the Germans, but he received required medical treatment, which resulted in the amputation of both his legs. He went into a prisoner camp in Zittau and was subsequently released back to Soviet forces in early May as part of Koniev's offensive toward Prague. He died of his wounds on May 3rd.[12]

German losses were light. Reportedly around 216, with 57 confirmed killed during the forest fighting to the northeast. A number of the casualties came from supporting units of *Division Nr. 464* that established a cordon to the north and east. The only known casualties in *'Brandebourg'* were *Gefreiter* Alexander Gajados (killed the 23rd), Georg Schmidt (*2.Kompanie/II.Bataillon* killed the 23rd), and *Gefreiter* Raimund Köttendorfer (*II.Bataillon* wounded on the 22nd and died on the 24th) all from *Jägerregiment 2 'BR'*. In addition *Hauptmann* Fritz Königstein, commander of *Panzerjäger-Abteilung 'BR'* was severely wounded in the head by a splinter from an enemy mine on the 24th and died of his wounds two days later.[13] The victory completely disrupted all Polish and Soviet operations further east as the final preparations were being made for the follow-on attack on Bautzen.

We pick up with *Leutnant* Grosser:

We drove into the town, passing a minefield. The buildings and the basements were searched. The first civilians showed up on the street. Prisoners were herded.

Jägerregiment 2 'BR' took over the entire sector for defense. Our regiment marched on further to Gröditz into the calm area.

I went to the *Division* command post with the commander, passing the building in which I had nearly gotten lost the evening before.

A short in and out visit at the headquarters of *Jägerregiment 2 'BR'*. To celebrate our reunion, a bottle of wine had its neck broken and then on we went.

Thousands of discussions at the *Division* HQ, a lot to handle. The *Division* was moving to Bautzen. It was supposed to kick off the next morning. There were a lot of preparations to be done. Maps had to be set up for the new area.

In the evening, we were back in Gröditz. Our orderly had prepared a wonderful celebratory meal, and *Leutnant* Schmidt wasn't entirely without a role in setting it up.

Roast goose, and a bottle of champagne. A good Schnapps in advance and then a proper cigar. And all of that from the captured Russian supply column. And a truck with civilian goods that had fallen into our hands was still down below in the part; all the men could have a nice evening.

---

11   Grzelak et all, p. 276.

12   Information on Maximov was drawn from Berndt, *Band 5. Spurensuche*, p. 37. Maximov is buried in Boleslawiec, Poland. An obelisk monument marks his burial site.

13   Ibid., pp. 37, 90.

With Weißenberg secured, *Panzergrenadier-Division 'BR'* was reunited under its *Divisional* command staff for the first time in nearly a week. The reestablish *4.Panzer-Armee* frontline at Kodersdorf now extended northwest. The second phase of the operation began as *'Brandenburg'* moved west to assemble with several other divisions in preparation for the attack on Bautzen that had served as the vital supply terminus for the *4.Panzer-Armee*.

Hans Spaeter's *Ib* Headquarters was reestablished in Rennersdorf and the accompanying supply units of the *Division* had consolidated in nearby Ruppersdorf. Spaeter was busy pushing supplied and ammunition out to the combat battalions in preparation for the coming assault. Like other parts of the *Panzergrenadier-Division 'BR'*, many elements had been dispersed behind Soviet lines the last few days, but managed to fight their way back to German lines. As Spaeter related: "There the remnants of the *Verwaltungs-Kompanie 'BR'* under Senior Paymaster Meyer (in civilian life, a pastor in Lübeck) arrived after having pushed their way through by foot from the north through the woods to friendly troops after the battles near Klitten. They told terrible stories about the Russians' [and Polish] actions among the civilians." The atrocities committed blindly against unarmed civilians observed by the men of *'Brandenburg'* during these days certainly galvanized their will to continue to fight.

18

Counterattack at Bautzen and Battles
East of Dresden, April 25th-30th

(Reference Maps 87, 88, 89, 90, 91, 92, 93, 94, 95, 96, 97, 98, and 99)

As soon as Weißenberg was recaptured the reassembled *Panzergrenadier-Division 'Brandenburg'* deployed west for an immediate attack against the Soviet and Polish forces operating around Bautzen. The bulk of the *Division* maneuvered northwest of the city as a blocking force while its armored units joined with *Kampfgruppe Wiethersheim* to clear Bautzen of Soviet forces. General Świerczewski finally understood that his army was in peril. A moment of panic and confusion likely swept through his command once it was understood his supply route back to the 52nd Army was cut. Most of his artillery units were scattered or destroyed. Communication with several of his divisions was non-existent and he had already lost the bulk of the 7th Polish Infantry Division and the reserve 16th Polish Tank Brigade. No one at Koniev's headquarters knew the exact tactical situation due to Świerczewski's lack of coordination with the 5th Army to his north and the 52nd Army to the east about his intentions to capture Dresden. Świerczewski immediately called a halt to his advance on Dresden. He ordered the 9th Polish Infantry Division to establish a defensive position in Bischofswerda with the assumption that the offensive west toward Dresden would resume after he reestablished a link to the 52nd Army. Next, he ordered the 1st Polish Tank Corps to turn around and head back toward Bautzen where fighting was ongoing since April 18th.[1] This order left the 9th Polish Infantry Division exposed.

The local defense of Bautzen was organized under the command of *Oberst* Dietrich Hoepke. Hoepke commanded *Infanterie-Regiment 371* as a *Major* during the invasion of the Soviet Union in September 1941 and was severely wounded. How long it took him to recover from those wounds and what his follow-on assignments are not entirely clear. What is known is that he was appointed commander of *Kampfbesatzung 'Ortsstützpunkt Bautzen'* (Local Combat Garrison Bautzen). Under his command were some 3,000 men that consisted of the following combat formations: *Festungs-Infanterie-Bataillon 1459, 1461*; *Landesschützen-Bataillon 393, 992*; *Flak-Abteilung 363* (12 x 8.8 cm Flak); *Örtliche Polizei* (45 men); a section of the *10.SS-Panzer-Division 'Frundsberg'* (200 men whose vehicles had no petrol and were left in the city when their division deployed north toward Spremberg); section of *Hitlerjugend* (70 boys); under the command of *Kreisstabsführer SA-Standartenführer* Ziegis were *Volkssturm-Bataillon 32, Volkssturm-Bataillon 33* (with attached *Panzerjagd-Kommando 186 Kp./I.Btl.* under the command of *Kompanie-Führer* Zeller), *Volkssturm-Bataillon 34*, and *Volkssturm-Bataillon 704*; a Transport Battalion; and a Cavalry Squadron. His main force was lightly armed *Volkssturm* whose average age was 47. Armed with captured French bolt-action rifles and MG34s, each battalion numbered 600 men and was organized with a headquarters company and three line companies (*1-3 Kp.*). His heavier force of *Festung-Infanterie* numbered 695 men per battalion who were armed with 12 heavy machineguns, 36 light machineguns, 54 *Panzerschreck*, 70 *Panzerfaust* and 12.8cm mortars.[2]

---

1   Grzelak et all, p. 276.
2   Berndt, *Kriegsschauplatz Sachsen 1945*, p. 54, 55, 61.

Image 13. The city of Bautzen and Ortenburg Castle looking east from the western bank of the Spree. Bautzen was no stranger to battle as it saw heavy fighting and destruction during the Thirty Years War and even during the Napoleonic Wars. During April 1945 the picturesque medieval city was besieged by the forces of the 7th Guards Mechanized Corps that attempted to reduce its defending garrison before the arrival of German reinforcements. The German defenders held out in Ortenburg Castle long enough for *Kampfgruppe Wiethersheim* and *Fallschirm-Panzergrenadier-Division 1 'HG'* to arrive and defeat the Soviet forces within the city. Author's collection.

Despite its status as a "fortress" the city of Bautzen had no modern fortifications. The city itself resides on a rising plateau that overlooks the Spree down a sharp bluff. At the top of the plateau is the Ortenburg Castle surrounded by medieval city walls. Just east of the castle is the medieval waterworks and church of St. Michael, fortresses in their own right, followed by the Rathaus (town hall) with its commanding tower. Further east is the Reichenturm tower, commanding the entrance to the old city. Outside of the city to the south was the Bahnhof (rail station). To the north west of the station was the König-Albert-Infanterie-Kaserne (military training base). Just north of Löbauer Straße and south of Muskauer Straße was the town brewery, a commanding structure that dominated the east-west roads into the city center. These were among the main areas of fighting for the small city. Starting as early as February 15th, prisoners-of-war, forced laborers, and others were put to work under military authority to build trenches and other defensive works around the outskirts of the city. Soon the local Party Officials became involved and with minor exceptions put the majority of the local population to work building trenches as well. Several concentric bands of fortifications were established along natural defensive terrain like the Spree River, and manmade structures like the Kaserne. *Oberst* Hoepke placed his command post in the Ortenburg Castle on the hill. During the following months, training and defensive preparation continued with the knowledge that the final Soviet assault on Germany was near.

Bautzen is by all accounts one of the most picturesque and historic towns in Saxony. Established

König Albert Kaserne, Bautzen i. Sa.

Image 14. König-Albert-Infanterie-Kaserne on Löbauer Straße, Bautzen. This building complex dominated the eastern approaches to the city and was heavily defended alternately by *Volkssturm* and Soviet infantry during the fighting. Author's collection.

in 1000, the town was no stranger to war. It was fought over and destroyed numerous times by fires during the 30 Years War in 1620 and 1634. After the battle of Lützen during the Napoleonic Wars, a combined Prussian force under the command of Count Gebhard von Blücher and Russian forces under the command of Prince Peter Wittgenstein, withdrew to Bautzen where they set up a defensive line along the heights, extending north-south following the curves of the Spree River. The combined Prussian and Russian force was defeated by Napoleon over the two day battle from May 20th-21st, 1813. Napoleon himself is said to have entered the fortress city after the battle. At the time the city's fortifications were designed to defend against an attack from west to east using the river and high bluffs as a bulwark. Now, 132 years later, the attack was coming from the opposite direction were there were little natural defenses.

On April 16th the 7th Guards Mechanized Corps' assault against the *Volkssturm* and *Fahnenjunker* battalions in Rothenburg, as well as *Jägerregiment 2 'BR'* was very successful. Jänkendorf was reached within the first 24 hours, followed by Weißenberg at 9:30 a.m. on April 18th. After leaving behind the 294th Rifle Division to set up a defense in Weißenberg, the rest of the Soviet force continued its uninterrupted drive west to the outskirts of Bautzen. Alerted to the approaching Soviet force, *Oberst* Hoepke activated the "tank alarm" that mobilized his defensive force. *Volkssturm-Battalion 33* deployed along the northern part of the town in an arc to the eastern approaches at the forest in Am Schafberg, just west of Niederkaina and the *Flugplatz Litten* (airfield Litten). At the airfield a section of *Flak-Abteilung 383* deployed to provide protection as approximately a dozen *Luftwaffe* aircraft were operating against Soviet forces from the airfield on a continuous basis (these may have been *Stukas* from Rudel's *Schlachtgeschwader 2*). The Cavalry Squadron deployed further east to Klein Bautzen to provide early warning along *Reichstraße 6*. Zeller's *Panzerjagd-Kommandos* deployed to the area between Bautzen and Weißenberg with orders to engage any Soviet tanks. *Volkssturm-Battalion 32*

Image 15. König-Albert-Infanterie-Kaserne on Löbauer Straße, Bautzen 1945. The scars of two back-to-back battles are evident. Photo by Kurt Arno Lehnert. Courtesy of Museum Bautzen.

Image 16. Husaren Kaserne, Bautzen. This building complex dominated the southern approaches to the city and was heavily defended alternately by *Volkssturm* and Soviet infantry during the fighting. Author's collection.

deployed along the southern approaches of the city to defend the König-Albert-Infanterie-Kaserne and *Hussar* Kaserne. The *1.Kp./V.St.Btl. 32* went further east to man the tank traps along the main road into Bautzen, likely near Pließkowitz. To the southeast at Rabitz deployed a section of *Landesschützen-Bataillon 393* along with a section of *Flak-Abteilung 383*.

By late afternoon the first elements of the 24th and 26th Mechanized Brigades reached the eastern outskirts of Bautzen near the airfield at Niederkaina. Zeller's *Panzerjagd-Kommandos* managed to knockout two T-34/85s earlier in the day, and subsequently withdrew under the support of the section of *Flak-Abteilung 383* located at the airfield. Several sharp engagements occurred followed by the defenders blowing the ammunition storage and main hanger before withdrawing. The Soviets managed to knock-out three anti-aircraft guns and some twenty aircraft still remaining on the runway. In the city, *Oberst* Hoepke ordered an evacuation of the civilians, though few actually left the city.

Soon after the airfield fell T-34/85s of the 13th Guards Tank Regiment under the command of Major Alexander Lukitsch Fomenko reached Am Schafberg with mounted infantry of the 24th Guards Mechanized Brigade. Fighting broke out with the defending *Volkssturm* and by midnight of April 18th/19th the village was captured. Between 2:00-3:00 a.m. elements of the 24th Guards Mechanized Brigade moved south and reached Nadelwitzer Straße across the Albrechtsbach stream. Opposite them was the König-Albert-Infanterie-Kaserne. Along Johann-Sebastian-Bach-Straße just outside the Kaserne was a defensive trench manned by *Hitlerjugend* armed with 2-3 *Panzerfausts* each and backed up by two 8.8cm Flak guns. The Soviets held back as the final attack plan on the city was prepared.

The city streets of Bautzen were racked by Soviet artillery shells and occasional aerial attacks. The streets soon clogged with wounded soldiers, staff cars, and refugees. The cries of the wounded mingled with those of the babies and children through the first night of the Soviet assault. The Soviets were aided in the formulation of their attack plan by former Yugoslavian prisoners that had been released from the local prison. These men knew the German defensive positions, likely because they had helped build the trench system earlier in the year. Soviet reconnaissance patrols began to infiltrate through German lines and reached all the way to the city, mapping German positions and possible movement routes.

Lieutenant-General Korchagin concluded his reconnaissance in force and quickly devised a plan to take the city by storm. The 26th Guards Mechanized Brigade was ordered to attack across the *Autobahn* through Burk-Teichnitz, then south to envelop the city from the north, while the 25th Guards Mechanized Brigade and 57th Tank Brigade enveloped the city from the south. Both forces were to establish a bridgehead over the Spree and block any German relief forces. The main assault into the city was led by the 24th Guards Mechanized Brigade. This force received orders to attack across Weißenherger Chaussee straight down Löbauer Straße to the castle. The infantry regiments of the arriving 254th Rifle Division were assigned to support the main assault.

That attack commenced immediately at 4:00 a.m. Soviet artillery and mortar batteries conducted a 15 minute bombardment of German positions across the eastern approaches of the city. Upon the bombardment's conclusion Soviet tanks rolled forward and began the attack on Bautzen. On the left wing the 26th Guards Mechanized Brigade ran into heavy fire from a battery of 8.8cm Flak and was temporarily halted. Its 215th Tank Regiment did capture Niederkaina then swung northwest to reach Burk by mid-morning. To the south the 25th Guards Mechanized Brigade and 57th Guards Tank Brigade advanced at high speed across the Hussar Kaserne and reached the Bahnhof at Neusalzaer Straße. The Soviet attack along the southern defenses was rapid and unexpected. Gaps in the German line opened up as platoons and squads were cut off further to the south. The right wing of *Volkssturm-Battalion 32* was ordered to evacuate the Hussar Kaserne and remove the horses back toward the city. German soldiers tried to make their way back to friendly lines as the Soviets established their own defensive perimeter. By 9:00 p.m. the *Festungs-Infanterie-Bataillon 1461* advanced to the south of the

Image 17. Bahnhof and Vorplatz, Bautzen 1945. The Bahnhof was briefly defended by *Volkssturm* and *Landesschützen Bataillons*. A number of Soviet tanks and assault guns were knocked out in the Vorplatz by *Panzerfausts* during the fighting, though they were cleared by the time this photo was taken. Photo by Kurt Arno Lehnert. Courtesy of Museum Bautzen.

Image 18. Bismarckstraße (Bahnhofstraße) looking northwest from the Bahnhof, Bautzen 1945. The buildings in this area show signs of heavy fighting as noted by the rubble and several roof collapses. It is unclear if the damage was caused by artillery, aircraft or direct fire. In the foreground is what appears to be a dead soldier with a tarp or camouflage smock covering their upper body. This late in the war both German and Soviet soldiers often used components of each other's uniforms due to frequent breakdowns in supply so it cannot be known with any certainty if this is a German or Soviet soldier. Photo by Kurt Arno Lehnert. Courtesy of Museum Bautzen.

Image 19. Catholic Seminary on Stiftsstraße (Friedrich-List-Straße), Bautzen 1945. Elements of the Soviet 254th Rifle Division advanced in this area of the city. It appears that the Seminary experienced a roof collapse during the fighting, possibly caused by shelling or aerial bombardment. German soldiers, likely *Volkssturm*, can be seen in the foreground after the fighting. Photo by Kurt Arno Lehnert. Courtesy of Museum Bautzen.

Image 20. Justizgebäude (Justice Department) as it looked in the early 1900s. Elements of the *Festung-Infanterie-Bataillon 1459* and *Volkssturm-Bataillon 33* conducted a defense of the building that began on 19 April. The defenders were soon cut-off from the rest of the German defenders by the Soviet 254th Rifle Division. *Oberst* Hoepke sent a relief force to the building complex that failed to get through Soviet lines. The garrison capitulated on 22 April after three days of fighting. Author's collection.

Image 21. Kronprinzenbrücke looking north, Bautzen. This was the main bridge across the Spree between Bautzen and Seidau on the western bank. The far left tower marks St. Petri Dom at Fleischmarkt, followed by the Rathaus tower, and finally the Lauenturm that marks the entry into the inner city. Author's collection.

city and reestablished a solid German line.

In the early morning darkness 10 Soviet T-34/85s rolled forward firing their machineguns against the positions of the *3.Kp./V.St.Btl. 32* along Nadelwitzer Straßer. The Soviet infantry jumped off the tanks and stormed the trench line killing 30 *Volkssturm*. They pushed forward into the König-Albert-Infanterie-Kaserne where a mix of about 100 German soldiers from the *Flak-Abteilung* staff and other units put up an ad hoc defense. The Soviet advance was up a gradual sloping hill toward the city center that gave the defenders a clear view of the forces maneuvering against them. *Hitlerjugend* of the *Panzer-Kommandos* armed with *Panzerfaust* fired at the Soviet tanks from their positions along Johann-Sebastian-Bach-Straße. Machinegun tracers and flames of discharging *Panzerfausts* crisscrossed the Kaserne in the early morning hours of April 19th. By 9:00 a.m. the 24th Guards Mechanized Brigade had pushed down Löbauer Straße in fierce street fighting and overran the remaining 8.8cm Flak guns defending the Kaserne. The defenders in the Kaserne were split in two groups and were slowly forced to withdraw west several blocks by noon. Soviet mortar, artillery, tank and sniper fire continued to take their toll on the mix of German defenders, who again withdrew, this time north to Taucher Cemetery by mid-day. At approximately 2:30 p.m. the remaining 5 officers and 20 men of the *Flak-Abteilung* staff and other survivors of the fighting at the Kaserne joined *Major* Schober and several companies of his *Volkssturm-Bataillon 32* in a counter attack down Löbauer Straßer. The attack did not make much progress and *Major* Schober became mortally wounded when a *Panzerfaust* he fired at a T-34/85 exploded on a nearby fence and tore his left arm off.

In the early morning hours of April 20th *Oberst* Hoepke ordered the withdrawal of his defense back to the inner ring of the city. At 4:00 a.m. the Soviet infantry of the 26th Guards Mechanized Brigade captured Teichnitz from a company of *Volkssturm-Bataillon 33* after a sharp artillery barrage.

Image 22. The destroyed Kronprinzenbrücke looking southwest from the eastern bank of the Spree, Bautzen 1945. The bridge was wired for demolition and detonated by the German defenders. Photo by Kurt Arno Lehnert. Courtesy of Museum Bautzen.

The men of *Volkssturm-Battalion 33* were well armed with *Panzerfausts* and Italian hand-grenades, but their captured French Rifles only had five cartridges of ammunition each. They had little choice but to conserve ammunition and withdraw back toward the city. Their main defensive position at the Fichteschule near the base of the castle plateau. The Soviet tanks were able to cross the Spree during the night and setup their defensive line astride the *Autobahn* as previously ordered. They deployed snipers to keep the *Volkssturm* at the Fichteschule occupied and immobile. By the evening the Soviets were reinforced by the 26th Polish Infantry Regiment, which subsequently forced the *3.Kp./V.St.Btl. 33* to withdraw back to Ortenburg Castle. In the south the 57th Guards Tank Brigade continued its attack west. It crossed the rail line bridge across the Spree River, where it captured Stiebitz by the afternoon. Further west the 25th Guards Mechanized Brigade reach Grubschütz by 2:00 p.m.

Fighting raged house-to-house along the eastern approaches. The German defenses along the inner ring were aided by the medieval walls and fortifications. The 24th Guards Mechanized Brigade reached the entrance to the inner city in the earlier morning hours at the Holzmarkt. Soviet T-34/85s were brought up to blast holes in the walls and barricades the crossed the roads into the city center. A Soviet platoon stormed the Post Office, but the Secondary School remained in German hands. Attacks and counter-attacks continued. *Major* Rohr, commander of the *Ersatz-Bataillon 704* was killed in the fighting. Fighting raged at the Brewery to the east. Soon the hospital was overrun and 400 wounded captured. The Landesstrafanstalt (State Prison) complex along Breirscheidstraße was cut off. Attempts by *Oberst* Hoepke to re-establish connection with the prison failed. Soviet mortar fire reigned down along the northern approaches to the castle grounds and inner city as the first Soviet infantry attacks along *Am Standwall* were repelled at Schützenplatz. Defending Schützenplatz were 10 men that consisted equally of *Landesschützen, Volkssturm*, and *Hitlerjugend*. Losses were typically replaced by the *Hitlerjugend* located at the Ortenburg Castle above the Schützenplatz and by *Landesschützen-*

Image 23. Bautzen looking north from the rail-road bridge. 1. Kronprinzenbrücke. 2. Medieval Water Works. 3. Ortenburg Castle. 4. City Water Tower. 5. St. Petri. 6. Rathaus. 7. Lauenturm. 8. Äußere-Lauenstraße. This represented the area of advance of *Kampfgruppe Wiethersheim* and the attached elements of *Panzergrenadier-Division 'BR'*. Author's collection.

Bataillon 992 that was defending along the eastern bank of the Spree at the base of the castle.

The last operational bridge across the Spree from Bautzen was blown at 7:15 p.m. Inbound supplies were stopped as did the flow of refugees and wounded out of the city. Before the bridge was blown elements of *Oberst* Hoepke's defensive force had withdrawn, to include the 200 soldiers of the *10.SS-Panzer-Division 'Frundsberg'* whose vehicles were left in the city due to a lack of petrol, as well as nearly 2/3rds of his *Volkssturm*. Fighting raged hose-to-house during the night. In the early morning hours of April 21st *Oberst* Hoepke ordered his defensive line withdrawn back along the streets Lauengraben, Kornmarkt, Wendischer Graben und Seidau. Sometime between 7:00 p.m. and 8:00 p.m. negotiations were conducted with the Soviets to surrender the Luther School that was packed with wounded. After the successful negotiations were completed and the school occupied, the Company Commander of the *2.Kp./V.St. Btl. 32* was singled out by the Soviets and executed. To delay the Soviet advance, the secondary school, corner buildings and shops between Kesselstraße and Kornstraße were set on fire. When the Soviets encountered resistance at the new German defensive line between Hauptmarkt-Fleischmarkt they brought up T-34/85s and assault guns to blast out the defenders at pointblank range. *Oberst* Hoepke's force was now running low on ammunition and *Panzerfausts*. He had no heavy weapons at his disposal. In desperation he ordered that the entire Seidau section of the city be set on fire to slow Soviet progress. The members of the *3.Kp./V.St.Btl. 33* attempted to minimize the order's destructive intent, but even with their conscious effort the west wing of the castle burned down. *Oberst* Hoepke organized small bands of "assault troops" and sent them out of the castle grounds to engage the Soviets in hit-and-run attacks. Pockets of German defenders held out in various parts of the city as urban combat raged through the day. As the fighting shifted to the medieval part of the city the streets became too narrow for Soviet tanks to operate effectively. Soviet infantry attempted to assault the Ortenburg castle grounds unsupported by heavy weapons. By the evening of April 21st

Image 24. The destroyed Tuchfabrik on Mühlstraße, Bautzen, 1945. This row of buildings was located at the base of the Ortenburg Castle plateau along the Spree and witnessed extensive fighting between *Volkssturm* and Soviet forces. Photo by Kurt Arno Lehnert. Courtesy of Museum Bautzen.

the Soviets were driving a truck through the streets asking the remaining defenders to capitulate, while in the castle a radio message was received from the HQ of the *4.Panzer-Armee* "Hold on. We are coming." During the early morning darkness of April 22nd a *Luftwaffe* airplane dropped replacement 0.58 ammunition into the castle grounds to assist the defenders. Other attempts to drop supplies were hampered by poor weather.

Inside and outside the city atrocities were committed. Soviet soldiers frustrated at the continued German resistance, took their vengeance out on the civilians hiding in basements and churches throughout the city. Their looting and raping was fuelled by the stocks of captured alcohol. A captured group of approximately 100 *Volkssturm* and *Luftwaffe* men, presumably captured from the airfield days earlier, were placed in a barn in Weigersdorf under Polish guard. The Polish guards subsequently opened fire on the barn with machine guns and threw hand grenades into the building. At least 48 were known to have been killed.[3]

On April 22nd, under orders from the 52nd Army, Lieutenant-General Korchagin dispatched his 57th Guards Tank Brigade and 25th Mechanized Brigade to defend the 294th Rifle Division around Weißenberg (see Chapter 17). He also dispatched the 26th Mechanized Brigade to the northeast around Pließkowitz to maintain the road north toward the 2nd Polish Army open. Inside the city Korchagin readied his defense. He deployed the 933rd Rifle Regiment along the eastern approaches of the city, while the 929th Rifle Regiment secured the western side and *Reichsstraße* 6 south to Rattwitzer Strasse. An engineer company secured the city center along Schillerstraße. Meanwhile elements of the 24th Mechanized Brigade and 936th Rifle Regiment continued to block *Oberst* Hoepke and his forces defending the castle. Localized fighting continued across the city where 5,000 civilians remained

Image 25. The destroyed Gaswerk in Seidau on the western bank of the Spree. Damage here was likely caused during the counterattack of Polish forces and those of *'Hermann Göring'* around 24-25 April. Photo by Kurt Arno Lehnert. Courtesy of Museum Bautzen.

Image 26. Kaiserstraße (Karl-Marx-Straße), Bautzen 1945. This photo is looking northwest from a position in front of the Knaben-Bürgerschule that was surrendered along with the wounded through negotiations to Soviet forces. This was a main avenue of advance for the Soviet 24th Guards Mechanized Brigade and signs of street fighting among the buildings are evident. Photo by Kurt Arno Lehnert. Courtesy of Museum Bautzen.

Image 27. Kornmarkt with the Commercial Building and Dresdener Bank, Bautzen 1945. The fighting in the Kornmarkt was particularly fierce as noted by the destruction and signs of direct action among the pictured buildings. The Soviet 24th Guards Mechanized Brigade fought stubbornly to take this area, and likewise defended it against *Fallschirm-Panzergrenadier-Regiment 1 'HG'* it before it withdrew north out of the city. Note the German Büssing-NAG 4500 A trucks in convoy. The truck one in the foreground appears to have a hole in the driver's side windshield that might signify a sniper's bullet. Photo by Kurt Arno Lehnert. Courtesy of Museum Bautzen.

trapped between the two combatants.

On April 23rd, the lead elements of the *20.Panzer-Division* and *Fallschirm-Panzer-Division 1 'HG'*, staged in the open farm fields between Weißenberg and Bautzen, after a redeployment from the area near Kodersdorf. *Kampfgruppe Wiethersheim* was reorganized to lead the attack and consisted of the armor elements of the *20.Panzer-Division* and the attached *Sturmgeschütz-Artillerie-Brigade 'GD'*, the *I.(gep)Bataillon* of *Jägerregiment 1 'BR'*, and the *1.Pionier-Kompanie* of *Panzer-Sturm-Pionier-Bataillon 'BR'* (which was reorganized into an armored company with tracked *SPWs*), and the *schwere-Panzerjäger-Abteilung 88*. The force contained some 40 *Panzers* and *Sturmgeschütze* (*Jagdpanzers* in the case of the attached '*Großdeutschland*'). The *Panzergrenadiers* were mounted in *SPWs* and trucks. No first person accounts of the fighting in Bautzen by elements of '*Brandenburg*' were located, so where they fought and what they experienced inside the city are not known. The *4.Panzer-Armee* also attached both *Sturmgeschütz-Brigade 300* and *301* to *Fallschirm-Panzer-Division 1 'HG'* in support of the counterattack.

Elements of the *20.Panzer-Division* led the initial advance on Bautzen from the northeast, reaching a point just outside the villages of Kreckwitz and Burk. A small, but well entranced section of the 26th Guards Mechanized Brigade that had not been deployed to Weißenberg, occupied former *Volkssturm* positions in the hills to the north and presented a problem to the German units advancing on the city. An artillery regiment and Rudel's *Stukas* were called in to attack the Soviet positions. A follow-on attack did not break the Soviet defense, so it was decided to shift the force slightly south. The goal was to capture the city before the German defenders in the castle fell, and not to engage in a pitched battle along the outskirts. Simultaneously, elements of the recalled 1st Polish Tank Corps reached the northern outskirts of Bautzen during the course of April 22nd-23rd.

Within the city the Soviets continued to squeeze the defenders of the Ortenburg Castle into a compressed defensive position around the castle's main square that measured about 150x150 meters. The fighting was personal, face-to-face with knives and hand grenades. The Soviets tried to rush the German defenders. The order of the day from *Oberst* Hoepke was simple "Who leaves their position will be shot!" A second defense bastion of *Hitlerjugend* remained to the northeast in the Schützenplatz.

General-Lieutenant Korchagin was not aware of the stunning defeat his Mechanized Corps just suffered at Weißenberg. He had no idea that three German divisions were bearing down on Bautzen. His focus was on employing the 24th Guards Mechanized Brigade to reduce the German garrison. His first alert that something was wrong may have been from whatever wireless communication existed from the defensive elements at Burk. He did not have enough forces to defend the city and was not prepared for the coming attack. Only the 254th Rifle Division was arrayed as a screening force along the western, southern and eastern approaches of the city.

A general assault on Bautzen commenced on April 23rd. Attacking west into the city from Niederkaina was the bulk of the infantry and support assets of the *20.Panzer-Division*. On the division's left flank, attacking northwest between Auritz and Falkenberg, was the majority of *Generalmajor* Lemke's *Fallschirm-Panzer-Division 1 'HG'*. Advancing directly north along *Reichsstrasse 96* was *Kampfgruppe Wiethersheim* and *Fallschirm-Panzergrenadier-Regiment 2 'HG1'*. *Kampfgruppe Wiethersheim's* attack was delayed until late on April 23rd as the force waited for the arrival of the attached elements of *'Brandenburg'* that were completing their movement from the battlefield of Weißenberg.

The joint *Kampfgruppe Wiethersheim* and *'Hermann Göring'* attack initially encountered little resistance along the outskirts of the city. It appears that General-Lieutenant Korchagin had not expected an attack from that direction. The *7.Kompanie* of *Fallschirm-Panzergrenadier-Regiment 2 'HG1'* quickly established a bridgehead across to the western bank of the Spree River over the still intact rail bridge that allowed elements of *Sturmgeschütz-Brigade 300* to cross. This force would link up with *Kampfgruppe* of *'Frundsberg'* on the following day that had advanced from the southwest to screen the approaches and act as a blocking force from the direction. The defensive positions of the 254th Rifle Division and elements of the 24th Mechanized Brigade along the rail-line were soon identified and immediately attacked by the *Luftwaffe*. By 5:00 p.m. the *Panzergrenadiers* and accompanying *Panzers* broke through the Soviet defensive line along the rail-line and reached the Hussar Kaserne. The Soviet infantry caught in the attack were surprised by the momentum and withdrew into the interior of buildings, particularly the basements. Pockets of Soviet resistance were by-passed in an attempt to reach the defenders in Ortenburg Castle. By evening they reached Muskauer Straße and cut the east-west road out of the city. The counterattack made surprisingly progress quick as the Soviet soldiers in the city were caught unprepared.

Along the western approaches *'Hermann Göring'* and the *20.Panzer-Division* fought through the positions of the defending 254th Rifle Division and also made quick progress. According to one account the vanguard of the *'Hermann Göring 1'* advanced from the east down Löbauer Straße fighting hand-to-hand against drunken Russian soldiers. As it neared the city center a last minute Soviet counterattack by some 20 Soviet T-34/85s and assault guns was defeated in fierce short range combat among the burning buildings.[4] The *Panzers* of *'Hermann Göring'* used incendiary rounds in the city, starting fires throughout many buildings. *Generalmajor* Lemke was under the impression that the city had been evacuated of all German civilians and that everyone inside was a Soviet. His men were surprised when they came across the first civilians in the city, almost shooting them, thinking they were Russian.

---

4   Hinze, p. 182.

Image 28. Lauengraben with Wendischem Haus, Bautzen 1945. The Wendischem was the seat of the highest judicial authority in Oberlausitz. It was demolished after the war due to its damage. This building may have been one of those destroyed by *Volkssturm* under orders from *Oberst* Hoepke who believed that by setting fires in buildings near the castle district he could hold off the Soviet advance. Note that the building was cordoned off after the fighting as it likely was near collapse. The jeep to the right is of a British Morris C8 FAT (Field Artillery Tractor) Quad produced by the Guy Motor Company. This vehicle was likely captured at Dunkirk in 1940. It shows signs of modification with added armor protection along the roof and rear. A number of these vehicles were assigned to the German garrison and used during the fighting. Photo by Kurt Arno Lehnert. Courtesy of Museum Bautzen.

After swinging south in a wide arc, *Kampfgruppe Wiethersheim* advanced into the city at night along with *Fallschirm-Panzergrenadier-Regiment 2 'HG1'*. Quick progress was again made by the combined German force. *Generalmajor* Hermann von Oppeln-Bronikowski of the *20.Panzer-Division* arrived and accompanied a small patrol through the streets to Ortenburg Castle in order to link up with the remaining garrison and coordinate the clearing of the city.[5] He expected to find some 1,200 soldiers, but instead found 400. The remaining men, many of whom were sleeping off the exhaustion of the last several days of battle, revealed to the General that some ⅔rds of their force had taken the opportunity to leave Bautzen during the initial Soviet attack. *Generalmajor* Oppeln-Bronikowski was not amused by the news. The irate *General* organized the remaining men and sent them out into the streets.[6] As *Kampfgruppe Wiethersheim* began to retake the districts, German deserters and looters who were identified were summarily executed on the spot.

General-Lieutenant Korchagin now found himself in a very difficult situation by the evening of April 24th. He ordered the small reserve force of the 24th Mechanized Brigade that consisted of three

---

5   *Generalmajor* Hermann von Oppeln-Bronikowski was the 142nd Recipient of the Swords to the Knight's Cross, which was received by teletype on April 17th, 1945. He received this award for the defense fighting along the Oder River in March.

6   Interview with *Generalmajor* Hermann von Oppeln-Bronikowski. Cornelius Ryan Collection, Section: German Forces (Box 66/Folder 11).

T-34/85s, three anti-aircraft guns and a Reconnaissance Company to block a German breakthrough to the castle. Meanwhile the staff of the 24th Mechanized Brigade that was holding a defensive position in the Town Hall quickly withdrew north to the City Clock Tower to avoid being completely surrounded. A radio message from Koniev's headquarters was received that night: "Fight to the death, but do not give up the city!" Despite the radio message, Korchagin issued orders for the Soviet defenders to withdraw to the northern suburbs. Several buildings outside the Castle were set on fire, possibly to mask his movements. With the exception of occasional machine-gun fire the city became eerily quiet.

Outside the city the 1st Polish Tank Corps arrived to relieve both Bautzen and Weißenberg. The 2nd Polish Tank Brigade led the counterattack down *Reichsstraße 6* to relieve Bautzen in the early morning hours of April 25th. They reached Stiebitz, but were repulsed by elements of *'Frundsberg', Fallschirm-Panzergrenadier-Regiment 2 'HG1'*, and *Sturmgeschütz-Brigade 300*. The haphazard counterattack of the 1st Polish Tank Corps to relieve the city without infantry or artillery support failed as elements of *Fallschirm-Panzer-Division 1 'HG'* intercepted the attack, knocking out 17 Polish tanks, killing 42 and wounding 120 Polish soldiers in the process.[7] As the weight of the German counterattack focused north of the city, many Polish units now found themselves isolated and exposed. Polish tank units advanced on Burk and Malschwitz, reaching as far as Hill 182 at Belgern halfway to Weißenberg, but no further. They began to realize the gravity of the situation as Polish units encountered pockets of German soldiers along the way. No quarter was given to these men when captured. On the evening of April 25th Polish forces captured 26 German soldiers, possibly *Volkssturm*, in the village of Burk that had since been occupied by German forces since the day before (after the Soviet forces evacuated under orders), and summarily shot them.[8] In Niederkaina, 195 men of *Volkssturm-Bataillon 33* were rounded up and massacred (see Introduction). Given the lack of infantry and motorized transport that marked the Polish Tank Corps counterattack, the German prisoners may have been shot given the lack of means to secure them. Overextended and behind German lines, these relief elements of the 1st Polish Tank Corps withdrew northwest. They initially attempted to stay ahead of the attacking German forces that moved north from Bautzen. Then the Polish force turned around to stand and fight on orders of Koniev's Chief of Staff who was sent to bring order out of chaos.

Inside the city the Red Airforce conducted a heavy raid to assist their ground forces in the counterattack. The *Luftwaffe* also made an appearance and intense dog fights broke out between German and Soviet fighters in one of the few late war aerial engagements along the East Front. Pockets of Soviet soldiers continued to offer resistance. Lemke's *Fallschirm-Panzer-Division 'Hermann Göring'* was ordered to attack north-northwest out of the city to engage the Polish relief force and Soviet remnants. *Kampfgruppe Wiethersheim* remained in the city for another 24 hours to assist in the mop up as Soviet soldiers that did not receive the order to withdraw held out through April 27th. Most Soviet soldiers fought stubbornly to the death. Those that tried to surrender were often shot on the spot, given the visible brutality they dealt out to the civilians of the city. Medical personnel and some wounded of the 254th Rifle Division that were left behind in the northern district of the city presumably fell into the hands of *Kampfgruppe Wiethersheim* and were summarily executed (see Introduction). Overall the 7th Guards Mechanized Corps and attached 254th Rifle Division suffered heavy losses during the brief fighting for the city. Exact numbers are not known, but based on cemetery records, nearly 900 Soviet soldiers are buried in marked graves in Bautzen. Many more Soviets were buried in unmarked trenches when the Germans retook the city. Total Soviet dead likely total over 1,500. The burnt hulks of 20 Soviet T-34/85s and four assault guns were strewn across the city streets after the battle. The records for the 7th Guards Mechanized Corps clearly show that by April 26th this Soviet force was destroyed after the recent battles at Weißenberg and Bautzen. Each mechanized brigade had

7   Grzelak et all, p. 276.
8   Berndt, *Kriegsschauplatz Sachsen*, p. 66.

lost on average between 80%-90% of its assigned personnel and armor. Its losses continued among the pastoral farm fields of Saxony.[9] German losses in terms of the original defense and counterattack are not known with any accuracy, but were far less than their Soviet counterparts. If the victims of both Burk and Niederkaina are combined with combat deaths, then there are about 388 German soldiers buried in Bautzen cemeteries. Another 333 soldiers, to include 201 *Volkssturm* are listed as missing and presumed killed in action while fighting outside of the city in the northern and western towns.[10] If we look at official damage and casualty statistics reported by the city of Bautzen the numbers are as follows: 10% of the city's residential buildings were destroyed representing 34% of the town's living space; 18 bridges were destroyed, more than 100 public and commercial buildings were damaged or destroyed; 6,500 soldiers from both sides were killed, and 350 civilians lost their lives.[11] While the fighting was brief, it was fierce.

Panzergrenadier-Division 'BR' reassembled to the north of Bautzen. On its right flank was the bulk of the *20.Panzer-Division* (minus its *Panzers*). On the left flank was *Fallschirm-Panzer-Division 1 'HG'* and *Kampfgruppe Wiethersheim* (attached *'Brandenburg'* elements were being released back to the *Division*). A general counterattack north began against the 2nd Polish Army and remnants of the 7th Guards Mechanized Corps' brigades. *Jägerregiment 1 'BR'* moved out immediately on the 25th. Despite the chaos of battle, the basic routine of military life continued, especially in the generation of awards, and the accompanying paperwork as *Leutnant* Grosser relates:

Soon after midnight, the regiment started moving out toward Bautzen in individual movement columns. I had stuff to do nearly the entire night in order so that I could finally get the whole paper war won, and yet again the *Stabskompanie* made themselves unpleasantly noticed in this regard. All of the clerks came up to me with thick folders of documents to be signed. There was lots of writing getting done. Promotions and awards were processed, and the first Iron Crosses showed up while it was still night. In addition, the orders for the movement had to be prepared. Petrol, ammunition and replacement personnel had to be put in. My head was spinning. In the meantime, an officer came and took me to the motor pool. There were a whole bunch of captured vehicles taken there. I was asked what we should take with us. The other equipment had to be blown up.

During the morning, the regimental headquarters moved out. I had to stay back because I was not yet through the paper war. Shortly before departure, I gave the *Krad* messenger staff the Iron Cross 2nd Class as a unit. They guys had behaved outstandingly in recent days and shown themselves to be extremely reliable.

Finally, I could leave. I went alone with my *Horch*. There were thick columns on the movement route. There were continually enemy aircraft over our heads. I went on side roads where there were no German soldiers to be seen—no man's land. It was, all things considered, a funny situation. We were going along the Eastern Front headed "west" against the enemy!

We got to the *Division* command post shortly after noon. To the adjutants; promotions and awards discussed. The *General* was lying in his room and not feeling particularly well with his wound. The Iron Crosses were stuck behind in the motorcycle-sidecar that I still had. I set up a few maps, figured out the situation and the views and then went further behind the regiment. The signs were bad. I got lost and wound up with the *Jägerregiment 2 'BR'*, which was just getting ready to attack. I and my thick vehicle were suddenly in the middle of the battlefield. An awkward situation. So I turned around fast. Finally, I found the regimental command post in an isolated farmstead. A very beautifully set-up manor house. *Hauptmann* Metzger was also there with some of his *Jagdpanzers*. In front it was relatively calm. The Russians were running around a lot to our

9   Berndt, *Band 5. Spurensuche*, pp. 12, 46.
10   Berndt, *Kriegsschauplatz Sachsen*, p. 67.
11   www.bautzen.de

Image 29. Domstift St. Petri and Petridom, Bautzen 1945. This image was taken near Fleischmarkt just a few blocks from the Ortenburg Castle. Looking down An der Petrikirche the signs of street fighting along the building facades are visible. In the distance is the top of the entrance way into the Ortenburg Castle on Schloßstrasse. It appears to have sustained direct fire damage from a Soviet tank or assault gun. Photo by Kurt Arno Lehnert. Courtesy of Museum Bautzen.

front with tanks. There were supposed to be more attacks during the evening.

The afternoon passed with plans for the upcoming undertaking. Artillery and *Jagdpanzer* crews were going in and out. In the meantime, some *Pioniers* and Signals personnel got their Iron Cross 2nd Class. The *Pionier* platoon leader had his Iron Cross 1st Class lent by the *Division* Commander.

Evening fell. The beginning of the attack was set for midnight. The *Division* was pushing a lot. During the evening, *Major* Bansen gave me the Iron Cross 1st Class. The *Ia* came at about 10:00 p.m. There was not enough time for all the preparations, so the beginning of the attack for the first stage was postponed to 1:00 a.m.

I felt bad the entire evening, and about midnight, I was really bad. I had to vomit and lay down, and I then fell into an unconscious and exhausted sleep. The *Major* ordered me to stay at the command post. He himself went forward with the *Ia*.

Hauptmann Steidl's *II.Bataillon* of *Jägerregiment 2 'BR'* followed behind *Jägerregiment 1 'BR'* on the 25th:

We were moved to the Bautzen area in a rather long motorized movement. The Russians had possession of the city itself and had strong forces in the vicinity. There were also rather strong forces facing us, including some well-equipped tank divisions. We started on a flank attack from some distance away headed north in order to head off an enemy push to the west. In a quick attack with heavy fighting, we went through Bolbritz and Uhna to Schmochtitz. Here before night fell,

Image 30. Schloßstrasse. This gateway marked the entrance into Ortenburg Castle. It was heavily fought over as the Soviet tried repeatedly to break into the castle grounds and eliminate the German garrison during this modern day version of a medieval siege. Once they did, the garrison withdrew across the courtyard into the remaining tower. Author's collection.

we were in front of an ornate palace in which there were still strong enemy units; I took the palace in a night attack and moved in. But during the night, the enemy set the roof supports on fire by firing on it. We moved into the stables.

The initial counterattack of *Fallschirm-Panzer-Division 1 'HG'* to the north of Bautzen was very successful. The Polish and Soviet units were simply unorganized in their defense tactically, and perhaps demoralized by the recent string of defeats. They had expected their advance towards Dresden to continue against little or no resistance given the war was all but over. Perhaps many did not want to lose their lives with overall victory so close at hand. Whatever their psychological state, they were on the defensive against violent German counterattacks. The *II.Btl./Fsch.Pz.Gren.Rgt 1 'HG'* attacked the 929th Rifle Regiment along the brickyard and around the transformer station in Rattwitz. After a day of heavy combat, the Soviets gave ground and the survivors withdrew north. To the west the *Panzer-Aufklärungs-Abteilung 'HG'* attacked into Bloaschütz where they defeated a Polish reconnaissance unit and captured a courier who was in possession of a map with the withdrawal routes of the 9th Polish Infantry Division (see below). The men of the *Abteilung* pushed further northwest to Bolbritz where they joined with Steidl's battalion from *'Brandenburg'* to force out the defenders. As Steidl noted above, his men were ordered northwest to cut off the withdrawing Polish infantry based on the map captured that day. With Rattwitz secure, the *II.Bat./Fsch.Gren.Rgt.1 'HG'* attacked due north and defeated the handful of survivors from the 24th and 26th Guards Mechanized Brigades defending in Teichnitz. By the end of April 25th *Kampfgruppe Wiethersheim* and their attached elements of *Panzergrenadier-Division 'BR'* left out of the northern districts of Bautzen and launched their attack northwest on the left flank of *Fallschirm-Panzer-Division 1 'HG'*.

The newly arrived *Fallschirm-Panzergrenadier-Division 2 'HG'* of the reconstituted *Fallschirm-Panzer-Korps 'HG'* established a security line to the west and southwest of Dresden, blocking the approaches to the city.[12] Both *Panzer-Korps 'GD'* and *LVII.Panzer-Korps* organized a general offensive north against the 2nd Polish Army to stabilize the front as reported by *H.Gr. Mitte* to *OKH* on April 24th.[13] General Świerczewski and his staff were likely completely overwhelmed by events on the battlefield.

Far to the north near Berlin, Marshal Koniev grew concerned about his southern flank as all communications between Koniev's command and the 2nd Polish Army had ceased days earlier. The sporadic reports that did reach Koniev's command from the 52nd Army and 7th Guards Mechanized Corps were alarming: Soviet and Polish units defeated ... mounting casualties and tank losses ... Weißenberg lost ... Bautzen lost ... connection to the 52nd Army cut ... German units on the offensive north. Koniev ordered his Chief of Staff, General Ivan Yefimovich Petrov and his Chief of Operations General Vladimir Ivanovich Kostylev to determine what happened and fix the situation. Koniev wrote after the war:

> On these days I was chiefly at my forward command post, and the chief of staff of the front, General of the Army Ivan Yefimovich Petrov, was at the main command post of the front. I appointed him to go to the troops of Koroteyev and Świerczewski and help to organize the cooperation of the troops on the spot, which, with the support of the units of the 5th Guards Army, should not only repulse the assault of the Germans, but also in turn inflict a blow on them.
>
> Simultaneously with this—since after the arrival of the Germans in the rear of the 2nd Polish Army, I had lost communications with its army commander, General Świerczewski—I gave a particular assignment to the chief of the operational command of the front, General Kostylev: he was to go to the 2nd Polish Army and establish communications with Świerczewski.[14]

When Petrov reached Świerczewski's headquarters he relieved the Polish General of command immediately. Kostylev was placed in command of the 2nd Polish Army.[15] The unauthorized advance on Dresden was called off and the remaining Polish units were ordered to withdraw northwest and reconsolidate. Koniev felt enough concern about the German attack north that he ordered the 5th Army's 4th Guards Tank Corps, reinforced by the 14th and 95th Guards Rifle Divisions to divert southeast and reinforce the battered 2nd Polish Army and remnants of the 7th Guards Mechanized Corps. Despite the steps Koniev took to stabilize the situation, the tactical disaster confronted by the 2nd Polish Army continued to unfold.

On April 25th a courier from the headquarters of the 9th Polish Infantry Division heading to the headquarters of the 2nd Polish Army was captured by *Panzer-Aufklärungs-Abteilung 'HG'* in Bloaschütz. The courier had in his possession a map of his division's planned withdrawal route from Bischofswerda back to friendly lines. The 9th Polish Infantry Division had previously halted its drive on Dresden in Bischofswerda on order from General Świerczewski. Colonel Aleksander Łaski initially ordered his men to set up a defense, but soon realized he was cut off and exposed.[16] Low on ammunition, with no artillery or tank support, the division had to withdraw or face possible destruction as new German units in the form of *Fallschirm-Panzergrenadier-Division 2 'HG'* deployed into the frontline between his position and Dresden. With the captured map, *Panzer-Korps 'GD'* set up an ambush with units of *Panzergrenadier-Division 'BR', Fallschirm-Panzer-Division 1 'HG'* and *Kampfgruppe Wiethersheim*. The Polish divisional commander Colonel Łaski was completely unaware

12 NARA T78/304/6255200.
13 NARA T78/304/6255185.
14 Koniev, p. 124.
15 Świerczewski was given back command shortly before the Prague Offensive began in early May.
16 Kaczmarek, p. 70.

of the seriousness of the tactical situation to his rear. He had spent the last 72 hours advancing 50 kilometers west almost unopposed as the rest of the army was being defeated in detail to his rear. He was so unaware of his dire predicament that he did not wait until the cover of night to conduct his movement. On April 26th his infantry division headed back east in three columns. His handling of the movement was tactically unsound. No screening units were sent out to establish security along the flanks and he ordered no forces to reconnoiter ahead of the main column. The columns were subsequently ambushed and many of the Polish soldiers were killed or wounded. The 26th Polish Infantry Regiment was ambushed in what became known as the "valley of death" near Crostwitz, likely by elements of *Kampfgruppe Wiethersheim* and destroyed, losing 75% of its soldiers. A group of 200 wounded arrived in Horka in trucks, just to the north of Crostwitz, where they were captured and executed in an incident likely attributed to the *20.Panzer-Division* (see Introduction).[17] There was only a single survivor, Chaplin Jan Rdzanek. Colonel Łaski was captured.[18] Hundreds of withdrawing Polish soldiers were killed by German artillery. Burning vehicles littered the horizon. Survivors made their way to Polish lines and were incorporated into the Soviet 14th Rifle Division over the course of April 27th and 28th. The 9th Polish Infantry Division was destroyed.[19]

In the early morning of the 26th Steidl's men continued to attack through heavily defended towns.

> In the early morning twilight, we met to do an additional attack on Milkwitz via Brossen. There were bitter battles with lots of losses. There were dead people in the ditches to the left and the right of the street. The town of Milkwitz was freed. In the command post, a piece of shrapnel from a shell hit the wall right next to me. An embittered ringing was sounding from the hills before us. During the night, the moveout order came from the regiment. I slept through the night ...

We now turn to *Jägerregiment 1 'BR'* during the early morning hours of April 26th. *Leutnant* Grosser:

> About morning, I woke up somewhat refreshed. The nausea was over. The communications officer who had watched the equipment reported to me that the attack was well underway. I got up and went forward because there wasn't anything to do here, after all. While en route, we were fired on by low-flying aircraft again. I should have grown out of my inability to distinguish friendly and hostile aircraft; I was always so naive and thought that it must be a German. To my surprise, however, the beasts mostly started spitting into the area in a most unfriendly way, so I had to dive out of my vehicle.
>
> I was totally lost and had no idea anymore where forward and rear were. The trip went right through the meadows. There were shot-up Russian and German tanks in a village. A lot of Russian and German armament. But it seemed it had been there for a long time. It was evidence of previous heavy battles. Our units were going through the town. No one could say where the regimental commander was. So onward we went, forward and back, hither and yon. I couldn't manage to get my bearings in the terrain. I stopped in a village on the hill in order to finally figure out where I was. There was a whole bunch of *SPW* in front of me. There were two long columns of prisoners in the valley. Suddenly, though it didn't touch me, there was a whistling in the air and

---

17 Polish sources cite 300 wounded were killed. Based on *'Brandenburg'* veteran accounts we know that shortly after the battle of Bautzen *Panzer-Sturm-Pionier-Bataillon 'BR'* advanced north to Doberschütz, which represented its left most flank. Just beyond that flank, about a kilometer to the southwest, was the village of Horka where the shooting of Polish prisoners reportedly occurred. This village resided squarely in the area of operations of *Kampfgruppe Wiethersheim* and the *20.Panzer-Division*. A large stone memorial now marks the site. The date on the memorial records 28.4.1945 as the date of the massacre.

18 A large Polish memorial now stands on the spot where the massacre took place. The date 28.4.1945 is etched in the granite's side.

19 Grzelak et all, p. 276.

an artillery round hit the crossing in the village. I flew into the dirt. With the next round, roofing tiles and other hard objects flew around my ears. I looked up. There were three Russians in front of my running out of a building. Damn it again, what did I get myself into? Has everything been conspiring against me since yesterday evening? The two messengers and I jumped behind the Ivans and finally caught them in a basement. The brothers were trembling all over. They clearly knew just as little as we did about what actually was going on. They had just given up earlier. Well if they had been a bit more alert, we would have been dead. What a coincidence!

I found the commander of the *Panzer-Sturm-Pionier-Bataillon*, *Hauptmann* Müller-Rochholz, with the *SPWs* in a [mill north of Dreikretscham]. He wasn't able to tell me where my commander was, either. Somewhere over there to the right, he thought. Otherwise he didn't know anything more about the situation. He had enough to do to pull his bunch together. A real chaotic situation, I thought; hopefully, the Russians weren't coming because we weren't packed up.

The trip went on. A company was digging in in a meadow. I took my *Krad* right along their holes. Careful, *Oberleutnant*, there's shooting going on here from the edge of the forest. He also set up an antitank gun there. I found it rather muggy because I was in the middle of the fresh meadow with my *Krad*. Even so, I managed to maintain my composure, at least on the outside. However, I was pleased as punch when my wheels had laboriously made their way through the damp meadow and I was standing safely behind the first building, but no shots were fired anyway.

After going hither and yon for a while, I had finally reached the commander where he was sitting in the kitchen of a building between an omelet and a map. His head was spinning. Otherwise, everything went very well. Now we had gotten a wide sector, a very wide sector, to defend. In addition, the terrain wasn't very great. Plus Ivan had made himself noticeable again with his tanks. What were we supposed to set up with just our couple of *Jagdpanzers*?

We made ourselves at home in another building in the living room. The artillery lived above us and *Hauptmann* Metzger was on the other side. As I imagined, the world had again become crowded. The *I.(gep)Bataillon* was taken away from us again and was subordinate to *Major* von Wiethersheim as an armored group. *Hauptmann* Metzger was also provided to this unit. So we were there again like poor infantry pawns.

The focus of our defense was on the right flank, the town of Neschwitz. *Hauptmann* Hunhold had his command post in the town. The town was in a sunken valley and was crossed by a large road coming from the northeast. From Neschwitz, it was possible to hold the terrain from the edges of the forest to the edges of the valley, which was where our sector ended. The enemy was also aware that it was making desperate efforts to take possession of the town again within the next few days, so there were bitter struggles.

Hauptmann Müller-Rochholz's *Pioniers* were also on the move on the 26th:

In the morning, *Leutnant* Koch (*2.Pionier-Kompanie*) and I were in Storcha. From there, we were using 2cm to fire from the foot of the church at enemy movements on the Weidlitz estate. I ordered Koch to take the small forest on the northern slope near the church in his sector and to search it, because that was the only endangered site in his sector. I myself went to see Oesterwitz (*Jäg.Rgt. 2 'BR'*), who had supposedly come in to our right toward Schmochtitz. When I was in Dreikretscham, we heard loud battle noise from the *2.Pionier-Kompanie*. I immediately went north from Dreikretscham and saw the *1.Pionier-Kompanie* under Michaelis—which was coming back from its deployment with *Kampfgruppe Wiethersheim*—hitting the flank of the Russians retreating out of the forest from Koch. It was determined in the process that the field barns in front of Koch's sector were full of enemy. Most of them were Poles! They were soft. The *1.Pionier-Kompanie*, with their *SPWs* mounted with MG42 mowed them down. There were a lot of enemy dead with no losses of ours. Bravo, Michaelis. You immediately grasped the situation and conducted a classic attack. In the meadow north of Dreikretscham, we assembled 600 prisoners, who were put en route to the Sollschwitz estate. The escort was only the wounded.

Because now it was time to take advantage of the situation. *Jägerregiment 2 'BR'* (I think it was Oesterwitz) was at that point being fired on by T-34s from the vicinity of Luga and by Luga, meaning from the flank.

It took some effort to get the young soldiers who had cut loose after a battle and unexpectedly great success back into order quickly and set them up for an immediate assault on Luga. The *2.Pionier-Kompanie*, formed up a few minutes later, advanced on Luga through the meadows. The *1.Pionier-Kompanie* assembled and attacked with two *Sturmgeschütze*, which I had found from another division and taken to Pannewitz. The two towns were taken quickly and easily. The Poles ran and were shot down like rabbits. The battalion command post was in Luga (a warehouse). The civilians came crawling out of the basements shuddering.

We went on against Luga. The enemy was there in spades. From north of Luga (Uebigau estate), T-34s were going into Luga. We set up contact with artillery (not our division's) in Sollschwitz. They wanted to support us.

We spent a half hour in Pannewitz and Luga. Then we attacked: the *1.Pionier-Kompanie* from the west via Krinitz and the *2.Pionier-Kompanie* from the south. We went straight to Luga and had it firmly in our hands after half an hour of house-to-house fighting. However, the Russian T-34s and a JS-IIs were standing in the forest on the hill 300 meters northeast of Luga and they could not be attacked across the open space without *Sturmgeschütze*. We got ready and failed with our first attempt at strong shots at the heavy tanks. It got dark and we went into Luga. This day brought over 600 prisoners and the Poles lost an awful lot of dead.

The prisoners were likely survivors from the ambushed 9th Polish Infantry Division making their way east and had joined elements of the 1st Polish Tank Corps. This successful attack was one that caught the attention of Soviet authorities after the war. *Hauptmann* Müller-Rochholz lamented in his postwar account given to Hans Spaeter after his return from Soviet forced labor in 1970 that: "I received 25 years in Russia for this battle. I should have given the order to shoot 300 prisoners of war!!" But he didn't shoot them. Other units of 'Brandenburg' also took prisoners during these days, often in large numbers. They were not rounded up and shot, despite all the brutal treatment of German civilians witnessed by the men of the *Division* in recent days. They were sent to nearby prisoner of war camps behind the *4.Panzer-Armee* lines. While specifics are not known, many were released within days after the start of Koniev's drive south into Czechoslovakia in early May as in the case of Lieutenant-General Maximov.

Attacks continued as new defensive line was reestablished across the northern flank of the *4.Panzer-Armee*. *Panzergrenadier-Division 'BR'* HQ moved to the east of Dresden while the *Division's* supply units moved farther south to Schirgiswalde where they were more secure. To the east of *'Brandenburg'* advanced *Fallschirm-Panzer-Division 1 'HG'* for several days before it was redeployed west on April 28th/29th. *Kampfgruppe 545.Volksgrenadier-Division, Division Nr. 464, 17.Infanterie-Division* and *72.Infanterie-Division* continued to hold a solid line further east running from Spreefurt-Klitten-Neudorf. This line was well north of the Rothenburg-Weißenberg-Bautzen line of advance used by the 7th Guards Mechanized Corps. To the west of *'Brandenburg'*, *Kampfgruppe Wiethersheim* of the *20.Panzer-Division* advanced north recapturing Kamenz. *Fallschirm-Panzergrenadier-Division 2 'HG'* held a defensive position between Dresden and Kamenz while *Kampfgruppe 10.SS-Panzer-Division 'Frundsberg'* set up a defensive position north of Dresden.

Over the next four days units of *'Brandenburg'* continued to fight pitched battles against scattered Polish and Soviet units. Below continues *Leutnant* Grosser's account of *Jägerregiment 1 'BR'* during

Image 31. The town of Bischofswerda represented the closest distance to Dresden achieved by the 2nd Polish Army. It was here that the 9th Polish Infantry Division and 1st Polish Tank Corps reached in their drive on Dresden before being ordered to turn around and head back northeast. The 1st Polish Tank Corps was ordered to relieve Bautzen and failed. The 9th Polish Infantry Division, recognizing it was now isolated, withdrew and was destroyed by *Panzer-Korps 'GD'*. *Fallschirm-Panzergrenadier-Division 2 'HG'* led the counterattack that cleared the town of any remaining Polish or Soviet forces on 24/25 April. The image is also a good representation of the terrain in western Saxony; small tightly grouped towns surrounded by cleared, rolling hills. The terrain was excellent for tanks but often exposed them to direct fire and aerial attack. Author's collection.

this time period.

April 26th Continued

The day was once more characterized by improvisation and rapid assistance. The Russians fought extremely fiercely to take possession of Neschwitz. Particularly at the northern end, the palace and the palace grounds frequently changed hands. But the men of the *II.Bataillon* repeatedly managed to throw the enemy out and take over the town. Many tanks were knocked out. About 15 of them were in the foreground. Two or three of them were taken out in close combat on the palace grounds. One of them was handled in a particularly bold way. A Grenadier clambered up the tank while it was moving, opened up the turret, threw a hand grenade in and let it fall into the vehicle.

The commander was mostly en route. I myself was in Neschwitz around noon in order to see the stores in front. I had a lot to do to bring the supply, which was again torn away, back to us. In the afternoon, we got a couple more replacements. Almost all of them were old *'Brandenburgers'*.

In the evening, at *Major* von Wiethersheim's invitation, *Hauptmann* Metzger and *Hauptmann* [Müller-Rochholz] met us for a drink. It had also become quiet up front, so the evening went very nicely.

Image 32. The town of Kamenz. Remnants of the 7th Guards Mechanized Corps and the 10th Polish Infantry Division attempted to occupy Kamenz as they withdrew north to rejoin the lines of the Soviet 5th Army. A small German garrison of *Volkssturm* and assorted other units defended the town. On 27/28 April the *20.Panzer-Division* advanced into the town and cleared out any remaining Polish or Soviet forces. This represented the furthest advance north achieved by *Panzer-Korps 'GD'* during its counterattack against the 2nd Polish Army. Author's collection.

April 27th

During the morning, a prisoner was taken. I interrogated him. He was a senior sergeant. Blond, blue-eyed and good-looking. A man next to me said, well, how many German women he had done bad things to. Initially, the Russian was very intimidated, but he opened up when I offered him a cigarette. He said that his unit was very broken down and everyone thought that Russia would lose the war. The fighting spirit was consequently bad. Okay, the usual stuff, of which only the opposite could be believed, as shown to us every day anew. The prisoner also said that he was an enemy of the Bolsheviks. He would like to go to the Russian division fighting on the German side. Yeah, that's all chitchat. [AN: the prisoner was referring to the *600.Infanterie-Division (r)* organized with former Red Army prisoners-of-war under the command of General Andrey Vlasov].

There had been a bit of firing for a while on our town. A shell went into the roof of a barn in which *Leutnant* Pietsch and my draftsman were. Pietsch was wounded, and the draftsman died from a piece of shrapnel in his head.

More hard battles broke out near Neschwitz [AN: to the west near Casslau]. The Russians were fiercely holding on at the edge of the town. Well, we suddenly got a report that *Hauptmann* Hunhold was seriously wounded. The commander went forward immediately. It turned out that our artillery from the neighboring sector of *Fallschirm-Panzer-Division 1 'HG'*, assuming that Neschwitz was occupied by the Russians, had fired shots into the town at a group that actually consisted of Hunhold and a few men. That just happened to be the first hit that was right on target. *Hauptmann* Hunhold's entire lower jaw was torn off. The *Division Ia* [Erasmus] was foaming at the mouth and wanted to have all our artillery tubes aimed at the *Fallschirm-Panzer-Division 1 'HG'* command post. He needed some seriously harsh words [to prevent his proposed action].

After 2 hours, *Rittmeister* Sandmeyer, formerly head of a squadron of the *Panzer-Aufklärungs-Abteilung 'BR'*, came into the command post [AN: he replaced *Hauptmann* Hunhold as commander of *II.Bataillon*]. A very active and adventuresome man. He had loaded up his *Krad* with Schnapps. The commander, who was still in front with the battalion, let him come forward immediately. On the road forward, Sandmeyer flipped his *Krad* and the Schnapps broke. Rotten luck!

Drinking in the evening.

Friendly fire is an unfortunate reality in war and no side is immune. By all accounts, however, the conduct of *Fallschirm-Panzer-Division 1 'HG'* during the relief of Bautzen and attack north was highly aggressive and lacked situational awareness. They used incendiary shells in Bautzen and nearly shot the first people they came across in the city before they realized that German civilians were still there. Now, knowing that they were operating in close proximity with neighboring German units, they committed to opening fire first before confirming their targets.

April 28th

In the morning, there were more heavy battles around Neschwitz. The commander went down so he could lead as he saw fit. From the division came a call that released Russian units were skulking around in the rear after having broken out of their pocket. Soon after that, we could hear shots and tank noises behind us. I mobilized the regimental headquarters and anything else still in the town. As soon as I tried to get out the door of my building, it buzzed outside and I thought I was seeing things; there was a T-34 in front of the door. I thought I had been hit. Back inside and grab the *Panzerfaust* on the table. When I was back outside, the tank was going full speed toward Neudorf. Off to the wireless radio so that the soldiers down below could get ready to meet it appropriately. Two of the pursuers in Neschwitz were immediately let loose on Ivan, who went into a streamed out of fear when he took fire. The unease in the rear came back soon.

At noon, I was ordered to the *Division* to get some more orders. The *Division* headquarters was in a big isolated estate. A lovely manor house with big rooms. This was also where the other adjutants were assembled. We found out that the *Division* would be moved to the Dresden/Meissen area in order to be deployed from there. With orders and maps under my arm, I went back to the regiment a half hour later. The march out was supposed to take place that evening. We were supposed to be relieved in this sector by an infantry unit.

When I arrived at the regiment, there was naturally an endless list of things to do in order to set up everything in the short time remaining. I had already ordered the battalion adjutant by telephone to get back to the regiment. The movement was supposed to take place in individual movement groups. Movement could only be done at night. At daybreak, everything that had not yet reached its new home had to be set up to move. The new battalion headquarters, which was moving into our housing, arrived in the afternoon. Only parts of the troops had arrived when we moved out that evening at the time ordered.

We left at 10:00 p.m. I had to lead a movement group while the commander moved on his own. So we separated soon after that. The movement initially went quite well, but shortly after midnight there were continual bottlenecks. I had serious problems in going forward.

April 29th

When it became light, I moved into Domnitz, where quarters were taken in a farmstead. An hour later, the commander was there as well. We fell into a deep sleep in white beds until noon.

In the afternoon, I made a visit to the *II.Bataillon* in Leppersdorf [east of Dresden] and stayed there for a short Schnapps. We did not hear anything from the division or the other people in charge all day, so we had ample quiet. Because the *Stabskompanie* was in the same town as we were, we were able to jazz up our stuff again and I checked the supplies and such. I had things issued to the troops in an orderly manner. In addition, we were able to finally eat in peace again.

Around evening, we rolled out again in order to get to our deployment area. Our forward elements were about a kilometer away from Lomnitz, when an administrative officer from the *Division* came with an order that everyone would remain in quarters, the old orders were revoked, the regiment would prepare for transport by rail, and additional orders would follow. I ordered the movement column to turn around and go back into their old quarters. All of the young men waved at me with a smile. I was also able to determine that there were still some nice girls remaining in our town. Well, that made the joy understandable, of course.

During the night, orders came for railway transport and the work that had to begin immediately.

April 30th

In the morning, we moved to Wachau in order to be closer to our transloading rail station at Dresden-Radebeul. In Wachau, we set up quarters in the palace. The count and the countess were still living in old times although the Russians had already been halfway into the village barely a week before. They wanted to take a few officers, but no enlisted personnel under any circumstances, and, by the way, did we want to do any work in the palace? Good God, the palace was protected as a historical site, after all. It was very difficult to make it clear to the people that we weren't a band of robbers and, second, that we weren't going into the palace because of its beauty but rather because of its central location and the large amount of space. In addition, we weren't planning to dream the war away for three weeks here; we were planning to move away as soon as we could.

The commander and I were underway a lot during the day. The commander held short formations with the troops in order to thank the men for their work and their willingness to sacrifice. I had a lot to do to set up the transportation away. This day that had become hot anyway was spared by pouring rain that soaked me and my travel plans to the bone.

In the evening, I fell into a deep sleep in my bed with white linens on it. I paid another short visit to the division to get a few more railway cars loose and complete my travel plan. *Major* Lau offered me a *Fahnenjunker Unteroffizier*, whom I gladly took on the way back. He was a former 'Brandenburger'.

Panzer-Sturm-Pionier-Bataillon 'BR', the *II.Btl./Jäg.Rgt. 2 'BR'*, and the *Division's* remaining self-propelled guns were positioned a few kilometers to the northwest of *Jägerregiment 1 'BR'*. Here they fought a series of battles with a Soviet Guards Tank Brigade before they received their orders to move toward Dresden for assembly, and rail movement. *Hauptmann* Müller-Rochholz believed that this was the 22nd Guards Tank Brigade, but its identity is not clear. His account of those days of fighting follows.

April 27th

At an extremely early hour, the battalion moved to the Spitzberg area via Neupuschwitz [road]. Doberschütz [southwest of Casslau] was occupied with little enemy resistance. The *I.Btl./Fhj.Gr.Rgt. 1244* was subordinated to the battalion, as were *Sturmgeschütze* from *Panzerjäger-Abteilung 'BR'* (*Leutnant* Freiburger?). Mission: Take Casslau, heavily occupied by the enemy! The battalion sector was from the edge of the forest south and southwest of Casslau (with *I.Btl./Jägerregiment 2 'BR'* on the right) via the northern edge of Doberschütz to the patch of forest north-northwest of Doberschütz. Contact was supposed to be set up to *Kampfgruppe*

Wiethersheim of the *20.Panzer-Division* there.

Reconnaissance showed that Casslau was covered with T-34s, JS-Stalin IIs and the new Russian super-heavy assault guns.

It is not clear what units were in defense at Casslau. According to *FHO* estimates they placed the 2nd, 3rd, 5th Polish Tank Brigades and the 1st Polish Mechanized Brigade of the 1st Polish Tank Corps clearly in the area between Casslau on April 26th. Elements of the 4th Guards Tank Corps had been directed into the area and likely started to arrive by the 27th. Given that the disparate remnants of the 7th Guards Mechanized Corps combined at this stage of the fighting to hold the frontline south of Königswartha, the exact composition of the defensive force is difficult to discern.

From right to left, the following were in the sector: *I.Btl./Fhj.Gr.Rgt. 1244, 1.Pionier-Kompanie, 2.Pionier-Kompanie* (The Reconnaissance Platoon was holding in Doberschütz with a good field of fire to the north.)

The first attack was at 4:00 p.m. The intention: The *1.Pionier-Kompanie* and *I.Btl./Fhj.Gr.Rgt. 1244* would attack from the forest south of Casslau through the orchards and take the buildings on the southern edge, while the *2.Pionier-Kompanie* with its subordinate *Sturmgeschütze* would attack from the sand pits about 700 meters west of Casslau.

What happened: The *Magen-Bataillon (I.Btl./Fhj.Gr.Rgt. 1244)* did not get out of the forest. The *1.Pionier-Kompanie* took two buildings on the southwestern edge of Casslau.

The *2.Pionier-Kompanie*, especially the three *Sturmgeschütze*, did not go forward because several JS-IIs and T-34s kept us down from the western edge of Casslau.

The *1.Pionier-Kompanie* could not hold the two buildings and retreated with losses.

The *Division* designated Casslau as the focus of the *Korps* sector. Casslau had to be taken.

Leutnant Puls arrived to the battalion with about 25 men of the *3.Pionier-Kompanie* that we had not seen since April 16th! They were sent to the vicinity of the command post in Doberschütz as a reserve.

The arrival of the *3.Pionier-Kompanie* was certainly a surprise to *Hauptmann* Müller-Rochholz as these men were last seen shortly after the start of the Soviet attack on April 16th. What odyssey they might have endured behind Soviet lines during the last 20 days can only be guessed at as no account was found that covered the *3.Pionier-Kompanie* specifically. *Hauptmann* Müller-Rochholz's account continues:

The second attack was at 10:00 p.m. The intention: The *Sturmgeschütze* would fire on the northwestern part of Casslau from the west. The *1.Pionier-Kompanie* and the *2.Pionier-Kompanie* would attack the southwestern part. After the *1.Pionier-Kompanie* and the *2.Pionier-Kompanie* broke through, the *I.Btl./Fhj.Gr.Rgt. 1244* would go in from the south.

What happened: The *1.Pionier-Kompanie* and the *2.Pionier-Kompanie* took four or five buildings in the southwest in close combat. The *Sturmgeschütze* (with one platoon of the *2.Pionier-Kompanie*) could not get near because the Russians immediately started firing with at least 10 tanks on the western edge of Casslau. The *I.Btl./Fhj.Gr.Rgt. 1244* did not get out of the forest again. The Russians were too strong. Three tanks were knocked-out among the buildings taken by the *1.Pionier-Kompanie* and the *2.Pionier-Kompanie*. The last *Panzerfaust*, shot by *Hauptmann* Michaelis, fell short of a JS-2 in the darkness. The tank was downright shooting us down in the buildings near them. We had to go back and we had a lot of wounded.

During the night, *Oberstleutnant i.G.* Erasmus arrived and made a recommendation to contact the *20.Panzer-Division* in Nausslitz to determine whether they might like to work with us.

I was there at dawn. The commander was a *Major* Möller.

My recommendation was to do an old-style *Panzer* attack from the northwest, attacking right across the open fields to Casslau—with 'Nashorns' moving north that would fire right in front of the point and stir up the Russians, while we would break through with all the units from the south. The recommendation was accepted.

Hauptmann Müller-Rochholz now prepared for the third attack on Casslau that was scheduled to start at 10:00 a.m. He was called upon to attack the Soviet unit now moving into the area between his positions and those of the *Jägerregiment 1 'BR'* at Neschwitz.

April 28th

Right on time, the first shells fell on the northwestern buildings of Casslau. The *1.Pionier-Kompanie* and the *2.Pionier-Kompanie* attacked from the edge of the forest south of Casslau. Now the men of the *I.Btl./Fhj.Gr.Rgt. 1244* were going with them as well. We were too weak during the first attacks. On our left flank, I advanced in the *SPW* with *Sturmgeschütze* and we gathered in the village with the gutsy people of the *20.Panzer-Division*. The Russians had undoubtedly not been expecting a third attack. In 15 minutes, the village was in our hands. Fifteen Russian tanks were captured, including one super-heavy assault gun, one JS-2 and four T-34s ready for action. Lots of trucks, cars and prisoners. The Russians had an awful lot of dead and were almost all shot down during the flight over the tapered slope to the north and northeast. The officers taken prisoner were sent to the *Division*. We had destroyed the 22nd Guards Tank Brigade. Only three tanks made it out of there.

After the defense was set up, I took a recaptured Steyr-Kübel, which the Russians had already painted green, to the division.

The *Bataillon*—as a regimental group—was given a battery of the *Heeres-Flak-Abteilung 'Voshage'*. Our new sector: from right to left: east of Casslau *I.Btl./Fhj.Gr.Rgt. 1244* adjoining *I.Btl./Jägerregiment 2 (1.Kompanie)* and a battery of the *Heeres-Flak-Abteilung* in Casslau—*2. Kompanie* in Nausslitz. Battalion command post at Doberschütz estate.

3:00 p.m. Russian attack by low-flying aircraft on Doberschütz. A bomb hit the command post. I flew through the door into the next room. The stairwell was completely destroyed. Our command clerk, *Feldwebel* Fischer, was dead. *Leutnant* Puls was wounded very seriously and several men were killed in action as well. *Leutnant* Koch from Nausslitz reported heavy attacks.

There was a panicky feeling. (The Schnapps that *General* Jauer had sent after his call—acknowledgment by the *Heeresgruppe*—had become a pile of broken glass, an entire box that could no longer be split up.)

On to Nausslitz with the Reconnaissance Platoon. The Russians were in and around Nausslitz with many T-34s. There were tanks and antitank guns and grenade launchers coming from the edge of the forest northeast of Nausslitz. With their heavy machine guns, the Russians held the open ground around Nausslitz.

The *General* sent us the *Kampfgruppe* under *Major* von Wiethersheim. Even he considered an attack on Nausslitz with our forces to be senseless. I wanted to at least help the *2.Pionier-Kompanie*.

At 5:00 p.m., the Reconnaissance Platoon and parts of the *2.Pionier-Kompanie*, which had crawled to us in the patch of forest southeast of them through the water ditches from Nausslitz, the remainder of Puls' platoon and von Wiethersheim's *Kampfgruppe* started on the attack on Nausslitz. We remained lying down in the heavy fire. Only the Reconnaissance Platoon and a few men from the *2.Pionier-Kompanie* got to the first buildings on the southeastern edge of Nausslitz. T-34s showed up in bunches. The *Panzerfausts* were soon out of ammunition. The T-34s were running around among us. We went back into the drainage ditches. I personally had to pull a young *Pionier*, who refused to go back because he still had a *Panzerfaust*, back through the ditches.

A courageous, bullheaded kid.

We now went into position on the edge of the forest southeast and south of Nausslitz. Nausslitz was lost.

6:00 p.m. We buried our dead on the Doberschütz estate grounds. *Leutnant* Puls was transported away. He looked very bad.

At about 7:00 p.m., the order came to turn the sector over to the *269.Infanterie-Division*. An advance team (artillery commander, two infantry battalion commanders) reported to Doberschütz. It was turned over during the night.

Those were two hard days and we lost a lot of comrades.

With dawn on April 29th, *Jägerregiment 2 'BR'*, *Panzer-Sturm-Pionier-Bataillon 'BR'* and other units of the *Division* began their movement toward Dresden and embarkation points for rail-movement. No one in the *Division* knew their final destination at that time. The movement south was kept secret. *Hauptmann* Müller-Rochholz recorded that "Even before daybreak, there was movement out of the Doberschütz area. First we went on the highway through Spreefurt to Seifersdorf, than finally to our quarters in Ottendorf-Okrilla. The battalion got three days of rest."

Starting on the evening of April 28th and through April 29th the *4.Panzer-Armee* redeployed its *Panzer* assets along the left flank of its new frontline. *Kampfgruppe 545.Volksgrenadier-Division* took over the sector of *Fallschirm-Panzer-Division 1 'HG'*, the *269.Infanterie Division* took over for *'Brandenburg'* and the *Fallschirm-Panzergrenadier-Division 2 'HG'* replaced the *20.Panzer-Division*. A new counterattack was launched under the command of *Fallschirm-Panzer-Korps 'HG'* north of Radeburg (north east of Dresden) that consisted of the *20.Panzer-Division*, *Fallschirm-Panzer-Division 1 'HG'*, and elements of the newly arrived *2.SS-Panzer-Division 'Das Reich'*. *Kampfgruppe 10.SS-Panzer-Division 'Frundsberg'* (as it was named after surviving its trek from Spremberg through Soviet lines) maintained a defense north of Dresden at Bärwalde for the time being. The Headquarters of *Panzer-Korps 'GD'* moved to Dresden, its final command of the war over, as *Panzergrenadier-Division 'BR'* prepared for its last deployment.

Hauptmann Steidl recorded that heavy artillery fire continued in his sector through the day. "We were glad that we were able to get out of the holes in the forest. Our own losses were substantial." Steidl's account continues:

Monday, April 30th. We went off with the vehicles while it was still night. There was a movement over a long distance. We went toward Dresden. We settled in Leppersdorf to rest on the morning of the 30th. The quarters were good. In the afternoon, we went on to Berbisdorf, a bigger town in the vicinity of Dresden. We were housed in ornate villas and hoped for quiet. But after an hour, we suddenly got an order to move. I laboriously sought out the *Landser* in the city and went with the vehicles in the late afternoon to the trans-loading railway station in Radeburg. Because I wasn't able to do any trans-loading until the next morning, we moved into the buildings in the city to the left and the right. I lay down in a cafe to rest. Where were we going? Our destination was unknown. Hopefully to the west.

Hauptmann Müller-Rochholz's account continues:

Rest. The vehicles, equipment and weapons were put in order. Teams were sent to Dresden to look for personnel released from our battalion, particularly survivors of the *3.Pionier-Kompanie*, at all offices. No luck.

Unteroffizier Seeliger (the fuel NCO for the *Versorgungs-Kompanie*) wanted to look for his family in Dresden. He was the oldest person in the battalion. He and two additional people from

8

8

the company who were at home in Dresden were sent out with the necessary papers. "Anyone who stops them will be prosecuted by *Panzer-Korps 'GD'* in a court martial." I told Seeliger, "If you find Schörner, tell the truth!" They found *Generalfeldmarschall* Schörner on the bridge over the Elbe. He took the papers and issued a certificate of his own that they were permitted to search for their family members in Dresden and the area within 100 kilometers of there and would have to be back at the *Bataillon* on May 1st. Seeliger came back on time, bringing his 15-year-old son to the *Bataillon* and said, "We ran into Schörner and he can be human."

The reference to Schörner is revealing. Here is the commanding general of *H.Gr. Mitte* checking papers of soldiers crossing the Elbe River in the rear area instead of conducting the business of operational level planning and warfare. While this might seem contrived, according to the *H.Gr. Mitte* Chief of Staff *Generalleutnant* Natzmer, *Generalfeldmarschall* Schörner was in fact out inspecting the frontline near Dresden on April 28th.[20]

The German victories between Görlitz and Dresden were remarkable at this stage of the war. *Panzer-Korps 'GD'* was rescued from encirclement and possible destruction for a third time. Bautzen and dozens of German villages and towns were liberated. General Świerczewski's goal of capturing Dresden for Polish glory was thwarted. His 2nd Polish Army suffered heavy losses and the Soviet 7th Guards Mechanized Corps was destroyed as a fighting force. Polish sources, particularly those written during Poland's Communist period, talk about the battle of Bautzen as a Polish "victory". These accounts cite that their forces stopped a German advance north to relieve Berlin.[21] This claim is likely based on two sources. A single wireless transmission from *Generaloberst* Alfred Jodl at 2:30 a.m. on April 25th was sent to *H.Gr. Mitte* that requested the offensive between Dresden and Bautzen continue north to relieve pressure on Berlin.[22] This wireless message was followed up by a phone call the following night from an audibly weak Adolf Hitler. In Appendix B *Generalleutnant* Natzmer describes the telephone call with Hitler in the *Führerbunker* on the night of April 26th/27th where Hitler asked *H.Gr. Mitte* to try to attack north with the *4.Panzer-Armee* toward Berlin. Natzmer informed Hitler that such an attack was simply impossible under the current conditions. There was never an attempt made by *H.Gr. Mitte* to enter directly into the Battle of Berlin. The attacks of the *4.Panzer-Armee* were conducted to destroy as much of the Soviet and Polish forces operating in the area between Rothenburg and Bautzen, prevent Dresden's capture, and stabilize the *4.Panzer-Armee* by reestablishing a continuous front with *Panzer-Korps 'GD'*. Jodl's wireless transmission and Hitler's request by telephone were little more than cries for help in the night at a desperate hour for the doomed Reich capital, hundreds of kilometers to the north. Even Koniev remarked that an attack north to relieve Berlin by *Panzer-Korps 'GD'* "was already not within their strength."[23] Not even Koniev saw such an attack as likely, or even a threat. In the final analysis the 2nd Polish Army was soundly defeated and it failed in both of its operational objectives. The 1st Ukrainian Front set the initial objective for Polish forces to screen the southern flank of Koniev's advance north toward Berlin. They failed to do so and were actually forced north out of their allotted zone of advance into that of the Soviet 5th Guards Army. General Świerczewski modified his assigned objectives and ordered his formations to advance recklessly west to capture Dresden. His effort failed and assured the destruction of the 9th Polish Infantry Division and thousands of casualties. Finally, Koniev had to relieve Świerczewski of command and redirect forces and commanders away from the battle of Berlin to stabilize his southern flank. There can be no doubt that whatever the individual courage of its soldiers and officers displayed on the battlefield, the 2nd Polish Army achieved none of its operational objectives and can hold no claim to thwarting a German

20   Tieke, p. 409.
21   Kaczmarek, p. 58.
22   NARA T78/305/6256419.
23   Koniev, p. 123.

attack north to relieve Berlin.

The tragedy of the 2nd Polish Army is rooted in its lack of training, discipline, and experience necessary to achieve the objectives it was given. Poor coordination between General Świerczewski's forces and the Soviet 52nd Army to the south also provide a decisive factor in the defeat. Koniev's commentary on the fighting, while politicized, reflects these observations with uncommon candor by a Soviet era general.

> Speaking of the first unfortunate period of the battles for us, I have already remarked on the inadequate experience and inadequate "blooding" (i.e., inadequate degree of having been under enemy fire) of the Second Polish Army. To this I must add that the commander of the 52nd Army, General Koroteyev, who, generally speaking, was an aggressive and experienced commander, in the given case did not show adequate concern about his junction with the Poles, which also led to the enemy breaking through on a flank that was known to be threatened.[24]

Koniev later remarked on the "viciousness" of the German attack north, which was possibly an allusion to the heavy losses suffered at the hands of the men of *Panzer-Korps 'GD'* and the *LVII. Panzer-Korps*.

The numbers recorded in the *Luftkommando 6* report on April 27th are telling of the joint Polish/Soviet defeat east of Dresden: "During the battles of the *4.Panzer-Armee* between April 20th-26th the Soviet 94th Infantry Division was destroyed, while the 7th Guards Mechanized Corps, the 1st Polish Tank Corps, the 16th Tank Brigade, the 5th, 7th, and 8th Polish and 254th Soviet Infantry Divisions were heavily defeated. 355 enemy tanks were destroyed, 320 guns of all calibers were destroyed or captured, and approximately 7,000 enemy were killed and 800 taken prisoner."[25] This German wartime assessment was incredibly accurate, if not conservative in its appraisal of enemy losses. As previously reported Lieutenant-General Korchagin's 7th Guards Mechanized Corps lost some 3,500 men and between 80%-90% of their armor. Two additional Soviet divisions, the 254th and 294th were destroyed totaling thousands of additional casualties. Polish sources cite losses for the 2nd Army as 4,902 killed, 2,798 missing, and 10,532 wounded totaling some 20% of their army. 57% of their tank force was lost (over 200 tanks and assault guns were destroyed or captured), and 20% of its artillery assets (over 120 artillery and mortars were destroyed or captured). The 2nd Polish Army's combat debut was disastrous. Infantry fought without the benefit of any combined arms from its artillery and tanks, while the artillery and tanks operated independently without infantry support.[26] The command staff failed its soldiers in the field. The desire to capture Dresden, motivated more by political or even patriotic goals of General Świerczewski, failed and cost him dearly. The combat debut of the 2nd Polish Army can be considered the worst Polish military defeat during the war since 1939. The Soviet advance south did not resume until after the Battle of Berlin was over and 48 hours before the Third Reich capitulated. Dresden was ultimately occupied by Soviet and not Polish army units.

What is remarkable is that this last German operational victory of the war was arguably of Koniev's own making. The lack of coordination between Koniev and Zhukov during the Vistula-Oder Strategic Offensive Operation allowed the combined remnants of *Panzer-Korps 'GD'* and the *4.Panzer-Armee* to escape west instead of being destroyed in the rear of their combined Fronts back in January. Koniev tried to dismiss the fact that he made no concerted effort to destroy these formations by stating they were defeated in detail, yet he admits that they caused him serious concern:

> Having concentrated in the approaches to the city of Kielce, the Germans fought stubbornly,

---

24   Ibid, p. 126.
25   Von Ahlfen, pp. 204-10.
26   Grzelak et all, p. 279.

and this at first slowed down the rate of advance of Gordov's 3rd Guards Army and Pukhov's 13th Army.

Having received a report of this, we, without losing time, turned the 4th Tank Army of Lelyushenko that was in motion, directing it to by-pass the city of Kielce from the southwest. As a result of this maneuver on the fourth day of the offensive, 15 January, the city of Kielce was taken, and a great part of the German troops resisting in the approaches to it were defeated, and their survivors were pushed into the forests north of Kielce.

Later on the remains of these troops [*Gruppe Nehring*], having joined other groupings [*Gruppe von Saucken*], retreating under the pressure from the First Belorussian Front, combined into one quite large grouping, consisting of several divisions. This grouping remained deep in our rear, pressed between the flanks of the First Ukrainian and First Belorussian fronts. *A* characteristic features of the Vistula-Oder operation, and even of the last period of the war in general, was noted in this. We already were not worried about creating a double front—inner and outer—around each surrounded enemy grouping in spite of everything. We considered—and considered correctly—that if the advance in depth was developed at an adequately fast rate, these groupings of the enemy remaining in our rear were of no danger to us. They would be defeated and destroyed in some way or other by the second echelons of our troops.

Thus, in the final analysis, it also occurred with this large grouping [*Gruppe Nehring* and *von Saucken*], which included several divisions, about which I have spoken. It twice suffered a defeat from us in the rear, under attacks from units of our Front and the First Belorussian Front, and twice after the battles sought ways to get out of the encirclement, then, half-scattered, these troops went in individual groups to the southwest through the forests, behind our troops, and finally were destroyed utterly in small skirmishes.[27]

Gruppe Nehring and *Panzer-Korps 'GD'* were not destroyed by Koniev. They were not even defeated in the sense that once their withdrawal west began they were able to out maneuver Koniev's forces and deflect all attempts at stopping their movement. In the end both formations reached German lines relatively intact. The depleted units that reached German lines were rebuilt by the *Ersatzheer* in March and April. Their survival was due to a large measure to the poor operational coordination between Zhukov and Koniev as well as Koniev's seemingly dismissive approach to cut off German formations. These once cut off formations later delivered a significant defeat to his forces and also to those of the 2nd Polish Army. The efforts of *Panzer-Korps 'GD'* brought the establishment of a solid frontline across the now north facing *4.Panzer-Armee* by April 30th. This defensive line was held until the start of Koniev's Prague Offensive a week later, the day before final surrender of Nazi Germany. What the operational impact on the battlefield might have been if Koniev and Zhukov had destroyed *Panzer-Korps 'GD'* and the bulk of the *4.Panzer-Armee* when the opportunity was presented during the Vistula-Oder Strategic Offensive cannot be precisely known. All that can be said is that the removal of some 100,000 German soldiers from the battlefield—the equivalent of 10-12 divisions in 1945— would have had a measurable effect on the war's length.

---

27   Koniev, p. 25.

19

The End in Czechoslovakia, May–June

(Reference Maps 100, 101, 102, 103, and 104)

The strategic situation at the end of April and beginning of May was fluid. Berlin had fallen. U.S. Forces had advanced into the Soviet postwar zone of occupation in both southern Germany and western Czechoslovakia, where they were informed by the Soviets to "hold".[1] Stalin wanted to ensure a postwar Czechoslovakia squarely in his Communist sphere of influence and Supreme Allied Commander General Dwight D. Eisenhower did not want to take any more risks than required in the final days of the war.[2] Stalin's political goal was to capture the capital of Prague and ensure he had as many Soviet forces within the country as possible at the time of the German capitulation to ensure there was no question of control.[3] Elements of the U.S. 4th Armored Division and 2nd Infantry Division had advanced from Plzen to the outskirts of Prague. Their main force was less than a two-hour drive from the city when word of a ceasefire reached their lines on May 7th. They were subsequently ordered to withdraw in keeping with Soviet wishes.[4] Stalin ordered Koniev to prepare for a general offensive south to begin on May 7th. Czechs were already organizing into armed bands. Resistance against the Germans, however, initially started as simple defiance that included covert acts of sabotage along the railway lines and roads to impeded German movement. Then an open revolt occurred in Prague and other locations. In Prague in particular, the situation bordered on chaos. Armed Czech civilians rose up on May 5th and occupied key sites throughout the city as they expected the imminent arrival of U.S. Forces. Open battles began in the city with German forces, particularly the *SS*, which resulted in horrific atrocities among both sides. The 1st Division of the Russian Liberation Army (known as ROA from *Russkaya Osvoboditel'naya Armiya*) established in 1944 under the command of the former Soviet General Andrey Vlasov, joined forces with the Czech

---

1   Rona Mendelsohn, *Liberation*, (U.S Embassy: Prague, 2010), p. 17. According to Erickson, Eisenhower initially gave the green light to plan for an advance to Prague. When this intent was communicated to Koniev he responded that no assistance was necessary and not desired. John Erickson, *The Road to Berlin* (Yale University Press: New Haven, 1999), p. 633-34.

2   According to Mendelsohn "Eisenhower was strict in ordering Bradley to stop Patton. On May 4th, Eisenhower had spoken to General Alexei Antonov, Chief of Staff of the Soviet Army, suggesting that after the Third Army had occupied Pilsen it be allowed to move to the western suburbs of Prague. Eisenhower waited for Antonov's reply. Antonov rejected the plan, urging Eisenhower "not to move the Allied Forces in Czechoslovakia east of the originally intended line" — to avoid, in his words, "a possible confusion of forces." Eisenhower agreed to Antonov's proposition and now ordered Bradley to inform Patton that under no circumstances was he to go beyond the Karlovy Vary-Pilsen-České Budějovice line. In addition, the city of Prague was not to be touched", p. 14. It should be noted that the Third Army had reached the German-Czech border on April 25th. Patton's offensive into Czechoslovakia did not commence until about May 5th/6th. For almost 10 days his forces were paused, along with most of the U.S. Army along the pre-determined demarcation line between the Western Allies and the Soviets. Had General Patton been given the authority in April to continue his offensive, there is no telling how far into Czechoslovakia he would have advanced and *H.Gr. Mitte* would likely have evaporated into pockets of surrendering men all along the frontline.

3   Erickson, pp. 625-30.

4   According to one U.S. veteran: "As we drove around the outskirts of Prague, the whole goddam Nazi Army came up out of nowhere. They were screaming, howling, crying, laughing ... . During the week, 80,000 Germans attempted to give themselves up, and we had to take them, all of them." Mendelsohn, p. 16.

Image 33. Views of the picturesque city of Olmütz (Olomouc), Czechoslovakia where *Panzergrenadier-Division 'BR'* conducted its final defense against Soviet forces during World War II. It was through Olmütz that the remnants of the *1.Panzer-Armee* withdrew to avoid being surrounded and cut off by Soviet forces of the 4th Ukrainian Front. Sharp street fighting occurred in early May between elements of *'Brandenburg'* and Soviet forces. Author's collection.

partisans against their former German allies. Their goal was to gain favor with the U.S. Forces they expected to advance from Plzen. U.S. Forces, however, never came. With the political situation in Czechoslovakia now escalating, Stalin ordered Koniev to commence his offensive a day earlier, on May 6th. The Offensive, officially known as the Prague Strategic Offensive Operation, lasted six days from May 6th-11th and had two military objectives: capture Prague and destroy *H.Gr. Mitte*.

Generalfeldmarschall Schörner was holding a large expanse of territory across most of southern Germany and Czechoslovakia at the end of April. According to Natzmer, his Chief of Staff, Schörner pursued separate and competing goals. Based on conversations with the neighboring *H.Gr. Süd* he was under the allusion that the territory he controlled could be used in negotiations to ensure his forces capitulated to the Western Allies and not the Soviets. At the same time he devised a plan known as Operation *Blumen* (Flower) where each of his armies would slowly withdrew toward the west in an organized fashion. His efforts were likely influenced by *Generalfeldmarschall* Albert Kesselring's independent surrender of the remaining German forces in Northern Italy to the Western Allies on May 2nd.

Schörner's main concern remained his overextended eastern flank. Already on April 30th elements of the Soviet 4th Ukrainian Front launched attacks against the *XI.Armee-Korps* along the *1.Panzer-Armee's* northern flank in the direction of Neu Titschen. Further southwest, elements of the 2nd Ukrainian Front pushed against the *XXIV.Armee-Korps* and *XXIX.Armee-Korps* toward Prosznitz, followed by Olmütz (Olomouc). A successful Soviet offensive meant that the *1.Panzer-Armee* would be cut off and unable to continue its withdrawal west. The protection of the Mährisch Ostrau industrial region now grew in significance as it was the last source of ammunition and other industrial output

Image 34. Prague, 9 May. This press photo was taken on the morning of 9 May from behind the Monument of St. Wenceslas looking northwest toward Wencelaus Square as the first armor elements of the Soviet 1st Ukrainian Front arrived in the city. Around the square is the debris of recent fighting caused during the Czech revolt that started on 5 May. In the foreground are members of the Czech partisans wearing captured German steel helmets. Photo by H. Fritsche. Author's collection.

to *H.Gr. Mitte*. With the death of Adolf Hitler, Schörner instructed Natzmer to fly north to Mürwik and meet with the new Reich *Führer*, *Großadmiral* Karl Dönitz as well as *Feldmarschall* Wilhelm Keitel and *Generaloberst* Alfred Jodl to request that no ceasefire begins until May 18th. He needed time to allow the rest of *H.Gr. Mitte* to withdrawal west. An immediate ceasefire left his soldiers well beyond the reach of U.S. Forces. There were no assurances given to Natzmer during the meeting. Back in *H.Gr. Mitte* everything was being done to prevent the *1.Panzer-Armee* from being cut off. This amounted to the deployment of the newly formed *10.Fallschirmjäger-Division* to the threatened southern sector around the *XXIV.Armee-Korps*, as well as the *8.Panzer-Division* and *Panzergrenadier-Division 'Brandenburg'* to Olmütz where they were ordered to hold the east-west withdrawal route open as long as possible.

Deployment to Czechoslovakia, May 1st-6th

Panzergrenadier-Division 'BR' shifted back to *Panzer-Korps 'GD'* control after the fighting around Bautzen, likely by April 26th. The *Panzer-Korps 'GD'* command post was established at Moritzburg Palace near Dresden, while the headquarters of *Panzergrenadier-Division 'BR'* was nearby in Bärnsdorf. However, this reunion of commands was short-lived. All elements of the *Division* were trans-loaded onto rail cars except for attached *Pionier-Bataillon 500 'GD'* that returned back to *Korps* control, *Panzer-Artillerie-Regiment 'BR'*, *Feld-Ersatz-Bataillon 'BR'* (if it was not disbanded at this point and its remaining cadre absorbed into the combat battalions) and *Korps-Sanitäts-Kompanie 'GD'*. They all remained behind with the *Korps* HQ.

A new *Heeresgruppe* order was received at *Division* headquarters on April 30th stating that

Panzergrenadier-Division 'BR' was to deploy by rail as quickly as possible to the vicinity of Olmütz in Czechoslovakia. No archival documents have been identified to date that can provide insight into this order from *H.Gr. Mitte*. What is known is that Olmütz was both a central transportation hub that had to remain open to allow the *1.Panzer-Armee* to withdraw west from the area of the eastern Czechoslovakia and the Carpathian Mountains, and also a gateway to the remaining industrial region under German control (see Appendix C). The Soviets were closing in from the north and the South, and it was decided that *'Brandenburg'* must rapidly deploy hundreds of kilometers to the southeast in response. In its current area of deployment near Dresden the *Division* was only a few hours' drive from the lines of U.S. Forces where a relatively easy surrender and end to World War II could be secured. Now they prepared to travel hundreds of kilometers further east where they would be all but surrounded by the Red Army.

In the early morning of May 1st the *Division* units moved to the north of Dresden, where they began transloading onto trains for their deployment by rail. During the morning the death of their *Führer*, Adolf Hitler, was announced over the radio. Dr. Braune was waiting with *Heeres-Flak-Abteilung 'BR'* to be loaded onto their trains when he heard the news of Hitler's death:

> *Heeres-Flak-Abteilung* in Ottendorf-Okrilla. Calm.
> News came that Hitler had died!
> The commander of the *Heeres-Flak-Abteilung 'BR'*, *Major* Voshage, mustered his troops and announced Hitler's death. The oath administered under him would be transferred to his successor, *Grossadmiral* Dönitz! "We will continue to fight as long as it is demanded of us!" To ourselves, we all thought about it. Our *Division* was still intact; it would continue to fight except for perhaps a few individuals. But the others?
>
> At about 4:00 p.m., an order went to the *Heeres-Flak-Abteilung 'BR'* to go to the transloading railway station. Transloading was supposed to be at midnight in Radeburg near Dresden. Transloading would occur on the night of May 2nd/3rd, 1945.
>
> The *Panzergrenadier-Division 'BR'* would be loaded up 24/7 in Dresden (suburb: Klotzsche) in order to move to Olmütz, Czechoslovakia (via Bautzen, Görlitz, Lauban and Hirschberg). The *Ib*, *Major* Spaeter, went ahead by car. The *Ia*, wounded, remained with the transports, and the *Division* commander was going along in a vehicle next to the railway line.

Sturmgeschütz-Artillerie-Brigade 'GD' received a full complement of *Jagdpanzers* while *Panzerjäger-Abteilung 'BR'* was reorganized and received a shipment of *Sturmgeschütze* before their respective deployments. Even this late in the war the *Ersatzheer* continued to function without interruption. The *1.Panzerjäger-Kompanie* and *2. Panzerjäger-Kompanie* of *Panzerjäger-Abteilung 'BR'* were both outfitted with *Sturmgeschütze* while the *3. Panzerjäger-Kompanie* received tractor drawn *PAK*. The *3. Panzerjäger-Kompanie* commander, *Oberleutnant* Meier (also known as "monocle Meier") went mysteriously missing before the rail movement. Both units were rail loaded and rolled south shortly after both *Jägerregiments* on May 1st.

Hauptmann Steidl was already on the train with his battalion rolling south when news of Hitler's death reached him. Here were his thoughts during the train ride:

> Tuesday, May 1st: Transloading began in the early morning. It went quickly and in the morning, the first transport train was moving east. Okay. But where? There was now a big "funnel" in the protectorate; Ivan was pressing from all sides. During the trip, I found out on the radio in the morning that our *Führer* had died in Berlin. All of us knew what that meant for us. Should we surrender for that reason like miserable cowards after years of struggle against forces many times our size? No! And again no! Now more than ever, they shouldn't have it easy with us old hands.

We would prove that.

It should be noted that the death of Adolf Hitler meant little to the men of the *Division* at this point in the war. It did not alter their strategic prospect of an unconditional surrender or better their tactical situation opposite the Red Army.

Steidl's train passed to the east of Prague. The country was split under Nazi rule and the half that contained Prague was known as the Protectorate of Bohemia-Moravia. Steidl likely recorded what he had heard, as there is no indication that he witnessed any of the following events he reported. He notes that the Czech revolt in Prague began on May 1st/2nd. But this is not correct. The revolt began a few days later. The Czechs, like all Slavs, were considered racially inferior by their Nazi masters. Resentment to the Nazi occupation had been simmering across the country since 1938. This was certainly true within the capital where many viewed the occupation in the long vein of history going back to the 1600s when the Bohemian nobility was decisively defeated in the battle of White Mountain by the armies of Holy Roman Emperor Ferdinand II. In Prague, a city where Germans had lived in the tens of thousands even before the war, anti-German feelings had reached a boiling point and mob rule took control. Starting on May 5th the mood of Czechs in Prague changed like the flip of a light switch and without notice. Czech national flags were waved in all quarters. People surged into the streets yelling "Death to the Germans! Death to all Germans! Death to all occupiers!" while German civilians went about their daily business, and others walked in the open wearing their *SS* and *Heer* uniforms. Almost everyone in the city, it would seem, took up arms against anyone that spoke German or looked German, whether they were actually a German or not. No one was spared vicious mob vengeance, especially not the city's long-standing German citizens who lived and worked there since the turn of the Century.[5] As noted above, the 1st ROA Division of General Vlasov initially joined the Czechs in taking control of vital parts of the city. When they realized that U.S. Forces would not advance to the Czech capital, they switched sides and entered into an uneasy truce with the German forces. On May 8th both the Czechs and German forces entered into a loose cease-fire that allowed the *Wehrmacht* and *SS* to start an evacuation of the city in an effort to get back to German lines. Outside the capital armed bands of Czech partisans sprouted across the countryside where they attempted to thwart all German movements by rail or road. We continue with Steidl's account:

May 1st/2nd. In Prague a revolt of the Czechs. Only Lazarett 14, which was Swiss property, was spared. The Swiss also sent a committee that took care of food and the wounded.

Everything else that occurred in Prague was terrible.

SS men and *SS* female auxiliaries were tied together naked, horribly whipped and thrown into the Moldau.

Others had their Achilles tendons cut with axes and sharp knives. The creeping people were administered the most severe tortures.

... . .

Wednesday, May 2nd. We rolled through Bohemia, steadfastly to the east. Our expressions were earnest; we expected the hardest battles and we were aware that it could not last much longer. The fall of Berlin was announced on the radio. *Grossadmiral* Dönitz had taken over command of the German *Wehrmacht* that was still fighting.

We went to Olmütz via Glatz (Kłodzko). We got unloaded in the evening in the pouring rain. Heavy fire roared from the nearby front. While we were unloading, I received my deployment orders and was supposed to occupy my position/fill in a gap in the front while it was still dark. I moved out with motorized assets before midnight. After a lot of wrong turns, I reached the edge of the city and went off into the unknown darkness. Shortly before my deployment location, I

5   Macdonogh, pp. 130-38.

moved into a dugout until dawn. We were wet to the bone. Our mood was not good. There were loud rumors about the end of the war.

Elements of *Jägerregiment 2 'BR'* were among the first combat units to arrive in Olmütz. The men of the battalion had little knowledge of the area or the overall tactical situation. As in so many situations in the past five months, they followed their orders to prepare a defense against a possible Soviet attack.

Jägerregiment 2 'BR' was followed by *Jägerregiment 1 'BR'*. *Leutnant* Grosser's account starts on May 1st. He made no mention of the *Führer's* death.

In the morning, the last preparations for the transport were made. As far as I could determine, we were supposed to go to Olmütz. We moved in three transports.

In the afternoon, we went to the loading ramp in Radebeul. Transloading took place right away. It initially went smoothly, but then there was a shortage of railway cars, so we were not ready until after midnight.

The commander and I went into a Sanka that the doctor had graciously provided to us.

May 2nd. In the early morning, we finally got a locomotive and shortly after that went into Bohemia to face a new fate. The trip went on without any disturbance from the air. There was a lot of sleeping and we played a lot of Skat and *Doppelkopf*. In addition, there was some serious poker playing.

May 4th. Once we had to go a long ways back; we were already in the Protectorate because we had been given bad directions.

Finally on May 4th, we couldn't go any further forward and we stayed stuck for hours at a railway station. The stretch was stopped up. Czech railway workers were directing the traffic, knowing that the Russians were in the vicinity and seeing their chance. They clearly wanted to mess everything up. To some extent, the railway telephones were also destroyed. There were German field railway personnel there, but they did not know how to push their way through. So I then got onto a handcar with two men and went off. At the next railway station, the first Czech one, it was really crazy, but the Czech railway workers spoke no German, so all our questions and talking was for naught. I got back onto my unique vehicle and went further on. We finally managed to get through back to our transport.

Grosser's regiment was turned out by Czech rail workers who attempted to misdirect the movement of *'Brandenburg'* trains as they rolled south. A trip that should have taken a single day turned into three.

Dr. Braune recounts the railway trip of the *Heeres-Flak-Abteilung 'BR'* that began on May 1st.

At about 3:00 a.m., I woke up when Clemens Koch was taking the vehicle from the ramp onto the trolley. It was damned cold outside; the blooms on the fruit trees were frozen everywhere. In order to avoid it, we did a lot of sleeping. At 11:00 a.m., the train was in the vicinity of Pirna with us in it, and about noon, it was south of Bautzen. It was snowing, raining and hailing, really messed up. We attempted to heat the inside of the ambulance with a soldering iron, but that was only successful for a short period. Because we had an entire car full of things to eat, we had no emergency in this regard. At about 5:30 p.m., I finally fell asleep; we were in Zittau. The weather improved, so the trip from Zittau to Görlitz could be done in the open. The radio reported the fall of Lübeck, the place I had chosen as my home, without heavy battles. The area was again very nice; my general impression of East Saxony, the Upper Lausitz and western Lower Silesia was an area pretty as a picture, pretty girls and a nightmarish dialect.

The transport train remained in the railway station in Görlitz until about 10:00 p.m. Then we went on. Starting at 10:30 p.m., we went back to sleep.

May 4th. We heard that Hamburg fell without a fight. It was not until 2:00 p.m. that the train set off again toward Glatz. The area was very pretty. During the trip, the adjutant came to us after exercising. He reported how dire the general situation was. The western front had collapsed, and the eastern front was here. There were still units fighting in Mecklenburg and the *Heeresgruppe Mitte* in Bohemia. There the Russians had broken through the Moravian Gate and threatened Olmütz. Supposedly the Western powers did not take eastern front soldiers as prisoners; they sent them back to the Russians. It was certain that things would only last a few days more. It was dumb that we had to go so far south.

Outside it was somewhat warmer; there was brand new snow on the Altvater.

In the evening, we reached Mittelwalde (Międzylesie). We stayed there with other *Division* transports next to us for a very long time. Next to us was the *Verwaltungs-Kompanie*. I inherited a big basket of sausage from the butchers, something we had been lacking in our hell.

The fabled Czech partisans who were supposed to be endangering the transports reached us. The commander ordered that the *Vierling* (4 barreled, 20mm anti-aircraft gun) be shown clearly; it would be a shame if it were let loose. Just when I wanted to go to sleep, further on we went.

Dr. Braune's reaction to the events along the Western Front at the time was muted. His home town was occupied without a serious battle, he notes, gaining some comfort from that. The rumor that the Western Allies will turn over to the Soviets all German soldiers who surrender to them, clearly induced concern among many of the men. They knew the Western Front had collapsed and that the war could not last much longer. But at the time they simply had no incentive to surrender. Their only recourse was to continue to fight and hope that senior leadership might navigate their way through the terms of unconditional surrender into a U.S. prisoner-of-war-camp.

Hauptmann Müller-Rochholz's *Panzer-Sturm-Pionier-Bataillon 'BR'* left later than the other units of the *Division*. Unfortunately this delay cost them dearly.

May 2nd. *General* Schulte-Heuthaus visited us in Ottendorf-Okrilla. The battalion was supposed to be the last unit (except for supply units) to be loaded so that the calm order could be maintained. (On May 3rd, it turned out that this was a Trojan horse because the Russians had already made their way south from Königsbrück. The Reconnaissance Platoon was again being used all the time.)

Noon: The battalion arrived in the friction plate factory south of Ottendorf-Okrilla. The *Führer* is dead; *Grossadmiral* Dönitz is his successor. We will not swear a new oath. We are a sworn-out bunch! The war can't last much longer. There will be chaos. During these days we want to remain true to ourselves and live through our fate until the end. The battalion's spirit, our comradeship and our dead obligate us to do that. Our shield must remain clean until the last moment. No one is leaving! All of the battles have proven that we will not be defeated if we stand together as one. That is how it will remain until the last order!

Some *Panzerjagdkommandos*—all young guys, mostly *Hitlerjugend*—asked permission to join us. They stayed with the battalion.

May 3rd/4th. Transloading in the Dresden area became more and more questionable. While the *1.Pionier-Kompanie* was already providing security to the north of the Ottendorf-Okrilla area, we were attempting to get railcars from all the railway stations in Dresden. It was often hard to do that.

The *Versorgungs-Kompanie* and the *2.Pionier-Kompanie* were moved by motor vehicle to Tetschen-Bodenbach. (Petrol was found in the friction plate plant and all the gas tanks were filled.) Then we had the first train together and we sent it to Tetschen-Bodenbach. The two *Pionier-Kompanien* were transloaded and they left. If only we knew where the *Division* had gone. We were put on a rail car with the headquarters and the *1.Pionier-Kompanie*. With a lot of effort, the second train was put together—pistols had to be used. On May 5th or 6th, the remainder of the battalion moved out. During the trip, we had contact with Graf Egloffstein on multiple occasions.

There was a longer stop in Glatz, with the entire trip being a huge stroll. It seems that the Czech railway workers were already sabotaging things. Glatz: *Oberarzt* Dr. Perkhoff was sent with all the amphibious vehicles to the food warehouse there and was supposed to follow the train by vehicle and then be loaded again. It worked. At least we had reserves of food. The amphibious vehicles were reloaded at a small railway station south of Glatz (only by hand).

At every stop, an effort was made to find out the destination of our transport from the railway personnel. It didn't work. Our radio operators attempted continually to reach the *Division*. That didn't work either. Instead, we heard Prague I and Prague II, radio stations that contradicted each other.

Just 5 kilometers to the north of the transloading platforms in Ottendorf-Okrilla units of the Soviet 4th Guards Tank Corps started to push south toward Dresden from Königsbrück. Clearly many German workers and civilians in the area knew the war was all but over. Many rail workers likely wanted an opportunity to get out of the area before the Soviets arrived and were not too happy to have to remain and complete the transloading of *'Brandenburg'*. According to Müller-Rochholz's comments there was a breakdown among the German rail workers sometime around May 3rd or May 4th as he had to use the threat of violence as a means of motivation ("pistols had to be used"). The contradictions in the Prague Radio I and II station broadcasts were caused by the fact that the Czechs that revolted had acquired one radio with the help of Vlasow's troops, while the *SS* remained in control of the other.

On the 7th, there were already units moving on the roads next to the railway to the north and west. Some of the *Landser* had put on civilian clothing and top hats and told us that we were crazy to still be going off to deployment singing. Our mood was quite good. We definitely wanted to get to our *Division* in this last phase.

During the night of May 7th/8th we reached Hannsdorf (Hanušovice) and the railway personnel refused to go any further. The next railway station was in the hands of the Russians. There was still a train going west from Hannsdorf with railway personnel. That was the end of the war for the railway.

The last unit of the *Division* to be transloaded was *Fahrschwadron 'BR'* on May 4th/5th. The transloading officer, *Oberveterinar* Dr. Heln, was provided with three transport trains by the *Reichsbahn*. The schedule was as follows:

1st transport: *1.Schwadron* Departure at 10:00 p.m.
2nd transport: *2.Schwadron*. Departure at 2:00 a.m.
3rd transport: Headquarters and *3.Schwadron*. Departure at 8:00 a.m.

SS-Sturmbannführer Graf von Egloffstein recounts the initial departure of *Fahrschwadron 'BR'*:

It was clear that our *Division* would no longer be moved into the eastern part of Bohemia. Our *Pioniers* were loaded as the next-to-last unit, then the *1.Schwadron* and then half of the

2.Schwadron of the *Fahrschwadron* and, as the last *'Brandenburg'* unit, the other half of the *2.Schwadron*, the *3.Schwadron* and the *Stab-Schwadron* of our *Abteilung*. Transport was from Dresden-Klotzsche via Neustadt, Zittau, Görlitz, Hirschberg, Glatz and Mittelwalde into the area of Grulich (Králíky), Bohemia. Our train was hit by three shells in Görlitz, but they did not cause any damage. They were the only three shells fired into the city of Görlitz. We were indeed the last transport that rolled over the viaduct over the Neiße in Görlitz. We had radio contact with our *Pioneers* one day more. Then it was gone. We didn't even have any more contact with our *Schwadrons* (that is, with the *3.Schwadron* and half of the *2.Schwadron*).

Separated from the rest of the *Fahrschwadron 'BR'*, the train carrying part of the *2.Schwadron* and all of the *3.Schwadron* never made it out of Germany. The train traveled via Görlitz, Hirschberg and Mittelwalde until the former border of the Protectorate of Moravia (Czechoslovakia) was reached. Then the train was turned around and made a trip back to just outside of Mittelwalde Międzylesie, where there were already white flags flying. Without any guidance from the *Division*, the men decided to make their way west. Their exact fate is unknown, but the men were suspected of making their way to U.S. lines.

Defense of Olmütz (Olomouc), May 5th-8th

As the last units of *Panzergrenadier-Division 'BR'* continued to load onto trains north of Dresden, the first units of the *Division* unloaded at Olmütz and headed into battle. The trains had taken different routes depending on when they left and how crafty the Czech rail workers were in mid-directing them. In Olmütz the *Division* was subordinated to the *XLIX.Gebirgs-Armee-Korps* under the command of *General der Gebirgstruppe* Karl von Le Suire. The *Korps* was defending the Mährisch Ostrau industrial region, just to the east of Olmütz.

Major Spaeter arrived by auto first in Olmütz with an advance party to setup a receiving station for the *Division*. He established contact with neighboring units in the vicinity of the city. The *Ia*, *Oberstleutnant i.G.* Erasmus, who was wounded by a piece of shrapnel during the fighting around Bautzen, boarded a later a train and had not yet arrived. *General* Schulte-Heuthaus was also still in transit. *Major* Spaeter, acting as the *Division* commander, the *Ia* and the *Ib*, conducted the unloading and deployment of the first units that arrived. His immediate mission was to provide security for the westward transit of German troops of the *1.Panzer-Armee* from the Mährisch-Ostrau area. All evidence suggests that he received almost no guidance from his *Korps* command or *H.Gr. Mitte*. *Panzergrenadier-Division 'BR'* was operating largely on its own, but from local unit liaison it was clear the Soviets were pushing from the south and that Olmütz was on the frontline.

This was indeed a desperate deployment. While the rest of the Reich was surrendering, here the men of *'Brandenburg'* deployed to hold a defensive line and allow other German units a chance to withdraw west in the hope of escaping Soviet captivity. Spaeter captured the mood: "It was also not courage that impelled a man to get up and carry on; it was simply desperation, a desire to somehow get away from this inferno, to find a place where his life was not in danger."[6] The veterans continued to stay together and fight while the new recruits that filled their ranks in March and early April began to disappear in small groups. Why the majority of the men of *'Brandenburg'* continued to stay together was a question Spaeter wrestled to answer in the 1950s when we wrote his history. "No one asked why—it really didn't matter. They fought, carrying those who wavered with them, held the positions—and remained together, one way or another" Spaeter opined.[7]

The order for the *1.Panzer-Armee* to withdrawal from its position east of Olmütz was given back on May 2nd/3rd by Schörner before *'Brandenburg'* arrived. The Soviets detected the westward

---

6   Spaeter, *The History of Panzerkorps Großdeutschland, Volume 3*, p. 482.
7   Ibid., p. 483.

movement and launched an attack to take the city from the south and cut off the *1.Panzer-Armee*. It was still not clear decades after the war why *Panzergrenadier-Division 'BR'* was ordered to this position and not some other division. Spaeter raised this question in his published history, believing that this decision might have rested in the desires of *H.Gr. Mitte's* Chief of Staff, *Generalleutnant* Oldwig von Natzmer. Seventy years after the war the decision still remains obfuscated by the veils of time.

The trains carrying *Jägerregiment 2 'BR'* under the command of *Oberstleutnant* Oesterwitz arrived at their destination ahead of the rest of the *Division* and Spaeter quickly ordered them deployed to the town of Tscheltzitschitz (Čelčice) south of Olmütz. This was a small town on the north-south rail line to the southeast of Prosznitz (Prostějov). The men moved forward along muddy roads, receiving constant fire by Soviet mortars and artillery. As Steidl recalled: "With great losses, we reached and occupied the town of Tscheltzitschitz. The Russians had just gotten there in superior numbers and were slogging away into the town. Ceaseless attacks were repelled with some effort." Fighting continued around the town through May 4th. By the end of the day the Soviets finally broke through the defenses of the *I.Bataillon* on their eastern flank, forcing them to withdraw back to Tschehowitz (Čehovice) along the rail line.

Panzer-Aufklärungs-Abteilung 'BR' was among the next units to arrive. Spaeter deployed them to the north of Olmütz. Located at the *Division* HQ on site were only the radio platoon, and the *O2*. On May 5th the trains carrying *Heeres-Flak-Abteilung 'BR'* finally arrived. Soon after, the first trains carrying *Jägerregiment 1 'BR'* reached Stefanau (Štěpánov). The offloading platforms in Olmütz had just been destroyed by Soviet shell fire and no more off-loading could occur in the city. *Jägerregiment 1 'BR'* deployed along a 15 kilometer stretch of rail-line that ran from Olmütz-Stefanau-Hohenstadt. *Major* Bansen, set up his command post near Nakel and met with the arriving *Jagdpanzers* of *Sturmgeschütz-Artillerie-Brigade 'GD'*. The *Division* commander and *Ia* finally arrived on May 5th and the *Division* headquarters began to resume normal staff functions. According to Spaeter there were only 3,000 *'Brandenburgers'* that deployed into Czechoslovakia.

Generalfeldmarschall Schörner's last order to the *Heeresgruppe* was issued on May 5th.

OB H.Gr. Mitte   5 May 1945
Soldiers of *Heeresgruppe Mitte*!
After six years of bitter struggle the superior strength of our enemy has succeeded in bringing about the fall of one part of our fronts. The front held by the southern army groups on the Eastern Front alone still stands unbroken. This is due to your bravery and steadfastness.

The war is approaching its end In keeping with the order from the Führer's chosen head of state and supreme commander of the German armed services, Grossadmiral Dönitz, we are to fight on until the most valuable German people have been saved.

After completing this mission it is my intention to send you, my soldiers, back to the homeland together and proudly. This noble mission of command can only be accomplished with an obedient and capable force. In these most difficult days of our Reich we must not lose our nerve or our courage, most of all we must not listen to the enemy's skillfully distributed rumors. We must have faith that our command is doing the right thing in this situation.

For six long years we have stayed together and defied the enemy. In the final weeks we must not show the world a picture of disintegration and thus shatter the negotiations that have begun. Every unauthorized absence, every attempt to find a way home on one's own, is an honorless betrayal of comrades and our people and must be punished accordingly.

Our discipline and the weapons in our hands are our pledge to exit this war decently and bravely. Our honor and the heroic deaths of so many of our comrades obligate us to do this. Only someone who gives up on himself is truly lost.

Soldiers of my army group!

Together we have mastered so many serious crises in many sectors of the east. You can trust in me to lead you out of this crisis too; and I have faith that you will stand by our people, state and head of state. But we must stand together and in spite of some traitors and cowards employ our last strength in these final hours of this war for the fulfillment of our mission. Only iron unity, unshakable will to resist and an always continuous front will lead us straight and true on the soil of the protectorate to the homeland.

Schörner
Generalfeldmarschall

Operation *Blumen* was now in full swing with the withdrawal of the *1.Panzer-Armee* setting the pace for the *Heeresgruppe*. The withdrawal quickly became a race as the Soviets pursued the German formations with purpose.

On May 5th Steidl was promoted to *Major*. According to the daily report issued out by the *Wehrmacht* that day, the withdrawal of the *1.Panzer-Armee* out of the region was progressing well. It noted that the Soviets were pushing from the north and that fighting broke out in Olmütz.[8] Steidl picks up the days' activity noting the increased desertions among the new recruits:

I moved my command post to Bedihorst (Bedihošt). Some *Landser* were AWOL. Mostly the new ones. The old ones continued to be made of iron.

Other units, such as the *Division 'Feldherrnhalle'*, reported a number of AWOL. The first evidence of breakdown. But we were in a gallows humor mood. There was *Flak* in the town. There were some good-mannered jokes with the guy in charge of the *Flak* at the celebration of my promotion to *Major*. Breitkreiz and Sonnenberg were great at this! People were drinking until it was late. Tomorrow was another day.

Dr. Braune reveals how his unit deployed south behind the *Jägerregiment 2 'BR'*, then quickly back north of Olmütz to support *Jägerregiment 1 'BR'* as the somewhat confused, and rapidly changing tactical situation dictated.

May 5th. I woke up at 5:30 a.m., when we were just getting into Olmütz. At about 7:00 a.m., we were pushed to the ramp, and 10 minutes later, the *Abteilung* was rolling through Olmütz, which was still asleep, and taking the road [south] toward Brünn (Brno). A short time later, we moved into local quarters in Blatze (Blatec). The front had to be somewhere a few kilometers to our east. The *Abteilung* did security against air threats. We cleaned out the ambulance and did a thorough cleaning of it. In addition, an opulent meal was prepared. In the middle of it, there was an alert at about 3:00 p.m. We went back the whole way until we were north of Olmütz and moved into Krönau (Křelov-Břuchtin). It was raining cats and dogs. Unfortunately, the Volkswagen had problems with the engine and had to be towed. The housing in Krönau was primitive. We were told that the Reich government was in Prague. Dönitz wanted to make peace. In the evening, the wrong field post number reported that all of the German troops fighting in the west in Germany, Denmark and Norway had surrendered.

Leutnant Grosser picks up his account with the arrival of *Jägerregiment 1 'BR'*. While he did not find the *Division* headquarters, he was able to make contact with *Sturmgeschütz-Artillerie-Brigade 'GD'* and *Panzer-Aufklärungs-Abteilung 'BR'*.

At 6:00 a.m., we arrived in the railway station at Stefanau near Olmütz. We were met there with

8   *Die Wehrmachtberichte 1939-1945, Band 3* (Biblio Verlag: Osnabrück, 1985), p. 567.

the news that no more trains could go to Olmütz because the railway station had been destroyed. In addition, the station was even in the area where there was enemy infantry fire. The Russians could also show up here at any moment.

The commander gave the order. Unload immediately! I had never experienced an unloading that went so quickly. Barely two minutes had passed and the majority of the vehicles were already off the train. The *Stabs-Kompanie* was allocated one town back as housing. The commander and I went forward to Stefanau, which was about 2 kilometer from the railway station.

In Stefanau, we found a sleepy, partially resigned, *Division* headquarters that was already waiting for us, wringing their hands. My commander was immediately given a wonderful broad sector to defend and be responsible for. Our *Division* headquarters wasn't there yet. A wonderful surprise! Five minutes later, we determined to our relief that our *II.Bataillon* was already on site and in position. Well, at least a consolation in this barren area, we found *Hauptmann* Metzger [*StuG.Art.Brig. 'GD'*] in the town. He had also found his way here with his *Jagdpanzers*. So at least we had a bunch of them with us again.

In Nakel (Náklo), we came across *Rittmeister* Sandmeyer and his staff. So we finally found out what things were like and that the results were totally without any consolation.

The commander was further on in order to set up the sector a bit, while I set up the regimental command post in a settlement on the other side of Nakel. The communications men had to keep running all the time to set up the telephone lines as quickly as possible.

The situation was that the Russians were pushing further west. They were coming from the vicinity of Sternberg (Sternberk) in the Sudeten, which could clearly be seen, given the good weather that day, and even better at night, when the enemy columns rolling in with their headlights on all the way looked line chains of lights coming down from the mountains. A really threatening feeling. With our right flank, we were right up against the band of fortifications around Olmütz. From there, our sector stretched about 15 kilometer wide toward the northwest. The mountains were in front of us, and there were swamps and water behind us in the left part of the sector. Most of the Russians, however, appeared to be rolling by south of Olmütz. But Ivan was making his presence in front of us unpleasantly dense. Mostly there appeared to be a lot of tanks here.

An ancillary field hospital train rolled into the railway station in Stefanau from Olmütz during the afternoon. All of them severely wounded. The locomotive uncoupled and steamed off. Ivan was right by the railway station. Two bursts from a Stalin organ went right into the middle of the train and caused appalling things to happen among the wounded. The physicians had disappeared with the locomotive into the secure hinterland. A terrible situation overall.

The medical staff of *'Brandenburg'* attempted to attend to the wounded, many of them in horrible condition.

By the next evening, our men, under the supervision of our physicians, managed to transport those still living away. It wasn't all that seamless, because the Russians were continuing to attack the railway station and could only be kept away from the shot-up hospital train with difficulty. The physicians and medics had to work under the most difficult conditions. Every car was hit at least once by Stalin organs. The cars were full of corpses and those that were still alive were half crazy and hardly conscious of the horror and terror.

On May 6th the Soviets attacked with heavy JS-2 tanks that penetrated the lines of the *Panzergrenadiers*. Temporary havoc ensued in the rear area as described by *Leutnant* Grosser:

Throughout the day, there was feverish work on improving defenses. In the *II.Bataillon* sector, there was relatively little pressure from the enemy. There was, however, heavy fighting around Stefanau. The commander and I were also frequently there. They enemy had a lot of tanks and continually penetrated into the town using tanks.

We were right at *Hauptmann* Metzger's command post when the alert notification came: Tanks in town! There were a couple of vehicles patrolling on the street. We were in our *SPW* with one leap. The three *Jagdpanzers* in front of the building jumped into action with a thud.

Behind a barn, one could clearly see from the flank that three enemy tanks, including a Joseph Stalin tank, were rolling out onto a road. A *Jagdpanzer* was moved forward. There was a trip through the barn and it got into position behind a corner of a building. The shots rang out, but initially everything went by terribly. *Hauptmann* Metzger ranted. The rest of us stood casually around the *Jagdpanzer* that was now moving out freely. It was like an exercise. The enemy tanks were not paying any attention to us. Finally, the first Ivan was hit and the second one was set on fire right after that.

The command post of the *Panzer-Aufklärungs-Abteilung 'BR'* was further on in the village. We made a call on them. We were hosted on the first floor with a small stack and a Schnapps. In the meantime, the Stalin tanks were showing up again below. With an incredibly loud engine noise, it went rattling through the town.

Everyone felt something incredible, but it wouldn't do anything to us. It didn't take long until the harassers were handled using two *Panzerfauste*. A great success!

On May 6th *Major* Steidl's *I.Btl./Jäg.Rgt. 2 'BR'* was ordered to deploy north and strengthen the line held by the *3.Batterie* of *Heeres-Flak-Abteilung 'BR'* along the far right flank of *Jägerregiment 1 'BR'*. The Soviet attacks south of the city appeared to taper off, while the in the north they increased. Desertions continued from the ranks of 'Brandenburg'. Initially it began from the ranks of the support personnel who had easy access to transport and could justify their presence in the rear areas. Then desertions now began from the ranks of the frontline combat soldiers. Steidl's recounts his movement north:

We started a motorized movement in the early morning. How many more times would we get into our faithful vehicles? The big funnel in which we were sitting was slowly turning into a big pocket. There was street fighting in progress in Prague. Russian enemy tank armies were advancing north from Vienna. Americans were coming into our rear from the west. But we were still keeping our cool. Everything was still going okay. We reached the town of Stefanau, which had a railway station.

Dr. Braune observed the absurdity of the situation. Around him the divisions of the *1.Panzer-Armee*, numbering tens-of-thousands of men were withdrawing without an apparent desire to fight. Yet the order from *H.Gr. Mitte* to 'Brandenburg' was clear: "hold your position and defend!"

Rotten weather, and Ivan is coming closer. In the morning, the news came that the first 'Brandenburgers' had absconded with trucks and machine guns. Was that happening to us as well? The other divisions here seemed to be already in the throes of dissolution. Everyone was attempting to get a vehicle and abscond.

I didn't have anything in the way of physician work to do. The Russians were now seriously attacking where they weren't finding any resistance. They were apparently very cautious toward us.

Generalfeldmarschall Schörner had again fired off an order, which indicated that we were to stay here until the divisions were out of Slovakia. According to the order, he wanted to break through to the west with the *Heeresgruppe*.

In the evening, I visited *Leutnant* Heyer, the commander of the *3.Batterie*.

The tactical situation was growing unstable around Stefanau. The command post of the *Heeres-Flak-Abteilung 'BR'* was in Krönau for the past several days along with two of its *Batteries*. Soviet artillery began to strike the area on the night of May 5th. The quarters for the battalion were hit causing some casualties. At the time only the *3.Batterie* was deployed forward in an area that had little cover itself. As Dr. Braune noted "it was like in the training area". About 2:00 p.m., there was a change in position of the *Abteilung* from the vicinity of Krönau to local quarters in Nakel as *Major* Steidl's men simultaneously moved into position. The move was forced by the increased pressure of the Soviets from the north.

On the night of May 6th the rest of the *Division*, to include the *II.Bataillon* of *Jägerregiment 2 'BR'* still screening to the south, moved north of Olmütz. The Soviet offensive from the south appeared to have been stabilized for the time being, and the *Division's* defense was bolstered with the arrival of *8.Panzer-Division* on May 5th. *Panzergrenadier-Division 'BR'* was now in a defensive position on May 7th west of the rail line of Stefanau. They had done their duty and held the gate at open for 48 hours. The *Wehrmachtberichte* reported that despite heavy fighting on May 6th the Soviets gained little ground around Olmütz. On the 7th the fighting grew desperate north of the city, as the Soviets were able to make a deep penetration between Olmütz and Freudenthal (Bruntál) at Sternberg.[9] The last elements of the *1.Panzer-Armee* slipped west along through the tightening neck south of Olmütz and further on near Wischau (Vyškov).

Major Steidl's men went into combat at the Stefanau rail station during the day. He likely had orders to hold it in case the *Division* had the opportunity for rail movement back north, however desperate this thought may have been at the time. Steidl recalled that "at the railway station, I dealt with my fateful position. A few meters from us, there were Russian tanks on the other side of the causeway. But our lines held firm. The Russians didn't go a step forward. I and my staff were in the railway station building." At 6:00 p.m. *Oberst* Oesterwitz, the commander of *Jägerregiment 2 'BR'*, went to see the *Division* commander in order to receive further orders and take up a new initial position. *Oberleutnant* Schmalbruch was sitting at the time in the vehicle belonging to *Oberleutnant* Brauschmidt, the communications officer for *Jägerregiment 2 'BR'* listening to news on the vehicle's radio. There he heard that a general surrender was announced and he was just about to get out of the vehicle when *Oberst* Oesterwitz came back. Schmalbruch told Oesterwitz about the radio broadcast regarding the surrender of the *Wehrmacht*, and in response, Oesterwitz did an about face and went back to see the *Division* commander in order to give him this news.

On the night of May 6th the *Wehrmacht* signed the articles of unconditional surrender. On May 8th all *Wehrmacht* forces were supposed to lay down their arms and surrender. It was on May 8th that *Oberst* Wilhelm Meyer-Detring, a liaison officer from *OKW*, was escorted through U.S. lines to meet directly with Schörner. He informed Schörner that formal capitulation was imminent and that no movement west of any large scale units would be allowed after the cease-fire was put into effect. The only option left was for German soldiers to make their way west independently.[10] Schörner apparently remained skeptical of his soldiers' ability to make their west safely as individuals without the benefit of an organized combat formation to protect their withdrawal. He stated that he would order his forces to observe the cease-fire but could not guarantee that every formation would obey the orders. Schörner already decided on May 7th that he personally would not surrender to either Soviet or Western forces. He informed Natzmer of his decision that evening. Following his discussions with Meyer-Detring, he turned over command of *H.Gr. Mitte* to Natzmer (see Appendix B). He ordered all the *Heeresgruppe* documents burned then boarded a small Storch aircraft and flew to Austria where he

9   Ibid., p. 568.
10   Ziemke, *Stalingrad to Berlin*, p. 134.

was later arrested and turned over to U.S. Forces on May 19th.

At 6:05 p.m. on May 7th the decision was made to reach Bistrau (Bystré) as a unit then completely disbanded the *Division*. On May 8th *Panzergrenadier-Division 'BR'* began an organized withdrawal west, nearly 100 kilometers. *Panzer-Aufklärungs-Abteilung 'BR'* was left to cover their withdrawal by defending the area along both sides of Stefanau.

Leutnant Grosser mused over the absurdity of the situation from his rooftop perspective on May 7th.

A wonderful clear day. On the roof of our building, a bar, I had a gap put in. There was a wonderful view of the terrain. From the mountains, one could look down at endless columns of enemy rolling in, recognizable through the flashing of windshields and the clouds of dust. A pretty picture, but also a really unpleasant and weird one.

In the early morning, the battles directly around the city of Olmütz had begun. The enemy was fighting persistently. Olmütz was actually a fortress, but the fortress troops had been withdrawn about 10 days before. The fortress artillery was only manned with a few men. Some of the bunkers and the battle stations in the foreground were still locked. There was no way to get a key. A real mess. In the city, a big food warehouse was closed off until the last minute. Now the paymasters didn't know where to put the stuff. The first appearance of dissolution and clear sabotage or confusion in the higher leadership became apparent.

Even in the regiment, the first cases of desertion showed up. First some clerks from the support units. This morning, it was an entire infantry gun crew that left their gun and went west.

A daily order came from *Generalfeldmarschall* Schörner. First: stand fast in the east and don't surrender. Then: Jodl and Keitel betrayed us and also surrendered for the east. Dönitz is with our *Heeresgruppe* in the Protectorate. We gradually moved to the American lines, with all the foot troops and German civilians coming along. The *Panzergrenadier-Division* remained near the enemy pointed east.

In the afternoon, orders were issued to report to the *Division* to receive more orders. At 6:00 a.m. the next morning, the movement initially began with a big leap (about 100 km). For the regiment, this leap went to Neustadt.

There was more feverish work to do before morning came. So I wasn't entirely conscious about what was going on right then. I was therefore not at all in a position to recognize that we had lost the war, nor were the comrades in my vicinity. Fortunately the Russians left us in peace to some extent, so all the preparations could be made carefully. The *Panzer-Aufklärungs-Abteilung 'BR'* occupied the entire division sector and was to keep the enemy at bay until the afternoon.

At 5:00 a.m. on May 8th everything was ready to move out. At 5:30, I went forward to the *II.Bataillon* to see whether everything was working okay with the moveout. The Russians fired 17.5cm on the road and I was just a hairbreadth away from being hit. Everything was working up front, but there were incredibly strong enemy concentrations seen. The bridges in the town were prepared for demolition. The demolition team was on site.

The demolition team was on site. Back again. The blown-up *Infanterie-Geschütze* were on the road. Orders had been given to blow up all *Geschütze* and excess vehicles so that the movement columns would be shorter and unnecessary obstacles would not be created. A sad sight.

At 5:45 a.m., I went back with the regimental headquarters. In Willimau, all the roads were full, and the regiment's movement columns formed up and moved out. Behind us, there was lively artillery fire. The Russians seemed to be starting on their morning attack.

We turned onto the main road. The *General* was at the *Division's* point of departure and he had the *Division* pass by him. It was supposed to be the last time. The commander got up in the vehicle and accepted the salute. The men sat upright in their vehicles and looked the general right in the eye. Trusting him now more than ever, we knew that the war was coming to an end, the war that had led to a wound for almost everyone, the war that had taken so many good comrades from us. We still didn't want the word "lost" to cross our lips. Everyone hoped, though silently, that weapons would not be taken out of our hands; instead there was a high degree of hope that the English and the Americans would join us in fighting the Russians. There were rumors to the effect that people supposedly knew that the divisions that had surrendered in the west were still armed and ready for combat against the Russians. More than ever, everyone trusted the *General* to get us safe and sound to the Americans, because no one wanted to fall into the hands of the Russians. We frequently talked about that in the vehicle. The Russians wouldn't get us—it would be better to put a bullet through our heads first—that was the general opinion.

The trip went on without any problems. Minor obstacles were quickly removed. In the afternoon, we arrived in Neustadt, our destination. The *Bataillons* were in the surrounding towns. We were in the Bohemian-Moravian highlands. The terrain was very similar to the Black Forest. Very narrow, deep-cut valleys. Neustadt was on the valley floor, surrounded by high mountains.

Suddenly very heavy firing could be heard from further on. Right after that, it was clear to us. Partisans! The brothers seemed to be seeing their chance. Further forward on the route of the *I.(gep)Bataillon*, a regular battle had developed. There was also machine gun fire and even mortars coming from the partisan side.

Our vehicles were moved. We were standing on the street talking when a bunch of machine guns drove among us. We ran in all directions. A couple more shots were fired from the mountains, and then it was quiet. The town mayor was taken as a hostage. Loudspeaker announcements were made in the town that the mayor would be shot if there was shooting during the night. No residents, except for the local police, would be permitted on the street.

The *Division* advanced to Bistrau. Travel was done in column, due to the increased activity of Czech partisans. In the evening of May 8th the *Division* set up a command post in the Svitava Valley. The night the *Wehrmachtberichte* reported that both Olmütz and Sternberg had been lost to the Soviets.[11] The next day, on May 9th came the final *Wehrmacht* broadcast at the exact time that *H.Gr. Mitte* commander *Feldmarschall* Schörner was making well his escape west. The final *Wehrmacht* report was broadcast throughout the defeated Reich:

The last German *Wehrmacht* report!
From the *Grossadmiral* headquarters
The *Oberkommando der Wehrmacht* announces:
In East Prussia, German Divisions were even yesterday courageously defending the mouth of the Weichsel and the western part of the Frische Nehrung, with the *7.Division* especially distinguishing itself. The Commander in Chief, *General der Panzertruppen* von Saucken, was awarded the Diamonds with Swords for the Knight's Cross on the Iron Cross in recognition of the exemplary conduct of his soldiers.

As a forward bulwark, our armies in Kurland tied down superior Soviet rifle and tank units under the proven command of *Generaloberst* Hilpert for months and gained immortal fame in particularly large battles. They refused any premature surrender. In a completely proper fashion, they were transported out with the aircraft transporting only disabled people to the west and later a number of children. The headquarters and the officers remained with their troops. At midnight, the German side stopped fighting and any movement in accordance with the conditions signed.

The defenders of Breslau, who withstood the attack from the Soviets for over two months, fell to enemy superiority at the last moment after heroic fighting.

---

11 *Die Wehrmachtberichte 1939-1945*, Band 3, p. 568.

In the southeastern and eastern front from Brünn to the Elbe near Dresden as well, all higher command offices have received the order to stop fighting. A Czech insurgency movement—which encompasses all of Bohemia and Moravia—might endanger the implementation of the surrender conditions in this area. The *Oberkommando* still has no reports about the conditions in the *Heeresgruppen* Lohr, Rendulic and Schörner.

The defenders of the Atlantic strongpoints, our troops in northern Norway and the occupiers of the Aegean Islands courageously upheld the fighting honor of the Germans in obedience and discipline.

Since midnight, weapons have been silent on all fronts. By order of the *Grossadmiral*, the *Wehrmacht* has stopped the fight, which has become hopeless. That brings the nearly six years of honorable fighting to an end. It has brought us great victories, but great defeats as well. The German *Wehrmacht* in the end honorably fell to a powerful superior force. The German soldier, true to his oath, has provided something unforgettable forever in his best deployment for his people. His homeland has supported him to the end with all its might with the most severe sacrifices. The unique service by the front and the homeland will find a final evaluation in a later good verdict of history. The service and the sacrifice of German soldiers on water, land and in the air will not fail to be noticed by the enemy either. Every soldier can therefore lay down his weapons standing proud and tall and courageously and confidently go to work for the eternal life of our people in the most difficult hour of our history.

In this difficult hour, the *Wehrmacht* thinks of its comrades left behind in front of the enemy. The dead obligate us to unconditional faithfulness, obedience and discipline toward our fatherland, bleeding from innumerable wounds.

At 8:30 p.m. on May 9th *Generalmajor* Schulte-Heuthaus issued his final an order to the *Division*:

All vehicles, weapons, ammunition, *Panzers*, etc. are to be destroyed immediately! *Panzergrenadier-Division 'Brandenburg'* will retain only the most necessary vehicles for transportation of people and small arms, and will assemble near Bistrau to break through into the Bavarian forest!

Generalmajor Schulte-Heuthaus planned to assemble the *Division* in a reception camp in the Fichtelgebirge in order to surrender *'Brandenburg'* to American forces. Explosions could be heard as vehicles and heavy equipment was blown; the assault guns of *Sturmgeschütz-Artillerie-Brigade 'GD'* and *Panzerjäger-Abteilung 'BR'* were now driven into a ravine.

H.Gr. Mitte's organized defense came to an end on May 9th. Many of the members of *'Brandenburg'* felt betrayed by Keitel and Jodl's announcement of capitulation. They was hope for an organized surrender to U.S. Forces, but that hope was now gone. The remaining men of the *Division* now left Bistrau for Deutschbrod (Havlíčkův Brod), which was to the southeast of Prague. "At the crossroads on the hill before Deutschbrod, in the middle of an open field, the end came for *Panzergrenadier-Division 'BR'* as one veteran later recalled. The remaining members dispersed to make their home; initially in small groups, then eventually as individuals.

The Race West, May 9th–June 1st

The *Division* began its movement west as an organized column. During the morning it broke up into its component battalions. Continued Soviet artillery and aircraft attacks on the clogged streets sowed panic. At a road junction northeast of Deutschbrod the remaining columns of the *Division* scattered. Some went further north toward Prague, others went west, and many went into the countryside. Koniev's 3rd and 4th Guards Tank Armies of the 1st Ukrainian Front raced south some 150 kilometers over the last three days and reached Prague at 3:00 a.m. on May 9th. From the south the 6th Guards Tank Army from the 2nd Ukrainian Front also reached the Czech capital, completing the encirclement of what remained of *H.Gr. Mitte*.

What follows are the remaining accounts of the units of *Panzergrenadier-Division 'BR'* as they fought their way west. We start with *Leutnant* Grosser's account of the *Jägerregiment 1 'BR'* withdrawal starting on the morning of May 9th:

It was 5:00 a.m. when the *Ia* came. He was very excited and distracted. He was coming from *Korps* and looking for *Major* Bansen. However, he came right back out of the room and ordered the *Major* to see him immediately. He then immediately had him get into his vehicle and then they left. My commander went right behind them and was back immediately.

Moveout in an hour. The Russians were attempting to cut off our road back. Blow up all excess vehicles. The only vehicles to be taken along were the ones that were absolutely necessary for transporting personnel. The object was to get 3,000 *Brandenburgers* home! That was how this last order from the *General* ended.

Twilight had fallen. There was an endless column of vehicles rolling along. It was not until after a heavy battle that we were able to form up. Reaching the point of departure on time was now out of the question.

It became dark. We had only proceeded a few meters. The road was unutterably clogged. There were two columns standing next to each other on the street, which wasn't all that wide anyway. There was a weird light over this whole picture that was full of pushing and shoving and to some extent even panic. The Russians were on our heels and "Save yourself if you can" and "We have been betrayed and are lost" were slogans passing from one person to another ominously. The embankment to the right and the left of the road was overwhelmed with burning vehicles that had been left behind after being destroyed. At one place, there were 27 assault guns, the entire *Sturmgeschütz-Artillerie-Brigade 'GD'*. A gruesome scene. The beginning of a "The Lord has smote them, their men, their steeds and their wagons." But it wasn't completed.

Finally we managed to free up the road by showing pistols. Vehicles posing an obstacle were pushed down the embankment. The terrible knot of vehicles slowly unraveled and rolled out. In the next town, I hear the voice of *Major* Lau, the *Division Adjutant*, in the pitch black darkness. We gave each other a short greeting. Lau was there, though he had doubts, to order the *Division* to move. However, he was not successful in reining in the stream of outside vehicles that had gotten glued among us.

We went further on slowly through the night. There were more and more bottlenecks. Standing around again and again. I was walking more than I was riding. I went by 30, 40, 50 or more vehicles until I could determine the reason for the bottleneck and get rid of it. A bridge that was too narrow, a defective vehicle or a driver that had fallen asleep. There was always something new, always some more cursing, always more urging on and lending a hand.

The night progressed. At one entrance to a village, there was a bottleneck without a break. No one could go forward or backward. I managed to snake my way through part of it with the Krad, and then it was all behind me. I couldn't fight my way forward by foot. The road was narrower along a causeway. To the right was an open field, and there were some vehicles with tracer rounds burning in it. The munitions caught on fire and the tracer rounds sputtered all over the place. There was also a column of horses on the road. The animals were so scared by the fireworks, some of which went between their legs, that it was almost impossible to hold them. There were teams and wagons all over everywhere on the road. In addition, there were again two columns right next to each other. It took over an hour for the clog to be broken up and for us to go on.

The *General* was there. We turned onto a side road because there was no way we could go forward at all on this road. At first we made good progress going forward and then we got lost and could not find the way again. There was a tank obstacle closed at the entrance to one town. "Made in Germany". We went by it. Further on again. Another tank obstacle, over half an hour of work, and then the road was free. But it was a mistake; we still didn't go forward. Right behind it, there were about 10 really thick trees cut down on the embankment to the right of the road such that they interlocked and lay right across the road. Shit!! With hellish curses, we set ourselves to chopping up the tree trunks and sawing them up and then pushing them aside. Finally we made it through and went on.

Finally after not much time had passed, we were behind a standing column again that contained a number of *'Brandenburg'* units. I was completely exhausted and fell asleep in the vehicle. The commander had also been shot. Finally I pulled myself together and went forward. I found *Hauptmann* [?] of our artillerymen sleeping in his vehicle. He didn't know anything and had been there over an hour. He had been yelled at by the *General* for not having done anything to go any further. He was now offended and resigned. I took a *Krad* from him that was right next to his vehicle. It was a one-person machine. I wouldn't have gotten by the column with a sidecar. I passed over 100 vehicles and then our *I.(gep)Bataillon* came. It was already getting light. There were forests on both sides of the road. Finally I got to the site of the disaster. The Czechs had cut trees to fall right across the road on a stretch of over 300 meters. Except for a small piece, it was possible to clear up the road with hard work. The column was rolling through again very soon after that.

Thank God, we had the regiment together again. The *I.(gep)/Bataillon* was moving in front with the *II.Bataillon* right behind them. We were standing/sitting on the edge of the road and let our forces roll right by us. A whole bunch of single stranger vehicles were, however, still among the regiment. But that wasn't all that worrisome.

We had come to a nice broad paved road. The long trip could go on. So we put a respectable number of kilometers behind us between 5:00 a.m. and 7:00 a.m.

There were a few *SPWs* on the road that had broken down due to engine damage or lack of fuel. The crew was milling about getting ready to blow them up. Onward we went. I found the *II.Bataillon* again and soon came across *Rittmeister* Sandmeyer's vehicle, in which *Leutnant* Drenger his adjutant, and *Leutnant* Hasse the administrative officer, were sitting. They had a bottle of Schnapps and were in the best of moods. I spent a little time sitting with them on their vehicle. The radio was playing, and it was like I was on a summer trip.

May 10th. Midnight was past. With frequent bottlenecks, the column pushed through further to the southwest. *Oberleutnant* Mücke and I traded off on orienting ourselves on the map and the frequent determinations that we had stopped. No Russians or armed Czechs showed up. So the trip went quickly, at least in this regard.

The tiredness after such an eventful and exhausting, at least mentally, day now affected everyone. People temporarily stopped continuing to fight against the overwhelming tiredness. Their eyes starting closing involuntarily. And although there wasn't much clarity about our situation and our near future, and even the next moment could bring a new dramatic event for which lightning-fast action and major alertness came, and everyone was overcome with an overwhelming nodding off. When I looked around in our vehicle that was occupied by about 10 or 12 men, I actually would have had the same impression as if we were going back to garrison after a field exercise if there weren't in every face of the stressed platoon a reflection of the great events in the middle of which we were moving.

At about 3:00 a.m. in the morning, the trip stopped entirely. Everyone was asleep. After we had stayed in the same place for about a half hour, I got up and went along the column. I counted over 200 vehicles just in front of us. No estimate could be made about what was behind us. At a bridge swinging high over a river, I reached the head of the column. The first vehicles were facing the flow of traffic or were right across the road and apparently wanted to go back. But that was completely out of the question on a road that is narrow anyway, going in switchbacks through the mountains. Even passing was impossible.

I quickly managed to figure out what was going on. There were already rumors flying in the column that the Russians were in the next town. A Russian lieutenant had supposedly gone there and, it was said, had provided assurances of free passage on our vehicles to our homeland via Tabor. All that anyone could say about that is that anyone who believed that must be blessed. Further on at the place it occurred, I determined that although there wasn't a Russian lieutenant, there was a German *Oberst* who came out of the darkness and held a stirring talk indicating that the Russians would take us with open arms—a typical "Seydlitz" officer!

When I was back with the commander and could tell him what I had determined, all the officers in the column were rounded up. The entourage gathered directly behind our vehicles. A *Luftwaffe General*, for whom it couldn't be determined whether he was real or not, took the floor. He considered it best to lay down our weapons and be captured by the Russians. There was no way out anyway, and otherwise he spouted all the optimistic drivel that I had already come across at the top. We were naturally most emphatic that we should not surrender to the Russians without any blood and without a whimper. We also were not shy about expressing our opinion. However, the *Luftwaffe General* ordered that we remain and surrender. The commander gave me a signal. I jumped in the vehicles and gave the order to turn on the engines. Right after that, the commander came and jumped into the vehicle. He left the *Luftwaffe General* behind, telling him that he didn't take orders from him.

As soon as the commander was in the vehicle, we got out of the column and went to the right across the road trenches onto the open slope that ended at the edge of a forest. We held a short war council there about what was to be done. At any rate, we would not surrender here before we had used all our tools to get out of the situation somehow. On the issue of whether we should proceed with vehicles or without them, the decision was made: with vehicles! Up in the forest in which we initially wanted to disappear before it became completely light, the dawn had already progressed substantially and there was already shooting. Some people were also coming back from there and told us that there were partisans hiding in the forest. In addition, there was a clattering of tank chains or heavy towing vehicles audible on the other side of the forest.

But nothing ventured, nothing gained. Get through, without consideration of losses, was the watchword. Everyone picked up his weapon so that we could get rid of anyone in our way why we were still traveling. And off we went. Unfortunately, the engineers and their vehicles were crowded out by us so they couldn't do anything with us. They were further behind us distributed in the column.

We were able to get out of the column without any problem; we quickly got out of there overland over the hill and lost sight of the column. What fate must be facing the men who remained behind and surrendered to the Russians. For us, the competition with the Russians for the Moldau began again. The last stage. Would we manage it or would we still be caught so close to our goal? We had 60 to 70 kilometers still to go. But now we had free rein again and we were alone as the column went on. Everyone was fully awake again. Our senses were sharpened to the max. Our fingers were pressing hard on the maps. Just don't lose our bearings. Up in an edge of the forest, we stopped again and got our wind back for the last sprint. Then off we went. Down in the valley, individual vehicles were going back and forth on the road. We couldn't tell whether they were Russians, Czechs or our people. But what did that matter; onward to our task. Everything had to be put on a map.

Off we went in a quick trip. The commander showed himself again to be a master of orientation and to have a nose for things. The road signs en route were put to the side or, even more often, turned around. But we figured that out quickly. We bypassed the bigger towns. If we had to pass a village, all of the weapons we had were extended over the edge of the deck. On every hill, at nearly every road junction, there was a single Czech, usually with a bicycle, who immediately disappeared into the next village as soon as he could when he saw us to report us. So the brothers must have branched their warning and reporting service over the entire area. The question was now whether they were doing this only for their partisan bands or, which of course would have been much more dangerous, whether these reports were passed on to the Russians. At any rate, there was always a need for speed if another scout showed his face again. But we were still able to get to the town before the reporters every time, so the brothers there were never warned in advance. Our armored vehicles contributed even from far off with their chains that clearly and penetratingly hit things and rattled. So we were constantly changing our direction so that the Czechs couldn't get an overview of the direction in which we were going.

We were traveling in the formation that had already been proven. We went with the *SPW* in the front. Then the motor vehicles and finally the second *SPW*. This sequence was good, because the Czechs wouldn't dare to attack the wheeled vehicles behind us, because they could still hear the second *SPW* rolling in.

Most of the towns we passed through were almost dead when we went through them, but we involuntarily felt the eyes and perhaps even rifle barrels behind the windows and doors. All that was needed was for one shot to go off, and then all hell would break loose. But the Czechs weren't confident against our armored vehicles, which they apparently thought were *Panzers*. In some towns, the male residents were assembled on the street, but even there, we wouldn't be encumbered. In a small city, there was a real Volksfest at the road junction in the middle of the town. A loudspeaker had been installed and a band was also playing Czech marches. We were also not encumbered or stopped here. A policeman cleared the way for us.

It was a wonderful day. Ascension Day, as only we can have it. It went great, we determined, because now we were doing the traditional boys' day out. The mood became wonderful with this motto. Some people on some vehicles were even singing. Everyone had the feeling that it couldn't be bad anymore, that we were free. This feeling was so much one of relief that no one really thought of the lost war anymore, and people had turned outdoorsy over the years that people had gotten into the moment without thinking about what the situation actually was and what was coming up.

And in fact, everything went smoothly. At 10:00 a.m., we went down the switchbacks on the steep bank. When we got to the river, we were struck with terror once again. The bridge on our maps was not there at all. But thank God, there was a ferry run by some Czechs.

So as soon as we were 50 meters over the river, everything was okay. We were already thinking about bathing in the Moldau. A very nice educated Czech handled the translation with the ferry. He also confirmed to us that the American zone began on the other bank. There were problems in taking the *SPW* across. They were too heavy for the ferry, which only carried 12 tons. The Czechs refused to move these two vehicles across and wanted to make it clear to us that we should leave them for them, because we couldn't possibly need *them* anymore. Finally, however, they said they would be willing to attempt to get the *SPW* across. Almost all the radio equipment, which was after all very heavy, was removed in advance, broken up and then thrown into the middle of the Moldau. The attempt to get across was successful, although the ferry threatened to almost capsize. After half an hour, everything was on the other side.

God, that's a great mood, just as if we had won the war ourselves. A big bathing party began and we were head over heels about how the Lord God had managed to get us into the cool green waters of the Moldau. Then we washed, shaved and did our major grooming. And then we basked in the sun on the beach. It was wonderful. A wonderful feeling that we were out of hell and now the homeland was in our grasp. Like a bolt of lightning, the news came into our peaceful picture that the Russians were now coming down the western bank of the Moldau from Prague. So now off we went. In a feverish haste, everything was packed on the vehicles for our trip to become prisoners. Now it was urgent that we get to the Americans before the Russians caught us. After a few minutes, we were off. The commander and I went in my rust bucket. I got behind the wheel myself in order to drive my vehicle myself on this last trip. A Czech on a motorcycle went at the front of our small column. Slipping along, the road went up the steep bank. Once we got up to the top, our Czech escort left us and used his hand to point out in which direction we should continue. We rolled slowly on in the warm noonday sun. It was a difficult trip for us, this last trip. On the way, we met a group of *Landser* with a wounded man. They asked us to take them with us. They were stuffed in on our vehicle that was overcrowded anyway. Onward we went. After traveling about 20 minutes, we came across a big cross street on which there were one vehicle after another to the left and right as far as the eye could see. Mostly they were soldiers who managed to make it out of Prague and go south in time. We later heard that the column was 20 kilometers long.

An *Oberstabsrichter*, or something like that, who came to see us brought the great word. Hook up behind, always behind, the Americans will probably be coming during the evening. So far they had not yet taken the column. In fact, there was not an American to be seen for miles.

"The Russians are also moving west of the Moldau," was still ringing in our ears! No, that wasn't the right thing for us, getting onto this endless column. It could happen that this evening it would not be the Americans showing up, but rather the Russians. We didn't go this far for that; we could have had that much more comfortably. Here we'll push on, said the commander. We went off right through the column. The people stared at us but no one attempted to stop us. Pisek was where the most forward prisoner-of-war camp was and also the headquarters of the American General Patton. So the nest had to be avoided, so it was decided that we would make a wide circle around the town.

So we moved about 5 kilometers further west through some towns where we were subjected to strange stares from the inhabitants. Sometimes it seemed as if the civilians wanted to band together against us. We quickly sought to give them a wide berth. Finally we disappeared in a big forest. There we stopped and tried to take a rests first. The vehicles were stopped. Two hours of rest were prescribed and sentries were allocated.

I first had a little snack and then I got into the shade and studied the map. However, I was overcome by exhaustion when I did this tasks and I fell into a deep sleep over the map.

May 11th. When I woke up, the allotted time had passed and the sun had gone a substantial bit further to the west. I went over to the commander and woke him up. Everywhere our men were the way they had gotten out of the vehicles, strewn on the ground sleeping like logs. After the most recent days and nights, it was really no wonder that the strongest man could no longer withstand his need to sleep.

The *Major* and *Hauptmann* Metzger picked themselves up and we got into a war council. After everyone had had some sleep, everyone looked optimistically into the future again and so we now were in no way inclined to go to the nearest American prisoner-of-war camp. Good, at any rate we would attempt to get to Reich German soil. Here among the Czechs it was really a bit dicey for us after all. So Schüttenhofen (Sušice) was chosen as the first goal. But our thoughts went much further. First we would go to Cahm, a bit into the Bavarian woods, where our *Division's* food storage site was. And then, because the war was after all at an end, we would go home. The commander wanted to go with Metzger in Metzger's Volkswagen to southern Germany and I and my rust bucket would take an additional five men to central Germany. We had enough gas to get to Hamburg and back. So why not? The war was over, after all. What optimists we were at this moment, how clueless we were about what was going on in Germany and what awaited us.

With glad courage and our hearts full of big plans, we got back into our vehicles. Our slogan wasn't to go to the Americans but to get home going through the Americans. Our trip started and we got good land under our feet. We didn't run into any Americans. Our trip always went behind things on narrow field and forest roads. And now we ran into really strange situations.

We came into a village. Red flags in all the windows and pictures of Stalin in the windows. A gate with Hammer and Sickle at the entrance to the village. The street was swarming with people. Good God, it was just about to collapse. Everyone involuntarily reached for his weapon. But what was going on; had the world gone crazy? The people cheered for us. With smiling faces, they raised their fists to us. And then all of a sudden flowers, flowers and more flowers. Had the world gone crazy? And then it hit us. They considered us to be the Russians, and they were apparently expecting them to arrive. We looked at ourselves. Of course, no wonder. Look at how we were dressed; hardly anyone had on a real German uniform. Someone had a camouflage coat, someone else a flight suit, and others like me had an English coat. So we lifted our fists and joyfully returned the greeting. It was a situation that really made us laugh. I looked around. The vehicles behind us were also covered in flowers. Our men were sitting on the vehicles and greeting people with balled fists on all side. A real Hussar rick. But we were still happy when we got out of the party because the whole thing was a bit uncomfortable even so. The Czechs would have been quite unpleasant to us if they had known who we really were. In the next few towns, nothing changed. Once we were met en route by a single man who yelled out, "Good by my darling." Aha, now we were being confused with Americans. That's really great. We yelled a few phrases in broken English to the man, who acted as if he were overjoyed. In the next town, we were Russians again. When we went around a corner, a woman next to my vehicle said suddenly, "My God, Germans!" So worried and yet so happy. I waved to her and then I was gone. In the next town, we were greeted again. The road branched in the town. We didn't know where to go and we stopped. Suddenly people were staring at us and in the next minute, the street was cleared out. Damn, we were recognized, best get out before being swarmed. We had not gotten far out of the town before an air raid siren went off. Back and forth, back and forth. Tank alert! Other towns in the vicinity took up the warning signal. Shit, now it's ticklish if the guys are using the bells to spread news of our presence. We disappeared as soon as we could into a small piece of forest. What was to be done? If we continued to run around with weapons it would be dirty for us if the Americans grabbed us, because anyone who was still carrying a weapon after May 8th would be considered a partisan and handled accordingly. That was an excessive risk. So orders were given to destroy the weapons. The officers kept their pistols. It all happened in a very short time. The rifles were broken up, the machine guns, submachine guns, hand grenades and *Panzerfausts* were taken apart, covered in dirt and thrown into a pond. Then we went on.

We saw that the Americans were on the road between Strakowitz (Strakonice) and Horadschwiz (?). If we could get by them without being noticed, we would make it. We chose the small town of Kattowitz (Katovice) along this road to go through. Shortly before we got there we picked up yet another old friend. *Feldwebel* [?], our liaison officer to the *Division*. He was cruising alone through the terrain on a *Krad*. And now on to the last sprint that would take us to Germany and, we thought, to freedom.

And then we were in Kattowitz. The residents cheered for us as usual. Shit, the nest was bigger than one would have thought from the map. Suddenly we were among a bunch of strange soldiers. What kind of people were they? Russians? Good God, don't make trouble at the last minute. We were in the middle of it and we heard a clear quack, quack. Aha, Americans. There were vehicles everywhere along and in the street. We greeted people to our left and our right. And wonder of wonders, no one stopped us. We got out of the town and were back on the open road. There were Czech partisans traveling in front of us. We had gone a good bit further and an American vehicle came up behind us. There was a First Lieutenant in it. He stopped us. Where did we want to go? To Germany! We were on the wrong road; this was an American supply route. He wanted to show us the right way. We were very glad; after all, we didn't have any other options. I got into the American's vehicle.

We went back to Kattowitz and stopped. The American battalion commander showed up on the road. He had a better idea of what was going on. What were we doing running around here? We answered that we had been sent from the prisoner-of-war camp in Pisek to Schüttenhofen because of overcrowding. After a short exchange, we were informed that we would be escorted to the nearest prisoner-of-war camp. I got back into the American's vehicle. And now we were actually on our way to captivity.

The Czechs were changed completely. Threatening us with their fists, they cursed and wanted to spit on us. We were extremely furious and at the same time were feeling a great letdown. We stopped in front of the town. There was a vehicle missing. It was our *SPW*. The officer told me that the vehicle didn't want to start. The troops were put onto an American vehicle. In fact, I found my orderly later and he told me that the vehicle didn't want to start. The Czechs were threatening them so the Americans wanted to get them out of the place as quickly as possible to protect them. They couldn't take any of their things with them and they went to a different camp than we did.

After a trip that wasn't all that long (6 km), we were in Strakowitz and were turned over to a big prisoner-of-war camp. Our trip was at its end and so was our dream of getting home more quickly. But we had escaped the Russians and had managed to make our way through to the Americans, which only a few had managed to do during these last few days. So even though our freedom had been taken from us, we were glad, proud, and thankful as well that we had gotten this far. The Ascension Day boy's day out was at its end!

Major Steidl's *I.Bataillon* of *Jägerregiment 2 'BR'* pulled out of their positions and began their withdrawal west. Here is his final account:

Tuesday, May 8th. We came out of our holes in the morning fog for the last time. Muddy, freezing and aware that this great war had come to an end. With heads hung, the individual groups went to the assembly areas, machine guns over their shoulders, ammunition boxes in their hands. We got into the vehicles that had been prepared and rolled off. Many other divisions went with us. The point was to get to the Bavarian forest in order to get away from the Russians. We were still strong enough to fight and we had our weapons. We wanted to get to the German border by passing to the south of Prague via Iglau (Jihlava). But we were still separated from there by many hundreds of kilometers. We rolled uninterrupted to the west until the evening, everything in order. In the evening, we were housed in a small town. Foot troops with their long baggage trains passed without stopping. The *Gebirgsjäger-Regiment 138* was also there and I met an acquaintance who had been in Poland with me. In the evening, the battalion commanders met at the command post. We decided immediately to break out so as not to lose any time. We moved out in the darkness and after a short trip, we were stopped by a tank obstacle. Hundreds of vehicles had to carefully be guided on the narrow road in order to go around the obstacle. We only went forward into the cold night slowly, fired upon by the Czechs, through burning towns.

An account of what happened during May 9th and 10th was not located in the available documents. What can be surmised based on a below account by another member of the regiment is that on May 8th Steidl and his men reached an area north of Deutsch Brod. At that point they disbanded under unknown circumstances and that most of *Jägerregiment 2 'BR'* and members of the *Division* staff were captured. They were subsequently marched south under guard by armed Czechs. This is the only time in any account by a veteran of *'Brandenburg'* that the word "Jew" is used in any form. Steidl, writing in the early 1950s, juxtaposed what was then known about the killing of Jews during the war (the term Holocaust did not come into universal use until the late 1960s and early 1970s) with his own treatment by a "Czech Jew" who may well have been extracting a small amount of vengeance against his prisoners. I left Steidl's commentary intact as it does show his struggle with rationalizing his military service against the backdrop of the genocidal war unleased by Nazi Germany—a struggle many of his comrades likely had.

Friday, May 11th. The first night went by without any sleep. Now was when the tiredness of the past stress broke out, hunger made itself known and thirst became a torment. So we hunkered down on the pavement, watched by Czech Jews and scalawags. There were a few hundred men in this courtyard. There were also women there. Everyone was in a good mood. The Czechs were not supposed to notice what was going on in our hearts. In the morning, we were ordered to "form up." We were put in ranks of three, watched like hardened criminals—or were they still afraid of us? Out of the courtyard, a bit through the city to get into another courtyard, which was larger this time and where some of our people were hunkering down. We were promised food. A well-fed, drunken Jew and a few thugs who didn't know how to still handle their rifles formed our "guard force." The courtyard was surrounded by buildings, and the big gate in front was closed.

The sun shone hot on our heads; we didn't get any food or water. However, the drunken Jew often had us form up, held a picture of Hindenburg in front of our faces, and gave everyone a strong lashing on the face with his riding whip. Don't talk to me just about atrocities by the evil Germans! Even the women were not spared this abuse. But icy hate and the deepest disgust affect the Czech Jewish creature.

In the afternoon, some Russian privates came to see us in the courtyard. They gave us cigarettes and were friendly toward us. Some people had their boots removed and their watches taken—many people didn't have them anymore—but otherwise we were left in peace. In the afternoon, we formed up in the courtyard. We thought we were going to get some food—but even our last possessions, such as pictures, money, bread bags, etc. were taken from us. Thirst slowly became a torment, hunger would not have been so bad even though there were some comrades lying unconscious on the stony ground already.

Night broke and it was quite cool; I hunkered down next to Braunschmid and stared into the clear, starry sky. Outside, there were Russian columns moving by without interruption. It was not until then that I became conscious of the entire weight of being a prisoner. I was firmly determined to risk everything to get away from these creatures. Better to risk everything than to go along with this farce. I was able to sleep for a few hours.

Saturday, May 12th. Nothing had changed by noon. Instead of food there were more blows with whips and sticks.

In the afternoon, we were taken out of the courtyard. We marched through the city and arrived at a big camp in a meadow at the edge of the city. The guard force consisted of Russians. There were tens of thousands of prisoners assembled there. We breathed a sigh of relief that we had gotten away from the Czechs. To my joy, I met a few acquaintances from my division, including *Oberleutnant* Kopp and *Sanitäter* Wichmann. Wichmann even still had something to eat and he gave me some. As evening approached, Ivan brought us a can of something. Braunschmid and I shared the contents—it was a sausage that tasted excellent. We were initially glad to have the plaster under our backs removed and get rid of our hunger to some extent.

On green meadows, we started resting, and on the nearby road, Russian tanks thundered by, headed toward Prague.

Sunday, April 13th. The sun shone hot in the morning sky when we had already marched east in endless columns for several hours. No one knew where we were going or how far it was.

Like an enormous herd, the grey stream surrounded by a cloud of dust and with Cossack sentries swarming around it moved forward, pushing itself forward carefully while motorized columns and columns of horse-drawn vehicles moved by it quickly without interruption toward the west—our homeland.

There was a short rest at about noon.

A Russian colonel told us that we would get into a nice camp near evening and that there would be a cafeteria, a bath, delousing and discharge there. There was a small ray of hope and until the evening came, it let us forget the pain of our feet that had been used until they were wounded. We had marched 60 kilometers, without food and without any water although it was very hot. What met us in the evening wasn't a cafeteria or a discharge point; it was a stockade surrounded by barbed wire and sentries. We fell down on the gravelly ground. I happened to find a piece of cardboard and lay down on it so that it wouldn't hurt so much. There was again no food.

The night became a torment. It was raining cats and dogs on our uncovered bodies. Many *Landser* were completely apathetic when faced with hunger and stress. A number of them had previously lain down in the ditches at the side of the road the day before and were released by the accompanying sentries using a shot to the back of the neck.

Shooting of German prisoners-of-war who could not walk on their own by the Soviets was unfortunately commonplace immediately after the end of the war. While no specific document exists that shows this was official Red Army policy, the multitude of German veteran accounts from this time do relate similar experiences, suggesting this practice was not unique to Steidl's situation.

Monday, May 14th. During the morning, we were told the same thing "with a straight face" about delousing, food and discharge. I "finally had it" and had definitely decided not to be a part of this circus any longer.

I took the first opportunity [to escape] even though I was already completely exhausted.

In the morning, we stopped at a pool. We undressed and took a bath. But right after that, we were herded together again. The heat and the dust were unbearable. We were no longer a swaying mass—gradually more and more people fell out. If we weren't given something to eat soon, everything would be over.

We jumped onto a few raw potatoes that had been freshly planted along the road. The sentries fired into the column now and then, but so what: hunger is terrible. In the afternoon, they let us rest in a clearing in the forest. We cooked up spinach found in the grass. Our stomachs once again had something. During the entire march, I had already thought about the possibility of getting away.

The sentries and the mounted Cossacks were too thick and the terrain was exposed everywhere. For the time being, it would be suicide to cut loose.

In the evening, we bivouacked in a long depression along the road. The smoky fire reached up into the sky. We were heavily watched. During the night, I discussed with Kopp, Wichmann, [Helmuth] Spaeter and a few other *Division* comrades my plan to book the next day regardless of the circumstances.

I was convinced that we could not stand it two more days under these circumstances and that we would wind up in the ditches at the side of the road as many thousands had. Better a small chance or a bullet in honor than to slowly kick the bucket.

Breakout to the homeland!

In addition, I indicated that we would reach the forested area of Humpoletz (Humpolec) the next day, where there were thick forests reaching south along the road. From there, we could make our way through to Austria. We all thought about it; Braunschmid hesitated. He had reached the end of his inner strength. We dozed off. Would the next day bring us luck?

Tuesday, May 15th. We intentionally stayed more toward the rear of the long column. Luckily I had been able to hide a map of this area and I made glances at it now and then; in an hour, we would have to be in the forest near the town of Humpoletz, where according to the map, the road went through the forest. We could also clearly see the enormous forests to our south, which could give us cover.

Soon the time had come. The Russian sentry was a few steps in front of us and the next one was on a horse 100 meters behind us. In a few minutes, the time would have come – one way or the other.

Braunschmid didn't go along. I said a short goodbye. The rest of us stayed close together. I turned around; the sentries couldn't see us at that moment—it was a curve—and with our last strength, my comrades and I jumped into the bushes with a cold feeling that we would be in the cross hairs for a bullet at any moment. We ran and crawled further into the forest—minutes became an eternity—but there was nothing behind us. A few hundred meters later, we threw ourselves into thick brush. We were free—and this feeling gave us hope of seeing our homeland again. I took over command and Wichmann gave me his compass. No we wouldn't fail anymore. The movement plan was determined—we could only move at night, avoiding towns and roads to the maximum extent possible.

We pushed ourselves a bit further south and waited for evening—for darkness. From the distant road, we heard "coups de grace" every now and then. Poor comrades that had to continue onward there extremely exhausted toward a terrible future—or a certain end. In front of us were the dark forests of the Bohemian/Moravian heights. Twilight fell slowly. We broke out. We only went forward slowly. The communication between one man and another had to be carefully maintained. Often there were extended stops before roads so we could wait for the Russians to have a gap in their columns so that we could get through one at a time like a hunted rabbit.

There were dogs barking from the nearby villages or shots from Czechs howling through the night while we were slogging through foggy meadows, damp with dew, with our tired eyes, almost drunk from lack of sleep. We refreshed ourselves at small pools and brooks. During the day, we ate young tree sprouts or raw potatoes that we had stolen from the fields during the night. So we slogged on for our 20-30 kilometers every night, working with lots of effort in terrain without any paths or catwalks; valuable hours went by, but the drive to have the Czech land behind us as quickly as possible kept our courage from going down. During the day, we crawled into thick bush and fell asleep. Often we were blessed as well, and we lay soaked to the bone in the bushes, while there were often Czech farmhouses a mere 100 meters away. We couldn't light a fire even once. Every civilian was armed and the Germans were "fair game."

Steidl and his group worked their way south toward Austria.

Thursday May 17th. We crossed what had been the Protectorate boundary. However, we were still in territory occupied by the Czechs. We tracked down a farm woman who was working nearby in the fields. She spoke German and sent us bread and potatoes during the afternoon. We were in "seventh heaven" and ate with a rare appetite. Because we did not want to move further in such a big group for security reasons and for food-supply reasons as well, we split up and moved on separately. *Hauptmann* Gabel from Leipzig took over one group and I took over the other one.

On Friday, May 18th. We passed the customs office, the actual border. We made a detour. At the edge of the next village, we were shot at. We spent hours crawling on our bellies through a field of grain. The bullets whistled above our heads. Not far from Zlabings (Slavonice), we crossed the border. We reached Dobersberg on the Thaga north of Waldhofen. The first civilians with red-white-red armbands came into view. Oh yes, in Austria there was an "upheaval," but even so, people were good to us ragged guys and gave us bread. We slept in hay until it was evening.

In the evening, we started off again.

We went across the Thaya. We wanted to pass Waldhofen on the east; there was a big Russian prisoner-of-war camp there. "In addition, the Russians are grabbing all the men they can find and sending them to Siberia," the civilians told us. Regardless of how it was, we were careful and did not want to be "collected" at the last minute before we reached our homeland. We got through the night.

It was Sunday, May 20th. In the morning we lay down in an isolated hay storage area. It was really a bit dicey for us; the road was close enough to be risky.

We arrived in a large farmstead during the afternoon; the people there were very nice and friendly. We had a wonderful meal and went off further during the evening. We passed Groß-Sieghards, Mesern, Idolsberg and Daubitz and on May 24th, we had reached the Danube at Weinzirl. We spent the night in an inn and were living well.

We went further the next day. At Krems, we saw the stream. We hunkered down in a vineyard. Former *Major* Helmut Spaeter, who had been the *Division Ib*, no longer had any shoes. He was walking in the cut-off pockets of his field blouse. There was a lot of traffic in the city. I went with Cerny into the city dressed as a civilian and looked around for a way to cross. No luck. We "tiptoed" further toward Spitz. Outside the city, we stopped in a tunnel. We took a look into the city. It was crawling with Russians. During the night, we went around the city and crossed the Danube in a primitive rowboat during the early morning. So on May 26th, one of the greatest obstacles had been overcome with lots of luck. After several incidents, we managed to get to a farmhouse in Eck. Mr. Fuchssteiner and his family gave us a really friendly reception. We crossed the heights on Sunday, May 27th and went on to Frankenfels. We saw Mt. Ötscher. For me, there was a particularly homeland-type feeling; the place is, after all, on the boundary with Steiermark.

Monday, May 28th. We reached Sulzbichl, near Mariazellerbahn.

There we separated from Spaeter, Kopp and Sinter. They wanted to rest with the famers there for a few days more and then get to Bavaria via Salzburg, Tyrol. When it was still afternoon, I moved on with Cerny, Busse and Wichmann. We reached Buchenstuben.

Tuesday, 29th. We reached Erlauf. We fought our way through the chasms of Mt. Ötscher on across the communal meadow and reached the Erlaufsee during the night. We asked for bread in a villa. We had to go on; there was a Russian camp in the vicinity. We went on a bit until we were south of Mariazell.

Wednesday, May 30th. We had a lot of luck and crossed a road south of Mariazell.

It was again a steep uphill climb. Exhausted, we found a bit of flour in a ski lodge. It was cooked. In the afternoon, we reached an alpine dairy not far from Gußwerk.

In front of us was the Hochshwab massif. That area was restricted. SS units were supposedly still putting up resistance there and the Salzachtal was swarming with Russians. My last friends left me—they had to go west to go back to their homeland. A last handshake—good luck—they left and I was alone. I went down the slopes into the valley. When evening came, I had reached the road in the Salzachtal. There was a lot of traffic. I waded through the Salza in the darkness. It was raining cats and dogs. I looked for a place to stay on the steep wall of the cliff on the other side. I could not go on because I was tired. I stayed there for a few hours soaked to the bone. I heard noise all night below me. I was not until the dawn of May 31st (Thursday) that I saw that it was an enormous Russian camp. I clattered over impassible terrain and reached a small alpine pasture outside of Weyscheid, where I cooked me some raw potatoes and dried off a bit.

But the Russians in the vicinity caused me to break out again immediately.

During the evening, I crossed the road from Weyscheid to the Seeberg.

In fog and rain, I crossed a high mountain crest and reached an isolated hunting lodge in Rotsohl at the foot of Hohe Veitsch during evening. I was able to dry off a little and I got milk and bread. I got myself familiarized with the general conditions after the changes. In the late evening of May 31st, which for me was actually the last day of the war, I lay down soaked to the bone in the hay of a small stable, in the happy but simultaneously anxious expectation that the next day would be the day I went home. I left in the early morning of June 1st. In the fog, I went uphill steeply to the Rotsohlersattel on Hohe Veitsch.

A strong stormy wind blasted me in the face; my thin torn trousers flapped in the wind. I had a bit of rest in the mountain hut.

But I hardly got any rest—my homeland was there—and I wasn't home yet.

I went on downhill over talus slopes, clumps of pines—into the forested area – to a farmhouse. A hot cup of coffee did me good. My road took me along the Veitsch valley. On the heights west of there, I reached the Hubertushof—I quickly went across the road and up to the Troiseck slopes. Once I had made it up—it was already afternoon—I saw the Mürztal, also known as the Stanyalm, in the sunshine—my homeland. I sat down on some moss and let my past roll through my mind. It all came across to me like a fairy tale—the long years of the war—the comrades—the far-off countries—the collapse. Machine gun fire interrupted my reflection. Right, there were Russians in my homeland—the war was lost—and it appeared that we had bled for nothing. Who knows? I didn't have any time to think. I had to see how to get across the Mürztal safely with its big bivouac sites in order to get to the Stanzertal. I had a farmer lend me a rake so that I could go through the Russians as an "agricultural laborer" with one leg limping, marking me as a "village idiot." I wanted to disguise myself that way so as not to run the risk of being pulled away before I even got to my house door. It worked. Even while I was on my way from the slopes of the Troiseck, I ran into a Commissar and he let me go on my way unnoticed. In Hodersdorf, I was back on the road after many days. My uncle was working in the meadow. He initially didn't recognize me at all. I shaved at his house, had something to eat and found out that everything was fine with my family at home… I breathed a sigh of relief. My uncle accompanied me. In Aumühl, Mama Glatt met me with my little daughter Marliese. I couldn't stay there long—I was passing the big camp in Kindbergdoerfl, which was swarming with Ivans. A horse-drawn cart came by Hanslwirt, one just like the thousands of others that I had often seen going through the steppes during the war, often retreating, then going forward. My wife was sitting in it. She jumped out, we hugged each other, and went on to Stafz—my mother collapsed on me. I knew it was worth it; I was home.

Writing in 1948, *Oberleutnant* Schmalbruch, commander of the *3.Kompanie* of the *I.Btl./Jäg.Rgt. 2 'BR'* provides an account of his final days starting May 8th.

New orders; try to get to Budweis (Ceske Budejovice). According to intelligence reports, the Americans were there. The roads for retreat were completely clogged or made impassible by blown-up tanks in the middle of the road. We only managed to get ourselves toward the west during the night with some effort. Through Saar, we reached the area north of Deutsch Brod, where the order to disband was given in the vicinity of Casslau and then everyone faced his luck on his own. That was the beginning of a road of misery for most people that will remain unique in military history.

I would like to note that I myself was selected by the Americans in Austria as part of the modern slave trading and was turned over to the Russians with thousands of other soldiers. In the Soviet Union, the *'Brandenburgers'* were among the most hated soldiers are were at the top of the blacklist. They were subjected to the most shameless interrogation and harassment. I would also like to point out that I experienced them showing behavior that can only be wondered at.

Many old comrades are even now in the faraway prisoner-of-war camps of the USSR because they belonged to 'Brandenburg'.

Elements of *Panzer-Sturm-Pionier-Bataillon 'BR'* finally arrived in Czechoslovakia. They had unloaded in Hannsdorf (Hanušovice) and more than 50 kilometers north of Olmütz. As they unloaded, they found themselves out of contact with the *Division* and along a deserted frontline. *Hauptmann* Müller-Rochholz describes what happened:

May 8th: In the early morning, the headquarters and the *1.Pionier-Kompanie* (2nd transportation train for the *Bataillon*) unloaded in Hannsdorf. There was no way to figure out where the *Division* was! It was a damned shame that in this situation we had no contact with our bunch. The radio stations were set up on the mountains. It was looking for the *Division*. The Reconnaissance Platoon and all its vehicles were en route in order to somehow pick up the tracks of the *Division*. They soon returned unsuccessfully. All of the roads and field paths were blocked by columns indicting moving in a panic to the west.

I used a pistol to force the railway personnel to give up a locomotive and two rail cars and we took the tracks further south. At the next railway station, there were shots with infantry weapons, antitank guns and machine guns. However, it only appeared to be Czechs. We would soon handle them. There was a train full of fuel on a side track. While we held the Czechs down, we forced the locomotive driver to uncouple the fuel train and we drove back to Hannsdorf.

The captured fuel from Ottendorf-Okrilla—special diesel—was going down the roads near the railway station and the *Bataillon* was filling the last containers with this *Krad* from this armored train.

A *Rittmeister* from a *Panzer-Division* [likely the *17.Panzer-Division*] brought a supposed order that the *Bataillon* was subordinate to his division and was supposed to be moved southeast of Hannsdorf in order to maintain a position there until noon on May 9th. I asked for a written order from my *Division* or a higher echelon about the subordination.

The headquarters, the *1.Pionier-Kompanie* and the *Panzerjagdkommandos* (motorized by us) moved to the western exit to Hannsdorf. I went with the *Rittmeister* and—after it was made clear that they wanted to deploy us and move out themselves—made myself available and said that my *Bataillon* was going along in our *Division's* retreat columns to the west and it was impossible for them to return against the flow. When I offered the people the armored train, they were happy and abandoned the attempt to grab us.

With the platoon of railway workers abandoned in Hannsdorf headed west, we created a convoy of five full petrol-transport vehicles, which totaled over 200 cubic meters. They were supposed to turn over this petrol to Graf von Egloffstein, who was moving behind us [by train], so that when we ran into the *Division*, we could at least bring along the fuel that they would surely need desperately.

The Soviets had attacked west between Hannsdorf and Olmütz beginning around May 6th preventing *Panzer-Sturm-Pionier-Bataillon 'BR'* and the *Fahrschwadron 'BR'* from reaching the rest of the *Division* by rail. Forced west, these cut-off units of *'Brandenburg'* faced the same stark choice as their comrades farther south—surrender to the Soviets or make your way hundreds of kilometers west. They chose the latter course of action.

At noon on May 8th we moved in as the only intact unit in the wild melee going west. It was a test of nerves. Everyone was doing what he wanted in this chaotic escape. We brutally kept our column intact. There was no other way to do it. Otherwise we would have been all bogged down in an hour and incapable of doing anything anywhere.

At a railway station [at Grulich], we found von Egloffstein's *Schwadron*. The armored cars also came in right then. They were turned over to Egloffstein. The men in this team were glad to be back with the bunch.

After passing through Grulich, we reached the area of Chrudim (Pardubice) that day. Troops were coming from everywhere and reporting that the Russians were already there, no one could go any further, etc. etc. It was impossible to get a picture of the situation. The Czechs were waging partisan warfare. Supposedly, there were shots being fired out the windows in the villages. Our intact *SPW* columns didn't run into anything like that. The people with armbands fled into the buildings as soon as we showed up. Graf von Egloffstein wanted to try to get through to Kolin with his transport train. We wanted to meet there. Reconnaissance showed that German columns were moving south from also the direction of Kolin. So it was crowded there.

This night Müller-Rochholz and Graf von Egloffstein's forces parted in their separate efforts to reach Kolin.

While it was still night, we went further west on secondary roads. No one was able to give us any information in response to our continued questions about 'Brandenburg'. Damn it, where could the *Division* be hiding?

In the last days of the war, we all didn't believe that it would end this soon. Everywhere that 'Brandenburgers' attacked, the Russians retreated. The mood of the soldiers and officers was great. Everyone definitely wanted to kill some tanks.

At 6:00 p.m., we moved into the area of Schlapens. There we were stopped by a Russian reception line. Our intent was to break through by force. A Commissar told us, however, that if we did, anyone who came behind us would simply be destroyed. "In order to avoid bloodshed, we put down our weapons!"

At the airfield near Chrudim *Hauptmann* Müller-Rochholz requested each member of the *Bataillon* write down a "last wish" and had them placed, for example, in blue envelopes with addresses at the *Kompanien*. Soon *Hauptmann* Müller-Rochholz surrendered with his most of men. Others, however, were not ready to give up.

From Schlapens, our path to captivity began. The Russians did promise us that we would be back in our homeland in four weeks at the latest. We officers were separated from our soldiers. We first went to Groß-Meseritsch and were taken by truck from there to Brünn. In Brünn, people started plundering us. The boots, watches, wedding rings, gloves and in some cases even trousers were taken from us officers. Anyone who objected to that was simply killed. One officer whose wedding ring wouldn't come off his finger had his ring finger shot off. We were not given any food at all during the first few days. We had to live off of what the Russians let us keep. After 10 days, we got the first hot meal; it consisted of a very thin watery soup. Three of us officers attempted to escape. Unfortunately, we were caught again after the first few hours. We were in an officer camp and were guarded particularly strictly. After about four weeks had passed, they started to divide us up into work groups. We had to undress and walk by two Russian female physicians. The two women looked at everyone individually and then determined the work groups based on their judgment. The groups were 1 to 4. Anyone who wound up in Group 1 had to get ready to be transported to the east immediately. Groups 1 and 2 had barely left and then the rest of us had to report for examination again. So it could happen that one was initially in group 4, the handicapped, and then gradually into groups 3, 2 and 1. But as soon as one got into Group 1, one had to get a haircut—and then off to Russia.

The Soviets lied and never kept their word regarding POWs. Time and time again, they offered the Germans any conditions they wanted to get them to surrender. Once they surrendered, many were murdered. Captivity lasted decades.

Hauptmann Müller-Rochholz's comments on treatment in Soviet captivity were not unique to him. Under prior agreement with the Western Allies, German prisoners-of-war could be employed as a "ready workforce" to rebuild damage Germany caused in other countries during the war, a.k.a. slave labor, skirting the Geneva Convention. Their treatment in Soviet camps was particularly harsh.[12] Avoiding Soviet captivity at all costs providing a strong motivation to the men of *'Brandenburg'* in the final weeks of the war.

Unteroffizier Hans Stübling was with a group of *Pioniers* and others that chose to fight their way west.

Our small remnant, with *Leutnant* Clemeur, *Leutnant* Küper, *Feldwebel* Müller-Otterbach (taken prisoner), *Obergefreiter* Schnafel and a few people from the Reconnaissance Platoon, plus *General* Klatt, a *Division Ia*, and men from strange units, a total of 40 men, pushed their way through to the west, motorized until the 11th, through villages and small towns occupied by the Russians with waving and roars of peace. Then the vehicles were destroyed and the maps drawn. Compasses were allocated and people went on by foot in four groups. It was uninterrupted patrolling against Cossack units hunting us, hateful Czech gangs and a damned fast. On May 21st, 1945, the last seven men and I were made prisoners of the Czechs at Pzibrans, east of Pilsen.

The last members of *Panzer-Sturm-Pionier-Bataillon 'BR'* went into captivity nearly 20 days after the surrender of the Third Reich.

SS-Sturmbannführer Graf von Egloffstein along with the trains carrying the *1.Schwadron* and part of the *2.Schwadron* arrived in Grulich right as *Panzer-Sturm-Pionier-Bataillon 'BR'* passed through from Hannsdorf to Chrudim. Below is his recollection of his unit's arrival and final days:

The transport rolled out of Klotzsche on the night of May 7th, and on the next day (May 8th), we were already outside of Grulich. There was already retreat going on around us. We were not transported by railway staff and we took over the train ourselves with our own railway personnel from the *Abteilung*. Because I had loaded primarily of all ammunition, not in the usual way, but rather placing it in each *Schwadron* with Spaeter's permission in anticipation of deployment being bogged down, I wanted to get to the western border of Bohemia by force of arms. According to a railway official, however, the Czech militia had already occupied all the signal boxes, so we had our train only on to the Reich border and there sat stuck between two other trains at noon on May 9th. That was where we first found out about the surrender at noon on May 9th, 1945. Because the Russian units were only a few kilometers away and machine gun fire was approaching, I called the NCOs together and released them from their oath to the flag and—still acting in accordance with regulation—gave them permission to take anything usable off the train and advised them to move west through the Sudeten in small groups. At the boundary near Rocknitz, we were assured of free passage through Bohemia and we went to Ross headed west with the remainder of our rolling stock. At about 7:00 p.m. on the evening of May 11th, we were picked up in Jaromer by Ivan. After the famous *coup de grace* march to Glatz, I saw the officers of my staff and the commander of the *1.Schwadron* again.

---

12   Giles, p. 392-396, and 420-425. Some German POWs were kept in Soviet camps until the mid-1970s, thirty years or more after they were captured.

In the end, Eggolsheim did not escape Soviet captivity. What is meant by the "famous *coup de grace* march to Glatz" can only be guessed at. It was likely a foot march similar to the one experienced by Steidl, where members of the *Division* who could no longer walk on their own were shot and left on the side of the road.

Dr. Braune provides a final accounting for the *Heeres-Flak-Abteilung 'BR'*:

May 8th. Woke up at 4:00 a.m. The *Division* has ordered that all excess luggage, office supplies, etc. are to be destroyed. In response, we burned the entire paper war effort. The *Abteilung* burned all the personnel records. Then movement began on a large scale. In the loveliest weather, we spent the entire day going through Moravia to the west. Initially the roads were good, but about noon they became very bad and at one point went through deep sand. The towing vehicles had to help out here. The ambulance, a Steier, was the only thing that made it through well everywhere. At about 6:00 p.m. we reached Heinzendorf (Henčov). We took local quarters. I first took a wounded man after to the medical company using the vehicle. The company was somewhere to our west on a path covered against aircraft. I met *Stabsarzt* Dr. Daum there. He said that we were supposed to surrender that night. The *General* had radioed to *Korps* that we should not accept any more orders. Schörner had already absconded the day before (see Appendix B).

When I was got back to Heinzendorf, the *Abteilung* was destroying all excess vehicles and all the heavy weapons. The small arms and light Flak went on as well as any PAK in the *Abteilung*. My ambulance was also destroyed.

Shortly before we moved out, I was invited to dinner by my darling hosts, two extremely elderly Czechs. They had formerly been in Vienna and still loved the old imperial Austria. When I said goodbye, they wished me a happy journey home, and the old mother, a former nurse, blessed me with a calming gesture. We moved out into the darkness. I was in a personnel transport vehicle at the *Abteilung* headquarters. Eggen and Koch were going behind in the column in a Volkswagen. Prager had been at some repair facility with my Volkswagen for days. I never saw him again.

May 9th. Cold trip at night, warm trip during the day. We were making bad time because the Czech had closed off the tank obstacles we had built, and they always had to first be blown up by the engineers going in front of us. Strong Russian air activity, some bombing, but nothing happened to us. As the day went on, traveling became more and more difficult because strange units were clogging up the roads with their undisciplined travel and penetrating our column. At about noon, we went through Deutsch-Brod. There was a wild shooting spree when a shot was fired somewhere. We stopped in the window. As far as I could see and hear, no one among us was wounded. At about 3:00 p.m. we determined north of Deutsch-Brod that we were sitting in a kettle. The big road west of us from Brünn to Prague was occupied by the Russians. The commander entrusted the commander of the *1.Batterie*, which was traveling with us, with the reconnaissance. Contact with large parts of the *Abteilung* had been lost. We were sitting in a forested area and the mood was very bad. The reconnaissance determined that the road was secured by tanks and light anti-aircraft weapons. (To this day, I have not lost the feeling that the *Oberleutnant*, whose name I have forgotten, didn't make it all the way to the road.) We initially stayed in our patch of forest and started to destroy the light canons of the *3.Batterie* that we still had. I destroyed most of my luggage and started moving by foot. Suddenly there was news that there was still a gap open. Everyone jammed into the few still intact vehicles and roared off to the northwest. We went as far as being right outside Tschaslau (Caslav). This city itself was occupied by Russians. En route we picked up a few wounded from the *Division*. Because I had no way to provide thorough medical care anymore, we went to see the Czech Red Cross in Tschaslau. Whatever happened to them? I have not retained the names.

May 11th. At 2:00 a.m., we abandoned our vehicles. They were destroyed. With our small arms, we attempted to cross the road from Brünn to Prague on foot. We managed to break through at about 3:00 a.m. There were still about 30 of us in the Abteilung, which included the commander, the adjutant, the administrative officer and me. The other ones, I knew little of, if I knew them at all.

We continued moving by foot to the west. When it was getting light, we reached a big patch of forest, where we rested until noon. Then we decided to continue the movement during the day in order to get through to the west as quickly as possible. Because our formation was too big, the commander split it up. He kept about half of it; the adjutant and the administrative officer stayed with him. I then moved out with the other half. We spent the entire day moving. There were soon people who had problems with their feet.

My *Abteilung* and I reached Wlaschim (Vlašim) the next day, May 12th. The town was heavily guarded and occupied by Russians. We did not manage to go around it without being seen. We had to go into the town. There was many thousands of German *Landser* on the streets there. I was separated from my group there. I was taken to Brünn by a Russian column, but was separated on route. A few days later, while I was trying to get to the Moldau in the west by myself, I was put into the Tabor assembly camp.

From there, after breaking out of the camp in early September 1945, I managed to get by foot to my home in Haidmühle on the Czech-German border via Moldautein, Netolitz, Prachstiz and Volary, along with Dr. Geinitz, an *Assistentarzt* from another division.

Dr. Braune ultimately escaped Soviet captivity and made his way into the U.S. Zone of occupation. On May 8th *Rittmeister* Frey received his final mission. For the next 24 hours *Panzer-Aufklärungs-Abteilung 'BR'* was ordered to hold the defensive line at Stefanau so that the rest of *Panzergrenadier-Division 'BR'* could gain a head start in its withdrawal west. After 24 hours Frey's forces were to disengage from the Soviets and head toward Schüttenhofen (Míčov-Sušice). As ordered, the men of the *Abteilung* deployed into the frontline near Stefanau, north of Olmütz, and conducted the *Division's* final wartime combat action. There is no identified account for what happened next. In the end *Panzer-Aufklärungs-Abteilung 'BR'* was broke up or destroyed in their withdrawal with any survivors going into Soviet captivity with the knowledge that their sacrifice bought the rest of the *Division* precious time to withdraw west.

While many of the men of *'Brandenburg'* went into Soviet captivity, others managed to cross the expanse of Czechoslovakia, dodging roving armed Czech bands and Red Army soldiers to reach U.S. Forces. The five month combat odyssey of *Panzergrenadier-Division 'BR'* was finally over.

20

Conclusion

The accounts by *Panzergrenadier-Division 'Brandenburg'* veterans that make up this book are insightful for their tactical description of the fighting at war's end and unique impressions of the milieu of that time. Their memoirs are made all the more important given the lack of operational war diaries and primary documents available for *Heeresgruppe Mitte* during this same time period. The end of the war in the East was unimaginably ferocious. The devastating Soviet firepower unleashed on each square kilometer was greater than anything experienced by *'Brandenburgers'* earlier in the war. Quarter was not expected and often not given between combatants. Atrocity was unfortunately ever present on the field of battle. The defensive fighting in the east that began in January 1945 had no strategic intent and no operational objectives. Adolf Hitler simply continued to pursue a war of resistance in the hope that "providence" might intervene on his side against the Grand Alliance's call for unconditional surrender. His intent of continued military resistance was made possible only by the improvisations of the *Ersatzheer* that continued to form, re-form, and field a constant stream of combat formations into the frontline in ways that allowed basic primary group bonds to flourish under the right conditions. Caught between a draconian military justice system and a real fear of Soviet captivity, the *Wehrmacht* formations continued to fight in the east and resist capitulation as there was no other choice. *'Brandenburg'* was not alone in this regard.

Will Berthold, one of the most successful German literary writers in the postwar period, published a book titled *Division Brandenburg: Die Haustruppe des Admirals Canaris* in 1959. He published this book less than a year after Spaeter's self-published three volume history of *Panzer-Korps 'Großdeutschland'*, but as a popular novelist Berthold enjoyed a much wider distribution across Germany. Part spy novel, part combat memoir, this work of historical fiction explodes with the exploits of Germany's *Sonderkommandos* from beginning to end. It is not surprising that it is still reprinted today in multiple languages. Berthold certainly did not have access to the war diaries and other primary documents available to modern researchers when he penned his work. Despite this historical shortcoming he summarized the final transformation of *Division 'Brandenburg'* into *Panzergrenadier-Division 'BR'* more accurately than Spaeter:

> Now the end was near. Everyone knew it, though a few dared say so. But the end of the Brandenburg Division was to be other than as conceived by those who had originally recruited the crack force. It neither fought to the last man, nor disintegrated into anonymity at the capitulation. It was in fact destroyed by the bomb placed in Hitler's headquarters on July 20th 1944, by Colonel von Stauffenberg. The S.S. established the fact that Canaris and a number of his officers were party to the plot... .
>
> The Admiral had in fact lost much of his authority over the Division before July 20th, but after that, the Division itself was dissolved. Those soldiers who wished were allowed to join Skorzeny's group. The others were absorbed in the Grossdeutschland Division where they spent the rest of the war. After the capitulation, a few of them offered their services to the espionage organizations, as a consequence of which Brandenburgers of the west fought Brandenburgers of

the East. Thus ended this elite body.[1]

The origin of *'Brandenburg'* is inseparable from the 1938 reorganization and expansion of the *Wehrmacht* under National Socialist Germany. Yet, the man who organized the elite commandos of the Third Reich, *Admiral* Wilhelm Canaris, attempted to steer his organization away from direct involvement in the ideologically driven policies of mass murder supported by the *Wehrmacht's* chief, Willhelm Keitel, and establish an anti-Hitler circle that ultimately cost him his life. The failed July 20th, 1944 assassination of Adolf Hitler was a catalyst for *'Brandenburg'*. In the wake of Canaris' arrest and dissolution of the *Abwehr*, the ongoing transformation from elite *Sonderkommandos* capable of worldwide special operation missions, into a conventional force of *Panzergrenadiers* built upon a core group of combat-tested officers and non-commissioned officers, was complete.

This transformation followed the Reich's strategic fortunes and the political rivalries driven by the rise of Himmler's influence. Through 1943 *'Brandenburg'* could claim a quasi-independent status under the *Abwehr* command, but by 1944 the *Division* had to make a choice. Either continue its commando work in the *SS*, or become regular frontline soldiers in the *Heer*. The *Division's* command chose that latter course. Many of the "old hands" that had joined as commandos and survived the brutal combat in the Balkans during the fall of 1944 saw the transformation as a "sell out". Few understood at that time the overall political implications of the deal that spared them from mass conversion into Himmler's *SS* where they would have fallen under the command of the notorious Otto Skorzeny (as some members from the *Division's* training and replacement organization did). Despite the "sell out" the men of *'Brandenburg'* maintained a high degree of cohesion and combat effectiveness through the last days of the war, and in some cases beyond.

The men that made up the new *Division* were raw recruits and veteran commandos. Whole battalions and regiments from more than a half-dozen different *Heer* combat formations fed the ranks and built out the divisional organization thanks to the efficient *Ersatzheer*. What welded this composite force together was the camaraderie forged during the initial deployment in Poland. Trust was built. Friendships emerged. Officers like Oesterwitz, Hunhold, Metzger, Müller-Rochholz, Voshage and their men learned to rely on and support each other. Their bonds transcended the different experiences and military backgrounds that distinguished them. In the end, the announcement of Adolf Hitler's death came and went with little fanfare. The *Division* did not fall apart or disintegrate. The men would not let down their comrades at this late hour. Only when capitulation was imminent do the accounts relate the start of desertions. They occurred first from the ranks of new recruits and then from some "old hands". With final capitulation and unconditional surrender looming over the heads of the men, no one wanted to surrender to the Soviets. They knew their only chance was to head west and reach the lines of U.S. Forces. The majority of the *Division* maintained their cohesion until the end and beyond. The overall experience of the men of *Panzergrenadier-Division 'BR'* retold through their wartime dairies and post war letters, serve as a reminder that men in battle will fight first and foremost for their comrades, followed next by their individual survival, regardless of the political apparatus that initially directed them onto the field of battle.

1   Will Berthold, *Brandenburg Division* (Mayflower Books Ltd: Frogmore, 1973), p. 146.

Afterword

It was inevitable that new source material pertaining to the topics contained in this book became available before publication. The rate of research on World War II by academics and avocational historians alike has only increased with the passing of seven decades since the end of the war. *Prelude to Berlin: The Red Army's Offensive Operations in Poland and Eastern Germany, 1945* was released as *Panzergrenadiers to the Front!* was under final preparation for publication.[1]

The source material for *Prelude to Berlin* consists of a series of extensive postwar studies prepared by the Soviet General Staff in the immediate decade after the war. Some were written for public consumption while others for distribution to internal military channels. The perspective contained in the collected articles offer a unique Soviet view into the situation opposite *Heeresgruppe Mitte*, and in particular *Panzer-Korps 'Großdeutschland'*, from the period January-Mach 1945. Germane operational and tactical observations from two separate articles in *Prelude to Berlin* are discussed below to enhance the historical narrative in the proceeding chapters.

The initial deployment of *Panzer-Korps 'Großdeutschland'* to Litzmannstadt (Lodz) and the defense by divisions *'Brandenburg'* and *'Hermann Göring'* south of the city was adversely impacted by the Soviet's 16th Air Army. This fact figures prominently in the Soviet understanding of their operational success around Litzmannstadt (Lodz) and is worth noting. *'Brandenburg'* veterans recalled air attacks during the first days of deployment to the city during mid-January 1945. Due to difficult weather conditions the window for air operations was limited at the start of the Vistula-Oder Strategic Offensive, but when the weather cleared the Soviets wasted no opportunity. During the critical three days from January 18th-20th the Soviet 16th Air Army of the First Belorussian Front flew between 700-900 sorties per day. Their optimal configuration was to group 2-4 ground attack aircraft into a wing that ranged low over the ground with orders to destroy "... the enemy's retreating forces along the roads, especially from the Kutno and Lodz areas, as well as against concentrations of his forces along the western bank of the Warta River, in the Sieradz area, while preventing the enemy from consolidating along the Warta defensive line."[2] Undoubtedly this level of Soviet air activity helped prevent a solid German defense from being established around the city where *Panzer-Korps 'Großdeutschland'* deployed and presumably gave valuable tactical intelligence to Soviet armored forces now advancing at break-neck speeds behind the main German line.

In none of the articles written about the Vistula-Oder Strategic Offensive in *Prelude to Berlin* did the Soviets mention their failure to identify the deployment of *Panzer-Korps 'Großdeutschland'* to the area. They make the point that the Western Allies allowed the movement of the *6.Panzer-Armee* from the Western Front to the Eastern Front for postwar political reasons, but they also identified the German shifting of divisions from *Heeresgruppe Süd* to justify in part the stiffening of German resistance opposite their forces. Nowhere do they mention the ordered deployment of *Panzer-Korps 'Großdeutschland'* by Guderian from its reserve status in East Prussia to Poland by rail. The articles leave the reader to assume that this *Korps* was always part of the *4.Panzer-Armee* before the winter offensive began. This is an important fact given how prominent *Panzer-Korps 'Großdeutschland'* factors into the

---

1   Soviet General Staff, Edited and Translated by Richard W. Harrison, *Prelude to Berlin: The Red Army's Offensive Operations in Poland and Eastern Germany, 1945* (Helion & Co in cooperation with the Association of the Unites States Army: Solihull, 2016).

2   From the internal work by Colonel A.D. Bagreev, *The Vistula-Oder Operation. The defeat of German-Fascist forces in Poland by Soviet Forces in January 1945* issued by the Voroshilov General Staff Academy in 1957. p. 77.

Soviet reasons for both operational and tactical failures of the First Ukrainian Front.

Once *Panzer-Korps 'Großdeutschland'* did deploy it became a source of continued frustration to the Soviets. A lack of inter-front Soviet cooperation was a major reason why this German formation and others were able to withdraw westward and reconstitute. Yet, the Soviet General Staff lauded both the pace of operations and cooperation between the First Belorussian and First Ukrainian Fronts. The initial success of the offensive led STAVKA to issue orders directing both Fronts to ". . . increase the pace of the offensive" and to accomplish this ". . . mobile forces were ordered to bypass powerful centers of resistance."[3] An increase in operational speed only exacerbated the need for close cooperation.

In the Soviet analysis of the first stage of the offensive from January 12th-24th by Colonel A.D. Bagreev in his *The Vistula-Oder Operation. The defeat of German-Fascist forces in Poland by Soviet Forces in January 1945* it was noted how the First Belorussian Front had to "adopt special measures for securing the flanks" due to the slower pace of the First Ukrainian Front.[4] Bagreev, however, concluded that one of the most important factor in the success of the operation was ". . . the organization of the close cooperation of the two *fronts*, which carried out the same task of defeating the German-Fascist forces in Poland."[5] As an example of this coordination Bagreev cites "for example, in order to eliminate the enemy's Kielce-Radom group of forces, the actions of the First Belorussian Front's 33rd Army and the First Ukrainian Front's 3rd Guards and 6th armies were scrupulously planed and coordinated according to place and time . . ."[6] Yet we know that those German divisions escaped the planned Soviet encirclement only to form the roving pocket known as *Gruppe Nehring* that remained a major problem for the First Ukrainian Front. This was the only attempt at joint tactical coordination between Zhukov and Koniev's forces during the winter offensive.

This Soviet operational perspective of the Vistula-Oder Strategic Operation is rooted in the concept of deep penetration and avoidance of any offensive delay caused by defensive fighting. From this perspective the Soviet winter offensive was a resounding success. However, from a strategic perspective the destruction of German formations would have gone a long way to collapsing the Eastern Front and ending the war sooner as these formations were successfully reconstituted by the *Ersatzheer* in March and April.

The bypassed *Gruppe Nehring* and *Panzer-Korps 'Großdeutschland'* became a noted problem for the First Ukrainian Front as discussed in Lieutenant-General S.P. Platonov, *The First Ukrainian Front's Lower Silesian Offensive Operation (8-24 February 1945)*. Platonov noted that " ... in our troop's rear the struggle continued against so-called wandering 'pockets,' which represented the remnants of the enemy's units and formations defeated in the January-offensive, which in dispersed groups, often large ones, were attempting to break through to the west and southwest in order to link up with their forces that had retired behind the Oder. They attacked our transports, headquarters, depots, and airfields, seriously interfering with the normal work of the front's rear organs."[7] This is a strong counterpoint to Bagreev's statement that "good coordination" between the Fronts existed. Rather, this quote is a statement to the contrary as noted in previous chapters of *Panzergrenadiers to the Front!* Platonov goes on to state that Koniev issued special directive No. 0028/op on January 27th to his army commanders ". . .to clean out their areas of hostile bands and ensure normal conditions for the rear's work."[8] This order was not effectively carried out as the German forces operating in Koniev's rear and flanks adversely impacted the First Ukrainian Front's offensive operations in February. Platonov concluded

---

3   Bagreev, p. 75.
4   Ibid, p. 80.
5   Ibid, p. 90.
6   Ibid.
7   Colonel N.A. Fokin, edited by Lieutenant-General S.P. Platonov, *The First Ukrainian Front's Lower Silesian Offensive Operation (8-24 February 1945)* that appeared in the *Sbornik Voenno-Istoricheskikh Materialov Velikoi Otechestvennoi Voiny (nos. 10-11) [Collected Military History Articles of the Great Patriotic War]*, p. 347.
8   Ibid.

that these forces ". . . to a certain degree complicated the situation in the front's rear and distracted attention and forces from the resolution of the main combat tasks."[9] We now know that the majority of German forces cut off in the initial offensive—in particular *Gruppe Nehring* and *Panzer-Korps 'Großdeutschland'*—did indeed make their way back through porous Soviet lines to the Oder River. The German forces that withdrew between the flanks of the First Belorussian and First Ukrainian Front established a strong defense along the Oder in the area of Glogau and were in turn able to halt the First Ukrainian Front's ". . .high offensive pace at which the operation was developing".[10]

As the fighting paused along the upper Oder at the beginning of February, *OKH* worked to quickly re-establish a solid defensive line. Barely trained new recruits were sent to the frontline in *Marsch-Battalions* while *Volkssturm* units were raised in local areas. Platonov's assessment of the stiffening resistance is an interesting look at the situation from their perspective. He identified that there was a high level of desertion from German units at this time. Screening lines were placed behind the Oder to halt deserters.[11] Platonov states that orders were initially issued to create whole new units from the retreating German stragglers, but that this order was quickly changed to send soldiers back to their parent division, presumably to ensure a cohesive combat force. This latter practice only served to reconstitute combat power quickly by grouping soldiers who were already familiar with each other (see discussion of Primary Group in Chapter 4 above).

Platonov correctly points out that German divisions now numbered between 2,000-7,000 men with the average being 4,000 in the wake of the Vistula-Oder Strategic Offensive. He makes a point of stating that a significant proportion of the frontline combat divisions were little more than *Kampfgruppen*.[12] The relatively low combat power of each German division raises the question as to why they presented such a formidable blocking force along the upper Oder despite having been defeated in the field and cut-off behind Soviet lines for nearly three weeks. The Soviet answer to this is very intriguing. Perhaps one of the most critical factors on the stiffening defense by defeated German combat units identified by Platonov was the immense fear of the Red Army reinforced through "Goebbels lying propaganda". The Soviet General Staff Study states that "the [German] soldier had been scared by fairy tales about the atrocities committed by Soviet forces against the peaceful population, about mass executions of prisoners, about exile to hard labor in Siberia, etc. On that score, in the minds of the German soldiers Siberia was associated with the idea of hell on earth. Many soldiers were ready to undergo the heaviest suffering under the bullets and shells on the front, if only not to end up in Siberia."[13] This was indeed a major factor in continued resistance unfortunately nourished by the real atrocities perpetrated by the Soviets and witnessed by the German soldier on the battlefields in Poland and in Silesia. The feelings of fear and hatred stirred up by Soviet atrocities were only exacerbated by the increased draconian punishment German soldiers now lived under in the final year of the war. The threat of being shot for desertion followed by the possible imprisonment of family members in concentration camps or their possible execution served to focus frontline soldiers on continued resistance.[14] Platonov assessed that these measures combined to foster a change in morale along the German frontline of the upper Oder. The First Ukrainian Front was ". . . no longer faced with an enemy running away in panic, as had been the case in the latter half of January, but a more or less organized combat force."[15]

The First Ukrainian Front was given the objectives of developing their offensive across the upper Oder River and Neisse Rivers to capture Dresden and reach the Elbe River in February. However, the stubborn resistance encountered along the Oder River halted all future offensive planning beyond

9   Ibid.
10   Ibid, p. 361.
11   Ibid, pp. 373-74.
12   Ibid.
13   Ibid, p. 378.
14   Ibid.
15   Ibid, p. 379.

the Oder-Neisse River line. Platonov concluded that "the underestimation of the enemy's forces and his capability for stubborn resistance along the Oder defensive line was one of the material reasons for the failure of the front's center and left-wing armies to carry out their assigned tasks and led to significant changes in the conditions for developing a general offensive beyond the Oder."[16] This again demonstrates the failure to coordinate between the two Soviet Fronts and the belief that German forces left behind the advancing tank armies would be destroyed by follow-on forces. The Soviets admit that their offensive plans were thrown off by "stubborn resistance" that came from the very German divisions they supposedly "cleaned up" behind the lines.

In discussing the stubborn defense of the upper Oder, *Panzer-Korps 'Großdeutschland'* is continually singled out in several articles contained in *Prelude to Berlin*. Concerning the operations in February, Platonov states that "The 'Brandenburg' Panzergrenadier Division, 'Hermann Göring' Panzer Division and the 20th Panzergrenadier Division, which were part of the *Grossdeutschland* Panzer Corps, were engaged in stubborn defensive fighting opposite the left flank of the 3rd Guards Army and the right-flank formations of the 13th Army."[17] He notes that the First Ukrainian Front attempted to encircle and destroy the German formations of *Panzer-Korps 'Großdeutschland'* in a planned offensive launched during the first week of February[18]. This offensive, while successful in pushing back the German formations in the area of Sagan, failed to destroy the *Korps*. In particular, Platonov notes that "as before, the most stubborn fighting unfolded along the front's central sector in the 13th Army's attack sector. Units of the 'Großdeutschland' Panzer Corps, which were defending here, were better armed and proved to be more resilient than the remaining German formations."[19] As detailed in Chapters 9-11 in *Panzergrenadiers to the Front!* this particular Soviet observation is not necessarily true. *Panzergrenadier-Division 'Brandenburg'* and *Panzer-Division 'Hermann Göring'* were not better armed, and in some cases, were actually weaker materially than other German combat divisions located along the front.

Panzer-Korps 'Großdeutschland' and its subordinate units, *Panzergrenadier-Division 'Brandenburg'* and *Panzer-Division 'Hermann Göring'*, proved to be formidable combat formations even when severely weakened. Once reconstituted along the Neisse River in March and April both divisions ensured the destruction of the 2nd Polish Army and 7th Guards Mechanized Corps at the start of the final offensive into eastern Germany.

The Soviet perspective outlined above, contributes to a broader understanding of the fateful events during the last six months of combat along the Eastern Front, which accelerated the defeat of Nazi Germany and reshaped Europe in the post-war world.

---

16   Ibid, p. 399.
17   Ibid, p. 375.
18   Ibid, p. 404.
19   Ibid, p. 405.

Appendix A

Analysis of the Retreat of *Gruppe Nehring* by *Generalmajor* Hans von Ahlfen

Generalmajor Hans von Ahlfen wrote his observations of *Gruppe Nehring's* retreat along with a brief analysis of Soviet operations during the Vistula-Oder Winter Offensive as part of the manuscript he prepared for the U.S. Historical Division while in post-war captivity. His remarks offer insight into the tactical and environmental factors faced by *Panzer-Korps 'GD'* and *Panzergrenadier-Division 'BR'* during the four week period that spanned the end of January and the beginning of February 1945. Several comments on Soviet operations that contributed to the ability of such a large German force to survive a 250 kilometer withdrawal from behind enemy lines should be highlighted. Von Ahlfen notes how Koniev's forces never purposely tried to eliminate German pockets as they were focused on a westward drive, corroborating Koniev's statements presented in Chapter 8. This created opportunities for German commanders to exploit tactically, as noted by von Ahlfen, despite operating against a better motorized and more lethal opponent, in terms of firepower. There was an observed desire by the Soviets to minimize losses that made them less inclined to invest in a pitched battle unless absolutely necessary. It would seem that luck also played a part. The unintended meeting of several cut-off German groupings at Bialaczow on January 18th/19th served to solidify *Gruppe Nehring* and give it the added strength required to cross the Pilica and reach *Panzer-Korps 'GD'*. Weather also aided the German movements as persistent fog prevented Soviet aerial attacks or reconnaissance. The snow aided in night navigation as units could easily follow the tracks of other vehicles, and the extreme cold froze swamps and rivers that allowed for easy passage along secondary tracks that were used to avoid Soviet forces operating along main roads. The Germans for their part proved adept at ad hoc reorganization of their units. They established a clear chain-of-command among disparate units that continued to function expertly while cut-off. Discipline and morale remained intact. Aided by favorable weather, and insufficient Soviet operational attention, the forces of *Gruppe Nehring*, and *Panzer-Korps 'GD'* maximized the limited tactical advantages to reach the main German lines and survive.

One question indirectly addressed in von Ahlfen's commentary is whether or not *Gruppe Nehring* could have survived its trek west without the deployment of *Panzer-Korps 'GD'*. What von Ahlfen states under "Friendly Forces" is that *Gruppe Nehring* linked up with von Saucken's forces at "just the right time", though this idea is not developed further. Von Saucken's *Korps* deployed to Litzmannstadt on order of Guderian into a disastrous situation. Both *'Brandenburg'* and *'Hermann Göring'* went on the defensive immediately and suffered heavy losses. *Panzer-Korps 'GD'* had no choice but to withdraw. While it did hold long enough to achieve a link up with *Gruppe Nehring*, it became obvious that the link-up brought more benefit to von Saucken then to von Nehring who quickly provided their "rescuers" with needed petrol, for example. While there was probably some benefit of having more combat troops attached to *Gruppe Nehring*, even if new and somewhat inexperienced as in the case of *'Brandenburg'*, von Nehring's roving pocket of 100,000 soldiers likely would have made it back to the Oder River on its own. The reverse cannot be said with any certainty for the approximately 15,000 troops *Panzer-Korps 'GD'*.

I. The retreat was possible because of the following:

Enemy
1) Most of the enemy motorized and armored units maintained their attack direction to the west without being disturbed.
2) Only weak units got through, and generally they were repelled with high enemy losses.
3) So far, the enemy has refrained from pressing on pockets even in locations that are advantageous for it, such as the Pilica crossing north of Sulejów.
4) The enemy, when sure of victory, is not cautious, which is something we also know about as well from the Polish and the French campaigns:
     A lack of reconnaissance and security. Therefore there are frequent surprise successes that cripple enemy initiatives to tackle us, even though they are limited in time and space.
5) In addition, for the first time, we can see among the Russians the intent to spare losses in penetrations it has achieved, in the belief that the war is about to be won.

Friendly Leadership
1) The coincidental meeting at Bialaczow of the retreating units on January 18th—and in particular Nehring's *Panzer* units that survived the crisis at Paradyz at noon on January 19th—made it possible to break through at Paradyz and cross the Pilica. Otherwise, most of them would have been annihilated and taken prisoner while still to the east of the Pilica.
2) It was just the right time to be picked up by *Panzer-Korps 'Großdeutschland'* from the area south of Lask.
3) The separation of motorized and armored units under *General* von Saucken from the foot units under *Generalleutnant* Hohn tied up the enemy with the portion that was dangerous to it, von Saucken's troops, thereby giving the very exhausted foot columns some breathing room.

Logistics
Petrol supply continues to always come at the last moment, though not in sufficient quantities.

Weather
1) Cold weather: Almost all the movement that was possible was on insignificant side roads; without a load-bearing layer of ice on the Pilica, the movement to the other bank would not have been successful.
2) The layer of snow made navigation during the night movements significantly easier.
3) Thick fog prevented enemy air reconnaissance and the use of bombers and fighter-bombers and made enemy ground reconnaissance more difficult.

Population
1) The Polish population in the Government General and the Warthegau willingly helped feed the troops. Even separated units were rarely betrayed to the Russians except in the vicinity of large cities (Litzmannstadt and Petrikau).
2) The population appeared to be afraid of the Russians.

II. Evaluation of the performance, combat value and behavior of the troops
1) When the great battle began, the troops were not as rested and fresh as one would have wished. Reasons:
   a) The Weichsel position occupied in mid-December 1944—after a Hungarian reserve division was relieved—required lots of fundamental improvements and required continued hard

labor, particularly because of the frozen ground.

b) On December 27th, the ice on the Weichsel was trafficable. The results were friendly and enemy attacks every night, which put a heavy demand on the troops conducting them and defending against them. In addition, a number of ice mines were lost, which put heavy demands not only on the engineers, but also on the troops defending them.

c) The training status of the replacement battalions required continued combat training under front-type conditions.

d) The way the Hungarian reserve division was relieved by the *4.Panzer-Armee* and the relief of the *Pionier-Brigade 70*, which required regrouping three times, which substantially stressed the troops.

2) The order from the *Korps*, which arrived very late, to evacuate the position on short notice created extraordinary demands, particularly in regard to moving the numerous ground-based and immobile antitank guns and light machine guns as well as large amounts of ammunition. Because the rear area close to the front was already bled dry due to the battles in the late summer and the autumn of 1944, it was only possible to take a very small number of vehicles along on short notice. Mostly the population drove their few horses into the forests. Although the heavily-packed troops managed to save weapons and ammunition by carrying them out of the position, continuing to move with such quantities was out of the question.

3) The successful battle in Ilza, which was decisive for the retreat south of Ilza, strengthened resolve and combat power yet again.

However, the initially unbroken movement by day and night with significant distances, standing around on blocked roads, a lack of proper food, a lack of sufficient quarters while it was getting colder, a complete shuffling of the units resulting in the lack of a single commander, bypassing several unoccupied friendly well-constructed rear positions (such as the Pilica position) without a battle, and finally the increasing images of a defeat (shot-up columns of vehicles, burned and blown-up combat materiel of all types) increasingly gnawed on morale and physical strength.

The nighttime attack on Paradyz on January 18th-19th was the last tightly controlled combat action by troops on foot. Later troops on foot were assembled without orders into endless movement columns with the intent of getting further to the west and not being captured without a fight.

There were enough small arms, ammunition and close combat materiel for immediate close combat defense, and the will to fight was unbroken.

However, after January 19th, only motorized and armored troops had any significant combat value for conducting operations.

4) Petrol shortage. *4.Panzer-Armee* command had fully equipped all its units before the big battle began so that it could form strongpoints in a situation of overall shortage. The rapid enemy penetration put the enemy in possessions of the gasoline reserves quickly. The results are clear.

On the morning of January 17th, the *Sperrverband* burned all the vehicles not being used directly for combat and their contents (such as all the luggage and all the orderly room materials). The Commander's command *SPW*, for example, was loaded only with weapons, ammunition, rations and soldiers—no personal luggage at all.

It is thanks to this measure that, for example, that the *lFH Abteilung* still had 12 tubes ready to fire until January 20th and 6 until January 24th and arrived in Glogau still having two firing-ready tubes and that the command *SPW* served in the last days of the retreat as what was frequently the decisive reconnaissance and combat vehicle.

For three days, the *SPW* formed a transport and combat group with one Wespe (10.5cm self-propelled artillery vehicle) to save petrol.

Not all the units let their useless deadweight go soon enough; they traveled for days with stuff that was useless for battles and then had to leave or destroy vehicles whose gasoline was used up uselessly in addition to these vehicles.

But even if there was planned saving of fuel, they were still forced to destroy combat vehicles. There was much too little petrol.

Appendix B

Final Days of *Heeresgruppe Mitte* by *Chef der Generalstabes Generalleutnant* Oldwig Otto von Natzmer

The below account of the last days of *Heeresgruppe Mitte* was written by *Generalleutnant* Oldwig Otto von Natzmer at some point after the war, likely the early 1950s. Von Natzmer's account of the late war was certainly important to Hans Spaeter from both a historical perspective and likely from a lineage perspective because von Natzmer had previously been part of the family of '*Großdeutschland*' combat units. After serving in various posts in the *161.Infanterie-Division*, the *XXXIX.Armee-Korps*, and *26.Panzer-Division* during the first 18 months of the invasion of the Soviet Union, he was appointed in mid-December 1942 as the *Ia* (Operations Officer) of *Infanterie-Division* '*Großdeutschland*'. This was a prestige appointment for any German officer given the stature of the division. The division saw combat actions around Rzhev while serving with *Heeresgruppe Mitte*, and during the heavy fighting around Kharkov in the spring of 1943 with *Heeresgruppe Süd*. He was an *Oberstleutnant* at the time, and he soon earned both the Iron Cross 2nd and 1st Class. On April 2nd 1943 he was awarded the German Cross in Gold, followed by a promotion to *Oberst* on May 1st 1943. On May 19th, 1943 *Infanterie-Division* '*Großdeutschland*' was reclassified as *Panzergrenadier-Division* '*Großdeutschland*'. Von Natzmer now served as the division's *1.Generalstabs Offiziere*. The division saw heavy combat during the fighting at Kursk and Von Natzmer earned the Knight's Cross, which was awarded to him on September 3rd, 1943. On July 1st 1944 he was promoted to *Generalmajor*, and re-assigned as the *Chef des Generalstabes* of *Heeresgruppe Nord* under *General* Schörner. He served there until the end of January of 1945. He was reassigned with Schörner to the staff of *Heeresgruppe Mitte* at the end of January 1945 as the East Front commands were reshuffled with the creation of *Heeresgruppe Weichsel* after the start of the Soviet Winter Offensive. He remained in *Heeresgruppe Mitte* through the final capitulation of the Reich, serving as the *Chef des Generalstabes* and earning a promotion to *Generalleutnant* in March. His account starts in April 1945 and continues through the end of the war. He offers insight into the operational decisions that affected *Heeresgruppe Mitte* during those final days.

Von Natzmer does not provide an explicit answer to the situation that drove the decision to deploy *Panzergrenadier-Division* '*Brandenburg*' to Olmütz. What his comments do reveal is that the situation of the *1.Panzer-Armee* became difficult due to increased Soviet pressure and that the victory at Bautzen, which stabilized the *4.Panzer-Armee*'s left flank, made possible the transfer of '*Brandenburg*' to assist in its withdrawal. More detail on the decision about the final deployment of '*Brandenburg*' is related in Appendix C.

Short report on the last days of *Heeresgruppe Mitte*
In late April 1945, the *Heeresgruppe Mitte* frontline ran roughly as follows: southwest of Brünn (there a loose border with the northern flank of *Heeresgruppe Süd*, *8.Armee*)-Olmütz-March-Freudenthal (up to there, *1.Panzer-Armee*, Commander in Chief *General der Panzertruppen*

Nehring, Chief, *Oberst, i.G.,* Freiherr von Weitershausen)-Glatz-Hirschberg (*17.Armee,*
Commander in Chief, *General der Infanterie* Hasse, Chief *Oberst, i.G.,* Gartmair)-Görlitz-
Bautzen-Dresden-Freiburg (*4.Panzer-Armee,* Commander in Chief *General der Panzertruppen*
Gräser, Chief, *Oberst, i.G.* Knüppel, *Generalmajor* starting May 1st), and continuing a loose
security front against the English and the Americans generally along the Chemnitz-Eger-Weiden
line (Commander in the Erzgebirge, *Generaloberst* Hoth and *7.Armee,* Commander in Chief
General der Infanterie Obstfelder, Chief *Generalmajor* von Gersdorff).

There were still land line connections in early May with our neighbors to the right
(*Heeresgruppe* and *Armee*), to *Heeresgruppe* Kesselring and to the *Führungsstab Süd* of the
Oberkommando der Wehrmacht, General der Gebirgstruppen Winter. Through relays, there was off
and on radio contact with the Reich government and *Führungsstab Nord.*

General observations: Everyone was fully aware of the hopelessness of the overall war
situation. Fighting was continued because 1) there were orders to that effect; 2) there was still
a vague political hope that there was discord in the enemy coalition (a hope that was also fed by
allusions from the *Führungsstab Süd* in late April); 3) because it was believed that if (2) were true
and there was a cease fire in which we would still be able to participate as a party to negotiations,
that a pledge in the form of Czechoslovakia, the heartland of Europe with all its untouched assets
would have to be held and could be held; and 4) it was the intention of the *Heeresgruppe* to use
the retreat movements already in progress to surrender as many troops as possible to the Western
powers and as few as possible to the Russians in any surrender.

In addition, there were a large number of medical facilities of all sorts with thousands of
wounded in the Czech area and disclosure of them was to be avoided as long as possible.

On the scale of the overall situation, the condition of the troops in the *Heeresgruppe* could
be considered good. It was the only *Heeresgruppe* that still had a somewhat cohesive front and
the troops' willingness to fight was unbroken. Though cases of desertion of small units and
shirking increased daily, overall there was no serious danger for combat effectiveness. The orders
continued to be carried out, the troops were in their commanders' hands, and things were in good
order in the rear (which was particularly due to the Commander in Chief of the *Heeresgruppe,*
Generalfeldmarschall Schörner). There was a shortage of ammunition and fuel, but there was
enough for the necessary combat operations. The railways were in operation; even in early May,
units were seamlessly moved by rail. There were also shortages in supplies and food for the troops,
but there was enough.

The enemy attacked in the area of Brünn and near Mährkisch-Weisskirchen with much larger
forces, forcing the *1.Panzer-Armee* to a slow retreat though it couldn't achieve any overall success.
The army in general managed to carry out the retreat movements ordered by the *Heeresgruppe,*
albeit with some corrections forced by the enemy. Nevertheless, the situation of the *1.Panzer-*
Armee caused concern because of the extraordinarily great demands placed on the troops. The
17.Armee, not pressed by the enemy and weakened by expenditures of all sorts for its two
neighboring armies, retreated according to plan. It and its center were the ones deployed furthest
to the east and that dictated the speed at which the *Heeresgruppe* retreated. The pressure on the
4.Panzer-Armee had been reduced after the favorable battle near Bautzen, but it continued to
increase slowly in the Dresden area. No one there assumed that there would be a Russian attack
seeking to be decisive until the Russians released significant forces from the battle for Berlin,
which they had more or less won already, and wanted to move them into the Dresden area for an
attack on Prague in early May. The *7.Armee* was not involved in the retreat movements.

The Czechoslovakian resistance movement was initially little noticed and was limited to the
Prague area.

The *Heeresgruppe* did not have a clear mission; it took over the general mission it had before, which was to maintain their current position as long as possible. The retreat movements begun were not officially authorized; they had simply been assumed.

In this regard, two events are worthy of note:

In the last days of April, either the night of April 26th/27th or the night of April 27th/28th, I was called [radio or telephone] from Berlin. Adolf Hitler himself badgered me to put together all possible forces, particularly *Panzers*, immediately on the left flank of the *4.Panzer-Armee*, advance to the north and get involved in the battle for Berlin, which would thereby be able to be turned into a victory.

Hitler could be understood only with difficulty; the second part of the conversation was with *General* Krebs, while Hitler listened and dictated the answers to Krebs. I explained to Hitler that it was impossible to carry out his demands. The forces he was counting on were not available and a thrust northward could not be made either because of the materiel, fuel and ammunition situation. In addition, I depicted the enemy situation and told him that such a thrust, even if it were undertaken, would at best reach to about Cottbus, but would stop there, so in any event it would be without any influence on the events around Berlin. Hitler had a hard time understanding this news; *General* Krebs finally responded to me that Hitler had the impression that the *Heeresgruppe* could but didn't want to. Once again, I referred to the main military reasons as to why such an advance would never have the desired effect; it would just cause unnecessary losses. That ended the conversation. In addition, a radio conversation from the *Oberkommando der Wehrmacht* came with instructions from *Major* Johannmeyer, Hitler's adjutant, to immediately pick up a personal and very important document from Hitler to *Generalfeldmarschall* Schörner on the Pfaueninsel (Peacock Island) near Potsdam. All of the attempts made to carry out these instructions failed. Two *Störche* and a bigger airplane came back without having accomplished anything. It later turned out that the document in question was the *"Führer's* Last Testament" in which Hitler named Schörner as the Commander in Chief of the *Heer*.

In this situation, which was described in brief above, I flew to Mürwik on May 3rd, 1945 to see Dönitz's Reich Government in order to: 1) be instructed about the overall situation and the intentions of the Reich Government; 2) to inform the government about our situation and an evaluation thereof; and 3) to request that a cease fire not be entered into under any circumstances until most of the troops of the *Heeresgruppe* had gained enough ground in the course of continued retreats to the west that they could surrender to the Western Allies rather than to the Russians. By our calculations, that would be the case about May 18th.

In any event, Commander in Chief Schörner had not made a decision that the *Heeresgruppe* would continue to fight. I only had the mission of insisting on a time for a cease fire of sometime around May 18th and emphasizing the Commander in Chief's intent of not laying down arms prior to the end of the retreat sometime around the time indicated.

After a long search, I found the Reich Government and the *Oberkommando der Wehrmacht* in the naval school in Mürwik. From the *"Oberkommando der Wehrmacht* camp" (*Generalfeldmarschall* Keitel, *Generaloberst* Jodl with a large circle of employees and advisors), to whom I presented the situation of *Heeresgruppe Mitte* after and our requests, nothing resulted except for a picture of general confusion and helplessness. The same could be said about a long conversation with von Schwerin-Krosigk, who was the Prime Minister and Foreign Minister at the time. My presentation to *Grossadmiral* Dönitz that day was attended by other ministers, *Generalfeldmarschall* Keitel, *Generaloberst* Jodl and others in addition to von Schwerin-Krosigk. After a detailed depiction of the situation in the *Heeresgruppe* and the capabilities it still had, I again requested that no cease fire be made prior to May 18th because, by our calculations, it would not be possible to surrender the majority of the *Heeresgruppe* to the Western Allies until that time. My reasons were known to all those present, as were the attitude, battle conduct and intentions of the *Heeresgruppe*. With reference to the overall military and political situation (of which I didn't get a clear picture anyway), I was not given any solid assurances that the time frame I had asked for would be met. However, I was promised by the *Grossadmiral* and by *Generalfeldmarschall* Keitel that the Reich Government and the *Oberkommando der Wehrmacht* would make efforts to meet this time frame and—this was what made the decision for me—that I could assume that the requests of the *Heeresgruppe* would be met. Even though, based on the overall impression I had obtained, I was clearer about the helplessness of the Reich Government and the *Oberkommando der Wehrmacht* than I had previously been, I still flew back to the *Heeresgruppe* believing that there would be no cease fire prior to May 18th. That was also what I reported to *Generalfeldmarschall* Schörner.

The situation in the *1.Panzer-Armee* was even tenser during the first few days of May. The continued crises, however, could be overcome—if only with some effort and by bringing in new forces. The contact with our neighbors to the right was broken at times; there was no longer any clear overview of the situation at *Heeresgruppe Süd*. The danger of a penetration by larger Russian forces from the area southwest of Brünn headed toward Prague, which would separate the two *Heeresgruppen*, and the thread to the retreat routes to the west for *Heeresgruppe Mitte* were clear. The retreat movements of the *17.Armee* and the *4.Panzer-Armee* went according to plan, but the Russian pressure on the left flank of the *4.Panzer-Armee* on both sides of the Elbe increased and could be considered preparation for the expected major attack. The enemy proceeded more energetically than before against the Erzgebirge, which were secured only by weak units under the command of the Commander in Chief of the Erzgebirge, and the Americans were also more active against the *7.Armee*. The Czechoslovakian resistance movement had grown but did not yet constitute a serious threat. The situation in the city of the Prague was confusing. There continued to be contact with an additional connection to the headquarters of the *12.Armee*. The *Heeresgruppe* pressured the armies to speed up the retreat movements. Even though the speed of these movements was dictated to the *1.Panzer-Armee* by the Russians to a certain degree, the overall speed depended on the *17.Armee*, which was still deployed far to the east and had to be expected to do major movement efforts in the last days. The speed could not be sped up if these movements were not going to turn into a rout, thus endangering the continuity of the entire *Heeresgruppe*. Saving the *17.Armee* from being captured by the Russians, however, was the main thought.

At noon on May 7th, a radio transmission came from the *Oberkommando der Wehrmacht* indicating that there would be a cease fire at 8:00 a.m. on May 9th; in the evening, the time was corrected in another radio transmission to midnight starting May 9th. Because this news did not appear to be suited for transmission by telegraph and the *Heeresgruppe* was not yet clear about the decisions to be published, the *Ia* of each of [*H.Gr. Mitte*] armies were ordered to report to the *Heeresgruppe* at 10:00 a.m. on May 8th.

This decision of the *Oberkommando der Wehrmacht* undid the entire *Heeresgruppe* planning. The plan to surrender most of the troops to the Western powers was moot. The *1.Panzer-Armee*, the *17.Armee* and the right flank of the *4.Panzer-Armee* were still located far enough to the east that they could not reach their goal prior to the beginning of the cease fire. For the *Heeresgruppe*, this order from the *Oberkommando der Wehrmacht* was a great disappointment; it came across as a betrayal and a sellout. A number of thoughts were brought up during the night on how they could still reach the goal set.

The possibility of continuing to retreat toward the west without regard to the cease fire, including using weapons, played a great role. The troops' condition and the enemy situation would only have allowed that for a short time. At this state of the discussions, *Generalfeldmarschall* Schörner prepared correspondence to the Commander in Chief asking whether the troops would continue to fight under these conditions and with this goal and asked that an answer be provided by noon on May 8th after the commanding general was asked. As a conclusion to the discussions and computations, I proposed to the Commander in Chief during the night that the battle not be continued because:

1) the political consequences of this decision by the *Heeresgruppe* could not be avoided;

2) Russia and the Western powers would start attacking with superior force from all sides, if not on May 9th, no later than May 10th or 11th, with the perimeter already drawn for the *Heeresgruppe* on both sides appearing particularly dangerous;

3) the deployment of the combined enemy air forces appeared probable as early as May 10th;

4) there was no likelihood of holding onto the *Heeresgruppe* troops until around May 15th after a cease fire that had already been entered into and was generally known and consequently;

5) and the great losses that would certainly occur could not be supported. Even being a prisoner of the Russians appeared to be better under these circumstances than death. Only for the *4.Panzer-Armee* did it appear necessary for me to continue the fight on its left flank to at least the evening of May 9th in order to keep the way open to the west for additional units of the *17.Armee* and the right flank of the *4.Panzer-Armee* itself.

After a short presentation, the Commander in Chief approved my suggestion even though he did not appear to be particularly interested in a final solution; he was already heavily occupied with personal matters. He entrusted me with issuing the relevant orders.

On the morning of May 8th, I informed the *Ia* of the [*H.Gr. Mitte*] armies (except for the *4.Panzer-Armee*, whose *Ia* did not show up on time) that there was a cease fire and at the same time ordered that the fight be stopped at midnight on the May 8th/9th night and that, under the order, the troops were to remain at the places they had reached at that time. No more travel could be done after midnight on the night of May 8th/9th. All troops and headquarters had free rein to get as far west as they could under their own steam. I added that all efforts were to be made to get as many people as possible out of being prisoners of the Russians, without regard to the materiel. All of the vehicles available and every drop of fuel were to be used for that purpose. Particularly the *17.Armee* could not leave any effort unmade in the process. With the agreement of the Commander in Chief received again, I gave the *4.Panzer-Armee* instructions to prevent a penetration of its left flank even after May 9th so that the roads for its right flank and the *17.Armee* to get to the west would not be cut. However, the *4.Panzer-Armee* never got this order while it was still able to move and therefore the order was never carried out. I also informed the *Ia* that the *Heeresgruppe* would move its positions to Saaz on the afternoon of May 8th in order to be close to the point on the front where the decision was made to achieve the "flight to the west." Finally, I gave the *Ia* a few more words about the end of this war, the collapse of all our hopes and the future fate of our fatherland—which must be the most difficult task that can be given to a chief. *Generalfeldmarschall* Schörner said goodbye to the *Ia* with short words.

In front of the staffs of the *Heeresgruppe*, the Commander in Chief held a short goodbye formation on the evening of May 7th. During the night, I gave all the orders to destroy documents, prepare for moveout, etc. The moveout of the *Heeresgruppe* was delayed on May 8th by an officer's report of new instructions from the *Oberkommando der Wehrmacht* that had to be awaited. Around noon, *Oberst* Meyer-Detring from the *Oberkommando der Wehrmacht* appeared with an American escort brought from Prague, not with the expected new instructions, but with an explanation as to why the cease fire had to be entered into at this undesired early time and why the agreements with the *Heeresgruppe* could not be complied with.

In the early afternoon of May 8th, the vehicle convoy of the *Heeresgruppe* left the Hauptquartier Wolchow. The sequence was as follows: The Commander in Chief with an administrative officer, the *IIa*, the Chief with an administrative officer, then the *Ia* staff, followed by the radio staff. The speed, originally moderate keeping the length of the convoy in mind, was very quickly raised by the Commander in Chief to the point that the convoy fell apart. Because of the beginning of the Czech rebellion, the Josefstadt-Jungbunzlau-Leitmeritz-Saaz route was ordered for the move.

I had held to the pace of the commander in chief, leading to the column breaking up behind my vehicle. In spite of multiple stops by the forward elements that were made necessary by the congestion on the roads, the remainder of the convoy did not manage to move forward. I asked the Commander in Chief to set up a longer stop, which was not permitted or implemented by him until we were at the Saaz airfield, where the Störche had been ordered to go. At the Saaz airfield, which was right by the main street, the Störche were nowhere to be found but it was reported that Russian tanks were en route from the north. This report appeared to be improbable but was confirmed by several eyewitnesses. After waiting about an hour, we saw tanks firing along the northern edge of the airfield and also heard tank fire directly to our east. Because there could be no more thoughts of the remainder of the convoy meeting up with us under these circumstances and Saaz was no longer to be the main headquarters of the *Heeresgruppe*, we went on to Podersam in order to make an attempt from there to put the staff back together there. The three vehicles arrived in Podersam when it was dark, and one of the Störche that had been sent in advance was found in the vicinity of this town in a meadow.

The enemy tanks in the Saaz area showed that the order to hold the positions in the Erzgebirge could not be carried out by the *4.Panzer-Armee*. I already mentioned the reason for that, which I found out later. So no one can say that substantial portions of the *Heeresgruppe* were still fighting after the cease fire, a fairy tale that comes up repeatedly. The two right [flank] armies and the *7.Armee* immediately implemented the order to stop fighting, while the left flank of the *4.Panzer-Armee* did not get an order to continue to fight, so they couldn't follow it. I do not know whether individual units set up a way to get to the west by force.

Generalfeldmarschall Schörner informed me while I was still at *Hauptquartier* Wolchow on the evening of May 7th that he would fly away and attempt to reach the Bavarian mountains, where supposedly everything was set up for him to go underground, no later than the night of May 8th/9th. He indicated that the reason for that was that he was too prominent and incriminated a person to go into captivity. I answered him that, although I did understand his decision, I could not approve it because I assumed that a certain leadership or influence on the *Heeresgruppe* would still be needed on May 9th and 10th and that he could probably accomplish more through negotiations with the Americans than I could. However, Schörner stood by his decision.

In Podersdam, first quarters were set up in the *Ortskommandantur*, where soldiers of all ranks were milling about begging for accommodation. The *Generalfeldmarschall* had the *Ortsgruppenleiter*, whom he immediately summoned, fetch him a civilian suit, put it on immediately and then had the *Ortskommandant's* room cleared out. In the meantime I had determined that only one Storch had been found and that that was the only command and control equipment available. All of my attempts to get a radio station in order to set up contact with the armies were fruitless. I therefore decided to fly early on May 9th to the headquarters of the *1.Panzer-Armee* and the *17.Armee* to find out about the situation there. My request to have the Storch provided to me for this purpose was denied by the *Generalfeldmarschall* and after a serious confrontation with him, I told the *Generalfeldmarschall* that I would have the Storch guarded and would prevent him from using it to fly away. The *Generalfeldmarschall* left me without a word, turned over command of the *Heeresgruppe* to me saying, "Continue to command the *Heeresgruppe* as best you can," said a few more words thanking me for my work and went back into his room. While I was sleeping for a half hour as morning approached in my vehicle in front of the door of the *Ortskommandantur*, the *Generalfeldmarschall* flew off with the Storch after the guard force released the Storch at his orders.

It was therefore impossible for me to set up contact with the armies again because I had still not found a suitable radio station and also had no news as to where my headquarters was.

At about 10:00 a.m. when Russian tanks were approaching Podersam, I and my administrative officer, Graf Carmer, first went to Karlsbad on May 9th but we were not allowed to see a higher American headquarters located there; I was sent to Eger to see the headquarters of the American 1st Infantry Division. It was not until I was in Eger that I managed to get in contact with an officer on the Command Staff of the 1st Infantry Division on May 10th and present him with my request to take as big a piece of the *Heeresgruppe* as he could. He promised me his assistance. Based on the way he told me about it later, he also initiated the appropriate measures. The large number of members of the *Heeresgruppe* who were taken in by the Americans even on May 10th and 11th may be in effect the last thing I was able to do for the *Heeresgruppe*.

signed von Natzmer
Generalleutnant

Appendix C

The End of the *1.Panzer-Armee* by its last Commander in Chief, retired *General der Panzertruppe* Walter Nehring

Walter Nehring replaced *Generaloberst* Gotthard Heinrici as commander of the *1.Panzer-Armee* on March 20th 1945. He remained commander until the end of the war. The below account was written for the 10th anniversary of the end of the war in 1955. His account brings clarity to the confusion about the choice to withdraw or capitulate in place that swirled around the senior officers of *Heeresgruppe Mitte* in early May, 1945. He also provides some insight into why Olmütz was defended. More than just a gateway west for the withdrawal of the *1.Panzer-Armee*, the *XLIX.Gebirgs-Korps* had a mission to defend the Mährisch Ostrau industrial region as a potential redoubt based on rumors that the new *Führer*, *Großadmiral* Dönitz, and his government might fly to Prague. Given that Hitler's death was announced while the first elements of 'Brandenburg' were on trains and en route to Olmütz, this argument can be ruled out as a reason to justify the *Division's* late war deployment.

The *1.Panzer-Armee* front was part of *Heeresgruppe Mitte* (*Feldmarschall* Schörner) and in early May, it ran from southwest of Brünn in a generally northerly direction to somewhere in the vicinity of Böhmisch-Trübau. The neighbor to the right was the *8.Armee* (*General* Kreysing) of *Heeresgruppe Süd* (*Generaloberst* Rendulic); the neighbor to the left was the *17.Armee* (*General* Hasse, who died on May 9, 1945).

The *1.Panzer-Armee* had the following *Korps* under it (listed from south to north) with a total of 28 burned-out front divisions: *XXIV.Panzer-Korps* (*General* Hartmann). *XXIX.Armee-Korps* (*General* Röpke, wounded, Deputy *Generalleutnant* Philipp), *LXXII.Armee-Korps* (*Generalleutnant* Schmidt-Hammer), *LIX.Armee-Korps* (*Generalleutnant* Sieler), *XI.Armee-Korps* (*Generalleutnant* Hohn), as well as the *XLIX.Gebirgs-Korps* which had been deployed by order of the *Heeresgruppe* to protect the Mährisch Ostrau industrial area and at the time was ready to fight its way back under the dynamic leadership of its commander, *General* von le Suire (who died in 1955 as a prisoner of the Russians).

The strength for rations, in spite of all the casualties from the months of bitter, but successful, defensive battles and thus very low combat strength figures, was still about 400,000 men.

No communications with US troops

There was no communication with the Americans advancing from the west. They appeared to want to stop at the old border between Bavaria and Czechoslovakia in front of the weak formations of the *7.Armee*, so the rear of *Heeresgruppe Mitte*, and thus the *1.Panzer-Armee* as well, were initially not directly threatened by them. Reportedly, a US liaison officer was supposed to be at the *Heeresgruppe Rendulic*, the neighbor to the south, in order to agree on a general end to fighting, or so it was hoped, because the overall war situation was hopeless and it demanded an immediate cease fire. At this point, almost no one believed that there was an unconditional surrender—with surrender to the Russians in addition.

The division status, given the overall difficult situation, could still be labeled good. The front was cohesive, there was leadership, the will to fight was unbroken and there was order in the rear areas. Cases of desertion or defection represented an extremely small percentage because all the soldiers knew that in this critical final stage of the war, which could no longer be won, the only thing saving individuals and the group from death or forced labor in Siberia was staying together. The Armee Commander in Chief had already made a statement to that effect quite openly on April 20th before the assembled personnel of the Armee headquarters, and on the same day [it was heard] in a training session for *NSFO* troops in Frydek near Mährisch Ostrau.

Troop supply was limited, even special ammunition (including tank ammunition) and petrol, but it was sufficient even though the continual evasive movements in the last weeks led to the loss of large and valuable stocks.

The Czechoslovakian railways were in operation almost up to the last days and they took German units where their deployment was needed. For example, the *8.Panzer-Division* was provided with parts in the vicinity of Olmütz as recently as May 5th.

The Czechoslovakian resistance movement hardly showed up at all until May 9th; they did not constitute an obstacle for the troops.

Soviet penetration attempts unsuccessful

The Russians attacked at Brünn and through Olmütz with significantly superior forces, but because of the divisions always proving their worth yet again, they did not break through, so the retreat movements toward the American front that the *Heeresgruppe* had ordered were generally carried out according to plan. Their intention—which was apparently to penetrate the *Heeresgruppe's* line going from Brünn and Iglau to Prague quickly into the rear of *Heeresgruppe* Schörner, which had an extraordinary span both militarily and politically—was unsuccessful until the last day of fighting in spite of the continual tension and crises during the battles.

Even though the *Armee* leadership and their subordinate troops had to be satisfied with orders from the Heeresgruppe to carry out the mission they had been given as best they could, there were also additional imperative reasons that must have made it clear to every soldier that they had to hold on to the bitter end.

Hundreds of thousands of refugees

In the meantime, there were hundreds of thousands of Silesian and Sudeten German refugees on foot and horse carts, occupying all the roads and, given the sad experiences of recent years, it was obvious that they had no choice but to move west to save themselves from the Russian victors.

Similarly, no one could leave the middle of the *17.Armee*, which was the one that had moved its echelons the furthest back in the middle Silesian area, to its fate; they had to hang on until this unit arrived.

It was also a matter of protecting additional German land and German people from letting Russian armies come in, and the *1.Panzer-Armee* in the end managed to do that in their sector.

Finally, our own *Armee* had to be saved from becoming prisoners of the Russians.

All of that would only be possible if the superior Russian forces could be successfully resisted long enough for the Americans to enter into a favorable cease fire under the general conditions and conventions that were usual among military commanders.

In addition, *Heeresgruppe Mitte* considered holding on to Bohemia and Moravia with its industrial facilities of all types as a fortress retreat. It was probably based on these considerations that the *Armee* leadership was erroneously informed that the Reich government would move to Prague. The suggestive political hope for a joint front with the Western powers against Bolshevism may also have played a certain role.

Because the news in the last days of the war was overlapping and contradictory and the *Heeresgruppe* may not have wanted to bring up the subject of a cease fire on loudspeakers, the *Armee* commanders were not in the loop about the discussions that had been held in the meantime between the *OKW* and the Allies. The fact that something was going on in this regard could be determined from the radio reports they listened in on. But no one could figure out the facts from them. On about May 4th, the *Heeresgruppe* ordered a broad-based retreat that the *Armee* was to conduct by fighting its way back into the U.S. frontline until May 16th—a solution that appeared to be sensible.

On May 6th or 7th, a new order came in indicating new destinations for extraordinary movement efforts that were unattainable for infantry divisions. It was clear that an effort was being made to get away from the Russians at the last minute after the previous negotiations appeared to have collapsed somehow. However, once again, there was no indication of the imminent cease fire, and certainly not of the unconditional surrender, probably because it was feared that providing such an indication could lead to a disorganized mass flight into which the combat-ready enemy could insert itself without any risk but with terrible losses for our troops.

The same day, the commanding general with tears in his eyes asked the Hungarian divisions included in the movement of the *1.Panzer-Armee* to release their units from the *1.Panzer-Armee* due to the extensive German retreat movements to the Bavarian border. With a heavy heart, he had decided to await the forceful Russians right there in order to surrender. The *Armee* commander had allowed him to do so for reasons of expediency.

However, in order to support the morale of friendly troops during this critical and rumor laden situation that could be affected adversely by the new apparently overturned retreat order from the *Heeresgruppe* and by the withdrawal of Hungary, the *Armee* commander on May 7th ordered that leaflets be dropped on May 8th with the following content, which now appears really grotesque but which he considered proper based on the instructions he had at the time:

"1.   Dönitz is coming to Prague!

2.   Schörner will take us home!

3.   Surrender is out of the question!"

It is clear that even at the highest levels of command, there was a lack of clarity about intentions and goals until the last days of the fighting, because all three points had been overtaken by the dramatic development of events even when they were written down on May 7th at noon; they were false and of course it was not until May 8th when the leaflets were thrown over the roads being used by the divisions moving west while the order to surrender was already en route!

On the evening of this tense May 7th, the *1.Panzer-Armee* got an order to send the *Ia* (Operations Officer) to the *Heeresgruppe* headquarters at 10:00 a.m. on May 8th to pick up an important order. At about 10:00 p.m., there was another telephone conversation between the commanders in chief of the *Heeresgruppe* and the *1.Panzer-Armee* as well as their chiefs of staff, from which, however – probably for the reasons of camouflage already mentioned—no precise information could be gleaned except for the circumstances people knew about that an end to the fighting could be expected within the near future.

A completely unexpected order to surrender

At some time around noon on May 8th, the *Ia* for the *Armee*, *Oberstleutnant* Sauerbruch, returned by airplane with two orders from *Heeresgruppe Mitte*. The first order—in writing—contained instructions, totally unexpected based on previous statements, to surrender unconditionally and immediately to the Russians at 12:01 a.m. that very night! The second one—an oral one—was an additional order from the *Heeresgruppe*, which was just as surprised by the dramatic developments in events as was the leadership of the *1.Panzer-Armee* and felt that it had been politically trumped.

Although the surrender conditions required them to "stay put" and forbid destruction of weapons, Schörner's additional order provided for setting up a "mass escape westward" in order to get as many German men as possible out of the grip of the east. Continuing the fight was not ordered for the *Armee* by any office, because such an intention had no military hope and would thus have made no sense.

Thanks to the prescient steps taken by the *Armee* Chief of Staff (*Oberst* Freiherr von Weitershausen), it was possible to get the corresponding *Armee* orders to the front as the afternoon went on. The extent to which they had a practical effect could not be determined; probably the majority of the fighting troops fell into Russian hands anyway because it was a long way to the American front and in addition, an extensive encirclement by the Russians, from the general area northwest of Vienna across the former front of *Heeresgruppe Rendulic* north into the deep rear of the *1.Panzer-Armee* was already underway. At the same time, the Czechoslovakian resistance, which had previously been just smoldering, burst into flame. It blocked the roads and fought the German attempt to break out with all available means.

The fates of individual units are known. For example, the *16.Panzer-Division* broke up into three groups. One was set upon by Russian units and annihilated in battle. The other two reached the American lines, where one group was made prisoners of war by the Americans, while the other was turned over to the Russians to be shot except for some individual men who managed to escape again.

From the *8.Panzer-Division*, parts of *Panzer-Regiment 10* ran into Russian forces on the road from Iglau to Prague. Small groups of escapees—consisting of 1 officer and 10 men—were able to avoid them, while parts of the *Aufklärungs-Abteilung* of the same *Panzer-Division*, which still had *Panzerspähwagen*, were forced to surrender. Most of the commanders of this division are said to be prisoners of the Russians still.

The general staff of the corps on the left flank (*XI. Armee-Korps*) fought their way west as a unit, losing 22 officers and civil servants in a battle with partisans. *Heeres-Panzer-Korps 'Feldherrnhalle'*, which was deployed somewhere near the line separating the two *Heeresgruppen*, managed to get to the Americans almost as a unit, but a short time later substantial portions of them were turned over to the Russians.

The command staff of the *AOK* was in the sector of the US 26th Infantry Division, whose forward units got the report on May 9th that surrender had been ordered. For weeks, the nerve wracking issue of whether they would be turned over to the Russian army leadership, which had made a demand to that effect, remained open; the issue was not decided favorably until early June.

The fate of this famed *1.Panzer-Armee* is particularly tragic because its bitter end was caused in the end by its dutiful perseverance under particularly severe conditions against a strong and vastly superior enemy force. The fame of the *1.Panzer-Armee* was founded on the penetration at Sedan and the daring advance to the coast of the English Channel in May 1940 under the command of *General* Guderian (now dead) and *General* von Kleist (who died in 1954 as a prisoner of the Russians), who were the first to use the newly formed *Panzer* branch in independent operational *Armee* units and take them to overwhelming victories. Its fame increased in the difficult years of 1941-1945 on the battlefields in the Balkans, southern Russia, Slovakia and southern Poland under the command of *Generaloberst* von Mackensen, *Generaloberst* Hube (who died in 1944), *Generaloberst* Raus and *Generaloberst* Henrici and eventually reached its dramatic climax on the battlefields of Moravia.

During the last days of World War II, the divisions of this *Panzer-Armee* stood unbroken shoulder to shoulder after having done their duty for six long and difficult years, prepared to accept even the last and perhaps the most difficult order of this war—the order to surrender in open field battle.

The numbers of these 30 divisions were as follows: Infantry: *15, 46, 75, 76, 182, 253, 254, 271, 304, 371, 711, 715. Volksgrenadiere: 78, 320, 544. Fallschirmjäger: 10. Gebirgs-Infanterie: 3, 4. Jäger: 8, 97. Panzergrenadiere: 10, "Feldherrnhalle I", "Brandenburg." Panzer: 6, 8, 16, 17, 19. Ausbildungs-Divisionen: 154, 158.*

They should never be forgotten by their people!

Appendix D

4.Panzer-Armee Order of Battle, January 14th 1945

This order of battle is taken directly from the original *Lage Ost* operational maps derived from *H.Gr. A.*, *12.1.14* (evening), *Prüf. Nr. 57031* located in RG242/H.Gr. A/Box 507. Other relevant information is annotated from other primary and secondary sources. At this time, the *4.Panzer-Armee* was part of *Heeresgruppe A*. At the start of the Soviet Vistula-Oder Strategic Operation It reported a total of 543 operational tanks and assault guns, along with 334 anti-tank guns of all types. For comparison purposes, the entire *Heeresgruppe* reported 1,122 operational tanks and assault guns, along with 1,950 anti-tank guns of all types.

4.Panzer-Armee
   Commander: *General der Panzertruppen* Fritz-Hubert Gräser (through capitulation)
   Chef des Generalstabes: Oberst i.G. Christian Müller (through January 25th)
      Generalmajor Wilhelm Knüppel (through capitulation)
   1.Generalstabsoffizier (Ia): Oberst i.G. Klaus Müller (through capitulation)

XXXXII.Armee-Korps. Commander: *General der Infanterie* Hermann Recknagel (thorough January 23rd); *Generalmajor* Arthur Finger through capitulation)
   Heeres-Pionier-Brigade 70. Commander: *Oberst* Hans von Ahlfen
      Sicherungs-Bataillon 955
      Sicherungs-Bataillon 954
      Rdf. Sicherungs-Bataillon 226
      K.M.G. Bataillon 442
   342.Infanterie-Division. Commander: *Generalleutnant* Heinrich Nickel
      Sturmgeschütz-Kompanie 1342
   72.Infanterie-Division. Commander: *Generalleutnant* Dr. Hermann Hohn (Formed *Gruppe Hohn* 24 hours after the commence of the Soviet assault)
   88.Infanterie-Division. Commander: *Generalmajor* Carl Anders
      Sturmgeschütz-Kompanie 1188
   291.Infanterie-Division. Commander: *Generalmajor* Arthur Finger
      Sturmgeschütz-Kompanie 1291
   Panzerjagd-Abteilung 744

Gruppe Hohn was formed 24 hours after the start of the Soviet attack to counterattack south into the flank of Soviet forces.

Gruppe Hohn (72.Infanterie-Division) Commander: *Generalleutnant* Dr. Hermann Hohn
   Sturm-Regiment-Panzer-AOK4
   1x Regiment of the *168.I.D.*

Sturmgeschütz-Brigade 201
Sturmgeschütz-Brigade 322
Sturmgeschütz-Kompanie 1072

The *XXIV.Panzer-Korps* was centered on Kielce. Its divisions were assigned to reserve positions almost directly behind the frontline.

XXIV.Panzer-Korps. Commander: *General der Panzertruppen* Walther Nehring (through March 19th); *Generalleutnant* Hans Källner
> *Korps-Füsilier-Regiment 79*
> *Werfer-Brigade 3*
> *16.Panzer-Division.* Commander: *Generalleutnant* Dietrich von Müller (though March 1945)
> *17.Panzer-Division.* Commanders: *Oberst* Albert Brux (wounded and captured by Soviet forces on January 17th); *Generalmajor* Theodor Kretschmer (assigned on January 30th and remained until capitulation)
> *Kampfgruppe 10.Panzergrenadier-Division.* Commander: *Generalleutnant* Friedrich Freiherr von Broich
> *20.Panzergrenadier-Division.* Commander: *Generalmajor* Hermann von Oppeln-Bronikowski

By January 14th 1945, the below *Korps* was temporarily transferred to the *17.Armee* due to the changing battlefield.

XXXXVIII.Panzer-Korps. Commander: *General der Panzertruppen* Maximilian Reichsfreiherr von Edelsheim
> *168.Infanterie-Division.* Commander: *Generalmajor* Dr. Maximilian Roßkopf
>> *Sturmgeschütz-Kompanie 1248*
> *68.Infanterie-Division.* Commander: *Generalleutnant* Paul Scheuerpflug
> *304.Infanterie-Division.* Commander: *Generalleutnant* Ernst Sieler
>> *Sturmgeschütz-Kompanie 1304*
> *Sturmgeschütz-Brigade 300*
> *Panzerjagd-Kompanie 614*
> *Schwere-Panzerjagd-Kompanie 669*

Deployed from *OKH* reserves to Litzmannstadt (Lodz) on January 12th, 1945:

Panzer-Korps 'Großdeutschland'. Commander: *General der Panzertruppen* Dietrich von Saucken (through March 12th then relieved of command by *Generaloberst* Ferdinand Schörner); *General der Panzertruppen* Georg Jauer (through capitulation)
> *Panzergrenadier-Division 'Brandenburg'.* Commander: *Generalmajor* Hermann Schulte-Heuthaus
> *Fallschirm-Panzer-Division 1 'Hermann Göring'.* Commander: *Generalmajor* Hanns-Horst von Necker (through early February then resigned his command); *Generalmajor* Max Lemke (through capitulation)

Appendix E

4.Panzer-Armee Order of Battle, April 15th 1945

This order of battle is taken directly from the original *Lage Ost* operational maps derived from *H.Gr. Mitte.*, *1.4.14* (evening), *Prüf. Nr. 74090* and *H.Gr. Mitte.*, *14.4.14* (evening), *Prüf. Nr. 78246* located in RG242/H.Gr. Mitte/Boxes 356-7. Other relevant information is annotated from other primary and secondary sources. At this time, the *4.Panzer-Armee* was part of *Heeresgruppe A*. It reported a total of 181 operational tanks and assault guns, along with 118 anti-tank guns of all types. For comparison purposes, the entire *Heeresgruppe* reported 562 operational tanks and assault guns, along with 487 anti-tank guns of all types. This represented a 50% reduction in armor and a 75% reduction in anti-tank guns available just 90 days earlier.

4.Panzer-Armee
    Commander: *General der Panzertruppen* Fritz-Hubert Gräser (through capitulation)
    Chef des Generalstabes: *Generalmajor* Wilhelm Knüppel (through capitulation)
    1.Generalstabsoffizier (Ia): *Oberst i.G.* Klaus Müller (through capitulation)

Sperrverband 'Reichenberger Senke'
    Stab Heeres-Pionier-Brigade 655

V.Armee-Korps. Commander: *General der Artillerie* Kurt Wägner
    Panzer-Abteilung 2
    Kampfgruppe 35.SS-und Polizei-Grenadier-Division. Commander: *SS-Standartenführer* Rüdigen Pipkorn
        Ausbildungs-Regiment 561
        Korps-M.G.-Bataillon 405
        Alarm-Regiment 94
        Alarm-Regiment 97
    275.Infanterie-Division. Commander: *Generalleutnant* Hans Schmidt
    (Its regiments were divided up between other divisions in the *Korps* area)
    214.Infanterie-Division. Commander: *Generalleutnant* Harry von Kirchbach
        Alarm-Regiment 35
        SS-Gendarme-Bataillon 6
        Heeres-Pionier-Brigade 70
    Kampfgruppe 36.SS-Waffen-Grenadier-Division. Commander: *SS-Oberführer* Dr. Oskar Dirlewanger
    342.Infanterie-Division. Commander: *Generalleutnant* Heinrich Nickel

Panzer-Ausbildungs-Verband 'Böhmen'
    Führungsstab
    2x Panzergrenadier-Ausbildungs-Regiment Stabes with *Regiment-Einheiten*
    4x Panzergrenadier-Ausbildungs-Bataillon

> *1x Panzergrenadier-Ausbildungs-Regiment Stabs*
> *2x Panzergrenadier-Ausbildungs-Bataillon*
> *Panzer-Aufklärungs-Ausbildungs-Abteilung 8*
> *1x Flak-Kompanie*
> *Scharfschützen-Lehr-Gruppe*

Panzer-Korps 'Großdeutschland'. Commander: *General der Panzertruppen* Georg Jauer
> *Sturmgeschütz-Artillerie-Brigade 'Großdeutschland'*
> *Panzerjagd-Abteilung 3*
> *Panzerjagd-Abteilung 4*

Kampfgruppe 545.Volksgrenadier-Division. Commander: *Generalmajor* Hans-Ernst Kohlsdorfer
Division Stab zbV 615. Commander: *Oberst der Reserve* von Below was assigned as "temporary" commander)
> *Heeres-Pionier-Brigade 687*
> *Festung-M.G.-Bataillon 3093, 3094, 3104*
> *Festung-Infanterie-Bataillon 1485*
> *Bataillon 500*

Panzergrenadier-Grenadier-Division 'Brandenburg'. Commander: *Generalmajor* Hermann Schulte-Heuthaus
> *Sturm-Regiment-Panzer AOK 4*

Korps-Gruppe General der Artillerie Moser (still forming). Commander: *General der Artillerie* Willi Moser
> *Division-Nr.193 (Ersatz-und-Ausbildung,* possibly a *Schatten-Division)*
> *Division-Nr. 404 (Ersatz-und-Ausbildung,* formerly *Schatten-Division 'Dresden')*
> *Division-Nr.464 (Ersatz-und-Ausbildung,* possibly a Schatten-*Division)*

LVII.Panzer-Korps. Commander: *General der Panzertruppen* Friedrich Kirchner (?)
> *Korps-M.G.-Bataillon 457*
> *Panzer-Abteilung 1*
> *Panzerjagd-Abteilung 4*

72.Infanterie-Division. Commander: *Generalleutnant* Dr. Hermann Hohn (through April 20th 1945); *Generalleutnant* Hugo Beißwänger
> *Festung-Infanterie-Bataillon 1456, 1460*

6.Volksgrenadier-Division. Commander: *Generalleutnant* Otto Brücker
> *Alarm-Bataillon*
> *Panzerjagd-Abteilung 183*

Festung Görlitz
> *Festung-Infanterie-Bataillon 1459* and *1461*

Heeresgruppe Reserve located at the southern end of the *4.Panzer-Armee*:
> *21.Panzer-Division.* Commander: *Generalmajor* Heinrich-Hermann von Hülsen
> *Führer-Begleit-Division.* Commander: *Oberst* Otto-Ernst Remer
> *Fallschirm-Panzer-Division 1 'Hermann Göring'.* Commander: *Generalmajor* Max Lemke

OKH reserve:

> *10.SS-Panzer-Division 'Frundsberg'*. Commander: *SS-Brigadeführer* Heinz Harmel (relieved on April 27th 1945 by *Generalfeldmarschall* Schörner); *SS-Obersturmbannführer* Franz Roestel (through capitulation)
>
> *20.Panzer-Division*. Commander: *Generalmajor* Hermann von Oppeln-Bronikowski

Deployed on order of *OKH* after the start of the Soviet offensive:
600.Infanterie-Division (russ). Commander: *Generalmajor* Sergei Buniachenko
344.Infanterie-Division. Commander: *Generalleutnant* Erwin Jolasse

Deployed from the *4.Armee* in East Prussia:
Fallschirm-Panzer-Korps 'Hermann Göring'. Commander: *Generalleutnant* Wilhelm Schmalz
Fallschirm-Panzergrenadier 2 'Hermann Göring'. Commander: *Generalmajor* Erich Walther

Appendix F

Soviet Forces

Various units of the Marshal Ivan Koniev's 1st Ukrainian Front confronted Panzer-Korps *'Großdeutschland'* during its withdrawal across Poland and defense of in Silesia and Saxony during the period January-May, 1945. Below represents the key Soviet formations it fought during its combat deployment. The sources for this information are derived from German wartime intelligence, Koniev's memoirs and a variety of other primary and secondary source material.

Operating against *Panzer-Korps 'Großdeutschland'* during January-February 1945:
4th Guards Tank Army. Commander: Colonel-General D.D. Lelyushenko
    5th Guards Mechanized Corps
        10th Guards Mechanized Brigade
        11th Guards Mechanized Brigade
        12th Guards Mechanized Brigade
        24th Guards Tank Brigade
        379th Guards Heavy SP Artillery Regt.
        1 04th Guards SP Artillery Regiment
        1447th Self-propelled Artillery Regiment
        2nd Guards Motorcycle Battalion
        285th Mortar Regiment
        11th Guards Mortar Battalion (RA)
        763rd AAA Regiment
    6th Guards Mechanized Corps
        16th Guards Mechanized Brigade
        17th Guards Mechanized Brigade
        49th Mechanized Brigade
        28th Guards Heavy Tank Regiment
        29th Tank Regiment
        56th Tank Regiment
        1433rd Self-propelled Artillery Regiment
        1727th Self-propelled Artillery Regiment
        95th Motorcycle Battalion
        240th Guards Mortar Regiment
        52nd Guards Mortar Battalion (RA)
        427th Guards AAA Regiment
    10th Guards Tank Corps
        61st Guards Tank Brigade
        62nd Guards Tank Brigade
        63rd Guards Tank Brigade
        29th Guards Motorized Rifle Brigade
        1689th Light Artillery Regiment

72rd Guards Heavy Tank Regiment
1222nd Self-propelled Artillery Regiment
7th Guards Motorcycle Battalion
299th Guards Mortar Regiment
248th Guards Mortar Battalion (RA)
359th Guards AAA Regiment
68th Guards Tank Brigade
70th Guards Self-propelled Artillery Brigade
13th Guards Heavy Tank Regiment
119th Guards Engineer Tank Regiment
51st Motorcycle Regiment

Operating against *Panzer-Korps 'Großdeutschland'* during March 1945:
13th Army. Commander: Colonel-General N.P. Pukhov
    24th Rifle Corps
        350th Rifle Division
        395th Rifle Division
    27th Rifle Corps
        6th Guards Rifle Division
        117th Guards Rifle Division
        280th Rifle Division
    102nd Rifle Corps
        121st Guards Rifle Division
        147th Rifle Division
        172nd Rifle Division

Operating against *Panzer-Korps 'Großdeutschland'* during April 1945:
5th Guards Army. Commander: Colonel-General A.S. Zhadov (northern flank of *Panzer-Korps 'GD'*)
    32nd Guards Rifle Corps
        13th Guards Rifle Division
        95th Guards Rifle Division
        97th Guards Rifle Division
        9th Guards Airborne Division
    33rd Guards Rifle Corps
        14th Guards Rifle Division
        78th Guards Rifle Division
        118th Rifle Division
    34th Guards Rifle Corps
        15th Guards Rifle Division
        58th Guards Rifle Division
    4th Guards Tank Corps
        12th Guards Tank Brigade
        13th Guards Tank Brigade
        14th Guards Tank Brigade
        3rd Guards Motorized Rifle Brigade
        29th Guards Tank Regiment
        1660th Light Artillery Regiment
        293rd Guards SP Artillery Regiment

298th Guards SP Artillery Regiment
76th Motorcycle Battalion
264th Mortar Regiment
240th Guards Mortar Battalion (RA)
120th Guards AAA Regiment
150th Tank Brigade
39th Separate Tank Regiment
226th Separate Tank Regiment
1889th Self-propelled Artillery Regiment

2nd Polish Army. Commander: General Karol Świerczewski (center of *Panzer-Korps 'GD'*)
5th Polish Infantry Division. Commander: Brigadier General Aleksander Waszkiewicz
13th Polish Infantry Regiment
15th Polish Infantry Regiment
17th Polish Infantry Regiment
22nd Polish Light Artillery Regiment
7th Polish Infantry Division. Commander: Colonel Mikołaj Prus-Więckowski
33rd Polish Infantry Regiment
35th Polish Infantry Regiment
37th Polish Infantry Regiment
38th Polish Light Artillery Regiment
8th Polish Infantry Division. Commander: Colonel Józef Grazewicz
32nd Polish Infantry Regiment
34th Polish Infantry Regiment
36th Polish Infantry Regiment
37th Polish Light Artillery Regiment
9th Polish Infantry Division. Commander: Colonel Aleksander Łaski
26th Polish Infantry Regiment
28th Polish Infantry Regiment
30th Polish Infantry Regiment
40th Polish Light Artillery Regiment
10th Polish Infantry Division. Commander: Colonel Andrzej Czatoryski
25th Polish Infantry Regiment
27th Polish Infantry Regiment
29th Polish Infantry Regiment
39th Polish Light Artillery Regiment
2nd Polish Artillery Division. Commander: Brigade General Benedykt Nesterowicz
3rd Polish Anti-Aircraft Division. Commander: Colonel Ivan Krenkow
1st Polish Tank Corps
2nd Polish Tank Brigade
3rd Polish Tank Brigade
4th Polish Tank Brigade
1st Polish Motorized Rifle Brigade
24th Polish Self-propelled Artillery Regiment
25th Polish Self-propelled Artillery Regiment
27th Polish Self-propelled Artillery Regiment
2nd Polish Motorcycle Battalion
2nd Polish Mortar Regiment

26th Polish Anti-Aircraft Artillery Regiment
    16th Polish Tank Brigade (Independent)

52nd Army. Commander: Colonel-General K.A. Koroteyev (southern flank of *Panzer-Korps 'GD'*)
    48th Rifle Corps
        111th Rifle Division
        116th Rifle Division
        213th Rifle Division
    73rd Rifle Corps
        31st Rifle Division
        50th Rifle Division
        214th Rifle Division
    78th Rifle Corps (Both of its divisions were assigned in direct support of the 7th Guards Mechanized Corps)
        254th Rifle Division
            929th Rifle Regiment
            933rd Rifle Regiment
            936th Rifle Regiment
        294th Rifle Division
    7th Guards Mechanized Corps. Commander: Lieutenant-General I.P. Korchagin; Deputy Major-General Maximov later assigned commander of the 294th Rifle Division and the defense of Weißenberg
        24th Guards Mechanized Brigade
            13th Guards Tank Regiment Commander: Major Alexander Lukitsch Fomenko
        25th Guards Mechanized Brigade
            12th Guards Tank Regiment
        26th Guards Mechanized Brigade
            215th Tank Regiment
        57th Guards Tank Brigade
            3x Tank Bataillons
        355th Guards Heavy SP Artillery Regiment
        291st Guards SP Artillery Regiment
        1820th Self-Propelled Artillery Regiment
    306th Self-Propelled Artillery Regiment
    952nd Self-Propelled Artillery Regiment

Appendix G

Organization of *Panzer-Korps 'Großdeutschland'*

The following images are of the final reorganization order of *Panzer-Korps 'Großdeutschland'* date 13 December 1944.[1]

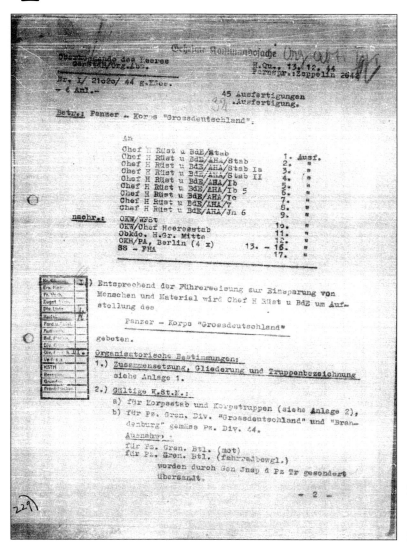

Image 35. Organization of *Panzer-Korps 'Großdeutschland'* 13 December 1944, page 1.

---

1   Located in NARA T78/533/232-44.

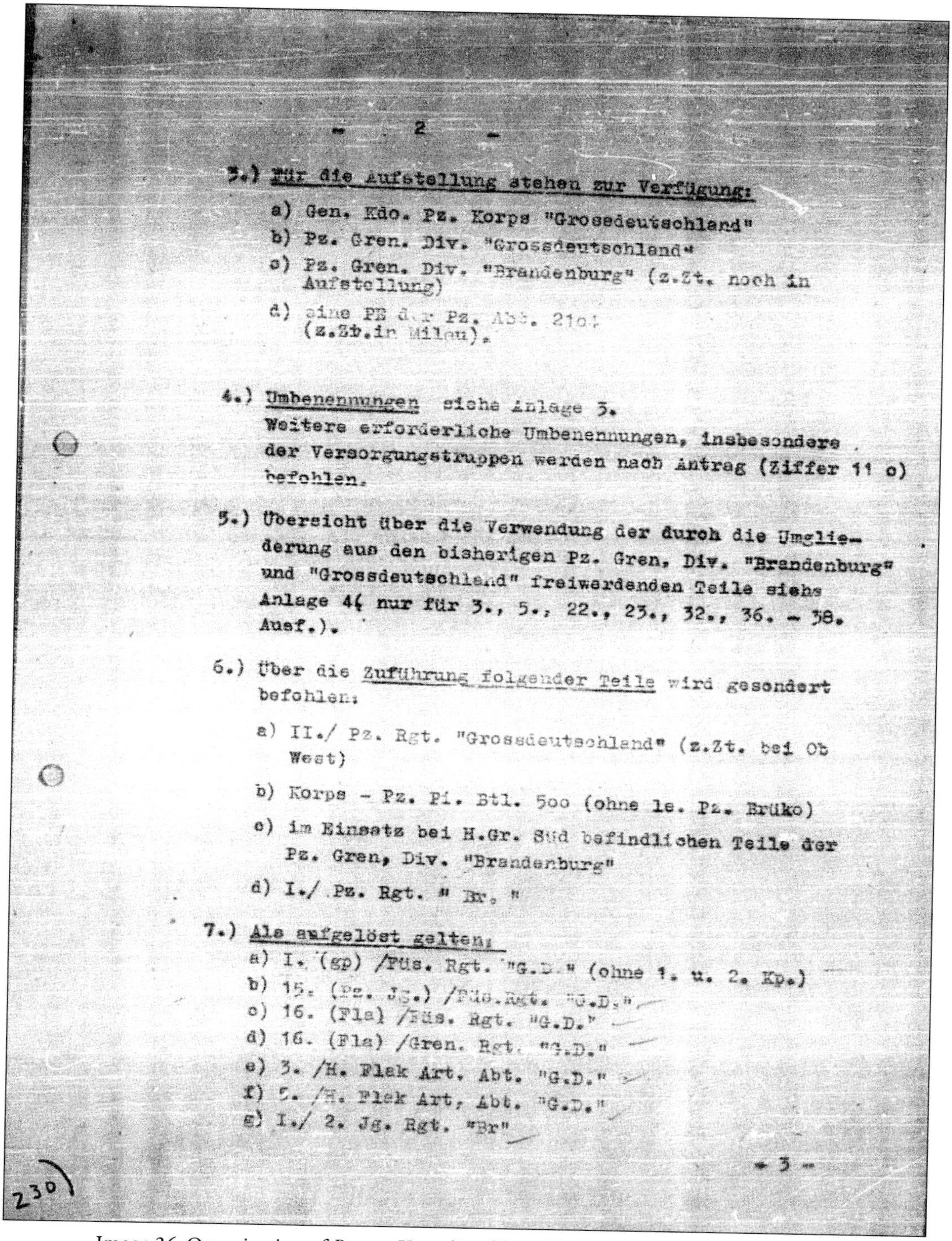

- 2 -

3.) **Für die Aufstellung stehen zur Verfügung:**

   a) Gen. Kdo. Pz. Korps "Grossdeutschland"

   b) Pz. Gren. Div. "Grossdeutschland"

   c) Pz. Gren. Div. "Brandenburg" (z.Zt. noch in Aufstellung)

   d) eine PE der Pz. Abt. 2101 (z.Zt. in Milau).

4.) **Umbenennungen** siehe Anlage 3.
Weitere erforderliche Umbenennungen, insbesondere der Versorgungstruppen werden nach Antrag (Ziffer 11 c) befohlen.

5.) Übersicht über die Verwendung der durch die Umgliederung aus den bisherigen Pz. Gren. Div. "Brandenburg" und "Grossdeutschland" freiwerdenden Teile siehe Anlage 4(nur für 3., 5., 22., 23., 32., 36. - 38. Ausf.).

6.) Über die **Zuführung folgender Teile** wird gesondert befohlen:

   a) II./ Pz. Rgt. "Grossdeutschland" (z.Zt. bei Ob West)

   b) Korps - Pz. Pi. Btl. 500 (ohne le. Pz. Brüko)

   c) im Einsatz bei H.Gr. Süd befindlichen Teile der Pz. Gren. Div. "Brandenburg"

   d) I./ Pz. Rgt. " Br. "

7.) **Als aufgelöst gelten:**

   a) I. (gp) /Füs. Rgt. "G.D." (ohne 1. u. 2. Kp.)

   b) 15. (Pz. Jg.) /Füs. Rgt. "G.D."

   c) 16. (Fla) /Füs. Rgt. "G.D."

   d) 16. (Fla) /Gren. Rgt. "G.D."

   e) 3. /H. Flak Art. Abt. "G.D."

   f) 5. /H. Flak Art. Abt. "G.D."

   g) I./ 2. Jg. Rgt. "Br"

- 3 -

230

Image 36. Organization of *Panzer-Korps 'Großdeutschland'* 13 December 1944, page 2.

— 3 —

8.) <u>Abzeichen:</u>

a) Das Abzeichen "G.D." auf den Schulterstücken wird von allen Angehörigen des Korps getragen.

b) Das Ärmelband "Brandenburg" wird von den Angehörigen der Pz. Gren. Div. "Brandenburg" und des FEB "Brandenburg" getragen.
Alle übrigen Angehörigen des Korps tragen das Ärmelband "Grossdeutschland".

9.) <u>Aufstellungsraum:</u>   L ö t z e n

1o.) <u>Aufstellungsendtag:</u>   31. 12. 44.

11.) Es wird um Mitteilung an GenStdH/Org.Abt. gebeten:

a) zum 2o. und 31. Dezember: Stand bzw. Beendigung
                                der Aufstellung,
b) zum 31. 12. freiwerdende Teile,
c) zum 31. 12. erforderliche Umbenennung.

II.) <u>Personelle Bestimmungen:</u>

1.) <u>Offz. Stellenbesetzung</u> regelt OKH/PA.

2.) <u>Uffz. und Mannschaften:</u>

a) Die bei der Auflösung der I. (gp)/ Füs. Rgt. "G.D." <u>freiwerdenden Spezialisten</u> stehen zur Auffüllung der gp.Teile der Pz.Gr.D."Br"zur Verfügung.

b) <u>Sonstiges</u> bei der Umgliederung der Pz. Gren.Div. "G.D." <u>freiwerdendes Personal</u> steht zur Auffüllung noch fehlender Teile der Pz. Gren. Div. "Brandenburg" zur Verfügung.

c) <u>Gestellung fehlender Spezialisten</u> aus Ersatzbrigade "G.D."

— 4 —

231)

Image 37. Organization of *Panzer-Korps 'Großdeutschland'* 13 December 1944, page 3.

- 4 -

d) Nach Abschluss der Aufstellung des Panzer-
Korps "Grossdeutschland" überzähliges Personal
ist zur Ersatzbrigade "Grossdeutschland" in Marsch
zu setzen.

IV.) Materielle Bestimmungen:

1.) Das Material der Pz. Gren. Div. "G.D." und "Br."
steht für die Aufstellung zur Verfügung.

2.) Über die Zuführung von Sturmgewehren folgt Son-
derbefehl.

3.) Gp. Kfz. werden ohne Anforderung durch Gen Insp
d Pz Tr zugewiesen. Stu.Gesch. der Pz. Gren. Div.
"G.D." werden von der Pz. Jg. Abt. "G.D." übernommen.

4.) Weiteres Material wird nicht zugewiesen.

V.) Die bisher für die Aufstellung der Pz. Gren. Div.
"Br" ergangenen Forderungen behalten sinngemass für
die Aufstellung des Pz. Korps "G.D." Gültigkeit.
(Umbewaffnung der Art. entsprechend Anlage 1)

J.A.

gez. G u d e r i a n
Generaloberst und Chef des General
stabes des Heeres

Für die Richtigkeit:

Oberstleutnant i.G.

Nach Abgang:
Op. Abt.
Gen Qu (4 x)
Gen Insp d Pz Tr
Gen d Art im OKH
Gen d Pi u Fest im OKH
Chef HNW
NSF - Stab
PA/1. St.
PA/P3

	18.Ausf.	Ausb. Abt.	30. Ausf.
19. - 22. "	Reichsf.SS, Feldkdo.		
23. "	St. IIe Heer		
24. "	Org. Abt. IK	31. "
25. "	IF	32. "
26. "	IH	33. "
27. "		34. "
28. "	Gr. II, III	35.u.56. "
29. "	K u B, Entw.	37.u.38. "
	Vorrat	39.u.45. "

232

Image 38. Organization of *Panzer-Korps 'Großdeutschland'* 13 December 1944, page 4.

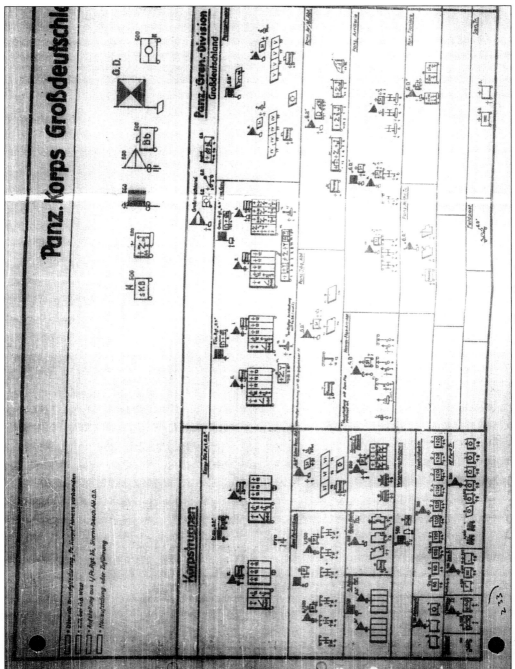

Image 39. Organization of *Panzer-Korps 'Großdeutschland'* 13 December 1944, page 5.

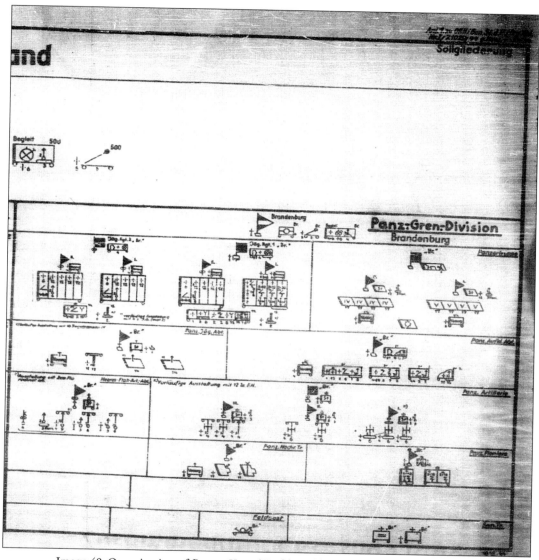

Image 40. Organization of *Panzer-Korps 'Großdeutschland'* 13 December 1944, page 6.

Anlage 2 zu OKH/GenStdH/Org.Abt. Nr. I/21o2o/44 g.Kdos. v.13.12.44.

K.St.N. - Gültigkeitsliste für
Stab u. Korpstruppen

Korps - Stab :

Stab Gen. Kdo.	K.St.N.	15 v. 1. 3. 42
Kps. Kart. Stelle (mot)	"	2o75 v. 1.11. 43
Kps. Begl. Kp.	"	126 v. 1. 2. 44
Kps. Aufkl. Kp.	"	1113 (gp.) (f.G.) v. 1. 4. 44
Stab Art. Kdr. (mot)	"	25 v. 1. 2. 41
Pz. Beob. Bttr.	"	3o5 v. 1. 9. 44
Pz. Pi. Rgt. Stab	"	7o1 v. 1. 4. 44
Feldgend. Tr. b (mot)	"	2o33b v. 1.11. 43

Korps - Füs. Rgt.:

Stb. u. Stbs.Kp.	"	11o4 v. 1. 4. 44
I. u. II. Btl.	"	wird durch Gen Jnsp d Pz. Tr. übersendt.
9. (s. J.G.)/	"	112o v. 1. 8. 44

schw. Pz. Abt.:

Stb. u. Stbs.Kp. schw.Pz.Abt. "Tiger" (f.G.)	"	11o7b (f. G.) v. 1. 6. 44
schw. Pz.Kp. "Tiger" (f.G.)	"	1176 (f.G.) v. 1. 6. 44
Versorg. Kp. "Tiger" (f.G.)	"	1151b (f.G.) v. 1. 6. 44
Panz. Werkst. Kp. schw. Pz. Abt.	"	1187b v. 1. 7. 44

- 2 -

235

Image 41. Organization of *Panzer-Korps 'Großdeutschland'* 13 December 1944, page 7.

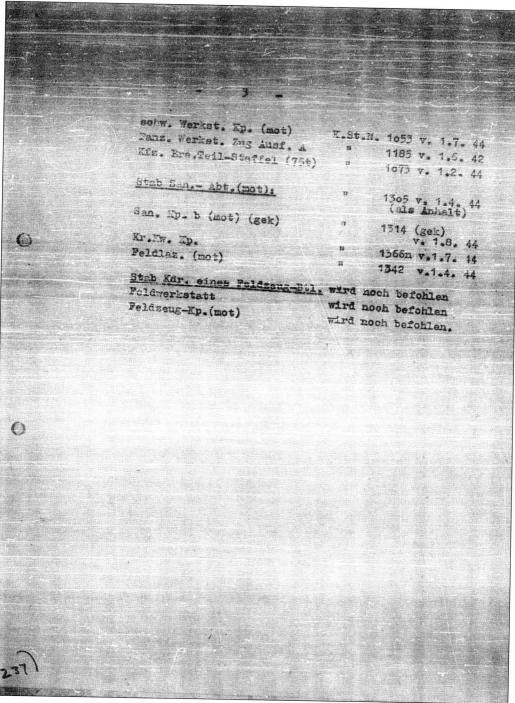

- 3 -

schw. Werkst. Kp. (mot)	K.St.N. 1053 v. 1.7. 44	
Panz. Werkst. Zug Ausf. A	" 1185 v. 1.6. 42	
Kfz. Ers.Teil-Staffel (754)	" 1073 v. 1.2. 44	
Stab San.- Abt.(mot):	" 1305 v. 1.4. 44 (als Anhalt)	
San. Kp. b (mot) (gek)	" 1314 (gek) v. 1.8. 44	
Kr.Kw. Kp.	" 1366n v.1.7. 44	
Feldlaz. (mot)	" 1342 v.1.4. 44	
Stab Kdr. eines Feldzeug-Btl.:	wird noch befohlen	
Feldwerkstatt	wird noch befohlen	
Feldzeug-Kp.(mot)	wird noch befohlen.	

237

Image 42. Organization of *Panzer-Korps 'Großdeutschland'* 13 December 1944, page 8.

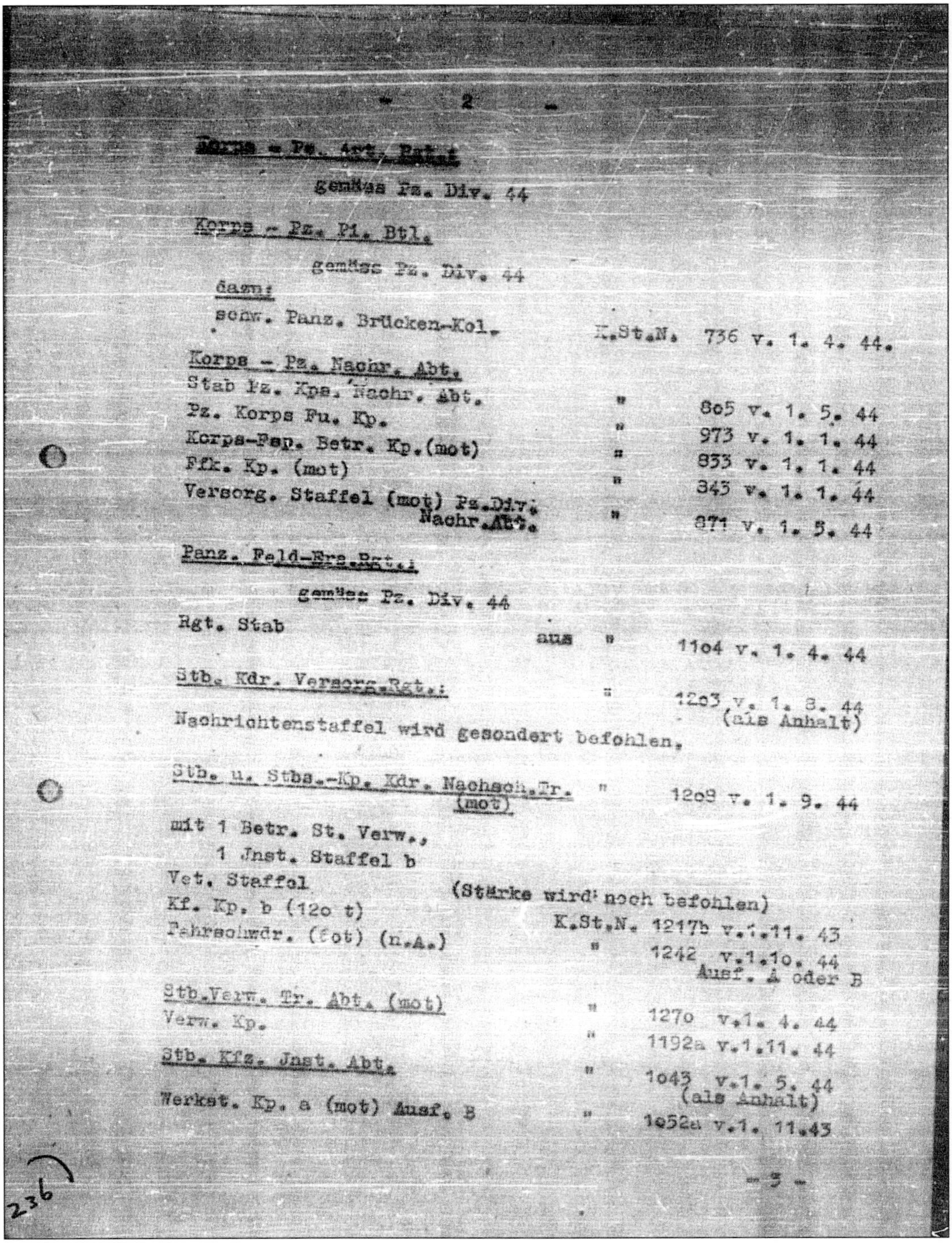

- 2 -

Korps - Pz. Art. Rgt.:

    gemäss Pz. Div. 44

Korps - Pz. Pi. Btl.

    gemäss Pz. Div. 44

dazu:

schw. Panz. Brücken-Kol.   K.St.N. 736 v. 1. 4. 44.

Korps - Pz. Nachr. Abt.
Stab Pz. Kps. Nachr. Abt.
Pz. Korps Fu. Kp.   "   805 v. 1. 5. 44
Korps-Fsp. Betr. Kp.(mot)   "   973 v. 1. 1. 44
Ffk. Kp. (mot)   "   833 v. 1. 1. 44
Versorg. Staffel (mot) Pz.Div.   "   343 v. 1. 1. 44
         Nachr.Abt.   "   871 v. 1. 5. 44

Panz. Feld-Ers.Btl.:

    gemäss Pz. Div. 44

Rgt. Stab   aus "   1104 v. 1. 4. 44

Stb. Kdr. Versorg.Rgt.:   "   1203 v. 1. 3. 44
                             (als Anhalt)
Nachrichtenstaffel wird gesondert befohlen.

Stb. u. Stbs.-Kp. Kdr. Nachsch.Tr.   "   1209 v. 1. 9. 44
              (mot)
mit 1 Betr. St. Verw.,
   1 Inst. Staffel b
Vet. Staffel
Kf. Kp. b (120 t)   (Stärke wird noch befohlen)
Fahrschwdr. (fot) (n.A.)   K.St.N. 1217b v.1.11. 43
                     "   1242 v.1.10. 44
                          Ausf. A oder B

Stb.Verw. Tr. Abt. (mot)   "   1270 v.1. 4. 44
Verw. Kp.   "   1192a v.1.11. 44

Stb. Kfz. Inst. Abt.   "   1043 v.1. 5. 44
                     (als Anhalt)
Werkst. Kp. a (mot) Ausf. B   "   1052a v.1. 11.43

- 3 -

236

Image 43. Organization of *Panzer-Korps 'Großdeutschland'* 13 December 1944, page 9.

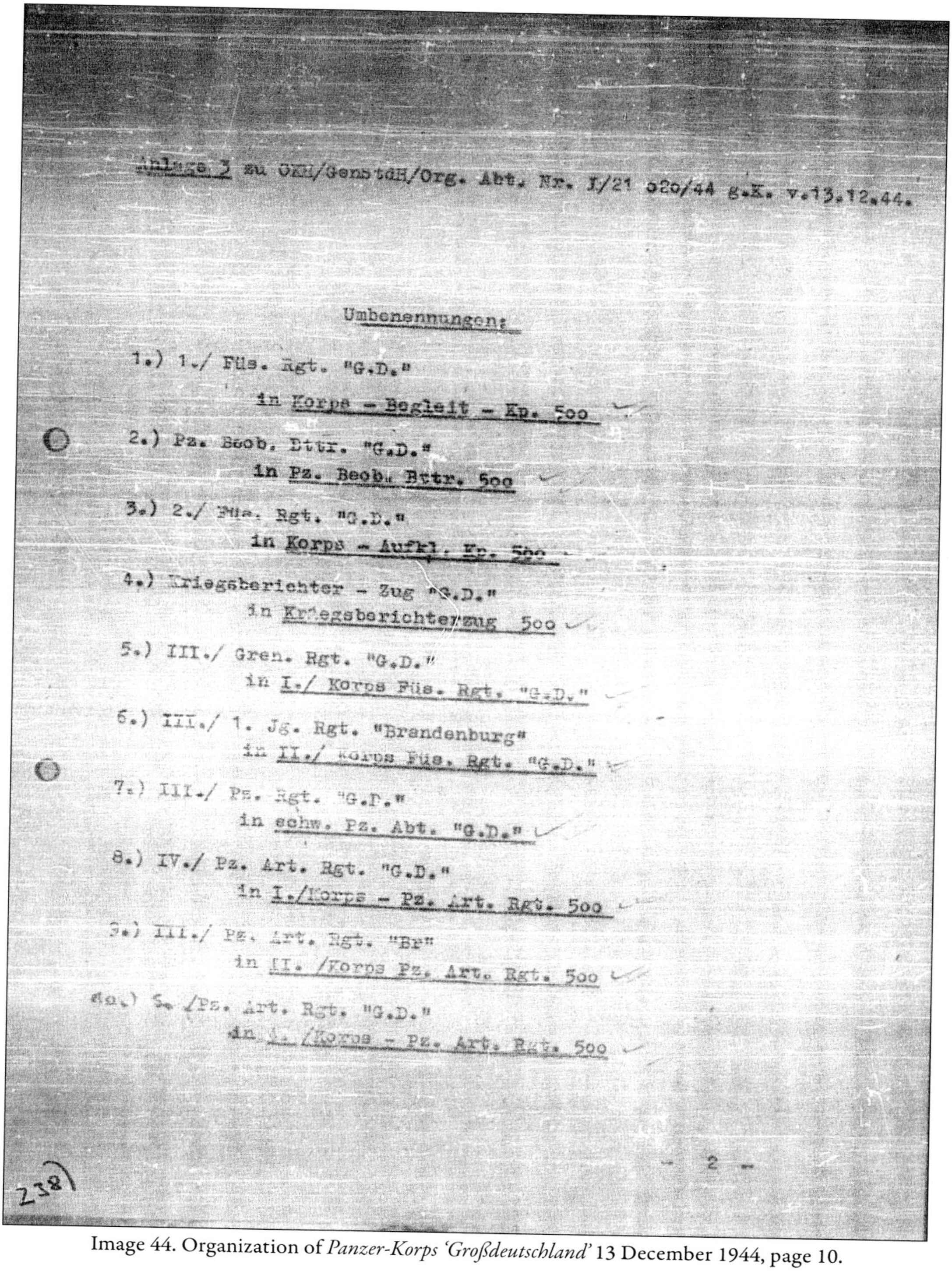

Anlage 3 zu OKH/GenStdH/Org. Abt. Nr. I/21 020/44 g.K. v.13.12.44.

Umbenennungen:

1.) 1./ Füs. Rgt. "G.D."
   in Korps - Begleit - Kp. 500

2.) Pz. Beob. Bttr. "G.D."
   in Pz. Beob. Bttr. 500

3.) 2./ Füs. Rgt. "G.D."
   in Korps - Aufkl. Kp. 500

4.) Kriegsberichter - Zug "G.D."
   in Kriegsberichterzug 500

5.) III./ Gren. Rgt. "G.D."
   in I./ Korps Füs. Rgt. "G.D."

6.) III./ 1. Jg. Rgt. "Brandenburg"
   in II./ Korps Füs. Rgt. "G.D."

7.) III./ Pz. Rgt. "G.D."
   in schw. Pz. Abt. "G.D."

8.) IV./ Pz. Art. Rgt. "G.D."
   in I./Korps - Pz. Art. Rgt. 500

9.) III./ Pz. Art. Rgt. "Br"
   in II. /Korps Pz. Art. Rgt. 500

10.) 5. /Pz. Art. Rgt. "G.D."
   in I. /Korps - Pz. Art. Rgt. 500

- 2 -

238)

Image 44. Organization of *Panzer-Korps 'Großdeutschland'* 13 December 1944, page 10.

- 2 -

11.) le. Pz. Brüko "G.D."
    in le. Pz. Brüko 500

12.)Stab Kdr. Div. Nachsch. Tr. "G.D."
    in Stab Kdr. Korps Versorg. Rgt. 500

13.) Kf. Kp. 1. - 6. /G.D."
    in Kf. Kp. 1. - 6. / 500

14.) Fahrschwdr. "G.D."
    in Fahrschwdr. 1./ 500

15.) Werkstatt- Kp. 1. - 3. "G.D."
    in Werkstatt- Kp. 1. - 3. /500

16.) Werkstatt - Kp. 1. u. 2. "Br"
    in Werkstatt - Kp. 4. u. 5. /500

17.) Ersatzteilstaffel "G.D."
    in Ersatzteilstaffel 1./500

18.) Feldlazarett "G.D."
    in Feldlazarett 500

19.) San.- Kp. 2./"G.D."
    in San. Kp. 500

20.) Stab Verw. Tr. Abt. "Br"
    in Stab Korps Verw. Tr. Abt. 500

21.) 8./Gren. Rgt. "G.D."
    in 9./ Gren. Rgt. "G.D."

22.) 14./ Gren. Rgt. "G.D."
    in 13./ Gren. Rgt. "G.D."

23.) III./ Füs. Rgt. "G.D."
    in I./ Füs. Rgt. "G.D."

239

- 3 -

Image 45. Organization of *Panzer-Korps 'Großdeutschland'* 13 December 1944, page 11.

3 -

24.) 13./ Füs. Rgt. "G.D."
        in 2. Füs. Rgt. "G.D."

25.) 14./ Füs. Rgt. "G.D."
        in 10. Füs. Rgt. "G.D."

26.) 4./ H.Flak Art. Abt. "G.D."
        in 3. /H.Flak Art. Abt. "G.D."

27.) 5./ Pz. Jg. Abt. "Br."
        in 7./Pz. Jg. Abt. "G.D."

28.) eine PK der Pz. Abt. 2104
        in 2./ Pz. Jg. Abt. "G.D."

29.) 15./ Gran. Rgt. "G.D."
        in 3./ (mot Z)/Pz. J. Abt. "G.D."

30.) San.- Kp. 1./ "G.D."
        in San.- Kp. "G.D."

31.) 1. Jäg. Rgt. "Br"
        in   Jäg. Rgt.1"Br."

32.) 13./1.Jäg. Rgt.   "Br."
        in 2. Jäg. Rgt.1"Br."

33.) 14./1.Jäg. Rgt.   "Br."
        in 10. Jäg. Rgt.1 "Br."

34.) 2. Jäg. Rgt. "Br."
        in Jäg. Rgt. 2 Br."

35.) III./ 2. Jäg. Rgt. "Br."
        in 1. Jäg. Rgt. 2 "Br."

95.) 13./2.Jäg. Rgt.   "Br."
        in 2./ Jäg. Rgt. 2 "Br."

240

- 4 -

Image 46. Organization of *Panzer-Korps 'Großdeutschland'* 13 December 1944, page 12.

- 4 -

37.) 14. /2. Jäg. Rgt. "Br."
    in 1o Jäg. Rgt. 2"Br"

38.) Stu. Gesch. Abt. "G.D."
    in II./ Pz. Rgt. "Br"

39.) 4./ Pz. Jg. Abt. "Br"
    in 3./ Pz. Jäg. Abt. "Br"

4o.) IV./ Pz. Art. Rgt. "Br"
    in III./ Pz. Art. Rgt. "Br"

41.) San.- Kp. 1./ "Br"
    in San.- Kp. "Br"

241)

Image 47. Organization of *Panzer-Korps 'Großdeutschland'* 13 December 1944, page 13.

Appendix H

Evolution of *Panzergrenadier-Division 'Brandenburg'*

The evolution of *'Brandenburg'* can be seen through these two different *Gliederung* (organization) diagrams.

This first image dated June 1944 reflects the final *Sonderkommando* organization of *Division 'Brandenburg'*.[1]

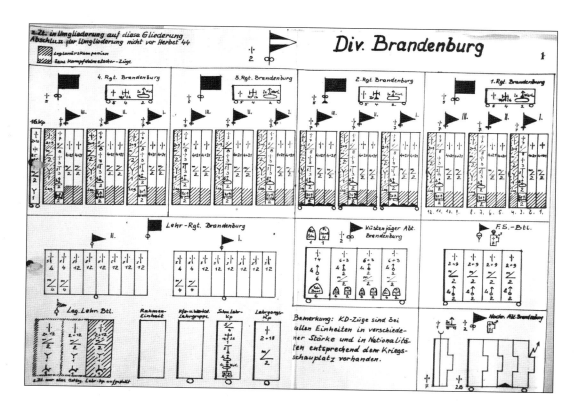

---

1   Located in BAMA RH20 1002-8.

This second image dated March 9th, 1945 is the final organization of *Panzergrenadier Division 'Brandenburg'* based on a *Panzergrenadier-Division 44* structure. Its composition changed little before the final Soviet offensive began on April 16th.[2]

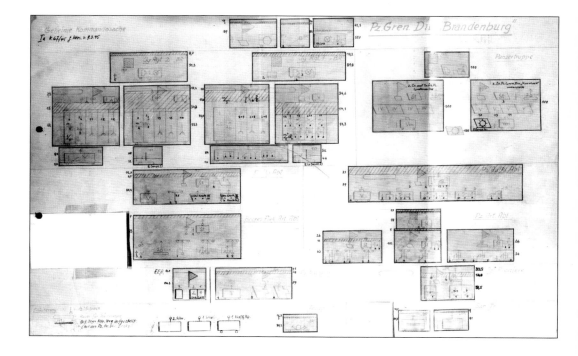

Appendix I

Knight's Cross and Higher Award Winners of *Panzergrenadier-Division 'Brandenburg'*

There were nine members of *zbv Division 'Brandenburg'* that received the Knight's Cross before the formation of *Panzergrenadier-Division 'Brandenburg'*. Four received the award posthumously, so they never served in the reformed *Division*. Two others, *Oberleutnant* Erhard Lange (1943 recipient) and *Oberleutnant* Wilhelm Walther (1940 recipient) that received the award prior to December 1944 do not appear to have served with the *Panzergrenadier-Division*. No mention of Lange was found in any accounts post-September 1944. Walther was severely wounded in the fighting around Belgrade and subsequently transferred out of the unit. Only three Knight's Cross recipients, *Leutnant* Werner Lau, *Major* Helmuth Spaeter and *Major* Konrad Steidl, who received the award earlier in their career, served with *Panzergrenadier-Division*. Of the three, Lau and Steidl were original *zbv Division 'Brandenburgers'*, as Spaeter served in *Panzergrenadier-Division 'Großdeutschland'* when he received his Knight's Cross on August 7th, 1943. The recipients discussed below received their Knight's Cross or higher awards as members of the reformed *Panzergrenadier-Division 'BR'*.

Not all the recipients of the Knight's Cross identified below received the award through the normal approval process. Several recipients fall into a potentially ineligible category. In three cases Knight's Cross awards were granted under the perceived authority of what is known as the *Dönitz Directive*. On May 7th 1945, *Großadmiral* Karl Dönitz, who became Hitler's successor as head of the Third Reich, upon Hitler's suicide on April 30th in Berlin, issued an announcement automatically approving all Knight's Cross awards that were prepared *properly*. Further analysis of this "Directive" in the past decade shows that it was not a "directive" but a "regulation" meant by Dönitz to be applied to awards that had already gone through the formal awards approval process, were positively endorsed, and sitting in his office awaiting his final review and signature.

The Knight's Cross awards for Wilhelm Bröckerhoff, Friedrich Müller-Rochholz, and Werner Voshage not only failed to meet the minimum standard set by the *Dönitz Directive* but were issued after the war without any qualifying documentation. It is simple fact that regardless of the individual acts of combat leadership achieved by the potential Knight's Cross recipients during the final months of war, their award cannot be authorized based on a strict application of qualifying criteria. For purposes of their inclusion here, they are annotated as "Contested". For those interested in understanding the Knight's Cross award process and the factors that contributed to a "contested" status see Viet Scherzer's *Ritterkreuzträger 1939-1945* for an in-depth discussion and analysis of the late war Knight's Cross recipients.

The information on the Knight's Cross winners below are derived from the accounts of *Panzergrenadier-Division 'BR'* obtained in the *Bundesarchiv* and translated for this book, Viet Scherzer's *Ritterkreuzträger 1939-1945*, Helmuth Spaeter's *Panzerkorps Grossdeutschland: A Pictorial History*, and from Ralph Tegethoff, *Die Ritterkreuzträger des Panzerkorps Großdeutschland*.

Recipients of the Knight's Cross and Oak Leaf

Afheldt, Eckart
>   Born: August 15th, 1918 in Neu Stettin, Pomerania
>   Died: December 3rd, 1999 in Munich
>   Awarded the Knight's Cross as *Oberleutnant* and commander of *II.Bataillon/Jägerregiment 2 'BR'* on March 17th, 1945.
>   Afheldt received the award for defeating a Soviet defensive position in Gross-Wiersewitz and securing a crossing point over the Bartsch River for the entire *Division*. His final attack west to reach German lines through Neu-Wiersewitz was believed to have surprised the Soviets sufficiently, that they hesitated in their own attack against the exposed flank of *Panzer-Korps 'GD'* along the Oder River. He was promoted to *Hauptmann* on February 1st, 1945.

Bröckerhoff, Wilhelm (Contested)
>   Born: September 3rd, 1907 in Essen
>   Died: July 16th, 1971 in Bochum-Linden
>   Awarded the Knight's Cross as a *Major* and commander of *Panzer-Artillerie-Regiment 'BR'* on May 8th, 1945.
>   Received the German Cross in Gold on October 9th, 1942.
>   Bröckerhoff was supposedly recommended for the award due to his leadership during the withdrawal from Poland from January 18th through February 20th. Specifically, he distinguished himself by establishing a defense that allowed the *Panzer-Korps 'GD'* to reform west of the Neisse River and stabilize a new defensive line between Guben and Görlitz.
>
>   Based on the accounts utilized in the research of this book, this award claim noted in Ralph Tegethoff's book is likely fictitious, as neither Bröckerhoff or his unit is singled out for any specific combat action during the mentioned time-frame. According to Veit Scherzer's research no proof exists in the Bundesarchiv that this award was ever recommended. Requests for evidence produced only recollections from *Generalmajor* Schulte-Heuthaus that a recommendation was sent to the *Korps* sometime during the latter half of March. However, *General* Jauer, Commanding General of *Panzer-Korps 'GD'* could not recall this case, and that no evidence exists that it ever reached the *Heer* Personnel Office. This case was brought by *General* Jauer to former *Grossadmiral* and Reich *Führer* Karl Dönitz in 1961 based solely on the recollection of *Generalmajor* Schulte-Heuthaus and Dönitz responded in a letter that "Very well, everything is in order!" and certified the award based on his May 8th, 1945 guidance. Bröckerhoff was an active member of the Award Association of the Knight's Cross in the postwar period.[1]

Brückner, Erich Von
>   Born: September 2nd, 1896 in Metz, Alsace-Lorraine
>   Died: April 1st, 1949
>   Awarded the Knight's Cross as an *Oberst* and commander of *Jägerregiment 1 'BR'* on March 11th, 1945.
>   Received the German Cross in Gold on March 25th, 1942.
>   After the initial deployment to Litzmannstadt, and the withdrawal west under Soviet pressure, part of the regiment and its headquarters element were encircled in the town of Lissa. The town was by-passed by the Soviets and declared a fortress. 2,000 German soldiers were now caught behind Soviet lines. After discussing the situation with the fortress commander, von Brückner

1   Viet Scherzer, *Ritterkreuzträger 1939-1945* (Scherzers Militaer-Verlag Ranis: Jena Germany, 2007), p. 124.

was given permission to lead a breakout west. On the evening of February 2nd, Brückner led the breakout and succeeded in reaching German lines at Glogau the next day without a single loss.

Leipzig, Hellmut Von
Born: July 18th, 1921 in Keetmanshoop, German Southwest Africa
Died: ?
Awarded the Knight's Cross as a *Leutnant* and platoon commander in *Panzer-Aufklärungs-Abteilung 'BR'* on April 28th, 1945.
It should be noted that Leipzig served as *Generalfeldmarschall* Erwin Rommel's driver for a period of time in 1942.
Von Leipzig was one of four soldiers of *'Brandenburg'* recommended for the Knight's Cross by *Generalleutnant* Schulte-Heuthaus during the intensive defensive fighting in mid-April after the start of the final Soviet attack west. On April 21st *Leutnant* von Leipzig was alerted to the Polish occupation of the town of Milkel, north of Bautzen. The Polish force had occupied the town's manor house. Milkel's occupation threatened the southward movement of *Panzer-Korps 'GD'* in preparation for the attack on Bautzen. *Leutnant* von Leipzig launched an immediate counterattack with his platoon mid-day. Under his command, the platoon knocked-out an enemy tank, assaulted the Polish force in the manor house, forcing them out. He subsequently engaged and defeated reinforcements that approached from the north via the Kleine Spree. His platoon reportedly used up most of their ammunition during the attack on the manor house and engaged the second Soviet force in hand-to-hand combat. His platoon suffered only three wounded in the counterattack while killing 20-30 enemy soldiers.
This counterattack was noted in *H.Gr. Mitte's* update to *OKH* (previously mentioned in the above text) as occurring on Aril 21st. A facsimile of the account, presumably used as the award justification contained in Spaeter's book *Panzer-Korps Grossdeutschland, A Pictorial History,* states the combat action took place on the 24th. Based on the general attack south of *Panzer-Korps 'GD'* that resulted in the destruction of Polish forces to the east at Förstgen on April 21st, this appears to be the correct date for the combat action.

Müller-Rochholz, Friedrich (Contested)
Born: February 16th, 1914 in Solingen
Died: May 5th, 2002 in Herzogenrath
Awarded the Knight's Cross as a *Hauptmann* and Commander of *Panzer-Sturm-Pionier-Bataillon 'BR'* on May 8th 1945.
Müller-Rochholz was one of several soldiers of *'Brandenburg'* supposedly recommended for the Knight's Cross by *Generalleutnant* Schulte-Heuthaus during the intensive defensive fighting in mid-April after the start of the final Soviet attack west. He was considered by both his subordinates and leaders as a *Pionier* who was dedicated with "heart and soul". He was nicknamed "Papa Müller" by his men and this was reflected in the various first person accounts presented in the text. Müller-Rochholz was recommended for the award for the defense of Niesky that he organized on his own initiative, and the successful breakout south with both the wounded and civilian population of the town during April 21st/22nd.
Of the three contested Knight's Cross recipients, Müller-Rochholz is likely the only one whose award might have been written given the frequent battlefield accolades identified by *Panzergrenadier-Division 'BR'* members during the research conducted for this book. However, according to Veit Scherzer's research, no proof exists in the Bundesarchiv that this award was ever recommended. Requests for evidence produced only recollections from *Generalmajor* Schulte-Heuthaus that a recommendation was sent to the *Korps* sometime during the latter half of April

along with several others. There is no evidence that the award recommendation ever reached the *Heer* Personnel Office. The date of the award was determined based on Dönitz's May 8th, 1945 guidance. Müller-Rochholz was an active member of the Award Association of the Knight's Cross in the postwar period.[2]

Oesterwitz, Karl-Heinz

Born: March 15th, 1914 in Innsbruck, Tyrol

Died: June 13th, 1999 in Pulheim, Rhineland

Awarded the Oak Leaf (Nr. 734) as *Oberstleutnant* and Commander of *Jägerregiment 2 'BR'* on February 10th, 1945.

Awarded the Knight's Cross as *Oberleutnant* and Commander of *7.Kompanie* of *Lehrregiment zbV 800 'Brandenburg'* on April 30th 1943.

Received the German Cross in Gold on December 13th, 1942.

Oesterwitz received the Oak Leaf to his Knight's Cross by leading his regiment to rescue a large supply column carrying, petrol, ammunition and rations under the command of *Major i.G.* Spaeter, which was surrounded by the Soviets in the area of Sprottauer Forest in early February 1945. The column was forced to repel repeated Soviet attacks, often at close range. The supplies were badly required by the withdrawing *Panzergrenadier-Division 'BR'*. Oesterwitz's attack was able to reach the column, and secure a withdrawal route. All the desperately needed supplies were successfully brought back to the *Division* lines.

While his Oak Leaves are not in contention, it is interesting that nothing was mentioned about this "rescue operation" anywhere in Spaeter's notes or in his own book.

Röseke, Erich

Born: January 24th, 1921 in Stuttgart

Died: May 2nd, 1994 in Leinfelden

Awarded the Knight's Cross as a reserve Oberleutnant and Commander of the *9.Kmpanie* of *Jägerregiment 1 'BR'* on April 14th, 1945.

Received the German Cross in Gold on March 22nd, 1945.

Röseke's award combined combat actions he participated in the fighting at the Soviet Bridgehead at Apatin, as well as for the defense of Kutno in Poland during the initial deployment of the *Division* to Litzmannstadt. His defense of Kutno reportedly allowed the evacuation of both civilians and wounded from the field hospital. While recovering in the field hospital in either late March or early April, Röseke was notified that he received the Knight's Cross, German Cross in Gold, and a promotion to *Hauptmann*.

Röseke's lungs would not heal properly during his hospital stay in February. He was released back home to Stuttgart in April but longed to return to his Division. He attempted to make his way to Silesia on his own but was unable to reach the *4.Panzer-Armee*. He did locate the *SS-Jagdverband Südwest* where he identified a number of former comrades from 'Brandenburg'. *SS-Jagdverband Südwest* was formed and staffed with some former 'Brandenburgers' after the transition of the *Division* from a *Sonderkommando* to *Panzergrenadier-Division* in September 1944. As Röseke recorded after the war "I rolled with them in the direction of the Alps!" He remained with them until capitulation and went into a U.S. prisoner-of-war camp.

It should be noted that in 1942 Röseke was in command of a Cossack Platoon that reached the Caspian Sea in the Soviet Union, earning him the reputation as advancing further east than any other soldier in the *Wehrmacht*.

---

2   Ibid., p. 160.

In the files from the BAMA was the following letter written by Röseke in reference to his Knight's Cross award:

October 24, 1954
Received October 26 [initials]
To:
Board of the 'Großdeutschland' Veteran's Association
c/o Mr. Hans-Joachim Krack
A question was asked in NFW no. 30 as to who had received the Knight's Cross after April 18th, 1945.

I received this award during the last weeks of the war—but I do not know the exact date it was awarded.

In late March/early April 1945, I received good wishes from various comrades in the field hospital where I was at the time. I later found out that *Feldwebel* Buhse, the administrative office for *II.Btl./Jägerregiment 1 'Brandenburg'* at the time, had undertaken to have the Knight's Cross and the German Cross in Gold, along with the certificates, given to me. But everything got lost in the chaotic last weeks of the war.

Now that it was asked in NFW who had received the Knight's Cross after April 18th, I assume that there are some documents somewhere that indicate who got the award prior to that date. I would like to find out whom I should ask to have someone take a look at that list.

In any event, I make the following report:

The award was for defending the cities of Kutno and Warthbrücken in January 1945 and for the withdrawals of the *6.Kompanie* and *7.Kompanie* of the *II.Bataillon* of *Jägerregiment 1 'Brandenburg'*. At that time I was an *Oberleutnant* (later a *Hauptmann*) and commander of the *6.Kompanie*. On February 8th 1945, I reported to *Oberst* von Brückner at the command post of the *Jägerregiment 1 'Brandenburg'*; I was told that I was supposed to be given the Knight's Cross.

Sincerely,
[signature]
Erich Röseke

Voshage, Werner (Contested)

Born: September 19, 1913 in Hanover
Died: Spring 1949 (reportedly shot in the area of Bad Hersfeld near the inter-German border)
Awarded the Knight's Cross as *Major* and Commander of *Heeresflak-Abteilung 'BR'* on May 9th, 1945.
Recipient of the German Cross in Gold on March 29th, 1944.
Voshage was supposedly one of several soldiers of 'Brandenburg' recommended for the Knight's Cross by *Generalleutnant* Schulte-Heuthaus during the intensive defensive fighting in mid-April after the start of the final Soviet attack west. He received the nomination because of his defense of Wehrkirch against repeated Soviet tank attacks. His *Flak* guns were responsible for reportedly knocking-out 40 Soviet tanks. Voshage's defense of the town allowed other units of 'Brandenburg' to withdraw west, to include all the wounded that were resident of the first aid station being cared for by Dr. Braune.

According to Veit Scherzer's research no proof exists in the Bundesarchiv that this award was ever recommended. The only documentation for this award came from a letter by Mr. Müller-Rochholz dated June 16th, 1980 where he stated that Voshage was recommend for the award in the middle of March. It should be noted that Müller-Rochholz was a member of the Award Association of the Knight's Cross at this time. There is no evidence that the award recommendation ever reached the *Heer* Personnel Office. The date of the award was determined based on Dönitz's May 8th, 1945 guidance.[3] It is interesting to note that his recommendation date of March noted by Müller-Rochholz pre-dates the supposed combat action that generated the award contained in Ralph Tegethoff's book. It is possible that Müller-Rochholz meant April and not March, but in any event, Voshage's award simply fails to meet the minimum criteria of the May 8th Dönitz's Guidance.

Wandrey, Max

> Born: April 8th, 1910 in Hamburg
>
> Died: February 21st, 1945 in a field hospital in Krauschwitz [Kroschwitz] (near Liegnitz, Silesia) after succumbing to his wounds.
>
> Awarded the Oak Leaf (Nr. 787) as *Major* and Commander of *II.Bataillon* of *Jägerregiment 1 'BR'* on March 16th, 1945.
>
> Awarded the Knight's Cross as a reserve *Oberleutnant* and Commander of *II.Bataillon* of *Jägerregiment 1 'BR'* on January 9th 1944.
>
> Received the German Cross in Gold on May 13th, 1942.
>
> Wandrey received the Knight's Cross for personally leading the assault on Hill 961 on the Island of Leros that resulted in the capture of British General Tilney and members of his staff prisoners. Soon after, most of the British forces surrendered and Leros fell into German hands on November 15th, 1944.
>
> Wandrey received the Oak Leaves to his Knight's Cross posthumously after he stepped on an improperly marked land mine on February 23rd in the area of Priebus while visiting his soldiers as Commander of *Jägerregiment 1 'BR'*. His award citation included a reference for leading a *Kampfmarsch-Bataillon* to rescue the *Feldersatz-Bataillon 'BR'* that was surrounded by Soviet forces in the Sprottisch-Waldau area in mid-February 1945. His counterattack, it was noted, rescued the new recruits, many without prior combat experience, while only suffering minor losses.
>
> Max Wandrey was originally a member of the *Allgemeine SS* where he served as a *SS-Hauptsturmführer* in Hamburg before he volunteered to enter military service after the outbreak of war in 1939.

Recipients of Higher Awards
Recipients of the German Cross in Gold

Becker, Dr. Theodor, January, 31st 1945, as *Oberarzt, Jäg.Rgt. 1 'BR'*
Glaser, Erich, March 22nd, 1945 as *Feldwebel, 6.Kp./Jäg.Rgt. 1 'BR'*
Gohlke, Karl-Heinz, March 30th 1945, as *Leutnant d.R., II.Btl./Jäg.Rgt. 2 'BR'*
Röseke, Erich, March 22nd, 1945 as *Oberleutnant d.R., 9.Kp./Jäg.Rgt. 1 'BR'*
Steidl, Konrad (Kurt), January 13th, 1945 as *Hauptmann d.R.*, Commander of *I.Btl./Jäg.Rgt. 2 'BR'*[4]
Streich, Willi, March 9th, 1945 as *Fahnenjunker-Oberfeldwebel*

Recipients of the Honor Roll Clasp of the *Heer*

Pansen, Hans-Gerhard, March 25th, 1945 as *Major, Pz.Aufkl.Abt. 'BR'*
Meschkeris, Wolf, March 5th, 1945 as *Oberleutnant d.R., Div.Begl.Kp./Pz.Gren.Div. 'BR'*
Stalf, Werner, [?] 1945, *Leutnant d.R., 7.Kp./Jäg.Rgt. 2 'BR'*

---

3   Ibid., p. 182.
4   This award was given for his actions around Belgrade, which technically constituted the transition period to *Panzergrenadier-Division 'BR'*.

Appendix J

Poems of the Damned

The veterans of *'Brandenburg'* who served since the early commando days of the *Division* shared a strong bond that transcended the chaos of war. Like most veterans of any nation or any time period, the war became a central part of their psyche. In the case of former members of the *Wehrmacht*, many went to prisoner-of-war camps for years, or even decades, and came home to a devastated country burdened with the collective guilt of Adolf Hitler's atrocities committed in the name of Germany. How they dealt with these feelings was as varied as the personalities of the men themselves. In the assorted papers of *'Brandenburger'* veterans collected by Spaeter were two poems that offer a glimpse into their attempt to assimilate their wartime experiences in a defeated, postwar Germany.

The first poem is by Eric Röseke who commanded the *6.Kompanie* of *II.Bat./Jägerregiment 1 'BR'* and the second is by Kurt Steidl who commanded *II.Bat./Jägerregiment 2 'BR'*. Their poems are not apologetic of their wartime experiences. Röseke's poem was written to his mother in the spring and summer of 1945 from the confines of a U.S. prisoner-of-war camp, while Steidl's was written in the early 1950s, a decade after he had returned home from the war. Röseke's poem is a brief chronological description of his varied combat deployments that the then 24 year old experienced since entering the war at the age of 18. It is light-hearted in its form and prose given its intended audience. Steidl's poem is heavy, and brooding. Two years older than Röseke when the war ended, he had more time to reflect on the past. His tone suggests he may have been conflicted with justifying the "sacrifices" his men made, and he hints at a struggle with survivor's guilt long after the war. The poems show how both men drew strength from the camaraderie they shared with other members of the *Division*—camaraderie that was a clear source of strength for them during the chaotic last months of the war.

Experiences during the war
by E. Röseke

I left you when I was a boy. The war began. I was called by the duty to march along unknown roads. Where to ... ? How long ... ? I didn't know. I followed the orders without saying anything. A holy fire burned in me. I was a soldier in body and spirit—a *Brandenburger Pionier*!

The army train went to France. We used Panzers to open up a path from Lüttich to the seashore, all the way to the Atlantic Ocean! How often my machinegun that I used in lots of combat spoke—before we proudly marched into Paris after long hot weeks.

We were already dreaming of new victories, of peace for the Fatherland—and then we saw England over there! The troops were ready to get going, but the guns were long silent. We soldiers had to get trained in bivouacs and garrisons, in drill and polishing and discipline.

We then went south and we were astonished to see the silver waves of the Aegean Sea, Mt. Olympus, the Acropolis and Athens ... And on we went into the distance. The battles that took place there were hard. The tropical stars shone for us many a night in Africa.

Time went by. The events of the war were like a tired, lethargic river. In the East, the armies were standing from the Arctic Ocean to the Caucasus. On hot days and cold nights, the front soldiers acquitted themselves in severe bloody battles as fighters and comrades.

I as well was with the army that went deep into Russia's steppes.

After getting off of armored vehicles, we marched through dust and muck. I learned to ride Cossack horses through salt marshes all the way to the Caspian Sea—and the expanses of Asia lay before me! My heart, it was so light,—so heavy ...

Months later, the sunshine of the Balkans shone on me again. I led the column as a young troop officer. Where Greece's ruins stand was where our battalion fought, in deep canyons, at the top of Mt. Parnassus and Mt. Helicon.

What beautiful pictures there were to see! Albanians with red fezzes, rich bazaars, Turkish women, mosques, pointed minarets ... —we faced time in a den of thieves or at the fire, laughed and drank wine.—Soldiers, the world belongs to us!

We went through the land of the black mountains over to the Adriatic Sea. We proudly called ourselves the "Panduren." It was a crazy life that humbled us there on the coast of Dalmatia for a long time, in the Karst Mountains and in the rocky wilderness in nameless solitude.

Stoßtrupps and *Jagdkommandos* pushed deep into enemy territory. We *Brandenburger Jäger* did not let them take a single step onto our ground! We fired doggedly—the enemy was tenacious—but we were more so! A lot of blood and sweat was shed there—the luck of the war fluctuated.

Two hundred men's hearts beat, and I as the head of the *9.Kompanie* bore the responsibility for them in good times and bad. But there were nice days again. The fire of war was forgotten and the soldiers' songs about love, luck and the homeland rang out clearly ...

Well our thoughts quickly turned to home ... The war still wasn't at an end. The fronts began to falter. The regiment was in Hungary. It rained. We dug in for weeks in the swampy forest at the Apatin bridgehead for weeks. Assault attack.—Close combat here and there.

Often during those hours where there are only real men, I had the luck of officers who know and love their troops. The commanders and generals led with an iron will, and in difficult situations they shared all our misfortunes.

Autumn landscape, the expanses of the puszta—the appearance of balls of light over the front ... Death comes along on our side; who will it take from among our ranks ... ?

Many a man stayed in front of the enemy.

Alone at night by candlelight, I wrote the reports to their loved ones in the home country ...

Then came the most difficult parts of the war. In the East, the divisions were on blood-soaked German soil; the nation was in a life and death struggle. Finally in the light of Christmas candles, I talked to my *Kompanie* about silent service and courageous hearts, and of unpretentious infantry.

We spent the winter campaign using hand grenades and pistols against the superior enemy forces fighting for a city in Poland. We kept our position. Then they overran us. The Russian armored tracks painted bloody trails on the land.

Pushed back in battle and penetrated! Two shots burned in my breast. I will never forget these weeks when I, weak from loss of blood, marched through deep snow on narrow paths with my comrades in a cold January through adventure and danger.

When I found my regiment again in Lower Silesia and was reporting to the colonel in the village on the bank of the Oder, we mutely shook hands and it was clear to us that the bitter end of the war, the defeat, had happened.

The front broke up. The masses of enemy tanks rolled through German land day and night on all the roads. Who would have thought it? Was our fight in vain? Was every soldier's grave in vain? Who can measure the pain of the people?

We silently accepted the steel helmet.

I keep with pride the simple cross from the German army made of black iron as the most beautiful ornament. It is to prove how courageously the troops fought! Brand new guys, fathers of families—I could rely on them! Everyone from my old *Kompanie* has grown close to my heart.

I have experienced a lot over the years and seen a lot. Soldier lives of danger! It was often difficult. But it was also beautiful! The war did leave me a lot of wounds, but luck never left me in the lurch. How often did you, Mommy, worry about me in difficult hours ... ?

I am now a prisoner. How bitterly I, as a front line soldier, find the view through prison bars, months behind barbed wire ...

Has fate managed to break me!—Never!—I am of firm resolve about that! And at some point, people will again talk of those who do their duty.

My gaze often goes towards my destroyed home city in the south; the war is over. We have peace. Work calls for new deeds!

I gladly look into the future, in spite of it all! I'll be with you soon. I want to trust in the old luck—life lies in front of me!

Our dead comrades
by. K. Steidl

Our dead comrades
Think of the dead. Everyone has their dead.
There is no German head to which at night no well-loved bloody head appears.
Fallen in the battle for the Fatherland.
Murdered by the executioner's hand. Erased by machines without pity or notice.
Think of the dead. If you yourselves are not strong enough to put yourselves in order, let the dead put your hearts in order and take the measure of their silent nobility.

When the month of fog comes upon us and the fields stay cold, when the grey fogs creep over the land, our thoughts go over endless level ground, over mountains and valleys in the north and south, over ice-covered oceans, all the way to their graves. We see the long lines of crosses that we have placed for them. On this side, however, we are again united with them in the German comradeship that was frequently proven to be a shield and a weapon.
The flames flicker and avidly eat one piece of wood after another.
I cannot ever forget the pictures of that heart ...
How many days we marched – together!
How many evenings we spent looking around a foreign land for the [illegible] – together!
How many nights we spent guarding – together!
We spent years fighting – together!
And today I am alone.
But suddenly it comes to me: when I see a [illegible] it seems that they're here! ...

... Lamentation of the dead is sad service for the dead! Did you want to make your dead into ghosts, or did you want them to go to Heaven? There is no third alternative for hearts that have been pushed into God's hand. Don't make us into ghosts; give us the right to go home! We would gladly be able to go into your district at any hour without hearing you laugh. Don't make us entirely senile serious shadows; leave us the damp spirit of exhilaration that lay as a gleaming and a shimmer over our youth. Give your dead the right to go home, you living people, for us to live among you and spend some time in dark and light hours. Don't cry for us, that every friend must avoid talking about us! Make joy grab a heart to chat about us and smile! Give us the right to go home, the right we won in life!

When life requires more and more sacrifice to argue for it, to the extent that we take an overview of nature and have been able to see its weapons in detail, so that it can give birth to new life and adds pain in order to heal wounds, then the soldier is the first representative of life. Because he represents the best selection of the peoples at all times and by using his life – and if necessary, by giving his life, enables the life of the remaining world and thus the environment and makes it secure.

However, he shows up in the hours in which fate puts a low value on the peoples, before the last judgment of the Almighty.

In it the nations are weighed and either found to be too light and erased from the Book of Life and History, or found to be worthy enough to have new life. Only someone who has himself had the opportunity to confront the most severe hardship in battle, who himself saw death reaching around him in years of effort, knows how to measure the size of the soldiers' use, to put a value on the entire weight of his sacrifice. From the instinct to affirm life, therefore, mankind has found generally valid measures to evaluate those who were prepared to sacrifice themselves in order to keep life for the community. Against the abominable egotists, the idealists stand, and when they condemn someone as a coward, they are thinking more from the unconscious knowledge of the sacrifice made for others.

They identify him as a hero and thus lift him up from the average indifferent events. No people, however, have more right and today, actually the duty to celebrate its heroes, than our entire German people.

Therefore, we praise those
>whom were at one time courageous and fighting in front with you and were able to go back, usually spread widely and half shot up, not infrequently only behind barbed wire and [illegible] cages newly made for today's eternal peace.

We praise you
>because you have kept your oath for the people and the fatherland until death,

We praise you again:
>Comrades! Your sacrifice is not in vain even though it might appear that way for the time being!

We want to be there all the time for you and your honor and hold up the ideals that [illegible] you.
>Let this be a sign of how proud we are of what you have done!

Anyone who does not render praise at your corpses and you at the same time is not a comrade!

Appendix K

The Battlefields of Weißenberg
and Bautzen Today

(Reference Maps 105, and 106)

In late March 2015 I had a brief opportunity (measured in hours) to visit both Weißenberg and Bautzen before I finalized this manuscript. What follows is my report of that impromptu trip.

The rolling hills and quiet towns that dot the picturesque landscape of Saxony do not reveal their violent wartime experiences willingly. There are no national battlefields. No historical markers exist to pin-point key events during the final fighting in April and May of 1945. There are war memorials—*Ehrenmals*—built during the early days of the defunct East German Communist State that can be found in most of the towns and cities fought over by the Red Army or Polish 2nd Army like Königswartha, Bischofswerda, Crostwitz, Kamenz, Uhsmannsdorf, Niesky, Weißenberg, and Bautzen.

Driving west today on the Autobahn 4 one can take exit 91 toward Weißenberg. As you turn onto the S55 Zufahrtstraße immediately on the left is a wide open farm field where the destruction of the 294th Rifle Division, 57th Guards Tank Brigade and 25th Guards Mechanized Brigade took place on April 24th, 1945. As the Soviet forces streamed out of Weißenberg heading northeast over two roads that today are known as Straße der Einheit and Nieskyer Straße, they had not anticipated the violent firepower the men of *Panzergrenadier-Division 'Brandenburg'* were prepared to unleash that day. The terrain favored the attackers who were positioned concentrically to strike the Soviet columns as they withdrew up the sloping terrain toward the Autobahn exposing themselves to *Jägerregiment 2 'BR'* positioned in defilade near Bucholz, then over the crest of the ridge back down the other side where they were exposed to the firepower of *Jägerregiment 1 'BR'* and supporting *Jagdpanzers* and *Sturmgeschütze*. Any Soviets on the ridge could be struck from both sides. There was no cover or concealment for the withdrawing Soviets expect for the pine forest to the northeast. Few reached the illusion of protection presented by the dark green woods.

There is no trace of the violence that took place that day in the field or along the dirt roads. The town of Weißenberg also has no overt indication that a fierce battle took place. The town's residents first experienced war on April 17th when Soviet artillery struck the Bahnhof. Soviet tanks entered the following day. There was fighting to the north of town when *Jägerregiment 1 'BR'* entered and reoccupied it on April 24th. Any remnants of the fighting have long since been repaired after the reunification with West Germany. The only reminder is the small Soviet cemetery that resides along the S11 in town directly across the street from the Middle School. There are 242 officers and soldiers buried there. The Cyrillic letters that adorns the stone archway to the cemetery reads "Eternal praise to the best sons of the Soviet Country". Each row of black marble grave stones is translated as follows:

First row

Here lies
Soldier
Kurchanskiy, Mikhail Ivanovich
1926-1945
Guards Lieutenant
Shkrigunov, Ivan Ivanovich
1921-April 23, 1945

Here lies
Lieutenant Colonel
Frankel', Boris Mironovich
1906
April 23, 1945
Bulavin, Petr Vladimir
Captain
1905
April 24, 1945

Here lies
Guards Senior Lieutenant
Lysenkov, Boris Dmitrievich
1914-April 21, 1945
Guards Captain
Mandrusov, Petr Ivanovich
1904-April 27, 1945
Private First Class
Shprikher, Mikhail Iv.
1918-April 18, 1945

Second row

Here lie
Guards Lieutenant
Magutov, P.A.
Guards Junior
Lieutenant
Loktionov, A.V.
Guards Captain
Zaikin, I.T.
They died the death
of the brave in the
battle for the Soviet
homeland
April 24, 1945 in
Weißenberg

Here lie
Guards Sergeant
Morozov, Nikolay,
born in 1925
Died on April 22,
1945
Senior Sergeant
Belnov, Ivan Aleks.,
born in 1923
Died on April 24,
1945
who died the death
of the brave for the
Soviet homeland
Junior Sergeant
Arzamastsev, Ivan A.
1918-April 20, 1945

Here lies
Guards Junior
Lieutenant
Gryazin, Aleksandr
Prokhorovich
Born in 1925
Died the death of
the brave for the
Soviet homeland on
April 25, 1945
Junior Lieutenant
Filatchenko,
Dmitriy Petrovich
Born in 1922
Died on April 23,
1945

Here lies Guards
Senior Lieutenant
Latyev, Nikolay
Andreevich
Born in 1910
Died the death of
the brave for the
Soviet homeland on
April 22, 1945
Senior Sergeant
D'yakonov, Ivan
Aleksandrovich
Born in 1914
Died April 17, 1945

Here lies
Guard Junior
Lieutenant
Khapilin, Mikhail
Nikiforovich
Born in 1913
Died the death of
the brave for the
Soviet homeland
April 17, 1945
Sergeant
Baryshev, Pavel
Yakovlevich
Born in 1923
Died April 18, 1945

Here lie
Guards Senior
Sergeant
Sotnikov, Sergey
Fedorovich
Guards Senior
Lieutenant
Rosov, Fedor
Davidovich
Guards Senior
Sergeant
Yukhtin, Ivan
Konstantinovich
Died the death of
the brave for the
Soviet homeland
April 21, 1945

Third row

Here lie Private Alekseev, Mikhail Pavlovich 1910 May 8, 1945 Soldier Kotsaga, Vasiliy Nikiforovich Born in 1914 Died on April 24, 1945

Here lie Junior Lieutenant Kireev, Vas. Vas., 1913 He died the death of the brave. April 18, 1945 Lieutenant Ovchinnikov, K. He died the death of the brave. May 8, 1945 Lieutenant Yur'ev, Filipp Am. 1900-April 26, 1945

Here lie Guards Senior Sergeant Sevost'yanov, A.N., 1922 Guards Junior Sergeant Arinichev, N.I., 1912 Guards Private Marchenko, A.A., 1923 Guards Private Podshivaylo, V.P., 1925 They died the death of the brave for the Soviet homeland.

Here lie Agafanov, Afanasiy, 1912 Ushkov, M.B., 1917 Zhmyrko, N., 1923 Taran, N.M., 1900 Shviridov, V.M. Tashanov, N. Nedlov, V.P. Grechok, E.A. Gmilakov, N. Sivonenko, L. They died the death of the brave for the Soviet homeland.

Here lies An unknown warrior girl She died the death of the brave for the Soviet homeland. Captain Vasin, Petr Lazarovich Born in 1912 Died on April 26, 1945 Lieutenant Kasatkin, Vasiliy Al. [illegible] 1924-April 19, 1945

Here lie Senior Sergeant Dmitritsev He died the death of the brave on April 18, 1945 Senior Sergeant Domnich, F.A. Senior Sergeant Shalanov, F.A. Senior Sergeant Zhdanov, N.A. She died the death of the brave for the Soviet homeland.

Here lie 4 officers They died the death of the brave in the fight for the Soviet homeland April 24, 1945 in Weißenberg and Private Korol', Vasiliy Iosifovich Born in 1902 Died on April 25, 1945

Back wall

Eternal praise to the Soviet soldiers/heroes who gave their lives for the freedom and independence of their homeland.

Here lie hero Guards soldiers who died the death of the brave in the fight for the Soviet homeland. April 24, 1945

Eternal memory for the best sons of the Soviet nation that died the death of the brave in the fight for a just cause.

The average age of the deceased is 29 years old. The relatively high age represents the manpower issues faced by the Soviet Union in the last twelve months of war. This required increasingly older recruits to serve in the frontline. It is not clear why so few officers and soldiers are buried here given the losses that occurred during the withdrawal on the 23rd. It should be noted that fresh flowers adorned the second and fifth graves of the third row during my visit in late March.

As one drives along the S11 winding through Weißenberg you descended down the western slope of this sleepy town and soon cross the Löbauer Wasser. Heading west one can follow the main route of advance of the Soviet 7th Guards Mechanized Corps toward Bautzen. After about 11 kilometers of country lane roads the dull gray wall with triple barbed wire running across its top marks the boundary of the Bautzen Airport and former East German Air Force base. The initial runway was built in 1910 and served military purposes through World War II. A permanent barracks was built in 1940 and a Pilot Training School opened in January 1945. Training elements of *Jagdgeschwader 1* and *Nahaufklärungsgruppe 15* were based there. The airfield was used extensively during the final weeks of the war until it was overrun by the Soviets. After the war the *Luftwaffe* buildings and runway were destroyed and the land turned into farm use. Between 1956 and 1957 a new concrete runway was built along with taxiways and parking areas for aircraft to support the newly established East German Airforce. YAK-18s, FAG-25s, L-29s, and MiG-21 all made appearances at the airfield. The routine sonic booms of the MiG-21s annoyed the local residents until the collapse of the East German Communist State rendered the airfield's military use obsolete. The entire airfield and supporting complex was upgraded in the 1980s along with a wide security zone that kept prying eyes from seeing anything more than the remaining concrete wall and barbed wire. Now the airport has been converted to civilian use, though the unmistakable, if not ominous, East German military construction is still present.

Four kilometers past the Bautzen Airport S11 ends. Make a right onto Löbauer Straße and head north uphill. Bautzen has grown in size since the collapse of East Germany. Areas that were open farmland outside the old König-Albert-Infanterie-Kaserne are now dotted with shops and service stations. Nothing apparently remains of the old Kaserne. There are no remnants of the fierce two days of fighting that occurred along this stretch of road toward the center of the city. Just past Fichtestaße on the right is the Taucherfriedhof Cemetery established in 1523 that also was the scene of intensive fighting from April 20th-21st. The next right on Am Ziegelwall will end at Muskauer Straße. Immediately on the left is the Soviet and Polish Cemetery where 3,000 soldiers are reportedly buried. In the center of the cemetery is a monument to the 13th Guards Tank Regiment of the 7th Guards Mechanized Corps that reads "Eternal praise to the heroes who fell in battles for the freedom and independence of our homeland". This memorial was likely established by the unit's commander Major Fomenko who received the title of Honorary Mayor of Bautzen in 1972.

The city of Bautzen was rebuilt quickly after the war. Much of the damage was repaired. Only the granite facades of a few buildings and several of castle walls retain the scars of the back-to-back modern sieges of the city's medieval quarter.

There is still much to see in Bautzen, and any visit should start at the Museum Bautzen to grasp the full impact of the city's rich history. From its Bronze Age origin, and subsequent destructive experiences during the Thirty Years War, Napoleonic Wars, and World War II, the city has endured and flourished through the centuries.

Image 50. East of Weißenberg, looking north. This image was taken at the intersection of the S55 on the left and the dirt road of Nieskyer Straße running along the right side, out of frame. *Panzergrenadier-Division 'Brandenburg'* concentrically attacked the withdrawing elements of 294th Rifle Division, 57th Guards Tank Brigade and 25th Guards Mechanized Brigade on 23 April destroying them in this open field and the one over the ridge to the northeast. The distance to the Autobahn is approximately 1000 meters. March, 2015. Author's collection.

Image 51. East of Weißenberg, looking southeast. This image was taken at the intersection of Straße der Einheit and S55. Behind the woods on the left is the town of Bucholz where *Jägerregiment 2 'BR'* initiated the destruction of the withdrawing Soviet formations on 23 April by attacking across the open field. The distance to the woods is about 1000 meters. Bucholz is another 1000 meters beyond. March, 2015. Author's collection.

Image 52. Soviet military cemetery, Weißenberg. March, 2015. Author's collection.

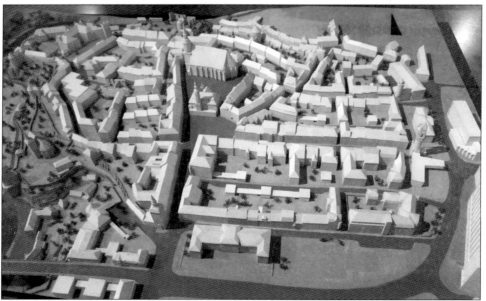

Image 53. 3D scale model of the medieval quarter of Bautzen. This model shows the two main avenues of approach toward the Fleischmarkt located in the center left by St. Petri, and Ortenburg Castle on the far left. The first avenue of approach runs from the Reichenturm (far right) west along Kesselstraße (Reichenstraße) into the Hauptmarkt. The second avenue of approach runs north from the Lauenturm (lower left) north along Lauenstraße. The narrow streets limited the use of armor in the medieval quarter. Museum Bautzen. Author's collection.

Image 54. Soviet War Memorial, Muskauer Straße, Bautzen. The memorial reads "Eternal praise to the heroes who fell in battles for the freedom and independence of our homeland". Undated internet photo.

Image 55. Facade of Museum Bautzen. The partially repaired facade shows the divot of small arms as well as the gouge of a larger caliber round. This building faces east and sits along Kornmarkt where heavy fighting occurred. March 2015. Author's collection.

Image 56. Lauenstraße looking south toward the Lauenturm from the Rathaus. It was along this avenue of approach that both the 24th Guards Mechanized Brigade advanced on 21 April, followed by the elements of 'Brandenburg' that were attached to *Kampfgruppe Wiethersheim* on 24/25 April. March 2015. Author's collection.

Image 57. Schloßstrasse. The street and entrance way to Ortenburg Castle has changed little through the centuries. March 2015. Author's collection.

Image 58. Beyond the gate at the end of Schloßstrasse is the sloping cobblestone road into the castle grounds. Fighting raged up this narrow street into the castle grounds. March 2015. Author's collection.

Image 59. Castle wall facing west. This partially original section of the old medieval wall in the castle square still bears the marks of fighting as noted by the near dozen divots caused by small caliber arms and possibly a larger caliber weapon. March 2015. Author's collection.

Image 60. Ortenburg Castle. The castle withstood numerous Soviet infantry attacks. The *Volkssturm* defenders managed to hold out in this building and across the 150 meter wide courtyard in the Castle Water Tower (directly behind where this image was taken). March 2015. Author's collection.

Image 61. Southern portion of the Ortenburg Castle. Looking east toward the Ortenburg Castle Water Tower along a section of castle wall that faces south. The remaining garrison under the command of *Oberst* Hoepke held out in the Water Tower and above this 20-25 foot stone wall in the castle grounds. This photo clearly shows the difficulty of the terrain and why the garrison was able to hold out in the medieval fortress as long as they did despite being outnumbered. March 2015. Author's collection.

Image 62. Bautzen, looking north. On the left is the Ortenburg Castle water tower; in the center foreground is the original medieval city water tower; just behind and to the right is the Michaels Church; between the two structures is the top of the rebuilt Ortenburg Castle; and to the far right is the spire of St. Petri. This image shows the defensibility of the castle district. March 2015. Author's collection.

Leader photographs

Image 63. *Generalfeldmarschall* Ferdinand Schörner (*H.Gr.Mitte*). Peter van Holstein via Mark C. Yerger.

Image 64. *Generalleutnant* Oldwig Otto von Natzmer (*Generalstab, H.Gr.Mitte*). Mark C. Yerger.

Image 65. *General der Panzertruppen* Fritz-Hubert Gräser (*4.Panzer-Armee*). Mark C. Yerger.

Image 66. *Generalmajor* Hans von Ahlfen (*Heeres-Pionier-Brigade 70*).
Bundesarchiv B 145 Bild-F016205-25, photographer unknown.

Image 67. *General der Panzertruppen* Walther Nehring (*XXIV.Panzer-Korps, Gruppe Nehring*). Peter van Holstein via Mark C. Yerger.

Image 68. *General der Panzertruppen* Dietrich von Saucken (*Pz.Korps 'GD'*).
Bundesarchiv Bild 146-1979-066-03, photographer unknown.

Image 69. *General der Panzertruppen* Georg Jauer (*Pz.Korps 'GD'*). Author's collection.

Image 70. *Generalmajor* Hanns-Horst von Necker (*'Hermann Göring'*). Author's collection.

Image 71. *Generalmajor* Max Lemke
(*'Hermann Göring'*). Author's collection.

Image 72. *Generalmajor* Hermann von Oppeln-Bronikowski (*20.Panzer-Division*) (left, with *Major* Gerhard Behnke, centre, and *General der Panzertruppen* Heinrich Eberbach, right). Peter van Holstein via Mark C. Yerger.

Image 73. *Generalmajor* Hermann Schulte-Heuthaus (*'Brandenburg'*).
Bundesarchiv Bild 183-R64062, photographer: Hans Lachmann.

Image 74. *Major* Erasmus (*'Brandenburg'*). Peter van Holstein via Mark C. Yerger.

Image 75. Marshal Ivan Koniev. Author's collection.

Image 76. Marshal Georgi
Zhukov. Author's collection.

Image 77. General Karol Świerczewski (2nd
Polish Army). Author's collection.

Bibliography

All quotes sourced to veterans of *zbv Division 'Brandenburg'* or *Panzergrenadier-Division 'Brandenburg'* that are not accompanied by a separate citation in the text are derived exclusively from the accounts located in the Bundesarchiv-Militärarchiv files of RH 26-1002. The reconstruction effort required to place the *'Brandenburg'* accounts in chronological order simply precluded the creation of individual citations. Doing so unnecessarily required some 1,000 end notes, all pointing back to this single record group. All sources noted below are cited in the body of the text.

Primary Documents
Bundesarchiv-Militärarchiv. Freiburg, Germany.
    RH 10 OKH Generalinspekteur der Panzertruppen.
        File 114. Panzergrenadier-Division "Brandenburg".
        File 121. Panzergrenadier-Division "Brandenburg".
        File 209. Panzer-Grenadier-Division "Großdeutschland".
    RH 26-1002 Sonderverband "Brandenburg"/Division "Brandenburg"/Panzergrenadier-Division "Brandenburg".
        File 1002-3. Materialsammlung zur Geschichte der Panzer-Grenadier-Division "Brandenburg" und ihrer Vorgänger. 1938-1943.
        File 1002-4. Materialsammlung zur Geschichte der Panzer-Grenadier-Division "Brandenburg" und ihrer Vorgänger. 1942-1945.
        File 1002-6. Einsatz der Division "Brandenburg".
        File 1002-8. Einsatz und Gefechtsberichte 1945.
    ZA1-2058 Der Feldzug Gegen Die Sowjetunion Im Mittelabschnitt Der Ostfront 1941-1945, Zehnter Teil by General der Infanterie a.D. Rudolf Hofmann
    ZA1-2759 Versorgungsführung der H.Gr. Mitte bei Rückzug und Verteidigung März-Mai 1945

Cornelius Ryan Collection. Mahn Center, Alden Library. Ohio University, Athens, OH.
    Section. Soviet Forces.
        Box 72.
            Folder 3. Koniev Memoirs.
            Section. German Forces.
                Box 66.
                Folder 11. Von Oppeln-Bronikowski, Gen, Notes on letter and telephone conversation.

Cornell University law Library, Donovan Nuremberg Trials Collection.
    Vol. IX. Witness: Erwin Lahousen/Office of U.S. Counsel for the Prosecution of Axis Criminality/Document Room Interrogation Analysis. "Atrocities against Military Personnel". 1945-09-15.
    Vol. XXXIII. Trial of the Major War Criminals before the International Military Tribunal. Nuremberg. 14 November 1945—1 October 1946.

Vol. XCIX 31. Seventh Army Interrogation Report. Generalmajor a.D. Alexander von
    Pfuhlstein. 10 April 1945.
Vol. CV 01. Office of Strategic Services Mission for Germany. United States Forces European
    Theatre. "Sections of the R.S.H.A. Possibly Involved in War Crimes". 23 June 1945.
Vol. CV 02. Office of Strategic Services Mission for Germany. United States Forces European
    Theatre. "Dissensions in German Intelligence Services". 7 July 1945.

United States National Archive Records Administration. College Park, Maryland.
    Record Group 242: National Archives Collection of Foreign Records Seized
        T77 Records of the German Armed Forces High Command (Oberkommando der
            Wehrmacht/OKW)
        Roll 852.
        Roll 788.
        T78 Records of Headquarters, German Armed Forces High Command (Oberkommando
            der Heeres/OKH).
        Roll 304.
        Roll 305.
        Roll 415.
        Roll 529.
        Roll 533.
        Roll 621.
        Roll 645.
        T311 Records of German Field Commands (Armies).
        Roll 167.
        Roll 168.
        German Armed Forces Operations and Situation Maps 1939-1945
            H.GR. Mitte.
        Box 351-358.
            H.GR. A.
        Box 507.

German Replacement Army Supplement, May 1945. Military Intelligence Division, War Department.
    Washington 25, D.C. [No Date].
Handbook on USSR Military Forces, TM 30-430. Washington, D.C.: U.S. War Department,
    November 1945.

Books
Von Ahlfen, Hans. Der Kampf um Schlesien, 1944-1945. Stuttgart, Germany. Motorbuch
    Verlag, 1963.
Bartov, Omar. Hitler's Army: Soldier, Nazis, and War in the Third Reich. New York. Oxford
    University Press, 1991.
_____. The Eastern Front, 1941-1945: German Troops and the barbarization of Warfare. New
    York. St. Martin's Press, 1986.
Beevor, Anthony. The Fall of Berlin 1945. New York. Viking Press, 2002.
Bergstrom, Christer. Bagration to Berlin: The Final Air Battles in the East: 1944–1945. Hersham,
    Surrey, U.K. Ian Allan Publishing. 2008.
Berthold, Will. Brandenburg Division. Translated from the German by Alan Neame. Frogmore, St
    Albans. Mayflower Books Ltd. 1973.

Berndt, Eberhard. *Band 5. Spurensuche. Die Kämpfe um Weißenberg und Bautzen im April 1945.* Eggolsheim. Dörfler Verlag GmbH, 2013[?].

_____. *"Die Kämpfe um Bautzen 18. Bis 27. April 1945"* in *Kriegsschauplatz Sachsen 1945. Daten, Fakten, Hintergründe.* DZA Verlag für Kultur und Wissenschaft GmbH. 1995.

Crofoot, Craig. *The Berlin Direction: April-May 1945. An extraction of the official Soviet Army Order of Battle of the Berlin Strategic Offensive Operation, April-May 1945.* West Chester, OH. The Nafziger Collection, 1999.

Die Wehrmachtberichte 1939-1945. Band 3. 1.Januar 1944 bis 9.Mai 1945. Osnabrück, Germany. Deutscher Taschenbuch Verlag GmbH & Co. KG. Biblio Verlag Reprint. 1985.

Erickson, John. *Road to Berlin: Stalin's War with Germany.* New Haven, CT. Yale University Press. Paperback edition. 1999.

Förster, Jürgen E. "The Dynamics of Volksgemeinschaft: The Effectiveness of the German Military Establishment in the Second World War," in *Military Effectiveness, vol. 3. The Second World War,* ed. Allan R. Millet and Williamson Murray. Boston. Unwin Hyman, 1988.

Frieser, Karl-Heinz, ed. *Das Deutsche Reich und der Zweite Weltkrieg - Vol. 8.* Karl-Heinz Frieser, Klaus Schmider, Klaus Schönherr, Gerhard Schreiber, Kristián Ungváry, Bernd Wegner. *Die Ostfront 1943/44 - Der Krieg im Osten und an den Nebenfronten.* München, Germany. Deutsche Verlags-Anstalt. 2007.

Fritz, Stephen. *Ostkrieg: Hitler's War of Extermination in the East.* Lexington, Kentucky. The University Press of Kentucky, 2011

_____. *Frontsoldaten: The German Soldier in World War II.* Lexington, Kentucky. University Press of Kentucky, 1995.

Gardner, Brian. *On to Kilimanjaro: The bizarre story of the First World War in East Africa.* New York. Macfadden-Bartell, 1964.

Glantz, Colonel David M., *Red Army Officers Speak! Interviews with veterans of the Vistula-Oder Operation (January-February 1945).* David. M. Glantz. 1997.

_____. *1986 Art of War Symposium: From the Vistula to the Oder: Soviet Offensive Operations, October 1944-March 1945.* Center for Land Warfare, U.S. Army War College. 19-23 May 1986.

Grzelak, Czesław, Henryk Stańczyk and Stefan Zwoliński, *Armia Berlinga, I Żymierskiego.* Warsaw, Poland. Wyadawnictwo Neriton. 2003.

Guderian, Heinz. *Panzer Leader.* Cambridge, MA. Da Capo Press. 2002.

Hinze, Rolf. *To the Bitter End: The Final Battles of Army Groups North Ukraine, A, Centre, Eastern Front 1944-45.* Translated with editing and minor revisions and additions by Frederick P. Steinhardt, MS PhD. Solihull, West Midlands, England. Helion and Company Ltd. 2005.

Johannesn, Hein. *Werner Mummert, Das Leben eines sächsischen Offiziers.* Gröditz, Germany. Verlag libergraphix. 2012.

Kaczmarek, Kazimierz. *Polacy w bitwie pod Budziszynem.* Warsaw, Poland. Wyadawnictwo Interpress. 1970.

Kahn, David. *Hitler's Spies: German Military Intelligence in World War II.* New York. Macmillan Publishing Co., Inc. 1978.

Kortenhaus, Werner. *The Combat History of the 21.Panzer-Division.* Solihull, West Midlands, England. Helion and Company Ltd. 2014.

Knop, Werner. *Prowling Russia's Forbidden Zone: A Secret Journey into Soviet Germany.* New York. Alfred A. Knopp. 1949.

Longerich, Peter. *Heinrich Himmler.* New York. Oxford University Press. 2012.

Macdonogh, Giles. *After the Reich.* New York. Basic Books. 2007.

Maslov, Aleksander A. *Fallen Soviet Generals: Soviet General Officers killed in battle, 1941-1945.* Translated and edited by David M. Glantz. Portland, Oregon. Frank Cass. 1998.

Mendelsohn, Rona. *Liberation. 65th Anniversary 2010*. Prague, U.S. Embassy. Global Printing Solutions. 2010.

Messerschmidt, Manfred. "German Military Law in the Second World War" in *The German Military in the Age of Total War*. ed. Wilhelm Deist. Dover, NH. Berg Publishers. 1985.

Miller, Charles. *Battle for the Bundu: The First World War in East Africa*. New York. Macmillan Publishing Co., Inc, 1974.

Mosley, Leonard. *Duel for Kilimanjaro, Africa 1914-1918: The Dramatic Story of an Unconventional War*. New York. Ballantine Books, 1963.

Naimark, Norman M. *The Russians in Germany: A History of the Soviet Zone of Occupation, 1945-1949*. Cambridge, MA. Harvard University Press Paperback Edition. 1997.

Noble, Alastair. *Nazi Rule and the Soviet Offensive in Eastern Germany, 1944-1945: The Darkest Hour*. Portland, OR. Sussex Academic Press. 2009.

Resse, Roger R. *Why Stalin's Soldiers Fought: The Red Army's Effectiveness in World War II*. Lawrence. University of Kansas Press. 2011.

Rudel, Hans Ulrich. *Stuka Pilot*. London. Bantam Books Paperback edition. 1979.

Scherzer, Viet. *Ritterkreuzträger 1939-1945*. Jena, Germany. Scherzers Militaer-Verlag Ranis. 2007.

_____.*Deutsche Truppen im Zweiten Weltkrieg. Band1. Formationsgeschichte des Heeres und des Ersatzheeres 1939-1945. Gliederung-Stärke-Ausstattung-Bewaffnung. Teilband A-B*. Jena, Germany. Scherzers Militaer-Verlag. 2007.

Seidel, Theodor. *Kriegsverbrechen in Sachsen. Die vergessenen Toten von April/Mai 1945*. Leipzig, Germany. Leipziger Universitätsverlag GMBH. 2013.

Sharp, Charles C. *Volume X. "Red Swarm", Soviet Rifle Division Formed from 1942 to 1945. Soviet Order of Battle World War II. An Organizational History of the Major Combat Units of the Soviet Army*. West Chester, OH. George F. Nafziger, 1996.

Shills, Edward A. and Morris Janowitz, "Cohesion and Disintegration in the Wehrmacht in World War II," *Public Opinion Quarterly* 12 (1948).

Spaeter, Hans. *The History of Panzerkorps Großdeutschland, Volume 3*. Translated by David Johnston. Winnipeg, Canada. J.J. Fedorowicz Publishing Inc. 2000.

_____. *Die Brandenburger, eine deutsche Kommandotruppe: zbV 800*. Düsseldorf, Germany. Karl-Heinz Dissberger. 1991.

_____. *Panzerkorps Großdeutschland. A Pictorial History*. West Chester, PA. Schiffer Publishing. 1990. Translated by Dr. Edward Force from *Panzerkorps Grossdeutschland Bilddokumentation*. Dorheim, Germany. Podzun-Pallas Verlag. 1984.

Stern, Fritz. *Frontsoldaten: The German Soldier in World War II*. Lawrence: The University Press of Kentucky, 1995.

Tessin, Georg. *Verbände und Truppen der deutschen Wehrmacht und der Waffen-SS im Zweiten Weltkrieg 1939-1945. Bearbeitet auf Grund der Unterlagen des Bundesarchivs-Militärarchivs; herausgegeben mit Unterstützung des Bundesarchivs und des Arbeitskreises für Wehrforschung. 14 Bände + 3 Registerbände in mehreren Teilen* (Osnabrück, Germany. Biblio Verlag, 1967-1998.)

Tieke, Wilhelm. *In the Firestorm of the Last Years of the War: II.SS-Panzerkorps with the 9. And 10.SS-Divisions "Hohenstaufen" and "Frundsberg"*. Translated by Frederick Steinhardt. Winnipeg, Canada. J.J. Fedorowicz Publishing Inc. 1999.

Trevor-Roper, Hugh, ed. *Final Entries 1945: The Diaries of Joseph Goebbels*. Translated by Richard Barry. Barnsley, South Yorkshire, U.K. Pen & Sword Military. 2007.

Van Creveld, Martin. *Fighting Power: German and U.S. Army Performance 1939-1945*. London. Arms and Armour Press. 1983.

Wette, Wolfram. *Deserteure der Wehrmacht. Feiglinge-Opfer-Hoffnungsträger? Dokumentation eines Meinungswandels*. Klartext Verlag. Essen. 1995.

Ziemke, Earl F. *Stalingrad to Berlin: The German Defeat in the East.* New York, NY. Barnes and Noble Books Reprint. No Date.

Index

Index of Places

Index of German Military Units